Coming Into Being
Among The
Australian Aborigines

Coming Into Being Among The Australian Aborigines

A STUDY OF THE PROCREATIVE BELIEFS OF THE
NATIVE TRIBES OF AUSTRALIA

Ashley Montagu

WITH A FOREWORD BY
Bronislaw Malinowski

A Fully Revised and Expanded Second Edition

ROUTLEDGE & KEGAN PAUL
London and Boston

First published by George Routledge & Sons Ltd in 1937
Second, revised edition published in 1974
by Routledge & Kegan Paul Ltd
Broadway House, 68–74 Carter Lane,
London EC4V 5EL and
9 Park Street,
Boston, Mass. 02108, USA
Set in 'Monotype' Baskerville
and printed in Great Britain by
W & J Mackay Limited, Chatham
© This second, revised edition, Ashley Montagu, 1974
No part of this book may be reproduced in
any form without permission from the
publisher, except for the quotation of brief
passages in criticism

ISBN 0 7100 7933 8
Library of Congress Catalog Card No. 74–80751

By Ashley Montagu

MAN'S MOST DANGEROUS MYTH: THE FALLACY OF RACE

THE HUMANIZATION OF MAN

MAN IN PROCESS

HUMAN HEREDITY

THE CULTURED MAN

MAN: HIS FIRST TWO MILLION YEARS

EDWARD TYSON, M.D., F.R.S. (1650–1708): AND THE RISE
OF HUMAN AND COMPARATIVE ANATOMY IN ENGLAND

STATEMENT ON RACE

THE DIRECTION OF HUMAN DEVELOPMENT

THE NATURAL SUPERIORITY OF WOMEN

THE REPRODUCTIVE DEVELOPMENT OF THE FEMALE

ON BEING HUMAN

THE BIOSOCIAL NATURE OF MAN

DARWIN, COMPETITION AND CO-OPERATION

ON BEING INTELLIGENT

IMMORTALITY, RELIGION, AND MORALS

EDUCATION AND HUMAN RELATIONS

ANTHROPOLOGY AND HUMAN NATURE

INTRODUCTION TO PHYSICAL ANTHROPOLOGY

HANDBOOK OF ANTHROPOMETRY

PRENATAL INFLUENCES

RACE, SCIENCE, AND HUMANITY

LIFE BEFORE BIRTH

THE SCIENCE OF MAN

ANATOMY AND PHYSIOLOGY, 2 VOLS (WITH E. STEEN)

THE PREVALENCE OF NONSENSE (WITH E. DARLING)

THE IGNORANCE OF CERTAINTY (WITH E. DARLING)

MAN'S EVOLUTION (WITH C. L. BRACE)

TEXTBOOK OF HUMAN GENETICS (WITH M. LEVITAN)

THE DOLPHIN IN HISTORY (WITH J. LILLY)

SEX, MAN, AND SOCIETY

MAN OBSERVED

THE HUMAN REVOLUTION

THE IDEA OF RACE

UP THE IVY

TOUCHING: THE HUMAN SIGNIFICANCE OF THE SKIN

THE AMERICAN WAY OF LIFE

THE ANATOMY OF SWEARING

THE ELEPHANT MAN

Editor

STUDIES AND ESSAYS IN THE HISTORY OF SCIENCE AND LEARNING

The object of true investigation, whether in philosophy or natural science, is to make unsparing discovery of existing contradictions and to question the facts until our conceptions are cleared up, and if necessary the whole theory and general view is replaced by a better.— JULIUS VON SACHS, *History of Botany*, Oxford, 1890.

Contents

Figures

Foreword

Is the savage really a savage? This question covers the fundamental problems of the modern Science of Man. It might, perhaps, be put in a less epigrammatic and less paradoxical form: are simpler cultures of the same nature as the more developed ones? Is the 'primitive' man's mind built on a different pattern from that of his more civilized brother? Could human institutions, such as the family and the state, property and marriage, have been in their beginnings almost the opposite of what they are now—or have they always been essentially the same? Such questions dominate recent discussions among the relevant schools of anthropology.

According to one of these two modern divergent views, cultures in general, and primitive cultures more especially, are not to be compared with each other. They have to be studied intuitively, by individual appreciation of each. According to the other view, the 'savage', the 'primitive', the 'aboriginal' is a human being like any other. Every culture is in its essence built on the same pattern. To speak about tribal or cultural 'genius' is no more than a metaphor. And all this means that there can be a really scientific approach to the study of human cultures by the comparative method, aiming at the discovery of general laws of culture. On this last view, which is shared also by the present writer, the savage is not really a savage, not any more, that is, than you or I. Humanity is one throughout, and the science of culture is possible.

Older anthropology was a detached and leisurely pursuit. In the good old pre-war days, the collection of curios in a museum and of curiosities in the ethnographer's notebook formed the delight of those who could afford to collect, to travel, and to read at leisure. In those days anthropology was concerned with a world in parts at least genuinely exotic. The aeroplane, the wireless, and film technique had not yet effected the paradoxical give and take which makes us now doubt when listening to an apparently native tune in Central Africa whether it had been born there or imported from some far away tribe, or had arrived there on the short wave, via New York or Los Angeles and London, from some old African slave colony in the U.S.A.

Pre-war anthropology was also aristocratic, as most leisurely pursuits must be. It was concerned with man's pedigrees, origins, and antecedents. It firmly believed in Evolution; in the rise of man from a lowly beginning to an exalted station in life. Dr Ashley Montagu has many interesting and enlightening things to say on this subject in his first chapter.

About a quarter of a century ago there came the first change towards a more rigidly scientific point of view. We then became aware that anthropology had an important task to fulfil as the foundation of the science of culture. The results of ethnographic observation were the nearest approach to what the physicist, the chemist, and the biologist obtained through experiments in a well-equipped laboratory. In order to obtain scientific laws of correlation, it was necessary to survey the widest range of cultural variation, and this was only possible through the work of the field anthropologist. Instead of building vast edifices of reconstruction, diffusionist or evolutionary, it seemed better to turn to the analysis of each culture as a going concern. In a subsequent comparative computation, this led us to the discovery of laws in cultural process, and the definition of the fundamental concepts underlying all cultural reality. This 'functional' approach was nothing but the vindication of a strictly empirical inspiration in theory, and conversely, the demand that observation should be guided by knowledge of the laws and principles of culture as a dynamic reality. The general tendency of this school was to make the savage essentially human, and to find elements of the primitive in higher civilizations. In the last instance, functional analysis aimed at the establishment of a common measure of all cultures, simple and developed, Western and Oriental, arctic and tropical.

Quite recently there has appeared yet another school of thought, this time in reaction against the scientific claims and efforts at standardization of the Functional method. The Functional theory of culture maintains that the general scaffolding of culture, more concretely the fundamental institutions and aspects, are the same everywhere. To a certain extent Functionalism tends to neglect, or at least to underrate the diversities of cultures, as well as the individualities of what is sometimes called the 'tribal genius', or 'racial' and 'national' characteristics.

In reaction to all this, and under the influence of Psychoanalysis and Behaviourism, of Spenglerian metaphysics and the Marxian conviction that social engineering is more important than social philosophy, the new theory has crystallized its principles. Its adherents emphasize the incompatibility and the incommensurability of human cultures. 'No common measure of cultural phenomena can be found', we are told by Dr R. Benedict. The attempt to make the study of cultures scientific, in the sense of postulating the existence of generalizations and universally valid laws, is deprecated. Professor Kroeber, championing the historical method, tells us that 'all historical definitions are in their very essence subjective'. In the same article (*American Anthropologist,* 1935) he emphasizes the subjective, artistic, and intuitive approach. Professor Boas himself has recently expressed his view that, since 'the relations between different aspects of culture follow the most diverse patterns', they 'do not lend themselves profitably to generalizations' (Introduction to Dr Ruth Benedict, *Patterns of Culture*). On an earlier occasion in his monumental article *s.v.* 'Anthropology' in the *Encyclopædia of the Social Sciences*, he has clearly stated his opinion that 'the laws of cultural process are vague, insipid, and useless'.

In all this I see the foundations of a new theory; it might be described as 'Cultural Monadology'. Each culture has a unique individuality of its own. It is the creation of its 'tribal genius', an objectivized expression of some collective entity, which spins its realities out of its inner determinism. Since each culture is a law unto itself, the inner determinism is so individual that to tackle it with an abstract apparatus of universally valid concepts, laws, and generalizations, must remain futile. A theory of culture with a world-wide validity, such as implied in attempts of the functional school, must from the very outset be rejected as fruitless.

Personally, I think that this new reaction—for as far as Professor Boas is concerned, the utterances quoted represent a new phase in his outlook—goes a little too far. I am still convinced that the search for general laws of cultural process and of cultural reality will remain the scientific task of anthropology. There is no doubt that, when in field-work we pass from one culture to another, we come to feel that some new 'tribal genius' or 'national spirit' is taking sway of us. I myself have confessed that

what interests me really is the study of the native is his outlook on things, his *Weltanschauung*, the breath of life and reality which he breathes and by which he lives. Every human culture gives its members a definite vision of the world, a definite zest of life. In the roamings over human history, and over the surface of the earth, it is the possibility of seeing life and the world from the various angles, particular to each culture, that has always charmed me most, and inspired me with real desire to penetrate other cultures, to understand other types of life (*Argonauts*, 1922, p. 517).

This I would now like to correct in the sense that—to quote again from the same context—'the love of the final synthesis . . . and still more the love of the variety and independence of the various cultures' constitutes the personal and artistic inspiration of the field-worker.

His scientific task lies elsewhere. It consists in translating this variety of cultures into the language of science, which must needs be universally human. The analysis of strange, hypertrophied, exotic customs and institutions into their constituent elements has convinced me that the foundations in each of them are essentially universal. The love between man and woman and the greed for material wealth; the lust for power and jealousy of sex; the selfless devotion of the mother and the antagonism between people who compete at close quarters—all these are to be found everywhere. And besides human passions, propensities and appetites, there are other determining factors equally universal and amenable to scientific observation and analysis. There is the environment, which acts upon man with an almost physical determinism. There are such factors as the territorial bases of all forms of human grouping. There is the need of using material apparatus in the most spiritual pursuits, and, in turn, of giving the imprint of the human mind to all matter shaped for human use.[1]

Although I do not altogether agree with the tendency represented by Professor Boas, Dr R. Benedict, Professor Kroeber, Dr Margaret Mead, Mr Gregory Bateson, and Dr Géza Róheim, I have nevertheless to acknowledge its extreme importance and the value of the corrective which it provides to the Functional Method. I therefore welcome the present book, in which Dr Ashley Montagu gives perhaps the most lucid, scientific, and convincing, as well as most consistent and moderate expression of this latest point of view in anthropology. The book may, in my opinion, turn out to be a bridge between the two methods. There is perhaps a partial failure on the part of the 'functionalist' to recognize that intuition must be more fully used in anthropology; and on the part of the 'cultural monadologist' to admit that generalizations are necessary even for the simplest description of an exotic culture.

I regard it as a great honour to have this book dedicated to myself, in conjunction with Edward Westermarck, to whose personal teaching and to whose work I owe more than to any other scientific influence. I am also glad to write this unconventional preface to an unconventional book: as far as I know, it is not usual to act both as prefacer and as dedicatee.

This admirable book is unconventional in that it does not fall readily into any of the current categories; it is neither a textbook, nor an evolutionary study, nor yet a piece of plain description. Yet I would recommend Dr Ashley Montagu's book as the best introduction to anthropology, indeed, to the study of social science. It deals with the question of primitive nescience of paternity—the most exciting and controversial issue in the comparative science of Man.

This question leads the author directly into the study of kinship and social organization, which are here very fully treated. The problem also implies the analysis of the 'savage' mind, and the author, a born philosopher, displays a width of outlook and precision of analysis which make his book an excellent prolegomena to primitive psychology. Mythology and religion, questions of early knowledge and technology, come one and all under discussion. Every topic is treated with a clarity of vision and lucidity of style which will render the book attractive as well as useful to layman and college student alike.

In one respect, the work is even better than a textbook. It is a model of how ethnographic material should be surveyed, critically digested, and reframed in clear convincing conclusions. There is perhaps nothing more instructive for the beginner, whether preparing for field-work or for theoretical study in social science, than practice in dealing with sources. The use of sources is in many ways more difficult and baffling in ethnography than in history. It certainly is more important; we cannot send any chronicler back into the reign of Charlemagne or Louis XIV, but new field-workers are still pouring into the remoter parts of the world among the remnants of primitive peoples, and they can make good where their predecessors have failed.

The reader will have to follow the detailed analyses of chapters II–VIII in order to appreciate the excellent handling of material and the manner in which Dr Ashley Montagu discusses the procreative beliefs of the Aborigines within the relevant context. In following the author, we also acquire the collateral knowledge about kinship and social organization, religious beliefs, systems of totemism, and magical ritual, all of which is related to the ideas concerning paternity, maternity, and descent. In chapter IX the summing up of the evidence shows how much our knowledge has developed on this subject since the original discoveries of Spencer and Gillen. The writer's verdict [in the first edition] 'that in Australia practically universally, according to orthodox belief, pregnancy is regarded as causally unconnected with intercourse' will, I think, remain the ultimate conclusion of science. It is supported by an irrefutable body of solid fact. A few apparently dissentient views are effectively dealt with by Dr Ashley Montagu. The psychoanalytic findings of Dr Róheim that the natives have a knowledge of physiological paternity which they subsequently 'repress' seems to me untenable. As Dr Ashley Montagu argues, it is not likely that the Central Australian should have in childhood a full knowledge of the physiological process and gradually grow up to 'repress' it into an adult belief in spirit children. 'Repression' may be a valid concept when applied to strong emotional tendencies. It can hardly take place with regard to a solid, well established, empirical piece of knowledge. The evidence of Dr Thomson has already been effectively 'repressed' in a brilliant critical article (*American Anthropologist*, 1, 1937, pp. 175–83) by Dr Ashley Montagu. I think that most will agree with the final sentence of Dr Ashley Montagu's article: 'I submit that the facts lead to quite an opposite conclusion to that arrived at by Mr. Thomson' (*loc. cit.*, p. 183).

Professor Lloyd Warner's account may have regional validity with regard to his own area, which lies on the periphery of Australian culture. To me, however, it appears that he also suffers from the confusion between what Dr Ashley Montagu calls 'orthodox belief' and random statements of irrelevant opinion. But Dr Ashley Montagu himself deals with his data so carefully and conclusively that there is no need to enlarge upon the issue.

I personally find the summary given by the author as convincing and well-balanced as any piece of comparative analysis and critical examination of sources can be. Equally conclusive, and theoretically more interesting, because wider in scope, are the author's arguments in the next chapter. In discussing the various theories of Frazer and Andrew Lang, Professor Westermarck and the late Dr Carveth Read, the author is able to develop his views on the fundamental questions of primitive kinship, social organization, and the beginnings of human marriage and the family. His arguments throughout are scholarly and critical, and they confirm all the sound findings of modern science. He unhesitatingly rejects the theory of promiscuity, group marriage, the existence of a primitive matriarchate and economic communism.

In a science like anthropology, with its word-fetishism and its hypertrophied concern with terminology, Dr Ashley Montagu's important *obiter dictum* about the use of words is to be welcomed. He disagrees with Frazer's theory of 'conceptional totemism', and criticizes the implications of this expression. But he has the good sense to add: 'The term has, however, assumed a definite place in the literature of ethnology, and it would be the cause of needless confusion to attempt to substitute some other for it at this date' (p. 226). It will be a happy day for anthropology when students give up inventing new terms and enlarging our jargon, and instead work on the analysis of facts and the clarification of concepts.

The several score new neologisms for the time-honoured expression 'bride-price', which had been suggested in the course of a prolonged correspondence in *Man*, is an example of this word-hunting waste of time. After all, we use the word 'savage' though we know that 'savages' are not savage; or the word 'native', though we know that we are natives of sorts; and the word 'aboriginal' though no race ever lived where it does now from the very beginning. Words such as 'culture' or 'civilization', 'race' or 'society', 'marriage' or 'kinship', 'religion' or 'magic' would be found one and all after etymological examination to be 'inappropriate'. Lord Raglan some time ago published an article in *Man* in which he accused me of using the term 'family' in a sense in which a great many lawyers, ladies at tea-parties, and taxicab drivers would never use it. Lord Raglan is quite correct in his argument. But then a physicist uses the words 'matter', 'space', 'time', and 'force' in a sense and with implications entirely absent from either etymological or colloquial usage.

In chapter X the author combines his knowledge of biology with his extensive reading in Australian ethnography. In his real métier he is a physical anthropologist, a great advantage to anyone dealing with sociology of procreation. I was naturally interested in his treatment of the puzzle why there are so few illegitimate children among such people as the Aborigines or Trobrianders. In that latter region, for instance, I found that, in spite of a good deal of prenuptial inter-course and the absence of contraceptives, pregnancy of unmarried girls hardly ever occurs. The author gives collateral instances: the observations of Rivers in the Solomon Islands and those of Dr Hogbin in an island off the north coast of New Guinea. Whether Dr Ashley Montagu's physiological solution (pp. 262 *sqq.*) will be final or not, his whole treatment of the subject constitutes an immense advance in our knowledge.

At one or two points of his argument I come in for adverse criticism, which, let me admit at once, is very much to the point. I am accused of inconsistency in my treatment of native beliefs concerning the reproduction of pigs (p. 292, n. 46). I think that Dr Ashley Montagu is completely correct here, and that his discussion of these facts supersedes my analysis.

The other point on which Dr Ashley Montagu criticizes my much earlier treatment of Australian kinship is the 'failure to recognize . . . that there was also the more important non-recognition of such a tie between mother and child' (p. 329). The author is quite correct in maintaining that maternity and paternity are both subject to cultural re-interpretation. I would urge, however, that I did note and comment on this underrating of maternity among some Australian tribes.[2]

At the same time I think that the role of mother and father in reproduction is fundamentally different. This difference may in certain cases be almost obliterated by native belief; the physical significance of maternity ruled out either by the excessive prominence given to paternity in reproduction, or else by animistic ideas. Nevertheless there is the fact that the infant is intimately and for a long time connected with the maternal organism before birth and afterwards, during lactation. This must have permanently influenced all human ideas of kinship. I would still repeat my earlier view that the foundations of the human family are to be found in the biological fact of maternity, and in the social fact that each community assigns a man as the protector and helpmate of a woman during pregnancy and lactation. But this in no way contradicts the general conclusions of the present book (pp. 349–51)—a lucid summary of the results of social anthropology, with Dr Ashley Montagu's own original contribution thrown in.

The last chapter is perhaps the most important, brilliant, and valuable of the whole book. But it is here, in the last round, that I feel tempted to join issue with the author. Perhaps in the process I might even be knocked out, that is, converted.

The author here links up the functional view of social anthropology with the new behaviouristic or monadological school. In discussing traditional experience and belief, the author takes his main stand on the behaviouristic view rather than on that of the functionalist. Culture is taken as the main determinant, not only of belief and mystical attitudes, but also of perception, experience, and common sense. 'We perceive the world according to the kingdom that is within us, and the kingdom that is within us, the content of our minds, is determined by the culture which has constructed and furnished it, hence, what reality is conceived to be is culturally determined . . .' (p. 382). And again, in criticism of 'common sense', which we are told 'does not perhaps have a real but a putative existence', Dr Ashley Montagu writes: 'Common sense represents a process of inference. What the nature of that inference will be depends largely on what happens during the passage of whatever it is that passes through the alembic of the mind . . . Common sense is a culturally conditioned trait' (p. 386).

All this is excellent behaviourism. It is good Lévy-Bruhl. It is all in line with the Margaret Meads and Ruth Benedicts of this modern world. It also is in many ways quite true. There is no doubt that on many points the common sense of a Central Australian differs from that of a New Yorker, and what is perfectly obvious to a Samoyed or Patagonian might appear absurd to a Londoner. In some cases the Londoner and the New Yorker are right, in others they are mistaken. But is there not one distinction to be drawn in order not to confuse the issue? I mean, the distinction between common sense in matters open to observation which are also of practical importance to a community on the one hand; and on the other, such subjects as illness and nutrition, death and birth, love and hate, chance and luck. In these latter the practical issues involved are primarily determined by social organization, by emotional relations between human beings and by factors which lie entirely beyond the limits of rational control.

And then there is the second question. Admittedly, culture determines our mental processes and even our common sense and apperception of fact. But is not culture itself in turn determined by environment, as well as by real categories of human experience and human life? In other words, are there not in every culture universal institutions, certain principles of practical knowledge, certain canons of art and craft which are a norm to every man and woman alive?

The two questions really hang together. A simple survey of ethnographic fact shows that, when it comes to certain aspects of behaviour, men do not differ, whatever their culture, nurture, or level of civilization. No man, woman, or child-once-burnt, pokes his finger into the fire unless he, she, or it wants to be burned. When hungry, human beings, unlike ostriches, do not swallow stones. The most highly civilized European stranded in the deserts of Central Australia would, after his canned goods had been exhausted, have to take lessons from the *lubra* how to use the digging stick in order to gather edible roots or tubers. He would have to be instructed by the men how to catch, prepare, and roast kangaroo or wombat. He would have to learn the relevant chapters of the Australian's unwritten natural history in order to avoid starvation. Common sense and powers of observation, the sense of reality are the same in Australian Aboriginal and sophisticated Westerner alike. What differs are the circumstances of concrete application, the traditional rules derived from this working of universally human common sense within the given circumstances and at a specific level of culture.

Those of us who have followed native agriculture in Melanesia or Africa, taken part in fishing expeditions in the Pacific or the Indian Ocean, or witnessed anywhere hunting or tracking, fire-making or the primitive woman-potter at her work, realize quite well that human knowledge in such matters is correct and precise. Its canons are of a universal validity. Common sense, in the fullest meaning of the word, almost to the verge of scientific refinement, exists among Aborigines when it comes to practical pursuits of a vital nature.

The Australian boomerang obeys the dictates not only of common sense, but of differential calculus. It does so because the Aboriginal has empirically discovered the principles governing the boomerang's flight and embodied them in his tradition of production and use of his implement. Were the native to swerve the fraction of an inch in the making of the boomerang, this would not fly its curved course. The fact that it does, bears witness to the truth that, when it comes to technology, a cultural trait is fully determined by natural conditions and the function which it is meant to fulfil. The same holds true of all technical apparatus and processes, canoes and spear-throwers, methods of making fire and of preparing the soil for cultivation.

Thus it is perhaps going too far to say that in all aspects of human experience and tradition, culture can be considered as an autonomous centre of specific determinism, completely unaffected by the real categories of objective reality and of adequate human behaviour. This emphatically is not the case with regard to those aspects of man's activities where, in a technological process he has to achieve definite practical results by the work of his own hands, legs, and body, and in which his brain acts as the main co-ordinating agency.

Let us turn to the other side of human behaviour. Let us consider how uncertainty, risk, uncontrolled elements, enter forcibly into a situation in which man has to act, not on his knowledge, but in spite of his ignorance. A fleet of perfectly built canoes starts on a fishing expedition, or on a distant trading voyage. All has been well constructed, prepared and foreseen—except, that is, the wind, the weather and the vicissitudes of chance. And there remarkably enough it is again experience which teaches man that here he has no knowledge to use; that he cannot foresee a tornado or a tidal wave; that he can be met with a thunderstorm or be dashed against an unknown reef. Experience teaches him that at this stage of his enterprise, he can only hope and fight against fear; that he has to act on his confidence of success and not on his despair and apprehensions of failure.

This is where knowledge and experience mingle with emotional attitudes. The play of hope against fear, of confidence against apprehension, produces a different type of mental process from that which is at the foundations of primitive knowledge. And we enter here the domain of magic and religion, of moral convictions and ritual activities. Culture here asserts definitely her autonomous power and determinism. We know of some cultures which rely entirely on magic, and others where ancestor-worship provides the dominant note. We know of totemic communities and others controlled by belief in shamanism, by the mythology and ritual of Culture Heroes, or again by the rule of Divine Kings. Yet even here there are certain general principles, certain fundamental realities, which make possible a comparative science of religion and of magic, of ritual and of ethics.

It may be best to apply these general considerations to the Aboriginal ideas about conception and birth. We have to register here two facts: first, exact knowledge about the physiology of birth is to these natives entirely irrelevant; second, neither experience nor common sense, that is, logic, can really be applied to the crucial issue. As regards this last point, the author himself shows conclusively that the Aborigines have not opportunities for relevant observation; that they cannot apply the *experimentum crucis*.

The conditions under which physiological paternity can be easily discovered are those in which marriage takes place rather late in life; girls are kept under strict control after puberty; and chastity is regarded as an essential virtue. Under such conditions a breach of the rule, that is, sexual intercourse of a nubile and unmarried girl, would normally give rise to conception. The discovery of the causal connection would be a matter of common sense experience and logic.

What, on the other hand, would be the conditions under which the discovery of physical paternity would be well-nigh impossible, while the affirmation of social paternity would be the natural outcome of experience and logic? Imagine a community in which girls are not only allowed, but ritually forced to have intercourse before puberty, that is, at a physiological stage where they cannot conceive; and at the same time where at puberty they are made to marry, that is, obtain a sociological father to any child which might appear. In such a community we could almost speak about an artificially set experiment which would force the observers to draw an erroneous inference. Dr Ashley Montagu expresses it cogently. Unequivocally clear facts, well known to everyone, confirm 'the belief . . . that only with marriage can children be born . . . to the Aboriginal . . . intercourse . . . has nothing whatever to do with pregnancy' (p. 389).

The author then proceeds to point out that quickening, which takes place some time after conception, and which is regarded as *the* 'direct and immediate experience' of the entry of a spirit child, is almost inevitably perceived near one of the sacred spots, regarded as the deposit of spirit children. For these spots are so thickly scattered that wherever quickening is perceived a spot nearby can be assigned as its source.

Let us note that Dr Ashley Montagu here uses such words as 'experience', 'common sense', 'observation', and 'knowledge', not in the sense in which he has defined them previously, that is in a sense culturally determined and essentially relativistic. On the contrary, the 'crucible of experience' mentioned on page 388, and all the expressions just enumerated, are used with a meaning almost borrowed from a scientific laboratory.

His whole argument to the very end of the book is conducted on lines, in my opinion, unimpeachably correct, on the assumption, that is, that the powers of observation and reasoning of the aborigines are identical with our own. Their mental equipment is entirely independent of any cultural dictates.

Dr Ashley Montagu's firm belief in absolute common sense, a universally human power of observation and logic, is shown also in his discussion of the fact that in aboriginal Australia pregnancy is first diagnosed by quickening. 'When something enters something else it usually makes the fact quite plainly known immediately, thus, a fly in one's nose, eye, ear, mouth, or any other place, the moment it enters any of these structures it makes its presence known immediately by producing unmistakable sensations . . .' (p. 389). No one would controvert this brief and adequate summary of a whole body of experience to which every man, primitive and civilized, scientific and mystical, has often been subjected. But obviously the author here applies conclusions drawn from human experience in general to that of the Aborigines. He assumes, in fact, that under certain conditions the American girl, the Chinese matron, and the Australian *lubra* react in exactly the same manner, and that this is also the case with any human being with a fly in his nose.

We may ask where does the bee in the bonnet, that, is the specific cultural dictate, come in. It certainly does so, in that culture suggests to the Aboriginal woman that a ready-made spirit child has entered her womb, and does not suggest to her that a male spermatozoon has entered her ovum and fertilized it. In its fullest scientific version of course, this suggestion was made rather late in the development of human knowledge. In a simple form, as the knowledge that intercourse produces pregnancy, the realization is very old. Indeed, as Dr Ashley Montagu has shown in this book, in a very crude, simple, and irrelevant form it exists even in Australia.

And here comes the second point: to the Aborigines an exact knowledge of physical paternity is not relevant. Concern about fatherhood as a physical reality depends, as far as I can see, on the standardized sentiments of sexual jealousy and, in close relation with this, on the emotionally determined value of direct lineage in the male line. The so-called primitive ignorance of paternity is nothing else but a very imperfect knowledge that intercourse is a necessary though not sufficient condition of the woman being 'opened up' as my Trobriand friends put it. This is always combined with some form of animistic superstructure, which in fact we find even in the Christian doctrine of the new soul being created concurrently with the body. The problem therefore is really one of emphasis and value.

In communities where intercourse between anyone except husband and wife is regarded as morally sinful; where infidelity affects the honour of the husband and degrades the woman to the lowest level, the value of chastity and the knowledge of paternity are obviously but two aspects of the same moral dictate. In Semitic cultures, for instance, we have a standardized and institutionalized system of watching the girl before she is married; of documenting her virginity at marriage; of guarding her with extreme care after she is married; and of punishing her for any breach of chastity, married or unmarried. In such a culture the emphasis, to be sure, will not produce an exact embryological knowledge, but certainly an acute interest in the relation between intercourse and pregnancy. In Semitic or Hamitic cultures patriliny and patriarchy are the dominant canons of kinship. It is easy to see that a positive doctrine about the bodily identity, as well as social continuity between father and child, must develop. It would be interesting if the sociologist would turn to such societies and make as minute a study of their overemphasis of paternity as Dr Ashley Montagu and others have made of its disregard in Australia. I venture to foretell that in such communities knowledge in the scientific sense is as much affected by cultural elements and re-interpretations as is the case in Australia.

I hope it is clear by now that I do not minimize the importance of cultural determinism. I only insist upon the distinction between those types of human behaviour where correct knowledge is indispensable for the business of life and those where knowledge must inevitably be affected by emotion, desire, and value. Sexual jealousy belongs to the latter class of human interests. It is a highly complex and often self-contradictory factor, and it has essentially social and emotional foundations. Men and women differ profoundly even within the same culture. One culture as against another can here rule attitudes which in some cases are almost diametrically opposite.

We could exemplify this variety of cultural rulings from the norms obtaining with regard to suicide. This is a virtue, even an absolute duty, to the Japanese nobleman, a sin to a Christian, and a felony under English law. When it comes to the causes and treatment of illness, we have in some cultures the belief in witchcraft and counter-magic; in others a conviction of natural ætiology and trust in scientific treatment. But here again no culture however rationalistic will ever completely banish the craving for miracles and supernatural means of treatment of disease. In our rational moods we in our own culture know that illness is strictly subject to natural determinism. But when medicine fails, we still resort to magic. I am fairly convinced that today, what with Christian Science, faith-healing, the various 'psychological' treatments, not to mention Lourdes, bed-side manner, and the laying on of hands by clerics or Harley Street specialists, we civilized Westerners have as much belief in the non-natural causes and methods of curing illness as any cannibal tribe in Africa, Australia, or Melanesia.

Thus the subject of conception and birth, so deeply entangled in sexual passion, jealousy, and the emotions associated with paternity and maternity, is one where observation and logic have not a fair chance of play. We are dealing here with a human attitude where observation will always be warped by emotions, and logic affected by passion. In contrast to this, we can find, even among the Aborigines, mental attitudes where the native is as rigidly scientific and fully governed by experience and the memories thereof as anyone of us so-called men of science.

In all this, however, I am but restating from a slightly divergent point of view the substance of Dr Ashley Montagu's excellent analysis. The only suggestion that I would like to make to the author is, that perhaps it is not necessary to throw overboard common sense, experience, and logic in order to prove his case. Indeed, in his actual handling of the subject, he does still apply the scientific categories of the human mind to the mental activities of the Aboriginal and to his behaviour. All that he needs to add is that, with an entirely different social organization, common sense in matters of emotional and social concern will necessarily reach somewhat different conclusions from those reached in our culture.

I have already mentioned that in one way the present book may lead to a compromise, or perhaps even more than that, to a cross-fertilization of Functionalism, on the one hand, and on the other, the School who insist on supplementing the rigidly scientific analysis of culture by a more intuitive approach. Some of the arguments, in which I have done nothing more than to restate Dr Ashley Montagu's analyses, may be taken as a specimen of this cross-fertilization. I think Functionalism will be able to vindicate its claims that there is a common measure to all cultures; that there are laws of cultural process, and valid generalizations as to the mutual dependence of the various aspects of culture.

After all, Professor Franz Boas would be the last to disagree with me in the contention that any racial theory which would make the human mind different as from one type of humanity to another, is not scientific. Neither Dr Ashley Montagu nor Dr Ruth Benedict would whole-heartedly subscribe to some of the arguments of Professor Lévy-Bruhl and others who ascribe to the Primitive a somewhat different logic from our own. But if the primitive mind does not differ from ours, then surely in all practical matters, where man constructs and handles tools, or initiates and supervises natural processes, culture will submit to the functional laws which define adequate means by the ends to which they are used. We have therefore one large aspect of culture, the one dealing with man's progressive mastery over his environment, in which determinism controls cultural processes in a way universally human and amenable to scientific laws. And let me be clear. I speak here not only of technology and the beginnings of science, but also of what might be called the economic aspect of civilization, in the widest sense of the word.

Functionalism will perhaps claim yet another sphere for its applicability. It is true that various cultures solve the same problems through different institutions. Thus reproduction is carried on in various forms of family, based on different types of marriage, and associated with dissimilar types of descent and kinship. Nutrition is satisfied through a great range of foods, differently produced, differently prepared, and differently eaten. Safety from enemies, from wild animals, and from the inclemencies of the weather is satisfied by a wide range of dissimilar organizations, methods of protection, and architectonic structures. But the functions which each one of such cultural mechanisms fulfils are comparable. The identity of function in reproductive institutions, for instance, imposes certain conditions which allow us to speak about the human family and human marriage; which make it possible to sum up all the facts of kinship and descent in a brief theoretical account; which in short make possible a general science of social anthropology.

But the Functionalist will, I think, be forced to the recognition of the fact that the concrete contents of each culture have to be defined and described with a fuller measure of artistic and intuitive talent than has often been employed in the past. Anthropology must become more vivid and more real; more concerned with living men and women, rather than with abstraction and mere generalization.

I think also that in the study of Primitive folk-lore and native decorative art, of dancing and of music, we shall find elements which may prove almost completely refractory to scientific analysis and yet will have to be recorded. Here the anthropologist may have to cease to be a mere analytic man of science. He may have to become almost an artist.

From this point of view the dictum of Professor Franz Boas that the work of the anthropologist 'requires a deep penetration into the genius of the culture' receives a new meaning and a new justification. Anthropology, after all, has to deal with human beings. It is almost a truism to say that man cannot be reduced to a mathematical formula—and woman is notoriously even more refractory. The excellent work of Dr Ashley Montagu on a theme equally related to man as to woman, to primitive science and to the emotions of a savage race, has required a treatment in which intuition and scholarship, artistic craftmanship and scientific precision had to be well blended and balanced. The author has acquitted himself of a difficult task in a masterly manner and produced a book of which both the Functional and the Intuitive School can be equally proud.

B. MALINOWSKI

NOTES

1   I have developed this argument briefly in my article 'Culture as a Deter-
     minant of Behaviour' in *Factors Determining Human Behaviour*, Oxford Univer-
     sity Press, 1937; and at greater length in the article 'Culture' in the *Encyclopædia
     of the Social Sciences*, ed. E. R. A. Seligman and A. Johnson.

2   Dr Ashley Montagu recognizes, indeed, that 'Malinowski was not altogether
     unconscious of the possible significance of the facts relating to "maternity"
     in Australia' (p. 330). The reference is to my earliest book, *The Family Among
     the Australian Aborigines*, written 1910–12, published 1913.

Preface to the second edition

This book, originally published in October 1937, has been out of print for many years. Since its publication, much field work has been conducted in Australia and new information made available relating to the procreative beliefs of the Australian Aborigines. This has been incorporated in the present edition. The book has been completely revised and rewritten, and although it has unavoidably increased in bulk, I hope it has improved in quality.

In this book I have not set out either to prove or to disprove anything. What I have been concerned to do is to discover what the facts are, what the various Australian aboriginal peoples really believe(d) about the genesis of babies.

Some Australian aboriginal peoples believed and understood that intercourse was the cause of conception, while others did not. My principal task in this book has been to answer the question: How is it possible that so intelligent a people as the Australian Aborigines can be ignorant of physiological paternity?

What does one mean when one speaks of 'ignorance of physiological paternity'? It is a question that has not always been asked by those who have discussed the subject. It is, therefore, necessary to make quite clear that by 'ignorance of physiological paternity' is meant lack of knowledge of the fact that a particular male is the biological *genitor* of a particular child.

Genitor means *begetter*. In its earlier forms genitor referred solely to the male parent, *genetrix* referring to the female parent. The latter form is now rare, and genitor is now commonly used for both male and female parent. What is implied in the word is that the parents are the biological *generators*, meaning those who cause to come into being, generate, beget, produce, procreate, engender, offspring from the stuff and being of the parents' own material bodies.

My purpose has been to inquire whether it is indeed a fact that, in this sense, there were any aboriginal peoples in Australia who had no knowledge of physiological parentage. And, to repeat what I have already said, if such peoples did exist, since they were far from unintelligent, what could possibly be the explanation of their apparent ignorance of so 'obvious' a connection? In the attempt to throw some light on these matters it has become clear that the concepts of biological and social parenthood are two quite different things, and that while in some human societies the first may not be recognized the other always is. The fact is that all classificatory or kinship terms and relationships are social. Such socially based and structured conceptions of relationship are, in fact, less arbitrary than is the decision to make biological parentage the basis for all kinship and classificatory relationships.

When, in the civilized world, whether they are married or not, persons—legally or not—adopt a child, they become the parents of that child by *social parenthood*. The important relationship between parent and child is not biological but social. This is true in every society, no matter whether or not it chooses to emphasize biological kinship, for the significant human relations between human beings are social, not biological. The biological consequences of their relations flow from their social, not their biological, interactions. Biology may influence, but it does not determine the social arrangements which any social group creates for itself.* Generation is one thing, parenthood is another. No matter who the genitor may be, the father of the child is the husband of the woman who gave it birth. That is a *social* fact, not a biological one.

In societies in which biological parentage is understood and recognized the kinship system is usually based on the biological relationships arising from the union of husband and wife. But kinship systems of the most elaborate kind are quite possible without any knowledge of biological relationships.

In approaching the study of Australian kinship beliefs we must avoid the error of attempting to see them through the distorting glass of our own idea of kinship relations; we must try to see them through the eyes of the Aborigines themselves. Having done that we can bring our own critical apparatus to bear upon the examination of what is in this way perceived.

It was my original intention to publish as an Appendix, with their kind permission, Dr Edmund Leach's Henry Myers Lecture on 'Virgin birth', together with the replies to this. Unfortunately, budgetary conditions have made this impossible. Had I been aware of this impediment I would have discussed this material in the body of the book. As it is, I can only urge the reader to consult these valuable contributions for himself. They are the following:

Edmund Leach, 'Virgin birth', *Proc. RAI*, 1966, 39–49; Melford E. Spiro, 'Virgin birth, parthenogenesis and physiological paternity: an essay in cultural interpretation', *Man*, n.s. 3, 1968, 242–61; P. M. Kaberry, 'Virgin birth', *Man*, n.s. C, 1968, 311–13; E. G. Schwim-

* Ashley Montagu (ed.), *Culture: Man's Adaptive Dimension*, Oxford University Press, 1968.

mer, 'Virgin birth', *Man*, n.s. 4, 1969, 132–3; P. J. Wilson, 'Virgin birth', *Man*, n.s. 4, 1969, 286–7.

I owe many thanks to my editor, Mrs C. J. Raab, for the skill with which she handled a difficult manuscript. To Dr Philip Gordon I am indebted for his careful reading of the proofs.

I am grateful to the following authors and publishers for permission to quote copyright material: C. P. Mountford and Angus & Robertson (Publishers) Pty Ltd, *Brown Men and Red Sand*; Blackie & Son Limited, J. R. B. Love, *Stone Age Bushmen of To-day*; Harper & Row, Publishers, Inc., W. L. Warner, *A Black Civilization*; Phyllis M. Kaberry, *Aboriginal Woman, Sacred and Profane;* Oceania Publications, C. P. Mountford, A. Harvey, and Andreas Lommel; The University of Chicago Press, M. J. Meggitt, *Desert People*; The University of Washington Press, J. C. Goodale, *Tiwi Wives*; C. M. and R. M. Berndt and the Wenner-Gren Foundation for Anthropological Research, *Sexual Behavior in Western Arnhem Land*.

ASHLEY MONTAGU

Princeton, N.J.

Preface

There is probably no more difficult subject in the whole field of the anthropology of the lower races than that concerning the ideas they have about the phenomena of generation and conception.—R. KARSTEN, *The Civilization of the American Indians*, 1929, 414.

In the spring of 1929, at the suggestion of Professor Bronislaw Malinowski, and the kindly connivance of Professor Edward Westermarck, I was persuaded to read a paper at the latter's seminar in Cultural Anthropology at the London School of Economics, which was afterwards published in the *Realist* (October 1929) under the title 'The Procreative Theories of Primitive Man'. This essay, according to some of my friends, should more properly have been entitled 'The Sexual Life of Neanderthal Man'! In that paper I very briefly considered the types of ideas and beliefs which various primitive peoples held concerning the process of coming into being. Having classified them I cursorily proceeded to discuss those theories or beliefs in which the procreative process appeared to be in no way associated in any causal manner with the act of coition. My purpose was to show, in the short time at my disposal, that the ignorance of the relationship between coitus and conception exhibited by such peoples as the Australian Aborigines and the Trobriand Islanders of North-western Melanesia was a perfectly comprehensible one, and perfectly compatible with all that was comprised within the native's own experience. My paper was very kindly received, and naturally the presence of both Professor Westermarck and Professor Malinowski—whose own book on the *Sexual Life of Savages* was just then off the press—made the discussion which followed a very lively one. It was, however, evident to me from this discussion that a fully worked out, though more narrowly concentrated, account of the subject of my paper would be well worth undertaking, and I therefore resolved as soon as circumstances would permit, to embark upon such a study. Academic duties and somewhat more urgent studies in other fields have, however, prevented me from acting upon that resolve until the present time. Now that I have completed this study it is obvious why it should be dedicated to Professors Westermarck and Malinowski, two scholars who were my first preceptors in Cultural Anthropology.

Professor Westermarck, more than a quarter of a century ago, in a prefatory note to a now classical work by G. C. Wheeler, *The Tribe and Intertribal Relations in Australia*, wrote:

Next to sociological field work . . . there are, within this branch of study, no other investigations so urgently needed as monographs on some definite class of social phenomena or institutions among a certain group of related tribes. A comparative treatment of some social institution as it exists throughout the uncivilized races of the world undoubtedly has its value. It bears out general resemblances as well as local and racial differences. It also, in many cases, enables the specialist to explain facts which he could hardly understand in full if his knowledge were restricted to a limited area. But at the same time the comparative study suffers from certain defects which seem to be wellnigh inseparable from the prosecution of so great a task. A social institution is not an isolated phenomenon, but is closely connected with a variety of facts. It is largely influenced by local conditions, by the physical environment, by the circumstances by which the people in question lives, by its habits and mental characteristics. All these factors can properly be taken into account when the investigation is confined to a single people or one ethnic unity.

Following the principles laid down in this passage, there appeared in 1913, Professor Malinowski's admirable study, *The Family Among the Australian Aborigines*. Since that time both Professor Malinowski and his students have from a similar viewpoint investigated a variety of social phenomena in Oceania and in Africa, with the most fruitful results.[1]

In the present work a single 'social phenomenon' as it is found expressed in a single 'ethnic unity', namely, among the Australian aborigines, is investigated in detail. The social phenomenon is here represented by the procreative beliefs of the Australians, their doctrines and the beliefs which they hold concerning the nature of what we call conception and pregnancy. In short the process of coming into being, their embryology.

Ever since the publication in 1899 of Spencer and Gillen's *The Native Tribes of Central Australia*, in which it was for the first time made known that there were aboriginal peoples in existence in Australia that possessed no knowledge whatever of the relationship existing between coitus and pregnancy, there has been a great deal of discussion concerning the nature of this ignorance. By some, like Professor Westermarck,[2] or Professor Carveth Read,[3] the reality of this alleged nescience has been virtually denied, while others, like Andrew Lang, have admitted the existence of the nescience, but have considered that it represents a purely secondary structure developed in accommodation to certain cultural requirements. There have been other theories too, and there has been some disagreement concerning the actual state of the beliefs held by particular tribes or hordes, so that there exists at the present time not a little confusion and a great deal of uncertainty concerning the real nature of the pro-creative beliefs held by the native tribes of Australia. In the present study an attempt has been made to gather together all the available evidence which in any way bears upon the procreative beliefs of the Australian Aborigines, and to subject that evidence to an examina-tion which may serve to provide an accurate estimate of the real nature of those beliefs.

Naturally, the bare examination of the beliefs themselves would hardly be sufficient to render an understanding of their character more than superficial. The wresting of such a belief from its cultural, that is to say, its functional context, and the study of it as an isolate would be to do violence to it, as if one were to attempt to study the physiology of an organ dissociated from the body of which it is a part. In the present work the ideas of the Australian Aborigines concerning procreation are studied in relation to the culture of which they form an integral part. Fortunately the Aborigines are both culturally and physically distinguished in rather more than a general way by a relative homogeneity, an 'ethnic unity', which greatly simplifies the task of the student of these matters. Moreover, their physical environment, not excepting the coastal as compared with the inland tribes, is relatively much the same. There may be more vegetation and water in one region than in another, but within a certain range of variation the sunlight and temperature,[4] the rocky formation of the land, and the kinds of plant and animal life are to a large extent similar. To study a belief or group of beliefs in relation to the culture of which it forms a part to the exclusion of any con-sideration of the framework, the environment, in which that culture functions, would be, in the present connection at any rate, to deprive oneself of many valuable aids in the attempt to throw some light upon the various problems which we shall have to consider, if not to commit a fault so egregious as the study of the belief apart from its cultural context. The conditions under which cultural events come into being and are developed and integrated, may or may not reflect the influence of environmental factors, but however this may be, the investigator cannot afford to neglect their study in relation to such events. This is particularly the case in the present inquiry where the biological and physical factors, even though the most strictly perti-nent of them may not be consciously recognized by the natives themselves, provide the materials out of which, upon the woof of imagination and myth, their beliefs are woven. These elements. in-deed, in their larger extension form the greater part of the native's physical environment, the rocky promontories, the water-holes, the rivers, the sea, the winds, and the clouds. And there is, of course, the person himself, and all other persons, and the variegated natural phenomena of life associated with them. All these things, and more, are intimately and virtually indissolubly bound up with the social life of the Aborigines so that the study of any single trait must necessarily involve the study of both its cultural and physical relationships, the whole system of related co-ordinates, as it were, of which that trait is but a single ordinate.

While I have endeavoured to assemble all the available data having any bearing upon the procreative beliefs of the Aborigines, I have, of course, been most concerned to arrive at its correct meaning. The observations here brought together have for the most part been taken from the accounts of first-hand observers, and as far as possible, an attempt has been made to present them in the order in which they were first reported and in relation to the territories concerning the tribes of which they were made. Thus, the central tribes are treated first, the northern next, and so on. In this way the historical as well as the geographical relations of the evidence may be seen in some sort of perspective. In discussing the observations reported by so many observers it has been quite impossible to put each one into the framework of the particular culture in which it functions, but as I have already pointed out, the relatively great cultural homogeneity of the aboriginal tribes of the Australian continent helps to simplify matters very considerably, for in virtue of this relative cultural unity it has been possible to take a single tribal culture as a type for the greater part of Australia, and having described it, treat of its procreative doctrines and beliefs in relation to that culture. Concurrently, without directly referring to them, it will become apparent how the similar beliefs of each tribe must similarly function within the context of their own culture.

The culture which I have selected as most typical is that of the Arunta of the Alice Springs district of Central Australia. The reason for this choice will become clear in the text. With the description of that culture in outline, the observations as given in the various accounts of our authorities concerning the beliefs relating to conception held by a large variety of Australian tribes are then presented in the manner already indicated. These observations are then summarized and examined in relation to the critical literature which has grown up about them.

The critical examination of all those objections which have from time to time been urged by different students of the subject against the too-ready acceptance as a fact of the *real* ignorance of many Australian tribes concerning the allegedly obvious facts of procreation occupies a large portion of the second part of this volume. This examination has involved the consideration of the biological, physical, and demographic evidence, and also the analysis of certain time-honoured theories, which are, in these connections, currently accepted by many ethnologists.

In a final chapter I have made an attempt at an analysis of the psychological background of the procreative beliefs of the Aborigines, of the mechanics by means of which these beliefs are maintained, and of the apperceptive processes which make the reception of the ideas involved not only easily possible, but necessary and inevitable. My procedure has been, as far as possible, to allow the facts to speak out boldly and unprejudicedly for themselves. I have, of course, endeavoured to bring the relevant facts into proper relation with one another in order that the effective meaning of the events they represent may be unambiguously understood. Beyond what the facts themselves have rendered cogent I have not thought it necessary to go.

Evolutionary generalizations concerning the facts discussed have for the most part been avoided, not that there is in principle any objection to such generalizations, but because in a work which is primarily devoted to the purely objective historical study of the facts as they exist in one fairly homogeneous cultural group there can be no room for such speculations.

Whether there exists evidence in the beliefs and myths of other peoples which indicate that they, too, were at one time ignorant of the facts of procreation, is a matter which falls outside the scope of the present volume. Sir Sidney Hartland very fully dealt with this aspect of the subject in his *Primitive Paternity*. The reader interested in the evolutionary treatment of the procreative beliefs of mankind is recommended to consult that work, and also the earlier work by the same author, *The Legend of Perseus*. In the first chapter of this book, however, in presenting the historical background of the events which have led to this study, a conspectus of the subject is taken which necessarily makes clear its broad evolutionary implications, and in chapter X the subject is briefly touched upon.

It must be understood from the outset that the procreative beliefs of the Aborigines represent but a special case of the belief in supernatural birth, a belief which assumes a large variety of forms and has a wellnigh universal distribution. The general structure of the Aborigines' beliefs is by no means unique or peculiar to them, but what is peculiar to them is the emphasis which is placed upon certain elements and the total lack of emphasis associated with other elements in that structure. These matters we shall consider in some detail.

It is perhaps necessary for me to state here that in this book I have no particular axe to grind nor any method of procedure to vindicate, unless it be the method of the objective historical investigator who observes, uncovers contradictions, resolves them, states the facts, analyses and classifies them, and presents the most probable conclusions to be drawn from them. By the use of such processes as these, errors of judgment can arise only either from the limitation of the person making use of them or from the limitation of the material itself. In the present instance the material available is, on the whole, as satisfactory as one has a right to expect, so that any shortcomings in its treatment, and unhappily I am aware that there are many, must be laid entirely at the author's door.

In quoting from the original sources in the pages which follow, I have adhered strictly to the author's text; no attempt has been made to reduce the spelling of native names and terms to a uniform scheme, each author is allowed to give his own rendering of native words—the resulting differences will not cause the reader a moment's trouble. Phonetic signs have, however, been reduced to their common equivalents.

To Professor Franz Boas and particularly to Professor Ruth Benedict, both of the Department of Anthropology, Columbia University, I owe thanks for a number of valuable criticisms and suggestions which have served to make this book a far better one than it would otherwise have been, but who, it must be said—in the time-honoured but very necessary disclaimer—are not responsible for views with which they may well disagree.

To Professor Bronislaw Malinowski, my teacher and friend, I am indebted for the original stimulus which led me to undertake the present work, and I am particularly grateful to him for the excellent Foreword which he has contributed to this volume.

Thanks are due to the following publishers for permission to quote lengthy excerpts from the works published by them: Macmillan and Co., Ltd, London, Spencer and Gillen's *The Arunta* and *The Native Tribes of Central Australia*, B. Spencer's *Native Tribes of the Northern Territory of Australia*, A. W. Howitt's *The Native Tribes of South-East Australia*, and Horne and Aiston's *Savage Australia*; Mrs Herbert Basedow and F. W. Preece and Sons, Adelaide, Herbert Basedow's *The Australian Aboriginal;* George Routledge and Sons, Ltd, B. Malinowski's *The Sexual Life of Savages*. I am also greatly obliged to the editors and publishers of the scientific journals from which I have allowed myself to quote freely.

ASHLEY MONTAGU

East Jaffrey, N. H.
13 *June*—18 *August* 1935
18 *June* 1937

NOTES

1 B. Malinowski, *Argonauts of the Western Pacific*, London, 1922; *The Sexual Life of Savages; Coral Gardens and their Magic*, London, 1935; R. Firth, *Primitive Economics of the New Zealand Maori*, London, 1929; I. Hogbin, *Law and Order in Polynesia*, London, 1934; R. F. Fortune, *The Sorcerers of Dobu; Manus Religion*; L. Mair, *An African People in the Twentieth Century*, London, 1934; H. Powdermaker, *Life in Lesu*, London, 1934; Audrey I. Richards, *Hunger and Work in a Savage Tribe*, London, 1932; and numerous others.

2 'I must confess that I have some doubts as to the present existence of any savage tribe where childbirth is considered to be completely independent of sexual intercourse.' *History of Human Marriage*, i, 293.

3 'No paternity', *JRAI*, 48, 1918, 146–50.

4 C. E. P. Brooks, *Climate*, 154–62.

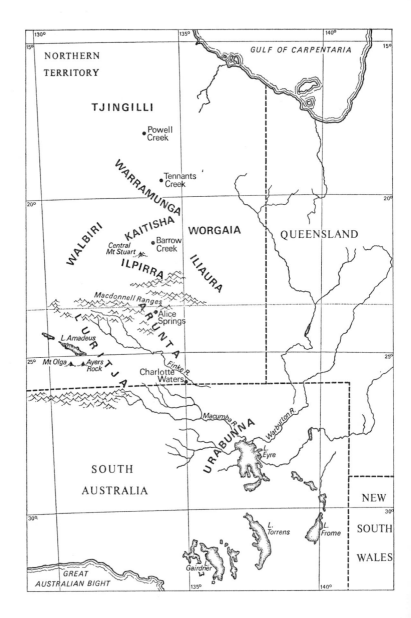

1 Outline map of Central Australia

CHAPTER I

Introduction

I have never myself imagined that any amount of evidence of law or usage written or observed, would by itself solve the problems which cluster round the beginnings of human society.—SIR HENRY MAINE, *Dissertations on Early Law and Custom*, p.205.

In the first volume of his book *The Legend of Perseus* which appeared in 1894, in which the 'world-wide-story-incident of Supernatural Birth' was examined, Hartland made the suggestion that the myths, stories, superstitions, and incidents relating to supernatural birth originated during that period in the development of human society when the physical relationship between father and child was imperfectly understood, or rather, not understood at all. The suggestion thus made represented a conjecture based upon a large number of accounts of almost universal provenience relating to the belief in supernatural birth. Finding this belief so widely distributed, Hartland further conjectured that it must also at one time have been common to all mankind.[1] Both these conjectures were stated in the form of suggestions or hypotheses, which, with the progress of knowledge, it was supposed might some day receive either proof or disproof. Reasoning of this kind was in the best tradition of the evolutionary school of thought. The methods of thought and investigation which had yielded such rich results with respect to the problem of the origin of species could not fail, it was considered, to be equally fruitful and revealing when applied to problems relating to the origin and development of social institutions. Animal and social structures were regarded as amenable to the same methods of analysis, such differences as they exhibited were thought to be due solely to the differences inherent in the materials from which they were constructed, and in the different organization of that material. In short, the world presented series of recurring phenomena which, allowing for the differences in their structural bases, differed from one another only in respect of the degree of complexity of their organization. The method which had so efficiently solved the problem of organization and development in one field could, it was considered, surely be relied upon to solve the same problem in all other fields. Those who thought thus committed the error of mistaking the result or effect of a method for the method itself, for the *principle* of evolution is not a method, but a generalization of great heuristic value. Darwin, to whom we owe it, arrived at it by means of a vast number of objective circumstantially detailed *historical* observations, which when fitted together gave him his generalization of evolution. The method he used was the method which all those whose work is based upon the observation of facts must use, the objective historical method, which, in brief, consists first of the collection and ordered arrangement of detailed observations of *facts*, the statement of these, and only secondarily, in the analysis of their meaning. After 1859 (when *On the Origin of Species* was published), evolution became a catchword, a phrase, and finally a method, *the evolutionary method*, so that even to-day it is still not unusual to find prominent thinkers speaking and writing of 'the evolutionary method'. But there never was such a thing. No single method applied to the solution of problems so diverse has been as successful as the method used by Darwin in arriving at his generalization of evolution. In the past this has been particularly true of the problems of the experimental sciences, sciences which have become experimental chiefly because they were informed by the heuristic principles of the evolutionary theory. Nineteenth-century sociologists grasping the immense significance of the *result* of Darwin's method, the principle of evolution, but not the method by which it was arrived at, at once set about showing that human societies had evolved in the same or in a similar manner as animal species. Their method in a sense was indeed evolutionary, for it consisted in forcing all social facts into a framework which would conform with their conceptions of evolution. This practice, of course, may now be recognized as an example of the manner in which the cart should not be put in relation to the horse.* In the social sciences, including ethnology, the use of the so-called 'evolutionary method' has had the effect of stimulating speculation and argumentation about ideas and theories upon the basis of generalization rather than upon the solid groundwork of fact. Since in the social sciences the experimental control of the material is for the most part impossible, it was easy for generalization to take the place of experiment and, in most cases, of fact itself. By the end of the nineteenth century this type of ratiocination had become so endeared to the hearts of thinkers like Herbert Spencer that Huxley could justly remark of them that their idea of a tragedy was a beautiful theory killed by an ugly fact! The great error of such thinkers, it is now obvious, was the assumption that the development of social structures proceeded upon the same mechanistic lines as animal evolution, development, and growth; that every society represented some stage in the process of this development, the exact progression of which could be determined upon analysis, and that human nature being everywhere the same, similar stimuli were naturally productive of similar responses. Upon the basis of such

---

* Or as wittily remarked by one critic of the manner in which the evolution of the horse was misconstructed, 'putting the chart before the horse'.

ideas it was possible to provide a complete picture of the origin, evolution, and development of human society, for all that was necessary was the eclectic selection of the pertinent facts from the literature descriptive of particular social groups, and the synthesis of these facts drawn from every quarter of the globe into one unified whole, as if one were dealing with stone artifacts. The works of Herbert Spencer, and later of Sir James Frazer, are excellent examples of this type of linear methodology. Supported by an encyclopædic range of facts, they presented a composite picture of the evolution of society, as it were, in a continuous straight line. In reality human societies are characterized by the discontinuity of their development, by a diversity of development which makes their equation to any one common pattern quite impossible.[2] Even the forms of expression of what we call human nature are seen to differ according to the societies in which they function.[3] To lump such discontinuities together and to attempt to educe an evolutionary line of development from them is to obscure the existence of the fact that at whatever comparable levels of cultural development we may take them societies differ from one another enormously, and present a virtually infinite variety of patterns.

There are no universal laws governing the development and progress of human societies, and there are no inherently determined stages of development through which they must necessarily pass. The forms of societies are for the most part the product of accidental factors, and in this sense every society is a law unto itself, and as such it must be studied. Before everything else then, each society must be investigated as a whole in itself, and not from the outset merely as a part of an assumed greater whole, namely world culture. In truth, there is no world culture, but only culture 'worlds', each of which calls for specific investigation, without benefit of so-called heuristic general laws into the framework of which each culture may be made to fit. When we have completed our specific studies, only then may it be possible to bring them together as so many clues towards the solution of the problem of the growth and development of cultures.

It is quite impossible to say of any society that because it now displays certain traits in some particular connection it must therefore, at some earlier time, have displayed some other trait, one perhaps more primitive than those now existing. Thus, to return to the reason for this preamble, Hartland's suggestion that the wide distribution of the beliefs relating to supernatural birth indicates the prior existence of a nescience of the physical relationship between father and child, and that this nescience must once have been common to all mankind, cannot be proven by an appeal to any group of cultural facts. Nor is there anything in such cultural facts which would justify the assumption that such a nescience necessarily represents a primitive stage in the development of ideas concerning the nature of conception. Indeed, as we shall see in a later chapter, the very opposite has with some force been argued.

When, however, Spencer and Gillen published their great work, *The Native Tribes of Central Australia*, in 1899, and for the first time made it known that the tribes investigated by them possessed no knowledge of the relationship between coitus and pregnancy,[4] Hartland felt that his suggestion of a few years earlier had been thoroughly substantiated.

Not long after the publication of Spencer and Gillen's work there appeared in January 1903 W. E. Roth's famous *Bulletin* no. 5,[5] in which a similar nescience of the relationship between coitus and pregnancy was described for certain of the tribes of North Queensland.

In the following year Spencer and Gillen published their work on *The Northern Tribes of Central Australia*,[6] in which the same nescience was demonstrated for the more northern of the Central Australian tribes.

The same year, 1904, witnessed the appearance of A. W. Howitt's long-awaited study, *The Native Tribes of South-East Australia*, a work of the first importance, but recounting disappointingly little concerning the native beliefs relating to conception. There were, however, a few statements which stirred the curiosity, and which doubtless suggested rather more than their author thought fit for them to do. Like so many of the early ethnological observers, Howitt, in all matters that touched upon the sexual life of the natives, preserved a scrupulous silence.

In the early part of 1905 Mrs K. Langloh Parker's delightful book on *The Euahlayi Tribe* of north-western New South Wales made its appearance with an introduction by Andrew Lang. In this introduction Lang briefly discussed Mrs Parker's findings concerning the conceptional beliefs of the Euahlayi in relation to the conceptional beliefs of the Arunta.

In September of the same year appeared Sir J. G. Frazer's arresting article on conceptional totemism among the Australian Aborigines.[7]

Later in the same year Andrew Lang's *The Secret of the Totem* made its appearance. In this book a chapter was devoted to a critical discussion of the conceptional beliefs of the Arunta in connection with Frazer's then newly postulated theory of conceptional totemism which had appeared only a few weeks before the publication of Lang's book. This and related matters were further discussed by Lang in an article which appeared still later in the same year.[8]

Early in 1906, Hartland reviewed Lang's book,[9] in which though he found much to admire in Lang's handling of his theme, he also discovered much with which he could not agree. To the criticisms made in this review, Lang replied in the next issue of the journal in which they were published.[10]

In the same year Mrs Daisy M. Bates published an interesting account of some Western Australian tribes, and briefly described some of their beliefs relating to conception.[11]

In this year was also published A. van Gennep's *Mythes et légendes d'Australie*, and also an article by the same author,[12] in both of which works the ideas of the Australians relating to conception were discussed. Van Gennep's book was made the subject of a very critical review shortly after its appearance by Andrew Lang.[13] To this review van Gennep made a spirited reply,[14] which served to elicit an equally spirited rejoinder from Lang.[15]

In 1907 appeared the first part of a work on the Arunta and Luritja of Central Australia, by Carl Strehlow, a Lutheran missionary stationed at the Hermannsburg Mission.[16] In this work certain of Spencer and Gillen's statements concerning the nature of the Arunta nescience of the procreative processes were seriously questioned, for Strehlow could not obtain any confirmatory evidence from his informants in support of these statements. Mortiz von Leonhardi, the editor of the greater part of Strehlow's work, had already discussed some of these matters in the light of Strehlow's communications to him in an article earlier in the same year.[17]

Also in this year appeared the original communications of Basedow,[18] and H. Klaatsch,[19] descriptive of the beliefs held by the native tribes of the Northern Territory of Australia, and also a general discussion of great originality by Andrew Lang of the Aboriginal conceptional beliefs.[20]

In 1908 the missionary, Jos. Bischofs, very briefly, reported upon the conceptional beliefs of the Nyul-Nyul of north-west Australia,[21] and in the same year W. Schmidt published a discussion of the Aranda notions of conception.[22]

Extending between the years 1904 to 1908, a series of interesting papers describing the conceptional beliefs of various Australian tribes was published by R. H. Mathews in various journals.[23]

In the light of these important contributions relating to the conceptional beliefs of the Australian Aborigines, as well as much other material of a similar nature but of a less striking kind, descriptive of the similar beliefs held by other peoples, Hartland, in 1909, was able to publish the first volume of his study of *Primitive Paternity*, in which he ventured to lay before the reader the case for the conjecture which he had made some sixteen years earlier in *The Legend of Perseus*.[24]

The beliefs [wrote Hartland], customs, and institutions of tribes in a low degree of civilization are our only clue to those of a more archaic condition no longer extant. They are evolved from them, and are in the last resort the outgrowth of ideas which underlay them. When, therefore, we find a belief, a custom, or an institution—still more when we find a connected series of beliefs, customs, and institutions—overspreading the lower culture we may reasonably infer its root in the ideas common to mankind and native to the primitive ancestral soil. The inference is greatly strengthened if vestigial forms are also found embedded in the culture of the higher races. It is raised to a certainty if unambiguous expression of the ideas themselves can be discovered to-day among the lower races. The advance of even the most backward from primeval savagery has been so great that a large harvest of these ideas is not to be expected. But the researches of the last few years have yielded enough, it is hoped, to afford a satisfactory solution of, among others, the problem under consideration in these volumes.[25]

During the years which have passed since Hartland's *Primitive Paternity* was published a great deal of evidence bearing upon the subject of the procreative ideas of primitive peoples has accumulated, and numerous general discussions of this evidence in relation to such problems as the origin of totemism, mother-right, father-right, kinship, and the family, have appeared. Professor Malinowski's full and illuminating accounts of the Trobriand Islanders' ignorance of the relationship between coitus and pregnancy have served to draw a certain amount of attention to the subject, resulting in many discussions of interest and value. Also Professor Radcliffe-Brown's important studies and those of his students on the social organization of Australian tribes have thrown a flood of light upon an extraordinarily large number of matters of interest in our present connection which had previously been either erroneously understood or not understood at all. In the present study advantage will be taken of all this new material in the attempt to discover what the nature of Aboriginal procreative beliefs is, and how those beliefs function in their particular context. There is a mistaken notion widely prevalent in ethnological circles to the effect that the Aborigines' nescience of the causal relationship between coitus and pregnancy takes the form merely of an ignorance or nescience of the physical relationship between father and child. In many regions this is indeed the case, but in quite a large number of other regions the truth is that a very real endeavour is made to recognize the physical father, whereas the status of the physical mother is reduced to that of a wet-nurse, a sort of convenient medium for the transmission of the incarnated or reincarnated individual into the tribe, but a person who actually, that is in socially construed physical actuality, plays no more part in the production and formation of that individual than a wet-nurse would. But what is of far greater importance is the widely distributed belief in other parts of Australia that *neither malen or female parent contributes anything whatever of a physical or spiritual nature to the being of the child.* Thus, the whole process of maternity is esteemed to be a rather secondary matter upon both these views. Actually the existence of physiological maternity as well as of physiological paternity is, as such, ignored. As we shall see in a later chapter, the allegedly obvious relationship between mother and child is not as obvious to many Australian Aborigines as it is to ourselves, not because there is any biological difference between the two groups, but because there is a very profound social difference, the psychological effects of which render such a relationship very far from being obvious to the natives.

It should at once be apparent that the view of the maternal processes which such notions lead to must have very wide implications indeed, yet because the actual evidence has been neglected in favour of catchwords and time-honoured clichés like the phrase *ignorance of physiological paternity*, discussions and controversies respecting the priority of mother-right and father-right have been able to enjoy a licence as broad and as long as the whole range of the unbridled human imagination would allow, without once approaching, be it said, to within a really fact-proof theory, one, that is, which could withstand the test of the facts as they are available to us. But these are matters which will be discussed in a later chapter. Here it is important to point out that the usage of such a phrase as 'the ignorance of physiological paternity' as a universal to denote what are supposed to be the conditions as they are found in Aboriginal Australia is a procedure which in view of the facts is both invalid and incorrect, as well as misleading, for it obscures such pertinently fundamental facts as the existence of the concept of non-biological maternity as well as non-biological paternity. What precisely the meaning of this last statement is cannot be fully comprehended until the whole of the evidence has been considered, although it should be evident from what has already been said that if there exists a nescience of the biological relationship between mother and child, or an underestimation of that relationship of such a character as to render it as a notion virtually non-existent, the whole concept of the biological family as it is usually understood must fall to the ground, for it should be apparent that the actual biological family is always at best no more than it is socially allowed to be. The so-called biological family among the Australian Aborigines is, as we shall have occasion to see, simply a socially determined group, and never more than that. If all this is true, it will readily be seen that the foundations of almost every theory of mother-right that has ever been propounded must quickly collapse, for all such theories are based primarily upon the purely hypothetical notion that the primordial family consisted essentially only of mother and child, for the reason that the relationship between mother and child was inescapably obvious in the physical system of correlates terminating with parturition whereas between father and child there exists no such immediately observable physical system of correlates.[26] As Maine put it, maternity is matter of observation, paternity matter of inference.[27] The truth is, however, that what is matter of observation and what matter of inference depends not upon the matter itself, but upon the character of the perception by means of which it is apprehended. What in one framework of reference is matter of observation becomes in another framework matter of mediate inference, and vice versa.[28] Observation and inference are not innate faculties of the mind, but highly cultivated formal processes which are in all societies developed along the lines laid down by, and in conformity with, the cultural pattern, and as the patterns differ so will the nature, the character, of these processes. When, for example, an Australian Aboriginal observes his totem animal and asserts that 'He same as me',[29] what he means is that there exists a very close physical relationship between himself and that animal. It is a kangaroo and so, too is he a kangaroo. When questioned he will maintain that physically he resembles the kangaroo, and that he can recognize the totem affiliation of any member of his tribe at once since each individual in some way resembles the animal or plant with which he is totemically identified. This fact of observation (or is it inference?) is by no means surprising since it is upon every hand supported by a cultural framework which renders it necessary. Individuals are something more than mere units in an aggregate of persons, each one possesses a certain distinct individuality which he owes chiefly to the totemic class to which he belongs, and which serves to distinguish him from other members of the tribe, and, at the same time, to identify him with a certain group of individuals of the same totemic group.[30] The individuality thus bestowed upon each member of the tribe becomes matter of observation and not of inference, for to the Aboriginal it is something which is immediately given in experience, something that is more often than not known to every member of the tribe long before the individual is born, for from the moment the woman feels herself with child the totemic place from which the child emanated and entered her is generally quickly settled, so that even before the child is born it is recognized to belong to a particular totemic group and none other by every member of the tribe. In all this there is nothing very remarkable; these facts merely illustrate

8

the point that what matter of observation or inference shall be is simply culturally determined. It will be shown, however, and this is a matter of the first importance, that observation and inference are processes which are not, among the Aborigines, organized upon the same plan that our own formal systems of valid reasoning demand. This is not to say that the Australian Aboriginal is a being mentally inferior to ourselves or that he is incapable of our particular kind of reasoning, or that he has a pre-logical mentality, or what not. The facts point clearly in the opposite direction, namely that the Australian Aboriginal native endowment is quite as good as the European's, if not better. In support of the latter statement there exists a certain amount of evidence of the weightiest kind, such, for example, as the opinions of observers who have lived among them for many years and who are not by any means inclined to be prejudiced in their favour.[31] Then there is the more direct evidence of the effects of schooling, the rapidity with which the native learns, and, what is more important, the consistency with which he generally maintains that learning, as is abundantly borne out by such a fact as the achievement of a school in Victoria whose scholars comprised entirely Aborigines, and which for three successive years was ranked as the highest standing school, from the point of view of scholarship, in Australia.[32] The ease with which the natives acquire good English when it is spoken to them as compared with the difficulty with which the white man acquires the native language has often been remarked upon by white observers.[33] Such a fact as that a pure-blooded Aboriginal who had learnt to play the game of draughts, by watching over the shoulders of players engaged in the game, who in 1926 decisively beat the ex-draughts champion of Australia in a series of matches, is also worth mentioning.[34] Instances of this kind could be greatly multiplied. Finally, there is the evidence of the intelligence tests which point strongly to an excellent native mental endowment.[35] So far as the evidence goes there can be little doubt that in the Australian Aborigines we are dealing with a group of mankind which is endowed by nature with a brain that is exceptionally good, so that such differences and peculiarities of mental functioning as the Aboriginal exhibits from the standpoint of civilized man must be accounted as due to nurture rather than nature, to culture rather than biology. As Professor A. A. Abbie has stated: 'Given equal opportunity, the average aborigine is quite the equal of the average European.'[36]

The processes of ratiocination which our own kind of thought demands differ from those of the Aborigines because the demands of their particular kind of organized thought differ from ours. It is quite as simple as that. The operations and processes of thought are determined by the nature of each culture, and ideas have their existence chiefly as cultural artifacts. Perception, the *meaning* with which we invest the sensation which we experience, is the instrument as well as the raw material of thought, and what meaning each sensation shall have is rigorously determined by the universe of thought, the social structure, into which the individual is born. Our percepts are as culturally determined as our institutions. In different cultures the identical experiences are responded to in quite different ways because the perceptual background against which they are evaluated differs according to what is considered obligatory in each culture.

The difference in the mode of thought of primitive man and that of civilized man [writes Boas] seems to consist largely in the difference of character of the traditional material with which the new perception associates itself. The instruction given to the child of primitive man is not based on centuries of experimentation, but consists of the crude experience of generations. When a new experience enters the mind of primitive man, the same process which we observe among civilized man brings about an entirely different series of associations, and therefore results in a different type of explanation.[37]

The conception of the relativity of mind, of mind as a function and dependable variable of culture, is indispensable for a proper understanding of the way in which members of different cultures may come to think. The thought processes of other peoples may differ so widely from our own, that they may, in a certain very definite sense, be said to live in an entirely different world from our own, for the world of all human beings is a world of conceptual thought, of culturally determined mental constructs, the categories of which may differ from others as the poles apart. It is impossible to judge the particular type of minds that different cultures create by standards which take no cognizance of the standards and categories of the cultures to be judged, and it is for this reason upon all counts completely incorrect to assert that what are for us in particular cases necessarily acts of observation and of inference must likewise be so for all other peoples. Maine's statement that maternity is matter of observation and paternity matter of inference is a case in point. The statement is almost always quoted in connection with discussions of 'physiological paternity', as if it were perfectly self-evident and quite beyond dispute, and it is, of course, quite true that judged from our own particular standpoint the statement, did it but refer to conditions which were functions of our own culture, would be self-evident, but as a description of the state of affairs in cultures other than our own, the statement deserved no more than the rank of a suggestion, not what it has subsequently become, an incontestable axiom. It is, it must be granted, a state exceedingly difficult to envisage in which it were possible that maternity was anything but a matter of observation, the observation of a cause and an effect so exclusively linked together as mother and child. The difficulty, however, arises solely from our misunderstanding, or rather inadequate knowledge, of what the individuals chiefly concerned habitually regard as *cause* and *effect* in this connection, and from our substitution, instead, of what *we* regard as such. In reality, as we shall have abundant opportunity to observe, in Australia the native observes in the process of pregnancy and birth matters which are perfectly consistent with his view of the world, but which do not conform to the requirements of our particular conceptual system. Cause and effect the native observes readily enough according to his own physical system, but that system is very different from our own. It is a quite illegitimate procedure, therefore, to generalize the terms of our own physical system and to expect them to hold good for a culture which functions according to *laws* that differ widely from our own, and to draw a conclusion for the *different* culture upon the basis of laws which hold good for ourselves but not for the members of that different culture. The simplest logician could be trusted to detect the fallacy here were the matter but stated in such terms, but unfortunately it is not often stated in this way.

It is perhaps one of the chief values of a study such as this that it renders the concept of cultural relativity more readily understood than a mere narrative account of any particular culture or a group of cultures could do, by treating of one central belief and the constellation of emotions, sentiments, thoughts and behaviour which revolve about it in all their functional interrelations, the culture actually as it works from the inside.

NOTES

1   *The Legend of Perseus*, i.
2   For an excellent exposition of this view, see Ruth Benedict's *Patterns of Culture*.
3   See Margaret Mead, *Sex and Temperament*; G. P. Murdock, *Social Structure*.
4   pp. 122–5.
5   'Superstition, magic, and medicine', N. Qld Ethnography, *Bulletin* no. 5.
6   pp. 281–332.
7   'The beginnings of religion and totemism among the Australian Aborigines', pt 2, *Fortnightly Review*, 78, 1905, 452–66.
8   'The primitive and the advanced in totemism', *JAI*, 35, 1905, 315–36.
9   'The secret of the totem', review, *Man*, 6, 1906, 27–8.
10 'Questiones totemicae', *Man*, 6, 1906, 51–4.
11 'The marriage laws and some customs of the West Australian Aborigines', *Vict. Geogr. J.*, 23, 1905, 36–60.

12 'Les idées des australiens sur la conception', *Mercure de France*, 61, 1906, 204–20.
13 'Mythes et légendes d'Australie', review, *Man*, 6, 1906, 123–6.
14 'Questiones totemicae, a reply to Mr Lang', *Man*, 6, 1906, 148–9.
15 'Questiones totemicae, a reply to M. van Gennep', *Man*, 6, 1906, 180–2.
16 *Mythen, Sagen und Märchen des Aranda-Stammes in zentral Australien*, pt 1, i-iii of Foreword by von Leonhard, and 50–7, pt 2, 53–60, pt 3, x-xii.
17 'Über einige religiöse und totemistische Vorstellungen der Aranda und Loritja in zentral-Australien', *Globus*, 12, 1907, 285–90.
18 'Anthropological notes on the western coastal tribes of the Northern Territory of South Australia', *Trans. Proc. Rep. Roy. Soc. S. Aust.*, 31, 1907, 1–62.
19 'Some notes on scientific travel amongst the black population of tropical Australia in 1904, 1905, 1906', *Report, 11th meeting Australas. Assn Advmt Sci.*, 1907, 580; 'Schlussbericht über meine Reise nach Australien in den Jahren 1904–1907', *Zeit. Ethnol.*, 39, 1907, 635–90.
20 'Australian problems' in *Anthropological Essays presented to E. B. Tylor*, 205–18.
21 'Die Niol-Niol, ein eingeborenstamm in Nordwest-Australien', *Anthropos*, 3, 1908, 32–40.
22 'Die Stellung der Aranda unter den australischen Stämmen', *Zeit. Ethnol.*, 40, 1908, 886–901.
23 'Ethnological notes on the Aboriginal tribes of Queensland', *Qld Geogr. J.*, n.s. 20, 1905, 49–75; 'Notes on some native tribes of Australia', *J. Proc. Roy. Soc. N.S.W.*, 40, 1906, 110; 'The totemistic system in Australia', *Amer. Antiquarian*, 28, 1906, 144; 'Notes on the Arranda tribe', *J. Proc. Roy. N.S.W.*, 41, 1907, 147; 'Notes on the Aborigines of the Northern Territory, Western Australia, and Queensland', *Qld Geogr. J.*, n.s. 22, 1907, 74–86; 'Marriage and descent in the Arranda tribe', *Amer. Anthrop.*, n.s. 10, 1908, 98.
24 Preface, v.
25 Ibid., v-vi. Vol. 2 was published in 1910. These views were reaffirmed by Hartland in his *Primitive Society*, 18–24.
26 For an exposition of this view, see R. Briffault, *The Mothers*.
27 *Dissertations on Early Law and Custom*, 203.
28 A. I. Hallowell, *Culture and Experience*.
29 B. Spencer and F. J. Gillen, *The Arunta*, i. 80.
30 I know of no work in which this is more beautifully realized than Eleanor Dark's remarkable novel, *The Timeless Land*, London and New York, 1941.
31 R. Brough Smyth, *The Aborigines of Victoria*; F. Bonney, 'On some customs of the Aborigines of the River Darling', *JAI*, 13, 1884, 122–37; T. Ward, *Rambles of an Australian Naturalist*, 278–307.
32 'In schools, it has often been observed that aboriginal children learn quite as easily and rapidly as children of European parents. In fact, the aboriginal school at Ramahyuck, in Victoria, stood for three consecutive years the highest of all state schools of the colony in examination results, obtaining *one hundred per cent of marks*', J. Mathew, *Eaglehawk and Crow*, 78–83 (author's italics); C. E. C. Lefroy, 'Australian Aborigines, a noble-hearted race', *Contemporary Review*, 135, 1929, 222–3.
33 M. M. Bennett, 'Notes on the Dallebura tribe of northern Queensland', *JRAI*, 57, 1927, 413; C. Pickering, *The Races of Man*, 142.
34 From the *Daily Express*, London, 27 May 1926: 'Draughts Sensation. Self-Taught Native Beats an ex-Champion. Jacob Harris, a full-blooded native from the Point Mcleay Mission Station, gave an astonishing performance in the Adelaide (South Australia) draughts championship. Harris has never seen any books on the game, and his knowledge rested solely on his natural play and skill acquired by playing other natives at the mission station. He astonished the champions by defeating N. McGregor (New South Wales) and R. Holmes (Western Australia) in the winner's class. Holmes was 1917 champion, and a recognized master of the game. Harris was defeated in the second round of the winner's class by J. Boyles (Victorian champion).'
35 S. D. Porteous, *The Psychology of a Primitive People*; 'Mentality of Australian Aborigines', *Oceania*, 4, 1933, 30–6. 'I have the highest opinion of the Australian social intelligence,' writes Professor Porteous (p. 36), though he finds the

auditory rote memory of the natives very deficient, but this there is every
reason to believe is an educable quality; how otherwise could we account for
the achievement of the native scholars referred to above? See also H. K. Fry
and R. H. Pulleine, 'The mentality of the Australian Aboriginal', *Aust. J.
exp. Biol. med. Sci.*, 8, 1931, 153-67.

36 *The Original Australians*, 54-5; on the intelligence of Australian Aborigines see
the following: S. D. Porteous, *The Psychology of a Primitive People*; H. K. Fry,
'Aboriginal mentality', *Med. J. Aust.*, 12, 1955, 353-60; Ashley Montagu,'The
future of the Australian Aborigines', *Oceania*, 8, 1938, 344-50; H. K. Fry and
R. H. Pulleine, 'The mentality of the Australian Aboriginal', *Aust. J. exp.
Biol. med. Sci.*, 8, 1931, 153-67; R. M. and C. H. Berndt, *The World of the First
Australians*, 8-11; R. M. and C. H. Berndt (eds), *Aboriginal Man in Australia*;
F. D. McCarthy, *Australia's Aborigines*; Abbie, op. cit.; G. Phelan, 'Aborig-
inal children in New South Wales schools', *Integrated Education* (Chicago), 3,
1965, 36-41; I. Schulz, 'The place of Aborigines in Australian society', *News-
letter*, Australian Institute of Aboriginal Studies, Canberra, 2, 1969, 28;43–
G. E. Kearney, P. R. de Lacey and G. R. Davidson (eds), *The Psychology of
Aboriginal Australians*.

37 *The Mind of Primitive Man*, 203. See also U. McConnel, 'Mourning ritual
among the tribes of Cape York Peninsula', *Oceania*, 7, 1937, 364; Claude Lévi-
Strauss, *The Savage Mind*.

CHAPTER II

The Arunta, the type pattern of Australian culture

Every human being, without choice on his own part, but simply in virtue of his birth and upbringing, becomes a member of what we call a *natural* society. He belongs, that is, to a certain family and a certain nation, and this membership lays upon him definite obligations and duties which he is called upon to fulfil as a matter of course, and on pain of social penalties and disabilities, while at the same time it confers upon him certain social rights and advantages.—W. ROBERTSON SMITH, *The Religion of the Semites*, 1894, p.29.

In order that we may have a clear conception of the framework of the cultures in which the belief we are to study functions, it is imperative at this stage to consider a type of such a cultural framework. For this purpose no Australian culture can serve to better advantage than that of the Arunta tribe of Central Australia. This tribe was for the first time fully described in the pioneer work of Australian ethnology by Baldwin Spencer and F. J. Gillen,[1] and it is upon the revised version of that work[2] that the following descriptive account is for the most part based. In what follows I have attempted to provide the background for our future discussions of the conceptional beliefs of the natives, and have of necessity been constrained to limit myself to categorically put essentials.

The Arunta, by virtue of their central position, were relatively untouched by white influence at the time (1896) when they were first studied by Spencer and Gillen. It is generally agreed that their isolated position in the heart of the continent of Australia, where they can have had but little contact with other tribes, enabled them to preserve their cultural structure in a form that has been relatively unaffected by foreign influences. The extraordinary homogeneity of Australian cultures, of which I have already spoken, renders their common origin a matter of practical certainty. There are, of course, considerable variations in many aspects of each culture, but these are, as a rule, readily understandable, so that any particular culture may, in a general way, be taken to represent the pattern of aboriginal Australian culture, the type of which is represented by the culture of the Arunta.

THE ARUNTA

The Arunta, consisting of some six local groups or hordes, are a tribe or nation which numbered about two thousand individuals when they were originally studied by Spencer and Gillen in 1896, a number which probably represented somewhat less than the optimum of their population. To-day, owing chiefly to the destructive effects of missionary and other white influences, the population of the Arunta is reduced to some 350 souls, whilst their culture is practically destroyed.[3] The Arunta live in the very heart of Australia, occupying a territory which extends from the Macumba River on the south to 70 miles north of the Macdonnell Ranges, a distance of about 400 miles, and lying between longitude 131–136° and latitude 23–27°, actually in the region described by the intersection of the Tropic of Capricorn by the 134th degree of longitude.[4] Thus, the Arunta are the most centrally situated of all the native tribes of Australia. To the north of the Arunta live the Ilpirra, the Kaitisha, the Warramunga, and the Tjingilli tribes; to the north-east live the Iliaura and the Worgaia, to the north-west the Walbiri, to the west the Luritja, and to the south-east the Urbunna (see Map, Fig. 1). The territory occupied by all these tribes extends for a distance, from north to south, of some 700 miles, and from east to west for some 450 miles. The nature of the country in this area varies much. At Lake Eyre, in the south, in what is known as the Dead Heart of Australia, the land is below sea-level, and as one proceeds northwards for a distance of between 300 and 400 miles the land gradually rises until it reaches an elevation of 2,000 feet. The southern portion of the area constitutes the Lower Steppes; the elevated plateau running northwards of this, the southern limit of which is roughly outlined by the James and Macdonnell Ranges, which extend from east to west for a distance of some 350 miles, constitutes the Higher Steppes. It is in the Higher Steppes region, in the vicinity of the Macdonnell Ranges near Alice Springs, that the Arunta dwell. Flowing through this immediate region are the main water-courses, the Finke, Todd, Hugh, Ellery and Palmer Rivers, with their tributaries which originate on the northern side of the main ranges of the Higher Steppe lands, the Macdonnell, James, Waterhouse, Kirchauff, Gill, Levi, and Strangeway Ranges. These quartzite ranges often rise to a height of nearly 5,000 feet, being separated from one another by deep gorges and valleys, in the latter of which the soil is hard and yellow and but thinly covered with exhausted scrub, with occasional patches of pines or cycads, and stray gum trees with pure white trunks. Away to the south and west of the Steppe lands lie the great true desert regions.

In 1950 a series of wet seasons caused serious floods in Australia. Among the astonishing results of the floods was the filling of the usually empty Lake Eyre to form an inland sea of 3,000 square miles.[5] Again, in 1954 Lake Eyre filled with water and teemed with fish. Where the fish came from remains a complete mystery.[6]

The only streams of any importance in the Arunta country are the Alberga, Stevenson, and Hamilton, which traverse the land from the west and unite to form the Macumba River, which at flood times empties itself into Lake Eyre towards the south-east. It is only very rarely that the rainfall is sufficient to fill the beds of these streams; but generally a local flood will occur in one of them, or on rare occasions a more widely distributed rainfall than usual may fill the creeks and also the Finke River, which flows south from the Macdonnell Range far away to the north. At such times the rising waters will overflow their banks and flood the low-lying lands adjacent to them, converting what for many months has been dry and parched land into a single sheet of water. The change, however, is of short duration, the rainfall ceases as suddenly as it appeared, and the water sinks. The water will continue to flow in the creeks for a few days, and then cease, only the scattered deeper holes retaining any.

The sun once more shines hotly, and in the damp ground seeds which have lain dormant for months germinate, and, as if by magic, the once arid land becomes covered with luxuriant herbage. Birds, frogs, lizards, and insects of all kinds can be seen and heard where before everything was parched and silent. Plants and animals alike make the most of the brief time in which they can grow and reproduce, and with them it is simply a case of a keen struggle, not so much against living enemies, as against their physical environment.[7]

The transformation is, indeed, striking, and it does not fail to leave its impress upon the mind of the native.

During the greater part of the year the larger number of watercourses are for the most part dry, except, as has already been stated, at flood times, the only available water being generally found in deep waterholes and gorges sheltered from the rays of the relentless sun which beat down upon the earth at a temperature of 115° in the shade. At night-time the temperature often falls below freezing-point. The native finds both extremes of temperature far from comfortable. During the day-time he tends to avoid the sun by keeping to such places as are in the shade, under some rocky promontory or in the umbrage afforded by the branches of a tree, or under the simple lean-to built of a few sticks and shrubs, which he builds as his only form of shelter from the elements. At night-time the cold is more or less successfully kept at bay by means of a small fire made of twigs, around which the native curls himself, and keeps the fire going by replenishing it with twigs as the necessity arises. His idea is to be as comfortable as possible, to have a fire which smoulders just sufficiently enough to keep his body consistently warm, not to make a fire, as the white man does, so large that it is either too hot to approach, or too cool to be of any use without danger to the sleeper. As it is, almost all natives bear signs of burns sustained during sleep whilst curled around their slow fires at night.

In time of drought, when even the waterholes and gorges no longer yield any water, the native is able to secure water from such sources as tree roots, or by digging in certain likely spots, often to a great depth, or he may satisfy his thirst by opening a vein in his arm and drinking the blood which issues from it. Under ordinary circumstances, kangaroos, rock-wallabies, emus, and other forms of game are not scarce, and there is an ample supply of water, which the native is careful to keep free from pollution. The men procure the larger game, while the women catch the smaller animals such as rats and lizards, also gathering large quantities of grass seeds, tubers, and fruits, and with their digging-sticks secure the grubs of various insects and such burrowing animals as small marsupials and various species of lizards.

The Arunta are organized into a large number of small local groups or hordes, each of which owns and occupies a given area of land, the strictly demarcated boundaries of which are well known to every Aboriginal. The Aborigines generally speak of themselves by the name of the locality which they inhabit. These local groups are composed largely, though not entirely, of individuals who describe themselves by the name of some animal or plant; almost every animal or plant having its representative amongst the human inhabitants. These groups may, therefore, be considered as local totemic land-owning groups. Such groups were never very large, the largest known to Spencer and Gillen were the witchetty grub people, consisting of some forty individuals occupying a territory of about 100 square miles, and the smallest a member of the plum tree people, of one individual with but a few square miles of territory.[8]

Local groups of the same designation may be found in many parts of the territory occupied by the tribe.

Each local group has a head man or *Inkata*, who assumes the lead in carrying out the functions of the totemic group. Outside the local group he does not, as a rule, possess any special powers by virtue of his position in that group, and such weight as his or any other man's opinion may have in tribal matters depends entirely upon his individual reputation, though in certain cases an *Inkata* may obtain some generally recognized authority within the tribe because he happens to be the head of a numerically important group. The *Inkata* is not in any sense a chief, and there exists nothing akin to the office of chieftainship among the Aborigines. The *Inkata* has no power over anyone. He is not chosen for the position of *Inkata* because of his ability; the office is hereditary, and passes from father to son, providing the son is of the same totemic group, which is not always the case. In a kangaroo group the *Inkata* must, of course always be a kangaroo man. Should the *Inkata* have no son to succeed him he will generally nominate his successor, who will always be either a brother or a brother's son. It is the *Inkata* who calls the elder men together for the purpose of discussing important business, but his chief function is to act as custodian of the sacred storehouse, which is called the *Pertalchera*, and is generally situated in a cleft in some rocky range, or special hole in the ground, in which, concealed from view, the sacred objects of the group are kept. To these sacred storehouses no woman, child, or uninitiated man may approach on pain of death. The women know the general situation of these storehouses and on their wanderings give them a wide berth. So sacred is the area of the *Pertalchera* that anyone who is being pursued, no matter how grave his offence, may, should he take refuge within the boundaries of the *Pertalchera*, claim the right of asylum, and so long as he stays within those boundaries he will remain unharmed. It is the *Inkata*, too, whose task it is to determine at what time certain ceremonies, such as the increase ceremonies, shall take place, the object of these ceremonies being to increase the supply of the animal or plant bearing the name of the particular group that performs the ceremony.

The only other classes of men of any importance in the group are the so-called medicine-men, of whom there are three distinct grades, the highest of which are capable of communicating with the tribal spirits, the *Iruntarinia*, and are also able to see spirit-children. The medicine-men are not hereditary classes, but men who have undergone special and severe forms of initiation into the profession under the supervision of other medicine-men, nor are they, unlike the *Inkata*, necessarily to be found in every local group, nor yet have they any special powers outside their purely magical functions, though in virtue of being possessed of these magical abilities they are regarded as superior to other men.

The general government of the tribe is carried out by an assembly or council which is usually drawn from the ranks of the older males, for these will generally be of greater experience in all knowledge pertaining to the tribe than the younger men, though younger men learned in the lore of the tribe are sometimes to be found in the assembly, to the exclusion of older men not so learned as they are. Age is not the important thing, but wisdom is.[9] The assembly has no fixed constitution nor is any definite name applied to it, and its deliberations are carried out in a perfectly informal manner. There are no definite times at which it meets, and it is convened only at such times when there arises some important matter affecting the tribe which requires consideration. Normally, the attention of the assembly is devoted to the arranging of corroborees, and the initiation ceremonies. Dates have to be fixed and the programmes discussed and outlined in detail, so that those who are to take part in them may be fully prepared in advance. Law-breakers are tried before the assembly, and the proper punishments are prescribed by it.

The Arunta have an extraordinarily highly developed conception of justice, and punishments, with an admirable balance of good sense and equity, are devised to fit the crime. The form which the punishment for various crimes and misdemeanours takes is traditionally prescribed. The offender is always encouraged to state his case and to defend himself against the charges brought against him, but once a sentence is pronounced it is always carried out, although an individual may seek to evade it by leaving the tribe for a time in the hope that when he returns the feeling against him may have calmed down, and the punishment perhaps not be carried out with the severity which would originally have characterized it.

In all matters whatever the judgment of the assembly is respected and supported by the horde as a whole.

The native generally camps near a waterhole, and when the advantages of this have been fairly exhausted he moves on to another; he cultivates nothing and domesticates nothing; the half-wild dingo, and the mongrels resulting from interbreeding with the introduced dog, which are to be found in large numbers in every native camp, have not been trained, as in many other Australian tribes, to assist in the hunting of game, and agriculture is totally unknown, as also is the storage of food, except for immediate ceremonial occasions. As a general rule food is merely gathered and then immediately consumed, everything that is edible being regarded as food.[10]

The members of each local group wander in small parties, often, for example, two or more brothers with their wives and children, over the land which they own, camping at favourite spots where the presence of waterholes, with their usual accompaniments of vegetable and animal food, enables them to supply their wants.

Each family, consisting of a male and one or more wives and children, accompanied by dogs, occupies a *mia-mia*, or lean-to, constructed of sticks and shrubs, in the foreground of which a small fire is kept burning. This constitutes the family hearth upon which all cooking is done, and round which the family, and perhaps a visitor or two, will gather to enjoy the social amenities during the day-time, and sleep during the night.

In summer the occupants of the camp are early astir, in winter rising only when the sun is well up. If food be plentiful, the men and women will lounge about while the children romp and play. If food be required, the women will set out with their digging-sticks, and *pitchis* or wooden troughs, in search of small animals, vegetables, and grubs. And the men will perhaps set off, armed with spears, a spear thrower, and boomerangs,[11] in search of larger game, such as emus and kangaroos.

Cooking is performed by the use of hot ashes, and the preparation of the animal for the hearth is done by means of knives and scrapers fashioned of stone, these implements being supplemented by the carver's teeth whenever necessary.

The hunter neither cooks his catch nor has anything to say about the disposition of its parts. The distribution of food is left to the older men. In the long run, however, each person receives an equal proportion of food, for the hunter of one day will be the cook or recipient of another. Mountford points out that there is much wisdom behind this method of food distribution. 'The government of the tribe', he writes, 'is in the hands of the old men, and it is they who have the power to make decisions and ensure their enforcement. Were the skilled hunters, who are generally young, allowed to apportion their own catch, they could, by bartering their game for privileges and power, upset the authority of the old men, and so, the social balance of the tribe. But under aboriginal law the successful hunter, young or old, can gain no advantage. His skill is of more value to the tribe than to himself; his only return is the joy of achievement, and the approbation of his fellows.'[12]

The natives have no pottery. Water is carried in the wooden *pitchi*, but it cannot be heated in this or in any other utensil that they possess, hence, hot water is ordinarily unknown to them.[13] Food collected on foraging expeditions is carried in bags woven of grass or rushes.

The natives pay little attention to time, though this is not to say that they have no conception of it. Time is counted by sleeps, moons, or phases thereof, and, for longer periods, by seasons. The various periods of the day are distinguished by definite names. Not having any great necessity to count in terms of large numbers, they count up to five by the fingers of the hand, anything above four or five is generally denoted by the term *oknirra*, meaning much or great.

Among the important functions of the local totemic groups is the performance of certain periodic ceremonies. Whereas these local groups represent a fundamental feature of the social organization of the tribe, perhaps its most fundamental feature, as in the majority of Australian tribes, is represented by its division into two exogamous intermarrying groups or *moieties*, each of which, among the Arunta, is further divided into two *sections*; among the northern Arunta the four sections thus resulting are further subdivided into two *subsections*, the total number thus obtaining being eight subsections, four in each moiety.

These various divisions are concerned with the regulation of marriage. The totemic organization, unlike the conditions in other Australian tribes, has nothing whatever to do with the regulation of marriage. A simple diagram will serve to illustrate how these marriage regulations work in practice.

The two moieties A and B consists of two sections each, A of sections *Panunga* and *Bultara*, B of sections *Purula* and *Kumara*, thus:

Moiety A	Moiety B
Panunga	*Purula*
Bultara	*Kumara*

A Panunga man must marry a Purula woman, but his children will not belong to his own section, Panunga, but to the other section in his moiety, the sub-section Appungerta of the section Bultara. When a Bultara man marries a Kumara woman their children will belong to the other section in the father's moiety, that is Panunga, and when a Kumara man marries a Bultara woman their children will belong to the Purula section, and it is the same for the eight subsections. Actually a man may only marry into a specific one of the subsections of his marriage section, according to the following arrangement:

Thus, a Panunga man marries a Purula woman, and their offspring will belong to the Appungerta subsection in the section Bultara, and so on. A man, therefore, can never marry a woman of his own local group but must take a wife from another local group belonging to the opposite moiety, and to the section which is the complementary of his own in that moiety. This kind of local exogamy, as Radcliffe-Brown was the first to point out,[14] is the result chiefly of the regulation of marriage by relationship, for not only is a man required by these regulations to marry into a particular subsection of the opposite moiety, but above all else he is required to marry a woman in that subsection who stands in a particular genealogical relationship to him, namely the daughter of his mother's mother's brother's daughter, that is, his cousin on the mother's side once removed. Should there be no such immediate genealogical relative available, then he may marry any one of the potential 'wives' in the proper complementary section who is thus closely related to him.

Marriage among the Arunta is then plainly determined by relationship and relationship alone: an individual can only marry his or her cross-cousin once removed.

A girl is frequently allotted to her husband in marriage even before she is born, but possession of her is not taken until she is of marriageable age, a period generally determined by the onset of menstruation, which is said to occur at about twelve years of age.[15] The manner in which the allotment takes place is by the mutual arrangement between two men, standing in relationship to one another of man and his mother's mother's brother's son, that the daughter's daughter of one becomes the wife of the son of the other. Since the arrangement is entered into when the boy and the mother of the girl (yet unborn) whom he is to marry are about the same age, it is obvious that the actual wives of the men will be considerably younger than themselves.

The betrothal is simply a formal matter into which no love or sexual element enters. The arrangement entails certain obligations on the part of the future husband towards the father of the girl and the relatives on her side. He must also ever afterwards avoid his mother-in-law, and never speak to her or even look at her.

From the standpoint of the male, marriage means the acquisition of a helpmate and a servant, who will carry his possessions for him when they are on the march, since he himself must travel unburdened in order that he, as the hunter, may be free and unhampered in his movements. The woman will prepare his food for him, make herself generally useful, and look after his children when he is away. In virtue of these functions a woman is regarded as something of an economic asset, and the more wives a man has and the younger they are, the wealthier is their owner esteemed, for women may be used in barter, and exchanged for certain commodities. It is not true that the married woman, as Frazer has remarked,[16] is treated like a domesticated cow, who is owned as property along with all her products, natural or otherwise. Nevertheless she together with all the fruits of her labours may be disposed of by her husband, her lord and master, down to the children that come from, or rather through, her. The women appear to be quite happy under this arrangement, and they are, on the whole, treated very decently by their husbands.

The Arunta male looks upon marriage chiefly as an economic arrangement and not as a sexual one, the latter factor, indeed, playing the least important role.[17] A wife is indispensable for the purpose of bearing children, and children have a certain economic value, for the children of both sexes from a very early age are encouraged to assist as far as they are able in supplying the needs of the family, the girls generally accompanying their mothers with their own little digging-sticks on their foraging trips, whilst the boys set off either alone or in small bands, usually independently of their fathers, to try their luck with the larger game for themselves. The economic is the dominant motive in marriage. Since uninitiated individuals of both sexes are forbidden to eat of a very large number of animals and plants, all of which are well known to them, upon pain of being visited by certain very unpleasant afflictions which would inevitably follow upon the consumption of such forbidden foods, much of what the little ones bring in will go to their parents, whilst such things as they are permitted to eat they are required to share. Children are not, as a rule, bartered, though on rare occasions they may be so exchanged. All children are treated with exceptional kindness and affection and an extraordinary amount of consideration, and only very rarely, and upon the greatest provocation, are they chastised physically.[18]

Thus far we have been using the term 'relationship' without giving any indication of the sense in which it is understood by the Arunta. To this matter we may now turn our attention.

Among the Arunta, as in every Australian tribe, there exists a complicated system of relationship terms expressive of the relationship of every individual to every other individual member of the tribe, as well as to such individuals who are not members of the tribe but with whom it is possible to have social relations. These terms bear with them an obligatory system of reciprocal rights and duties which are observed between the individuals to whom and by whom the term is applied. These terms themselves do not possess the limited connotation that our own intimate relationship terms possess, as when we speak of 'wife', 'father', and 'mother', and thereby denote a particular individual, but they are extended among the Arunta to embrace a much wider group of individuals whose status is genealogically determined, that is, determined by means of descent and marriage, or birth and affinity. In short, these terms refer to individual relations arising out of the solidarity of the family. Thus a man is always classed with his brother and a woman with her sister; so that if a given term of relationship is applied to a man by a particular individual the same term is applied to his brother, and a particular term to their children, and so on. A father's brother is a 'father', and the latter's children are my brothers and sisters. Within the immediate family distinctions are recognized and expressed by the use of suffixes of the order of birth of the children of the family, thus the term *arulkalinia* is applied to the first or oldest child, the idea of seniority is described by the term *chorla*, the youngest child is *kaindinia*, the idea of juniority is expressed by the term *chorlda*, and allowance is made for the description of intermediate siblings by the use of the term *orldinia*, meaning in the very middle; the term *mbuppa* being used to describe siblings on either side of the middle one. Similar terms are in use with respect to the father's brothers and the mother's sisters and their children. In this way, it will be seen, every individual ultimately comes to be distinguished by a definite term of relationship from every other individual. The fallacy of treating such relationship terms as if they served to define groups of individuals and nothing more is obvious.

A second principle which is characteristic of the Arunta, as well as all other Aboriginal relationship systems, is that which brings relatives by marriage into the class of consanguineal relatives. Thus, the wife of any man I call 'father' becomes my 'mother', and the husband of any woman I call 'mother' becomes my 'father'.

It must, however, be quite clear that cross-cousin marriage whether associated with the four- or eight-class system produces a reciprocal equation between affinals or relatives by marriage and consanguineals. As Fortune puts it, the marrying male line a has a lien in perpetuity on the sisters of another male line b, b to c, and so on until z is to a as line a is to b.

The most interesting social consequence of this system, as Fortune shows, is that a man cannot marry a woman without creating a lien in perpetuity upon the male line from which she comes in favour of his male descendants. The women who are sisters of a male line are, as it were, in entail to an opposite male line.[19] It should be quite clear then that upon such a system the marrying partners and their respective relatives actually belong in the class of consanguineals even before marriage.

A third principle, called by Radcliffe-Brown the principle of non-limitation of range, is the characteristic recognition and classification of relationships between every member of society, whether of one's own or of another tribe, with whom one is likely to have any social relations whatever.[20]

Such a relationship system is in reality very much more precise and thoroughgoing than our own relationship system, for while one of its characteristics is that it embraces under a single term a number of individuals who fall into status groups according to the above-mentioned principles, it also serves to define the individual relations, the rights, duties, and forms of behaviour, obtaining between the individuals constituting the various kinds of relatives very much more particularly and significantly more nicely than our own system does. Thus, for example, an individual, among the Arunta, behaves to all individuals to whom the same general term is applied, such, for example, as father or mother, in a certain general way, but he does not behave in *exactly* the same way to each of these individuals, for he makes a conscious distinction between near and distant relatives who fall into the same terminological class. Hence, he will pay more particular attention to the observance of his duties in relation to his near relatives than to his more distant ones, for example, his own father and the latter's brothers, junior and senior, as distinguished from a distant cousin of his father. Clear degrees of relationship are recognized, and these distinctions which have so definite an effect upon the individual's behaviour are based, it must be apparent, upon the recognition of the closeness of the ties existing between the members of the immediate family.

Such facts have been too often overlooked in the theoretical discussions concerning Aboriginal systems of relationship, the usual procedure having been to assume that the classification of certain individuals into relationship groups distinguished by a common term signified that for all practical purposes no distinction was made between the members of such 'groups', but as we have already seen in connection with but a single institution, namely marriage, such distinctions have the very practical effect of determining which particular woman among his potential 'wives' a man may actually marry. Indeed, more attention is paid to the recognition of distinctive individual relationships among the Arunta than is the case among ourselves. Every individual *must* stand in a definite relationship to every other individual, or, put in another way, the relations between individuals must be precisely and clearly defined, for without the relationships thus defined it would be impossible for the individual to regulate his conduct in the ordinary course of social life in any workable manner. Hence, as Radcliffe-Brown has pointed out, such a statement as that of Frazer that the Aboriginal terms of kinship 'designate relationships between groups, not between individuals',[21] is inaccurate and misleading.

In the relationship system then, we have a series of *functional* relationships which regulate the social relations between individuals, and form, among other things, the basis upon which the marriage sections operate. Thus, all individuals of one's own generation bear a relationship to a particular individual which is reflected in the subsection to which that particular individual belongs, so that one's actual blood brothers and sisters will belong to one's own subsection, but one's father will belong to another subsection of another section in the same moiety, as will one's father's brothers and cousins; one's mother's brother will belong to yet another section in the opposite moiety, as will one's maternal cousins and one's eligible wives. One's father's brothers and his cousins will all be denoted as fathers, like-wise one's mother's sisters will be called mothers. It should be under-stood that these terms are in use regardless of whether or not the individual is married. All these relationships exist for the individual from the moment he is born. From an early age he learns into which subsection he may marry and into which he may not, and he knows that death is the penalty prescribed for those who violate the rules, which, of course, are equivalent to laws. He learns, too, the various duties, restrictions, obligations, and privileges which are associated with each degree of relationship, and the penalties which will inevit-ably follow upon their neglect or violation. He is expected to provide his classificatory father with a share of the game he obtains, to avoid, and neither to speak to nor look at, his classificatory mother-in-law, and so on.

Kinship determines the fundamental form of all social behaviour in relation not only to one's own kin, to the members of one's own group, but to individuals of other groups belonging to other tribes, and to whom there can be no conceivable blood relationship.[22]

Whilst it is of the first importance for a proper understanding of the Arunta relationship system to realize that it is based essentially upon the relations holding between parents and children, and be-tween the children of the same parents and their offspring within the immediate family, it must be clearly understood that the question of *blood relationship* does not play any part whatever in the natives' conception of relationship. Such a thing as blood relationship, or consanguinity, is not recognized by the native; for him, instead, all relationships are *social*, and are based upon clearly distinguished social factors. The distinction which the native customarily makes between individuals is not as between blood relatives and 'others' (not-relatives), but between near and distant relatives.

Every member of society is, as we have seen, a relative of one kind or another, and each individual is so by virtue of the genealogical connection which exists between himself and others, a connection which may always, even though on occasion there may be some difficulty in doing so, be traced back to every family in the group. But in all this, no question of blood arises. The family itself, consisting of parents and children, is not regarded as a blood group, as a biological or physiological unit, but as a social group. The conditions of necessarily intimate and peculiar family association—prolonged over a long period of time—produce of themselves the very definite and far-reaching effect of socially binding the members of the family together in a unique manner, a manner which receives the fullest individual as well as social recognition. It is the psychological con-ditions arising out of the social relations which necessarily exist between individuals living in close and continued association with one another which give the family its peculiarly integrated and well-defined status in every kind of community whatever—even among ourselves, where the biological or physiological relationships are assumed to play a dominant role.

The fact that a number of individuals, from their earliest days, have grown up together, in association with a particular man and his wife or wives, to whom they are under a large variety of obligations, whose duty it has been to care for, to educate, and to instruct them during their early years, will naturally be operative in producing certain sentiments between the individuals thus associated which will differ very appreciably from such sentiments as may result from association with one's classificatory fathers and mothers. These sentiments do not, however, involve any conception of a biological relationship or affinity between the individual, his siblings, and his immediate father and mother. It should be remembered that everywhere the association of any child or children with a particular group of individuals is not a biologically but a socially determined matter. There is nothing in the simple fact itself of a child being born into a family or social group which renders it necessary that that child shall remain associated with the family or the group into which it is born; were it not for the fact that it is considered *socially* the best possible arrangement that the pattern set by the physical conditions, but not determined by them, should be followed socially, the arrangement would unquestionably not exist.[23]

It should be clear, then, that the Arunta understand by relationship not biological affinity but social affinity.

Among the Arunta, fatherhood and motherhood are conceptions which possess a somewhat different meaning from that which they possess among ourselves. Among ourselves the emphasis is placed upon the biological fact of relationship. We think of our father and mother fundamentally and essentially as the individuals who generated us, one particular man and one particular woman, and it is this fact, the fact that they are the individuals who generated us, which determines at least our terminological and genealogical relationship to one another. In reality, of course, fatherhood and motherhood among ourselves are conceptions no less socially founded than they are among the Arunta. Where social relations have not existed between parents and children, fatherhood and motherhood are terms which from the sociopsychological standpoint can have no meaning for the individuals concerned. Just as there cannot be a family without social relations between the members constituting it, so there can be neither fatherhood nor motherhood in any but the narrow, and relatively unimportant biological and legal senses, without social relations of a very definite kind. It so happens that in our particular kind of social organization the biological or physiological relationships between individuals receive a special emphasis, whereas among the Arunta, biological relationships as we view them are not understood and therefore never considered. Among the Arunta there is no question of any one man or woman conceiving a particular individual. Individuals are simply not physiologically conceived at all, and a particular man and woman are never thought of as having anything whatsoever to do with the actual generation of a child; this, indeed, is something which is known to have been determined in the far distant dream-time, the *Alchera*, and men and women, according to Arunta belief, have nothing to do with the matter.

According to Arunta tradition, in the early dream-time in the far distant past, or *Alchera*, in that time when there were neither men nor women, there dwelt in the western sky two beings, of whom it is said that they were Numbakulla, that is, self-existing beings who came out of nothing. And it happened one day that they discerned, far away to the east, a number of *Inapertwa*, that is, rudimentary human beings or incomplete men, who possessed neither limbs nor senses, who did not eat, and who each presented the appearance of a somewhat amorphous human being, all doubled into a rounded mass in which just the vague outlines of the various parts of the body could be seen. These *Inapertwa*, who were destined to be transformed into men and women by the Numbakulla, represented the intermediate stage in the transformation of animals and plants into men, so that when the Numbakulla came down to earth and fashioned the *Inapertwa* into men, each individual so fashioned naturally retained an intimate relationship with the animal, plant, or other object, of which he was indirectly a transformation, and with which he was at one time identical. It is in this way that men came into being, and it is for this reason that men necessarily possess totems, that is an animal, plant, or other object or thing, such as water, wind, sun, fire, cloud, or whatnot, with which each individual is closely identified, since it is to that plant, animal, object, or thing that the native believes himself to owe his original creation. Spencer and Gillen write of the relationship between the individual and his totem:

At the present day a very definite relationship is supposed to exist between the individual and his totem. A man will eat only very sparingly of the latter, and even if he does eat a little of it, which is allowable to him, he is careful, in the case, for example, of an emu man, not to eat the best part, such as the fat. The totem of any man is regarded, just as it is elsewhere, as the same thing as himself; as a native once said to us when we were discussing the matter with him,

'That one', pointing to his photograph which we had taken, 'is just the same as me; so is a kangaroo' (his totem.)[24]

The *Alchera* ancestors of the Arunta possessed powers far exceeding those of their living descendants: it is they, for example, who created the various natural features of the land inhabited by the tribe today, the gorges, the rivers, the gaps, and so forth.

The *Alchera* ancestors were originally banded together in totemic companies who wandered over the land in various directions, as recorded in the traditions associated with them. Each ancestor carried with him one or more sacred stones, which were associated with the *Kuruna*, that is, the spirit-part of the individual, and which are called by the Arunta *Churinga*. Wherever the ancestors originated, and wherever they camped during their wanderings, there were formed *Knanikilla*, or local totem centres.

At each of these spots—and they are all well known to the old men, who pass the knowledge on from generation to generation—a certain number of the Alchera ancestors went into the ground, each leaving his Churinga behind. His body died, but some natural feature, such as a rock or tree, arose to mark the spot, while his spirit part re-mained in the Churinga. These Churinga, as well as others, which the wandering parties left behind them, were stored in *Pertalchera*, or sacred storehouses, that usually had the form of small caves and fissures in the rocks, or even a hollow tree or carefully concealed hole in a sand-bank. The result is that, as we follow their wanderings, we find the whole country is dotted over with *Knanikilla*, or local totem centres, at each of which are deposited a number of Churinga, with *Kuruna*, or spirit individuals, associated with them.[25]

Each totem centre is, of course, associated with a particular species of totem. Thus, for example, in one locality there will be wild-cat spirit individuals, in another a group of emu, then a group of kan-garoos, and in another a group of hakea flower, and so on. At each of the spots at which a *Churinga* was deposited the natural object which arose to mark its site, such as a tree or rock, became the abode of the *Knanja*, which also means totem. It is this conception of spirit individuals associated with *Churinga* and resident in certain definite spots, determined by the situation of the *Knanja*, that lies, according to Spencer and Gillen, at the root of the Arunta totemic system.

We may take the following as a typical example of how each man and woman gains a totem name. Close to Alice Springs is a large and important witchetty grub[26] totem centre or *Knanikilla*.[27] Here there were deposited in the Alchera a large number of Churinga carried by witchetty grub men and women. There are numerous prominent rocks and boulders and certain ancient gum trees along the sides of a picturesque gap in the ranges, that are the *Knanja* trees and rocks of these spirits, which, so long as they remain in spirit form, they usually frequent. If a woman conceives a child after having been near to this gap, it is one of the spirit individuals which has entered her body,[28] and therefore, quite irrespective of what the mother's or father's totem may chance to be, that child, when born, must of necessity be of the witchetty grub totem; it is, in fact, nothing else but the reincarnation of one of the witchetty grub people of the Alchera. Suppose, for example, to take a particular and actual instance, an emu woman from another locality comes to Alice Springs, and whilst there becomes aware that she has conceived a child, and then returns to her own locality before the child is born, that child, though it may be born in an emu locality, is an Udnirrin-gita or witchetty grub. It must be, the natives say, because it entered the mother at Alice Springs, where there are only witchetty grub *Kurunas*. Had it entered her body within the limits of her own emu locality it would as inevitably have been an emu. To take another example. Quite recently the lubra or wife of a witchetty grub man, she belonging to the same totem, conceived a child while on a visit to a neighbouring Quatcha or water locality, which lies away to the east of Alice Springs—that child's totem is water; or again, an Alice Springs woman, when asked by us as to why her child was a witchetty grub (in this instance belonging to the same totem as both of its parents), told us that one day she was taking a drink of water near to the gap in the Ranges where the spirits dwell when suddenly she heard a child's voice crying out, '*Mia, mia!*'—the native term for relationship, which includes that of mother. Not being anxious to have a child, she ran away as fast as she could, but to no purpose; she was fat and well favoured, and such women the *Kurunas* prefer; one of them had gone inside her, and of course it was born a witchetty grub.[29]

The natives are quite clear upon this point. The spirit children are supposed to have a strong predilection for fat women, and prefer to choose such for their mothers, even at the risk of being born into the wrong class.[30]

In support of the belief in this predilection of the spirit-children for fat women the natives can point to the fact that the fat strong women are actually much more fertile than the thin weaker ones who are very frequently sterile, or rarely bear children.[31] The incapacity to produce children is generally explained by the natives as having been brought about by the woman in her youth, in consequence of her having playfully or thoughtlessly tied a man's hair waist-band around her waist. The latter so used, if only for a moment or two, has the effect of cramping the girl's internal organs and rendering them incapable of the necessary expansion.[32]

Another way in which a woman may be entered by a spirit-child is the following:

If a man, for example, be hunting an emu and, whilst he is chasing it, runs into a wallaby *Knanikilla*, a wallaby *Kuruna* may go into it. If the man spears it near to the *Knanikilla* and gives some of it to his wife to eat, the wallaby *Kuruna* will go into her. She does not eat it, but, as is supposed always to be the case, it enters by her loins. Later on she becomes sick, and then knows that the *Kuruna* has given rise to a *Ratappa* inside her, which, when born, belongs to the wallaby *Knanja*. It is definitely said that she does not actually eat the *Kuruna*.[33]

'*Ratappa*' is the term applied to the child within the mother's womb, and is also used to describe a new-born baby. The spirit-child, or *Kuruna*, always enters the woman through the loins, never through the vulva. The *Kuruna* represents an earlier stage of development than the *ratappa*. The *Kuruna* is described as being of shapeless form, having neither arms nor legs, nor head, and resembling a very small round little pebble of a red colour. After entering a woman it develops into, or gives rise to, a *ratappa*. It does not enter as a *ratappa* but as a *Kuruna*, and it only changes into the former within the womb or *ilpa*.[34]

Although Spencer and Gillen nowhere explicitly say so, it would seem probable that the *Kuruna* are regarded as actually representing that stage in the evolution of men and women when the latter were all *Inapertwa*, away back in the far distant Alchera. The description given by the natives of the physical form of the *Inapertwa* corresponds exactly to that which they give of the physical form of the *Kuruna*,[35] and since it is the spirit of *Alchera* origin which actually enters the woman, it enters in its original form and subsequently undergoes development as a *ratappa* in the womb of the mother. In this way the identification of a man with his totem animal and his undoubted recognition of some physical difference in their respective appearances would be accounted for.

So clear and unequivocal is the native conception of the form of the *Kuruna* and of the *ratappa* that they will reject every phenomenon which may offer itself as such unless it fully agrees with their conception of it; thus, on the rare occasions when, owing to some accident, a child is born at a very premature stage, nothing will persuade the natives that it is an undeveloped human being, for it is nothing like either a *Kuruna* or a *ratappa*; 'they are perfectly convinced that it is the young of some other animal, such as a kangaroo, which has by mistake got inside the woman.'[36]

In North-Western Australia, among the Drysdale River tribes, the belief is identical. Thus, Dom Hernández writes: 'Most if not all the cases of abortion were due to . . . ignorance. For, thinking that the pains and inconveniences that usually accompany gestation were caused by blood congestion or by *djákolo* (charm or object introduced by magic into the human body) women tried to get rid of them by some of their barbarous methods—striking or hard kneading of the belly—and the result was, naturally, abortion. Thus when, on one occasion, a bush woman was reprimanded at the mission for having killed her unborn child, she replied innocently that what she had ejected was not a child but a rat!'[37]

We have, in this rejection of the premature fœtus by the natives, a striking instance of something that many students have found it somewhat difficult to understand, namely, the denial of a relationship so apparently obvious as that which, in the present case, exists between the premature fœtus and the child. But, as we have seen, according to native orthodox belief, which is firmly based on what is believed to be the true history of the world of the Arunta, there is room only for a *Kuruna* and a *ratappa* in the complete embryological canon of the Arunta. It would, therefore, not only be unorthodox, but perfectly pointless for the native to look upon the premature fœtus as anything more than the material form of an error on the part of the *Kuruna* of some animal, which has mistakenly entered into the wrong host.

It is to be noted here that every animal has a *Kuruna*, and that the *Kuruna* enters the female animal of the group with which it is associated in the same manner as the *Kuruna* enters the human female. 'An emu *Kuruna*', for example, 'goes into an emu, who lays an egg containing the little emu *Kuruna*, which is very small and cannot at first be seen, but it grows into an emu inside the shell and hatches out from this just like a little kangaroo or human baby grows inside its mother's *ekura*, or baby bag, and hatches out.'[38]

Still other ways in which a woman may be entered by a *Kuruna* are associated with the so-called *ratappa*-stones. These stones, as their name implies, are the *Knanja*, or the abodes of the *Kuruna* of young children; actually there are no *ratappa Knanja*, but the *Kuruna* inhabiting these *Knanja* enter women and give rise to *Ratappa* which become children. These *ratappa*-stones, of which there are but a few, are associated with detailed traditions relating to their origin, which here, as elsewhere, are faithfully mirrored in the tribal ceremonies, and which, as we shall see, naturally give them their meaning. Such a ceremony was in the keeping of an *Inkata* of Alice Springs, and was at his request performed by a Panunga man, who enacted the part of a woman with a new-born child, the child being represented by an oval mass of twigs and grass stalks encased in hair string and white down, upon which two black spots were left to indicate the eyes. Holding the supposed child in his hands the performer sat down swaying and quivering, while the other men sang and danced around him. This over, the child was pressed against the stomach of the *Inkata*, who then took and pressed it against that of the old Purula *Inkata* in charge of the Engwura[39] totemic ceremonies.

The tradition associated with this ceremony is characteristic of the consistent detail upon which the native beliefs are based. The tradition is as follows:

In the locality of a plum-tree totem about fifteen miles S.S.E. of Alice Springs is a special rounded stone which projects from the ground amidst mulga scrub for a height of about three feet. This stone is called *Perta ratappa*. In the Alchera a man named Intatirkaka, who belonged to the plum-tree totem and was not an *Ulpmerka*,[40] came from a place called Kulla-rata, a water-hole out to the north of Mount Heuglin, in the Western Macdonnells, and, crossing a depression in the latter range close to Mount Gillen, he proceeded to Uk-ang-wulla, which means the hollow or hole, and lies close to Quiurnpa, where he found a *Nurtunja*[41] erected, but could not see any people to whom it belonged, so he proceeded to appropriate it; but when he tried to pull it up out of the ground, all that he could do was slightly to loosen it; seeing that he could not secure it whole, he broke it off at the butt, and down it tumbled with a loud crash. The *Nurtunja* was the property of a plum-tree woman, named Unkara, who, with her new-born baby boy (*ratappa*), was out hunting for the plums on which they fed. She had originated at this spot and had lived alone here, having nothing to do with the plum-tree *Ulpmerka* men who lived not far away. When she heard the crash she came quickly back to her camp, and there she saw what had taken place, and was greatly grieved; as the natives say, her bowels yearned after her *Nurtunja*. She put her baby boy into the hollow where the *Nurtunja* was broken off, just below the surface, and leaving with him a large number of Churinga, went in pursuit of the thief. The boy went into the ground, and the *Ratappa*-stone arose to mark the spot. Each of the Churinga which the Alchera woman left with the boy had a *Kuruna* or spirit belonging to it. The former were placed in the *Pertalchera* at Quiurnpa twaidja, a gap in the Macdonnell Ranges, now know as Pine Tree Gap.[42]

Increase ceremonies (*Mbanbiuma* or *Intichiuma* ceremonies) are performed at the *Knanja* of the *Ambaquerka* (young child) which results in the departure of the *Kuruna*, whose *Churinga* are now in the *Pertalchera* at Quiurnpa, to enter women. Under ordinary circumstances any woman who passes by such a *ratappa*-stone is likely to be entered by an *Ambaquerka Kuruna*. Should a young woman who does not wish to have a child pass by the stone, she will disguise herself, and walk and limp like an old woman, whose voice she will imitate muttering, 'Don't come to me, I am an old woman.' A malicious man may cause women to become pregnant by clearing a space round the stone and, while rubbing it, exclaiming, 'Plenty of young women, you look and go quickly.' A man who wishes to punish his wife for supposed unfaithfulness performs the same ritual, whilst pronouncing the words 'That woman of mine has thrown me aside, and gone with another man, go quickly and hang on tightly'— meaning that the child is to stay within the woman for a long time, until by so doing it may cause her death. Again, the husband of the childless woman by using a different formula at a *ratappa*-stone may cause a *Kuruna* to enter his wife.[43]

From the above account we see that every individual is regarded as the incarnation of an *Alchera* spirit or ancestor, and that as such the individual cannot possibly be *generated* by other living individuals, and that parentage must then be, necessarily, a purely social matter and not a biological one.

When a *Kuruna* enters a woman and a child is born, the old men determine what particular *Kuruna* has undergone incarnation, and then assign to the new-born individual the *Churinga* the spirit part of which gave him being. This *Churinga* is always kept in the *Pertalchera*, necessarily of the region in which the mother was entered by the *Kuruna*. The fact that the *Churinga* are kept in the *Pertalchera*, which literally means *Alchera* rock, is explained by the fact that when a *Kuruna* enters a woman it drops its *Churinga*, and this, when found by the father, or father's father if living, at the place described by the mother, is then deposited in the *Pertalchera*. Sometimes, however, the *Churinga* is not found, in such an event a new one is made from mulga, or some hard-wood tree, near to the *Pertalchera* of the child, which is then marked by the *Arunga*, or paternal grandfather of the child, with a design belonging to the child's totem. When this has been done the *Churinga* is then placed in the *Pertalchera* and is regarded as the child's *Churinga Knanja*, with which its *Kuruna* is associated.[44] With each *Churinga* is also associated another spirit element which is the twin or double of the individual's own *Kuruna*: this is the *Arumburinga* which remains associated with the *Churinga* and spends a great deal of its time in and around the *Pertalchera*. The *Arumburinga* is conceived to be a kind of guardian spirit of the individual, but only in a very general way. The *Arumburinga* does not watch over the individual continuously, and may, upon occasion, even be unfriendly towards him, though generally an individual's *Arumburinga* is considered to be a friendly spirit. The *Arumburinga* is immortal, and the loss of the *Churinga* usually means that the *Arumburinga* has followed it.[45] In such a case the native does not mourn the loss very seriously, though he may have a vague idea that some ill may befall him.

One tradition tells that the *Churinga* came to be placed in the *Pertalchera* for safe-keeping, another, that Numbakulla originally fashioned large numbers of *Churinga* belonging to all *Knanjas*, or totems, with each of which he associated a *Kuruna* which he had previously made. He then sent out *Inkatas* or *Knanja* groups with numbers of these *Churinga* and *Kurunas* which each gave rise to men and women, their *Churinga* being deposited at certain spots, which subsequently became the *Pertalcheras* of the various totem centres.

Each man and woman has a *Churinga knanja* and men, but not women, may possess others by inheritance.

When a person dies his *Kuruna*, now called *Ulthana*, returns to its *Churinga* in the *Pertalchera*.

It remains but to say that whilst the totem is quite clearly not inherited in the sense of descent from parent to offspring, the totem of the child should, however, be that of its father's moiety. The majority of the members of one totem belong to the same moiety of the tribe, although there are always a certain number of totemites who belong to the opposite moiety.

Occasionally a local totemic group may die out, in which event their *Churinga* will pass into the custody of a neighbouring group together with the land defined by the boundaries of the *Pertalchera*; the group into whose custody these things pass must be *Nakrakia* to the extinct group, that is, it must belong to the same moiety of the tribe as the latter.

Such an extinction of a group is, however, always only temporary, for sooner or later some woman is bound to be entered by a spirit-child in the locality of the group no longer represented by living individuals, for the spirits of the *Alchera* ancestors still inhabit the locality, and are always on the look-out for women through whom they may be reincarnated, and the group in this way resuscitated.

It is evident, therefore, that every totemic group is in a very special sense a biologically determined unit, the material elements of which are represented by the *Knanja* or abodes of the *Alchera Kuruna*, which by their presence ensure the continuity of the totemic group, and secondarily by means of the *Churinga* with which the *Alchera Kuruna* are associated. The *Knanja* cum *Churinga* are, as it were, the material cellular elements of the germ-plasm of the totemic group, and as long as they exist, it is impossible for the totemic group to become extinct. The biological continuity of the totemic group is thus as real a biological continuity as any social apparatus devised for the purpose could possibly secure. In reality, of course, the continuity is no more than socially determined, but this is as we see it and not as the native does; for him these things are *in rerum natura*, and are made clear to him by the traditions of his tribe and the everyday events of his social life, a life which embraces the complete totality of his experience.

As well as ensuring the continuity of the totemic group itself, the continuity of the species of the animal or plant with which the group is identified is likewise secured and maintained by the same powers that operate in the case of man, except that in these connections the powers are usually manipulated by the performance of certain ceremonies. These ceremonies are performed at particular seasons of the year, well known to the *Inkata* and often announced to him through the medium of a dream as the most appropriate time at which to secure the increase of the totem animal or plant over whose increase ceremony he presides. Since these times are the seasons of natural increase of these animals and plants, the increase ceremonies are usually followed by the visible increase of the particular totemic animal or plant, and such an immediate response to the performance of these ceremonies does not fail to impress the native as a very forceful demonstration, if such were needed, of the truth of his beliefs.

INITIATION

Every member of the tribe must during the course of his life pass through a certain number of ceremonies of initiation before he can be admitted to full membership within it. These ceremonies constitute, primarily, a re-enaction, for the benefit of the novice, of the complete history of the tribe as handed down in its traditional lore, and both in a psychological and a physical sense are calculated to make a man of him. The initiation ceremonies through which a girl must pass are brief, though they are impressive, being much less so, however, than in the case of the youth, for whom they extend over a long period of time and for whom they are much more severe and trying.

The initiation ceremonies commence when the boy is between ten and twelve years of age, before puberty, the final ceremony taking place when he is about twenty-five or thirty. The ceremonies are four in number, as follows:

(1) Painting and throwing the boy up in the air or *Alkirakiwuma*.

(2) Circumcision or *Lartna*.

(3) Subincision or *Arilta*.

(4) The *Engwura* or fire ceremony.

ALKIRAKIWUMA

In the first ceremony the boy is taken to a central spot near the main camp where the men, and in this case, the women also, are assembled. The boy is then tossed in the air several times by the men, whilst the women dance round the group singing and shouting. Any old man to whom the boy has not in the past paid the proper amount of attention may avail himself of the opportunity now afforded him of physically impressing upon the boy the necessity of conducting himself as he should in the future. The boy is then painted with certain designs on chest and back by the proper relatives, and whilst being so decorated he is told that this will promote his growth to manhood, and he is also told by the tribal fathers and elders that in the future he must not play with women and girls, and that he must henceforth go and live in the men's camp or *Ungunja*, away from his family from whom he is henceforth separated.

During this ceremony his nasal septum is bored through, and thereafter he begins to wear the nose-bone. Before his ceremony the boy is known as an *Ambaquerka*, the term applied to a child of either sex. After this ceremony, and before that of circumcision, he is called *Ulpmerka*.

LARTNA

The ceremony of *Lartna* or circumcision may take place at any time after puberty, and many years may elapse after the first ceremony before the second is entered upon. Preparations are usually made for this ceremony, all unknown to the boy, by his elder male relatives (usually his elder brothers); these preparations consist chiefly of the collection of a large amount of food material to be used during the period of the ceremonies, since these extend over several days and are attended by *corroborees*.

At a pre-arranged time the boy is suddenly set upon and seized in the men's camp by certain of his classificatory brothers, and carried off despite his struggles to the ceremonial ground or *Apulla*, which is situated at some distance from the camp and so placed that it cannot be seen by the women when in camp. Women are, however, present during the early part of this ceremony, and the proceedings are opened by their enaction of an *Alchera* scene.

During the proceedings which follow the boy is told certain of the secrets of the tribe and warned on pain of death never to reveal them, or anything he witnesses during the ceremony, to anyone. Should he do so, he and his relatives would surely die. He is then informed that he is no longer an *Ulpmerka*, but a *Wurtja*.

Following a ceremony in which the *Mura tualcha* of the boy, that is, the woman whose eldest daughter, born or unborn, has been assigned to him as his future wife, hands him a fire-stick with the injunction to hold fast always to his own fire, that is, not to interfere with other women, the *Wurtja* and his ceremonial guardians together with the women followed by a number of shouting boys then leave the ceremonial grounds and return to the main camp, where the women and the boys must remain during the rest of the ceremony.

On the fourth day the *Wurtja* is brought out within a short distance of the ceremonial ground and placed behind a brake of shrubs, from which he may not move without the permission of his guardians. At midnight his eyes are bandaged and he is led back toward the ceremonial ground, where, his bandages removed, he witnesses the performance of certain totemic ceremonies in the meaning of which he is carefully instructed.

On the fifth and sixth days similar performances are given, and on the seventh day he is taken out hunting by his ceremonial guardians; the night being spent in the chanting of songs telling of the deeds of the *Alchera* ancestors, to which the *Wurtja* is required to listen attentively. On the following day a particularly significant totemic performance is given for his benefit which relates to a tradition, in which he is fully instructed, of the wanderings of the kangaroo in the *Alchera*. After this performance those who are to assist at the circumcision are selected in council. On the succeeding day a similar performance is gone through in connection with, let us say, the rat totem, and during the next few days performances in connection with the other totems are given.

During all this the *Wurtja* must not speak unless he is spoken to, he must pay careful attention to everything that occurs during the ceremonies, while the impressive experiences through which he passes under such unusual circumstances, and which are surrounded by such an aura of mystery, are allowed to sear themselves into his mind. He learns about the origins of the totems and the meaning of the ceremonies associated with them, and, finally, that he has now reached the stage preliminary to his full initiation into the tribe.

Following the performances of various other impressive ceremonies, the women return once more to the ceremonial ground, and the boy, concealed by the bodies of his ceremonial guardians, runs the gauntlet with them through the ranks of the women, the ceremonial guardians the while pelting the women with pieces of bark carried for the purpose, a final volley being the signal for their hasty departure to their own camp, their pace accelerated by the vehement shouting of the men.

This ceremony is intended to represent a stage in the dissociation of the *Wurtja* from the influence of the women. Following the performance of certain other ceremonies, the women again return to the ceremonial ground, and those who stand in the relation of mother's mother to the novice assist in the performance of a special ceremony, following which they return to their own camp where they must hereafter remain. Immediately the ceremonial ground is filled with the sound of bull-roarers, and so loud is the noise made by these that they can easily be heard by the women and children in camp, who believe that the roaring is the voice of *Twanyirrika*, the spirit who enters the body of the novice after the operation of circumcision and takes him away until he is recovered.

At a certain signal the novice is laid upon his back, the assistant of the operator grasps the foreskin and pulls it out as far as possible, whereupon the operator with a quick movement severs it with a small stone knife. The blood from the wound is allowed to flow into a shield, and, in a dazed condition the *Wurtja* is taken back to his brake where he receives the congratulations of the men, who inform him that he is now a proper man. While he is still bleeding his ceremonial guardians bring up the bull-roarers, and pressing them against the wound, inform him that it was these and not *Twanyirrika* which made the sound he had heard, that these are sacred *Churinga* which must never be shown to or talked about to the women and children. Meanwhile the youth stands over a dampened fire the smoke of which is supposed to be efficacious in healing the wound. After the ceremony he is now an *Arakurta*. Soon, other recently initiated *Arakurta* are brought on to the ceremonial ground, and the backs of all of them are scraped with a *Churinga*. Finally the *Arakurta* is taken to the camp of the other *Arakurta* escorted by his ceremonial guardians, where he remains until his wound has healed and he is ready for the ceremony of *Arilta* or subincision.

ARILTA

The *Arilta* ceremony takes place shortly after the recovery of the youth from the effects of the first operation. At this ceremony no women may be present. Here, too, ceremonial performances are given relating to the totems and their *Alchera* origins, and these are prolonged far into the night. Upon a certain day before dawn everything is ready; the novice is not told what is about to happen to him. When he arrives at the ceremonial ground he is told to lie down flat upon a living table formed by two initiated men; as soon as he is in position another man sits down astride his body and grasping the *Arakurta*'s penis puts it on the stretch, the operator then quickly approaches, and with a stone knife lays open the penile portion of the urethra. This operation over, the *Arakurta* is now regarded as having passed to the stage of an *Atua-kurka*, or initiated man.

The blood from the wound is allowed to flow into a shield, which is then emptied into a fire which has previously been prepared for the purpose. If the wound be painful the initiate puts some glowing pieces of charcoal into the ashes and then urinates upon them, meanwhile holding his penis above the glowing embers; the steam arising from the fire is said to ease the pain. Until the wound is healed the *Atua-kurka* must lie upon his back, otherwise it is believed his penis will grow crooked.

It often happens that at the conclusion of the *Arilta* operation, other intiated men who are present and who have therefore already been operated upon on some previous occasion, will voluntarily offer to undergo a second or third operation. In such cases the old incision is enlarged.

When certain other ceremonies have been performed and the *Atua-kurka* is completely recovered, he, together with the other men who were present at the ceremonies, assemble at some little distance from the main camp and begin to sing loudly. The women, hearing the singing, approach and begin to dance as they did at the ceremonial ground. The men discontinue singing as soon as they are near to the women, shouting '*Tirra, tirra, tirra*', a sound which resembles that made by the whirling bull-roarers, and which is immediately taken up by the women. The now undecorated *Atua-kurka* emerges from the midst of the assembled men, and running up close to the women, who continue dancing, suddenly turns upon his heel and runs away into the bush where he is followed by a number of men who spend the night together with him singing all the while until daybreak. Shortly before it is light the *Atua-kurka* is accoutred by his ceremonial guardians in the full regalia of a member of the tribe and provided with a shield and spear-thrower. Around daybreak he sets out, in the centre of a group of men led by the individual who removed his decorations at the conclusion of the *Arilta* ceremony, while all again shout '*Tirra, tirra, tirra*'. When within about fifty yards of the women, the *Atua-kurka* proceeds alone, hiding his face behind his shield, up to the women, when one or two of his immediate family and tribal sisters throw their wooden bowls or *pitchis* at his shield, and pressing their hands upon his shoulders, and rubbing their faces against his back, they cut off some locks of his hair, which they keep to make up afterwards into ornaments for themselves.

After this ceremony the *Atua-kurka* is free to go into the presence of the various elders who participated in the ceremonies, though he must not speak to them until several months have elapsed, nor must he speak loudly in their presence.

At daylight on the morning of the next day the men provide themselves with fire-sticks and, surrounding the young man, conduct him to the women, who are again waiting to receive him. He is fully decorated, and carries a shield and boomerang and some twigs of Eremophila. When the party is within a short distance of the women the men throw down their fire-sticks and halt, and the young man steps out from the centre of the group and throws his boomerang high up in the direction of the spot at which his mother was supposed to have lived in the Alchera. This throwing of the boomerang in the direction of the mother's Alchera camp—that is, of course, the spot at which the Alchera individual of whom his mother is supposed to be the reincarnation lived—occurs during the performance of other ceremonies, such, for example, as those which accompany the knocking out of the teeth in eastern groups of the Arunta and also in the Ilpirra tribe. It seems to indicate the existence in the Alchera, the far past times, of some special relationship between a man and his mother. Nowadays it may perhaps be regarded partly as intended to symbolise the idea that the young man is entering upon manhood, and thus is passing out of the control of the women and into the ranks of the men. The fact that he is using the boomerang is indicative of this, and his throwing it towards his mother's camp is an intimation to her of the fact that he is passing away from her control.[46]

After this ceremony the initiate must seat himself upon a fire upon which he is pressed down by the women who have made it. This ordeal over, he returns to camp, where he is forced to keep silence for three days, following which he becomes a fully initiated member of the tribe, though it is not until he has passed through the *Engwura* ceremonies that he becomes an *Urliara*, or a fully developed man.

THE ENGWURA CEREMONY

The *Engwura* is characterized by a long series of ceremonies each of which is occupied with the performance of ceremonies re-enacting the history of the totems of the tribe, and terminating with ordeals by fire which form the last of the initiatory ceremonies. The performance of the various totemic ceremonies need not here be described, a very full account of them occupying 130 pages will be found in *The Arunta* by Spencer and Gillen.[47] At the majority of these performances the young men who are to undergo the final processes of their initiation are present, but from a certain number of these ceremonies they are driven by the elders into the bush, where it is their duty to obtain supplies of food for the sole consumption of the elders. Throughout the whole period during which the ceremonies are taking place, and those observed by Spencer and Gillen lasted from the beginning of September well into January, the *Ilpongworra*, as the young men are collectively called, after having taken part in a certain ceremony, are under the strict care of a delegated elder, who sees to it that they obtain as little to eat as possible, and that they are none too comfortable. When out hunting for the benefit of the elders the *Ilpongworra* are supposed to abstain from eating any of the game they secure, but must bring it all back to the elders who may, or may not, give them a small share of it.

On three separate occasions on three separate days it is the duty of the women to assault the *Ilpongworra* with fire-sticks which they throw at the young men's heads as the latter pass by the women's camp. The *Ilpongworra* defend themselves against injury as best they can with their shields, but not infrequently one of the *Ilpongworra* is very severely scorched as a result of the experience. It is of interest here to note that during this procedure the women make certain unmistakable beckoning motions to the men, which they, of course, must disregard. Returning to the camp, after the final fire-throwing ceremony of the women, and following a number of other exhausting ceremonies, which need not be detailed here, with the exception of the mention of one in which the *Ilpongworra* with lighted fire-sticks rush towards the women and children who are assembled outside for the purpose and hurl their fire-sticks over the heads of the women, they, in a body, return to the *Engwura* ground, from which they are not allowed to move upon any pretext whatsoever. After lying silent all night the *Ilpongworra* are sent away into the bush for two days, during which preparations are made for their ordeal by fire.

A secluded spot amongst the ranges some two miles away from Alice Springs was selected, and here, while the young men rested by the side of a water-hole in the bed of the Todd, the *Urliara*, who were in charge of them, went to the chosen spot and made a large fire of logs and branches about three yards in diameter. Then the young men, of whom forty were present, were called up, and putting green bushes on the fire, they were made to lie down full length upon the smoking boughs, which prevented them from coming into contact with the red-hot embers beneath. The heat and smoke were stifling, but none of them were allowed to get up until they received the permission of the *Urliara*. After they had all been on once, each one remaining about four to five minutes on the fire, the old men came to the conclusion that they must repeat the process, and so, making up the fire again, they were once more put on in the midst of dense clouds of smoke, one of the older men lifting up the green boughs at one side with a long pole so as to allow of the access of air and ensure the smouldering of the leaves and green wood. There was no doubt as to the trying nature of the ordeal, as, apart from the smoke, the heat was so great that, after kneeling down on it to see what it was like, we got up as quickly as possible, and of course the natives had no protection in the way of clothes.[48]

Finally, after a ceremony in which the *Ilpongworra* kneel down for some seconds in fires prepared by the women, who again beckon to them with various unmistakable sexual motions, and the removal of the ban of silence from them, the *Ilpongworra* are admitted to full manhood and standing in the tribe, and are hereafter regarded as fully initiated *Urliara*.

These ceremonies are, of course, of great interest in themselves, for they are manifestly a celebration and ritual enaction of the phylogenetic history of the tribe as represented today chiefly in its totemic organizations and the traditions associated with them, their celebration being calculated to keep impressively fresh and alive the social and 'biological' foundations upon which that history rests. We have briefly seen how gradually and impressively the individual is initiated into the secrets of his society and into a knowledge of the manner in which it came into existence, as well as the nature of the means by which that existence is ensured both for the present and the future. We have seen how the individual is gradually led from childhood to full manhood, step by step through the history of the tribe, how, in his social ontogenetic development he repeats, in a crude way, the phylogenetic history of the tribe, and learns to esteem and respect the elders, who, by their conduct of the ceremonies and their regulation of the totemic performances, and their conveyance of the traditions associated with these, have impressed upon him their true worth and significance, upon which he could not have put quite the proper valuation before his initiation.

The majority of these ceremonies are generally each associated with the most detailed traditions which effectively serve to give them their meaning. Practices, however, such as circumcision and subincision seem to be conspicuously lacking in any traditions which would serve to explain their meaning to the natives. Circumcision and subincision were, according to tradition, introduced in the *Alchera*, the first by Numbakulla, who used a fire-stick for the operation,[49] and the second by the *Achilpa* or *Alchera* ancestors of the men of the wild-cat totem—for what, if any reason, no one knows; to a query concerning the matter the native will invariably reply that these rites were practised in the *Alchera* and must therefore be so practised today. In other parts of Australia there are, however, definite traditions which purport to give these rites a meaning, and these traditions, to which we shall later have occasion to refer, though quite clear rationalizations, may none the less be quite as good explanations of the significance of the practices as any other that could be offered, though this is to be strongly doubted. The fact that these practices exist does not, of course, necessarily imply that they ever had a meaning among the Arunta, for they may have been taken over from some other tribe for any number of different reasons, but whatever the origin of these practices may have been, however irrational the reasons for their adoption, they must, at any rate, have given rise to some sort of philosophy which would give them a congruency with such beliefs and practices as already formed part of the existing background of native philosophy. The discussion of this matter may, however, profitably be deferred until a later chapter.

The foregoing much compressed account of Arunta culture must, for the present, do service as a general background against which the procreative beliefs of the numerous other tribes inhabiting Australia, as well as of the Arunta themselves, may be seen. It has already been pointed out that no great violence will be done to the facts should we thus perceive these beliefs against the background of Arunta culture, for although these beliefs unquestionably vary in details from tribe to tribe and even from horde to horde, they are on the whole so strikingly similar in nature as to render such a procedure much less objectionable than would conceivably be possible in any other case.

Our real purpose, however, is to avoid committing so egregious an error of method as the study of the procreative beliefs of these other tribes as if they were functions of Arunta culture, but rather to endeavour to discover what the Aborigines really believe about procreation wherever in Australia their beliefs in connection with this subject have been reported upon, and to utilize the forms which this belief assumes in our study of the similar conditions in relation to, and within the framework of, the culture of the Arunta.

NOTES

1   *The Native Tribes of Central Australia.*
2   *The Arunta.*
3   For a trustworthy and dispassionate account of the state to which the Arunta as well as other Australian tribes have been reduced, see S. D. Porteous, *The Psychology of a Primitive People.* See also Spencer's preface to the *The Arunta.* The conditions but cursorily referred to in these works tell but one fraction of the story which has everywhere in Aboriginal Australia, wherever the white man has penetrated, been the same. A story of ruthless cruelty, injustice, dispossession, and wholesale murder of native populations, in too many cases by officially constituted bodies such as the white police force. Another writer

puts the case differently. 'The Australians', he says, 'were one of the most amiable and kindly of savage races, and the European settlers became interested in them and befriended them; they were soon decimated by tuberculosis and other diseases which were spread by the old clothes given them by the colonists. The reduction in numbers of the aborigines has been often attributed to systematic murder; but that view is one of the libels which have been widely circulated regarding Australia', J. W. Gregory, *The Menace of Colour*, 150. See also A. Moorehead, *The Fatal Impact*, London, 1965; M. Reay, 'The background of alien impact', in R. M. and C. H. Berndt (eds), *Aboriginal Man in Australia*, 377–95; A. A. Abbie, *The Original Australians*, 230–63. For a brief account of the brutal murder of some thirty innocent natives by the police some years ago, see C. E. C. Lefroy, 'Australian Aborigines, a noblehearted race', *Contemporary Review*, 1929, 222–3. For an early account of similar depredations, see G. C. Mundy, *Our Antipodes*, chapter v, 104 sqq. One of the most sympathetic writers on Australia, who knows Australia as few people know it, has remarked: 'It is to be noted that the whites are always murdered and the blacks just killed', C. T. Madigan, *Central Australia*, 252. The same writer tells the following story: A station manager asked his aboriginal stockman to ride a rather refractory colt. The black fellow did not relish the idea. After a little thought he said, 'Mine tinkit you better ride 'im boss. Blackfellow getting very scarce now', ibid., 254; C. D. Rowley, *The Destruction of Aboriginal Society*.

4　An excellent account of the physiography of Central Australia is to be found in C. T. Madigan, op. cit.; but the best of all such accounts is B. Spencer's *Wanderings in Wild Australia*.

5　*Illustrated London News*, 127, 19 August 1950, 272–3.

6　*Science*, 120, 1954, 205.

7　*The Arunta*, i, 3.

8　Ibid., 9.

9　*The Arunta*, i, 12; Basedow, *The Australian Aboriginal*, 125; see also W. E. Roth 'Notes on government, morals, and crime.', N. Q ld Ethnography, *Bulletin* no. 8, and [James Tucker], *Adventures of an Outlaw*: the Memoirs of Ralph Rashleigh, 312–13.

10　On the mobility, and on the possible origin of the domestication of the dog, there is an interesting passage by the naturalist Le Souëf who writes: 'I used to wonder why the natives shifted their camp so often, but I don't now, as, although we were only in ours three days, the amount of evil-smelling refuse that the natives had thrown away close to the camp was considerable, and the odour was perceptible on the third day before the camp even came into sight, and being in thick scrub there was not much breeze to carry it off, and flies and ants were attracted in numbers. If we had had several dogs, instead of only one, it might not have been so bad.' W. H. D. Le Souëf, *Wild Life in Australia*.

11　Boomerangs among the Arunta are not of the *returning* variety as they are in other parts of Australia. For an account of the boomerang, see D. S. Davidson, 'Australian throwing-sticks, throwing-clubs, and boomerangs', *Amer. Anthrop.*, n.s., 38, 1936, 76–100.

12　C. P. Mountford, *Brown Men and Red Sand*, 122.

13　There is no evidence that they have ever happened upon the notion of heating water by the use of hot stones.

14　Radcliffe-Brown, 'Three tribes of Western Australia', *JRAI*, 43, 1913, 159.

15　Since white observers generally underestimate the age of natives, it is probable, that at least one or two years should be added to this figure.

16　*Totemism and Exogamy*, i, 236.

17　H. Basedow, *The Australian Aboriginal*, 222.

18　B. Malinowski, *The Family Among the Australian Aborigines*, chapter vii.

19　R. F. Fortune, 'A note on some forms of kinship structure', *Oceania*, 4, 1933, 1–9.

20　A. R. Radcliffe-Brown, 'The social organization of Australian tribes', *Oceania*, 1, 1930, 44.

21 J. G. Frazer, *Totemism and Exogamy*, i, 303.

22 For a clear discussion of this see A. P. Elkin, 'Kinship in South Australia', *Oceania*, 9, 1938, 69, and 10, 1940, 333–4.

23 We may notice here that this arrangement has in our own time come to be considered as hardly the best possible one, and at least one communist country, the USSR, at one time officially declared its intention of ultimately abolishing the family and the sanctioned custody of the beings born into it to the parents. The State in Russia entrusted the biological parents of the child with its care, but this was considered a temporary expedient. The theory being that the family of its very nature stands in opposition to the State, that the individual is essentially a member of the State, and not of a particular unit like the family, an institution which was regarded as an arbitrary arrangement. The Russians appear long since to have abandoned this view. In Israel, however, such community guardianship of the children who live entirely apart from their parents, has been successfully realized in the Jewish *Kwuzah* or community. Magnus Hirschfeld gives a sympathetic account of the *Kwuzah* in his *Men and Women*, 286–92. See also E. Tauber, *Molding Society to Man*; M. E. Spiro, *Kibbutz* and *Children of the Kibbutz*.

24 *The Arunta*, i, 80.

25 Ibid., 75–6.

26 The witchetty grub is the larva of the big Cossos moth, and about the size of a large man's middle finger.

27 '*Knanikilla* means the place of the *Knanja* or totem. *La* is a suffix used to indicate position; thus *petala* means on a hill.' (S. and G.)

28 'The spirit or *Kuruna* always enters the woman through the loins.' (S. and G.)

29 '*Kurunas* are also supposed to be especially fond of travelling in whirlwinds, and, on seeing one of these, which are called Uraburaba and are very frequent at certain times of the year, approaching her, a woman will at once run away.' (S. and G.)

30 Ibid., 76–7.

31 Ibid., 39 n. 1.

32 Ibid.

33 Ibid., 78.

34 Ibid., 363.

35 See p. 29 above.

36 *The Arunta*, 39.

37 T. Hernández, 'Children among the Drysdale River tribes', *Oceania*, 12, 1941, 125.

38 *The Arunta*, i, 85.

39 Name applied to a special series of totemic ceremonies shortly to be described.

40 One who is *not* uncircumcised.

41 A sacred pole connected with a totemic ceremony.

42 Ibid., 270–1.

43 Ibid., 272–3.

44 Ibid., 106.

45 *The Native Tribes of Central Australia*, 138n.

46 *The Arunta*, i, 213.

47 Ibid., 175–303.

48 Ibid., 294.

49 The fire-stick was still used for this operation in the twenties by the Yantowannta tribe of the Cooper Creek district of the Lake Eyre region. See H. Basedow, 'Subincision and kindred rites of the Australian Aboriginal', *JRAI*, 57, 1927, 126.

CHAPTER III

The procreative beliefs of the Central Australian Aborigines

Nothing that is shall perish utterly,
But perish only to revive again
In other forms . . .
    LONGFELLOW

In the present chapter the relevant evidence relating to the procreative beliefs of the tribes of Central Australia is presented and discussed in some detail.

In this place it is desirable to point out that before the publication of Spencer and Gillen's account of the Arunta theory of conception in 1899, in spite of an earlier considerable literature of a rather desultory kind on the natives of Australia, with the exception of such general assumptions as were made by Hartland, there had previously existed no suspicion of the facts as they were made known to the world by these investigators. The scientific literature dealing with the Australian Aborigines was almost entirely confined to short accounts, published in various periodicals, of certain aspects of the social organization of the tribes reported upon. The interesting and in many ways invaluable compilations of contemporary knowledge relating to the Australian Aborigines, such as the works edited by R. Brough Smyth,[1] G. Taplin,[2] J. D. Woods,[3] and E. M. Curr,[4] assembled mainly by means of the questionnaire method from missionaries, police troopers, and similar sources, represented almost the sole attempts to record in some sort of systematic way something of the manners and customs, the folklore and linguistics, of the Aboriginal tribes. But in almost all instances, such was the delicacy of the feelings of the correspondents or the editors that rarely were they able to permit themselves to make more than the briefest reference to those customs and beliefs which it was their habit to dismiss with some such decorous epithet as 'disgusting' or 'bestial'. Characteristic in this respect is the great work of an investigator who belonged to this period, namely, A. W. Howitt, in whose numerous writings on the native tribes of South-East Australia, and in his monograph by that title,[5] which was not published until 1904 and represented the fruits of forty years of labour among these tribes, there is not to be found a single reference to the sexual life of the natives, and but two or three of the most cursory references to the native procreative beliefs.

Thus it is that in every sense of the word Spencer and Gillen's account of the Arunta represents the first and pioneering work of Australian ethnology; and, indeed, though it is by no means free of serious faults, it will always remain one of the best accounts of a primitive people available to the student of human culture and society.

In an account of the Arunta preceding the appearance of that by Spencer and Gillen by some eight years, which actually includes the first description, brief and incomplete though it is, of the conceptional beliefs of the Arunta who live towards the south-east of Spencer and Gillen's hordes on the Finke River, the Rev. L. Schulze, a missionary attached to the Mission at Hermannsburg, writes of the native conceptional beliefs:[6]

These natives believe that the souls of the infants dwell in the foliage of trees, and that they are carried there by the good mountain spirits, *tuanjiraka*, and their wives, *melbata*. The nearest tree to a woman when she feels the first pain of parturition she calls *ngirra*, as they are under the impression that the *gurunna*, or soul, has then entered from it into the child. Such a tree is left untouched, as they believe that whoever should happen to break off even a single branch would become sick. But if the tree should be injured or broken down by winds or floods that person would get ill whose *ngirra* the tree was.

This account, as far as it goes, is in essential agreement with that given eight years later by Spencer and Gillen, with something of which we have already become acquainted in the last chapter. It will perhaps be recalled that we encountered the *tuanjiraka* as *Twanyirrika* during the circumcision ceremonies, though there was no occasion to hear of their wives, the *melbata*. *Ngirra* is the *Knanja*, and the *gurunna* the *Kuruna* of Spencer and Gillen.

Obviously, Schulze's is a very limited account of the native conceptional beliefs. The points to be noticed here are three. First, that the abode of the *souls* or spirits of infants is limited to the foliage of trees; second, that the mountain spirits *tuanjiraka* and their wives, *melbata*, carry them to their abodes in the foliage of the trees; and, third, that the soul is said to enter a pre-existing child already within the mother.

The first point, the restriction of the abodes of spirit-children to the foliage of trees, may, I think, most plausibly be attributed to Schulze's limited information, if what Spencer and Gillen write is also true for this southern group of the Arunta. The second point, namely, that the souls of the infants are placed in the foliage of trees by the *tuanjiraka* and their wives, actually throws some light upon a matter which, as reported by Spencer and Gillen, is not very clear and will be discussed in some detail in the succeeding report, namely why it is that the *Churinga Twanyirrika*, which is made by the paternal grandfather of the new-born child from some wood taken from a tree close to the *Pertalchera*, has no *Kuruna* associated with it.[7] Among the Arunta there is a tradition with respect to the origin of the *Churinga* which has it that an *Alchera Inkata*, deputed by a superior *Inkata* acting upon the command of *Numbakulla*, arranged for the birth of children by placing *Kuruna*—always in pairs—in many of the mulga trees. These trees are called *Tidja*.[8] According to this tradition the lesser Alchera *Inkata* (*Inkata kupitcha*) then said to the *Oknirrabata*, the wise old man,

I . . . have put Kuruna, or spirits, in the mulga trees. You take a log of mulga wood and split it. The Kuruna are everywhere in the trees; make the Churinga for them smooth and good and cut the *Ilkinia*[9] on them with an opossum tooth. Make the *Indulla-irrakura*.[10]

In the early days the old Oknirrabatas often made these *Tidjanira*. The old men are supposed to have known, or at least to have been able to recognize, the particular mulga trees in which the Inkata had left the Kurunas. The Oknirrabata would see an *Iwupa* or Kuruna (both of these are names applied to spirits), in, perhaps, a specially large mulga-tree. It would disappear, but the man then knew that the tree was a *Tidja alchera*, in which the Inkata had placed Kuruna. He then cuts a log (*taga*) from the tree and splits it into two (*taga chiepa kuma tera*); out of each half he fashions a *Churinga tidjanira*, and thus makes a pair of mates, *unpora ninga*, ornamenting each with the Ilkinia, or mark of the totem. The two Kuruna mates, one *atua* [man] and one *arragutja* [woman], associate themselves with, and enter into the Tidjanira, which are then placed in the *Pertalchera*. These Churinga, made in the Alchera and even in later times by great Oknirrabatas, though of course wooden, rank as *Churinga indulla-irrakura*, along with those carried about by the original Inkatas. The old men are able to distinguish between the Churinga associated with the *atua* and that with the *arragutja* Kuruna.[11]

It would seem likely that the *Tidjanira* of Spencer and Gillen is but another version of the same thing called by Schulze *ngirra*, that is, the abode of the soul or spirit. *Tidjanira* is the name given to a *Churinga* made out of the wood of the *Tidja* or mulga tree, and we have seen how and for what reasons some of the original *Alchera Churinga*, the *Churinga indulla-irrakura*, were made in this way, and afterwards placed in the *Pertalchera*. Schulze's report is clearly either a garbled record of this tradition or the report of actual conditions which still follow the *Alchera* pattern. In either event, it is of interest to note that two *Alchera* ancestral men called *Twanyirrika* were created out of the first *Tidjanira* by the first great *Inkata* created by

Numbakulla, the *Inkata oknirra*.[12] The *Kuruna* associated with their *Talkara* (stone *Churinga*) and *Tidjanira* still give rise to men who are called *Twanyirrika*, but this is only a name.[13] The *Churinga Twanyirrika* which is made by the paternal grandfather of the child is a secondary *Churinga* and is never used as were the *Twanyirrika Churinga* referred to in the above tradition, which is part of the Achilpa tradition with which we shall shortly deal.[14] Nevertheless, the origin and meaning of these secondary *Churinga* seems clear, and in the light of Schulze's statements provides us with a clue to the actual origin of the *Churinga*. For according to the tradition of which we have just read, the *Kuruna* entered the woman directly from the tree, and it was from this tree that the original *Tidjanira Churinga* were made, and then placed in the *Pertalchera* with which their *Kuruna* are now associated. As Schulze points out, should anything happen to the tree, the individual whose *ngirra* it is would fall ill. In this we have what may possibly be the explanation of the origin of the *Churinga*. For if trees and rocks—stock and stone—were the original abodes of the spirits, then a portion of such a tree or rock would represent the immanent token of the individual's relationship to that rock or tree, the original seat of his spirit part to which, upon his bodily death, it will return. The *Knanja* or *ngirra* tree or rock is actually the original source of all the *Churinga*, each *Churinga* representing the complete spirit part of one *Alchera* ancestor whose abode that *Knanja* or *ngirra* originally was. The reason why the secondary *Churinga Twanyirrika* have no *Kuruna* associated with them is because the latter are already associated with the particular *Churinga Indulla-irrakura* of the *Alchera*.

With respect to the third point, that the *gurunna* enters the child when the woman feels the first pangs of parturition, there can be no doubt that as worded this statement implies that the child is already in existence before the soul enters it. The statement that the 'natives believe that the souls of the infants dwell in the foliage of trees' would support this interpretation of the phrase; in any case, Schulze writes 'souls of the infants' not 'infant souls', nor yet 'soul children' or 'spirit-children'. This statement then would imply that the spiritual and corporeal parts of the individual are at least of separate, if not of different, origin, that it is only an *Alchera* spirit or the spirit part of an individual ancestor which undergoes incarnation, and that the corporeal part of the individual in whom it is incarnated is of separate origin. This is, of course, a fundamental matter, but until we have considered the further independent evidence it will be of no advantage to pursue the matter any further here. We may therefore defer the discussion of this matter until the whole of the evidence has been surveyed.

The account of the Arunta procreative beliefs and the relevant observations concerning them which follows here is derived chiefly from Spencer's revision of the work originally written by him in collaboration with F. J. Gillen and published in 1899,[15] and in its revised form published in 1927 under the title *The Arunta*. This version has, after careful consideration, been selected in preference to that of the 1899 text, since it is in all essentials the same as the former except that much new and important material has been added, and where there has been any change in the text it has generally been in the interest of greater clarity. It is necessary here to make clear that the revision was made following a second study of the Arunta, some thirty years after the first, by Spencer, during which he paid particular attention to certain matters, his own report of which had been challenged from time to time, one such matter being the alleged native nescience of the real nature of the procreative process. In this connection Spencer writes: 'There can be no doubt as to the general correctness and wide distribution of the native theory of conception, as originally described by us'.[16] This statement applies specifically to such Central Australian tribes as the Arunta, Urabunna, Luritja, Ilpirra, Walbiri, Kaitisha, Worgaia, and Warramunga.

In the following excerpts from Spencer and Gillen's work a certain amount of repetition of material already presented in the preceding chapter necessarily occurs. In view of my intention to record verbatim each investigator's account of the procreative beliefs of the peoples studied by him, such repetition has proved unavoidable.

We have already seen how closely the totemic organization and the ceremonies associated with it are bound up with the whole past history of the tribe, and we have also seen how inseparably woven into the fabric of this organization are the procreative beliefs of the natives.

The whole past history of the tribe may be said to be bound up with these totemic ceremonies, each of which is concerned with the doings of certain mythical ancestors who are supposed to have lived in the dim past, to which the natives give the name of 'Alchera'.

In the Alchera lived ancestors who, in the native mind, are so intimately associated with the animals or plants the name of which they bear that an Alchera man of, say, the kangaroo totem may sometimes be spoken of either as a man-kangaroo or as a kangaroo-man. The identity of the human individual is often sunk in that of the animal or plant from which he is supposed to have originated. It is useless to try to get farther back than the Alchera; the history of the tribe as known to the natives commences then.

Going back to this far-away time, we find ourselves in the midst of semi-human creatures endowed with powers not possessed by their living descendants and inhabiting the same country which is now inhabited by the tribe, but which was then devoid of many of its most marked features, the origin of which, such as the gaps and gorges in the Macdonnell Ranges, is attributed to these mythical Alchera ancestors.

These Alchera men and women are represented in tradition as collected together in companies, each of which consisted of a certain number of individuals belonging to one particular totem.[17]

Each of these Alchera ancestors is represented as carrying about with him, or her, one or more of the sacred stones, which are called by the Arunta natives Churinga, and each of these Churinga is intimately associated with the *Kuruna* or spirit part of some individual. Either where they originated and stayed, as in the case of certain of the witchetty grub people, or else where, during their wanderings, they camped for a time, there were formed what the natives call *Knanikilla*, each one of which is in reality a local totem centre. At each of these spots—and they are all well known to the old men, who pass the knowledge on from generation to generation—a certain number of the Alchera ancestors went into the ground, each leaving his Churinga behind. His body died, but some natural feature, such as a rock or tree, arose to mark the spot, while his spirit part remained in the Churinga. These Churinga, as well as others that the wandering parties left behind them, were stored in *Pertalchera*, or sacred store-houses, that usually had the form of small caves and fissures in the rocks, or even a hollow tree or a carefully concealed hole in a sand-bank. The result is that, as we follow their wanderings, we find the whole country is dotted over with *Knanikilla*, or local totem centres, at each of which are deposited a number of Churinga, with *Kuruna*, or spirit individuals, associated with them. Each *Knanikilla* is, of course, connected with one totem. . . .

As we have said, the exact spot at which a Churinga was deposited was always marked by some natural object, such as a tree or rock, and in this the spirit is supposed to take up its abode, and it is called the spirit's *Knanja*.[18]

We may take the following as a typical example of how each man and woman gains a totem name. Close to Alice Springs is a large and important witchetty grub totem centre or *Knanikilla*. Here there were deposited in the Alchera a large number of Churinga carried by witchetty grub men and women. There are numerous prominent rocks and boulders and certain ancient gum trees along the sides of a picturesque gap in the ranges, that are the *Knanja* trees and rocks of these spirits, which, so long as they remain in spirit form, they usually frequent. If a woman conceives a child after having been near to this gap, it is one of these spirit individuals which has entered her body,[19] and therefore, quite irrespective of what the mother's or father's totem may chance to be, that child, when born, must of necessity be of the witchetty grub totem; it is, in fact, nothing else but the reincarnation of one of the witchetty grub people of the Alchera. Suppose, for example, to take a particular and actual instance, an emu woman from another locality comes to Alice Springs, and whilst there becomes aware that she has conceived a child, and then returns to her own locality before the child is born, that child, though it may be born in an emu locality is an Udnirringita or witchetty grub. It must be, the natives say, because it entered the mother at Alice Springs, where there are only witchetty grub *Kurunas*. Had it entered her body within the limits of her own emu locality, it would as inevitably have been an emu. To take another example. Quite recently the lubra or wife of a witchetty grub man, she belonging to the same totem, conceived a child while on a visit to a neighbouring Quatcha or water locality, which lies away to the east of Alice Springs—that child's totem is water; or, again, an Alice Springs woman, when asked by us as to why her child was a witchetty grub (in this instance belonging to the same totem as both of its parents), told us that one day she was taking a drink of water near to the gap in the Ranges where the spirits dwell when suddenly she heard a child's voice crying out, '*Mia, Mia!*'—the native term for relationship, which includes that of mother. Not being anxious to have a child, she ran away as fast as she could, but to no purpose; she was fat and well favoured, and such women the *Kurunas* prefer; one of them had gone inside her, and of course it was born a witchetty grub.[20]

The natives are quite clear upon this point. The spirit children are supposed to have a strong predilection for fat women, and prefer to choose such for their mothers, even at the risk of being born into the wrong class. . . .

There is a curious belief in regard to one method of conception. If a man, for example, be hunting an emu and, whilst he is chasing it, it runs near to a wallaby *Knanikilla*, a wallaby *Kuruna* may go into it. If the man spears it near to the *Knanikilla* and gives some of it to his wife to eat, the wallaby *Kuruna* will go into her. She does not eat it, but, as is supposed always to be the case, it enters by her loins. Later on she becomes sick, and then knows that the *Kuruna* has given rise to a *Ratappa* inside her, which, when born, belongs to the wallaby *Knanja*. It is definitely said that she does not actually eat the *Kuruna*.[21]

The members of each totem claim to have the power of increasing the number of the animal or plant, and in this respect the tradition connected with Undiara, the great centre of the kangaroo totem, just as the Emily Gap is the great centre of the witchetty grub totem, is of especial interest. In the Alchera, as we have already described, a special kangaroo was killed by kangaroo men and its body brought to Undiara and deposited in the cave close by the water-hole. The rock ledge arose to mark the spot, and into this entered its spirit part and also the spirit parts of many other kangaroo animals (not men) who came subsequently and, as the natives say, went down into the earth here. The rock is, in fact, the *Knanja* stone of the kangaroo animals, and to them this particular rock has just the same relationship as the water-hole close by has to the men. The one is full of *Kurunas* of kangaroo animals, just as the other is full of those of men and women. The purpose of the ceremony at the present day, so say the natives, is, by means of pouring out the blood of kangaroo men upon the rock, to drive out in all directions the *Kurunas* of the kangaroo animals and so to increase the number of the animals. The spirit kangaroo enters the female kangaroo in just the same way in which the spirit kangaroo man enters the kangaroo woman.

Every animal such as a kangaroo is supposed to have a *Kuruna* or spirit part, just like a human being has. As a *Kuruna* it has no legs or arms or head, but goes into its mother and grows into a kangaroo or rat or wild dog, as the case may be. An emu *Kuruna* goes into an emu, who lays an egg containing the little emu *Kuruna*, which is very small and cannot at first be seen, but it grows into an emu inside the shell and hatches out from this just like a little kangaroo or human baby grows inside its mother's *ekura*, or baby bag, and hatches out.[22]

Churinga is the name given by the Arunta natives to certain sacred objects which, on penalty of death or very severe punishment, such as blinding by a fire-stick, are never allowed to be seen by women or uninitiated men. The term is also applied to various objects associated with the totems, but the greater number belong to that class of rounded, oval or elongated, flattened slabs of wood and stone, varying in length from six or seven feet to two or three inches, to the smaller ones of which the name bull-roarer is now commonly applied.[23]

It must be remembered that the country occupied by the tribes, amongst whom the cult of the Churinga exists, is of great extent, so that, even in important respects, beliefs vary considerably. It is, however, possible to say that there is one fundamental Churinga belief according to which every individual possesses a special one of wood or stone with which his or her *Kuruna*, or spirit part, is intimately associated.[24]

The original Churinga are, one and all, connected with the *Knanjas* or totems. At the present day the whole country is dotted over with *Knanikillas*, or local totem centres, and each of these has one or more sacred storehouses in which the Churinga are kept under the charge of the head man of the local group. . . .

The general name for the head man, throughout most, but not all, of the totemic groups, is *Inkata*, and for the storehouse, *Pertalchera* (*perta*, a rock), in reference to the fact that crevices and caves in rocks are the favourite secreting places. *Pertalchera* thus signifies the Alchera rock. Each one of these contains, amongst others, the original Churinga of every individual that, in one way or another, came to be deposited there in the Alchera. With each of these, again, a *Kuruna* or spirit is associated. When the *Kuruna* goes into a woman and a child is born, the old men determine what *Kuruna* has undergone reincarnation. The Churinga is preserved in the *Pertalchera*, and there it remains in association with the *Arumburinga*, or double of the *Kuruna*. This Churinga is known as the *Churinga knanja* or *Churinga indulla-irrakura*. The *Arumburinga*, however, can travel about freely, and, in fact, often visits, and is supposed to watch over, its human representative. The spot at which the child is born and brought up, and at which it will probably spend the greater part of its life, has nothing to do with determining the resting-place of its Churinga. That remains in the storehouse or *Pertalchera* in which it was deposited in the Alchera, and to which the *Kuruna*—now called *Ulthana*—returns when the man or woman dies. In the case, for example, already quoted, in which a witchetty grub woman conceived a child in a water locality, or *Knanikilla*, twelve miles to the north of Alice Springs, where the woman's home camp is located, the child was born at the latter, but its *Churinga knanja* is deposited in the *Pertalchera* of the water group to which it belonged in the Alchera.

So far as the possession of the *Churinga knanja* is concerned, each man and woman has a personal one; men, but not women, may possess others by inheritance. The most detailed and important traditions relating to the origin of Churinga is that associated with the Achilpa [wild-cat] totem. . . . The tradition, so far as it deals with Churinga, is shortly as follows:

A great Being called Numbakulla made the first Achilpa Churinga with a *Kuruna* associated with it, from which the first Achilpa man originated. Later on, he fashioned very large numbers of Churinga belonging to all *Knanjas* or totems, drawing upon each the design or designs now characteristic of the *Knanjas*. Each one of these was associated with a *Kuruna* or spirit which Numbakulla had previously made. Leaders, or Inkatas, or *Knanja* groups, some Achilpa (wild cat), some Erlia (emu), some Arura (kangaroo), some Unjiamba (Hakea flower), etc., were sent out with numbers of Churinga and *Kurunas* that gave rise to groups of individual men and women, each with his or her own Churinga, all of which were deposited finally in various *Pertalcheras*. According to the Achilpa tradition, the original Churinga, made by Numbakulla and afterwards by the Achilpa Inkatas, in the Alchera, were all stone ones called *Churinga talkara*. First of all a number of these were made, then each of them was split into two, one of which was *Atua* or *uria* (male), the other *Arragutja* or *malia* (female). The pairs are now called *Chua ninga*, but the old Alchera name for them was *Unpora ninga*. According to the Achilpa tradition, the two forming a pair were tied together with hair string. Later on the *Inkata Achilpa kupitcha* transformed the female Churinga —that is, the ones with which a woman's *Kuruna* was associated— into wooden ones called *Churinga tidjanira*. Some of the latter had holes bored through them, and were called *Tidjanira alknarinja*. The women who arose, and still arise, from the *Kuruna* associated with these are called *Arragutja alknarinja*. This tradition accounts for the fact that at the present time only men have *Churinga talkara*—that is, stone ones. The stone ones are commonly spoken of collectively as *Churinga perta*, the wooden ones as *Churinga rola*. The special, personal Churinga belonging to each individual is also spoken of as his or her *Churinga knanja*. Each one of these original Churinga, wooden and stone alike, is also called *Indullairrakura*. In addition to these Churinga, that were carried by the Alchera ancestors, there are two other kinds. When the old Inkatas marched across the country they left *Kuruna*—always in pairs—in the Tidja (mulga) trees. In the Alchera . . . an *Oknirrabata*, wandering through the bush, would suddenly catch sight of an *Iwupa*, or spirit, in the form of a child playing about on one of the trees; it would suddenly disappear, and then the old man knew that it was one of the *Kuruna* left by the Inkata. Splitting a block of wood, taken from the tree, the *Oknirrabata* then fashioned from it a pair of Churinga, one associated with the male and the other with the female spirit. That tree was henceforth regarded as the *Rola knanja* of each *Kuruna* and of the human beings to whom they gave rise.

The Churinga thus made were placed in the local *Pertalchera* and were regarded as *Indulla-irrakura*, but, in this case, the man who arose from the *Kuruna* had a wooden and not a stone Churinga.

According to other traditions—and the traditions vary to a certain extent in different parts of the country and in different local groups— less stress is laid upon the Inkata, though there appears always to have been a leader of each travelling group. In some cases, as described in connection with the totems, the ancestors are stated to have arisen at a definite place and to have remained there. Each ancestor had one, and only one, original Churinga, carried either by the Inkata or by himself, or herself, because, quite unlike what happens at the present time, women were allowed, in the Alchera, to see and own sacred objects such as Churinga, *Nurtunjas* and *Waningas*. When he, or she, died, that Churinga, associated with its *Kuruna*, remained behind in the *Pertalchera*, in which it had been placed for safe keeping by the Inkata or the Alchera ancestor. According to another wide-spread tradition, the spirit is supposed to drop its Churinga when it enters a woman. On the birth of a child, the mother tells her husband the position of the tree or rock near to which she believes the child entered her, and the man, accompanied by one or two of the older men, and always, if alive, by his own father—that is, the *Arunga* of the child—goes in search of the Churinga. Sometimes it is found, sometimes it is not; in the latter case a new one is made from the mulga, or some hard-wood tree, near to the *Pertalchera* of the child, and is marked by the *Arunga* with a design belonging to the child's totem. The Churinga is then placed in the *Pertalchera* and is regarded as the child's *Churinga knanja*, with which its *Kuruna* is associated.

In some parts of the tribe, especially the Central and Northern divisions, whilst there is the same belief with regard to the existence of the original Churinga, the custom prevails of the *Arunga*—that is, the paternal grandfather of a child—going out into the scrub when a child is born, and making a wooden Churinga out of a tree close to the *Pertalchera*. This has nothing to do with the original one, which, according to this tradition, is left in the *Pertalchera*. It is called *Twany-irrika*, and is ornamented with a design belonging to the child's totem. The size—it is often a large one—and design are decided upon by the *Arunga*, but it has no *Kuruna* associated with it. A large number of these are stored in the *Pertalchera*; they are much used during totemic ceremonies, such as those shown at the Engwuta, and it is one or more of these that are placed in the youth's hands after circumcision. The natives say, *Churinga Twanyirrika, itja Kuruna*, that is, it is a Twanyirrika Churinga, but has no *Kuruna*.[25]

Each Churinga is so closely bound up with the spirit individual that it is regarded as its representative in the *Pertalchera*. Those of dead men are supposed to be endowed with the attributes and powers of their owner, and actually to impart these to the person who, for the time being, may, as when a fight takes place, be fortunate enough to carry one of them about with him. The Churinga is supposed to endow the possessor with courage and accuracy of aim, and also to deprive his opponent of these qualities. So firm is their belief in this, that, if two men were fighting and one of them knew that the other carried a Churinga, whilst he did not, he would certainly lose heart at once, and without doubt be beaten.[26]

We meet in tradition with unmistakable traces of the idea that the Churinga is the dwelling-place of the spirit of the Alchera ancestor.

The Achilpa belief is that the *Kuruna* or spirits were first made by Numbakulla, and, later, a Churinga for each one of them. One tradition relates that, when the Achilpa men were out hunting, they erected a sacred pole or *Nurtunja*, that they carried with them during their wanderings, and on this hung their Churinga and placed their spirit parts in them for safe keeping, taking them down when they returned to camp. Whilst this is so in regard to Alchera tradition, it must be pointed out clearly that the Arunta native, at the present day, does not regard the Churinga as the abode of his own spirit part, placed in the *Pertalchera* for safety, though at the same time it is intimately associated with himself, and more especially with his *Arumburinga*, which is really the twin or double of his own *Kuruna*, and the half of the original *Kuruna* of his Alchera ancestor. If anything happens to it—if it be stolen—he mourns over it deeply, and has a vague idea that some ill may befall him, but he does not imagine that damage to the Churinga of necessity means destruction to himself. The value of the Churinga lies in the fact that each one is intimately associated with, and is, indeed, the representative of, one of the Alchera ancestors, with the attributes of which it is endowed. It is also felt that the *Arumburinga*, which spends much of its time in and around the *Pertalchera*, in which the Churinga is kept, may follow it, and thus the individual will lose the guardianship of the spirit.[27]

[According to the Achilpa tradition] Whilst many leaders, locally known as Inkata, Alatunja, Chitchurta or Chantchwa, are associated with Alchera times and myths, Numbakulla, according to this tradition, is the supreme ancestor, overshadowing all others. He gave rise to all the original Kurunas, Churingas, and Knanjas, in fact to everything associated with the Alchera. He himself had no special Knanja or totem, but made and owned them all. During his long travels he created many of the main features of the country and decided upon the location of the central places now associated with the various Knanjas—Achilpa (wild cat), Erlia (emu), Arura (kangaroo), Udnirringita (witchetty grub), Irriakura (yelka), Emora (opossum), etc.

At every such place he put his foot down, saying, *Nana, Knanja Achilpa, Erlia, Arura*, etc.; here is wild cat, emu, kangaroo, etc., Knanja. Then he drew and left on some rock or ground surface what is called a *Churinga ilpintira*—that is, a special design or mark associated with the totem of that locality. Each of these designs now forms the distinctive mark or *Ilkinia* of the Knanja of that place.[28]

Numbakulla thus created all the original Kuruna and Churinga. He himself was full of Kuruna: as the natives say, *Kuruna injaira oknirra, kwanala mberka Numbakulla*; there were a very large number of Kuruna, inside the body of Numbakulla; and again, *Kuruna aradukka* (or *aradugga*) *kwanala, Numbakulla*; the Kuruna came out from inside Numbakulla.[29]

The first Churinga made by Numbakulla and placed by him on the *Churinga ilpintira* is called *Churinga indulla-irrakura* [totem design] *Numbakulla*. All of the original Alchera Churinga, made by Numbakulla and subsequently produced from them or made by the various ancestral Inkatas of the different Knanjas or totem groups, are also called *Churinga indulla-irrakura*. By the splitting of each of these original ones a pair was made. The pairs were at first tied together, and each man and woman had one of them associated with his, or her, Kuruna or spirit, which was originally placed in it by Numbakulla. One Churinga of each pair had an *atua* or man's spirit, the other an *arragutja* or woman's. Each Churinga had also an *Aritna churinga*, or sacred name, associated with it and its Kuruna, and all these names were given, originally, by Numbakulla. Later on, the Kurunas emanated from the Churinga, and gave rise to men and women, each of whom bore, as his or her sacred name, the one given to the Churinga by Numbakulla.

The natives are very definite in regard to the fact that the Churinga is not the changed body (*mberga* or *mberka*) of the man or woman: the original Churinga and Kuruna were made by Numbakulla before there were any men or women.[30]

It must be remembered that every one of the great number of Kurunas that gave rise to all the men and women of the various Knanjas was, according to this tradition, created originally by Numbakulla. Some of them, such as those associated with *Inkata Achilpa maraknirra, Inkata Achilpa oknirra, Inkata Achilpa kupitcha*,[31] Illapurinja, and the Inkatas of other Knanjas, emanated from Churinga in the Alchera and gave rise directly to human beings—without entering a woman. In all other cases the Kuruna entered a woman and, within her, gave rise to a child called *Ratappa*—the term applied to the child developing within the womb and also to the new-born baby. The 'spirit child' that enters a woman always does so, as a Kuruna, through her loins, never by way of the vulva. . . . The Kuruna is described as being very small, round, like a very little pebble, and red in colour. It is shapeless, and has neither arms nor legs nor head, but develops these within the mother and gives rise to a *Ratappa*. It does not enter as a *Ratappa*, but as a *Kuruna*, and only changes into the former within the womb or *ilpa*.[32]

The natives are quite clear on the point that in the case of all the Knanjas originated by Numbakulla, men and women of the same Knanja, or totem, were arranged in pairs as mates, and married one another. It followed that, at first, all the members of one local group, men, women and children, belonged to the same Knanja, but, when the Knanikillas and Knanjas had become established and the people increased in numbers and began to move about the country, visiting different camps and assembling at various places to perform ceremonies, the Kurunas of one Knanja group entered women of another, and so the present irregular local distribution of men and women of different totems or Knanjas was brought about. At the same time the majority of individuals in any one locality typically belong to the Knanja that has its Pertalchera there.[33]

When a man or woman dies, the spirit part, or *Kuruna*, immediately leaves the body and flies away to its *Pertalchera* in the form of a little bird called *Chichurkna*, whose whistling is often heard when there has been a death in the camp. As soon as it has joined its *Arumburinga* the latter hastens from its *Knanja* tree, or rock, or from its *Pertalchera*, to the grave, to protect the body against attacks by mischievous spirits called Eruncha. It remains there until the *Kuruurkna* or girdle, made of hair cut from the dead man, has been woven. During this short period of perhaps three or four days, it receives the special name of *Alknuriniata*. It then goes back to its *Knanja* tree, and the spirit of the dead man returns to the grave in the form of an *Ulthana* until the final mourning ceremony of *Urpmilchimilla* has been held, after which it returns to the *Pertalchera*, and there joins the *Arumburinga* and other spirit beings, assuming once more the form of a *Kuruna* that can enter a woman and be reborn.[34]

From this account of the *Alchera* and conceptional beliefs of the Arunta the following points emerge: (1) that each individual is the incarnation of an *Alchera Kuruna* or the reincarnation of an Alchera ancestor, (2) whose spirit part or *Kuruna* enters the prospective mother directly from its *Knanja* or abode, that is, the place at which it was deposited in the *Alchera*, (3) generally choosing a woman as its mother whose husband is of the correct moiety, that (4) on occasion a *Kuruna* may deliberately choose to enter a woman of the 'wrong' class and so bring it about that the living representative of an *Alchera* ancestor belongs to a class different from that of the ancestor whose incarnation he is, the totem, of course, remaining unchanged, (5) that the *Kuruna* therefore exhibits a certain amount of liberty of choice as to the woman, the moiety, and the class which it will enter, (6) that the *Churinga* represents the split half of the *Kuruna* of the totem ancestor, the other half being its guardian spirit, the *Arumburinga*, that (7) after his death the spirit part of an individual returns to its *Churinga* in the *Pertalchera*, (8) that the native does not regard the *Churinga* as the abode of his own spirit part, but rather of the *Arumburinga*, which watches over the *Kuruna*, the *Churinga*, and to a certain extent, himself, and finally (9) that intercourse does not play any causal part in the production of pregnancy, which is believed to be due to the entrance into a woman of a *Kuruna*.

There are a number of points in this account which are not very clear, and the most important of these is one that we have already encountered in our discussion of Schulze's report, namely whether the individual represents an incarnation of an *Alchera* spirit or the spirit part of an *Alchera* ancestor only, or a reincarnation of that ancestor *ab ovo usque ad mala*, soul and body. According to Spencer and Gillen's account, it would appear that the individual is, among the Arunta, regarded as a complete reincarnation of an actual *Alchera* ancestor, body as well as soul, though not necessarily of the *first Alchera* ancestors. The lack of clarity arises chiefly from Spencer and Gillen's carelessness in speaking at one time as if a *Kuruna* were merely a discarnate soul, the spirit part *only* of an individual, and at another time as if it represented the complete *Alchera* ancestor, the reader being left to choose, unassisted, between the two alternatives afforded. Nowhere, however, in Spencer and Gillen's account is there any explicit statement that the individual is the reincarnation of the spirit-part *only* of an ancestor, and not also of his corporeal part. As to the native's beliefs concerning the fate of the body and of the spirit after death, according to Spencer and Gillen it would be quite obvious to him that at death the body undergoes a physical dissolution, and that the spirit must therefore leave it and return to its abode. But the native, it appears, is no Platonic dichotomist, and we must avoid any confusion which would result here from thinking him so, for the spirit which leaves the body after death is not merely the spirit of that particular body, it is a *Kuruna*, the actual being of an eternally incarnable *Alchera* ancestor in spirit or quasi-spirit form, a spirit soul *and* body, for the *Kuruna* is described as having a definite, though it be a somewhat amorphous, structure, 'very small, round, like a very little pebble, and red in colour'. Further, 'it is shapeless, and has neither arms nor legs nor head, but develops these within the mother and gives rise to a *Ratappa*', developing from a diminutive little thing, the *Kuruna*, into a baby, a *ratappa*, within the mother.[35] It would seem then, that the *Kuruna* represents an already preformed individual who undergoes an unfolding only within the mother's womb, in which, before the entry of the *Kuruna* into her, no other soul *or* body could have been present: 'the *mberka*', that is, the body, write Spencer and Gillen, 'is supposed to be formed later when the *Kuruna*, having left the *Churinga*, enters a woman.'[36] Thus, the primitive or elementary anatomical structure of the *Kuruna* is developed within the womb of its mother into a proper body, which may be identical with the body of a particular *Alchera* ancestor who has already undergone repeated incarnations in the past. The body of the individual who dies is but the husk of a soul and a body which are immortal. A *Kuruna*, then, is properly the germ of a complete individual, being made up of the spiritual and corporeal parts of an *Alchera*, or more recent human, ancestor. It follows, therefore, that upon this view there can be no question of the incarnation of the spirit part alone of such an ancestor, nor can there be any question of an already pre-existing body within the mother into which the spirit part alone enters, for the body develops only *after* the *Kuruna* has entered the mother—from the *Kuruna*. Thus, the whole process of conception and pregnancy is due to no other cause than that the woman has been entered by a *Kuruna*. The *Kuruna* is the cause of conception.

A second point of importance which requires consideration here is the question whether intercourse plays any part, either as a condition or as a cause, in the production of conception and pregnancy. In answer to this question Spencer and Gillen state that 'we have amongst the Arunta, Luritcha, and Ilpirra tribes, and probably also amongst others such as the Warramunga, the idea firmly held that the child is not the direct result of intercourse, but it may come without this, which merely, as it were, prepares the mother for the reception and birth also of an already formed spirit child who inhabits one of the local totem centres. Time after time we have questioned them on this point, and always received the reply that the child was not the direct result of intercourse.'[37]

The statement that 'the child is not the direct result of intercourse, that it may come without this', may, as it stands, be taken to mean that the child is considered to be the direct result of factors other than intercourse, but that intercourse is assumed to have an indirect connection with the entry of the spirit-child into the woman; what this indirect connection consists in is briefly indicated in the phrase that intercourse 'merely, as it were, prepares the mother for the reception and birth also of an already formed spirit child who inhabits one of the local totem centres'. In other words, in some cases intercourse is regarded as an act not altogether unrelated to the entry of a spirit-child into a woman. Intercourse prepares the woman for the reception as well as the birth of a spirit-child, but intercourse is, apparently, not absolutely necessary, since the spirit-child may enter and be born of a woman as a *ratappa* 'without this'. Clearly therefore, intercourse is regarded as bearing a certain relationship to pregnancy, namely, as the preparer of the woman for the reception of the spirit-child, for though the preparation by intercourse is a dispensable process, without which the spirit-child or *Kuruna* will enter a woman in any event, it is nevertheless recognized that as a rule the preparation by intercourse is helpful.

It seems that Spencer and Gillen repeatedly inquired of the

natives whether pregnancy was possible without intercourse, and that the replies they received led them to believe that intercourse was regarded as having nothing whatever to do with conception *in the sense of being productive of it*. Intercourse merely opens the woman up, paves the way, but it depends entirely upon the will of the spirit-child whether or not it will enter her. Often enough a spirit-child will enter a woman without this preliminary preparation. Pregnancy begins with the entrance of the spirit-child, not with intercourse.

The Aboriginal world is essentially a spiritual world, and material acts are invested with a spiritual significance. Human beings have a long spiritual history behind them, and the spiritual source of every member of the tribe is known. The spiritual origin of children is the fundamental belief, and among the most important stays of the social fabric. It were absurd then to think, in the face of such knowledge, that an act such as intercourse could be the cause of a child. The investigator's questions on this point would perhaps strike the native as somewhat stupid, since from his earliest years intercourse has been an almost daily experience with him, so that while intercourse and pregnancy would generally tend to occur together, so would eating, walking, breathing, excreting, sleeping, and so on; there could be no reason for possibly associating the one with the other, excepting that the physical act of intercourse between the sexes would have the effect of 'opening up' the womb of the mother, and thus, in the event of a spirit-child electing to enter the particular woman, it would find ingress easy and everything in order upon its arrival. To their questions on this point, this, in effect, is the answer which Spencer and Gillen received, time after time.

Here it is necessary to emphasize the fact that the *Kuruna* does not enter the woman through the vulva, but either through the abdomen, the loins, the navel, or the mouth, so that the 'preparation' has no reference to the opening up of the vaginal canal itself, although, according to Strehlow, the natives regard the opening up as definitely physical as far as the womb is concerned, for without this opening up it is believed that the woman's womb would not be in a condition to receive a *Kuruna*. It is also quite possible that the operation is regarded as a ritual act which may promote the entry of a *Kuruna* into a woman.

It must be pointed out that the knowledge of anatomy which most primitive peoples possess is in most respects extremely rudimentary, whilst their knowledge of the function of the various structures of the body is in no better state. The Aborigines are no exception to this rule, nor, for that matter, is the average young man or woman of our own enlightened society. The Aborigines, however, are good observers, and since they do not indulge in intercourse between the sheets, nor snuff the candle when they do, but adopt a sitting face-to-face position which renders such observation inescapable, they cannot have failed to observe the relations which would easily enable them to deduce the position of the male organ during coitus within the body of the female. Such experiences would suggest that the male organ enters the abdomen, and hence, the notion might well come about that it is the abdomen which intercourse opens up, that is, renders commodious, and thus efficiently prepares for the reception of a spirit-child.

Again, we may observe here that intercourse happens to be the merest of accidents in its capacity as a preparer of the woman for the reception of the spirit-child, and we may also readily see that it would be objectionable from every point of view to allow the possibility of artificial manipulation of the proper parts to supplant the male organ in this connection. Upon this view of the matter it would almost seem to be the obvious function of the penis to prepare the female for the reception of a spirit-child, since, apart from its more ordinary functions of providing a passage into the external world of urine and ejaculatory fluid, it could hardly be imagined to serve any other more useful purpose. It is, indeed, in the very nature of intercourse that the penis serves as a preparer of the woman, both physically and psychologically, for the reception of an *Alchera*, a 'dream' child, and it would appear that Spencer and Gillen took the 'preparation' by intercourse of the woman to mean no more than this.

We may then, I think, reasonably conclude from Spencer and Gillen's account that among the Arunta pregnancy is considered neither a direct nor an indirect result of intercourse, nor, apparently, is it even considered as an indispensable condition thereof, as it is among certain neighbouring tribes, whose ideas on this subject we shall shortly have occasion to examine.

It is to be greatly regretted that no one up to the present time seems to have felt it necessary to question the Arunta upon their conception of the nature of the seminal fluid. The omission appears the more extraordinary in view of the important light which any notions that the native might have concerning the nature and functions of this substance would undoubtedly throw upon their procreative beliefs. Spencer and Gillen's complete silence upon this point, not to speak of that of so many other observers, upon the subject of the seminal or ejaculatory fluid, is, however, not altogether without its significance, for did the seminal fluid play any conspicuous role in the natives' conception of things it would unquestionably have become evident in some, at least, of the ceremonies and customs reported by them, but it has not done so, and I think, therefore, that we shall not be unjustified in assuming that the seminal fluid is not regarded as of any great importance in the native conception of its functions, whatever that may be, and that at most its function is conceived to be that of a lubricating agent, as it is regarded, for example, among the Trobriand Islanders.[38]

If, then, pregnancy is not the result of intercourse, who, then, if any, are the biological parents of a child? The answer would appear to be quite simple. Not the individual who stands in the relation of husband to the woman the child calls 'mother', his father, nor yet the mother herself, but Numbakulla, the maker of all the *Alchera* ancestors, the *Kuruna, Churinga, Pertalchera, Knanja,* and *Knanikilla.* It is essentially with Numbakulla as the central figure that the most important ceremonies of the Arunta are celebrated, for he is indeed the creator of every member of the tribe, in the sense that every member of the tribe is the incarnation or a reincarnation of an *Alchera* being created by him, and to whom he thus owes his existence; he is, as Spencer and Gillen write, 'the supreme ancestor, over-shadowing all others'.[39] The natives assert that in the *Alchera* Numbakulla was full of *Kuruna*, and that he gave birth to these *Kuruna*,[40] which 'gave rise to all the men and women of the various *Knanjas*',[41] some of them giving 'rise directly to human beings—without entering a woman'.[42]

From this it is quite evident that the only real biological parent recognized by the Arunta is Numbakulla, their actual *genitor.* The relationship is looked upon not as a supernatural one, but as a perfectly natural one, for every individual is the natural offspring of Numbakulla, that is, in the sense of having been directly or indirectly created by his command. He alone, therefore, can possibly be the biological parent of every Arunta. It must be remembered, however, that the *Kuruna* created by Numbakulla, or born of him, actually represent, as far as human beings are concerned, the transformations of various plants, animals, *Inapertwa*, and so forth. We may then consider Numbakulla as the host within whom the lower kind of *Kuruna* was transformed into the higher, just as the transformation occurs within the mother host today, that is, from a *Kuruna* to a *ratappa*.[43] Numbakulla, of course, created all the things he transformed, and likewise regulated their transformation and distribution. Women, it appears, were created in order to serve as hosts for the *Kuruna* after Numbakulla had disappeared. According to the Achilpa tradition, the first woman who served as a host, or mother, for the *Kuruna* was Illapurinja who was created directly from a *Churinga* according to the instructions left by Numbakulla to his *Inkata*.[44] The second woman, Lungarinia, was brought into being through the medium of Illapurinja.[45] In the *Alchera* large numbers of *Kuruna* entered first Illapurinja and subsequently Lungarinia, giving rise immediately to men and women.[46] These women were necessary because the *Alchera*

Inkatas were full of *Kuruna,* as were the *Churinga* in their possession, which had first to find a host before they could be born as men and women. Subsequently the *Churinga* were split into pairs, or mates, one half female, the other half male.[47]

According to this conception of the nature of 'coming into being', it is evident that the woman who gives birth to a child merely acts as the medium through whom it is conveyed into the proper moiety and section of the tribe, and in and through whom it undergoes the necessary transformation from a *Kuruna* into a *ratappa.* Sometimes a *Kuruna* enters the wrong woman in error, in such cases the child is invariably born dead.[48] When, however, it deliberately chooses to enter the wrong woman, all is well. Thus, the entry of a *Kuruna* into a woman, its development, and birth, are each matters which are completely independent of her in every physical sense. There is no symbiotic relationship between her and the developing *ratappa,* for once a *Kuruna* has entered a woman its development is of its own nature inevitable. From the physical standpoint, then, the mother of a child is no more than the host who has received and given birth to a child which has chosen to enter her. She is merely the medium through whom a *Kuruna* is transformed into a *ratappa,* and transmitted as an individual into the proper tribal group. Between herself and the child there can obviously be no physical relationship whatever, for in each case the ancestry of the individuals concerned is perfectly well known, both are incarnations of an *Alchera* spirit, and both independent beings in their own right; both owe their original existence to Numbakulla, and their present being to the initiative of the *Kuruna.* Hence, there cannot exist any physical, not to mention genitive, relationship between them.

Owing, however, to the difference in the generations to which they necessarily belong, and because the particular woman of whom the child has been born usually, though not always, nurses and cares for it generally, the social arrangement is that the child shall call that woman 'mother', in the same sense in which he calls those women who belong to the same generation as his own mother by the same term, for socially, that is to say, in particular relation to their own family group, the functions of these other women are precisely the same. The critically important point which requires to be emphasized here is that 'motherhood' is regarded as a purely social matter, and not as a biological one. The nature of the act of birth is in all its elements considered as something experientially and traditionally obligatory, it is the way in which a *ratappa* enters the tribe, and that the *ratappa* happens to come through the medium of a particular woman is, in this connection, due to no other virtue of that woman than that she usually belongs to a man, the *Kuruna* of whose totemic ancestors dwell at a spot near which this woman has passed, and at which one of them, seeing that she was comely, immediately entered her. Any one of the man's other wives might have fared equally as well or badly, depending upon whether or not they already had a sufficient number of young to care for, and assuming that they were sufficiently attractive.

Once the child is delivered the chief function of the woman through whose medium it has passed into the tribe is to nurse it and attend to its wants generally until that time comes when, at or shortly before puberty, the child departs from the family circle, and her parental duties are at an end.

The actual physical experience involved in giving birth to a child is so minimized, and the social implications of the result of the birth so magnified, that the former wilts away into the obscure background before the all-embracing consequences of the latter. It may be noted that childbirth among the Australian Aborigines, as among many aboriginal peoples who are relatively unmixed, is a comparatively light affair for the woman, who is usually up and about her regular duties within a few hours after the delivery of the child.[49] There is no period of confinement before the birth of the child, and there is no period of convalescence afterwards, so that the actual experience of birth is by no means the traumatically impressive experience that it generally is for the white woman. There is, therefore, no great affect normally associated with childbirth, nor is it in any way climactic, but it is cumulative, for it represents the culmination of a cycle of events all of which have been known and taken for granted for some months previous to the final event, and which, being known and taken for granted, have given rise to the expectation that a child will eventually make its appearance through the medium of the woman in relation to whom the appropriate signs have been observed. With the appearance of the child, there is an end of the whole matter.

This great lack of emphasis associated with childbirth tends, of course, to minimize any notion of the physical ties which might exist between a particular woman and an individual who has been transmitted through her medium into the tribe.

The inconsequence of the part which the woman plays in procreation follows, of course, inevitably upon the whole system of beliefs according to which the native lives, for sexual conception as a result of the intercourse between men and women is a notion which has no place in that system of beliefs. *There is, therefore among the Arunta, an ignorance of physiological maternity, as well as an ignorance of physiological paternity.* This is a point of the first importance, but one which seems to have been generally overlooked in the many discussions that have turned upon the procreative beliefs of the Aborigines. The truth seems to be that there is an ignorance of physiological or biological parentage altogether, and that, therefore, there can exist, at most, only a recognition of social parentage. The distinction is, of course, a very real one, and not merely the result of a piece of casuistical reasoning. The Arunta, naturally, never have any occasion to make the distinction for the reason that the conditions wherewith to make it have never arisen. Their ignorance of physiological parentage does not represent a failure to recognize certain conditions and relationships, nor does it constitute a positive rejection of such conditions and relationships, for these simply either do not exist or are not allowed to exist in the universe which they have constructed, or rather that tradition has constructed for them. The pattern of the materials with which they have to build necessarily determines the pattern of the resulting structure, and the resulting structure is from every point of view a perfectly coherent and well integrated edifice, within which and in relation to which everything functions with admirable efficiency.

With respect to the position of the father in relation to the child, from the conceptional standpoint this is naturally not less nor more important than the mother's. Socially, however, the paternity which results from a child being born into a man's family has the effect, owing to the far-reaching ramifications of the patriarchal organization of the horde or tribe, of giving a greater degree of meaning to the relationship between father and child than that which could exist between a mother and the child to which she has given birth, for the fact is that it is socially much less her child than it is that of her husband, since it is a *Kuruna* related to his own moiety which enters the proper moiety and class only because of that relationship, and not by virtue of any remote relationship that the *Kuruna* may bear to the mother, who, of course, is of another moiety. It is always the father's moiety affiliation which determines the moiety affiliation of the child, the totems have nothing necessarily to do with the matter. The dominance of the father in regulating the early tribal being of the child, together with the influence of the general affect associated with his position in the family group, as well as the general dominance of the male over the female, is yet another of the factors which serves to minimize the relationship between mother and child, and to ensure that a greater emphasis is placed upon the relationship involved in paternity. Naturally, these facts emphasize only the social relationship, and nothing more, for that is all that they are calculated to emphasize.

At this point we may turn to the report of the Rev. C. Strehlow, a missionary who for many years was attached to the Lutheran Mission Station in the western Macdonnell Ranges at Hermannsburg in Central Australia, and whose valuable monograph on the south-eastern Arunta[50] and Loritja has given rise to some controversy. The work, written in Hermannsburg, was transmitted in the form of notes to Germany where it was edited by Freiherr Moritz von Leonhardi, a fact which was in many ways fortunate, since it served to settle a certain number of points which would otherwise have remained doubtful. It is necessary here to state that Strehlow obtained almost all of his material from three or four native informants who were constant attendants at the Mission Station,[51] and who were therefore somewhat acquainted with the teachings of Lutheran Christianity. The fact that Strehlow's informants attended at the Mission does not constitute a reason for doubting either the value or the accuracy of the information obtained from them relating to the orthodox beliefs, yet upon this ground and in view of the following letter addressed by Sir Baldwin Spencer to Sir James Frazer the latter had declined to make use of Strehlow's work. Spencer writes:[52]

For at least twenty years the Lutheran Missions have been teaching the natives that *altjira* means 'god', and that all their sacred cere-monies, in fact even their ordinary corroborees, are wicked things. They have prohibited any being performed on the Mission station, and have endeavoured in every way to put a stop to them and to prevent the natives from attending them, and certainly they have never seen one performed. Under these conditions it is not altogether surprising that when S. questions the natives he discovers that *altjira* means god, and gets very doubtful information in regard to all sacred or secret matters. . . . Not only have the missionaries for years past sternly rebuked the members of their flock (whose presence in church and school is an indispensable condition to participation in the distribution of flour, tobacco, etc.) for any inclination towards the heathen and devilish beliefs and practices of their parents, but they have actually attempted to break these down to the extent *of marrying individuals of wrong groups*. It is rather late for any one of them, how-ever well he may know the language, to attempt an investigation into sacred beliefs and customs.

Certainly information obtained from natives who have been exposed to Mission influences should be treated with some circum-spection, but to disregard such information altogether were neither fair nor wise, especially since there is now every reason to believe that Strehlow is on many points more reliable that Spencer and Gillen.

Since Strehlow makes no use of the term 'God' in a theological sense, and since he has explained his usage of the term as having much the same meaning as that given by Spencer and Gillen for *Alchera*,[53] there can be little objection to Strehlow's introduction of the term, though I think it would have been better to have retained the native word.

With respect to certain fundamental points in their accounts Strehlow has been unable to confirm the statements of Spencer and Gillen, and as a consequence of this there has been a noticeable tendency in some quarters to damn his work for its unorthodox departure from the canon of Spencer and Gillen; it may therefore at once be said here that there is not the slightest reason to believe that Strehlow's report represents anything other than a perfectly dispassionate and unbiased account of what his informants themselves told him. In his foreword to part I of Strehlow's work the editor, Leonhardi, writes:

In primeval times the totem-gods (*altjirangamitjina*) wandered about the land and finally entered the earth, where they are believed to be living to this day. Their bodies were transformed into rocks, trees, bushes, or *tjurunga* stones and woods. The belief in an eternally repeated reincarnation of these totem-gods which Spencer and Gillen thought to have found, Herr Strehlow has not been able to confirm. According to him, the manner in which children originate is con-ceived in various ways; either a *ratapa* which resides in the trans-formed body of the totem-god enters a passing woman—such children are supposed to be born with narrow faces—or a totem ancestor comes out of the earth, throws a small *namatuna* (*tjurunga*) towards the woman, and this *namatuna* is in her body transformed into a child, which will subsequently be born with a broad face. Besides these two ways of coming into being, a few natives related (and the old men finally admitted) that in rare cases a totem god himself may enter a woman and be reborn. But he can undergo such a rebirth only once. The children thus originating are said to have light hair. As a matter of fact *Aranda* with light hair are occasionally encountered.[54] The totem god, who is believed to be related in one of the three ways mentioned, is called *iningukua*, and it is believed that he follows the human being as a sort of guardian spirit. In the third case, where the rebirth of the *iningukua* is assumed, the grandfather's totem-god is said to assume the part of the guardian. The Loritja have, on the whole, the same views (*Globus*, xci, 285 ff., and xcii, 123). In the first of these articles in *Globus* (p. 289) it was mentioned that a child may originate in the womb if the woman has seen an animal, or after she has partaken of a good amount of fruit. When I requested a con-firmation of this, Herr Strehlow answered, 'If a woman during her wanderings sees a kangaroo which suddenly disappears from her sight, and if she feels the first indication of pregnancy at this moment, then a kangaroo *ratapa* has entered her, not the particular kangaroo itself, but rather a kangaroo ancestor in animal form. Or a woman may find *lalitja* fruits and feel sick after eating plentifully of them; in that case a *lalitja ratapa* has entered her through her loins, not through her mouth. Both cases, therefore, should be classed with the first method of coming into being, that is by the entry of a *ratapa* into a woman passing by a totem-place.' As regards the Larrekiya tribe on the north coast, H. Basedow has recently published a similar account (*Trans. Roy. Soc. South Australia*, xxxi, 1907, 4). In view of the importance attached to this problem, it would be of the greatest value (see also A. Lang in *Anthropological Essays Presented To E. B. Tylor*, Oxford, 1907, 217) if further investigations could be made among the Larrekiya and the neighbouring tribes. Concerning the *tjurunga* we merely wish to mention that it is regarded as the 'secret body' [*verborgene Leib*] of the totemic ancestor as well as the body of a definite human being; it forms the connecting link between a human being and his *iningukua*. At the same time the *tjurunga* is magically related to a totemic animal or plant, the increase of which by means of totemic ceremonies is thereby made possible. Also concerning the *tjurunga* the views of the Loritja are fundamentally the same, though with characteristic differences in detail. They call the *tjurunga* 'body picture' [*Bild des Leibes*] (Loritja: *Kuntanka*), a name which must not be considered as at all symbolic. I shall not enter into further details here since the matter will be fully treated of later, and shall simply add that the Aranda as well as the Loritja definitely refused to regard the *tjurunga* as the seat of the soul or the life of a particular human being. This point has been made quite clear by the old men and by the medicine-men. Designations like '*Seelenholz*' or 'soul-box', etc., cannot, therefore, be applied to the *tjurunga* of the Aranda and Loritja.[55]

We may now turn to Strehlow. Following an account of the wanderings of the totemic ancestors of the Arunta essentially the same as that given by Spencer and Gillen, Strehlow goes on to say that:

. . . their bodies, however, were transformed into rocks, trees, shrubs. Some totem-gods are assumed to have entered a water-hole, etc., and are believed to be there to this day. In these rocks and trees, representing the transformed bodies of the ancestors, and especially in the mistletoe growing upon such trees, but also in water abounding in fish and similar places live the unborn children, *ratapa*, or spirit children. But not only the whole body, but also parts of the body of the totem-gods have become or turned into *tjurunga*; thus, for example, an eagle totem ancestor lost a long feather (*tjurungeraka*) which now forms a special totem: *eritja albala*. On the other hand, the body of an *alknarintja* woman was transformed into a *tnima* bush from which sap has flowed out and was congealed at the bark. This *trima* sap forms the totem *tnimamba*. The totem of the kangaroo fat is of the same character. The fat of a kangaroo totem-god is likewise *atjurun-geraka*, and so on. Very many totem-gods were transformed into *tjurunga*, which are now kept in the sacred stone caves. During their wanderings they lost some of the *tjurunga* which they carried about with them. These *tjurunga* were transformed into trees, rocks, etc., from which *ratapa* also originate. These *ratapa* are fully developed boys and girls of a reddish complexion, they possess body and soul. Ordinary mortals cannot see them, but the medicine-men maintain that they are able to do so. According as the particular totem-god from whose transformed body a *ratapa* originates is related to a definite natural object, the *ratapa* is likewise related to this object. In the gum-tree into which the body of a kangaroo ancestor (*ara*) has been transformed, a kangaroo *ratapa* resides. Likewise an opossum (*imora*) *ratapa* resides in a tree which represents the body of an opossum ancestor. (It is to be noted that in each tree, mistletoe sprig, or rock, etc., only one *ratapa* resides.) In water-holes abounding in fish are situated the totem centres of numerous fish ancestors who have entered the earth there. In some cases the totem-gods are not related to any natural objects, but are themselves designated as totems, such as the *ratapa* and *worra* totem. Since the Aranda are ignorant of the part that the man plays in procreation, the origin of human children is explained in the various ways described below. Sexual cohabitation is considered merely as a pleasure. I have not been able to confirm Spencer and Gillen's statement that it represents a sort of preparation for conception. I have been assured, by the way, that the old men are well aware that cohabitation is the cause of conception, but that they do not tell this to the young men and women. It is certain that the Aranda as well as the Loritja know the connection between intercourse and birth in animals, even children are taught that.

If a woman passes a place in which the transformed body of an ancestor resides—such a place is called *knanakala*—the *ratapa* that has been looking out for her and has recognized in her his class mother, enters her body through her loins, a process which causes sickness and quickening. When the child is born it belongs, as has been stated, to the totem of the totem-god in question. If the woman, for example, has passed an emu *knanakala* and has there noticed the first indication of pregnancy, an emu *ratapa* has entered her, so that the child will belong to the emu totem and will receive a name connected with that totem, such as Iliakurka (small emu), or Iliapa (emu feather).[56]

Thus, the Aranda assume that there are two ways in which children may originate. Either a fully developed boy or girl enters a passing woman from a mistletoe sprig, rock, fissure, etc., or a totem ancestor throws his *namatuna* towards a woman which then assumes the form of a child within the woman's womb. Both ways are said to be equally frequent. That a child has entered the mother in the first described way can be recognized by the fact that it has been born with a narrow face, in the alternative case the child will be born with a broad face.[57]

But in addition to the two ways mentioned, there is another and rarer way in which children may originate. That is to say, the *iningukua* may first throw his *namatuna* towards the woman and then enter her himself, and thus be reborn. The children thus originating are said to be born with light hair. This more uncommon way of coming into being was told me by certain natives; but the old men from whom I have received most information about the beliefs and legends of the Aranda denied this. However, when the natives who had told me about the origin of light-haired children according to the foregoing account persisted in their statement, the old men admitted that in rare cases the *iningukua* himself really entered women in order to be reborn. The soul of an *iningukua* reborn as a human being goes, after his death, like that of all other human beings, to the island of the dead, and there awaits its final annihilation by a stroke of lightning. A repeated reincarnation of a totem-god never takes place.[58]

The Loritja hold the same views as the Aranda concerning the way in which children originate. Either an *aratapi* enters the woman or a totem ancestor comes out of the earth and throws his *tjurunga* towards her, which within the woman changes into a child. The Loritja say that the latter method is the more usual.[59]

In rare cases the totem of a person may be uncertain. Concerning a woman who lives in Hermannsburg an old man maintains that she belongs to the totem of the wind, while her own husband says that she is a *tnima* woman.[60]

In the introduction to part 3 of Strehlow's work Leonhardi makes the following interesting remarks:[61]

Pater W. Schmidt in his interesting article ('Die Stellung der Aranda unter den australischen Stämmen', *Zeit. f. Ethnol.*, 1908, 866 ff.) has made a number of criticisms of Strehlow's report. On page 7, note 1, of the present work, Strehlow has attempted once more to clarify the *ratapa* theory, that is, the confusion which has arisen from the fact that a totem-god in the form of an *iningukua* accompanies, as a guardian, not only the human being whose *ratapa* has emanated from the tree, rock, or *tjurunga*, into which the body of the same totem ancestors was transformed, but also those human beings whose *ratapa* originate from the *tjurunga* which the *altjiran gamitjina* merely carried about with them and left behind in various places; this doubt does not seem to have been felt by the Aranda. Either the power of their logical thought does not extend so far, or, what seems more probable to me, they disregard this uncomfortable inconsistency. Schmidt is mistaken in attributing to the Aranda a two-soul theory. As far as can be ascertained, only one soul is recognized, the *guruna*, which after death is called the *itanana*. *Iningukua* is not in any way a totem spirit. Schmidt's most serious objection to Strehlow's statements refers to his remarks on the connection between cohabitation and conception; he objects primarily to the statement, 'I have been assured, by the way, that the old men are well aware that cohabitation is the cause of conception, but they do not tell this to the young men and women.' The statement is certainly not very aptly expressed. I understood it to mean, and Strehlow subsequently confirmed my opinion as correct, that the old men continue to teach the orthodox *ratapa* dogma to the young people, but that they themselves, or, at least, some among them, have arrived at a more rational view. But they conceal this, if for no other reason than that their influence and prestige would suffer if the old doctrine were undermined. It may be left undecided whether the particular *knaribata* have of their own accord found the correct connection between intercourse and birth, or whether the influence of the whites has made itself felt here.

There is no valid reason for denying to the old Aranda men the credit for having found the connection between coitus and birth since they recognize this connection in animals. Likewise, it is certain —and in this I agree entirely with Lang and with Schmidt—that it is not primitive ignorance which lies at the root of the conceptionalism of the Central Australians. It is rather the teaching about the totemic ancestors and their transformation into trees, rocks, and *tjurunga*, as well as about the *ratapa*, that has led to such artificial conceptions. This opinion of mine has not been shaken by the statement of Fr. von Reitzenstein (*Zeit. f. Ethnol.*, 1909, 644 ff.) who attempts to prove that the aforementioned belief of the Aranda and other Australian tribes goes back to the earliest times of mankind. To me it is certain that it is definitely established that the natural causal connection between intercourse and conception is unequivocally recognized. Reitzenstein passes this fact over somewhat too lightly. The other reason that has been adduced for the primitiveness of this belief, the ignorance of the nature of conception, namely that cohabitation is merely regarded as a pleasure, must be discarded, for Strehlow found that he was mistaken in this. Spencer and Gillen were right in reporting (*Nat. Trib.*, 265) that intercourse is regarded as a kind of preparation of the mother for conception. I confess that I felt some doubt concerning this point in Strehlow's report. This doubt, which I imparted to him, following a perusal of Schmidt's article, induced Strehlow to inquire into the matter once more. The result was to establish the fact that according to the Aranda as well as the Loritja, it is only by means of the sexual act that the woman's womb is put into a condition enabling it to receive a *ratapa*. The womb must be prepared for it; without preceding coitus the womb remains closed, *ilba worranta*. This also holds true for birth out of as well as in wedlock. Strehlow's statements about the connection between the eating of certain foods and conception still remain obscure to me. These beliefs do not seem to be compatible with the remainder of the *ratapa* theory. I have the impression that these beliefs have entered from a foreign source and have merely been superficially amalgamated. From Basedow's definite reports about the tribes of the Northern Territory we know that there the view is held ' . . . if a man, when out hunting kills an animal or collects any other article of diet, he gives it to his *gin* who must eat it, believing that the respective object brings about the successful birth of a piccaninny. In other words, conception is not regarded as the direct result of cohabitation'. (*Trans. Roy. Soc. South Austral.*, xxxi, 1907, 4.) J. G. Frazer has briefly noticed (*Man*, 1909, No. 86), according to the information of the Rev. C. M. Morrison, that in the tribes in the Cairns District, of North Queensland, ' . . . the acceptance of food from a man by a woman was not merely regarded as a marriage ceremony, but as the actual cause of conception'. This is, however, merely a brief note, and as far as it goes indicates that among these tribes the eating of certain foods is considered the cause of conception.

The most important points in Strehlow's account and in Leonhardi's commentary will be discussed here in the order of their occurrence.

First, with respect to the totem ancestors or *altjirangamitjina*.[62] These are consistently spoken of by Strehlow as 'totem-gods'. This requires explanation. The origin of the attachment of this meaning to the native term is given in a letter to Spencer and Gillen from the pen of the senior missionary at Hermannsburg, the Rev. H. Kempe. The letter was written in 1910.[63]

As regards the word '*Altjira*' in the language of the natives of Central Australia, I beg to tell you that, so far as I know the language, it is not 'God' in that sense in which we use the word—namely, as a personal being—but it has a meaning of old, very old, something that has no origin, mysterious, something that has always been so, also, always. Were *Altjira* an active being, they would have answered '*Altjirala*': the syllable '*la*' is always added when a person exercises a will (force) which influences another being or thing. We have adopted the word 'God' because we could find no better and because it comes nearest to the idea of 'eternal'. The people through the usage of a word often use it as a name for a person. This, according to my conviction, is the true meaning of the word *Altjira*.

The meaning of the native term as given here by Kempe is almost identical with that given to it in 1899 by Spencer and Gillen, who briefly defined it as 'the dim past'.[64] It is quite clear then, that for *totem-god* we should read *Alchera ancestor*. The fact is that the Aborigines have no gods.

Second, the statement that the *Alchera* ancestors were changed into *Churinga* which pass as their transformed bodies, and that many of them were directly transformed into rocks, trees, etc., is hardly in agreement with Spencer and Gillen's statement that according to the Achilpa tradition it is held that Numbakulla first made the *Kuruna* and afterwards the *Churinga*.[65] Spencer writes:[66]

As we pointed out many years ago, the connection between a man and his Churinga and totemic animal or plant is very intimate, but, so far as we have been able to study the matter, and after very careful and minute investigations amongst natives whilst they were actually performing ceremonies in connection with which hundreds of Churinga were used, we have never heard the Churinga referred to as the common body of a man and his totem.

Nor, as Spencer writes in this connection,[67] 'According, also, to all the traditions of the natives, as told to us, no animal, plant or human being ever actually became changed into a Churinga, nor did any human being become changed into a tree or stone. The latter arose to mark the spot at which the ancestor went into the ground—that is died.'

Yet, we may remark, it is none the less probable that the connection between the *Churinga* and the body of the totem ancestor exists.

Since there is very good reason to believe that Strehlow's represents a more accurate account of the native beliefs than that given by Spencer and Gillen it will be necessary to devote some space here to the consideration of the various contradictions and discrepancies in their respective accounts with a view to clarifying the issues involved.

It may at once be stated that if we had no other evidence than that provided by these writers, namely, Spencer and Gillen and Strehlow, it would upon the basis of their respective contributions render the whole picture a far more coherent one if we accepted Strehlow's statement of native belief that when many of the totem ancestors entered the ground their bodies died and were *transformed* into some natural feature which now marks the spot upon which they made their last appearance upon earth. Spencer has denied any knowledge of transformation. 'His [the totem ancestor's] body died, but some natural feature, such as a rock or tree, arose to mark the spot, while his spirit part remained in the *Churinga*.'[68] However, in the variety of traditions relating to the *Churinga* which Strehlow gives, the *Churinga* in every case represents the transformed body of a totem ancestor with which a spirit is in no way identified, excepting that spirit-children are believed to live in the totemic centres from which the various *Churinga* originated, and with which the *Churinga* are associated.

Actually Spencer and Gillen have themselves provided evidence of the existence of such a belief in their account of the tradition relating to the *Churinga Twanyirrika* which we have given on pages 57–8, at any rate, as far as the relation between totem centre and *Churinga* is concerned.[69]

Spencer and Gillen themselves state that in the *Alchera* large numbers of *Churinga* were deposited in the earth and that at these spots arose those natural features or *Knanja* in which the spirit-children took up their abode. If, as we could easily do, in spite of Spencer's negative evidence, we interpreted this to mean that where the *Churinga* were deposited there they were transformed into these natural features we would then have an account of native belief in all essentials agreeing with that given both by Spencer and Gillen and by Strehlow. We would then have a common source for these natural features, the *Knanja* and the *Churinga*, the one being convertible into the other, the *Knanja* being the transformed bodies of the totem ancestors of their *Churinga*, and the existing *Churinga* representing either a part or the whole of the transformed bodies of similar totem ancestors. Since every *Churinga* is associated with some definite totem, and every *Knanja* is likewise associated with a definite totem, and since these merely represent the transformed bodies of totem ancestors, an individual can derive his body only from such sources, his spirit must originate from some other source. This source is almost always the *Knanja* in which the spirits have their abode. Spirits do not have their abodes in *Churinga* but only in *Knanja* according to Strehlow, whereas according to Spencer and Gillen they would appear to have their abodes in both. There would be no great point to the citation of the many contradictions in which Spencer and Gillen have involved themselves in this connection, we need only cite that statement of Spencer and Gillen in which it is clearly shown that the *Churinga* is not regarded by the Arunta as the abode of the *Kuruna*. They write:[70]

We meet in tradition with unmistakable traces of the idea that the Churinga is the dwelling-place of the spirit of the Alchera ancestor. The Achilpa belief is that the *Kuruna* or spirits were first made by Numbakulla, and, later, a Churinga for each one of them. One tradition relates that, when the Achilpa men were out hunting, they erected a sacred pole or *Nurtunja*, that they carried with them during their wanderings, and on this hung their Churinga and placed their spirit parts in them for safe keeping, taking them down when they returned to camp. Whilst this is so in regard to Alchera tradition, it must be pointed out clearly that the Arunta native, at the present day, does not regard the Churinga as the abode of his own spirit part, placed in the *Pertalchera* for safety, though at the same time it is intimately associated with himself, and more especially with his *Arumburinga*, which is really the twin double of his own *Kuruna*, and the half of the original *Kuruna* of his Alchera ancestor. If anything happens to it—if it be stolen—he mourns over it deeply, and has a vague idea that some ill may befall him, but he does not imagine that damage to the Churinga of necessity means destruction to himself. The value of the Churinga lies in the fact that each one is intimately associated with, and is, indeed, the representative of, one of the Alchera ancestors, with the attributes of which it is endowed. It is also felt that the *Arumburinga*, which spends much of its time in and around the *Pertalchera*, in which the Churinga is kept, may follow it, and thus the individual will lose the guardianship of the spirit.

With this statement the fact may be regarded as settled that the *Churinga* is not among the Arunta regarded as the abode of the spirit.

What meaning the statement may have that 'The value of the Churinga lies in the fact that each one is intimately associated with, and is, indeed, the representative of, one of the Alchera ancestors, with the attributes of which it is endowed', it is difficult to imagine in view of Spencer's latter denials, unless it is assumed to mean what it is obviously intended to mean, namely, that the *Churinga* represents an *Alchera* ancestor, in which case it is difficult to avoid the conclusion that the *Churinga* is actually regarded as the transformed body of the ancestor,[71] which, of course, is precisely the explanation which Strehlow obtained from his informants.

Spencer and Gillen's difficulty was one that would easily arise out of the nature of the facts themselves. There is no doubt that a spirit is in a certain manner associated with a *Churinga*, but it is not necessarily an intimate part of the *Churinga*, just as the spirits inhabiting *Knanja* are not an intimate part of the *Knanja* though they are closely associated with it, they are all separate and distinct things. In other words, a definite distinction is made and recognized to exist between

Kuruna associated with transformed totem ancestors, *Knanja* and *Churinga*.

From the evidence available to us it is not quite clear why *Knanja* should be so much more closely associated with *Kuruna* than *Churinga*, but there are doubtless good enough reasons, even if we have not been made aware of them. On the face of the evidence it would appear that those totem ancestors who were transformed into *Churinga* are specially characterized by the fact that no *Kuruna* reside within them, and that only those totem ancestors and *Churinga* which were transformed into various natural objects are characterized by the fact that a certain number of *Kuruna* have taken up their abode within them, depending upon the number of *Churinga* originally deposited. That a particular *Churinga* is associated with a definite child is, of course, known by the fact that its *Kuruna*, that is, the child's spirit-part, was derived from a definite *Knanja* animal, food, or what not; the manner in which the exact *Churinga* is determined has already been made clear.

We have already seen that according to Spencer and Gillen's account we are led to infer that the *Kuruna* represents the corporeal as well as the spiritual part of an *Alchera* being, although we could not be quite certain upon this point. It would now seem more likely that the body is believed to be derived from the transformed totem ancestor, whether *Knanja* or *Churinga*, and that the *Kuruna* is derived from any one of the sources we have seen to exist. This is a view which is afforded some support by the findings of H. K. Fry who conducted some illuminating investigations among the tribes closely neighbouring upon the Arunta, namely the Luritja and Pintubi tribes.

The native belief . . . provides for the identification of his body with that of his totem ancestor, either in the form of a familiar spirit inhabiting a totem place, or in the form of a *tjuruna* representing the transformed bodies of the totem-ancestors of his mother and himself.[72]

The spirit part of a man, *kurun-kurun* (Pintubi), the equivalent of the Aranda *kuruna*, was stated by my Pintubi and Luritja informants to have nothing to do with the totems and *tjuruna*. They said that the *kurun-kurun* was formed in the berries (*nanta*, Luritja, *dzungurbma*, Pintubi) of the mistletoe (*natangini*, Luritja, *ndzinkininpa*, Pintubi), and then hangs down from the leaves of the mistletoe. When a pregnant woman passes, the *kurun-kurun* goes in. When a man dies his *kurun-kurun* goes west to a big water (*waleia*, Luritja, *apinti*, Pintubi; translated by my interpreter as 'the sea'); it goes into the water—'finish'.[73]

With such a belief it is easily understood how an individual may represent the incarnation of a totem ancestor and yet be the possessor of a *Kuruna* which is of entirely separate origin and as likely as not entirely new, for the individual derives his body alone from the totem ancestor, whereas his spirit is derived from a separate source, and at death the spirit is 'finish'.

Such views are not in harmony with those stated by Spencer and Gillen for the Arunta who, according to them, believe that the spirit is derived from an ancestral source and that it is eternal, undergoing repeated reincarnation, whereas the body undergoes disintegration at death.

In 1936 Miss Olive Pink found that the Arunta when questioned upon the matter denied any knowledge of a belief in continuous or repeated reincarnation. She writes:[74]

I should state that I found no evidence to show that the aborigines believed in reincarnation except in so far as the spirits of babies and very young children who die are concerned. These are said to be born again through the same mothers. But my informants, both sophisticated and unsophisticated, alone or in groups, emphatically denied it. The unsophisticated said a man '*finished altogether*' when he died; his body disintegrated and his spirit went away to the 'salt-water' (or as some said, into 'a cold country underground'), where they lived the same lives as blackfellows used to do, in so far as performing ceremonies, etc., are concerned. I then explained what was *supposed* to be their belief, namely continuous reincarnation; they retorted 'that white fellow talk—not blackfellow'. When I persisted, as I did, going back and back to the same subject on many occasions to see whether they would contradict what they had said either unknowingly or by implication, they said that the baby-spirit which a woman 'found' at the time of quickening was a new one, not that of some, previously deceased, adult blackfellow.

These findings fully corroborate those of Strehlow and of other more recent workers among the Arunta and neighbouring tribes, and clearly lend no support to the account of these matters as given by Spencer and Gillen.

Here it may be mentioned that the belief that the soul goes either to an island of the dead or to some water region after death where it dwells permanently or sojourns for some time is widespread throughout Australia.[75] Apart from Strehlow's report the belief in the destruction of the soul by lightning either among the Arunta or among other Australian tribes has not been reported by other investigators. The soul or spirit is said either to go and *live* by the shores of a lake or sea[76] or to enter it and 'finish',[77] or to return after a while to undergo reincarnation.[78] It is, of course, quite possible that a variety of beliefs of this kind may exist within the same tribe and perhaps horde, and it may be that the differences in the reports of these beliefs are due to this cause. Spencer's vigorous denial of Strehlow's statement is hardly to the point. Spencer writes: 'So far as our own investigations are concerned, this is absolutely at variance with the fundamental beliefs of the Arunta people. There is no such thing as the destruction of the soul by lightning. The *Kuruna* of each *Alchera* ancestor splits into two, giving rise to a new *Kuruna*, that continually undergoes reincarnation, and an *Arumburinga*, that is everlasting.'[79]

Clearly a belief in the destruction of the soul after death would appear to be quite incompatible with a belief in continuous or repeated reincarnation of the soul, but before continuing our examination of this matter we may proceed with the discussion of the subject of body and soul.

Spencer and Gillen in their accounts of the spirit beliefs state quite clearly that only *Kuruna*, that is, spirits, inhabit *Knanja*, but that when a *Kuruna* enters a woman it is known as a *ratappa*; thus, they write,[80]

The term *Ratappa* is not, strictly speaking, applied to a 'spirit child'. The spirit is always spoken of as *Kuruna*, and it is only after entering the mother that it gives rise to a *Ratappa*. Even at the *Ratappa* stone, so called because a small child went into the ground there, it is a *Kuruna* and not a *Ratappa* that enters a woman. The term *Kuruna* is always used in reference to the spirit itself, either before it enters the mother or after it leaves the body.

The term *ratappa* is also used for a child within the womb of the mother or a new-born baby. Hence it is clear that whatever a *ratappa* may be it is not merely a *Kuruna*, but a *Kuruna* to which something else has been added, that is, a body. This would suggest that the separate origin of the body and spirit is recognized, but, as we have already seen, Spencer and Gillen's statements would appear to mean that the *Kuruna* is already possessed of a body at the time when it enters the woman's womb. 'The kuruna is described as being very small, round, like a very little pebble, and red in colour. It is shapeless and has neither arms nor legs nor head, but develops these within the mother and gives rise to a *Ratappa*.'[81] But these words may just as well alternatively be taken to mean that a *Kuruna* is recognized to be a spirit only and not to be possessed of a body. '*The mberka*', that is, the body, Spencer and Gillen have written 'is supposed to be formed later when the *Kuruna*, having left the Churinga, enters a woman.'[82] May it not be that in the existence of these terms, *Kuruna* and *ratappa*, we have evidence of the recognition of the distinct and separate origin of spirit and body? That the *Kuruna* is spirit pure and simple, and the *ratappa* spirit *plus* body? And that, to repeat, the body is believed to be derived from a source other than that from which the spirit is derived? Certainly it is so according to Fry's Luritja and Pintubi, but they, it should be remembered, are not Arunta. Strehlow renders confusion worse confounded by speaking at times of '*guruna*' as meaning soul or spirit, and '*ratapa*' as meaning spirit-child in the sense in which Spencer and Gillen use this term; at other times Strehlow uses the terms '*guruna*' and '*ratapa*' interchangeably and with equivalent meanings. Moreover, according to Strehlow, it is the *ratappa* which reside in or are associated with the *Knanja*—the transformed bodies of the totem ancestors—and it is *ratappa* which enter women. Of these *ratappa* Strehlow has said that they are 'fully developed boys and girls of a reddish complexion possessing body and soul'.[83] Strehlow also states: 'According as the particular totemgod from whose transformed body a *ratapa* originates is related to a definite natural object, the *ratapa* is likewise related to this object'.[84] Here then body *and* soul originate from the transformed ancestor's body, and a spirit-child is a being with a body and soul even before it enters a woman. Does this mean that the body and soul is that of the totem ancestor himself? Strehlow has taken pains to make it clear that only one *ratappa* is associated with each transformed totem ancestor, the other *ratappa* which may be associated with the *Knanja* we are told originated from the *Churinga* which he carried with him when he went into the ground, the *ratappa* which are derived from other sources are said to have originated from the *Churinga* which they lost during the course of their wanderings. Hence only a few *ratappa* can be regarded as having originated from a totem ancestor himself, the numerous others, apparently inexhaustible in number, are merely regarded as of *Alchera* origin. The most reasonable explanation would appear to be that the body is regarded as being derived from the totem ancestor's body, whether a *Knanja* or a *Churinga*, and that the spirit may in some cases be derived from one which originated from the transformed body of a totem ancestor represented by a *Knanja* and in most cases from the spirits associated with it. Spencer and Gillen speak of the emanation of spirit-children from the *Alchera* ancestors who went into the ground, but this would appear to be only partially true, for spirit-children also originated from transformed *Churinga*, hence Leonhardi is quite justified in criticizing their continued references to the reincarnation of *Alchera* ancestors, since it is only a relatively small number of *ratappa* who are derived from the totem ancestors themselves. The incarnation of a totem ancestor, as Strehlow has shown, occurs in a quite different way.

We may now, I think, begin to see daylight. All those spirits, *Kuruna* or *ratappa*, which are found in the mistletoe berries, which among the Pintubi and Luritja are said to be formed there, and among the Upper and Middle Finke Arunta are said to be placed there or in the foliage of trees by the good mountain spirits and their wives, and by the *Alchera Inkatas* according to Spencer and Gillen, including those which occur in places where in the *Alchera* numerous *Churinga* were deposited—all these spirits were clearly placed where they occur by the *Alchera* ancestors themselves, while at those spots where they themselves entered the ground their bodies were transformed into rocks, trees, gorges, etc., and from them a single *Kuruna* or *ratappa* originated as there likewise did from each of the *Churinga* which they carried with them. Hence, at each incarnation a new individual is born who represents a being of *Alchera* origin, but who is not himself usually the incarnation of a totem ancestor, though he may be derived corporeally from one. Upon such a view a belief in reincarnation is quite unnecessary—all that is necessary is the belief in incarnation—and the notion that at death the spirit is either annihilated or goes to the island of the dead, or the shores of a great lake, becomes quite intelligible and by no means incompatible with such beliefs.

It has been urged against Strehlow's denial of the existence of a belief in repeated reincarnation among the Arunta that this is incompatible with the widespread Aboriginal notion that white men sometimes represent the reincarnation of deceased members of the tribe.[85] This argument is not, I think, of any great pertinence since in such cases we have evidence only of but a single reincarnation of a particular deceased individual and nothing more. Such an individual will originally have been the incarnation of a spirit-child of *Alchera* origin, his death and reappearance in the form of a white man is certainly an exceptional occurrence for it is not all white men who are regarded as the reincarnations of deceased blackfellows.[86]

What seems most likely is that the belief in single incarnations of spirit-children who were created in the *Alchera* represents the orthodox belief, and that at the same time there exists a belief which renders it possible that in certain cases a deceased individual may be reincarnated and reborn; we have already seen that it is believed that children who die young may be reborn again to the same mothers, but such a belief by no means implies the existence of a general belief in reincarnation for precisely the same belief exists among those Australian tribes which may be clearly shown not to have such a general belief. Clearly such statements as that at death the spirit 'finish' taken together with the *Churinga* doctrine and the beliefs relating to the origin of spirit-children can only be interpreted to mean that at death the spirit is either annihilated or goes away for ever to the island of the dead, and that therefore the spirit can never undergo more than a single incarnation. It is evident then that a belief in reincarnation as a general doctrine can hardly be said to exist among the Central tribes.

The absence of a belief in reincarnation or repeated incarnation of the same body and/or spirit does not, of course, in any way affect the question of whether or not these tribes are ignorant of the relationship between intercourse and childbirth, it is of value, however, to establish the most probably true beliefs of the natives so that, as nearly as possible, the actual manner in which those beliefs function may be properly understood.

I give here two accounts of the Arunta procreative beliefs by R. H. Mathews. Of this author Spencer writes: 'as he was never in Central Australia or in personal contact with the natives, and only rarely indicates the sources of his information, it is difficult to judge of the value of his evidence, some of which is certainly unreliable.'[87] Since, however, it is very likely that Mathews obtained his information from someone who had been in contact with the natives, and, moreover, since there is nothing in them which seems in any way doubtful I give his accounts here for what they may be considered to be worth.[88]

When a woman becomes conscious of the maternal function she reports that she had a dream somewhat to this effect: One night when she and her husband were camped near a certain spring or water-hole, she heard voices of infants laughing among the leaves of a tree growing near. Her husband may also say that he heard the infant coming down out of the tree just before daylight, when it came and pulled his hair, after which it vanished and was believed to have entered the woman's body through the navel or any other part. When the child is born it is assigned the totem of the locality where the mother or father had the dream.

The locality where either of the parents had the dream is, of course, the local totem centre of any particular local group. Mathews's remarks are perfectly consistent with both Spencer and Gillen's and Strehlow's account of these matters, excepting that these latter observers make no mention of the man or woman becoming aware that she has been entered by a spirit-child through the agency of a dream, but, as we shall shortly see, this is quite a common means of determining the totem of the unborn child among the Arunta.

In an additional account of the Arunta beliefs given by Mathews elsewhere, he states that:[89]

According to the Arranda belief, a woman may be camping with her husband close to a certain rock, soakage, etc., and a spirit child will come out of the ground, or from the rock, etc., and will throw a tiny *tjurunga* at her when she is lying asleep. This magical implement enters the woman's body and becomes a child. Another version of this belief is that a woman, whilst out walking in the bush, may pass near to a certain tree where a little spirit child is nestling among the leaves, and it throws a small invisible *tjurunga* with the same result. Clumps of mistletoe growing on the branches of gum trees are believed by the blacks to be the favourite dwelling place of spirit children in quest of a human mother. It is also believed that spirit children are borne along in whirlwinds, and if they pass close enough to a woman will cast a small *tjurunga* at her in the way described. These mythic infants are very diminutive and may be in the form of any sort of creature, or even invisible altogether.

The following account of the Arunta beliefs is from the pen of H. Basedow, an observer who enjoyed a very wide acquaintance with many Australian tribes gained during the tenure of various official posts, such as government geologist and Protector of the Aborigines. Certain of the fundamental conceptions which Basedow generalizes for the Aborigines as a whole he derives from the pattern set by the Luritja, whom he calls the Aluridja, the neighbours of the Arunta.

The fundamental conception of the *kobong* (or totem), so far as the Australian aboriginal is concerned, is of a religious nature. In the beginning of all things, the Aluridja say a number of exalted creatures of human form came out of the earth and were gracious to their tribes-people. Then appeared a menace in the shape of a gigantic dog which chased the good people from one place to another, until they decided to adopt the forms of various animals and plants, and thereby became either too fleet for the dog or were not recognized by it. Other good people now descended from the hills and drove the dog back to its hiding-place in a cave where the evil spirits dwell. The newcomers kindled a fire at the mouth of the cave and kept the evil beings in captivity whilst the original Deities re-assumed the human form. Ever after, however, these good creatures were able to alter their appearance from human to animal at will; but each individual in his choice adhered to the particular animal or plant which had saved him from the ravages of the great evil dog. Eventually they formed themselves into flat slabs of stone or wood, upon the surfaces of which they scratched the emblems of their animal representation and the tradition of their long wanderings on earth. The spirits of these Deities now live in the sky but can return at any time to re-enter the slab generally known as the '*tjuringa*'.[90]

All tribes recognize the existence of deified ancestors, now real or spiritual, whom they regard as sacred and worship accordingly. All ancestors stand in a definite, intricate, and intimate relationship to some animal, plant, water-hole, or other natural object which they have at some time or other represented; some indeed in the first place appeared as animals and later took human form. They are now looked upon as being those powers who by virtue of sacred ceremonial can produce the species they have at some time incarnated, in plenty, or allow it to proliferate. As a matter of fact, some of the sorcerers of the tribes often declare that they can see the inside of a sacred rock or *tjuringa* teeming with young, ready to be produced.[91]

Just as the 'totem' ancestor is connected with an animal, plant, or other natural object, and is embodied in the sacred form of the *tjuringa*, so the individual who traces his descent from such ancestor recognizes a close and mysterious affinity between himself and the *tjuringa* which has become his by heredity; henceforth it becomes his sacred talisman which protects him from evil and procures for him the means of maintaining his existence.[92]

The 'totem' is very dear and sacred to the native, and is religiously protected by him. I well remember on one occasion on the Alberga River I discovered a small black and yellow banded snake which I killed. An Aluridja man who was attached to the party at the time was greatly shocked at this, and, with genuine sorrow, told me that I had killed his 'brother'. Turning to an Arundta he lamented aloud: '*Kornye! nanni kallye nuka kalla illum*', which literally translated means: 'Oh, dear! This brother of mine is dead.'[93]

It had been talked among the old men for some time past that the *lubra* Maiyarra was giving cause for suspicion. Her husband Pitjala agreed; to his knowledge there had been no occasion for her to leave his camp for some moons past. His mother, old Indarrakutta, had told him that when she and Maiyarra were gathering roots down by the Womma waterhole many of the gum trees were covered with manna and they partook freely of the sweet meal, which, as he knew, does not often come to their district. The old woman had cautioned the girl and growled at her when she did not obey, because she knew Maiyarra was of the Yailliadni clan and should not be allowed to eat the manna. This disobedient *gin* had, however, not eaten much before she became sick and was obliged to lie in the hot sand of the creek where the bullrushes stand. Indarrakutta had stood aghast, Pitjala explained to the old men, when, unexpectedly disturbing a snake from the bullrushes, she observed that the creature, in gliding over the ground, touched the body of Maiyarra with its tail and, in its great haste to disappear, had left a portion of its glossy slough beside her. 'Yakai,' gasped the men, as if from a single mouth, 'then it is clear that the ever wakeful spirit of Womma has caught the neglectful Maiyarra sleeping and it is certain she is with child.'

Such was the history of the case as narrated to us. It corroborated previous observations from central and northern tribes. The recognition of maternity is not connected primarily with any conjugal liberties a husband or number of tribal husbands may be privileged to enjoy, but more with the recollection of any accidental contact with an object by which it is supposed a spirit child can enter the body of a woman. The spiritual ingress may take place in a variety of ways, but as often as not it is believed to be by means of a hollow object of some description. In the present instance it was a snake-skin.[94]

G. Róheim writes:

In Central Australia . . . the advent of the child is announced in a dream, which we shall call *the conception dream* (somewhat paradoxically as she dreams this about the time when she feels the movements of the child).[95]

The following dreams are those of an Aranda woman called Ngunalpa, wife of the famous Irriakura (Charley Cooper), one of Spencer's chief informants. Her husband's totem is *yalka*, hers is *yipatcha* (a kind of witchetty). Her mother's name and totem were *Ilia* (emu), her father was called Ilpirinja, and his totem was *indjalka* (another kind of witchetty, a green worm with a bad smell).

'In my dream I saw a *rubaruba* (whirlwind) with an *iwupa* (poisonous kind of witchetty worm). Next day I vomited my bread, and I knew that I was pregnant.' This was at Mount Andulja. She had had a fight with her husband before the dream. This was because he had *lolkuma* (refused to give her meat. He did this because she had not fetched water). The child was an *erritja* (eagle hawk), because Mount Andulja is an eagle hawk place and the wind blew from there. The *ratapa* was in the *iwupa*, and she had a headache because the cold went in through her head. The *iwupa* becomes a *chapa* or *chimacha*,[96] both being great delicacies of the Aranda menu. This girl's name was Erritja.

Her second daughter, Maud (she mentions only the white name. Contact with the whites was of old standing, even when she was a child at Alice Springs), belongs to the *renana* (snake) totem. It was near Katia, a *renana* place, that she was surrounded by a whirlwind, and she vomited.

Her third daughter's name and totem is *Erritja*. She was walking with her husband, near Andulja, when she saw a little girl with *kapita aralkara* (fair hair). The little girl came quite near, and then she disappeared. After this she felt the baby. The girl with the fair hair looked like her own sister Nelly, in fact she thought it was Nelly when she first saw it. As the vision approached from Andulja, the little girl was an *erritja*. Her own grandfather (*aranga*) and her father's brother are also *erritja*.[97]

Róheim claims that both Spencer and Strehlow

have very much exaggerated the facts when they stated that the Aranda did not know the causal relation between coitus and conception. It would be nearer the truth to say that some of them go so far in their acceptance of the official doctrine as to deny this connection. The staunchest advocate of the *churunga* doctrine was of course old Yirramba. He went so far as to say that even a man could give birth to a child if the spirit entered him. I knew enough about him from his dreams to understand why he was such a radical *churunga* believer. But in most cases coitus was regarded as a necessary preliminary. Some of the western Luritja (Pana, etc.), who had never seen a white man before, held views that were intermediate between the mythical and the natural explanation. They would say that the unborn child or embryo came out of the *kuntanka*,[98] but entered the father's body first and then penetrated into the mother through the penis. Or they would also say that sometimes the *kuntanka* had nothing to do with the whole thing; the child just went into the mother from the father's penis.

To make assurance doubly sure, I have seen the children of these western tribes enacting the whole process of coitus, conception, and childbirth. There was certainly no sexual ignorance in their case. We must not forget that the whole doctrine is esoteric and cannot even be properly revealed before initiation, i.e. before they are officially acquainted with the existence of *churungas*. After initiation the majority really believe that something else is needed besides coitus to ensure conception—that is, repression has set in, but not gone very far.[99]

The fact that Róheim observed children enacting 'the whole process of coitus, conception, and childbirth' does not, of course, mean that these children were aware of the fact, as Róheim implies, that intercourse is causally related to conception and childbirth, nor does it even necessarily mean that they recognized that intercourse was in some way connected with childbirth. The observed fact alone that in play they go through the 'whole process' tells us very little concerning their ideas about that process. If, as all observers including Róheim are agreed, it is generally known that intercourse serves to prepare the woman for the entry of a spirit-child into her, the role of intercourse will, in the case of the children's play, be quite clear—it is but the mirror of what is officially believed, namely that intercourse is usually a necessary preliminary condition of the entry of a spirit-child into a woman. Róheim's statements cannot be too easily dismissed. As an experienced psychoanalyst he could be relied upon to discover and faithfully report those nuances of meaning and behaviour which might perhaps escape others. His statements concerning the western Central tribes, namely, that they believe the unborn child to enter the mother through the penis are certainly somewhat novel, for no other investigator had been previously able to secure similar statements from the natives. These statements are, of course, not in question, and although they were secured from informants who had never seen a white man it is none the less possible for all that that some white influence had been at work here, though this is to be doubted. If then Róheim's report is to be relied upon it would seem probable that until the native is initiated into the social interpretation of the nature of things he is under the impression that intercourse is closely connected with childbirth; when, however, he has been initiated into the traditional teachings he discovers his former elementary knowledge to have been incomplete, and he gradually shifts the emphasis from a belief in material reproduction to one in favour of spiritual reproduction. The inference from this being that in certain groups the shift in emphasis, the displacement, may become so complete that any connection between intercourse and childbirth may eventually come to be altogether obscured. This precisely is what many students of this subject have claimed to have been the general process throughout Australia.[100] We shall have occasion to examine this claim in some detail in a later chapter.

The following extremely interesting account by H. K. Fry represents the relevant report of the findings of the Adelaide University Anthropological Expedition to Mount Liebig in Central Australia in August 1932.[101]

Representatives of the Pintubi and Luritja natives gave the following account of *tjuruna*: When a baby is born his or her ancestor place is known and a big *tjuruna* is made, this being the case for a boy or girl. It is kept in a cave *kolpinga*. When a boy has been initiated he is given a second *tjuruna*. This is his mother's. The two are then shown to him and he is told '*Anango ndzunto kutara nuntupa*'—'Body yours two *tjuruna*.' They tell the girls, 'We have your body over there,' but the *tjuruna* are never shown to them. When there are many sons the eldest looks after the mother's *tjuruna*, and for each other boy they make another one for the mother's body. It was also stated that a man could give away his first *tjuruna*, but must always keep the one given at his initiation. After a boy has been circumcised, but before he has been shown his *tjuruna*, he is given a *mataki* (Pintubi) *manabokma* (Ngalia). This is a small bullroarer, equivalent to the Aranda *namatuna*. The *mataki* is carried in the boy's hair, which is done up in a bulky chignon. . . . It is given by a man to his son. If he has no son he gives it to his sister's son.

The native belief, therefore, provides for the identification of his body with that of his totem ancestor, either in the form of a familiar spirit inhabiting a totem place, or in the form of a *tjuruna* representing the transformed bodies of the totem-ancestors of his mother and himself.

The narratives of women concerning the conception of their children give further information on this question. The following histories are quoted from notes taken at Mount Liebig.

1. *Waripanda.*—Ngalia women, speaks Pintubi. Female child. 'Find along Watulbi. She went for food—*ildzulpa* = gum from the small stems of the *warildzi* bush. After she ate that, she felt something in her belly. Does not know what happened. She fell down, she got up, went back to the camp, drank water and was sick. Baby's totem is *ildzulpa*. She dreamed that *induda* [the totem personality or spirit of a place] belong to Watulbi. That he threw a stick which hit her and she fell down. Then she went for food and the rest happened. She does not remember if the man in the dream was like anyone she knows. There is a boy *induda* at Watulbi now called Jarakula. This is her husband—*korei*—her actual husband.'

2. *Njiljimba.*—Pintubi. Male child. 'One place Namara. She was taking witchetty grubs (*ilkoara*) in the roots of witchetty bushes. She fell down. She got up, went back to camp, had a drink of water, then felt sick. She lay down. Then sick. The totem of the child is *tala* = honey ant. Someone threw honey ant, that was why she fell down. Stick fell from tree, and she thought someone threw it. Did not see anyone, but thought someone might have thrown it. She dreamed before she went out, then she went for honey ant. She dreamed she saw a baby in the bush, and it disappeared.'

3. *Larija.*—Pintubi married to Ngalia man. Female child. 'She went for water and *Ndzina* threw a little stick, which hit her in the stomach and went right inside her. She got up and went back to camp. After she went back to camp she was sick, then she felt something heavy inside. This happened, she did not dream it. She dreamed a man had a waddy in his hand and threw it and she fell down. After she came back from the water she dreamed this. The waddy went through the belly below the navel, not the vagina, and went up. The man was an old man with a white beard, a shortish man with a big stomach, he looked like Tuma, a Pikili chief from Watulba. She calls Tuma *korei*. He is actually her own eldest sister's husband. She went for the water at Taluwara—two days south of Walunguru (M. Leisler). *Ndzina* (= mirage) is the totem ancestor of the place. She saw him hazily even though he was standing in a clear place and not far from her. She did not get a clear view of him, just a glimpse. She felt the pain, fell down, the stick went in, and the fall drove it in farther. The totem of the child is *ndzina*.'

4. *Jatakalana.*—Pintubi. Female child. 'She went for *Ilkoara* (witchetty)—with a stick—someone threw at her. Old man threw it. She saw old man come up, she saw him throw the stick. She felt something hurt in her belly. She fell down, and lay on the ground, and felt nothing. The old man got into her belly while she lay down, and old man became baby. When she went back to the camp she was sick, and she knew the old man had gone in. They did not see the old man again when they went out, so he must have gone into her. The old man was like Tjinapurutuna—she calls Tjinapurutuna *kameru* (= mother's brother, Luritja); he calls her *dzundalpa* (= sister's daughter, Pintubi). The baby's totem is *taralpari* or *takiberi* = emu. She was at Wili west of Ilbilla, the totem of which is emu. The old man was the *induda*. She had a dream, old man came near, he threw a little stick at her. After that dream she knew she was pregnant. When she woke up she did not know she was pregnant, but in a couple of days she knew it.'

5. *Jankumbingi.*—Pintubi. Male child. 'She went for a big mob *lupulpa* (= jelka, Cyperus rotundus). While she was digging, an old man threw a little yam stick at her. She felt it hurt in the bottom of her abdomen. She fell down, she went back to camp and was sick. She felt a weight in her inside. After that the old man was not seen any more. She think that he be inside her, and become baby. The old man was like Tuma. She calls Tuma *kameru*, and he calls her *okari dzundalpa* (*okari* = sister's daughter, Luritja). She had a dream that old man Tuma came along. When he came near he threw a little waddy at her and he disappeared. She dreamed this after the above events. Baby's totem is *kaldzu*, water. Kaldjupimba is the place of the water totem, and is one day north of Walunguru.'

In each of these histories it will be noted that the throwing of a *tjuruna*-equivalent is given as the cause of conception, but in four cases the conception-idea is overdetermined. In cases 1 and 2 the eating of the totem is coincident, and in addition the agency of the totem-ancestor is brought in by case 1. Again, in cases 4 and 5 the totem-ancestor is definitely stated to become transformed into the baby, the 'old man' becoming a female child in the instance of case 4.

Róheim's interesting interpretation[102] of the visionary agent of impregnation as a father-substitute receives some support from these histories. But there is the complicating factor that conception occurs at a definite locality, the impregnating agent is the totem-ancestor of that place, and this totem-ancestor may be the person of a relative of the woman in question. This is illustrated most forcibly in the history of case 1. The woman certainly did not state that she recognized her husband in the person of the totem-ancestor, but the recognition must have been made. Here, then, is a case which should represent the happy marriage in which the father-image is merged in that of the husband, whereas in fact the accidental circumstance, that the totem-ancestor of the locality was also the woman's husband, appears to have been the determining factor in the case.

The complexity of the conception-idea, illustrated by the women's stories related above, was found to be even more complicated when the question was discussed with some of the older men. These informants stated that unless a woman had sexual intercourse at a certain locality she could not find her baby there. This statement was taken down verbatim in the Luritja language from the dictation of a Luritja and Pintubi man:

Watingo mura lianka kunkanka, tjitji mantjilia nindzani.
Man copulate not unmarried woman, child she gets not.

Wati ankuntala, kunka nura tjukutantanka dzinara, tjitji mantzilia nindzani.
Man gone away, woman place belong totem if sits down, child gets not sits down.

I was unable, in spite of many questions, to obtain any statement from my informants concerning any effect which sexual intercourse has on the woman such that pregnancy can occur. Concerning knowledge of pregnancy, however, they state that although a woman 'dries up' when she is pregnant, yet she does not know that she is pregnant until she feels something in her abdomen.[103]

Our information so far has been concerned with the origin and nature of the body. The spirit part of a man, *kurun-kurun* (Pintubi), the equivalent of the Aranda *kuruna*, was stated by my Pintubi and Luritja informants to have nothing to do with the totems and *tjuruna*. They said that the *kurun-kurun* was formed in the berries (*nanta*, Loritja, *dzungurbma*, Pintubi) of the mistletoe (*natangini*, Luritja, *ndzinkininpa*, Pintubi), and then hangs down from the leaves of the mistletoe. When a pregnant woman passes, the *kurun-kurun* goes in. When a man dies his *kurun-kurun* goes west to a big water (*waleia*, Luritja, *apinti*, Pintubi; translated by my interpreter as 'the sea'); it goes into the water—'finish'.[104]

It is to be noted here that the dream among the Luritja and Pintubi, as among the majority, if not all, of the Australian tribes, is a customary means through which the pregnancy of a woman is either announced or confirmed, either to the mother herself or else to some close relative, the manifest dream content being apparently thoroughly 'institutionalized'.

The fact that Fry's informants stated that unless a woman had had sexual intercourse at a certain locality she could not find her baby there, decidedly, as Fry says, renders more complicated the already complex conception ideas of the Luritja and Pintubi, we must therefore devote some space to the clarification of these ideas.

Each individual, it is clear from Fry's account, represents the reincarnation of a totem ancestor, who has a real existence 'either in the form of a familiar spirit inhabiting a totem place, or in the form of a *tjuruna* representing the transformed bodies of the totem-ancestors of his mother and himself'. It is to be noted that the corporeal and spirit parts of an individual are derived independently of one another and in different ways. The entry of the *body* of the totem ancestor into the woman is effected by the throwing of a *tjuruna* at the woman in the totem locality, the throwing of the *tjuruna* being regarded as 'the cause of conception', the spirit part or soul entering the reincarnated body of the ancestor already within the pregnant woman, subsequently, and in complete dissociation both of the *tjuruna* and the totems.

The important question now is this: If the throwing of the *Churinga* is the cause of conception, is it the sole efficient cause, or are we here dealing with a plurality of conditions, sexual intercourse within the totem locality being the other indispensable condition? This question does not, I think, present any insuperable difficulties. According to Fry's informants, a woman cannot be entered by a child unless she has previously had intercourse within the boundaries of the totem locality at which the spirit-child normally resides. It is to be noted that Fry's informants speak of 'intercourse at a certain totem locality', and of the abode of the totem ancestors as the 'totem place'. This, if it means anything, means that the local totemic group will generally live in the vicinity or locality of the abodes of its totem ancestors, so that intercourse will in any event generally take place within the boundaries of the totem locality of the group, and since there are a variety of totems represented within a local area, it is in the vicinity of one particular totem abode that the *Churinga* will be thrown, and the totem ancestor of that particular place enter the woman. This, indeed, is how the totem of the child is determined. Intercourse does not have to take place at the totem place or in the immediate vicinity thereof. If this interpretation is correct[105] then Fry's account is in essential agreement with Spencer and Gillen's findings, as when they write,[106]

we have amongst the Arunta, Luritcha, and Ilpirra tribes, and probably also amongst others such as the Warramunga, the idea firmly held that the child is not the direct result of intercourse, that it may come without this, which merely, as it were, prepares the mother for the reception and birth also of an already-formed spirit child who inhabits one of the local totem centres. Time after time we have questioned them on this point, and always received the reply that the child was not the direct result of intercourse . . .

We have already discussed the significance of these statements in the preceding pages, and we have seen that intercourse is regarded as a purely adventitious preparation of the woman for the possible reception and birth of a spirit-child among the Arunta; this would appear to be the situation also among the tribes of the Northern Territory and of Queensland. Among the Pintubi and Luritja, however, the belief seems to assume a more integrated form, for intercourse is regarded as an essential preliminary without which the spirit-child would not enter the woman.

Among the Pintubi and Luritja, however, intercourse is a *condition* of pregnancy but not the cause of it, the cause being the throwing of the *Churinga*. Intercourse may naturally occur without being followed by the entry of a spirit-child into the woman, but a spirit-child will not enter a woman without intercourse between her and a man having previously taken place within the general locality in which the abode of that spirit-child is situated.

Among the Arunta intercourse must at most have been regarded as a helpful though not as an absolutely indispensable preliminary to the entry of a spirit-child into a woman.

It should be noted here that the spirit-child does not enter the woman through the vulva, but through the loins, the navel, or the abdomen; the male organ is, however, probably assumed by the natives, as it is by many whites, to pass into the female loins, certainly into the abdomen, during intercourse, and thus the preparation may be regarded by the natives as a definitely physical one, and not in any sense as a ritual one. But such an act of preparation is a far cry from being either a direct or an indirect cause of pregnancy, for it would appear to be merely an act of accommodation, and not necessarily a premeditated one, towards the totem spirit who may happen to wish to enter a particular woman.

Now, since intercourse is virtually an everyday occurrence in the life of the Aboriginal woman, she is naturally almost always in a state prepared to receive a spirit-child, and the frequently observed fact that a woman may for years live without being entered by a spirit-child would render it perfectly evident that pregnancy depended upon the will of the totem ancestors, and not upon intercourse. There can therefore be, among the Pintubi and Luritja, no recognition of the part that intercourse plays in the causation of pregnancy, in the sense that intercourse is recognized as the act which touches off the spring which sets the whole cycle of events going which eventually terminate in the birth of a child; on the contrary, this last event is regarded as being due entirely to the entrance of a spirit-child into the woman.

Fry's remaining findings have already been discussed in the preceding pages.

Miss Olive Pink, to whose work on the northern and north-western Arunta we have already referred, has this to say of the pro-creative beliefs of these groups:[107]

Contrary to the usually accepted opinion, I found the Aranda natives do understand the part the father plays in procreation; they believe that the body of a baby comes from its father and mother conjointly. It is only the spirit part which enters the mother at the time of 'quickening', when she 'finds' it.

The totemic estate was also the place where the woman who was brought into the 'horde country' by marriage, usually, found her baby's spirit. To her this was a country of the opposite moiety, but to her husband and baby it was their own 'country'.

In a normally functioning community she would seem to have 'found' it, as a rule, in the correct ancestral locality, more often than do the women in the more disintegrated areas. But this is natural where freedom of movement over the country of the tribe is so un-restricted now, and she is more often away from her husband's own country than not. In some cases she has not even seen it; as a result of economic pressure.

When a woman 'finds' her baby's spirit elsewhere, the headman of that totemic area is told and he gives to him, or her, a name belong-ing to his estate. If the baby is a boy a name is given which is associa-ted with some water, tree, or stone near which he was 'found'. This feature indicates the place where some dream-time ancestor per-formed some act, and with which ritual songs and paint are associa-ted. Or he may have performed some ceremony and left *tjurina* there, and consequently baby-spirits awaiting incarnation.

Miss Pink is aware of the difficulty of obtaining the original beliefs of these natives who have been so greatly altered as a result of their continuous contact with the white man over many years. She has herself stated that 'among missionized natives it is extremely difficult to find out what the *original* beliefs really were, or even what their own *really* are now. The beliefs they recount are sometimes only such as they think the missionary would approve if he should hear them'.[108] Further, Miss Pink writes that 'In the Aranda tribe my informants were, of course, sophisticated natives, which fact, although it facilitated discussion with them, also made some of their statements "suspect". So there had to be a constant sifting of "wheat from chaff", and I have no doubt that some "chaff" may have escaped the winnowing'.[109]

We have already considered some of Miss Pink's findings in connection with the problem of reincarnation which, as we have seen, she found not to exist among the Arunta except in so far as children who have died young are concerned. Here there is only to be considered the statement that the Arunta do understand the part which the father plays in procreation, and that they believe the *body* of the baby to be derived conjointly from the mother and father, the spirit part entering later.

It is here necessary to point out that no one has previously described such a belief for the Arunta, or any other Australian tribe for that matter. Certainly the statement that the body is derived from the parents conjointly is incompatible with the *Churinga* doctrine, and certainly it could form no part of the traditional teaching.

What has probably occurred is that as a result of the breakdown of Arunta culture and the long association of the natives with the missionary and other whites, the traditional teachings have undergone a very considerable modification which, at the present time, is discoverable in such beliefs as Miss Pink has reported. Or it may possibly be that as a result of the weakening of the emphasis which was in the past placed on the traditional view of these matters that the simplest material interpretation of the facts has been arrived at by the natives themselves.

In view of these considerations it is doubtful whether Miss Pink's findings may be accepted as representative of the Arunta Aboriginal procreative beliefs.

With reference to the procreative beliefs of the northern tribes of Central Australia Spencer and Gillen state that:[110]

In every tribe without exception there exists a firm belief in the reincarnation of ancestors. Emphasis must be laid on the fact that this belief is not confined to tribes such as the Arunta, Warramunga, Binbinga, Anula, and others, amongst whom descent is counted in the male line, but is found just as strongly developed in the Urabunna tribe, in which descent, both of class and totem, is strictly maternal.

According to the traditions it is believed that in the far distant past certain semi-human ancestors wandered about over the country now occupied by the Urabunna tribe, and at various places performed sacred ceremonies. Wherever these ceremonies were performed there were deposited in the ground, or in a rock or water-hole, or other natural feature, which arose to mark the spot, a number of spirit individuals called *mai-aurli*.[111] These *mai-aurli* emanated from the bodies of the *Alchera* ancestors, and every living individual is regarded as the incarnation of such a spirit.

Among the Urabunna, as among the Arunta, the totems are strictly divided between the two moieties of the tribe. In general among the northern tribes descent both of class and totem is strictly paternal, a spirit-child, for example, is not supposed to enter any woman unless she is the wife of a man of the same moiety and totem as the spirit. Among the Urabunna, however, the case is different, the spirit can only enter a woman of the same moiety and totem as itself, should it by chance enter the wrong woman it will invariably abort. Associated with these ideas is the belief that in each successive incarnation the spirit changes its sex, moiety, and totem. This belief is also found in the Warramunga tribe.

The spirit of a dead man, now called *kumpira*, returns to the place where it was originally left by the *Alchera* ancestor, where it remains until it undergoes reincarnation. As a result of this peculiar belief each spirit, it is obvious, will, in the course of time, run the whole gamut of the totems, and alternate from side to side of the tribe, and at death always return to its original home.[112]

In most of the Northern tribes, but not in all, the totemic groups are believed to have arisen as the direct offspring of one great eponymous ancestor;[113] among the Urabunna the members of each totemic group are believed to have arisen as the direct offspring of one or two eponymous ancestors.[114]

According to these notions it is quite clear that we are not dealing here, among the northern Central tribes, with the reincarnation of the *Alchera* ancestors themselves, but rather with the *offspring* of these ancestors, a point which Spencer and Gillen do not seem to have succeeded in making sufficiently clear. It is evidently clearly recognized among some of these tribes that each individual is the incarnation of a spirit-child which was not the offspring of one of the *Alchera* semi-human ancestors or beings, but was merely in his keeping and deposited by him at a certain spot. Among other tribes, and according to Spencer and Gillen, the majority of the northern Central tribes fall into this category, the belief is that each individual represents the incarnation of the direct offspring of an *Alchera* ancestor. In no case is there a belief in the reincarnation of the *Alchera* ancestor himself. This point, it will be recalled, has already been made by Leonhardi *apropos* of the Arunta in connection with Spencer and Gillen's use of the phrase 'the reincarnation of totem ancestors', but, as I have endeavoured to show, Spencer and Gillen used the term 'ancestors' to refer to the original *Kuruna* left by the great *Alchera Inkatas* in certain spots, as well as to the *Inkatas* themselves. Certainly Spencer and Gillen's use of the term 'ancestor' is confusing, but there can be no doubt that whatever the case may be with respect to the northern Central tribes, the more southern Central tribes, or at least the Arunta, do believe that the *Inkatas* as well as the spirit-children they carried about with them are, at least occasionally, reincarnated. Strehlow has himself stated the fact. What does seem fairly certain is that the eponymous ancestor of the Arunta, Numbakulla, is never reincarnated, and this would appear to be true, too, of the eponymous ancestors of the totemic groups among the northern Central tribes.

In respect of the Warramunga tribe Spencer and Gillen note that 'the women are very careful not to strike the trunks of certain trees with an axe, because the blow might cause spirit children to emanate from them and enter their bodies. They imagine that the spirit is very minute—about the size of a small grain of sand—and that it enters the woman through the navel and grows within her into the child.'[115]

Referring to the problem of the meaning of the practices of incision and subincision they add: 'It will thus be seen that, unless the natives have once possessed, but have since lost, all idea of the association between procreation and the intercourse of the sexes, which is extremely improbable, the elaborate and painful ceremonies of initiation cannot in their origin have had any direct relation to procreation.'[116]

With respect to the Walbiri, Capell, writing in 1952, states that 'The concept of birth from a given spirit centre is similar to that reported commonly from the Central Australian region, although the information to hand does not justify one in saying that an Aranda type of conception idea is present. If one asks *njarbalaŋgu balga manu?*, "Where did he find you?" i.e. "Where were you born?", the answer is in terms of the spirit centre, *jugujudu* (from which comes the spirit child "*gurulba*").'[117]

In the first full report of the Walbiri, Meggitt in 1962[118] reported that

the Walbiri postulate the existence, not of spirit-children, but of *guruwari* spirit-entities, which are by no means the same thing. It is true the people believe that a *guruwari* determines the child's sex to the extent that, in each incarnation, the same *guruwari* animates a child of the opposite sex to that in the previous incarnation. But they also say that this is being wise after the event, for nobody can know which individual previously possessed a particular *guruwari*. The *guruwari* are impersonal, homogeneous entities, whose course of incarnations through the ages cannot be traced in the way that those of the Aranda spirit-children can be known.

All the older men with whom I discussed the matter held that

copulation and the entry of a *guruwari* into the woman are both necessary preliminaries to child-birth; but in general they thought the
action of the *guruwari* to be more important, because it animates the
foetus and helps to determine its future character or personality. A
few men expressed additional opinions on the matter. One maintained that the father's semen carries some of his patri- or lodge-
spirit into the child, which is partly formed from the semen. Another
said the semen mingles with the retained menstrual blood to create a
foetus that the *guruwari* vivifies—a view resembling that of the Ooldea
Pidjandjara (vide Berndt, 1945, p. 79).

The women, on the other hand, were emphatic that coitus is the
significant antecedent of parturition; the entry of the *guruwari* is a
secondary event that identifies the child formed of the menstrual
blood. Indeed, many of the women were surprised that my wife and
myself had to ask for such self-evident information. Warner had
the same experience with the Murngin of Arnhem Land (1937,
p. 24).

It seems to me unlikely that the variety of opinions is merely the
outcome of the people's limited acquaintance with Europeans, for
there is much evidence to demonstrate that desert Aborigines change
their beliefs very slowly on subjects that are important to them, no
matter how intensive European contact is. Consequently, I agree
with Warner and with Róheim (1945) when they say that the Aborigines' answers to questions about conception depend on who is
asked and in what circumstances. In ritual contexts, men speak of
the action of the *guruwari* as the significant factor; in secular contexts,
they nominate both the *guruwari* and sexual intercourse. The women,
having few ritual attitudes, generally emphasize copulation.

The people appear to make no use of contraceptive techniques
(if in fact they know of any apart from *coitus interruptus*), and most
married couples desire large families. As it is thought that many acts
of intercourse are necessary to lead to pregnancy, lovers do not worry
about the consequences of casual liaisons. For the same reason, the
inability of a married person to have children may be blamed on his
or her laziness; he has not copulated often enough to enable the
guruwari to act effectively.

Surely, if many acts of intercourse are considered necessary to
ensure pregnancy in order to make the *guruwari* act effectively, then
it is the *guruwari* that are the principal initiators of pregnancy?

Mountford, writing of the Pitjandjara as he knew them in 1940,
describes the mythological beliefs of this people, and gives an account
of Tjinderi-tjinderiba, the mythical willy-wagtail woman, with her
many children who made a dry weather camp on the northern side

of Ayers Rock.[119] In an adjacent shallow cave there are four boulders, the children of Tjinderi-tjinderiba. These four boulders contain

an inexhaustible supply of spirit children, the *yulanya*, little beings only a few inches high, with light skin and long black hair. When one of these little people desires to become a human baby, it leaves its *yulanya* stone and sets out on a search for a suitable mother. On seeing a woman with large breasts and a kindly face whom it thinks would make a good mother, it quietly follows her and, waiting until she sits down or goes to sleep, enters her body through the vulva and starts life as a human being. The two right-hand boulders in the small cave are *Tanamildjan* (the opposite moiety) from those on the left and, of course, *Nananduraka* (the same moiety) to each other. . . . A *yulanya* spirit child will only enter a woman who is *Tanamildjan* to it; in other words, the spirit child obeys the same laws, when choosing a mother, as a man does when choosing a wife.

Thus, it is clear that these tribes have a conception of the spirit-child which is identical, or almost identical, with that of the more central tribes.

NOTES

1   *The Aborigines of Victoria.*
2   *The Folklore, Manners, Customs, and Languages of the South Australian Aborigines.*
3   *The Native Tribes of South Australia.*
4   *The Australian Race.*
5   *The Native Tribes of South-East Australia.*
6   'The Aborigines of the Upper and Middle Finke River', *Trans. Proc. Roy. Soc. S. Aust.*, 14, 1891, 237.
7   *The Arunta*, i, 107.
8   Ibid., 370.
9   Ibid., 371, totem design.
10   Ibid. The original *Alchera Churinga.*
11   Ibid., 371.
12   Ibid., 365.
13   Ibid., 107.
14   Ibid.
15   *The Native Tribes of Central Australia.*
16   *The Arunta*, i, x.
17   Ibid., 72–3.
18   According to G. Róheim, the literal meaning of this word, *Knanja*, is *origin.* Cf. 'The psycho-analysis of primitive cultural types', *Int. J. Psychoanal.*, 13, 1932, 58.
19   'The spirit of *Kuruna* always enters the woman through the loins.' (S. and G.)
20   '*Kurunas* are also supposed to be especially fond of travelling in whirlwinds, and, on seeing one of these, which are called Uraburaba and are very frequent at certain times of the year, approaching her, a woman will at once run away.' (S. and G.)
21   *The Arunta*, i, 75–8.

22   Ibid., 84–5.
23   Ibid., 99.
24   Ibid., 102.
25   Ibid., 103–7.
26   Ibid., 110.
27   Ibid., 111–12.
28   Ibid., 356.
29   'The word *aradugga* or *aradukka* is generally used with the meaning of coming out of, or being born, as in the phrase, *Tmerga ratappa aradugga*, the child was born yesterday. The word *knailjalugga* is more often used when speaking of a Kuruna coming out of, or emanating from, a Churinga; for example, when a man is shown his own *Churinga knanja* he is told, *Nana Churinga indulla-irrakura ingwana; unta knailjalugga*; here is your Churinga indullairrakura; you came out of it. The Churinga is not regarded as the body, or *mberka*, of the man: the *mberka* is supposed to be formed later when the Kuruna, having left the Churinga, enters a woman.' (S. and G.)
30   Ibid., 358–9.
31   These terms refer to three of the first four Inkatas of the Alchera in order of importance, respectively, the very great Inkata, the great Inkata, the lesser Inkata, and the little Inkata (Lukata kurka).
32   Ibid., 362–3. 'The term *Ratappa* is not, strictly speaking, applied to a "spirit-child". The spirit is always spoken of as *Kuruna*, and it is only after entering the mother that it gives rise to a *Ratappa*. Even at the *Ratappa* stone, so called because a small child went into the ground there, it is a *Kuruna* and not a *Ratappa* that enters a woman. The term *Kuruna* is always used in reference to the spirit itself, either before it enters the mother or after it leaves the body.' (S. and G.)
33   Ibid., 369–70.
34   Ibid., ii, 423.
35   Ibid., i, 363.
36   Ibid., 358 n. 1.
37   *The Arunta*, i, 222.
38   *The Sexual Life of Savages*, 142.
39   *The Arunta*, 356.
40   Ibid., 358.
41   Ibid., 362.
42   Ibid., 362–3.
43   Pater W. Schmidt, in a study of the origin and significance of the conceptional beliefs of the Arunta as reported by Strehlow, has some interesting theories to offer in this connection. I give them here for what they are worth, but I do not propose to discuss them, since they represent the sort of speculative interpretation which I consider it would be impossible either to prove or disprove. To me it seems only that Schmidt's interpretation would make of the Arunta the kind of metaphysicians that I do not for a moment believe them ever to have been. Schmidt writes: 'among the Arunta it was the supernatural being Mangarkunjerkunja [this is the same being who among the more northern Arunta studied by Spencer and Gillen is called Numbakulla] that leads men from their imperfect formless state into the sociologically higher one of *tjurunga* totemism, for at that time he gave to every man a *tjurunga* and designated it as the body of the one connected with it. Thus, the *tjurunga* is the external symbol for this new higher existence, this process of being put into relation with a totemic ancestor. I must also point out that one of the two most frequent methods of conception in which the totemic ancestor plays the most important part because he himself appears in an active role [*selbsthandelnd Auftritt*], consists in the ancestor's throwing a small *tjurunga*, a *namatuna*, towards the woman, which is in her body transformed into a human form. Mangarkunjerkunja thus did not create men *ex toto* but found them already in a living state. Likewise the idea originally lying at the base of the conceptionalism seems to be that the totemic ancestor is not responsible for the entire existence of the subsequent being but merely grants it the sociologically

higher existence of which, however, they are absolutely in need, under present conditions, in order to exist at all. This higher existence was, so to speak, granted as a sort of sociological entelechy in a *materia prima, sociologice informis*, which in turn, originates from the procreative act, and therefore from the relation with the man. Since for special reasons . . . the connection with the totem of the male has been lost entirely among the Arunta, the attempt was therefore made of entirely denying by dint of consistent theorizing the importance of the male in conception, an attempt, however, which it seems cannot be carried out completely in view of the general knowledge and experience.

'It is impossible to object to this theory on the ground of Strehlow's statement concerning the nature of the *ratappa* (spirit child), "these *ratappa* are fully developed boys and girls of a reddish complexion, they possess a body and soul." It must be observed, first of all, that the other already mentioned method of conception knows only of the *namatuna* which assumes human form only within the body of the mother. Furthermore, it must be observed that the *rella maneriṇja*, the helpless beings of primordial times, received their final form and the free use of their limbs from Mangarkunjerkunja only, the founder of *tjurunga* totemism. Formerly their eyes were closed, their limbs firmly adherent to the trunk, all this being merely the mythical expression of a sociological and not a physical inferiority' (888–9).

'Elsewhere I have emphasized (*Anthropos*, 3, 1908, 623) that we are here dealing not with physiological stages of development, but with sociological stages of development, that the pitiful helplessness of the *rella maneriṇja* reflects, in the myth, the contempt of a race that, at least, in its own opinion is sociologically and culturally superior to the original inhabitants whom it found. Thereby this race indicates that it considers itself a stranger and an invader, that those who are responsible for the present cultural status of the Arunta, represent a later immigrant element . . .' (880) 'Die Stellung der Aranda unter den australischen Stämmen', *Zeit. Ethnol.*, 40, 1908, 866–901. It may here be remarked that there is nothing in any Arunta myth which may be interpreted as exhibiting the slightest degree of contempt for the *rella maneriṇja* or *inapertwa*. On the other hand, the Arunta consider them as their biological relatives from whom they are descended, since they were by Numbakulla transformed from them, and for whom therefore they possess an affection and respect which is abundantly displayed during the course of their totemic ceremonies. For a detailed criticism of the views expressed in this book by Pater Schmidt, see his 'Die Konzeptionsglaube australischer Stämme', *Int. Archiv Ethnog.*, 44, 1952, 36–81. For a discussion of Pater Schmidt's study see A. Capell, *Oceania*, 23, 1953, 240.

44 *The Arunta*, 362.
45 Ibid., 364.
46 Ibid.
47 Ibid., 361.
48 Ibid., 39.
49 For the authorities and the evidence in support of these statements for primitive peoples in general, see Ploss and Bartel's chapter in *Woman*, entitled 'Are Births Easier among Civilized or Primitive Natives?' ii, 580–96. For Australia, see J. Hooker, 'On child-bearing in Australia and New Zealand', *J. Ethnol. Soc.*, London, n.s., 1, 1869, 68–71, in which Hooker gives the statements of a number of first-hand observers of whom he had made inquiries concerning the facts relating to labour and birth. The statements thus obtained almost all agree that labour is short and birth easy among the Aborigines. Similar statements are made by R. Oberländer, 'Die Eingeborenen der australischen Kolonie Victoria', *Globus*, 4, 1863, 278–82, and by E. Palmer, 'Notes on some Australian tribes', *JAI*, 13, 1884, 280. Similarly, Basedow, who gives an account of labour and delivery as observed by himself among the Larrekiya of the Port Darwin district, also indicates that labour is brief and birth easy. 'The event', he writes, 'is almost invariably spontaneous. In my experience I have very rarely seen complications, and then usually when the *lubra* had

been living under civilized conditions' (*The Australian Aboriginal*, 63). Spencer and Gillen state that there is rarely any difficulty in child-bearing among the Arunta. *The Arunta*, ii, 487.

50   Spencer and Gillen dealt chiefly with the southern, central, and northern groups. Cf. *The Arunta*, ii, 590.

51   Ibid., 589.

52   Quoted in J. G. Frazer, *Totemism and Exogamy*, i, 186–7.

53   *Mythen, Sagen und Märchen des Aranda-Stämmes in Zentral Australien*, 2.

54   The fact is that in children of both sexes as many as 80 per cent have been found to be fair-haired. See A. A. Abbie, *The Original Australians*, 31.

55   Foreword (pages unnumbered), ii–iii, *Mythen, Sagen und Märchen*.

56   Ibid., 52–3.

57   Ibid., 55–6.

58   Ibid., 56. Leonhardi's note: 'Strehlow has not been able to substantiate Spencer and Gillen's statement concerning the Aranda and neighbouring tribes which definitely declared that all children are the reincarnations of totem ancestors, and that their souls are continually reborn. I corresponded with him about the matter on various occasions. (See *Globus*, xci, 288.) According to his investigations such a belief is not to be found among the Aranda and Loritja whom he questioned; he thinks that it would be entirely in opposition to the beliefs according to which the totem-gods are thought to be still living on earth. In the exceptional cases in which a totem-ancestor himself is to be reborn, only a single, never a repeated, incarnation takes place. Strehlow thinks that he must also contradict reincarnation theories attributed to the Aranda living towards the east as related by Spencer and Gillen. I should like to point out here that "the reincarnation of ancestors" reported by Spencer and Gillen as the general and only belief of the Aranda and the other tribes investigated by them is a designation which decidedly cannot be applied to a number of examples given by the authors. If one takes the expression literally, as one doubtless is intended to do in most cases, it can only be understood to mean that the particular totem ancestor himself is reborn again and again. But that is not at all compatible with all the beliefs reported for the different tribes; for example, not for the Urabunna. According to Spencer and Gillen only a few ancestors wandered about the Urabunna territory. From their bodies the spirit children emanated in various centres, and from these spirit children arose the first human beings who since that time have been continually reborn (*North. Trib.*, 146). Similar beliefs are reported for the Kaitish and the Unmatjera (ibid., 156–7, 158 n.) The same thing holds true for the Warramunga (ibid., 161). Surely in such cases one cannot speak of the rebirth of totem ancestors (*alcheringa* ancestors) but only of a reincarnation of the spirit children which originally emanated from them. For the totem ancestors are in certain cases definitely regarded as still living, as, for example, the Wallunga snake of the Warramunga. But also among the Aranda the assumed general reincarnation theory is not compatible with all the reported evidence; for instance, in not all these cases where we are told that the ancestors carried about with them on their wanderings many *tjurunga* (not only their own), and that spirit children emanated from those lost on the way (*North. Trib.*, 150). Likewise their beliefs that totem-ancestors still live, for example, in a water-hole (*Nat. Trib.*, 45) is incompatible with the assumed general theory. Very interesting are the reports of R. H. Mathews (*Proc. Roy. Geog. Soc. Queensl.*, xxii, 1907, 75–6) concerning the belief in incarnation or reincarnation of the Chingalee (Tjingilee of Spencer and Gillen). The various subdivisions of this tribe seem to disagree a good deal in their beliefs. One of them believes in the repeated reincarnation of the ancestors, in which case the sex changes each time exactly as among the Urabunna according to Spencer and Gillen (*North. Trib.*, 148). In a clan (*Unterstamm*) of the Kwarranjee such a change of sex does not occur, the souls of women not being reincarnated at all. This belief is found also among the Gnanji (*North. Trib.*, 170). Finally, the northern Chingalee do not believe in reincarnation at all, for in each case it is an entirely new spirit child that

emanates from a rock or tree and is born as a human being. After death the soul wanders about for some time and then goes northward. This belief would come quite close to that of the Aranda as reported by Strehlow. If these reports of Mathews are correct, they would prove that very different beliefs can exist side by side in a single tribe. In any case, according to what has been said above, Spencer and Gillen's statement that "in every tribe without exception there exists a firm belief in the reincarnation of ancestors", seems to me misleading.' Ibid., 56–7.

59 Ibid., *Mythen, Sagen und Märchen des Loritja-Stämmes*, 60.
60 Ibid., 53.
61 *Die totemistischen Vorstellungen und die Tjuringa der Aranda und Loritja*, x-xiii.
62 According to Spencer this should be spelt as two words, *altjiranga* and *mitjina*, *The Arunta*, ii, 585.
63 Ibid., 596.
64 *The Native Tribes of Central Australia*, 119.
65 *The Arunta*, ii, 585.
66 Ibid.
67 Ibid.
68 Ibid., i, 75–6.
69 Ibid., 370–1.
70 Ibid., 111–12.
71 This view is supported by Róheim's findings. 'Everything that an Aranda does is modelled on a pattern. There is nothing new under the sun; we are only doing what totemic ancestors did at the dawn of the world. They are the eternal ones of dreams, for all myths are dreams, and, as we see, some dreams are myths. Now the totemic ancestors always end their days by going into the earth and becoming *churinga*.

'However, although becoming *churinga* means death, it means something else besides. New life sprouts forth from these sticks and stones, and it is from these that the *ratapa* (unborn babies) swarm forth and enter the wombs of women', *Int. J. Psychoanal.*, 13, 1932, (52).
72 H. K. Fry, 'Body and soul', *Oceania*, 3, 1933, 251.
73 Ibid., 256.
74 O. Pink, 'The landowners in the northern division of the Aranda tribe, Central Australia', *Oceania*, 6, 1936, 288–9.
75 D. Collins, *An Account of the English Colony in New South Wales*, ii, 355–6; G. F. Angas, *Savage Life and Scenes in Australia and New Zealand*, i, 108; Ch. Wilhelmi, 'Manners and customs of the Australian natives', *Trans. Roy. Soc. Vict.*, 5, 1861, 188–9; G. Taplin, *The Folklore, Manners, Customs, and Languages of the South Australian Aborigines*, 18, 58; C. W. Schürmann, 'The Aboriginal tribes of Port Lincoln', in Woods, *The Native Tribes of South Australia*, 234–5; A. W. Howitt, *The Native Tribes of South-East Australia*, 434–46; R. H. Mathews, 'Ethnological notes on the Aboriginal tribes of New South Wales and Victoria', *J. Proc. Roy. Soc. N.S.W.*, 38, 1904, 349.
76 E. Eylmann, for example, states that the Western Arunta believe that the soul goes north after death where it lives for a time on the shores of a great lake (*Die Eingeborenen der Kolonie Südaustralien*, 189).
77 H. K. Fry, 'Body and soul', 256; O. Pink, loc. cit., 289.
78 Thus Elkin writes of some of the Dampier Land tribes who believe in reincarnation that 'During the period between incarnations, the spirit sojourns at one of the spirit-centres. Some spirits, however, are not reincarnated; they are said to go to Loman, from whence there is no return' (A. P. Elkin, 'Totemism in North-Western Australia', *Oceania*, 3, 1933, 439). See also A. P. Elkin, 'Beliefs and practices connected with death in north-eastern and western South Australia', *Oceania*, 7, 1937, 275–99.
79 *The Arunta*, ii, 588.
80 Ibid., 363n.
81 Ibid., 363.
82 Ibid., 358.
83 Loc. cit., 52.

84 Ibid.
85 B. Malinowski, *The Family Among the Australian Aborigines*, 221–2. The identification of white men with deceased members of the tribe has been reported by the following authorities: J. Morgan, *Life and Adventures of William Buckley*; [James Tucker], *Adventures of an Outlaw*; G. Grey, *Journals of Two Expeditions of Discovery in North-West and Western Australia*, i, 301–3; Ch. Wilhelmi, 'Manners and customs of the Australian natives', *Trans. Roy. Soc. Vict.*, 5, 1861, 188–9; A. W. Howitt, *The Native Tribes of South-East Australia*, 434, 445, 446; J. Henderson, *Excursions and Adventures in N.S. Wales*, 161; J. MacGillivray, *Narrative of the Voyage of H.M.S. 'Rattlesnake'*, i, 30; R. Brough Smyth, *The Aborigines of Victoria*, ii, 224; W. E. Roth, N. Qld Ethnography, *Bulletin* no. 5, 16; R. H. Mathews, 'Ethnological notes on the Aboriginal tribes of New South Wales and Victoria', *J. Proc. Roy. Soc. N.S.W.*, 38, 1904, 349, also 'Sociology of some Australian tribes', ibid., 39, 1905, 113–14; G. W. Earl, 'On the Aboriginal tribes of the northern coast of Australia', *J. Roy. Geogr. Soc.*, London, 16, 1846, 241; B. Spencer, *Native Tribes of the Northern Territory of Australia*, 265.
86 When the Drysdale River tribes of North-Western Australia first encountered white men they regarded them as *djimi*, supernatural beings. Those who first saw whites adopted the 'white-fellow' totem to commemorate their coming. See T. Hernández, 'Social organization of the Drysdale River tribes, North-West Australia', *Oceania*, 11, 1941, 216.
87 *The Arunta*, ii, 590, n. 8.
88 R. H. Mathews, 'Marriage and descent in the Arranda tribe, Central Australia', *Amer. Anthrop.*, n.s., 10, 1908, 98.
89 R. H. Mathews, 'Notes on the Arranda tribe', *J. Proc. Roy. Soc. N. S. W.*, 41, 1907, 146–63.
90 *The Australian Aboriginal*, 269–70.
91 Ibid., 271.
92 Ibid., 271–2.
93 Ibid., 217.
94 Ibid., 61–2.
95 G. Róheim, 'Women and their life in Central Australia', 63, *JRAI*, 1933, 241.
96 Róheim does not give the meaning of these words.
97 Ibid., 244–5.
98 The Luritja word for *churunga* (R).
99 G. Róheim, 'Psycho-analysis of primitive cultural types', *Int. J. Psychoanal.*, 13, 1932, 96–7.
100 For a more extended discussion of Róheim's views see pp. 353–76.
101 H. K. Fry, 'Body and soul', 247–56.
102 *Int. J. Psychoanal.*, 13, 1932, 57 sqq.
103 Loc. cit., 250–4.
104 Ibid., 256.
105 This interpretation finds support in Róheim's statement: 'When a man returns home from a *wamulu* (downshaking) ceremony, my Luritja informants told me he will have intercourse with his wife in the camp and the *wamulu* (down) will fly from his body into the woman. Thus a child is conceived, and the child's totem is determined in this case not by locality, but by the ceremony which preceded coitus'. Loc. cit., 65–6.
106 *The Native Tribes of Central Australia*, 256.
107 O. Pink, 'The landowners in the northern division of the Aranda tribe, Central Australia', *Oceania*, 6, 1936, 288.
108 Ibid., 280 n. 7.
109 Ibid., 277.
110 *The Northern Tribes of Central Australia*, 145.
111 Ibid., 146.
112 Ibid., 148–9.
113 Ibid., 175–6.
114 Ibid., 174–5.
115 Ibid., 330–1.

116   Ibid.
117   A. Capell, 'The Wailbri through their own eyes', *Oceania*, 23, 1952, 115.
118   *Desert People*, 272–3.
119   *Ayers Rock*, 148–52.

CHAPTER IV

The procreative beliefs of the native tribes of Northern Australia

Men shall cast their skins and live for ever, but lizards and serpents shall die.
—From a Zulu myth.

B. H. Purcell, writing of the initiation ceremonies of the Workii (or Worgaia) tribe, makes the following statements of interest in connection with the procreative beliefs of the natives:[1]

The Bora Ceremony. After the third initiation into this remarkable ceremony the youth is made to drink semen that is taken from 6 or as many young clean gins and blacks, as may be in the camp at the Bora ground. No gins are admitted to the ceremony other than these. When an old man is dying, they do exactly the same. They hold that as semen brought them into the world, it should keep them alive and from dying; and when a man dies they think that the semen germinates and even comes through the earth again and appears in the form of a white man or something else, often a star.

These statements suggest that the Worgaia are aware of the role that the semen plays in generation. In speaking of the operation of subincision Purcell writes as follows:[2]

The terrible rite of 'Micka' making, as it is known by the Workii Blacks, is either performed on the backs of men, as in circumcision, or else on the ground. . . . Before the natives, according to their legends, understood relationships, father and daughters cohabited; consequently deformities became numerous and the good spirit angry. The men then established totems, the deformities disappeared, but the people increased. Consulting again the good spirit, they were told to perform the mutilation. They all refused, but seizing one man, they made a 'Micka' of him and the way all the women ran after him, caused the others to become jealous of him.

From these statements it would appear evident that the Worgaia are aware of the relationship between coitus and childbirth, and, from Purcell's previously cited statements, the awareness presumably extends to the part that the semen plays in procreation.

Did Purcell's statement of the beliefs of the Worgaia stand alone they might strike one as rather surprisingly well informed for an aboriginal Australian people, but the fact is that precisely similar beliefs have recently been recorded by an independent worker who was probably quite unaware of Purcell's report. However, similar beliefs have been recorded recently for the tribes living farther to the east on Cape York Peninsula. About the Murngin of Arnhem Land, Northern Australia, Professor W. Lloyd Warner writes as follows:[3]

I have spent some time with the northern tribes of Australia in two different field expeditions. I was in very intimate contact with the natives of the region. During the first eight or nine months while I was there I was firmly convinced that the people had no understanding of physiological conception and believed in the spiritual impregnation of a woman by a totemic child spirit. All the fathers told me their children had come to them in dreams as totemic souls or in some extra-mundane experience and had asked that their mothers be pointed out to them. They had complied with the request of the children, who had entered the vaginas of the mothers. During all this time, although I was in constant relationship with a large number of the men and although there was practically no taboo in our conversations which were of the most intimate nature, I could find no indication of any knowledge whatsoever of physiological conception; yet in the study I was making of the people, and looking at the problem from the point of view of the 'total situation', that is, considering the whole of the culture, there were strong indications that the natives understood the true nature of the father's physical function.

The second time I entered the area I determined to go into this matter further, since the people I studied were but a continuation of the central tribes on which Spencer and Gillen had reported. An occasion arose in which I could inquire directly of certain old men just what the semen did when it entered the uterus of a woman. They all looked at me with much contempt for being so ignorant and informed me that 'that was what made babies'. I had not been able to obtain this information earlier because the ordinary savage is far more interested in the child's spiritual conception, which determines its place in the social life of the people, than he is in the physiological mechanism of conception. He had far rather talk about ritual and myth than he would the ordinary mundane affairs of life. The relationship existing between the primitive men of north-eastern Arnhem Land and me as a field worker would be the same as that between the traditional visitor from Mars who might have come to study the Puritans of Massachusetts in colonial days. Had he asked Cotton Mather or any other member of the community 'where babies come from', he would have discovered that they came from heaven and that God sent them and that it was the special duty of the church to look out for them. He might be told that the stork brought them and discover totemic 'spiritual conception'. He would have been told this for exactly the same reason that the ordinary anthropological field investigator is informed by the natives that the totemic spirit is what causes impregnation.

The father-son reciprocal is the solid bond around which ego's spiritual affiliations are organized, since by a mystical experience of his father he leaves the totem well as a tiny fish and is directed by his male parent into his mother's womb. The father's mystical experience is the expression of the creation of the family of procreation. It is in fact the first element in the filio-parental relationship, since it is the first moment when either parent is supposed to know the beginning of this new generation within his own family. The annunciation of the child to the father by a dream symbolizes the parents' sexual intercourse, and in Murngin thought both dream and intercourse are necessary for conception and birth.[4]

The ideas surrounding birth give the father a prominent part in the procedure. The various spirits of the unborn and the dead live with the clan totems in the clan wells. As stated, a father dreams that the child comes to him, asking where it can find its mother, and enters the mother's vagina. The next day the man informs the wife that she is going to have a child, or, if it is his first child, to test the value of his dream he may keep it a secret. The natives believe these dreams are always true since a wife usually tells her husband that she has felt the movements of a child within her. The husband knows then that his dream is true. He sharpens his spears, rewraps his spear-thrower, and prepares to go hunting, for he knows that he will be successful because his child has come from the totemic spirits within the water, bringing good luck with it. He kills an abundance of game and brings it home. A slight ceremony takes place, after which he may eat all food, for, according to Murngin thought his wife having conceived, he is now a father [otherwise a married man who has no children must observe a number of food taboos until his wife announces her pregnancy]. This removal of taboos on his diet furnishes one of the reasons for a man's eagerness to have children.[5]

Further north, on Melville Island, similar views are held by the Tiwi, described by Dr Jane C. Goodale:[6]

A woman will remain in the *murukubara*, young woman, classification until the day when a certain food 'no longer taste good'. Having been well instructed in the facts of life, she knows that she is carrying a child, and she becomes known as a *poperiŋnta*, a pregnant woman.

Much has been written about aboriginal conception beliefs. Knowing that this was an 'important question', I approached a group of men and women one day early in my investigations and quite seriously asked them, 'Who makes babies and how do they get inside the mother?' I was entirely unprepared for the reaction. The men and women stopped their talk and looked at me questioningly. When I said nothing, they looked at each other and began to giggle, then broke into uncontrolled laughter. They paused only to repeat my question to each other and to those who, hearing the uproar, came to investigate. Each time my question was repeated, the laughter resumed with renewed convulsions. Finally, one woman dried her streaming eyes and caught her breath enough to answer my repeated question. 'Boy make him', she said, and looked so contemptuous at my innocence that I feared for my future ability to get any useful information from these people. I did the only thing possible and joined in the continuing laughter, hoping that they would think that I had meant the question as a joke in the first place.

After a while I said defensively, 'I know boys make babies, but in America we tell little children a big bird brings them to the house.' A lengthy and quite serious debate ensued. Finally the woman who had given me the first answer said, 'They reckon Purakapali makes children.' 'Where does he get them from?' 'Oh, from anywhere.' 'What does he do with them?' 'Reckon he tells his wife Bima to bring them down to the women.'

I knew I had literally and figuratively asked for it, and it was six months before I asked a direct question again. However, by this time I had considerable information concerning Tiwi conception beliefs, and the direct question was merely to put the various facts in their proper perspective.

Without a doubt, the Tiwi today know that sexual intercourse between a man and a woman is likely to result in pregnancy, that husbands and lovers can *make* babies. Two instances will illustrate this. Accompanying the expedition to the island was a man who had been in Darwin for over a year. He was returning to see his wife whom he had left on the island and his newborn son. When I asked his wife who was the father of her child, she replied with the name of her husband, but when I asked her who *made* the baby, she gave me the name of another man. I asked a number of other women the same set of questions separately, and each gave the same two names in the same order of relationship. I asked the other women how they knew the name of the man who *made* the baby, and they said, 'That is easy. The baby looks like B, its mother's lover,' and indeed the infant was the image of its biological father.

The case of the only 'single' girl in the settlement is another instance. A was in her late teens in 1954. She was classed as 'single' by my informants, not because she did not have a husband (she had two, both of whom she had deserted), but because she preferred to live with her parents and accept the love of three young men simultaneously. The other women considered her to be very foolish, for they said it was hard enough to stay out of trouble with one husband and one lover at the same time, but with three lovers at the same time there was plenty of trouble in the bush. Lovers are considered to be more jealous than husbands, and they said that all three boys were following her in the bush and there was no opportunity to 'do business.' But evidently A and one lover did find time to be alone, as she became pregnant.

Again I asked two questions, who was the father and who made the baby. The women said. 'She got no husband. By and by when that baby get born, we see who make him, then she marry that one.' A solved this particular problem by having a miscarriage, whether induced or by accident I was unable to determine.

Although the Tiwi recognize that either a husband or a lover can make a baby by having sexual intercourse with its mother, they also assert that such activity cannot alone create a *Tiwi* child. A Tiwi must be *dreamed* by its father, the man to whom the mother is married, before it can be conceived by its mother. To the Tiwi there is no conflict between the two beliefs concerning conception. In fact, there is only one belief, while there may be two 'fathers.'

According to Tiwi belief, individuals exist in the universe before birth into Tiwi society. Unborn individuals are called *pitapitui*, and if conditions are right, groups of *pitapitui* may sometimes be seen by both men and women, playing about the locality with which they are associated. An interesting contrast was found between male and female informants' descriptions of the appearance of *pitapitui* in general. Male informants described the playing *pitapitui* as small individuals with human shape, while invariably my female informants told me that they looked like little birds that live in the pandanus. One woman, when given the opportunity, selected without hesitation a picture of the brown honeyeater from a book on tropical birds as representing the appearance of these unborn *pitapitui*. I thought it particularly appropriate that the proper designation of the brown honeyeater is *Glicophila indistincta*!

Regardless of the difference in appearance perceived by male and female Tiwi, both sexes agreed on the social characteristics of the *pitapitui*. The principal activity of these unborn children seems to be either playing or hunting for their parents. When I asked what was their life if they were never found by their fathers and thus not born into Tiwi society, my informants suggested that they undoubtedly married other *pitapitua* and had babies, hunted for their food, fought, and eventually died: in other words, lived a life similar to that of the living.

Individual *pitapitui* are affiliated with one or another of the matri-lineal sibs and thus must be born to a mother who is a member of its own sib. But evidently there is no direct communication be-tween *pitapitui* members of a sib and female members who will become their mother. *Pitapitui* do not know which woman in their sib is their particular mother and can only obtain this information from their father, whose identity they do not know.

A *pitapitui* lives in the country of which his father is an owner (not necessarily a resident). Each country has a number of known locali-ties inhabited by *pitapitui*. As part of my census data I asked individ-uals to name the place in which they had lived as *pitapitui*. Many of them had no idea, but others were very definite in giving the geo-graphical location and adding, 'That place is alligator, or flying-fox, or pandanus *dreaming*.' In every case obtained, the sib name given was not that of the informant's own sib, but rather the name of his or her father's matrilineal sib. In this instance, the word 'dreaming' is used in reference to a place owned by particular matrilineal sibs and inhabited by the children of *male* members of the *owning* sib.

The word 'dreaming' is also commonly used as a synonym for one's father's matrilineal sib in such statements as 'one should marry one's *dreaming*' as an alternate to 'one should marry a member of one's father's sib,' having exactly the same referent. It was some time before I became aware of this equivalence of an individual's *dreaming* with his or her father's sib so that in my data collection I asked in-formation separately until one day an informant, with whom I had been checking much of the data collected up to that time, turned to me and said with much impatience at my evident stupidity, 'But they are the same: one's dreaming and one's father's sib!' But they are not exactly the same. An individual is not a member of his or her father's matrilineal sib, nor are they owned by that group. They rather *possess* an essence of that sib as their *dreaming*.

Unborn Tiwi (*pitapitui*) do not possess a *dreaming*, and this is the essential difference between the unborn members of a matrilineal sib and the living member of that sib. A *dreaming* is the catalyst that transforms a Tiwi from the world of the unborn to that of the living. A *pitapitui* gets a dreaming by being found by, or finding, a father. The act of 'finding' is also called *dreaming*, and it occurs typically while the father is asleep. According to some of my male informants, a father can only 'find' a *pitapitui* while he is resident in his own country. If this is true—and exceptions to this occur in my case histories—then *pitapitui* have a pre-existent local corporate group affiliation as well as a sib affiliation. This concept is strengthened somewhat by the belief that should a man have difficulty in 'finding' a *pitapitui*, the man's own deceased father will locate one and bring it to his son. No living man can locate a *pitapitui* to send or bring to his son. Ideally, that is, if the son has married into his father's matrilineal sib and if there has been local corporate group endogamy, a man's father is member of the same localized matrilineal sib segment as is the *pitapitui* that he finds for his son . . .

The Tiwi today say that the *pitapitui* are 'stories' from *palinari* (dream) time, the past. As such they strengthen the position of an individual in his *ideal* social relationships with his local corporate group, his localized matrilineal sib segment, and his father's, mother-in-law's, and spouses' matrilineal sibs. It is for these reasons that fathers still dream their children, in spite of the fact that many of my informants could recognize conflict of this belief with their traditional knowledge of biological conception and with what knowledge they have acquired through contact with Western science and beliefs. The apparent conflict between the biological and sociological beliefs concerning conception is neatly resolved by discriminating between men who make babies and fathers who dream children, both of whom are necessary to conception and creation of a new Tiwi life.

Cases of father's dreaming their children were related to me in 1954.

'My father been die when I little boy. By and by I get wife. Father see I no got *pikanini*. He get *pitapitui* from Karslake Island in my country and bring them to me. One day I was out with Pablo. We are crossing a mangrove swamp, and the water was deep. Pablo go ahead. I couldn't cross so I go sleep in mangrove. Five girls come up. "Papa," they say, "I had five girls. Four been die Rosemary was behind." I say, "Come along." I go back to Darwin. One night I be asleep. A spear hit me on the head. I wake up. I think wife hit me on head. I slap her. "You been kill me," I say. "No," she say, "I been asleep." I point to my head and say, "Look here, I got hurt." She say, "No, no. I no hit you." I think then maybe *pikanini* and next morning I got *pikanini*.'

Ali had a dream in which he saw his unborn son in a canoe, killing a turtle, Ali then went to Darwin without his wife, and his dream son followed him and said, 'You are my father, but who is my mother?' If a man has several wives and particularly if they are members of different sibs, this is an important question. Ali told the *pitapitui* that his mother was Polly. Later, Ali told me, he received word from his wife, Polly, back on the island, that she was pregnant.

Women never see their children in dreams before they know they are pregnant, and so I questioned several women on whether they really believed husbands saw their children in dreams *before* their wives told them they were pregnant. One elderly lady related the following story as proof that husbands did indeed dream their children before their wives conceived.

'Bos saw his son in a dream. His son was in an airplane fighting in the sky. The son was shot down receiving wounds in his arm and leg. The injured *pitapitui* came up to Bos and said, "You are my father, but first I go to America to get good medicine. I send my sister to you first; I will come behind. In six years I will come back and you will know me." Six years later Bos's wife gave birth to a son. When Bos first looked at his son he said, "What is he? He is a man, but he has a crooked arm and leg. This is the son I dreamed." '

The relationship among dreaming localities, localized matrilineal sibs, and landowning groups is definitely not a simple, unambiguous one. Direct questioning of informants on localization of *dreamings* elicited a myth and a list. 'Back in *palinari*, Tokombini was the big boss. He called a big meeting at Muripianga in the Yeimpi country. He say to each one, "What are you going to be?" and they would say, "alligator," "water," and so on. The Muripianganila said to his sister Uriupianila, "You go make that place, Uriupi." And he went on and gave places to each one.' Mountford continues this myth and states that each was also instructed to 'create the aboriginal foods belonging to each place and then change themselves into the particular bird, reptile, fish or inanimate object with which that locality is now associated.'[7] The list that was given corresponded with separately obtained listings of localities associated with *pitapitui* and *dreamings* (father's sib), rather than origin places for particular matrilineal sibs. However, if sib marriage exchange and local endogamy were strictly followed, each locality should contain two *pitapitui* centers, each belonging to one particular sib and inhabited by unborn members of the alternate affinal sib. . . . Although Tiwi social structure has obviously changed over time, Tiwi mythology does not reflect these changes. We should not expect to see a complete congruence between mythology and fact, but it does seem that among the Tiwi there is far less acknowledged relationship of the past with the present than has been reported for other aboriginal peoples. Tiwi beliefs of conception *dreamings* appear to be almost completely disassociated today from mythology and philosophy concerned with the origin of life, activities of *dreamtime* ancestors, or continuity of descent through time. I do not believe that the disassociation is a recent result of the breakdown of Tiwi culture and loss of traditional philosophical teachings and faith. In Tiwi culture, there is little recognition of our dependence on the past as validation of the present, and this factor emerges as a dominant characteristic of Tiwi life.

Pregnancy. Once a *pitapitui* has been dreamed by its father and been told who is its mother, the women say that it enters their body through their vagina and goes into a little 'egg' located in the placenta (*anera*). There it grows big until it bursts out of the egg, at which point birth takes place.

When the baby begins to grow inside its mother's body, it makes some food taste bad to its mother, and by this sign women know that they are pregnant. (A husband evidently does not tell his wife he has *dreamed* a child and sent it to her.) A pregnant woman must observe certain precautions. Because she might offend the *maritji* (rainbow spirits), she cannot bathe in the sea or in large bodies of fresh water, particularly those in a strange country. Placing food on a fire (cooking) or spitting into the flames will cause a child to twist in the womb and give pain. Certain foods are also taboo. Pregnant women may not eat carpet snakes, fish, or hawksbill turtle, nor the eggs of crocodiles or snakes. During all the rainy season and for most of the dry season, pregnant women may not eat yams. Yams begin to grow during the wet season, and only when they have reached their full growth late in the dry season are they harmless to the unborn child. . . .

'In the old days,' I was told, a pregnant woman was not allowed to walk in the bush after dark. Another *pitapitui* might pass into her body and two babies would be born at the same time. In 1954, my informants insisted that this had never happened in the past, and that today only mission girls had twins . . .

This belief that a 'walk in the bush in the dark' will produce twins is, I think further proof of the recognition that sexual intercourse can result in pregnancy. No reason was given, but this seems to be consistent with the belief that menstruation is caused by sexual intercourse. Although a father will dream of several of his children at one time, he never sends them to the same wife at the same time. A *pitapitui* theoretically cannot get into its mother's womb without being sent by its father, but multiple births have occurred. Since a father is entirely innocent, a lover must have been responsible; hence, the 'shame' and probable concealment of the event from the mother's husband.

It does not, it seems to me, necessarily follow that the production of twins after a walk in the dark in the bush constitutes proof of the recognition that sexual intercourse can result in pregnancy. On the contrary, it might constitute even stronger evidence of the belief that the really important agency in causing a child to be conceived is the entry of a spirit-child into her, and that in the dark such spirit-children, not seeing well, will sometimes enter a woman who is already pregnant, that is, by mistake . . . a mistake that is usually rectified by killing one of the twins at birth.

Most valuable is the testimony of an English-speaking Aboriginal medical assistant, Waipuldanya or Wadjiri-Wadjiri of the Alawa tribe at Roper River in the south-east corner of Arnhem Land. He states:

We regard The Snake as the Boss. His symbol is the rainbow. He is the Roadmaker, bringing young girls to puberty, forming the roads to their wombs, so that the spirit-children may pass to be born of their flesh. My people do not believe that conception occurs through sexual intercourse. It is achieved immaculately by the spirits, much as happened to the Virgin Mary.[8]

I belong to the Kangaroo totem. We all know that the kangaroo made the coolibah tree, called Mutju. We all know that the Elders of the Kangaroo clan chew Mutju bark. When it is masticated they spit it out and chant, 'The wives of the Kangaroo totem are commanded to have children.'

A few months later the women will be pregnant. Every Alawa believes that his totem impregnates them after the Road has been made by the Rainbow Serpent.

In recent years I have had medical training and listened carefully to doctors who assured me that conception takes place through fertilization of female ova by male sperm following intercourse. That story would raise a great laugh among the Alawa.[9]

Chaseling reports on the Yulengor of Arnhem Land as follows:[10]

Theories of conception and birth have been severely jolted in recent years, for until recently it was not known that intercourse had any connection with conception, and Yulengor regarded it as being merely a natural and satisfying function. There are no virgins in aboriginal society, for at an early age a girl is handed over to her husband and is married for the rest of her life. In parts of western Arnhem Land, when hordes gather for ceremonies, their hosts provide them with food and also advance their wives for their visitors' wellbeing. The question of illegitimate children does not arise, for births are thought to be the work of a spirit.

At some time when the potential father is hunting the spirit of his prospective child comes to him and presents him with a large fish or turtle and enables him to spear it. Not yet comprehending the omen, the man returns to camp with the spirit at heel, and when all are asleep this spirit enters the mother and begins its preparations for birth. In a variation of this belief, the spirit follows the mother when she goes for water, and jumps into the water so as to enter the woman. When a man knows that his wife is to become a mother he endeavours to recall some unusual experience that has befallen him in hunting.

His mind dwells on any large fish he has caught, perhaps in the last month, or maybe several years previously, and he regards this incident as marking the coming of the spirit-child.

Half-caste children compelled a readjustment of these ideas. First it was assumed that eating the white man's food or the wearing of white clothing caused white-skinned offspring. An anthropologist visiting an Arnhem Land mission station at the invitation of a missionary of irreproachable character, asked an aboriginal why his normal full-blood son had a light skin. The father's startling reply was: 'The child's mother works in the missionary's house.'

According to a revised popular birth theory, intercourse is necessary only as an act of preparation. In itself it is an invitation to the new spirit to come to the mother from the spirit world. Ideas on the birth question are very vague and the time factor is ignored. Wogburra, who had been taught to read and write and had lived amongst white folk for twenty years, told me that his wife was about to give birth to a child, and gossip named Miniji as the father. He intended to spear Miniji! I asked when his wife had last seen Miniji, and he was certain that it had been two years previously, when Miniji left for his tribal country.

In an account of the Tiwi tribe of Melville Island, William Douglas[11] writes of Larry, an Aboriginal

[who] several years after his marriage to Dolly left her and Melville Island for some unexplained, impulsive reason, and went to the mainland city of Darwin, capital of Australia's Northern Territory. He was away from Dolly and Melville Island for two years. During that time, two important events occurred. Larry lost his right eye in a fight. Dolly became pregnant and gave birth to a daughter which she presented to Larry at the end of his two year absence.

One moonlight night on the beach at Jiberabu I came across Larry, holding the little black baby in his arms and singing tenderly to her. His one right eye fairly danced with excitement. He was delighted with Dolly; he was in ecstasy over the baby girl. He sang a strange melody and his thoughts were far, far away in the spirit land from which all people come and to which they return on death.

It was from the spirit world that the baby girl had recently come. Larry knew, for the baby had sought him out before her birth. She had come to him in a dream, touched him with a spear and asked for her mother. Larry, in Darwin, told the spirit child where to find Dolly at Snake Bay. And so the spirit entered Dolly's body and in due time the baby girl was born.

Writing of the Larrekiya of the Port Darwin district, Basedow states:[12]

According to the legends of the *Larrekiya* it happened many years ago that a baby boy rose suddenly from the ground out of the burrow of a bandicoot (*Perameles* sp.). He was seen by the people of the *Larrekiya*, who invited him to come to their camp, but he refused. Some time after, when he had become a man, they again met him. Again he was asked to join the *Larrekiya* men in camp, but once more he declined. Thereupon the men became angry, and dragged him to a waterhole, and threw him into it. The stranger immediately sank, and five bubbles of air arose to the surface as he disappeared. The men sat down and watched the water, when suddenly the face of the man reappeared. The *Larrekiya* hurled a spear at him, and he was killed, because he had no father and no mother, but was an accomplice of the evil spirit, who, it is asserted by the old men of the *Wogait,* makes big fire, from which he takes an infant and places it at night in the womb of a *lubra*, who must then give birth to the child.

In the ordinary course of events, if a man, when out hunting, kills an animal or collects any other article of diet, he gives it to his *gin*, who must eat it, believing that the respective object brings about the successful birth of a piccaninny.

In other words, conception is not regarded as a direct result of cohabitation.

Of the tribes of western Arnhem Land, Dr and Mrs R. M. Berndt write:[13]

In the Goulburn Island–Oenpelli–Liverpool area, which has been subjected to much alien contact, the Aborigines have some understanding of the importance of the sexual function in procreation, and of the formation of the foetus from substances related to both the male and female parents. It is so generally known, and has become so much an established belief, that Aborigines take for granted the process of foetal formation and growth.

In mythological texts, an Old Woman leaves actual children (not spirit children) at particular places, and from these have evolved the present Aboriginal groups. No mention is made in these stories of the facts relating to the formation of the child and to the part played by the father. When questioned on this aspect the Aboriginal informant, after discussion with older men, will answer, 'But we don't need to say all that. How else do you think human beings are made? We are not the mythical ancestral people who created themselves, or were never born but always there. Nor were we vomited from the mouths of our mothers who were virgins. Why does a husband copulate with his wife, and why does her menstrual blood stop upon conception? Aren't we part of our father and mother?'

But when pressed, informants describe the process of conception and pregnancy in the following way.

To impregnate a woman five to six ejaculations on successive days are required. During that period the woman must not have coitus with any but her own husband* nor herself eject the semen by bodily exertion, abdominal pressure, etc. This accumulated substance serves as a basis for the foetus, which is termed an 'egg' (i.e., *guladjulg*). At the stoppage of the menstrual flow, the blood which would normally be ejected goes now to help the formation of the 'egg'. This 'egg' receives nutriment from the food which the mother eats, and the milk which will later be given to the child flows internally to the advantage of the foetus.

About this time the father 'brings the spirit child' to his camp; this spirit child resides in the father from the time of its finding. He does not give the 'spirit child' directly to his wife, but awaits his opportunity. He first finds out if his wife has been constant in her affection for him, and whether her menstrual flow has stopped;† and when both his own and his wife's sexual desire is heightened, and he has refrained from coitus a short time, he goes to his wife. Then they indulge in erotic play, and the husband ejaculates into her congealed semen.‡ It is through this semen that the spirit child leaves the body of the father and enters that of its mother, and with the semen it goes into the uterus (termed 'woman's bag,' *wureiwurei*) and breaks the 'egg' which has been formed.§ This 'breaking of the egg' commences the formation of a foetus in human likeness. However, the spirit child does not remain in the uterus, and after breaking the 'egg' travels internally through the woman and resides in the upper part of her back just above the shoulders. The husband does not yet tell his wife about the spirit child's entrance.

When the foetus grows quite large and the mother begins to show her pregnancy, the spirit child leaves its position in her back, saying, 'Time for me to come in.' It travels round the right side and into the uterus, 'opens the egg and works it,' and becomes part of it, thus animating the foetus.

At this juncture, the husband tells his wife that his spirit child has entered her, mentioning its sex.‖ The wife's mother looks at her

* Some Aborigines say that it is alright for her to have coitus with *mamam* who stand in relationship to her husband as 'brother,' and are of the husband's *namanamaidj*; but not with her husband's 'brother-cousin' or other type of *mamam*, otherwise the continuity and 'building up' quality of the semen will be spoilt.
† After the cessation of her menstrual flow, the woman realizes that she may be pregnant.
‡ Semen coagulated through non-ejaculation over a short period, as opposed to liquid semen which is a result of continual or regular coitus.
§ i.e. 'the egg is hatched inside the uterus, as a fowl hatches an egg in a nest.'
‖ Some form of sex determination is practised widely among Aborigines in the

daughter and says, 'I think my daughter going to have a baby,' and continues with special information concerning pre-natal care: 'You not going to get water or carry wood, you just stay in your camp. You mustn't run about with other men now, but be quiet.'

Ronald Berndt found that among the Yirrkala in the far north-eastern corner of Arnhem Land a knowledge of physiological paternity existed concurrently with the usual dreaming beliefs. The ancestral wife of Mumuna (Lightning) as she travelled through tribal territories left spirit-children dreamings in each of them,

the spirit-children who animate the foetus in pregnant women to-day. While it was admitted that the foetus came into being through the natural sequence of sexual intercourse and conception, and that both the father and mother played an important role in its formation, it was necessary further that before the foetus became really 'alive' it should be animated by a spirit-child from a Centre like Mira-maridji; that is, from a Centre initially created by the Mumuna and by a spirit-child left by her.[14]

Similarly the natives of north-eastern and north central Arnhem Land studied by Dr Ronald Berndt believe that 'sexual inter-course is an essential preliminary to pregnancy. Children in this area, for instance, are called *judu* (*jutu*, usually employed in a singular sense), or *djamarguli* (plural). The former word means "semen"; that is, the child originated from the semen. The latter means "through (or from) work"; to "work" (*djama*) a female is to have coitus, and *djamarguli* is literally the "result of working (or coitus)"'.[15]

It was through the incestuous intercourse of the two ancestral sisters, Djanggawul, that human beings were produced, and the country through which they passed was populated. Berndt remarks: 'Even at that early period, the importance of sexual intercourse in relation to pregnancy must have been realized, for the part the male [i.e. the ancestral Brother of the Two Sisters] plays in this activity is heavily stressed: the emphasis is such that it cannot be a mere pro-jection of present-day knowledge.'[16]

I altogether fail to see why, in spite of 'emphasis', present-day knowledge has not been projected by them into the past. The em-phasis placed on a belief today can tell us nothing as to the character of its earlier forms.

Summarizing, Berndt writes:[17]

Northern Territory and elsewhere, and is a subject which has not been sufficiently investigated. Apart from the 'spiritual' knowledge of the sex of a child (i.e., either a male or a female spirit child will appear and enter the father), they say that they can determine its sex by observation of the mother's navel or nipples, the changing of her facial appearance, and the side of the abdomen upon which the child lies.

The Djanggawul Sisters, through their perpetual pregnancy, and their ability to produce great numbers of *rangga* folk, the ancestors of the present-day Aborigines, express their true function as Fertility Mothers. They define the physical differences between males and females, between the *rangga* and the mat; expressing this symbolically, they put the *rangga* boys who emerge from their wombs into the coarse grass, the *rangga* girls into the shelter of the *ngainmara*-uterus mat. By stressing the sacredness of womankind, this Aboriginal culture has enshrined motherhood, for it is realized that the continuity of the group is dependent primarily, and in a more spectacular way, on the female. To ensure this fertility, however, 'that the *rangga* within the *ngainmara* may remain plentiful', the contribution of the virile male is essential. The myth, therefore, acknowledges both physiological paternity and maternity. The *rangga* is as sacred as the *ngainmara*; and insemination (symbolically expressed in a variety of forms) is a biological necessity in the fertility sequence of coitus, conception, pregnancy and childbirth.

At Yirrkala, on the eastern side of Arnhem Land, according to Mountford,[18]

The people of the *dua* moiety believe that when *Tjambuwal*, the thunder-man, creates the rain clouds he places in them a number of spirit children, *jurtu*. These *jurtu*, who are so small that only the medicine-men can see them, descend on the raindrops to the land, or the sea. If on the land, the little *jurtu* enter one of the various *dua* yams, fruits, and especially the *dua jarapang* or *lirawar* wild honey; if the *jurtu* falls in the sea, it inhabits the *dua* fish or the green turtles. The little child spirits of *Tjambuwal* will not have anything to do with *jiritja* foods.

One day . . . two men catch a green turtle, bring it to the shore and cut it up so that everyone can have a meal. The cutting up of the turtle releases the *dua* spirit child living in its body. That night, when everyone is asleep, the spirit child, *jurtu*, visits one of the men in a dream and says:

'You are my father. *Tjambuwal* put me in the turtle you cut up today, so that I could find a mother. Where is she?'

The father points out one of his wives, whom he has been told has ceased menstruating; the child enters her body and starts a terrestrial existence. Next morning the father, if he remembers the dream (the aboriginal men said it was not often that they did), says to his wife:

'Last night a *jurtu* came and asked me for a mother, so I sent it to you.'

Within a short time the mother shows signs of pregnancy. . . .

The conception beliefs of the *jiritja* moiety vary somewhat from those of the *dua*. They believe that when a woman ceases to menstruate her blood goes into the sky and is there changed into a spirit child, *jurtu*. After some time the little *jurtu*, desiring an earthly mother, creates a thunderstorm and a rainbow, and using the raindrops as a vehicle of travel, descends to the earth. If the *jurtu* falls into the sea, it enters some *jiritja* creature such as a dugong, a hawksbill turtle or a queen fish; if on the land, a hive of *jiritja* honey, *kamou* or *barangit*, or the body of some *jiritja* creature. Should the aborigines spear a dugong and find that it is particularly fat, or locate a hive well stocked with honey, they know that the dugong or the hive is inhabited by a spirit child.

When, for example, the dugong is cut open, and the *jurtu* escapes, it visits the sleeping father and asks him which of his wives is to be his mother. As with the *dua* moiety, the father points out a wife who has ceased menstruating. The child enters her body through the vulva. If the father remembers next morning he tells the expectant mother about his dream. Soon afterward the woman feels the movements of the *jurtu* within her body. As soon as a woman ceases to menstruate, she must not eat meat or fish. Her diet is limited to grass-seeds, yams, the fruit of the cycad, shell-fish, and crabs.

Among the Gunwinggu people of western Arnhem Land the spirit-children do not occupy any visible habitation such as a rock or other external site, but are to be found in paperbark trees, meat-ants' nests, and in the jungle. When they see people they swim and splash in the water, and if people call to them they can hear the children calling back. 'If people light fires, the children cry out in fear and dive into the water. Young girls are not to go near there, and, if the ant nests are broken, children will come out in search of women'.[19]

'Spirit centres like this', write the Berndts, 'reflect the Gunwinggu belief that human beings are composed of two basic ingredients—material substance, plus something else. That something else is the animating spirit, ideally connected with a person's own father's territory.'[20] The same principle roughly appears to hold for the ancestral spirits, the *djang*, 'in so far as their spirits live on independently after the transformation of their physical bodies.'[21]

We have here a number of independent accounts of different tribes living in the same general region who appear to be aware of the role played by the seminal fluid in producing children and who, at the same time, possess conceptional spiritual beliefs which follow the same general pattern as those found elsewhere in Australia. May it not then be, in view of these findings, that a similar knowledge exists among the numerous other tribes in which this knowledge is said not to exist? Professor Warner says, 'I think there is a possibility that this knowledge does exist among the people but is not considered important and that the spiritual conception of the child looms so large in their thinking that the field worker obtains nothing but these facts when he investigates primitive peoples.'[22] This is, of course, a most important point, and, indeed, the very crux of the problem with which we are here concerned; moreover, as we have already seen, Róheim has stated that this is precisely what occurs among the western Central tribes investigated by him, and Strehlow has indicated that similar conditions existed among the Arunta and Luritja, although none of these investigators has indicated in any way whatever that the Central tribes possessed any knowledge of the nature of the seminal fluid. It would be a hazardous procedure to argue from the conditions found among the tribes living towards the coast on the north and to the north-east that similar factors were operative among any of the tribes living elsewhere in Australia, for the tribes living on the north and north-east have, it can be shown, been considerably influenced by Papuan contacts.[23] Moreover, these regions have for many years past been steadily infiltrated by white settlers and prospectors as well as by missionaries, so that it would have been of interest to know something of the actual cultural background of Professor Warner's informants in view of their remarks. The native is at all times exceedingly obliging, and the question one asks often determines the nature of the answer one receives. However, Purcell's account of the Worgaia beliefs indicates that they form an integral part of the native dogma, and I consider that here, at least, there can be no doubt that the connection between seminal fluid and birth is understood, though only, it would appear, in a magico-religious sense. It it also possible that the connection may be a purely adventitious one, but this, for the time being, must remain a speculation. That the Worgaia understanding of the relationship between the seminal fluid and childbirth is a magico-religious one, at least in one of its aspects, seems clear from the fact that they believe that when a man dies his semen germinates and even comes through the earth to appear in the form of a white man, a star, or something else. At the same time, however, they hold that the semen brought them into the world—but in precisely what way we are not told.

As we shall later see there is every reason to believe that the beliefs of the tribes of this general region are not strictly indigenous, that there is some evidence that foreign influences have been at work, and that for this reason they cannot be regarded as strictly aboriginal Australian beliefs. None the less, the points raised by Professor Warner and others must be borne in mind; we shall have occasion to refer to them again, meanwhile we may proceed with the further accounts. Concerning the tribes of the Northern Territory, Spencer writes:

Varied though these tribes are in regard to their organizations and customs, there is fundamental agreement on certain points. It was in the Central tribes that we first described the belief in the existence of spirit children who inhabit certain definite localities and enter women. It is interesting to see that this belief is universal amongst the Northern Territory tribes. A similar belief has been shown by Dr. Roth to exist amongst Queensland natives and by Mrs. Bates amongst certain tribes in West Australia. In regard to this matter there has been considerable difference of opinion, but I think it may now be regarded as established that some such belief was once widely prevalent over a large part of Australia. I am, myself, inclined to think that it was once universal, for the reason that it now exists amongst tribes so widely different from one another in many other respects as the Dieri, Arunta, Waduman, Mara, Kakadu, and Melville Islanders. The Kakadu beliefs are amongst the most definite that we have. Without going into details which are explained later, it may be said there was one great ancestor, named Imberombera, who was responsible, originally, for all the spirit children with whom, either directly or by means of individuals whom she sent out, the country was peopled. There were local spirit centres, just as in the Arunta, and it is these spirit children who have ever since been born again. With this belief is also closely bound up that of reincarnation. It is curious again to find that there is fundamental agreement in this matter right through the tribes and, further, that the Arunta in the South and the Kakadu in the North have remarkably parallel beliefs. In the former some of the ancestors are known by name, others are not. Every individual has his, or her, secret name, known only to the old men of his local totemic group. For some reason this is one of the most secret and most difficult things to find out in the Arunta. If the old ancestor is born again, then the human incarnation takes that ancestor's as his own secret name. In the Kakadu, on the other hand, the name of every ancestor is known and every member of the tribe bears that ancestor's as his or her name in common, everyday use. In some tribes, such as the Warramunga, each totem group had one great ancestor from whom, when he shook himself during the performance of ceremonies, numerous, but nameless, spirit children emanated. We have, in fact, an interesting series of stages beginning with the Arunta and its numerous original ancestors for each group, passing through the Warramunga with its one ancestor for each group, and then on to the Kakadu with its single great, original ancestor for all the groups.[24]

There are one or two points in connection with this belief to which attention may be drawn. In the first place it is essential to remember that there is no such thing as a virgin amongst the women of the native tribes from one end of Australia to the other. As soon as a native girl reaches puberty, she is handed over to her allotted husband and has continuous intercourse for the rest of her life. In that respect there is no difference between any two native women, and yet the native sees that some women have children, some do not. The intercourse is continuous, the bearing of children is sporadic. It is long after a woman has had intercourse before she becomes aware that there is a child within her. Seeing then that every woman without exception has continuous intercourse; that some have children, some do not; that those that have them bear them at varying intervals which have no relationship to the time of intercourse, and that the woman only knows she has a child when the quickening takes place, which, again, has no reference to intercourse, it is not a matter of surprise that the savage man, who is, according to his lights, a very logical being, should seek some other explanation of the origin of children than that of sexual connection.

There is one very interesting and suggestive point in this connection, and that is the common explanation of the existence of half-castes given universally by their mothers, speaking in pidgin English, viz., 'Too much me been eat em white man's flour.' The chief difference that they recognized between their life before and after they came into contact with white men was, not the fact that they had intercourse with white men, instead of or side by side with, blacks, but that they ate white flour and that this naturally affected the colour of their offspring. I have seen old natives in Central Australia accept, without question, their wives' half-caste children, making no difference whatever between them and the pure bred ones.[25] On the other hand, it is, of course, naturally, a belief that is one of the first to become modified when the natives have been for some time in contact with white men.[26]

One of the most striking features of the native tribes in Central and Northern Australia, whose customs were investigated by the late Mr. Gillen and myself, is their universal belief that children enter women in the form of minute spirits, the representatives of formerly existing men and women, who are thus reincarnated. This belief in reincarnation, and in procreation not being actually the result of sexual intercourse, has now been shown to be prevalent over the whole of the Central and Northern part of the continent—that is, over an area four and a half times the size of Great Britain—amongst many Queensland tribes and in a large part of West Australia. It is now too late to secure reliable information, in regard to matters such as this, from any part of Australia where the natives have been at all closely in contact with whites, but, though the belief was first described in connection with the Arunta tribe, it has now been shown to be widely prevalent over the continent, and I have little doubt but that at one time it was universally held amongst the Australian tribes. From my own personal experience I know that it is, or was, held by the Urabunna tribe inhabiting the country on the West and North-West of Lake Eyre; by the Arunta that extends to the north of the Urabunna up to and beyond the Macdonnell Ranges; by the Kaitish and Unmatjera tribes whose territory extends beyond Barrow Creek; by the Warramunga tribe inhabiting country north-wards to and beyond Tennant's Creek; by the large Worgai tribe out to the east of the latter, towards the Queensland border; by the Tjingilli tribe, whose country centres in Powell Creek; by the Umbaia, Nganji, Binbinga, Mara, Anula, Mungarai, Nullakun, and other tribes extending eastwards from the telegraph line to the Gulf of Carpentaria and occupying the vast area drained by the Roper, Macarthur, Limmen, Wickham and other rivers; by the Djauan and Yungman tribes, north of the Tjingilli; by the Waduman, Mud-burra and other tribes along the Victoria and Daly rivers running westwards; by the Kakadu, Iwaidja, and allied tribes inhabiting the northern littoral, and by the natives on Bathurst and Melville Islands.[27]

The Port Essington natives believe that, at first, there were no real human beings, but only alligators, sharks, turtles, cockatoos, etc., and that the present men and women are descendants of these. They also believe that the spirit child goes inside the woman at a spot which is frequented by such children and that natives who die are born again at a later period.

In the Mungarai tribe, in which I had more opportunity of in-quiry, the beliefs are very definite. The far past time—the equivalent of the Alcheringa in the Arunta tribe—is called *Kurnallan*. During this time the old ancestors walked about. Each one had his original home, called *Burnamandu*. As in the case of the snake Uruanda, they made the country with all its natural features as they walked along. Wherever they stopped they performed ceremonies, and, when doing so, shook themselves,[28] with the result that spirit children, called *Mall-mall*, who, of course, belonged to the totem (namarague) of the ancestor, emanated from their bodies. These spirit children now go into the right lubras, and are born as natives. Close to what is now McMinn's bar, on the Roper River, there is a large gum tree full of spirit children, all of them belonging to one of the totems associated with the Nakomara sub-class, and always, so my native informant told me, on the look out for the right lubra. Again, at Crescent

Lagoon, the old ancestor Namaran, the thunder man, deposited numbers of spirit children, and, if a Ngaritjbellan woman dips her toes in the water, one at once passes into her up her leg, or, if she stoops and drinks, goes down into her through her mouth. The spirit of a dead person, called *Anora*, goes back to his old home (*Burnamandu*), and sooner or later is born again, and in this tribe the sexes are supposed to alternate at each successive reincarnation.

In the Yungman tribe there is precisely the same belief in regard to the origin of children as in the Mungarai. For example, a *Nanung*, or sugar-bag (honeycomb) man arose at Opobinga, near the old Elsey Station. Here he is reported to have stayed without wandering about. He had numbers of spirit children, who now inhabit the trees and stones near his old camp, and out of these they come and enter the right lubras. He had, also, many bull-roarers, which the Yungman people call *Purdagiair*. In the Yungman, as in the Mungarai tribe, the sexes are supposed to alternate at each successive reincarnation.

In the Nullakun tribe the old times, during which the ancestors walked about the country, are called *Musmus*, and each of them has his place of origin, called *kundungini*. Like one of them, a rainbow man, called Kulakulungini, each of them is supposed to have had numbers of spirit children who emanated from them when they shook their bodies during the performance of corrobborees. It is these who are now constantly entering lubras, and being born. After death the spirit of the dead person, called *Maritji*, goes back to its old home, Kundungini, where it remains until it is born again. At each successive reincarnation the sex changes.

The beliefs of the Mara tribe are fundamentally identical with those of the Mungarai and Nullakun tribes. The old times are called *Djidjan*; each ancestor had his ancestral home, called *Wailba*, and, as he wandered over the country, he made the natural features and left spirit children behind him, who are continually entering the right women. After death the spirit, which is called *Padinia*, goes back again to its *Wailba* until such time as it undergoes reincarnation. At each successive reincarnation, also, the sex changes.

In the Waduman and Mudburra tribes, inhabiting the country between the Daly and Victoria Rivers, they have the same idea of spirit children, whom they call *Ngaidjan*, existing in the form of little frogs. The Waduman believe that, in the far past times that they call *Jabulunga*, there were two old men named Idakulgwan and Imumdadul. They were brothers, and came from the north-east. As they travelled along they met an old woman named Ibangalma, or Tjora, who came from the salt water country. She had no black-fellow, and her totem (*Gwaian*) was Eramerlgo, or sugar-bag. As they came along, the two men made country, creeks, yams, kangaroos, snakes, sugar-bags and many other things that the natives now feed on. They also carried with them plenty of *Ngaidjan*, or spirit children, and gave some of them to the old woman Ibangalma, telling her to take them away to other parts of the country and leave them there. They said, *Ya moinja laia lungin, Ngaidjan anoadja tjumba angebir*, which means, you go away to another country, where you stop leave *Ngaidjan* behind. She did so, and the natives say that, when leaving them behind, she gave them their totems. They grew up and were the first blackfellows, men and women. When they died their spirits became *Ngaidjan*, entered lubras, and were born again. Each *Ngaidjan* knows which is the right lubra to enter, and will not go into a wrong one. Each *Ngaidjan*, also, has one special place, called Poaridju, the equivalent of the Nanja [i.e., Knanja] of the Arunta, which is its normal stopping place, though, of course, if it chooses to do so, it can move freely about the country. Before going into a lubra each *Ngaidjan* enters, and stays for a time, in its mother's totemic animal or plant. If the mother be Eramerlgo, or sugar-bag, then it goes into this, if a yam then into a yam, and so on. Sometimes a woman, when digging for yams, hits one with her stick, and may hear the baby *Ngaidjan* crying out, or, if she hits a goanna, she may hear the child speaking inside it.

Ibangalma finally went to a place now called Hayward Creek, and, later on, the two brothers Idakulgwan and Imumdadul came up and stopped there. Tradition relates that Idakulgwan married Ibangalma, and that they had a great many children. First of all they had a boy named Giblongwa, and then another Widba, and a third called Ijubulma. Each of these three has been reincarnated and is now alive. The two old people lived a long time as, respectively, Maluka and Muluru. Their *Ngaidjan* have undergone reincarnation, but are not at present, represented in the tribe. The two old men Idakulgwan and Imumdadul remained at Hayward Creek, where they are now represented by two stones, whilst another, at the head of the Flora Creek, represents Ibangalma. It appears as if a generation, at least, is allowed to elapse between any two successive reincarnations. One of our informants, for example, called Alwairi, was the reincarnation of a brother of his *baba*, that is his father's father. Alwairi's young daughter, named Maidjangba, is the reincarnation of a woman of the same name who was her mother's mother.

In the Arunta and other Central tribes it is only, relatively, a few members of the tribe who actually bear the names of old ancestors, but in these more northern coastal tribes there is a constant succession of the names, and every individual, without exception, is the reincarnation of some special ancestor.

I was much interested in finding amongst the Kakadu and allied tribes not only a very firm and most definitely expressed belief in the reincarnation of ancestors and in the absence of any necessary relation between sexual connection and procreation, but also a curious parallel to the Arunta idea of Iruntarinia and Arumburinga.

As described in the legend associated with Imberombera, the Kakadu believe that the whole country was originally peopled with individuals and spirit children who are now continually undergoing reincarnation. What we may call the original spirit, the equivalent of the Iruntarinia amongst the Arunta, is called Yalmuru. If we take the case of any one individual the belief is as follows. When a man, and the same, precisely, is true of women and children, dies, the Yalmuru, that is the spirit part, after the final burial and mourning ceremonies are complete, keeps watch over the *benogra*, or bones. After a time the Yalmuru, as it were, divides into two, so that we have the original Yalmuru and a second spirit called Iwaiyu. The two are distinct and have somewhat the same relationship to one another as a man and his shadow, which, in the native mind, are very intimately associated. For a long time they remain together but, the Yalmuru desires to undergo reincarnation, the two leave the *benogra* or bones, which are always some distance out in the scrub—often miles away from the camp. They go forth together, the Iwaiyu in the lead, the Yalmuru behind. Out in the bush they find the natives, who of course cannot see them, hunting for food. The Yalmuru takes the Iwaiyu and puts it, in the form of a small frog called Purnamunemo, which lives under the sheaths of the leaves of the screw-pine or Pandanus, into some food such as fish or 'sugar-bag' that the man is searching for. If, for example, it be fish, the Yalmuru goes into the water and drives them into the man's *chipoiyu* or fishing net, if it be *mormo* or 'sugar-bag', he guides him to the tree in which the bees have made their hive. In either case, as soon as the man has secured the fish or *mormo*, out jumps the frog, unseen of course by the men. It is caught by the Yalmuru and, together, the two spirits return to their camping place. The food in which the Iwaiyu was placed will be the child's totem. The latter is thus always selected by the Yalmuru and may change from one reincarnation to another. As we have seen, when dealing with the totems, it often does. Sometimes, when an animal, such as a crocodile or fish, contains for a time the Iwaiyu and the animal is speared, then the *Bialila*, or child to which the Iwaiyu subsequently gives rise, bears the mark of the spear wound.

The natives return to their camp with the food that they have secured, quite unconscious of the fact that the Yalmuru and Iwaiyu have been out in the bush. At night time the two latter come back again to the camp and watch the men and women. The Iwaiyu is again in the form of a little frog. When all are asleep, the two come up to the camp and enter the mia-mia where the man and his wife are sleeping. The Iwaiyu goes up and smells the man; if he be not a 'right' father he says, *ngari koyada*, which means, not this one. He tries another one, finds him right and says, *ngari papa*, this one is my father. Then he goes and smells the latter's lubra. The Iwaiyu gets into her hair, then feels her breasts and says, *korngo ngari koiyu*, these are my mother's breasts; *nagari koiyu*, this is my mother. Then he comes down and goes into the woman. The Yalmuru returns to the old camp. Every now and then he comes and looks at the woman, but does not speak. When it is evident that the woman is going to have a child, the Yalmuru comes up to the camp at night time and tells the father that the child is there and what its name is and also its totem. He tells the father that he must not give it any other name except the one that he mentions, because that is the child within his wife.

Ungara, a Kakadu native, told us exactly what happened in his own case. When his father's brother died his *benogra*, or bones, were left for some time in a tree, not very far from the camp at which he died, but, later on, they were carried more than 20 miles away and placed in a Banyan tree overhanging a water pool. Ungara, who had his wife Obaiya and one child with him, was once camped near this place. He threw his *chipoiyu*, or net, into the water and left it there for some little time. Then he gathered long grass stalks and went into the water to drive the fish into the net. He did not know that the Yalmuru had already done this, and that the Iwaiyu was in one of the fishes. The net was so heavy that he called out to Obaiya to come and help him lift it out on to the bank. While they were doing this the Iwaiyu jumped out and was caught by the Yalmuru and then they both went back to the bones. Ungara and his wife Obaiya took the fish out and carried them to their camp in dilly bags. There were a good many other natives camped about. That night, while they were sleeping, the Yalmuru and Iwaiyu came into the camp, and, after examining the man and woman, as previously described, the Iwaiyu went into Obaiya. While telling us this Ungara mimicked exactly the actions of the Iwaiyu going first to the father then to the mother. Later on the Yalmuru came one night and whispered as follows in Ungara's ear; *chipoiyu nanjil yapo araji*, the fish went inside your net; *jibul widjeru*, it was full up; *mukara bialilla ngeinyimma*, your child was there; *brau Monmuna murakamora narama*, give it the name Monmuna murakamora; *jereipunga kunbaritja*, its totem is *kunbaritja* (a small fish); *balera koregora onje narama koyada*, by and by do not look out another name; *Monmuna murakamora ngeinyimma ingordua bialilla araji*, Monmuna murakamora is the child inside your lubra.

When the child is young the Yalmuru watches over it. If it strays away from camp and gets lost in the bush, the Yalmuru guides it back and, later on, when the child has grown into a man, the Yalmuru still helps it, in fact a good deal depends on the Yalmuru because, if it be not vigilant, some other hostile one may work evil magic against the individual associated with the Yalmuru's Iwaiyu. Finally, when the individual grows really old, the Yalmuru comes some night and whispers in his ear, *Iwaiyu ngeinyimma bialilla unkoregora, ngainma ngeimba, parda mornda, ngainma boro mornda moiyu, ngeinyimma jereipunga koregora*; which means, Iwaiyu, you look after a child, my back bone and thighs are no good, my eyes are no good and sore, you look after the Jereipunga (totem). In other words the Yalmuru is supposed to tell the Iwaiyu, that is, the spirit within the man, that he, the former, is worn out and that the Iwaiyu must take on the part of providing for a new child being born, and must also look after its totem. As the natives say, *baranga Yalmuru wariji ge*, the old Yalmuru is done for completely; *Iwaiyu nigeri Yalmuru*, the Iwaiyu is the new Yalmuru. It is really rather like a very crude forerunner of the theory of the continuity of the germ plasm. The old Yalmuru splits, as it were, into two, one half, the Iwaiyu, persists, the other finally disappears. In its turn the former becomes transformed into a Yalmuru which again splits; one half remains, and the other perishes, but there is an actual spiritual continuity from generation to generation.

It will be seen from the above how very definite the ideas of the Kakadu tribe are in regard both to the fact that the child enters the woman in spirit form without any reference whatever to sexual intercourse, and also to the fact that the child within the woman is the actual representative of one special individual amongst the old ancestors.[29]

The following account, by G. H. Wilkins, relates to an unnamed tribe living in Arnhem Land on the Gulf of Carpentaria.[30]

Among the natives polygamy is practised extensively, and wives are acquired as gifts from friends and in compliance with a complicated totemic system. It is generally arranged that young girls are given to old men, and young men get wives beyond the child-bearing age. . . . The belief about spirit children is thought by some scientists to be held by many of the aboriginal tribes. Several of the Arnhem Land natives told it to me as being true. They said that all children are first of all controlled by spirits which roam the bush, and that they are under the guidance of various controls, such as emu, crows, pandanus, turtle, etc. Women are not able to see these spirit children, but men can see them, and when a married man sees the spirit of a child under control of a suitable totemic guide, be it bird, tree, or fish, he will send his wife to the place where the spirit child was seen and the child will enter the woman, to be born in due time. Because the father was the first to see the child, he is in a position to know its totem, and he alone has the right to name the child after it is born.

Concerning the beliefs of the tribes of the Daly River district, the Mulluk Mulluk, Madngella, Marithiel, Nangiomeri and Moiil, Stanner writes:[31]

It is clear . . . that two theories of sex exist side by side: (*a*) a mystical theory of the type commonly found in Australian cultures, and (*b*) a barely understood, confused version of orthodox theory learned from whites. The emphasis in belief ranges from tribes like the Mulluk Mulluk and Madngella, which have completely forgotten their own mystical theory (which undoubtedly existed) to bush tribes with only the most imperfect knowledge of white beliefs. In tribes (like the Marithiel) where the beliefs co-exist in some definite form, the framing of the question governs the answer one receives. According to the Nangiomeri, *mambir*, or spirit children, enter a woman with certain types of food, or while she is bathing, or crossing a stream. *Mambir* originally came out of a rock from which a spring gushed in dream-times, and now are to be found in all permanent water. They sometimes invest trees, but always stay near water and near women. Old people sometimes see them, but never young people. An interesting distinction is drawn between (1) a child's father, *i.e.*, the social father, or husband of the child's mother, and (2) the man who 'finds' the child, *i.e.*, finds and gives to the woman the food considered to be responsible for her pregnancy. Many men can thus point out children whom they 'found', but who have other 'fathers'. The distinction approximates to that between *genitor* and *pater*. In the pure native theory the sexual act seems to have mostly an erotic significance, but in the altered belief it is considered to be in some way concerned with pregnancy. How or why is not known. Many natives think that *mambir* will not enter a woman who has had too much sexual association with white men, and they attribute to this the fact that so few women now have children. There has been and still is a great deal of sexual association of white men and black women.

Of the Djamindjung who live along the north-west coastal strip of the Northern Territory, Stanner states that they are characterized by a local patrilineal totemism, each patrilineal totem or *wabiri* having a local totem centre.

Conceptional beliefs of the spiritistic type are held, and 'water children' and 'leaf children', that is, spirit children, are common objects of conversation. In dream times *zurkban*, the rainbow serpent culture hero, put spirit children in water holes and rivers, but whether they inhabit totemic sites is uncertain. . . . It is certain, however, that the important factor determining descent of the *wabiri* is not the accidental location of conception. This may be in another man's *yagbali* [territory around a totem centre or locality, country; possibly horde country]. Commonly, however, it is within the father's *yagbali*. The natural species linked by dreams, by divination, or by some other method, with the realization of conception does not necessarily become the *wabiri*, although it may. Many of the Djamindjung natives seem to be 'found' in association with other species than the *wabiri*. One cannot fail to be deeply impressed by the way in which, when doubtful cases arise, natives turn for a solution and guide to the sheer principle of patrilineal local horde descent, and thus of totems within the horde country. Irregular marriages, conceptions and births in other than the *yagbali* of the father, tend to irregularize the totemic descent. Nearly always if doubt is felt about a person's totem, natives say: 'What was his father's *yagbali*?' When the *yagbali* is named they say: 'Well, his *wabiri* or *paniet* must be so-and-so,' naming one of the totems centred in the *yagbali*, irrespective of the place of birth or conception. Djamindjung children are 'found' in the customary spiritistic fashion of the aborigine. It seems to be true of the Djamindjung as it is certainly true of the Murinbata to the north that a child may be 'found' in association with a natural species, usually an edible, and perhaps a totemic species, but be 'given' another species for its *wabiri*. This is invariably a totemic species located within his father's *yagbali*, but the species associated with his 'finding' need not be. I was unable to determine with certainty if this associated species was a totem in the conventional sense or not. I could discover no specific term for it. Possibly it may be a separate conceptional totem, but natives seem to regard it indifferently, and in no way like the *wabiri*, which may, on the other hand, itself be the species associated with a 'regular' conception. This would seem in itself to be a reason for believing that the conception species which is not the direct patrilineal *wabiri* is not elevated to the rank of a separate totem, and a further such reason is that one's *wabiri* may be only a collateral totem of the father, in the sense made clear below. . . .

The *wabiri* totem is probably a cult totem.[32]

Clearly it is the *wabiri* which ties the child to the father's *yagbali*, whereas the conceptional object does not necessarily have any such function. It is Stanner's impression that this tribe, like those of the north and north-east, 'are in transition from one scheme of totemic and social organization to another'.[33]

In a subsequent report on the Murinbata,[34] the most important remaining tribe in the salt-water country west of the Daly River in the north-west of Northern Australia, Stanner has very clearly described the nature of the remarkable changes which are taking place in the social organization of this people as a consequence of recent continued contacts with neighbouring tribes who have moved into the district. The Murinbata are just beginning to adopt the sub-section system, and their ingenuity in adapting it to their own social structure is impressive as well as extraordinarily instructive. What is happening is that the kinship and marriage systems are altering in a very significant way, new totemic associations are being formed, and the subsection system is being superimposed on a tribal organization in which the major pre-existing groups were the local patrilineal hordes, patrilineal local totemic clans, patrilocal and patriarchal families, and two exogamous patrilineal moieties.[35]

The Murinbata believe in the pre-existence of *naritnarit* spirit children, which inhabit water, hollow trees, logs, the leaves of trees, even the wind. They are invisible, mobile, can be blown by the wind or ride its changing currents to distant places. They can leave their spirit centre to follow the woman they are to fertilize. Several different kinds of spirit children are distinguished. One such is *wakal mulunthuna*, or 'leaf (*mulun*) children', those born as a result of impregnation by a *naritnarit* from the leaves of certain trees. These are *wiya*, a term applied to anything undesirable, bad, deformed, or diseased. Such children are killed by being buried in the ground. Single girls are particularly liable to conceive from *wakal wiya*. Women will not shake the leaves or branches of trees for fear of disturbing and being impregnated by these *mulunthuna*. The *naritnarit* do not inhabit *nakumar* totem sites, but have their own spirit centre at Yangantha in the district called Wakaltjinung in Murinbata country near the Fitzmaurice River, a place where stones are said to be shaped like a child. The affixation of *wakal* (children) to the local name Tjinung is significant. The stones of Yangantha are inhabited by a *naritnarit* population which can be increased by the performance of the appropriate ceremonies. This is not apparently the privilege of a small cult group. Anyone by beating the Yangantha stones with a bunch of leaves and uttering three or four times the words: '*S-s-s-s! Thunudzi nata danai*' can assure the continuance of the child-spirits. These ceremonies are called *bangawar* or *nungawar* and seem to resemble the well-known *talu* and *intichiuma* increase ceremonies. These rocks are the mythological spirit centre of both healthy and sick *naritnarit*, who were placed there in the olden dream-time by the culture-hero of the Murinbata—Kunmanggur, the Rainbow-Snake Man, who is thus the giver of life in a real sense, the source of much tribal authority, and of traditional observances. Kunmanggur also placed *naritnarit* in the watercourses, where they associate closely with fish. When these fish are caught, the *naritnarit* are likely then to impregnate certain of the womenfolk of the aboriginal hunter, usually his wife or his sister. The spirit child does not enter the woman with food, or by the uterine passages, but under the toe nail. The *naritnarit* usually betrays its presence and its intentions, but more often to the father than to the mother. It may cling to his shoulder as he returns from a hunting or fishing trip. It will set his muscles twitching, or whisper in his ear, or tweak his hair. These are certain indications of the presence of *naritnarit*. It is thus that children are 'found' by the father or a near male relative. If the 'finder' of a *naritnarit* is the husband of the woman who gives birth to a child, the child will speak of the father as *lamala nai*, 'my shoulder'. A mother's brother is called by the child whom he found *minga nai*, literally 'my wood'. Sexual intercourse has an erotic significance only, and is not considered to have any essential relation to conception, except that only women who have been deflorated can conceive. Even before puberty sex experience in aboriginal children is common. Since all girls after puberty have continued sexual experience, all then are ripe in native eyes for motherhood, and can by accident, or carelessness in dealing with *mulunthunu*, be impregnated by *naritnarit*. This may happen within or at any distance outside the patrilineal *da* [a man's father's father's horde country, which is also his own]. A man's 'water' (his *nura*), the billabong or watercourse from which his *naritnarit* came, need not be in his own *da*. The location of the *nura*, and the natural species with which the *naritnarit* was associated when found by the father, do not seem to have any essential relation with *nakumar* [the patrilineally inherited local totem] inheritance. It is interesting to find that each *naritnarit* needs a father as well as a mother. Some man has to find it. Only *wiya* leaf children are fatherless.

When asked his 'dreaming', a Murinbata tends to give the names of several totemic species. These are all the *nakumar* of his *da*. There seems to be no belief that totem sites are inhabited by spirit children, so that children are not ancestors incarnated by totemic animism.[36]

The following native accounts throw much light upon the conception beliefs of the Murinbata.[37]

A native named Kulamburt and his brother were out shooting game for a white man when they saw suddenly the apparition of a *naritnarit* riding a horse. The spirit child called out and frightened the men, who ran away. Later they shot a turkey, wounding it in the mouth. The gun, which was defective, burst. The *naritnarit* was thought to have done this. Subsequently Kwuriyan, the wife of Kulamburt's brother, conceived and a girl, Kanbunin, was born three months later. Kanbunin speaks of Kulamburt as *minga nai*. Her teeth are slightly deformed, and this is thought to have been due to the wounding of the *naritnarit* by the exploding gun. Kanbunin's *nakumar* totem is the sugar-bag, *tfitai*, not the turkey (*mundurygoi*.) Both happen to be Tiwunggu totems, but *tfitai* is the *nakumar* of Kanbunin's father, and she thus inherits it. She could, informants say, have been found in association with a Kartjin species. This would not matter, because it could not be her *nakumar*. A Kartjin woman's child must be Tiwunggu, even when found in association with a Kartjin *nakumar*. Another Murinbata native who went to Darwin as a police witness took his wife with him. A wind sprang up from the south one night and blew his clothes and paper money outside his hut. Both man and wife immediately associated this event with the arrival of a *naritnarit* on the wind from Murinbata country. Later the woman became pregnant. The child was given the father's *nakumar*.

Three months before Kamoi was born a kangaroo (*kumbit*) was killed with a spear. The *naritnarit* associated with the kangaroo must also have been wounded for at birth Kamoi was seen to have a mark in the place where the kangaroo had been pierced. Kamoi's totem is not *kumbit* but *ninu*, the turtle, her father's *nakumar*.

From these two native accounts it is evident that the Murinbata do not consider it necessary for the species which becomes the patrilineal *nakumar* to be that which was associated with one's conception, although it may be. The conception agent is not regarded as a totem, or at least so it appears, and the place of conception may be anywhere, either within or outside the patrilineal *da*. The pattern is a common enough one throughout Australia, and is in essentials of a striking homogeneity in north-west Northern Australia.

There are several points relating to the procreative beliefs of the Murinbata which require to be noticed here. The first is the belief that the usual avenue by which a spirit-child gains entry into a woman is beneath her toe-nail, presumably her big toe-nail. There is apparently no belief relating to the entry of a spirit-child through any other part of a woman's body, or by any other means. As far as I am aware such a belief has only once before been reported in an Australian tribe, and it is of interest to note that this tribe, now probably extinct, was the far distant Nimbalda of the extreme north of South Australia, among whom the belief prevailed that the spirit-child entered the woman under the nail of the thumb or that of the big toe. Since the majority of investigators who have taken pains to enumerate the avenues customarily followed by the spirit-child in entering a woman among the various tribes described by them omit any mention of this particular one,[38] the occurrence of this same belief among such far separated tribes as the Nimbalda and the Murinbata is worth bearing in mind in considering the diffusion of cultural traits within Australia.

What is of more importance for our purpose is the fact that, according to Stanner, intercourse among the Murinbata is held to bear no essential relationship to conception or childbirth. It is also of great interest to note that in the case of the girl Kabunin the period, according to Stanner's informant, which elapsed from her conception to her birth lasted altogether three months. Such a statement certainly serves to lend support to the idea that the Murinbata are unaware of the relationship between intercourse and childbirth, although even under the conditions described this conclusion does not necessarily follow. It would not follow, for instance, if there existed a general belief that the parents of a child simply generate its body, but that the soul enters it at a subsequent time; there is, however, not the slightest evidence of the existence of such a belief among the Murinbata, and hence our original conclusion is on the available evidence a legitimate one.

The Aborigines of Groote Eylandt, off the east coast of Arnhem Land, are much exposed to winds. These winds, according to Mountford, together with their associated seasons, largely determine the life and customs of the Aborigines. Three main winds are recognized, the south-east *mamariga*, the north-east *timbura*, and the north-west *bara*. Each of these winds originates at a specific totem centre. The south-east winds carry spirit-children of the *wirinikapara* moiety to their mothers. The little spirit-children hide in the grass until the father dreams about one. A short while afterward his wife will be pregnant.

Except for the fact that the north-west wind originates in a wind-increase centre near Maitjunga, in the middle of Blue Mud Bay, and carries children of the *oranikapara* moiety, the conception beliefs are the same as those for the south-east winds.

The north-east wind does not appear to be associated with spirit-children, but largely with the production of cumulus clouds in the wet season.[39]

The Aborigines of Groote Eylandt appear to be quite aware of physical paternity, the processes of procreation, and so on. Worsley states: 'When questioned about the dual belief the belief in the spirit-children and their knowledge of natural processes—the women state that they know the natural processes perfectly well, and recognize the onset of pregnancy by the cessation of the menses, etc. At the same time, they say, we also accept the spirit-children idea. The ideas about spirit-children are thus a kind of theological dogma which is accepted although the natural processes are understood.'[40]

NOTES

1   B. H. Purcell, 'Rites and customs of Australian Aborigines', *Zeit. Ethnol.*, 25, 1893, 288.
2   Ibid., 287.
3   'Birth control in primitive society', *Birth Control Review*, April 1931, 15, no. 4, 105–7; *A Black Civilization*, 23–4.
4   *A Black Civilization*, 53.
5   Ibid., 68. See also 132, 280.
6   *Tiwi Wives*, 136–45.
7   C. P. Mountford, *The Tiwi, their Art, Myth and Ceremony*, 35.
8   D. Lockwood, *I, The Aboriginal*, 34.
9   Ibid., 113.
10 W. Chaseling, *Yulengor: Nomads of Arnhem Land*, 65–70.
11 W. O. Douglas, 'Jiberabu', *Colliers*, 134, 26 November 1954, 30.
12 H. Basedow, 'Anthropological notes on the western coastal tribes of the Northern Territory of South Australia', *Trans. Proc. Rep. Roy. Soc. S. Aust.*, 31, 1907, 4–5.
13 R. M. and C. H. Berndt, *Sexual Behavior in Western Arnhem Land*, 80–3.
14 R. M. Berndt, *Kunapipi*, 159.
15 R. M. Berndt, *Djanggawul*, 6–7.
16 Ibid., 51.
17 Ibid., 306.
18 *Art, Myth and Symbolism*, 308–9.
19 R. M. and C. H. Berndt, *Man, Land and Myth in North Australia*, 26.
20 Ibid., 27.
21 Ibid.
22 W. L. Warner, *A Black Civilization*, 24.
23 See, for example, Professor Warner's own article 'Malay influence on the Aboriginal cultures of north-eastern Arnhem Land', *Oceania*, 2, 1932, 476–95. Professor Warner considers that the Malaysian influence has not affected the social organization or beliefs of the tribes of north-eastern Arnhem Land to any very great extent, but the evidence he offers far from supports such a contention. Cf. 224 ff. See also R. C. Berndt, *Arnhem Land, its History and People*, Melbourne, 1954.
24 B. Spencer, *The Native Tribes of the Northern Territory of Australia*, 23–4.
25 In a letter to R. R. Marett, dated 17 June 1913, Spencer writes, 'It is a very remarkable thing that all over Australia when first white men come into contact with natives and half-castes appear on the scene, that their light colour is attributed by the women to eating the white man's flour. So far as they realize, this is the only change of importance that has taken place in their lives, and it, and it alone, explains the light colour of the child. At Alice Springs we had a couple of natives with a family of three black and two half-caste children, and the father regarded the latter as his children just as he did the former. The white man's flour was the only way in which they accounted for the difference. Of course after a little contact with whites, they very soon realize how matters stand, and this belief is one of the earliest to disappear. I am inclined to think that the first savage, living under the social conditions of the

Australians, who discovered the relationship between connexion and pro-creation, was an intelligent man.' R. R. Marett and T. K. Penniman (eds), *Spencer's Scientific Correspondence*, 158–9.

26 *The Native Tribes of the Northern Territory of Australia*, 25–6. That educated white men who have long been associated with the natives may firmly hold not dissimilar views, the following remarks of the Catholic missionary Jos. Bischofs taken from his article on the Nyu-Nyul tribe of North-Western Australia will somewhat touchingly show. Bischofs writes: 'After many years of experience it seems that the following statement can be made about the aborigines: A black woman will not, as a rule, give birth to a full-blooded child after she has once given birth to a half-caste child. In other words, even though she lives in a continuous and unbroken union with her black husband under the most favourable conditions, she will thereafter only give birth to half-caste children, even if she has only upon one occasion had intercourse previously with a white or coloured (Chinese, Malayan) man. I have already put this observation before several experts, without, however, any satisfactory explanation being arrived at (p. 37).

'I have observed several cases in which black women, of 35 to 40 years, after a single union with a coloured man have produced a half-caste child, when previously they were sterile, although they have been married to many blacks. I observed a similar case recently. A nineteen-year-old robust aboriginal lived for two years with a sixteen-year-old healthy girl from another tribe. When it came to childbirth, the newborn was not full-blooded, but half-caste, precisely as I had expected, inasmuch as I already knew from the black that the girl had had connection with an immoral white before she came to live with him. It follows from this that the black women are lost to their race once they have connection with an individual of another race, and in relation to their own race they remain sterile' (p. 37), Jos. Bischofs, 'Die Niol-Niol, ein eingeborenenstamm in Nordwest-Australien', *Anthrops*, 3, 1908, 32–40. In this connection it may here be remarked that it is a common belief among animal breeders, the world over, that once a pure-bred female has been mated with an impurely bred male, even though she is thereafter exclusively mated with pure-bred males, her progeny will never be quite as good as they were before the mating with the impure male. There is, however, no scientific evidence available in support of this belief. The American Black is, of course, the complete disproof of Bischofs's curious observations. There is even a case on record of a Black woman giving birth to twins, one Black and the other mulatto, the result presumably of separate fertilizations by a white and a Black. What is of real value in Bischofs's observations is the statement, concerning one particular girl, that despite previous continuous intercourse, she first conceived at sixteen years of age. The importance of this statement will be-come clearer in a subsequent chapter.

Of interest in connection with Bischofs's statements is the following para-graph culled from the first issue of the leading official popular medical organ of the Nazis, *Volksgesundheit*. 'The semen of a man of alien race is harmful. Such male semen is absorbed immediately and completely into the blood of the female in intercourse. Therefore, a single contact between a Jew and a woman of another race is sufficient to corrupt her blood for ever. With his alien albumen one also acquires his alien soul. She can never again, even if she marries an Aryan man, bear pure Aryan children—but only bastards, in whose breasts two souls dwell and in whose very bodies degeneration is clearly visible.' Reported in *New Republic*, 4 December 1935, 101, in an article entitled 'The Nazi war on medicine', by Ralph Thurston. The alleged influenc-ing of the later offspring of a single mother by her earlier pregnancies is known as *telegony*, a purely mythical phenomenon, for a short discussion of which the reader may be referred to Ploss and Bartel's *Woman*, ii, 379–81; for more detailed discussions see E. Rabaud, 'Telegony', *J. Hered.*, 5, 1914, 389–99, and A. Montagu, *Human Heredity*, New York, 1963, 73–5.

27 *The Native Tribes of the Northern Territory of Australia*, 263–4.
28 'This shaking of the body is a very characteristic feature in the totemic

ceremonies of many tribes. It was very much in evidence amongst the War-ramunga, who decorate themselves profusely with down when performing the sacred ceremonies during which they are supposed to simulate the old ances-tors. When they thus shake themselves, little bits of down tumble off just as the spirits used, originally, to emanate from him when he shook himself' (S).

29 Ibid., 266–74.

30 G. H. Wilkins, *Undiscovered Australia*, 197.

31 W. E. H. Stanner, 'The Daly River tribes: a report of field work in North Australia', *Oceania*, 4, 1933, 27–8.

32 W. E. H. Stanner, 'A note on Djamindjung kinship and totemism', *Oceania*, 6, 1936, 447–9.

33 Ibid., 451.

34 W. E. H. Stanner, 'Murinbata kinship and totemism', *Oceania*, 7, 1936, 186–216.

35 In view of Stanner's remarkable findings among the Murinbata it is of interest to note that they afford the first independent confirmation of D. S. Davidson's analytical study of Australian institutions in terms of the geographical distribution theory, at least, in respect of the subsection system (*The Chronolog-ical Aspects of Certain Australian Social Institutions*). Radcliffe-Brown has criticized the method of Davidson's study, but Stanner's findings provide at least a partial vindication of Davidson's method. Radcliffe-Brown has characterized David-son's method as one of 'conjectural reconstruction'; 'the scientific study', he writes, 'of such peoples as the Australian aborigines will make little progress until we abandon these attempts at conjectural reconstruction of a past about which we can obtain no direct knowledge in favour of a systematic study of the culture as it exists in the present for the purpose of reaching some understand-ing of what it really is and how it works' ('The diffusion of culture in Australia', *Oceania*, 1, 1930, 370). But clearly there is a place in ethnological science for a method of reconstruction which shows itself capable of arriving at conclusions which subsequent direct knowledge confirms. Where direct knowledge is lacking conjecture based upon such knowledge as is available may serve to light the way. Verification is our only means of determining the validity of a theory, and in one place, at least, Davidson's theoretical conclusions have been satisfactorily verified.

36 W. E. H. Stanner, 'Murinbata kinship and totemism', 193-5.

37 Ibid., 195–6.

38 The belief found among the Mungarai of the Roper River district (see p. 126) that a spirit-child may enter a woman through her toes is probably to be classed with the similar belief held by the Murinbata and Nimbalda (see p. 213). See also the belief of the Forrest River tribes (p. 195) that a spirit-child may enter a woman through the foot.

39 C. P. Mountford, *Art, Myth and Symbolism*, 95–7.

40 P. Worsley, 'The Changing Social Structure of the Wani Ndiljaugwa', 145.

CHAPTER V

The procreative beliefs of the native tribes of North-Eastern Australia, Queensland, and Cape York Peninsula

Before I was born out of my mother, generations guided me,
My embryo has never been torpid, nothing could overlay it.
For it the nebula cohered to an orb,
The long slow strata piled to rest on it,
Vast vegetables gave it sustenance,
Monstrous sauroids transported it in their mouths and deposited it with care,
All forces have been steadily employed to complete and delight me,
Now on this spot I stand with my robust soul.

WALT WHITMAN

W. E. Roth is responsible for the account of the procreative beliefs of the native tribes of North Queensland which follows here.[1]

Origin of Man. The first Aboriginals.—In the beginning Anjir was lying in the shadow of a thickly-leaved tree. He was a blackfellow with very large buttocks, but peculiar in that there was no sign of any orifice. Yalpan happened to be passing by at the time, and, noticing this anomaly, made a cut in the usual place by means of a piece of quartz-crystal, with the result that the evacuations were expelled and spread over the surface of the ground. All blacks were thus originally born from Anjir's dung.[2] Yalpan went southwards, and has never been heard of since. Anjir was buried underground after he had 'breeded'—the interpreter's expression—all he wanted to.[3] (The Koko-warra of Princess Charlotte Bay.)

It was out of the local river whence men and women originally sprung, but on their first appearance there was no specialization or differentiation of sex: the stiff spear-grass gave the males their distinctive attribute while the two labia majors remind the girls of their early peregrinations along the two river banks. (Tully River.)

The moon (kakara) made the first man and woman, the former out of the same stone used for manufacturing tomahawks, the latter out of box-tree. The man was completed by rubbing him all over with white and black ashes, and placing in his inside a stick of pandanus-root, which, when required can be brought into prominence. The woman was rendered subtle and soft by rubbing her with yams and mud: a ripe pandanus fruit was enclosed in her belly to produce her courses; to finish her distinctive features she was slit up with a sharp edge of a flat mangrove-root. (Proserpine River.)[4]

Sexual History. Conception not necessarily due to copulation.—Although sexual connection as a cause of conception is not recognized among the Tully River blacks so far as they are themselves concerned, it is admitted as true for all animals:—indeed this idea confirms them in their belief of superiority over the brute creation. A woman begets children because (*a*) she has been sitting over the fire on which she has roasted a particular species of black bream, which must have been given to her by the prospective father, (*b*) she has purposely gone a-hunting and caught a certain kind of bull-frog, (*c*) some man may have told her to be in an interesting condition, or (*d*) she may dream of having had a child put inside her.

By whichever of the above methods the child is conceived, whenever it eventually appears, the recognized husband accepts it as his own without demur. A similar belief holds good amongst the Kia blacks of the Proserpine River, but here it is the medicine-man (*warwinjala*), originally informed by *Mogari* [the spirit of a deceased person], who tells the woman's father or the woman herself that she is about to be with child. When twins occur, the second child is accounted for by the mother having been told to be in an interesting condition by a medicine-man belonging to another country, and with whom both parents are accordingly correspondingly angry.[5]

At Cape Grafton it is a particular species of pigeon which brings the already manufactured baby to the mother in the course of a dream.[6]

Infants may be fashioned by spirits and then inserted in the mother.—Nguta-Nguta, also known as Talpan, are the nature-spirits living in the dense scrub and undergrowth who send the babies along. The Cape Bedford blacks believe that these spirits have very long hair, with big ears, and two sets of eyes, one in front and the other behind, i.e. they hear and see everything: they are visible only to certain old men, but disappear into the ground whenever anyone else comes near: and are like human beings in that they have wives, children, and spears. The same natives say that babies are made in that portion of the west in which the sun sets, and in their original condition are full grown, but in their passage into their maternal homes take the form of a curlew (the spur-winged plover) if a girl, but of a pretty snake if a boy. When once inside the mother, baby takes on its human shape again, and nothing more is seen or heard of that particular bird or snake. When at night the blacks hear the curlew crying out, they will say: 'Hallo! there's a baby somewhere about.' In the case of a boy, the woman will probably be out hunting, and suddenly sing out that she sees the snake in question, and, as often as not, run away: her mates, even she herself, will perhaps join in looking to see where the serpent has got to, and turn over rocks, leaves, and logs in their fruitless search—it can nowhere be found, and that is a sure sign that it has reached its destination, and the future mother knows now that she is pregnant. It is the husband here who asks for the baby to be sent as a punishment when vexed with his wife.[7]

Anje-a, originally made by Thunder, is the individual, according to the Pennefather blacks, who fashions the piccaninnies out of swamp-mud, and inserts them in the bellies of the women. He is never seen but can be heard laughing in the depths of the bush, amongst the rocks, down in the lagoons, and along the mangrove swamps: when he is heard, the blacks say 'Anje-a he laugh: he got him piccaninny'. Women do not know when the infants are put inside them—they only feel them subsequently—because they may be placed in position during the daytime, at night, and in the course of a dream. Before actually inserting these mud-babies in the women, however, Anje-a makes the boys travel in a round-about way across the bush, their forms being already moulded into shape, whereas he causes the girls to pass over a piece of wood stretched crosswise, at a certain height, over the path he instructs them to travel by: as each girl stretches her legs over the cross-piece, she gets split in the fork and is now completed. For cutting the posterior orifice in both sexes Anje-a uses a piece of wood from the *Acacia rothii* Bail. Sometimes an accident befalls these infants before they get inside their human mothers, e.g., they may catch one of their feet in a log, and so be born with various deformities (club-foot, etc.). When the woman has plenty of room inside, twins are sent. Thunder, who can also make children out of swamp-mud, manufactures his all left-handed, which can thus be distinguished from Anje-a's, who are all right-handed. . . .

On the Proserpine River, it is Kunya who makes the babies out of pandanus-roots, and puts them into the woman when bathing. He is a nature-spirit most often dwelling in the ground, but he is also to be met with below the water-surface, as well as in the rocks and caves and in the quiet of the bush. When he inserts the infant in the mother, he puts in it the kuya or vital spirit.

When it is remembered that as a rule in all these Northern tribes, a little girl may be given to and will live with her spouse as his wife long before she reaches the stage of puberty—the relationship of which to fecundity is not recognized—the idea of conception not being necessarily due to sexual connection becomes partly intelligible.[8]

The Vital Principle: Spirit, Soul, etc.—On the Tully River, this is associated both with the shadow and with the breath. It goes away during sleep, fainting-fits, etc., and returns when the person awakes or recovers. It is of no tangible substance ('no bones' is the local description), and can be heard only at nights. Thus, for upwards of some days after it has taken its departure from the body, it can be heard tapping on the tops of their huts, creaking on neighbouring branches, etc. Every man has his own Koi, every woman her own Ku-inggan—one for each, and good or bad accordingly. After death, these can return to their old homes and friends. The Koi, etc., finally goes away into the solitudes of the scrub, where it can be met with everywhere; but it does not inhabit or become associated with any particular tree, clump of trees, cluster of rocks, cave, or stone, nor does it necessarily particularly haunt the burial ground or the locality where its late body was cremated. It is everlasting, so far as the blacks have any conception of the term, but, owing to the absence of tangible substance, requires no food, and hence no victuals are put aside or prepared for it. Koi (or Ku-inggan) is good or evil, according to the disposition of the individual whence it has been released. But if a man is alone by himself, day or night, the Koi of even one of his deceased relatives may come to do him harm. On the other hand, if it is seen or heard by several blacks together no harm arises, for it cannot injure the whole lot at once. Indeed, these natives are always taught, or, rather, have impressed upon them from childhood up, the many disadvantages of which an individual, when alone, renders himself continually liable at the instance of these spirits. Good fires are the only means these aboriginals have for keeping Koi away. . . .

Animals and plants are not regarded as having any Koi, etc.

The Bloomfield River natives have an idea of 'something' being associated with the breath or Wau-wu: that when a black dies, is unconscious, or delirious, etc., his wau-wu—and in this expression they apparently include his will, and thinking powers—leaves the body and travels about. After an individual's decease, apparitions of him may be seen by the survivors, and such a ghost or spiritual representation is called Wu-inggul, Winggul or Topo, but this, curiously enough, is apparently independent of the wau-wu. (R. Hislop.) Wu-inggul haunts its late home and present burial place where it can both be seen and heard, especially at night when the branches creak or whenever any sound, which cannot be otherwise accounted for, is rendered audible. Dogs are reckoned upon having thinking powers, etc., or wau-wu, and bear a sort of relationship to their masters, who will often speak of them as their mother, son, brother, etc., in addition to mentioning them by their proper names, these being conferred upon them according to the districts whence they have been obtained, or to the various tracts of country occupied by their owners. When talking about any live or dead shrub or food-plant, the Bloomfield blacks employ the same terms as are used to denote a live or dead individual, but they do not ascribe any breath, thinking, or will-power to it.

At Cape Bedford.—The belief is fixed in a certain vital principle or Wau-wu, associated with the breath, but differing from the 'something' to which a similar term is applied on the Bloomfield, in that it is part and parcel of the deceased's ghost or spiritual representation. This wau-wu is within the human body, both sleeping and waking, and only leaves it when death occurs: it may hover around its burial place for a time, and may be seen by and communicate with the living. Thus it often shows itself to one of the deceased's blood-relatives or intimate friends, to tell him who it was who sent him out of this life, and to ask for revenge. Again, if a man is travelling all alone, the wau-wu perhaps of his father or some friend bears him company to protect him from an ambuscade: he may probably see nothing, but his spiritual guide warns him to hide, and let his enemy pass by. It may, however, come with hostile intent, and make a person *wu-tchi* [a doom inflicted by a spirit]. When wau-wu finally ceases visiting its late owner's grave, it travels in the direction of the east, and enters a white person; these blacks will often look for a resemblance to some deceased tribesman amongst the Europeans, and often wonder how and why it is that we have forgotten all about our aboriginal ancestors. Nature-spirits (*Manya*) all come under the same category as wau-wu, in that they are originally derived from people deceased, and usually only leave their haunts in the forests and caves at night. The old men who are not afraid can both see and even spear, but not destroy them (as in the local burial ceremony): they can also converse with them, and be warned by them of various dangers: but women and children are afraid, and never see them. It is interesting to note that the lower animals possess wau-wu: for instance, if an individual happens to beat a dog—dogs have human names here—more unmercifully than usual, it is of common occurrence to hear a comrade say something to the following effect:— 'Look out! you are thrashing him as if he had no wau-wu.' Plants are not recognized as having any life or consciousness.[9]

On the Pennefather River, the vital principle, etc., the Ngai and Cho-i, are not connected with the breath but with the heart and after-birth. This ngai, which the blacks can feel palpitating, talks to them, and tells them when it is hungry or thirsty or wants to rest: it can even talk to them during sleep and thus causes dreams. It has nothing to do with the breath or *Wanji* (a term also applied to a gust of wind), which leaves the body first: it is only some time after death that the ngai takes its departure from the corpse, and if a male, passes into his children, both boys and girls equally. Indeed, not until a person's father dies does he or she possess an ngai: if the child dies before its father, it never has one: in the case of a female who might possess one it passes at her death from sister to sister, and when no more of these relatives are left to receive it, it goes 'along mangrove, finish altogether'. Again, not only does ngai separate from the body after death, but also during fainting-fits (e.g., those produced by collapse, loss of blood, etc.) and other forms of unconsciousness: to cure a fainting-fit, etc., the friends all around will start stamping with their feet to get ngai back again, just as they do with similar purpose in the case of a corpse. On the other hand, from the time when Anje-a puts him or her into the mother's womb, everybody possesses a cho-i, which occupies the same quarters and has similar subjective sensations as the ngai: it differs, however, from the latter in that a portion of it stays in the after-birth, the remainder leaving the corpse at death to wander about for ever in the bush. Freed thus at death from its connection with the body it can be sometimes seen, often heard, and certainly smelt. If interrogated as to the appearance or qualities of a cho-i, the natives will refer to their shadows, which, though called by another name, constitute the nearest approach they can get to rendering themselves intelligible. When the medicine-men go away for a spell in the bush they are believed to talk to these cho-i, with whose assistance they are supposed to control people's lives: it should be borne in mind that these wandering cho-i (i.e., those portions of them that were not left in the after-births) are all mischief-makers and evil-doers in that they can make a person sick, or even 'cranky'. And though these cho-i usually wander some-where in the bush, there are certain hollow trees, particular clumps, and others with unusually widespreading branches, etc., which they are believed more or less specially to haunt: thus at night, when the leaves are rustling, or the branches crackling, they can be heard. Furthermore, the presence of a cho-i can be recognized, day or night, by the nose. During one of my periodic visits to Mapoon, I was afforded a curious illustration of this. A few days after the death of a woman in one of the huts, and after the removal of the body, the Rev. N. Hey happened to be dressing with carbolic (in the same apartment) the wounds of a little boy who had suffered some trivial injuries, and in the course of his friendly offices spilt some of the acid on the floor: that same night the occupants were terrorised by the deceased's cho-i which they knew was present by the smell. But to return. It has been stated that a portion of the cho-i which Anje-a originally puts into the baby remains in its after-birth. Now, when the child is born into the world, the grandmother takes the after-birth away, and buries it in the sand, marking the situation by a number of twigs stuck in the ground in more or less of a circle, and tied together at their tops forming a structure resembling in shape a cone. Anje-a comes along, recognizes the spot, and taking the cho-i out carries it to one of his haunts where he places it, and where it may remain for years, in a hole in the rocks, in a tree, or in a lagoon. Three or four such haunts are known in the neighbourhood of Mapoon . . . Now, when Anje-a actually makes the mud-baby, which he inserts in the mother, he puts in a bit of the cho-i of his father if a boy, and that of his father's sister if a girl: when he makes the next little brother or sister, he put another bit in, and so on. And although the parents know whose cho-i their offspring possesses—whether its father's or its father's sister's—they are as yet ignorant of the particular spot where it has all these years been imprisoned, and whence it was finally released and put in the child's body by Anje-a. This information is obtained as follows:—When the navel-string is cut by the grand-mother (with a kangaroo-tooth, etc.) the different haunts of Anje-a are called out, and the name mentioned at the moment of breaking tells them when the cho-i was brought. (The navel-string curiously enough has two names here: *alinyi* for the portion left on the child, and *anombite* for that remaining on the after-birth.) The child's own country, its 'home', where it will in the future have the right to hunt and roam, is thus determined, not by the place of actual birth, but by the locality where its cho-i had been held captive—situations which may sometimes be many miles apart. Hence a baby is some-times spoken of as a *Ko* (tree)—*Akworra* (rock, stone, etc.)—or *Ngo-i* (fresh water)—*manu* (obtained or received from)—*agamo* (young infant). When an individual is finally dead, i.e. has no cho-i or ngai, the corpse as a piece of putrefying matter, 'all finish', is known as Pau-uto, or Ji-o.[10] Animals and plants have neither ngai or cho-i.[11]

Similar beliefs are to be found among the Proserpine River blacks on the eastern coast.[12]

The above account of the procreative beliefs of the natives of North Queensland provided the first confirmation of the surmise that the beliefs of the Central tribes of Australia were not peculiar to them alone, but were of very wide distribution throughout Australia.

From Roth's account we learn that the Koko-warra of Cape York Peninsula have an ancestor or culture-hero to whom they trace their origin, all blacks being originally born from his dung. We have already noticed that according to Taplin the Narrinyeri of South Australia have a belief that their culture-hero was born of his mother's dung without a father. Among the Koko-warra, however, we may look upon 'Yalpan' as the great 'father' who caused them to come into being, and the blackfellow Anjir as the medium through whom they passed into being, arising from his dung. Again, we see here that, as in the majority of the cases we have examined thus far, the actual individual from whom the first Aborigines are said to have arisen was of the male sex.

Writing some sixty-five years after Roth about the Tully River blacks, the Dyirbal, among whom he lived for more than ten months in 1963-4, and of whose language he made a profound study,[13] Dr R. M. W. Dixon's observations lead him to believe that the Dyirbal are quite aware of the basic facts of conception, and that they probably were so at the time Roth made his observations. Dixon spent most of his time working with old Aborigines who were, by and large, remembering back to the early years of the century, that is, to about the time of Roth. At what he calls the basic level of belief Dixon found that the Dyirbal were quite aware of the relation between intercourse and childbirth, and that what he calls the mystic level of belief may be the only level explicitly acknowledged, the basic level of belief being more implicit. 'The basic level of belief,' writes Dixon, 'is for instance implicit in the structure of language. Thus there is a verb *bulimbinyu*, "to be the male progenitor of", that has clear reference to the particular act of copulation that induced a conception. Explicit discussion is normally in terms of mystic belief, but basic belief is implicit in the reasoning, language and actions of the aborigines.'[14]

But if the explicit discussion is normally in terms of mystic belief, does this not suggest that the Dyirbal consider the mystic belief rather more important than the basic belief? Nowhere in aboriginal Australia was it denied that intercourse is a necessary condition if conception was to be produced. What was denied was that it was a sufficient condition. Furthermore, while regarding intercourse as a necessary condition, it was not really regarded as an agency in the production of conception—it merely prepared the way. The important conditions fall into the 'mystic' system of beliefs. Every aboriginal knows that intercourse produces conception in animals, and he also knows that while that is true of animals it is not true of human beings. Hence, Dixon's observations do not really successfully challenge the view that the Tully blacks do not understand the relation between intercourse and childbirth.[15]

Among the natives of the Proserpine River the moon is regarded as their original progenitor. A similar belief, we shall find, occurs also among such widely separated tribes as the Kariera in Western Australia and the Euahlayi in north-western New South Wales in the east.[16]

It is to be noted that the procreative beliefs of these Queensland tribes in general follow the pattern of the beliefs as recorded for the tribes living elsewhere in Australia, namely, the belief in the spirit origin of children. The variations in the details of these beliefs from tribe to tribe, or from horde to horde, in this region are of great interest. For example, among the Tully River blacks, and it is to be particularly noted that the statement is made explicitly with respect to them alone, the belief in the spirit origin of children is associated with the notion that animals come into being as a result of physical or sexual connection. Here only human beings have spirits, or *Koi*, animals do not have *Koi*. At Cape Bedford, however, animals are regarded as having spirits, *wau-wu*, just as men have, and although Roth nowhere explicitly says so his remarks would seem to imply that here, among the Cape Bedford blacks, animals are also regarded as being of spirit *origin*; it is difficult to read Roth otherwise. It is clear, however, that the Tully River blacks believe in the separate origin of men and animals.

The knowledge of the relationship between intercourse and pregnancy in animals said to be possessed by the Tully River blacks has excited a good deal of suspicion in the minds of some writers as to the reality of these natives' beliefs in so far as they apply to humans. If, it is argued, these natives recognize the relationship between intercourse and pregnancy in animals, how is it that they have failed to recognize the same relation as applying to themselves? The answer usually returned is that they have, but because the fact is incompatible with dogma it is not admitted, and even denied.

This view of the facts as reported by Roth is, of course, a reasonable one to take, assuming that we may rely upon the soundness of Roth's report; discussion of this viewpoint must, however, be deferred until a later chapter.

The deep and vivid reality which their procreative beliefs have for the Aborigines is well brought out by Roth's account of the behaviour of the Cape Bedford natives when they animatedly turned over rocks and leaves and logs in the endeavour to search out the snake which it was thought might have wished to enter some woman.

Among the Pennefather River natives we have two creators of babies, Anje-a and Thunder, Thunder in turn having originally been the creator of Anje-a. Anje-a makes the right-handed children and Thunder the left-handed. The efficient manner in which abnormalities such as deformities and twins are explained cannot but command one's admiration, for given the premises with which the native has to work, the route by which he arrives at his conclusions is faultlessly logical.

The bodies of the babies to be incarnated are apparently newly fashioned, and are something quite independent of the spirit; at death, as the natives say, the body is 'all finish'. The spirit is seemingly eternal, except among the Pennefather River natives who seem to hold a highly original view of the spirit, and the Cape Bedford natives who believe that the spirit part of a dead individual becomes incarnated in a white person—obviously a late development, but, as we shall see, an inevitable one under the given conditions—and lives on eternally as a ghost but does not undergo reincarnation.

The curious belief of the Pennefather River natives that the *ngai* of the father passes equally to his sons and daughters, but only after his death, before which his children do not usually possess one, so that should a child die before its father, it dies without an *ngai*, is extremely interesting. The woman may transmit her *ngai* to her sisters, should there be no relatives to whom to transmit her *ngai*, it disappears altogether. This belief is highly original, but quite impossible to explain on the evidence available. Anje-a and Thunder do not, so it would seem, have anything to do with the spirit part of an individual, apart from the secondary procedure already indicated. The *ngai* is something quite clearly inherited in the fashion described, contingent upon the death of a certain relative. The *ngai* part of an individual is merely an animating principle, a vital principle, of a somewhat shadowy nature, and possessing no very definite character, nor is it associated with any particular individual, it is simply a principle, a power. The *cho-i*, the spirit part of an individual, is inserted into his body when he is yet in the mother's womb, by Anje-a for right-handed, and by Thunder for left-handed children. A portion of the individual's *cho-i*, however, remains in the afterbirth, and it is from this source that Anje-a and Thunder take their supply of *cho-i* for the inspiriting of other relatives who may be born in the future. The determination by augury of the place to which Anje-a or Thunder had carried the afterbirth, *cho-i*, apparently serves to determine the totem of the child as well as its future hunting territory.

Spirit incarnation is the rule here and there is no evidence of a belief in reincarnation.

Sir James Frazer has recorded the statement made to him in conversation by the Bishop of North Queensland, Dr Frodsham, that the disbelief concerning the relationship between intercourse and pregnancy 'is not limited to the Arunta, but is shared by all the North Queensland tribes with which he is acquainted, and he added that it forms a fact which has to be reckoned with in the introduction of a higher standard of morality among the aborigines, for they do not naturally accept the true explanation of conception and childbirth even after their admission to mission stations'.[17]

R. H. Mathews writes of the Queensland tribes:[18]

In all the aboriginal tribes there is a settled belief in the reincarnation of the shades of their predecessors. Conception is supposed to be altogether independent of sexual intercourse. When a woman for the first time feels the movements of the child in the womb, commonly called 'quickening', she takes notice of the spot where this occurred, and reports it to the people present. It is believed that the spirit of some deceased progenitor has just at the moment entered the woman's body. The entry may have been through some one of the natural openings, or through any part of the skin. When the child is born, it will be assigned the totemic name of the mythic ancestor belonging to the particular locality.

The implication of these somewhat generalized statements is that there exists a definite belief in reincarnation among the Queensland tribes, at least the recognition of the 'quickening' as the moment of entry of a deceased progenitor's spirit is open to such an interpretation and, as it stands, to no other. It is, however, extremely doubtful whether the belief in reincarnation exists among any of the Queensland tribes, certainly such a belief has never been reported for any of them. Mathews's statement is therefore to be received with the greatest caution.

The following passages from Ursula McConnel's report of field-work among the Wik-Munkan tribe of the Cape York Peninsula on the Gulf of Carpentaria, who occupy a tract of land below the junction of the Coen and Archer and the Pretender and Holyrod Rivers, throw an interesting light upon the procreative beliefs of this tribe.

The *pulwaiya* [totem] has a sacred place of origin, its *auwa*, where it resides and whence it issues forth. These *auwa* or totem-centres are sometimes the nests and breeding places of birds, animals and plants concerned, and are always situated on the hunting grounds of the clan to which they belong, where the totemic species is abundant. Each *auwa* has its own peculiar characteristics. Trees, bushes, rocks, naturally or artificially arranged, ant-beds or holes in the ground in the vicinity of the *auwa* are sacred to the totems. There is always water near by in the shape of river, creek, lagoon, water hole, swamp, or well at the bottom of which the *pulwaiya* resides and into which the dead of the clan are believed to go. They are said to play about the vicinity of the *auwa* in the form of their totem. This is perhaps why plants or animals are protected near the *auwa* of their representative totem and why the killing of an animal or the injuring of a plant near its *auwa* is not only strictly forbidden but believed to be attended by grave consequences. It is to these ghosts or spirits that appeal is made during the ceremony carried out at the *auwa* to ensure a plentiful supply of the totemic object. That the clan should feel its economic dependence upon its forbears is natural, since it is from them that the knowledge and skill required for the pursuance of economic activities and their arts and crafts is handed down. This aspect is illustrated in the ghost clan, where the *pulwaiya* are human beings who are said to have taught men the arts of building the dams and fish-traps and cooking the fish in ant-bed ovens.[19]

A short distance from *Pantiauwa* [a small lagoon] is the baby (*puka*) *auwa*. Milkwood trees are hit for girl babies and gum trees for boy babies. Women who desire children take part in the ceremony and as the trees are hit their names are called:

'. . . Baby (*waiya*)! Babies go to all women everywhere! Go inside (a woman's name is called)! A girl baby first and a boy baby after! Baby (*waiya*)! A baby come to me!'

Women who do not want babies keep away from this ceremony, and are afraid to swim in the lagoon or drink the water in case they should become pregnant.[20]

There is here clearly no belief in reincarnation. We shall return to a consideration of the beliefs of this tribe somewhat later in this chapter.

In the following account by Donald F. Thomson of a study of the Koko Ya'o who live on the east coast on the Pascoe River of Cape York peninsula, occupying an area north of a line drawn from the mouth of the Mitchell River on the west, to Prince Charlotte Bay on the east, many features of novel interest both in regard to the social organization and to the procreative beliefs of this tribe are presented. In respect of the latter these are of such importance that a rather considerable amount of space will have to be devoted to the body of Thomson's report, in order that the nature of the peculiar procreative beliefs of this tribe may be fully understood.

The Koko Ya'o are a typical salt-water people, they are members of the Kwadji people of eastern Cape York. The tribe is divided into two exogamic moieties, called Koiyana and Karpeya. The Koko Ya'o are patrilineal, tracing their descent in moiety and clan through the father. The natives claim to be able to distinguish physical differences between the members of the two moieties in the eyes, face, hair, and skin. To Thomson no such differences were recognizable. It may be noted here that a similar belief prevails among the Arunta.[21]

THE YILAMO AND THE CULTURE HERO I'WAI

I'wai (the crocodile), the Culture Hero of the Koko Ya'o, was the leading figure among the Yilamo or Wulmpamo, the ancestors of the present race. These 'Big Men', as the natives call them in English today, were mythical ancestral beings who invented the present culture and traditional stock of knowledge. They lived at a time in the dim past, generally called by the somewhat nebulous term *omonoma*, literally 'in the beginning, at first', the favourite word on which to commence the telling of a legend.[22]

. . . the native conception of the Yilamo and their place in the scheme of life was expressed to me by a man of the closely allied Ompela tribe. . . . 'After the Big men, the Middle People lived, last we come and we find the white man,' *i.e.* the white man did not exist in myth or tradition, he has no antiquity, but has been 'found' by the fathers of the present generation.[23]

In the days of the Yilamo, *minya** (animals) were men. My informant stated that there were some exceptions to this, and *Apanyu*, the dingo, was never a man, and when speaking of *tauwa* (*Sterna fuscata*) he said 'long time *minya*'. Consistent with this is the occurrence of this name in the 'sings' of I'wai when carrying *kan'na* [an initiate, or novice] on his back. Implicit in the mythology and the Saga of I'wai is the belief that I'wai, as well as the other Yilamo, were once mortal, not supernatural beings, although they were endowed with powers not possessed by men to-day.[24]

It was I'wai who invented the initiation ceremonies; the others were merely spectators or 'helpers'; as my informant himself expressed it, all the others were 'working for him'. It was he who called meetings of the other Yilamo to watch him 'play', and the 'sings' in the present day ceremonies are those of I'wai. The belief of these people in the ancestry of the present race is particularly interesting. Like all primitive people who are dependent on memory and tradition alone, they have no definite ideas of the antiquity of their race; the present order reaches away into the dim past only a little farther than the memory of the oldest of the old men extends— to that dim, hazy period of which the old men were told long ago by their fathers' fathers. Beyond that were the Pama Yi'adji, the 'Middle People' of my old Ompela informant—the human ancestors who followed the Yilamo and who bridge the gap that they feel to exist between the Yilamo and the present day. The absence of the talk of white men from mythology, and the fact that their fathers can remember 'finding' him, are proof of his recent arrival upon the scene.

The Wulmpamo handed down their stock of knowledge to the Pama Yi'adji who have passed it to the present race. The old men in each generation are the guardians of traditional knowledge, which they pass on to the succeeding generation at initiation, in the form of 'sings' and legends. No Koko Ya'o man would ever think of doubting the reality of the Yilamo, for every day he has proof of

---

* *Minya* is a collective term for all animals, also for animal food, as distinct from *mai'yi*, plants and vegetable food (T).

their existence, in his totemism and *kintja* (tabu), as well as in every feature of the country, which he knows like a book, and each part of which is indelibly associated with the Culture Hero and the Totemic Ancestors. From his earliest childhood he has grown accustomed to meeting evidences of the activities of I'wai, and each day he is constantly seeing physical features in his own clan territory—boulders, headlands and islands—left by I'wai on his Odyssey, giving optical proof of the reality of I'wai, and the deeds recounted in the Saga that he has heard the old men, whom he has every reason to revere, tell and re-tell, with flashing eyes. He knows that these are full of *kunta* ('very *strong*, this one'); it is brought home to him almost from birth in a hundred ways—backed by *kintja* that mean death to break. To the old men, these things are so real that they frequently talk of the days of the Culture Hero as vividly as if they themselves had lived them.[25]

The totem centres or totemic stones, at which *Intichiuma* rites are carried out in the normal totemism, were left behind by the Yilamo—typical Australian totemic ancestors, mythical beings who first appeared in the form of men and later assumed animal form. These Yilamo performed extraordinary deeds the scenes of which are often marked by stones; sometimes the totemic ancestors were themselves turned to stone; but directly or indirectly they gave rise to the *kol'a watjaman*, the 'story stones' or totem centres of the present day.[26]

Every adult member of the society possesses two distinct kinds of totem which may be classed as follows:

(1) The personal totem, called *nartjimo norntadji*, which he does not inherit at birth, but which comes from the mother's moiety, and sometimes from her clan. Conceptional totemism is absent, and the natives have a knowledge of physiological paternity, evidence of which will be adduced later.

(2) Clan totems, called *pola* (father's father, man or woman speaking) of which each individual has several, and handed down from generation to generation in the patrilineal line. These are associated with the Yilamo, and are centred about *kol'a watjaman* or *mutta* (totem centres or 'story stones'), at which ceremonies of *Intichiuma* type may be carried out.[27]

Every individual, at birth, possesses two spirits. One of these, the *norntal*, is the '*poi'ya*' that pulsates on the head of an infant (the fontanelle). It resides in the body only during early childhood and with the closure of the frontal suture goes to a place in the mother's country called *nartji norntadji*, the place of the *norntal*. The other spirit, the *mipi*,* or 'ghost' as it is most frequently translated, remains in the

---

* *Mipi* or *kobi* is a ghost, a kind of non-material ego . . . It is generally used for ghosts of the dead (T).

body until death, when it goes to join the *norntal*, with which it has remained in intimate association during the dream-life of the individual.[28]

The personal totem . . . comes . . . from the mother's moiety by augury commencing soon after birth and culminating in the removal of an upper central incisor tooth. The avulsion of the tooth is not in any way associated with initiation.[29]

It has been stated that the *norntal* is intimately associated with the dream-life, and the *nartji norntadji* is also called the *nartji Mukkainan* (the dream place). It is therefore immaterial whether a man asks '*n'ka norntal wantuna?*' (where is your *norntal*?) or '*nono wantuna mukkainan?*' (where do you dream?). Throughout life, when a man dreams, his *mipi* goes to his *nartji norntadji* to join his *norntal*. For this reason he must not be awakened from sleep except by calling his name from a long distance. The natives' conception of sleep is very close to that of death; in each the *mipi* leaves the body to join the *norntal*, but in sleep *poi'ya* still animates the body. If a man has a lagoon or watery place as his *nartji norntadji* he may dream that he is swimming there with his *nartjimo*. If his personal totem is a bird he may dream that he is flying with it. A woman whose *nartjimo norntadji* was *pull'o* (pheasant coucal) told me that she dreamed that she was flying with *pull'o* and that she went with it to the grassy places that the bird frequents at Pull'onon. A man always knew where his *norntal* was from his dreams.[30]

It has been stated that when a man dies, his *mipi*, which is bound up with his *poi'ya*, goes to join his *norntal* in his *nartji norntadji*. Soon after death a lighted torch of *ontji* (*Melaleuca* bark) is passed over and around the body and limbs of the *korntoi* (corpse), and is then placed in the hand of the dead man—in the left hand if he is *tako*, and in the right hand if he is *minnijigo*.* He is told to take the torch and go home to his own *nartji*—the *nartji norntadji*. 'Norntallago bati!' To your *norntal* you go. When they see a 'shooting star' the people know at once that somebody is dead. They follow its passage across the sky, crying aloud: '*Mil'adji! Mil'adji! Mil'adji! Mil'adji! Mil'adji! Mil'adji!*' If, as of course most frequently happens, the star merely passes across the heavens, they say that somebody from another *nartji* has died, but if, as once occurred while I was camped with the Yintjingga tribe on the Stewart River, a report is heard, the watchers cry '*Mumpa!*' They know that somebody is dead and that his *mipi* has come to join his *norntal* in their own country. My informants stated that when a man died he was received in his *nartji norntadji* by the Wo'odi Mukkan, literally the 'big devil'. This does not imply the belief in a deity, nor is there any belief in a supreme being, but my

* That is respectively left-handed or right-handed.

informants always spoke of the Wo'odi Mukkan as a kind of presiding spirit in the world to which they go after death. There a man may be greeted by his mother, and as he comes she would tell him (in the case of Pornjogobi)* not to strike water (the usual *norntadji*) but to strike the *akanja*, his own *nartjimo norntadji*.[31]

Intichiuma rites are not performed in connection with personal totems. Pornjogobi belonged to Norlataltampany, a clan whose territory centred about Norlatal (Mosquito Point), from which it took its name. At this spot the *wote'i* (dugong) *kol'a* was situated. If the people noticed a falling off in the number of dugong, a ceremony to increase dugong was performed at this stone by the old men who claimed the dugong as *pola*. The stone was approached slowly, 'Go easy, not rough,' as Pornjogobi expressed it. The men then took leaves and struck the stone, spitting and hissing through their lips as they cried:—

Ampimbo!	*Ampi'!*	*Ampi'!*	*Ampi'!*
'You come plenty!	Come plenty!	Come plenty!	Come plenty!'

'You see dugong spout!' my informant cried.[32]

In the territory of the clan Porn'yinon on the Middle Pascoe River, there are a number of very important totem centres, including the Pai'yam', the Rainbow Serpent. He frequents a lagoon, the water of which is said to be *tonko-tonko* (black) in colour and hot, and is believed to be the urine (*kumpo*) of Pai'yam'. My informant told me that he had seen the water shoot up from the place of Pai'yam'. Sometimes Pai'yam' leaves this lagoon and goes inside a great stone at a place called Api. Pai'yam' is said to resemble a snake; he has marks of many colours on his body and a great crest on his head. Members of his clan might swim in the black lagoon, but not others, and the natives told me of a man who had gone to that place, and whose *mipi* (ghost) was taken by Pai'yam'. The victim became like a baby; he 'cried like a child', and returned from the place exhausted. But Yarrogobi, a medicine-man who belonged to Porn'yinon, recovered his *mipi* for him.[33]

The most unusual of all the totems is *wolmpilgobi*, sexual licence, which is associated with the 'woman story stone' at Tolnonoma. If they 'flash' the woman 'story thing' left by I'wai, they declare that the woman will 'go *wolmpilgobi*'.† My informants said that this story thing was once 'flashed' by a man who had been 'pushed' (coerced) by another who wished to obtain an 'outside' woman, *i.e.* a woman from another place, for women were difficult for a young man to

* Personal name meaning the one who likes honey.
† *Wolmpilgobi* is a loose or lewd person, generally a woman; one given to free sexual intercourse, a harlot. . . . Less frequently the term is applied to men (T).

obtain. He put on *porta* (red ochre), *matan* (white paint), and *normpa* (charcoal) and a special *keni* (medicine) used to attract women. The women all went *wolmpilgobi* and ran after the men. 'Everybody fight,' my informant added. Now they have stopped 'flashing' this stone. This abstract '*wolmpilgobi*' which possesses the women as a consequence of the painting of the totem centre, is also a totem of the clan of Tolnonoma.[34]

THE KNOWLEDGE OF PHYSICAL PATERNITY

I actually approached the present study with a firmly rooted belief that the natives were entirely ignorant of the fact of physiological fatherhood. It was only after I was repeatedly made aware of the facts stated here that I became convinced of the reality of the natives' knowledge.

Informants of the Koko Ya'o, Ompela, and Kanju tribes treated contemptuously any suggestion that the mother has any part in conception, and declared that *tall'all*, the seminal fluid of the male, produces the child. 'Mother nothing,' my informant, Tjaminjinyu, of the Ompela tribe, declared with finality.

In the Koko Ya'o, Kanju, Yankonyu, Ompela, and Yintjingga tribes, there is a firm belief in the contraceptive (not abortifacient) properties of certain plants. I was informed of this fact by both men and women in widely separated localities, and in each case the names of two plants that are used, *ka'ata* and *pi'ala*, were given to me. I had striking evidence of this belief when collecting genealogies from a group of Kanju people on the Batavia River. After writing down the names of a man and his wife that occurred in one of the branches of the pedigree, I asked, as usual, for the names of their children, and received the spontaneous reply, 'Not got, *Keni yankoi'n*, he shut mesel,' *i.e.* she has not got any, she has eaten medicine; she has shut herself. Those were the exact words volunteered by one of my informants— a woman with whom I had never discussed the question. The men, as usual, in all matters pertaining to women, such for example as childbirth, generally disclaim any first-hand knowledge of this medicine, but they freely admit that a '*keni* belong woman' is used, and declare that they would be angry if they found their women using it. Most of my information on this subject was obtained from old women. They stated that this *keni* was 'old-fashioned' and all agreed that when they used it 'piccaninny no more come out'.[35]

The two plants mentioned above, *tjarri* or *ka'ata* (*Dioscorea sativa* var. *rotunda*) and *pi'ala* (*Entada scandens*), are both good *mai'yi*, and are freely used as foods, the root of the former, and the bean of the latter, but in each case only after a tedious process of cooking and subsequent washing in frequent changes of water. When used as a contraceptive the *keni* is generally eaten raw, sometimes roasted, but in each case without the prolonged washing to which the same material is subjected when used as food. A very large *tjarri* rootstock, called *tjarri kalmpa*, a 'male' *tjarra*, is selected, and this either raw or cooked, is given to the young woman by one of the older women credited with a special knowledge of such matters. I was informed that this *keni* is taken in the early morning on an empty stomach, after which the woman lies down, refraining from drinking throughout the day, until sundown. The old women declared that once a woman had taken this medicine she would never have a child. One explanation of its action was that it 'dried them up', another that it closed the genital passages *so that the tall'all could not enter*. These are, of course, merely the speculations of my informants, for in such matters, which are not freely discussed, there is probably nothing that could be called an orthodox belief.[36]

All the people of the Kawadji, including the Ompela and Koko Ya'o recognize at once the footprints of every individual with whom they come into regular contact in the normal course of their lives. So closely allied is the footprint to the foot that made it, that the name *ta'o* is applied both to a foot and to a footprint or 'track'. It is therefore impossible to tell, except by the context, whether a man is speaking of a foot or a footprint. The footprint of a child is believed to resemble that of its father. When the paternity of a child in the Ompela tribe was in doubt the natives said, 'Look *ta'o*, *ta'o* belong Tjaminjinyu!' 'Look at the foot—the footprint is that of Tjaminjinyu!' Here then in a single phrase we have a clear statement of native belief. They not only recognize paternity by this very seeking for the physiological father of the child, but they express a definite belief in a physical bond, and even a physical resemblance between the father and child.

This idea of a physical resemblance between father and child is an interesting and important one, for it is very different from the belief generally recorded by ethnographers in Australia. Sir James Frazer[37] says of the Central Australian: 'fatherhood to a Central Australian savage is a very different thing from fatherhood to a civilized European. To the European father it means that he has begotten a child on a woman; to a Central Australian father it means that a child is the offspring of a woman with whom he has the right to cohabit, whether he has actually had intercourse with her or not. To the European mind the tie between a father and his child is physical, to the Central Australian it is social.'

But the phrase 'look *ta'o*' is incompatible with these primitive beliefs, since it shows the definite idea of a physical bond between parent and child. Moreover, the study of the sole of the foot and the footprint fits well with his own normal practice of studying tracks and identifying them with individuals, and forestalls the criticism that he has learned it from a white man. There is also a social aspect to fatherhood, but the social bond between a man and his father appears to be less strong than the bond with his *mukka* or *kala*, his mother's elder and younger brothers, respectively, either of whom may frequently act as his guardian.

Wife-lending, however, is not unknown, but the only form appears to be that between brothers (actual or classificatory), in which an elder brother may be 'sorry' for his younger brother and lend one of his wives to him, never in the reverse direction. This can be explained under the levirate and merely anticipates what normally takes place on the death of the elder brother (*yapu*), when his *ya'a'du* takes his wife or wives, and may adopt his children. That is what had actually occurred in the case that I have already cited, in which the paternity of the child was in doubt. The mother of the child had been lent to Tjaminjinyu by a classificatory elder brother, and when the child was born the father was decided by the examination of its feet. Even then the husband of the woman accepted the child as one of his own children, for although he was not the physical father, he was the social father, just as Tjaminjinyu would, in the event of his elder brother's death, have adopted the child of which he was the *actual* but not the *social* father. He would then have become the *social* father of his brother's children, to whom he was already a *classificatory* father and who already addressed him as *pipi* (father, father's younger brother).

There is in this society nothing approaching the sexual licence that Professor Malinowski found to be the regular thing before marriage in the Trobriand Islands. In the Koko Ya'o tribe a girl has normally no sexual experience before marriage, for she is married actually before puberty, even before she is physiologically capable of bearing children. Prior to this she lives at her parents' fireside, and even during the day she is under the constant surveillance of her mother, whom she accompanies in her daily quest for food. The reason that the natives give for this child-marriage is that the girl will not be afraid of her husband if she grows up with him.

I found no evidence of any beliefs either in reincarnation or in the entry of a spirit into the mother at conception. The existence of some such beliefs might have been expected, when, in a patrilineal society, the child possesses at birth a *norntal* or spirit that comes by augury from the mother's moiety.

In discussing the personal totemism of this tribe I suggested that the anomalous method by which the personal totem is obtained may be a heritage from a previous matrilineal condition. The meanings of the names of the two totems appear to support this, *i.e. nartjimo*, the name of the personal totem, *mother's father*, which might be expected in a matrilineal society, and the name of the clan totem, *pola*, meaning *father's father*, which is found in the existing patrilineal state.

Evidence is not lacking for the belief that there has been an extensive invasion, or invasions, of culture, and it seems probable that the natives of this area of Cape York were originally matrilineal and were invaded by a patrilineal people, possibly bringing with them a knowledge of physiological fatherhood.[38]

In this extraordinarily interesting account it will have been noted that the myths relating to the early history of the tribes as exemplified by the Koko Ya'o myth of the culture hero I'wai follow much the same plan as those of every other Australian tribe we have so far considered, the tribal ancestors here being definitely stated to have been mortals and not supernatural beings. And, of course, it will be recalled that the belief that animals were once men is not altogether unique in Australian cosmology.

I'wai does not appear to have had any connection with the creation of the totems nor with the creation of the members of the tribe, but he is said to have created the initiation ceremonies and many of the natural features of the land. The initiation ceremonies of the Koko Ya'o, which for reasons of space have not been described here, quite clearly represent a recapitulation of the activities of I'wai, the ceremonies being strictly non-totemic.

The actual ancestors of the tribe are the Yilamo or Wulmpano, who lived in the *omonoma*, 'in the beginning', and it is these ancestors who gave rise to the totem centres of the present day. From these totem centres the individual derives his clan totems, or *pola*, of which each individual has several and which are 'shared by all the members of his clan, and handed down from generation to generation in the patrilineal line'. Increase ceremonies of the Arunta type are practised at the totem centres. By 'totem centre' it seems that we are to understand merely a totem abode, and not a *Knanikilla*.

The personal totem or *nartjimo norntadji* possessed by any individual comes to him through the mother's moiety, and is determined by augury. Increase rites are not performed in connection with the personal totem.

The beliefs with respect to the vital and ghost spirits possessed by each individual are, it will have been observed, very similar to the beliefs held in the same connection by the Queensland and Cape York tribes described by Roth.

The totem of sexual licence, which may perhaps be understood also as the totem of excessive sexual desire, is certainly of interest here, such a totem we shall encounter at least once again on the opposite side of the continent, namely, among the Kariera of Western Australia.[39]

It is by no means clear what the totem centres are actually understood to be. The spirit-parts of an individual, we have already seen, are derived from other sources, and his totems are, in the case of his personal totem, indirectly determined by the mother's totem in many cases, and in the case of the *pola*, his clan totem, is associated with the tribal ancestors and the totem centres, but indirectly, since the *pola* are handed down from one generation to another, in the patrilineal line. This will mean that a particular individual may trace his totemic membership to a Yilamo ancestor, and thus to an association with a particular totem centre; he does not, however, derive his totem from the totem centre directly, but only indirectly from his father or father's brothers. Increase ceremonies associated with the totemic animals or plants, etc., may take place at the totem centres, but at no definite seasons, as among the Arunta, for example. Thomson's account of the simple increase ceremonies performed in connection with the dugong totem renders it fairly clear that the *kunta*, or power, within the totem stones is manipulated by the totem members for the purpose of increasing the supply of their totem animals.

Now, whatever the power within the totem stone is, it must clearly be of a spiritual nature. Are there then spirit dugong either actually or potentially present in the dugong totem stones, which, following the performance of the proper rites, emerge and subsequently appear in the desired shape and quantities? Or does this power merely cause the existing dugong to increase of themselves alone?

Thomson has stated that he could find no evidence of such beliefs. And from the description of the totemic rites themselves we derive but little assistance in the attempt to return an answer to these questions, but from the description of the sexual licence totem, and of two totems, the description of which has been omitted here, from Thomson's account, the heat and sickness totems, in which their essential essences emanate directly from the totem stones, it is likely that a similar conception either held or holds for the other totems too, that is to say that the totem animals are regarded as emanating directly from the totem stones themselves. Such a belief would not necessarily involve any associated belief such as incarnation, all that is necessary is that the totem animals should come directly into being from the totem centre, the transformation of the spirit form into the dugong form taking place after the spirits have emerged from the totem stone.

Thus, any doctrine of reincarnation or even of incarnation is upon such a theory rendered quite unnecessary.

It is not altogether surprising, therefore, to learn that the natives entertain some idea of physiological paternity, nor is it surprising to learn that the mother is 'nothing', having nothing to do with conception, and that the child is held to be the product alone of the seminal fluid of the male. In short, physiological maternity is unrecognized and physiological paternity is declared to be the only existing 'blood' relationship between parent and child.

The belief that the mother plays no part whatever in the generation of the child follows the general Aboriginal pattern, and the belief that the father is the sole genitor of the child, that the child is the product of the father's seminal fluid, is a belief which is limited to some of the tribes of this region of Australia alone.

So singular a belief combined with the other singularities of organization and culture of this tribe raises a strong suspicion that this and these other unusual features are not indigenous to it, but have been introduced from some external source.

This suspicion is converted into practical certainty when it is considered that the Koko Ya'o are situated on the eastern coast of the Cape York Peninsula, only 150 miles south of Torres Strait, and thus within reach of the peoples living on the islands within the Strait, and by this means within possible reach of Papua and the rest of Melanesia. Thomson has stated: 'There is strong evidence for the belief that the Cult of I'wai came into Australia through Torres Straits. It is non-totemic and is superimposed upon a totemic culture in which it belongs not to one clan or to one moiety, but to the tribe as a whole. The cult associated with it is practised by all the clans of the tribe, and thus forms a basis for tribal, rather than clan, solidarity.'[40]

The cult, as Thomson points out, together with the ritual dances and masks associated with it, bears a striking resemblance to the hero cults of Papua, and it is highly probable that these found their way to the Koko Ya'o through the western islands of Torres Strait.[41] The cultural affinities existing between Papua, Torres Strait, and Cape York Peninsula have long been recognized and it is known that the contact has been maintained by means of the dug-out canoe, which is in use all down the eastern littoral of the peninsula and as far south as the Batavia River in the Gulf of Carpentaria.[42]

The fact that the Koko Ya'o claim to be able to distinguish the members of each moiety by means of various anatomical characters might actually mean that in the remote past the tribe was composed of two racial varieties, or, what is possibly more probable still, two distinct cultural groups each of whom presented some real or fancied or artificial physical difference, upon the basis of which the members of the two groups could be more or less easily distinguished, and that the present beliefs merely reflect the remains of past realities which have ceased to be so as a result of the complete mergence of the physical differences, and the complete incorporation of the cultural ones. This is a view which has recently been given a new support by Haddon and by McConnel.[43]

It is, however, all things considered, highly probable that the procreative beliefs of the Koko Ya'o have been appreciably modified from their original state by some influence proceeding from a source outside Australia, and very likely Papuan. The procreative beliefs of the Koko Ya'o being so very different both in character and in form from what we have come to know as the Australian pattern, it is a fair assumption that they originated elsewhere than among the Koko Ya'o. Clearly they cannot have suffered this peculiar change as the result of contact with some other Australian tribe or tribes, for there is no tribe in any other region of this continent which possesses anything approaching the nature of the Koko Ya'o beliefs. The change, therefore, must have been introduced, as we have said, from some source outside Australia, and this source, there is abundant evidence to suggest, was most probably Papuan.

In view of these considerations it becomes impossible to consider the Koko Ya'o procreative beliefs as originally Australian, and, being thus foreign in origin, cannot be considered in the body of our discussion to follow of the general pattern of the procreative beliefs of the Australian Aborigines.

It is, however, to a large extent quite possible to distinguish the indigenous Australian elements both in the totemic organization and in the procreative beliefs, the analysis quite definitely pointing to the fact that prior to the Papuan contact the Koko Ya'o social organization and procreative beliefs were essentially of the North Queensland type described by Roth.

Thomson's statement, that there is a firm belief in the contraceptive properties of certain plants, which, 'given to the young woman by one of the older women credited with a special knowledge of such matters', has, according to some, the effect of drying up the woman, and, according to others, the effect of closing up the genital passages so that the seminal fluid cannot enter, is of great interest. It would seem at first sight difficult to reconcile such ideas with the belief that in procreation the 'mother nothing', for obviously the mother is an indispensable condition of the procreative process according to these beliefs; without the mother it would be more reasonable to say 'father nothing', for his *tall'all* (seminal fluid) cannot give rise to a child without the co-operation of a woman. But here a woman is considered as contributing nothing towards the formation of a child, the father does all that is necessary, but it would seem impossible to disregard the fact that a woman is a necessary adjunct towards the completion of the process. Yet impossible as it would seem the fact is disregarded. While pregnancy is not considered to be the fruit of the commerce of the sexes as we understand it, intercourse with a woman who has not been 'closed' against the reception of the *tall'all* is necessary before the *tall'all* can give rise to a child. There is, therefore, present among the Koko Ya'o a knowledge of the relationship between intercourse, male ejaculation, and pregnancy, but the pregnancy being obviously produced by the male, the female is regarded as playing a purely passive and thoroughly unimportant role in the whole process.

It would be interesting to know what the Koko Ya'o really think concerning the nature of the *tall'all*. Do they consider it as something spiritual in nature or merely physical? To these questions there is nothing in Thomson's account which would enable us to return an answer. *Tall'all* is, of course, something that they can see. Is it, however, a miniature child already preformed? Or is it an amorphous entity which undergoes development into a child during the period of pregnancy? The internal evidence would suggest that the latter hypothesis is the one generally accepted among the Koko Ya'o, for it is apparently to the body alone that the *tall'all* gives rise, and there is, as far as we are able to judge, nothing spiritual connected with it.

The native belief that the footprint of a child resembles that of its father, of course, proves nothing, for such a belief may well be a quite conscious rationalization manufactured to fit the apparently orthodox belief in the physiological paternity of the child, and in order to give social paternity a presumed physical validation.

Finally, it seems perfectly clear that the Koko Ya'o belief in physiological paternity and in the *tall'all* as the source of the child is as much in the nature of a superstition as is the spirit-child belief of the Arunta and other Australian tribes. The fact that the Koko Ya'o belief resembles our own more closely than does that of the Arunta and these other Australian tribes should not blind us to the fact that this is primarily an accident, and that the Koko Ya'o belief is obviously not based upon a reasoned solution of a difficult problem, but represents an orthodoxy of precisely the same nature as that relating to their totemic increase rites and their spirit beliefs in general.

In a subsequent communication Thomson states:

The extension of field work on the Gulf of Carpentaria subsequently has shown that the knowledge of physiological paternity is widespread in this region. The natives of the Wik-Monkan tribe of Archer River, and also those of neighbouring tribes, distinguish between physiological and sociological aspects of paternity by use of special terms, which are employed in conjunction with those of the kinship system.[44]

Thomson goes on to say:

The Wik-Monkan recognizes, and freely affirms, the fertilizing influence of seminal fluid (*tankarra*), but on the physiological aspect of conception and pregnancy his knowledge is less exact. He recognizes that pregnancy results from the introduction of seminal fluid, but as to how the embryo is produced his ideas are as vague as those of any white man who possesses no biological knowledge. His belief is that the seminal fluid enters the uterus (*po'o mompa*) and gradually builds up the body of the embryo, and thus he insists that a single sexual act is not sufficient to produce conception, which can result only from repeated intercourse.[45]

In spite of the existence of this knowledge, as Thomson points out, a baby totem centre exists in one of the clan territories of the Wik-Munkan at which ceremonies for the increase of babies are carried out.[46] We have already had an account of the beliefs relating to this baby totem centre from Ursula McConnel, but Thomson gives us the Wik-Munkan myth relating to the origin of this baby totem centre. This myth tells that in the beginning an ancestral 'little man' or 'little ghost' lived at what is now the site of the baby totem centre. 'At first there were only these two people, the man and the woman; no others. They went hunting together, and they copulated and copulated' until the woman was big with child. 'After this the man and woman made the baby totem centre.'[47]

A Wik-Munkan moon myth given by Thomson recounts that when the Moon was a man he one day went fishing. After spearing many fish he rested and sank down under the water; some women seeing some of the dead fish went after them. The Moon seized two of the young ones and began to rape them, exclaiming, 'Look at me; I am pouring out my semen for you all.' But the old men said, 'This is bad', and all the women and children came and looked at the semen and said, 'This is bad.'

'At length Moon spoke, "I shall eat it myself!" He picked up his own semen and swallowed it, and then cried, "You shall all die altogether. I shall lie down; I shall die, but I shall come up again. After that I shall rest, but each time I die I shall come back again." So after the old moon dies he rests awhile, but the new moon always appears again later.'[48]

Thomson concludes:[49]

The statement of the fertilizing power of semen and of its action in 'building up' the body of the baby, and the revelation of the life giving powers of seminal fluid that forms the theme of the Moon myth, are incompatible with ignorance of physical paternity.

Furthermore, the distinction in terminology in the kinship system between the physiological and the social aspects of fatherhood is in itself significant enough to place fatherhood in the Wik-Monkan tribe in a category very different from that recorded elsewhere in Australia.

The distinction in terminology to which Thomson refers is that the actual husband of the woman to whom the child is born is, after the child has been ceremonially presented to him, known as the *placer* or *begetter* of the child (*puk wunpun*).[50] 'The generic kinship term for father is *pip*, the reciprocal term, *nenk*. A child has only one *pip wunpun* although it may have many *pip*.'[51]

That the Wik-Munkan possess a knowledge of the relationship existing between intercourse, seminal fluid, and pregnancy there can be no doubt whatever. They recognize that cessation of the menses is indicative of pregnancy, they know that the genital passage is closed after conception, and they 'believe that there is a bag (*mompa*), the name applied to the fœtal membranes and also to the placenta, in which the seminal fluid is stored, and within which it assumes gradually the form of an egg (*tita*).'[52] That their knowledge of the relationship between intercourse and childbirth is not too vague, and that their recognition of the actual father of a child is not determined by purely social factors is further borne out by the account which Thomson gives of a young man (at the Mapoon Mission on the Batavia River) who bitterly complained to him that he had been induced to marry a girl, who had subsequently given birth to a child of which he was not the father. 'He admitted that he had had sexual intercourse with the girl before marriage, but he affirmed that as this had occurred only once, he was sure that the baby that had been born later could not have been his own. Nothing that I could say to him would shake his belief: married men, he declared, had told him that conception followed only after repeated acts.'[53] Thus, it is clearly recognized that a man, whether he is the husband of the woman or not, must have repeated sexual intercourse with a woman before conception can be produced. The necessity of repeated intercourse so that the body of the embryo might be built up would appear to afford the plainest proof of the fact that intercourse and the seminal fluid are considered to be the chief cause of conception and childbirth.

Yet in spite of this and of the myths relating to the creation of the baby totem centres it is, upon Thomson's account, difficult to see what precisely the function of these baby totem centres may be. With reference to the baby totem centre Thomson writes:[54]

The myth of its origin is typical of those that explain the origin of the totem centres of these people. The fundamental fact revealed in the myth is the discovery by the totemic ancestors (the man and woman who made the totem centre at Qrnyau'wa) of the fact that pregnancy resulted from sexual intercourse, and the importance of this is indicated by the fact that at Pantiau'wa the centre representing the female genitalia is regarded as the most important of the small centres (*au'wa many'*) that compose the whole totem centre. The increase rite, the thrusting of a yam stick or other implement into the symbolic vagina, is believed to give rise to babies in no more literal sense than the increase rites performed at any other totem centre give rise *directly* to animals. The belief is simply that a ritual state of well-being results, something like mana, and causes them to multiply.

On an earlier page Thomson writes:[55]

At the baby totem centre at Ark Qrnyau'wa increase rites (*au'wa kent'n*) were performed by men and also by women when they wished babies to go to other places. The centre itself is said to have sunk out of sight under water, but the breaking off of the tops of termite mounds close to the totem centre today constitutes the increase rite. As this rite is performed, the names of places to which it is desired to send babies are mentioned. Sometimes the names of individuals may be called, especially, my informants added, in the case of a woman who is *maritji*, 'too much run about,' and who will not remain with her own husband, in order to 'make a big row come out,' i.e. in order to bring down vengeance upon her head.

Certain inconsistencies in these passages are worth remarking. In the first place Thomson states that the increase rite is believed to give rise to babies in no more literal sense than the increase rites performed at any other totem centre give rise *directly* to animals, all it is believed that the increase rites achieve is a state of ritual well-being. In the second place Thomson states that as this rite is performed the names are mentioned of places or individuals to whom 'it is desired to send babies'. Clearly the latter statement would suggest that spirit babies actually exist at the baby totem centres; the account which Miss McConnel gives of them and the practices associated with them certainly lends some support to such a notion, and so, too, does Thomson's own account of the myth relating to the creation of these centres, for according to this myth when the baby totem ancestors had completed their task 'they left their children' at what is now the totem centre.[56] Further, it is believed that:[57]

Every living member of the Ornyau'wa clan is represented by a tree that springs up in the totem centre. This tree starts to grow as soon as a woman becomes pregnant, and continues to grow throughout the life of an individual. . . .

My informants cited an actual instance in which a tree associated with an Ornyau'wa man had been cut during his lifetime. The tree withered and gradually died; when it commenced to wither the man sickened, and as the tree dried up and slowly died, so the man declined and died too.

Such facts would indicate that there exists an association between the individual and this totem centre somewhat more profound than is suggested by Thomson's statement concerning the ritual state of well-being which causes the totem animal to multiply. Indeed, from Thomson's account it looks very much as if the individual is regarded as the incarnation of a spirit-child, and that the knowledge of the relationship between intercourse and childbirth is actually limited to the notion that the *body* and not the spirit is the result of intercourse. This, too, may be the explanation of Warner's discovery that along with the beliefs in spirit conception it is also believed that seminal fluid makes babies, that is, the body of babies. Upon such a view the picture which Thomson draws becomes a comprehensible one, however difficult otherwise. The evidence cited by Thomson relating to the Wik-Munkan understanding of procreation is conclusive on the corporeal aspect of the subject, but on the spiritual side it is quite inconclusive.

It may be pointed out here that the role which the seminal fluid is believed to play in building up the body of the embryo reads suspiciously like the New Guinea notion of these things, and similarly the belief that it is necessary for the father to lie repeatedly with the mother that the body may be built up during the prenatal period is a widespread New Guinea belief, occurring also over a wide area of Melanesia.[58] We have already discussed the matter of Papuan influences in this region of Australia in connection with the Koko Ya'o, and there can be no doubt whatever that similar influences have been at work among the Wik-Munkan, a fact which Thomson himself is careful to point out in his description of the culture as a whole.[59] It seems to me probable that the idea of the necessity of repeated intercourse for the building up of the body of the fœtus, the function of the seminal fluid, as well as certain other related ideas represents the Papuan contribution to the spirit conception beliefs which are still to be found in this part of Australia.

The following account by Sharp of the procreative beliefs of another Cape York tribe, the Yir-Yiront who live along the western coast of Cape York Peninsula in the vicinity of the mouth of the Coleman River, is also of interest because whilst on the whole following the general pattern of the procreative beliefs of other Australian tribes, there is some indication that some foreign influence has been at work here also.

For each clan there is one watery spirit centre situated on the clan domain in a lagoon, creek, or bit of the sea. Here a particular male or female ancestor of the clan resides, whose responsibility it is to send out all the 'spirit children' which will be born into the clan. These derive from an inexhaustible store, are transformed into some active natural object such as a leech, snake, small fish, whirlwind, turtle, etc., which can enter the body of the mother after it has been seen or 'found' by the mother herself or by the real or classificatory father, who sends it on to the mother. There is no dreaming associated with conception, which may or may not be one of the multiple totems of the child's clan. The native states that children are sent out from the spirit centres only when people copulate; but it is not the intercourse, but rather the immigration of the 'spirit child' which causes a pregnancy. 'Spirit children' are sent out without consideration of the regularity or irregularity of the parents' marriage. When a woman discovers her pregnancy, the circumstances of the 'finding' of the natural agent, which may have been several months previous, are remembered by the mother or by the father. Since the responsible ancestor sends 'spirit children' only of his own clan to the countries of his own clan in his own tribe, the resultant offspring is affiliated with the clan in whose country the natural agent was 'found'. With the aid of various obvious fictions, the 'spirit child' is usually found in the clan country of the child's real father.[60]

The present members of the clan mirror the past of the ancestors in names, personal characteristics, and relationships. An individual has his 'own' ancestor, a kind of *alter ego*, whose name he bears, who is physically like him, whose wife is his wife, and whose children are his children. A man calls his ancestral twin 'younger brother'; he also thinks of himself as his own 'younger brother', apparently unaware of the philosophical subtleties involved. The modern individual is not a reincarnation of the ancestor, they have no 'soul stuff' in common, nor has the 'spirit child' from which a man develops any connection with the ancestral double. The individuals and the relationships of present society thus recreate exactly the past society, just as the rites recreate ancestral activities.[61]

In an earlier passage Sharp states that the mother 'is the

disciplinarian, the father avoiding the responsibility by pointing out that the child belongs to the mother "by blood" '.[62]

The organization of the tribe follows a simple patrilineal pattern, yet paternity seems to be recognized as a purely social matter, while maternity is regarded as a primarily physical condition. The father it would appear has nothing whatever to do with the physical being of the child. Children emanate from an inexhaustible supply which the clan ancestors regulate. When they send out spirit-children these undergo incarnation in the proper women through the agency of some natural object, but only after they have been 'found' either by the mother herself or by the real or a classificatory father, in the latter cases the spirit-child is sent along to the woman by either of the men. Clearly then, the spirit-child is regarded as an entity quite independent in origin both of man and woman. The real father of a child is the man who 'finds' the spirit-child, whether he is the actual husband of the woman to whom it is born or not, but if he happens to be a classificatory father, he remains so, and the child is brought up in the family into which it is born, that is, the immediate family of the mother and her actual husband. The clan membership of the child's real father will, however, determine that of the child. And as Sharp remarks, 'The position of a given man's children is thus fixed as regards the kinship system, but [remains] variable as regards the clans.'[63] The mother of the child is obviously regarded as the host in which the spirit-child undergoes development, and this is apparently construed as a physical process which endows the relationship between mother and child with a value of a physical order, which cannot be the case in respect of the process of 'finding' which determines paternity. A most highly original set of views.

The belief that spirit-children are sent out from the spirit centres when people copulate is the belief I had in mind when I suggested that there was some indication that some external influence had probably been at work here in determining the beliefs of the Yir-Yiront. Obviously, however, this 'influence', whatever it may have been, can have been but of slight duration and produced but the slightest of effects; these effects, however, were sufficient to establish a connection between sexual intercourse and the sending out of the spirit-children from the spirit-centres. This is merely a suggestion, and as an explanation there is no very cogent reason for considering it as more probable than any other, for it is quite possible that the association was arrived at by the Yir-Yiront independently of any outside influences. We have already seen that intercourse regarded as in some way a preliminary to the entrance of a spirit-child into a woman is to be found among the tribes of the interior of Australia. Among these tribes, as among the Yir-Yiront, intercourse is not regarded as a cause of conception, but as an indirect condition thereof. It is even quite possible that the Yir-Yiront belief is also held by the Central tribes, but there is no actual evidence of this, although it may well be that the point has been overlooked.

Since the Yir-Yiront have no knowledge of the actual relationship between intercourse and pregnancy, it seems highly probable that the belief that children are sent out from the spirit-centres only when people copulate, represents the much modified form of a belief that was originally, in a much fuller form, introduced into the tribe by some extraneous people.

Elsewhere Sharp writes:[64]

I know of only one area in Australia to-day where it would be possible to get native ideas on procreation wholly uncontaminated by European concepts, and that area* has not been worked anthropologically and for a number of reasons probably won't be until mission influence reaches it. Elsewhere the natives, though they may never have seen a white man, know many of his beliefs, including those relating to the mechanics of reproduction. The missions especially, confronted with the problem of pregnant widows or unmarried girls who claim to have 'found' without having had any recent contact with males, in other words without having 'committed sin', have been at pains to explain the European point of view. Such a statement of fact by the all-knowing white has naturally impressed the native,[65] and is known even among the wilder bush tribes such as those I worked with my second season. This, of course, complicates the problem of the field worker investigating the matter, and means that his conclusions regarding the original, pre-European beliefs of the natives can be little more than a matter of his own opinion.

While details vary from region to region, the basic general belief of the various groups with which I have dealt is that conception occurs when a spirit baby enters a woman's body (not necessarily through the vagina), and materializes in the womb. Such a conception may be an entirely private experience on the part of the woman concerned. Nowhere was the male thought of as impregnating the female, as placing the spirit baby in the women through intercourse. There are no spirit babies in seminal fluid, any more than there are in other body fluids. Young girls and old women, as well as many of those of middle age, have regular intercourse with men, but have no babies, as everyone knows. In the community I know best, of 123 post-puberal females who have been regularly married more than a year, twenty-six have definitely never given birth to a child and, so far as could be discovered, never conceived. Women may thus have

* Bentinck Island at the base of the Gulf of Carpentaria.

intercourse with men, but they do not conceive unless a spirit baby enters them.

There is, however, a vague recognition of a very general relationship between intercourse and conception or the finding of a spirit baby. It is generally admitted that if a woman never had any intercourse, she would not find a spirit child. The people with whom I did most of my work believed that ancestral spirits sent out spirit children, and stated that these were sent only to women who have had intercourse. But they would be perfectly willing to believe it possible for a woman to conceive who had had no intercourse for several years. They know, however, that in the normal course of events it would be only the very young, the very old, or the diseased who would go for any length of time without intercourse, and there would be other more obvious reasons than the lack of intercourse to explain why such women did not conceive. An association between sexual activities and conception is found in areas where linked, multiple totems are in vogue, where subjects connected with sex and with birth and young children are normally linked together as totems of the same clan. Thus the Yir-Yiront Rain clan numbers among its totems the male and female genitals in their several parts and conditions, menstruation and menstrual blood, semen, urine, the anus, fæces, the act of defecation, the act of bearing a child, afterbirth, umbilicus, breasts and milk, and young children in general. Such a complex of associations may be based primarily on anatomical relationships. When it comes to a question of the cause of conception in animals, who have no spirit babies, the native simply gives up; but in discussing the matter, he always points out that animals copulate and that this must have something to do with the arrival of the young. In my opinion, the original idea of the natives with whom I have come in contact is that intercourse prepares a woman for conception, but does not in any specific instance cause it.

I myself have never thought these conceptional beliefs so amazing, and after working with aboriginals for almost three years I still fail to see why the fact that they lack precise information on the physiology of procreation should by some be considered as an indication that they must be moronic. Their ideas of many other natural processes are just as vague. For them sex is a pleasant and exciting pastime which goes on practically all the time between all adult men and all adult women, married or not. While all women participate in sexual activity, quite distinct is the business of having babies, which is peculiarly woman's own private mysterious affair, many aspects of which are tabu to males; and not all women have babies.

It is true that the spirit baby beliefs, in their various forms, have a definite sociological function in associating a child with a pater, actual or classificatory, that is with the mother's husband, irrespective of the genitor. This is especially the case where a child is linked to a patrilineal group through spirit baby beliefs. But whether, in this situation, the beliefs are cause or effect I certainly would not attempt to answer. I see no reason for believing that the aboriginals ever knew more about procreation than they do to-day, just as I see no reason for astonishment that they know as little as they do to-day.

In a later communication Sharp writes:[66]

I should think that the present general association of intercourse and infants might as well be interpreted as a move towards belief in a causal connection as away from such a belief. Either interpretation seems perfectly possible, and both equally hypothetical. Spirit conception beliefs do have the definite social function of linking a child with a particular totemic complex; but this and other aspects of aboriginal philosophy could be achieved, I believe, without the necessary repression of a knowledge of procreation. At least, I see nothing in the native philosophy which would demand such a repression.

Miss Ursula McConnel has reported a moon legend, which is of interest here, told her by one of the last of the older men of the Koko-yalunyu or Koko-yilbur tribe on the Bloomfield River in North Queensland.[67] The legend tells how the moon, Gidja, was a man in the olden days, and there not being any women he transformed a boy to be a wife unto him, and then,

By and by Gidja looked round for something with which to make a *boban* (piccaninny). He took bark from the bloodwood and milkwood trees and crushed them, extracting the red and white juices. These he put inside Yalungur* through the orifice which he had made and pushed them up as far as he could. The milk (*djiwan*) came up into Yalungur's breasts and made them swell like a woman's and the blood (*mula*) stayed where Gidja put it. Then Gidja picked the crimson flowers of the bottlebrush (*yumor*) that grows in the river bed and the scarlet blossoms of the flame trees (*nagun* and *waubara*) that grow in the scrub. He put them into a string dilly-bag (*ngunyan*), mixed them together with some yams. He took also a long-shaped yam (*bambaiyal*) and a round-shaped yam (*kauwa*), and all these he pushed inside Yalungur. Then Gidja worked away, worked away (*djambi*),† mixed and mixed, but no child (*kangal*) came yet. So Gidja tried another kind of yam (*maugadji*) and put that inside

---

* A young Koko-yimoji man (Endeavour River), whom Gidja converted into a woman.
† The use of the word *djambi* (penis) here, and the accompanying explanation that 'Gidja was naughty along that woman' reveals the nature of Gidja's activity.

Yalungur to make the passage slippery* and tried again. Then Gidja said, 'That's right now!—*kangal* come now all right!' And by 'sun-up' (midday) the Moon's *kangal* was big inside Yalungur. Gidja stayed with Yalungur all day, and by sun-down the Moon's *kangal* was 'close-up' born.

Gidja made a *kangal* in one day. No one else can make them like that. It takes other men many months to make a *kangal*. If Gidja had not made a woman like that, men would have no wives, no one to make *mara*† etc., and no children. Gidja made a woman the first time, and now men have all these things.[68]

Commenting upon this legend, the significant part of which I have alone given here, Miss McConnel writes:[69]

The introduction of the word *djambi* into this account of the Moon's creative activities shows that the sex-contact is considered a necessary part of the process. This is particularly interesting in view of the fact that in most cases the Australian aborigine is believed to be ignorant of this fact. The Koko-yalunyu quite definitely consider sex-contact to be necessary to child-bearing. They frankly admit, however, that they do not understand *in what way* it is necessary. Observation of plant and animal life is limited to processes that are visible to the naked eye, and I found nothing analogous to a theory of fertilization of the ovum.‡ The nearest approach to this idea appeared to be that the materials put into the woman by Gidja were created by sex-activity into the human form of the baby and that since Gidja used this means in the beginning, it is necessary to follow his example. Gidja is a *deus ex machina* who set the ball rolling and now things happen so. This explanation is, however, too remote and impersonal for the facts of more intimate personal experience. An 'accidental' element enters into individual cases which cannot be explained in terms of Gidja's established order. Men and women marry but they cannot bear children at will, Yalungur is requisitioned as a link with Gidja's creation. She sends the babies to their mothers and so is the mystic cause in individual cases. Thus women experience those mysterious visitations of the *mulgal-mulgal* (unborn babies)—butterflies, suggestively hovering as if seeking someone; an unexpectedly-filled dilly-bag when the mind is preoccupied; the sudden appearance and disappearance of a snake, and a quarrel in the camp. These experiences, followed by an awareness of pregnancy, are remembered and interpreted as the cause of pregnancy, being attributed to the presence of a *mulgal-mulgal* that was seeking and has now

---

* A comment 'to make it easy for the baban to be born' was volunteered here.
† A fine white flour from the fruit of the macrozamia.
‡ They said that they had heard that 'yarn', but whilst showing interest in the white man's ideas, they maintained a tentative attitude towards them (Mc).

found a mother. Such stories are easily credited and gain currency when other explanations are lacking, and the snake, the butterfly, and the quickly-filled dilly-bag, the quarrel, and the husband's beating are regarded as omens.

Miss McConnel tells us that 'the Koko-yalunyu quite definitely consider sex-contact to be necessary to child-bearing', but she adds that the moon-legend explanation is 'too remote and impersonal for the facts of more intimate personal experience'. These facts are the elements which Miss McConnel terms 'accidental', such as the association of pregnancy with the visitation of the unborn babies, the *mulgal-mulgal*, in the form of snakes, butterflies, etc. It is Yalungur from whom these unborn babies emanate, and it is she who sends them to the women. Thus, we have here the typical form of the Australian beliefs relating to procreation. Children are conceived not as the result of an act of intercourse, but as the result of the will of an ancestor, 'the mystic cause', from whom they originate and who causes them to undergo incarnation in the women. Sex contact is a condition of pregnancy, but not the cause of it. Gidja did thus in the beginning, and therefore one does similarly now, but it is quite clear that the Aborigines do not understand what the connection is between an act of intercourse and pregnancy, they do not know '*in what way*' intercourse is necessary. Intercourse has something to do with pregnancy, no doubt, but exactly what remains obscure, and would not, it would seem, be of much concern to the native. Apparently intercourse is regarded as a condition which makes the entry of an unborn baby into a woman possible, but clearly the unborn baby comes neither from the man nor the woman, but from the ancestral Yalungur.

Whatever their theories may be, the important point of course here is that these natives do not regard intercourse as the cause of conception but only as a condition thereof. And such a belief, in varying degrees, we have already encountered among other Australian tribes.

There is nothing, therefore, that is at all aberrant or extraordinary in the procreative beliefs of the Koko-yalunyu.

NOTES

1   'Superstition, magic, and medicine', N. Qld Ethnography, *Bulletin* no. 5.
2   Among the Narrinyeri of South Australia, the culture hero Warungari is said to have been produced from his mother's excrements. See Taplin, *The Folklore . . . of the South Australian Aborigines*, 38.
3   Roth, op. cit., 16.

4   Ibid., 17.

5   Ibid., 22.

6   Ibid.

7   Ibid., 23.

8   Ibid.

9   Ibid., 18.

10   Of the Kabi tribe of the Bennett district of Queensland J. Mathew writes, 'individual men would tell you upon inquiry that they believed that death was the last of them. In other words, a man's personality died with his body and was not continued in his ghost', *Eaglehawk and Crow*, 146.

11   Roth, op. cit., 18.

12   Ibid.

13   *The Dyirbal Language of North Queensland.*

14   'Virgin birth', *Man*, n.s. 3, 1968, 653–4.

15   For a lively and highly informative discussion of the subject under the title 'Virgin birth', see E. R. Leach, *Proc. RAI*, 1966, 39–49; D. M. Schneider, *Man*, n.s. 3, 1968, 126–9; P. M. Kaberry, *Man*, n.s. 3, 1968, 129; M. E. Spiro, *Man*, n.s. 3, 242–61; H. A. Powell, *Man*, n.s. 3, 1968, 651–3; K. O. L. Burridge, *Man*, n.s. 3, 1968, 654–5; E. Leach, *Man*, n.s. 3, 1968, 655–6; E. G. Schwimmer, *Man*, n.s. 4, 1969, 132–3; S. Montague, 'Trobriand kinship and the virgin birth controversy', *Man*, n.s. 6, 1971, 353–68; M. Spiro, *Man*, n.s. 7, 1972, 315–16.

16   See pp. 219–21.

17   J. G. Frazer, 'Beliefs and customs of the Australian Aborigines', *Man*, 9, 1909, 146.

18   R. H. Mathews, 'Ethnological notes on the Aboriginal tribes of Queensland', *Qld Geogr. J.*, n.s. 20, 1905, 73; 'Notes on some native tribes of Australia', *Amer. Antiquarian*, 28, 1906, 144.

19   U. McConnel, 'The Wik-Munkan tribe', part ii, *Oceania*, 1, 1930, 187.

20   Ibid., 200.

21   *The Arunta*, i, 31; ii, Appendix E, 597–9.

22   D. F. Thomson, 'The hero cult, initiation, and totemism on Cape York', *JRAI*, 63, 1933, 460.

23   Ibid., 461.

24   Ibid.

25   Ibid., 461–3.

26   Ibid., 492.

27   Ibid., 493.

28   Ibid., 493.

29   Ibid.

30   Ibid., 497–8.

31   Ibid., 498–9.

32   Ibid., 501.

33   Ibid., 501–2.

34   Ibid., 503.

35   Ibid., 506–7.

36   Ibid., 507.

37   *Totemism and Exogamy*, i, 3, 336, 337.

38   Thomson, op. cit., 508–9.

39   See pp. 204–5.

40   Ibid., 504.

41   A. C. Haddon, *Reports of the Cambridge Anthropological Expedition to Torres Straits*, 5, 1904, 220–1, 6, 1908, 45, 1, 1935, 272–8.

42   W. E. Roth, 'Transport and trade', N. Qld Ethnography, *Bulletin* no. 14; A. C. Haddon, op. cit., 1, 1935, 272–8; R. Hamlyn-Harris, 'Some anthropological considerations of Queensland and the history of its ethnography', *J. Roy. Soc. Qld*, 29, 1917, 1–44; U. H. McConnel, 'Totemic hero-cults in Cape York Peninsula, North Queensland', *Oceania*, 6, 1936, 452–77; W. Lloyd Warner, 'Malay influence on the Aboriginal cultures of north-eastern Arnhem Land', *Oceania*, 2, 1932, 476–95.

43 Loc. cit., i, 272–8; McConnel, loc. cit., 452 sqq.
44 D. F. Thomson, 'Fatherhood in the Wik-Monkan tribe', *Amer. Anthrop.*, n.s. 38, 1936, 374–93.
45 Ibid., 375.
46 Ibid.
47 Ibid., 390.
48 Ibid., 388–9.
49 Ibid., 391–2.
50 Ibid., 381.
51 Ibid., 384.
52 Ibid., 377.
53 Ibid., 375.
54 Ibid., 393.
55 Ibid., 391.
56 Ibid., 390.
57 Ibid., 391.
58 B. Malinowski, *The Sexual Life of Savages*, 176; M. Mead, *Sex and Temperament*, 31–2; G. Landtman, *The Kiwai Papuans of British New Guinea*, 230.
59 Thomson, loc. cit., 392, 509.
60 L. Sharp, 'Ritual life and economics of the Yir-Yoront of Cape York Peninsula', *Oceania*, 5, 1934, 23–4.
61 Ibid., 22–3.
62 'Social organization of the Yir-Yoront tribe', *Oceania*, 4, 1934, 426.
63 'Ritual life', 24.
64 In a letter to the author dated 16 June 1936.
65 It may here be noted that the Bishop of North Queensland, Dr Frodsham, was of another opinion, for he informed J. G. Frazer that 'by all the tribes with which he is acquainted both in North Queensland and in Central Australia, including the Arunta; not only are the natives in their savage state ignorant of the true cause of conception, but they do not readily believe it even after their admission into mission stations, and their incredulity has to be reckoned with in the efforts of the clergy to introduce a higher standard of sexual morality among them'. J. G. Frazer, *Totemism and Exogamy*, i, 576–7.
66 Letter to the author dated 3 July 1936.
67 U. McConnel, 'A moon legend from the Bloomfield River, North Queensland', *Oceania*, 2, 1931, 9–25.
68 Ibid., 11.
69 Ibid., 20–1.

CHAPTER VI

The procreative beliefs of the native tribes of North-Western Australia

The Great *Woolaston* has told me, that Animalcula are dispersed about in *opportune Places*, to be the Seed of all Generations; & the greater *Virgil* has told me, that certain Mares of his Acquaintance were impregnated by a West Wind, which therefore I concluded to be one of those *opportune Places*, & considered it as the proper Vehicle of these floating Embryos.—SIR JOHN HILL, *Lucina sine Concubitu*. A Letter Humbly Address'd to the Royal Society; In Which Is proved by the most Incontestible EVIDENCE, drawn from Reason and Practice, that WOMAN may conceive and be brought to Bed without any Commerce with MAN. London, 1750, 12.

Concerning the beliefs of the Niol-Niol (Nyul-Nyul), H. Klaatsch recorded the following observations:

It was very difficult to get absolutely accurate information from the Niol-Niol regarding their belief in the reincarnation of the soul. But, clearly enough, they accept the existence of the soul before birth. The name given to the soul in this stage is '*Rai*'. The *Rai* are supposed to be sitting in trees, like birds, and to enter the body of a woman independently of sexual intercourse. They also accept the existence of the soul after death, as spirits called '*Njer*' which may be useful to the living relations, but may also sometimes tease them. I never could find out if the *Njer* are transformed into *Rai*.[1]

According to J. R. B. Love the Worora 'believe that the man conceives the spirit of a child in a dream at Woongguru* and is from the original mythological being who is supposed to abide at the place where he went to earth. The man puts the child in the woman, and when the child is born it is named by the father with the name of the Woongguru where he conceived it.'[2]

Writing of the natives of the West Kimberley district of Western Australia, Mrs D. M. Bates states:

The Broome district natives believe that every baby must be dreamed by its father before it comes into the world, and this 'dream baby' is called *ngargalula*. If the *ngargalula* does not appear to its future father, and his wife gives birth to a child, the father does not believe that the child belongs to him, since the *ngargalula* did not come to him. Again, should a man have been separated from his woman for some considerable time, and while he is away from her a *ngargalula* comes to him in his dreams, and should the woman have a baby in the mean-

* A place where the spirit of one of the original creating men or beasts is supposed to reside.

time the man believes the baby to be his *ngargalula* baby, no matter what length of time may have elapsed during which he has been apart from his woman. Procreation does not appear to have anything to do with the birth of the child. A man sleeps, and while he sleeps he dreams, and in his dream a *ngargalula* comes to him, the ground on which he sees it being generally some known part of his father's territory. He sees on the ground near the *ngargalula* some vegetable or animal, or, if he is a sea-coast native, it may be part of the coast within his territory, and a turtle or some fish may be seen near the *ngargalula*. Whatever animal, bird, or fish is seen on the *ngargalula booroo* ('spirit baby's' ground) becomes the individual *jal'nga* or totem of the baby. The little *ngargalula* follows its future father to his camp, and, according to him, is merely 'carried' henceforth by his woman through her mouth or navel. It brings its own totem with it, but later it inherits its father's totems. Its special *booroo* is called its *ngargalula booroo*, and some function connected with the initiation of the boy will take place on the *ngargalula booroo*. Let us suppose that the long edible bean is the boy's *ngargalula* totem. When he has passed some stages of his initiation, he begins to dream the increase of his totem. He dreams his *ngargalula booroo*, and he picks up a branch of the bean and, chewing it, spits all the chewed portions all about him. When the ripening season for the bean comes around a very plentiful supply will ensure from the dream increase.[3]

A very similar account of the beliefs of the native tribes in the same neighbourhood has been given by Professor A. P. Elkin, with whose reports we may now proceed.

Writing of the beliefs of the Karadjeri tribe of the Kimberley Division of North-Western Australia, he states that

according to the theory of conception held by the Karadjeri and every other Kimberley tribe, the father 'finds' or sees in a dream, or may be in a waking vision, the child that his wife is to bear. The country in which he has the dream becomes the *nura** of the child, while a dream associates the child with its totem, its *bugari*.

. . . Karadjeri totemism is a variety of local totemism in that the various *bugari* are definitely associated with particular horde countries or localities, and . . . the dreaming on the part of the father associates the totem of his child, while still a spirit child, with the country in which he 'found' it, which normally should be, or is arranged to be, some part of his own horde country. But while fundamentally the totemism is 'local', the descent is almost always patrilineal.[4]

The following account of the procreative beliefs of the tribes of

* A term used to describe both the spirit-home and the horde country of a child, or any other individual.

Dampier Land is also by Professor Elkin. The tribes specifically referred to are the Djukan in the neighbourhood of Broome, the Ngormbal in the vicinity of Barred Creek, the Djabera-Djaber of Carnot Bay, the Nyul-Nyul from Beagle Bay to near Pender Bay on the west and across the Peninsula to King Sound, the Bardi in the northern corner of the Peninsula above the Nyul-Nyul, and the Djaui on the inhabitable islands at the mouth of King Sound.

The local organization is associated with the belief in pre-existence of spirits. Spirit children, *nagarlala*, sometimes referred to as *rai*, invisible, live in definite centres such as waterholes, springs, trees, and rocks on the land and in the sea. The medicine-men are said to know, through dreams, the whereabouts of these places which are, of course, *rai*. The entry of a spirit child into its mother's womb is always associated with a dream in which the father sees or 'finds' it. Further, according to Nyul-Nyul informants, the spirit child tells the father what its name is to be. It also tells the man that he is to be its father, and asks him where his wife is. Having given the information to the spirit child, he may then take it in his hand and put it down near his wife, or on her navel. It will enter her womb, though not necessarily at once. At the time of the quickening, the woman tells her husband that a child has entered her womb. He then remembers 'finding' the child in the dream.

The tribes of Dampier Land also believe in reincarnation. Some babies, at least, are believed to be the dead reincarnated. Such a spirit child comes to the father in a dream just as the *nagarlala* do, explaining that it wants to be born again, this time as his child, and giving the name it previously bore. The father then washes the spirit child and leaves it in fresh water for three days, after which he puts it near, or sends it to, his wife. It enters her just as a *nagarlala* would do. The washing is reserved for spirits which are being reincarnated. During the period between incarnations, the spirit sojourns at one of the spirit-centres. Some spirits, however, are not reincarnated; they are said to go to Loman, from whence there is no return.[5]

The relationship of the spirit child to the totem may be seen in the following examples: The Bardi informants said that a man sees a little boy or girl, the spirit child, about 10 inches high, on the ground, in a tree, or on a stone. Coming up to him it tells him that it wants the dreamer to be his father, and asks for the whereabouts of the dreamer's wife. Later on, the man dreams that the child is drinking at his wife's breasts. If the mother does not like or want the child, the latter, who realizes the fact, drops a little spear about 4 inches long, which the father, still dreaming, picks up and throws into some wood or a tree from which the spirit child cannot withdraw it. The child then stops with the spear. But some time after this, when the man and his wife are walking about seeking food, the former may throw his spear at a turtle, fish, kangaroo or some other game but when he pulls the spear out of what he believes to be a turtle or some other creature he sees the spirit child, who then passes between his legs and enters the wife, who is following not far behind her husband. According to my informants, the spirit child has grasped the turtle, *etc.*, which, however, really was not an animal at all, but a spirit child. This is somewhat contradictory; the general impression I received in the Kimberlies was that in such cases the spirit child took the form of the particular animal being speared.

Nangor, a Bardi man, dreamt of his eldest son, and later, when hunting, speared what he believed to be a large white fish, *berinan*, but which he discovered was a spirit boy. He told his wife his experience. She was at the time preparing *nalgo*, a native fruit, for eating. That night they both dreamt of the child, and Nangor told him that he did not want him. Later, however, while out collecting honey, Nangor saw a turkey which proved to be this spirit child again, who passed between his legs and entered into his wife. When this son grows up he will eat neither turkey nor *berinan*; they are his *rai*, that is, they were associated with his invisible or *rai* form, and further, they are forbidden, another meaning of the term *rai*; in other words, they are as good as invisible to him.

Nangor himself was conceived as follows: His father was fishing one early morning and picked up a green turtle, at which moment Nangor, then a spirit child, *nagarlala*, caught him by the wrist and followed him out of the water. After his father had dreamt of him several times he threw a spear under his father's leg while his father was asleep, and then entered his mother's womb.

Another Bardi informant calls the spirit child seen by a man after spearing game, *randza*. It follows the man home and enters his wife. A person will neither kill nor eat the species thus associated with his *randza*, for it is all one body and one blood with him. If he did eat it he would be ill. This informant and his father have one kind of fish as totem, while his mother and her father have another. His mother's brother, however, has a different totem from his mother's, namely, a mullet. The reason for this is that his mother's father was visiting another *bor*** where he speared a mullet and the male spirit child appeared. This means, said my informant, that his mother's brother really belonged to another 'father', a man of that *bor*, from whom he was thus 'stolen'. His mother's mother's totem was kangaroo.

---

* A definite subdivision of the tribal territory, each one of which is occupied by a patrilineal horde, the members of which enjoy the hunting rights of their own *bor*, and may not trespass upon the *bor* of others.

The last instance shows not only that the totem is local, but also that a person's totem depends on the place where his pre-existent spirit was 'found' or seen by his father, and that this is closely associated with the mother's experience of conception, for this usually happens in the *bor* of 'finding'. I did not get a similar case from my Nyul-Nyul and Djabera-Djaber informants, and apparently I did not discuss the possibility with them. They were, however, emphatic that the child's totem depends on the father—that the descent of the totem is patrilineal. But this seems to depend upon the patrilineal descent of the horde, or rather of the horde country, for these informants definitely associated the totem with the 'country' of birth, and implied that this was the father's country. In any case, the mother has nothing to do with the descent of the totem. In one case a woman's two children have different totems, neither of which is hers; the reason is that they were sons by different husbands, and were born in different 'countries', each inheriting the totem of the *bor* of his father, which was the *bor* in which he was born. As we have already noticed, the Nyul-Nyul belief regarding conception is that a father 'finds' in a dream the spirit child which is to be incarnated through his wife, and learns its name from it. This is probably the personal name, though it could be the totemic name, but at the time that I was informed of the fact I was unable to find any trace of totemism in the tribe. At the same time, I learned another Nyul-Nyul belief, namely, that a tribal brother might give food to a man's wife, and that a spirit child might follow this into the woman. In such a case the latter's husband will have a dream in which the spirit child tells him that he is not his real father, but that he will have to act as his father, for he, the spirit child, must, through the action of the dreamer's tribal brother, be incarnated through the dreamer's wife. Here again I was at the time up against a blank wall as far as totemism was concerned, but if totemism did exist among the Nyul-Nyul this would apparently mean that this child would have the totem of the tribal brother, that is, of the 'country' where the woman in question experienced conception. If, however, totemism did not exist there, it would, if acquired fit naturally, into the pattern of these spirit-children and conception beliefs.

I have already mentioned the belief in reincarnation. Nangor's second son came not from a *rai*, but from a deceased person, that is, he was a reincarnation. Nangor was returning from an 'inquest' held at the burial place of a man who was his tribal 'son'. On his way home, the spirit of the deceased pulled his belt from behind. He alone saw the spirit, and he did not tell anyone of the incident. The spirit followed him and appeared in several dreams. He watched it and it finally entered the wife, who had accompanied him to the 'inquest'. Again, unfortunately, I do not know definitely the association of this incident with totemism. But the distinction was obviously drawn between a child born from a *rai*, or totem, and one reincarnated. We would expect the person reincarnated to have the totem which he possessed in his previous existence, but the inference from Nangor's information is that a person has a totem only if his conception were associated with a natural species. It may be that Nangor and the Bardi in general had not yet elaborated a complete totemic philosophy. . . . [6]

SPIRIT-DOUBLE

According to Spencer and Gillen the Aranda associate this belief with reincarnation. Klaatsch, however, says that the Nyul-Nyul do not believe in reincarnation, but I, without knowing Klaatsch's conclusion, found that the belief was held by this tribe and also the Bardi, as already stated. Further, one Bardi informant gave me some particulars regarding a spirit-double belief, but he did not associate it with the *tjuruna*. It is connected with the placenta, and like the creature associated with the 'finding' of the pre-existent spirit child, *nagarlala*, is called *rai*. The placenta is interred at a person's birth, but the *rai* associated with it grows up just as the child does, keeping pace with the growth of the latter. It is always the age of the individual, gets sick when he does, and dies when he dies. It usually remains in the individual's own local country, *bor*, even when he is away. It may visit him in a dream and tell him if there is anything wrong happening in his 'country', for the *rai* can travel about, while the incarnated person is tied to one place. *Rai* are otherwise invisible except to medicine-men. They live in the sand—probably all the horde countries of the Bardi have beach frontages—and their sole food is their arm-blood, which, of course, is like themselves, *rai*, invisible and secret. This fact is known, for they are seen in dreams using their arm-blood for this purpose. Superhuman powers are attributed to them. Thus, if a *bindji-bindj*, a piece of pointed pearl shell, is found in a tree that has apparently been struck by lightning, it is believed that a *rai*, a spirit-double, really killed the tree with one of the shells which it keeps in its 'inside'. I suppose it would take a medicine-man to detect this piece of shell, for medicine-men also keep *bindji-bindj* in their 'insides'. Indeed, it is the *rai* of various kinds which gives a medicine-man his powers; thus Nangor said that his son would be a medicine-man, for he had three *rai*, namely, a turkey, a fish, and his spirit-double. This suggests individual totemism. Further, the use of the one term, *rai*, for the spirit-double and the totem associated with the finding of the spirit child, suggests that there might be some relationship between the two.[7]

The Ungarinyin tribe of the Hann River region believe that

A father always 'finds' his child in a dream in association with water, either in a water-hole or in the falling rain. Even if, in the first instance, as sometimes happens, he 'finds' his child in water in waking life, he will see it in a dream later on when he is asleep in his camp. In his dream he sees the spirit child standing at his head, and catches it in his hand, after which it enters his wife. If he be away from his camp at the time of this dream experience, he ties the spirit child in his hair, and so brings it home to his wife. This takes place at the time of the quickening. The 'finding', however, is not haphazard. It is always connected with definite spirit-centres which are *ungud*;* thus, spirit children belong to the mythical age. This is what natives mean when, for want of better command of English, they say that the pre-existent spirits are *made* by *ungud*; when pressed for further explanation, they can only deny that this action occurs up above, 'on top', on the sky, in spite of the fact that the rain comes down from above, and that the rainbow-serpent, also called *ungud*, as well as *wondzad*, is said to bring the spirit children. They feel that having stated that the matter is *ungud*, nothing more need be said.

Now, *wondzad* is also a term for a large quiet edible snake or python, which, however, is also mythical, that is *ungud*, and as such is said to be the *kian*, mate of *wondzina*. The latter is the main subject represented on the cave picture galleries of the Ungarinyin and Wurara tribes, one of which is situated in each *tambun*.† *Wondzina*, whether represented by a head only, or with part or all of the body as well, is always depicted with a nose and eyes, and a special headdress, but without a mouth. Primarily, he represents the source of rain, and if his painting is retouched, rain will fall, though this should not be done until the commencement of the normal wet season. It does not seem to matter in what *tambun* gallery the *wondzina* painting be thus retouched; rain will come. But one *wondzina*, the one in the gallery of the Kalarungeri horde which has for its totem *kolini*, rain, is of special importance in this regard. The headman is able to usher in the wet season by merely dreaming that he has visited this rock-gallery or *bandza*.

Wondzina, however, is not only causally conected with the rain, but also with the increase of natural species, and also of the human race. The belief is that if a species, the increase of which is desired, be depicted on a *wondzina* gallery, the increase is assured. But this is not done haphazardly. The species painted on the gallery of any

* The dim mythological past, the equivalent of the *Alchera* of the Arunta.
† An individual's horde country, usually that of his father. For an account of these galleries and a discussion of the *wondzina* beliefs, see A. P. Elkin, 'Rock paintings of North-west Australia', *Oceania*, 1, 1930, 257–79.

tambun are the totems of the horde, and, of course, the painting and retouching is done by fully initiated members of the horde, for the galleries are secret. Thus, the life and increase of any particular totemic species is causally associated with a *wondzina*. The latter may be a generalized life-giving power which is symbolized by the special *wondzina* paintings in each cave-gallery. On the other hand, the *wondzina* at the gallery of each *tambun* may be a different culture-hero of the *ungud*, to be compared with the various *mura-mura* heroes of the mythical age of the Dieri tribe, or the *altjira* heroes of the Aranda *altjiruna*. The natives speak of the *wondzina* of this centre, and the *wondzina* of that centre, and so on, and even compare them with one another with regard to their responses to man's requests. This point has yet to be definitely settled, but according to Mr. Love's interpretation of Wurara mythology, the 'Wonjuna' were the first men who wandered over the earth, making many of the natural features and going into the earth in spots, where their pictures re-mained and their spirits abide for ever.[8] The interpretation of the various *wondzina* as distinct individuals, and not as symbols of a generalized power, is supported by the fact that at three cave-galleries known to me, there are rounded stones which are said to be the testicles of *wondzina*, surely of an individual hero in each case. Further, the *wondzina* paintings at one cave are interpreted as female; if this be correct, they must refer to a culture-heroine whose spirit resides at this site. Incidentally, Mr. Love once heard the grammatical feminine form of 'Wonjuna', namely 'Wonjuninya', being used by Wurara folk. On asking them what it meant, he received the reply 'Woong-guja', which he translates as rock-python, but which he also says is the feminine form of 'Woongguru', an ancestral spirit-place, and 'Woongguri', an ancestral male being. . . .

The female *wondzina* gallery which I visited was said to be definitely associated with the increase of the human race. To touch up the painting results in the going forth of spirit children to be 'found' by fathers and incarnated through the wives. In this case the 'mechanism' for the increase of mankind is the same as for the in-crease of natural species. Other *wondzina*, whether classed as feminine or not, are also regarded as sources or guardians of spirit children. A particular *wondzina* may be asked in a dream for a spirit child, or a *wondzina* might offer one to a man as he is dreaming. Moreover, some *wondzina* are said to be more liberal in this regard than others. Thus, the pre-existent human spirits are intimately related to the *wondzina* represented on the rock-galleries of the various horde countries, but only a full knowledge of the tribal mythology will determine the nature of this relationship, whether, for example, *wondzina* brought the spirit children to the locality in the *ungud*, or whether they are emanations from him, and so on. However this be, each person has his *ungud* place or spirit-home, which is 'along water', and though this particular site may be some distance from the *wondzina* gallery, yet there is a causal relationship between the two; the pre-existent spirits are in the former because of their association with the *ungud wondzina*.*

An individual, therefore, belongs to his *tambun*, and possesses its totems, because his pre-existent spirit was associated with the *wondzina* of that *tambun*. Generally, his *ungud* place, or spirit-home, the water where his father 'found' him, is situated in his father's horde country, but it might be in another; in the latter case, a person does not seem to have any claim over this *tambun*, or over the *ungud* centre where he was 'found'. If this be correct, his connection with the *ungud* time, also called *lalan*, is through the cave-gallery of his own horde, with its *wondzina* and totems which are represented on it and through the various *ungud* sites of his *tambun*, including his own spirit-home and the 'homes' of the spirits of the totems of his horde. In the Forrest River district, however . . . a person does have the right of residence in the horde country in which his spirit was 'found', whether it be the country of his father or not. The solidarity of the patrilineal horde is apparently stronger in the Ungarinyin tribe than here.[9]

The Unambul, who live to the north of the Ungarinyin in the Kimberley division of north-western Australia, have been well described by Lommel. The members of the tribe have been exposed to missionary and other white influences. Their procreative beliefs are as follows:

All aboriginals refer to *sexual intercourse* as '*play*'. With regard to physical paternity, some deny any relation between the sexual act and pregnancy, while others admit that sexual intercourse has something to do with pregnancy among animals or even among white men, but still deny such a relation in their own case. The latter became clear in a long discussion between a missionary and some aborigines. The missionary wanted to raise the falling birth rate of his

---

* Mr. Love seems to think that in the Wurara tribe, the 'woongguru' or ancestral spirit-places are independent of the 'Wonjuna'. He says that 'every child has a Woongguru, that might be called the birthplace name, or conception-place name. Thus it will be seen that the Wonjuna, the human figures of the cave-paintings, are not the sole progenitors of the present race' (ibid., 4). 'Woongguru', however, is a place 'where the spirit of one of the original creating men or beasts is supposed to abide', and as such is applied to the picture-caves, the Wonjuna-places, as well as to striking natural features associated with the actions of mythical beasts of the past. Moreover, the masculine form of the noun, 'Woongguri', 'includes Wonjuna, and is almost equivalent to Wonjuna' (ibid., 3). As this is so, it may be that the Wonjuna are connected in some way with all spirit children centres (E).

people and was in his innocence admonishing the men to sleep more frequently with their wives. But these men could not see the connection between this sort of 'play' and the birthrate. Only after long discussions they agreed that there might be some connection. The cause of pregnancy in the opinion of the aborigines is a dream. In this dream the soul of the father wanders around in the country and meets somewhere—mostly at the water-place where his own soul has emanated—a so-called spirit-child. After having dreamt a spirit-child in this way, he hands it over in a second dream to his wife. Without a dream they say a woman cannot become pregnant. This dream is often more a vision which occurs during normal daily life. A man 'sees' a little snake or a small fish which disappears as suddenly as it appeared. In this way he becomes aware of 'having found a child'. It is not necessary that he gives this spirit-child to a woman at once, he may keep it for years by 'fastening it into his hair'. These dreams seldom do occur isolated. They are accompanied by others which involve the totemistic beliefs. In the 'child-dream' a man goes back to the place, the Wondjina, the Ungud, from where his own 'soul' originally emanated.[10]

[Lommel comments] The aborigines, ignorant of natural science, see psychic powers at work. They regard sex functions as 'play', and do not realize the consequences of the physical act, even if they admit some knowledge about these facts regarding animals. The necessity of a physical act as a cause of fertility goes unnoticed. They see and realize a psychic event which they call a 'dream'. Possibly fertility and pregnancy among them are not based on a physical act alone but on a psychic disposition as well. Modern research has shown that human fertility is dependent on psychic well-being also. Regarding the life of the aborigines, they are dependent on a psychic atmosphere which is mainly created and controlled by their medicine-men. It may be justifiable to regard psychic factors in their life even more important than modern research has shown them to be in ours.

Consequently the aborigines may be right in claiming that their falling birthrate in recent times is due to the mental disturbance which is caused by the news of the approaching civilization. According to their opinion they 'cannot find the proper dreams' any more which are necessary for fertility, and they explain that they either have to do too much heavy work at the missions and stations and sleep too deeply to dream properly, or that they 'think too much about white men' in their dreams. Possibly the aborigines in this way point out correctly the reason of the falling birthrate: the disturbance of their whole psychic life and their peace of mind by the facts and news of the approaching civilization. In a later phase of contact with civilization the falling birthrate may be easily connected with the infection of veneral disease. In this early stage it may be caused by the lack of the necessary psychic disposition.

On the other hand this dream may not only be a condition of fatherhood and pregnancy but at the same time a consequence of it. Instead of realizing the facts of pregnancy or fatherhood by way of the conscious mind, these realities may come by way of the subconscious, that is by dreams which express these realities. That there exists in their subconscious mind some idea of physiological paternity is betrayed by their language. The word for sperm, 'wondjir', is obviously connected with 'Wondjina', the god of rain and fertility.

So perhaps we can leave the question of knowledge about physical paternity to the division of the human mind into a conscious and a subconscious part. There is in this case no conscious knowledge of it, but a subconscious idea which expresses itself in dreams and symbols.[11]

In a later communication Lommel interestingly returns to the discussion of these points:[12]

Many conversations with aborigines suggested that rumours and tales of modern culture, as well as merely superficial contact with it destroy not only their concept of the universe but also upset their psychic balance enough to diminish their reproductive abilities. The missionary of Kunmunja, the late Rev. J. B. Love, who had concentrated around his mission almost the whole Worora of over 200 persons, clearly saw that it was dying out fast: only about one-tenth of the whole population was under 20 years. There were, however, no discernible material reasons for this state of affairs. Economic conditions were excellent and the mission kept a close eye on sanitary conditions. The missionary talked things over with the men and several times did so in my presence. It became clear that the aborigines regarded a special psychic disposition, which they called a 'dream', as the cause of pregnancy. Intimations to have more frequent intercourse with their wives remained meaningless to them. There, in the mission, the problem of ignorance of physical paternity did not exist. The physical facts had been brought to their knowledge by discussions with white persons, but still they regarded those facts from a different point of view. To them the physical act of generation was more or less insignificant; the accent was on a psychic condition—a dream—which they regarded as being of biological importance concerning their procreative disposition.

Men of the hinterland who had almost no contact with whites referred to those dreams as the one and only, or at least the main, reason of paternity. Those who had talked about these questions with white persons frequently still insisted on the dream as indispensable but admitted that intercourse had also a function. Moreover, they were always ready to state that things might be quite different amongst white people and animals.

These dreams involve all the mythical and totemic ideas. The first and creative beings of their Genesis transformed themselves, dreaming again and again, into the animals and plants which they were creating. One of these things is a mythical snake called Ungud which represents the water. From that snake originates an anthropomorphic called Wondjina, representing rain and fertility. In the depth of wells, which resist the heat of summer, these two beings are incessantly creating so-called spirit children, souls of children to be born.

To beget a child a man has to find such a soul or spirit child first. He finds it in a particular dream in which the name of the spirit child, containing the vital essence of the future child, comes to his conscious mind. The aborigines maintain that to make such a dream possible sleep must not be too heavy. The name of the spirit child goes first to the heart of the dreamer and later into his head; he then is thinking like a white man, that is, he becomes fully conscious of the name. A man lacking strength either in his heart or in his head cannot keep the name and therefore cannot pass on that spirit child to his wife. He then is incapable of begetting a child and will try to borrow a spirit child's name from a medicine-man.

The aborigines declare that such child-dreams have become very rare to-day. Those who work on stations say that heavy work exhausts them so that their sleep becomes too heavy. They cannot catch the name of the spirit child any more. Those of the hinterland say that all their dreams are too much troubled by visions of the white man, of aeroplanes and ships. So they always dream of these things and have no child dreams any more.

Lommel's account of conditions among the Worora, Ungarinyin, and Unambul should leave little doubt as to the nature of their procreative beliefs. Lommel's second account of these beliefs is, perhaps, the most enlightening. From this it is quite clear that the 'dreaming' of the child and the remembering of its name are the 'one and only, or at least the main, reason of paternity'. That this *must* be so was at the time (1950) more than ever evident to the Aborigines. Any suggestion that more frequent intercourse with their wives might put a stop to the calamitously falling birthrate was regarded as meaningless and demonstrably unsound in view of the fact that in spite of intercourse with their wives few children were born.

The remarkable fact is that the explanation given for their falling birthrate by the Aborigines is very much to the point. It is now well established that psychic factors play a significant role in fertility. Unfavourable life experiences, apathy, anxiety or stress may produce marked disturbances in the sexual functions.[13]

Culture represents man's adaptive invention for increasing the ease and rendering more gratifying the means of satisfying his basic and derived needs.[14] It is his adjustive adaptation to his total environment. When, for any reason, that gratification is threatened and the adjustive arrangements of the group are disrupted, its members may be seriously stressed, in the very real physiological sense, and subsequently suffer a profound depression of vital energy, which, in some cases, falling below a certain minimal level, may result in death. The depopulation of Melanesia following the advent of the white man is commonly attributed by authorities to such a cause.[15] The actual physiological changes in animals and human beings exposed to anxiety and alarm-producing conditions have been described by Cannon, Selye, Gantt, and others. Very briefly, the depressing action is produced mainly through the autonomic nervous system, which at first results in an excessive activity of the sympathetico-adrenal axis. This in turn results in exhaustion of the interrelated systems, with the consequence that the circulation begins to fail, with increasing permeability of membranes, separation of the serum from the red blood cells, the agglutination of the latter, passage of the serum through the membranes, with resulting failure of vital organs to receive a sufficient oxygen supply to enable them to maintain their functions. Derangement of protein synthesis and cell membrane pump function, together with large increases in lactic acids, amino acids, fatty acids and phosphoric acids in the blood, further complete a series of metabolic and other changes which may quickly lead to extreme debilitation and death.

The missionary referred to by Lommel, Mr J. R. B. Love, has given a valuable account of the procreative beliefs of the Worora, as follows:[16]

The Worora believe that a man conceives the spirit of a child in a dream. When a child is born, the father waits till it can sit up, to make sure that the child is going to live. He then thinks back to where he imagines he conceived the spirit of this child. There are certain marked localities all over the Worora country that are supposed to be spirit centres for all generations. Most of these spots are near prominent water pools, and so are likely to be used as camping places, though some of them are not near water. Some spots are considered as particularly likely places to get a child spirit. These places are called *wungguru*. In a dream the man sees the rock python coming to him, bearing a child in its mouth. The man takes the child; when the baby is born, the father remembers! where he had the dream that brought him the child. When the baby can sit up, the father tells the mother the name of the place where *he* conceived the child, and the name of this place forthwith is the child's name, and the place is called the child's *wungguru*. . . . The Worora say, when a man dies, he leaves his children behind him; if he has no children, he leaves his *wungguru* behind him. The idea is that a man's spirit is inseparably united to mother earth, at the spot where his father conceived him in a dream, and that this spot, which gave him his life, can give other lives too.

When travelling in the bush with Worora men, they will often point out a place as so-and-so's *wungguru*; and great is the pleasure shown by a man when I can tell him that I saw his *wungguru* in the bush. The whole country of these people is rugged and picturesque, and the *wungguru* is always a remarkable-looking spot, often being a place of rare beauty. Sometimes a man will catch the spirit of a child in a lightning flash, instead of in a vision during sleep.

Some few of the people say that their father saw a vision of his dead father in a dream, instead of the rock python, and the child will then bear the name of the father's father, or of the father's father's sister, if a girl. In this way names may be perpetuated.

The baby girl has a *wungguru* attributed to it, just as the baby boy has. The *wungguru* need not be in the child's own horde territory, but may be anywhere the father has been travelling. At least two men declared that their children were conceived by them in a vision at sea, on the lugger.

One or two men are said to have no *wungguru*, which unfortunate lack accounts for their feeble physique and failure to have properly developed. Tjarangala, the beardless weakling, who killed a kangaroo with a stone, as related earlier, was said to have no *wungguru*, which was the reason why he had not grown strong. Probably he had had a *wungguru*, like all the others, in his early infancy; then, as it became apparent that he was not growing up to the full strength of manhood, he was said to have none.

Love's account of the Worora procreative beliefs enlarges upon those given by Lommel and presents several additional ones not referred to by Lommel. The first of these is that a spirit-child may be caught by the father in a flash of lightning, instead of in a dream. The second is that the father waits till the child is able to sit up, thereby making sure that it is going to live, before he thinks back to where he dreamed it. He apparently had the dream before the child was born, but only remembers this when the child sits up, and it is then that he tells his wife the details of the dream. Finally, a person's *wungguru* may leave him because he is not strong enough. This would suggest that while it is through the *wungguru* that a child comes into being, once that has occurred the *wungguru* need not stay with the individual if it feels that it would be more usefully employed elsewhere. Neither the health, strength, nor body of the individual appears, upon this view, to be dependent upon the *wungguru*, for the body survives, even though it is weak, in these special cases, after the *wungguru* has departed. This, then, would further suggest that either the *wungguru* is not really responsible for anything more than the spiritual part of the individual, or if it is originally also responsible for his body, his physical being, it is not essential that it remain with the body if the individual is to continue to be. It is not the absence of a *wungguru* that weakens him, but rather his weakness that causes it to depart from him.

THE FORREST RIVER TRIBES

Among the Forrest River tribes examined by Elkin, namely the Yeidji, Arnga, Andedja, Wembria, and Wirngir,[17]

The horde country or *gra* is patrilineal; a person has the right of residing or hunting in his father's horde country and bringing his wife to live there, even if his spirit-centre be outside its boundaries. In the latter case a person has the right of residence in two horde countries, his father's, and also the one in which his father 'found' his pre-existent spirit. The term *gra* is used both to denote the horde country and a person's spirit-home, just as *nura* does in the Karadjeri tribe. The spirit *gra* is the place where a person's pre-existent spirit 'sat down along' water, where he was seen by his father, and from which he came when entering his mother at the time of her quickening. It is a small natural feature, always associated with water. The father might see the spirit child in the water when he is walking by, or when he is swimming or fishing. Thus he might appear a fish or crocodile, but when he brings his catch to land, he sees a spirit child instead, so he does not take it home, for it is not really a fish, *etc.* But he might take the spirit child home in his hand and put it alongside his wife, whom it enters, or it might crawl along like a small turtle to the woman who, in her dream, throws dust at it, but does not prevent its entry. The spirit child always enters the woman while she is asleep, but there is no certainty as to the point of entry.

A person's spirit *gra* may be outside the country of his horde, for his father may have 'found him' when on 'walk-about'. Such a person has the right of residence in two horde *gra*, that of his father by descent, and that to which his spirit belongs. Normally, however, a person's spirit-centre is in his father's horde *gra*. Each horde country has several spirit *gra*; for example, Umbalgari contains at least four-teen which I could map. Yura six, and Mararan three. . . .

These spirit-centres play no part in the arrangement of marriages. Probably, too, we should not speak of a spirit *gra* as belonging to a person, but rather of his belonging to it. Reincarnation is not associated with the spirit *gra*, nor, as far as I could gather, is the doctrine held, nor do the dead return to their spirit *gra*. The dead go to *niligu* (=somewhere) in the east. A great man, Bundulmiri, guards the road.

THE DRYSDALE RIVER TRIBES

Among the Unambul, Kambera, Pela, Miwa, Kuna, Uriat, and Taib tribes of the far north-west, the father dreams the spirit-child.[18]

It sometimes happens that one of two own or tribal brothers who of necessity are members of the same moiety and who have become very friendly, being frequently together, may have the spirit-child dream and so become the possessor of the child; but before he passes it on to his wife, if he has any, the other brother may come along and steal the 'spirit-child' from him, or may be followed by the child; this other brother will then give it to his own wife in whom the child will be incarnated. Incidentally even a man without a wife may have the spirit dream and may have his child 'stolen'.

Dom T. Hernández, who has lived among and reported on these seven tribes, states that he has 'known four or five cases of such supposed spirit-children thefts, and the curious thing about it is that the child, when born, belongs to the man who originally had the dream and bears his totemic name.'

Dom Hernández was unable to discover how the Aborigines know when a spirit-child has been 'stolen'. It seems not unlikely that the idea of 'stealing' was developed to account for the fact that while the wife of a man who had found a spirit-child in a dream failed to become *enceinte*, the wife of some other man, who may have had a similar dream a little later, did become pregnant. In order to clarify this point Professor A. P. Elkin 'suggested to Father Hernández that the spirit-child theft belief might be regarded by the aborigines as an explanation of the possibility that a wife might not become pregnant after her husband had dreamt of a spirit-child (i.e. 'found' one in a dream), but that instead, his brother's wife became pregnant. Father Hernández now tells me that this is precisely what is supposed to happen.'[19]

It is quite probable, as Professor Elkin has suggested, that the second man yields his claim to the paternity of the child which has been incarnated in his wife because he has merely dreamed that the child followed him or that his dream was later than the claimant's.

Although the idea of spirit-child 'stealing' has been thus far recorded for some of the tribes of North-Western Australia alone, it may well have occurred among other tribes in Australia, where it would serve as an explanation of the fact of a man's dream spirit-child being incarnated in a woman who was not his own wife. In any event, the concept of 'stealing' serves to underscore the un-physiological nature of the Aborigines' procreative beliefs.

As elsewhere in Australia, spirit-children, among the Drysdale River tribes, abound in specific localities associated with some natural phenomenon. 'No unmarried person can get any of those children, but those that are married have no limitations. The children are theirs for the taking.'[20]

Dom Hernández stated positively that the Drysdale River tribes 'are ignorant of the most elementary physiological aspects of conception'.[21]

THE TRIBES OF THE EASTERN KIMBERLEYS

Among the Djerag, Lunga, Djaru, Malngin, Mirung, and other tribes of the Eastern Kimberleys,[22]

A man dreams that a spirit child approaches him, announcing that it will be incarnated through his wife. Sometime later on he brings some food, such as kangaroo, emu, snake, fish, bird, *etc.*, to camp, but it is so fat that his wife refuses to eat it. Those near by, noticing that when someone else eats a bit of it he or she becomes sick, say that it is not food, but a baby. The spirit child enters the man's wife at the time of quickening, and when born has for its totem the animal, reptile, bird, fish or vegetable that had made the taster sick. This is apparently one of the totems of the particular sub-section to which the child will belong. This implies that the father will use discretion in choosing the food to offer to his wife after having seen the pre-existent child in a dream. The opinion of those around the camp is not really necessary, for a father often knows what his child's totem will be as a result of seeing the pre-existent spirit in the form of the creature which he spears. And apparently he sees what he is pre-disposed to see according to the sub-sectional totemism of the tribe.

Writing of the same tribes, P. M. Kaberry states:[23]

Generally the spiritual genitor (finder of the child) and pater (social father) are one and the same person, but if the genitor chooses to hand over the spirit child to a tribal brother, or if his wife runs away with another man while pregnant, then it is the pater who bestows on the child his own totems, and the right to live and hunt in his own horde country. The man finds the child either in the form of a spirit child or of some animal or fish in the pool. It asks him for a mother: '*Kaga nandaba gire*'; and that night the man dreams that the spirit child is playing with his spears and his wife's paper-bark. In making free with their possessions she may be giving expression to the fact that she is already a member of the family. In the dream, the child enters the woman by the foot, while the latter is asleep. The next morning the man tells his wife that—*yariri jilmi* or 'I bin dreaming spirit child'. Conception and finding do not necessarily coincide: in one instance a child was born four 'moons' or months after the finding.

In a subsequent valuable discussion of totemism in North-West Australia Miss Kaberry describes the spirit-child beliefs of the Wolmeri, Lunga, and Djaru tribes of East and South Kimberley. Miss Kaberry very graphically shows how thoroughly functionally integrated the procreative beliefs of the natives of these tribes are with their social and economic life.

Wandering from one water-pool to another constitutes a most important activity in the lives of the Aboriginal, one, indeed, upon which his life to a considerable extent depends. When the rains fail to come he is utterly dependent upon the scattered rock-holes and soaks in the river bed. Under such circumstances it is not difficult to understand how the dependence upon the fertility powers of rain came to be made the foundation of a rainbow serpent cult, for in this region the rainbow serpent is regarded as one of the most important of totemic ancestors. It was he who first gave man the gift of rain-making rites, and he is believed to dwell at the present time in some of the deeper rock-holes. Depending as much as he does upon the life-sustaining powers of the water in the pools, they have come to be for the black, literally, a source of human life, for in them are spirit-children, placed there by the rainbow serpent in *ŋaruŋgani* [i.e., the mythical past]. The blacks do not understand the true connection between sexual intercourse and conception. They believe that conception occurs only when a man has found a spirit-child in one of the pools, that it is either temporarily incarnated in some fish, bird or animal, or else remains with it, and that it follows the man back to the camp. If a man kills an iguana, and it makes his wife sick on eating it, this fact is attributed to the presence of a spirit-child. Later the man dreams that it has entered his wife, and it will be born as a child. Now a permanent association is established between the child and the food which the natives connect with his conception. Professor Elkin has called this a conception totem, and the native term for it among the Djaru, Lunga, and Wolmeri tribes is *djeriŋ*.

We must remember that to the Aborigine his existence before birth is just as real, in the sense of being an actual fact, as that afterwards. Because he lived in a pool as a spirit-child, and was found there by his father, that pool is singled out from all others as being called his 'little country' (*Wanyego:ara dam*—Lunga term) as distinct from his 'big' or 'horde' country (*noara:m da:m*). Sometimes he may take it as a personal name, but in any case it is a focal point for sentiments of a proprietary and intense character. So that within the circumference of the wide tract of country over which he wanders there is this one place which has a significance reaching back into his pre-natal existence as a spirit-child, and which links him as an individual with the rainbow serpent, who embodies within himself those powers of fertility on which man is dependent. In other words we are confronted once more with this belief in some quality shared by man and the natural forces—a belief which has its own inescapable logic. These spirit-children made by the rainbow serpent, half reptile and half human himself, still preserve their kinship as it were with natural species, in that they can inhabit temporarily the body of some animal, bird, or fish or anything else that is eaten as food. And the nexus between spirit-child and natural species persists through the lifetime of the individual. It is singled out from all other species by a single term—*djeriŋ*, and thus a social identity is bestowed on it.[24]

What is of great interest here is the recognition of sickness as an evidence of conception. Since sickness, vomiting or a feeling of malaise is often a first symptom of pregnancy, any animal that has been eaten immediately prior to its onset will be taken to be the cause of the sickness and of the entry into her of a spirit-child of the particular animal totem. It makes very good sense.

In her book, *Aboriginal Woman, Sacred and Profane*, Dr Kaberry reports her observations on nine Kimberley tribes, the Lunga with whom she spent six months, the Wolmeri with whom she spent three months, and for shorter periods with the Djaru, Miriwun, Malngin, Wula, Kunian, Punaba, and Nyigina.

Of the spirit-child beliefs of these tribes Dr Kaberry writes (pp. 42–5):

These spirit-children, *djinganara:ny*, are not ancestors, as is thought among the Arunta, but were placed in the pools by *Kaleru*, the rainbow serpent in the *ŋaruŋgani* or Time Long Past, before there were any natives. Often they are temporarily incarnated in animals, birds, fish, reptiles, but they also wander over the country, play in the pools, and live on a green weed called *ginda:l*. Descriptions vary; some say *djinganara:ny* are like little children about the size of a walnut; others, that they resemble small red frogs. Conception occurs when one of these enters a woman. Its presence in the food given her by her husband makes her vomit, and later he dreams of it or else of some animal which he associates with it. It enters his wife by the foot and she becomes pregnant. The food which made her ill becomes the *djeriŋ*, conception totem of her child. Scars, moles or dimples are the wounds where some animal or fish was speared by the man.*

Now these beliefs may suggest parallels with the stories of a stork occasionally told to children in our own culture. But they do not spring from any prurience or shame on the subject of sex, which natives were willing to discuss with freedom. They arise out of an ignorance of physical paternity. The husband of the woman is the social father of the child and as a rule its spiritual *genitor*, for it sometimes happens that the woman finds the *djeriŋ* herself or that it is given to her by another man. The latter, however, will not dream of the spirit-child, nor have access to the woman sexually, nor exercise any rights over the child, who will take the country and the totems of the mother's husband.† There were also instances where although the husband himself had found the *djeriŋ*, he did not afterwards dream of the child. But his wife would then assert that she had done so, with the result that the belief in 'spiritual conception' was practically logic-proof.

The relationship with the mother is both social and physical, though this point will be raised later, in view of its contradiction by Dr Ashley Montagu in *Coming Into Being Among the Australian Aborigines*. In this book he has weighed and summed up the evidence for an ignorance of physical paternity, and my own researches confirm his conclusions in this matter. I investigated the problem as exhaustively as possible, and these natives in spite of over thirty years contact with the whites had still no idea of the true relation between sexual intercourse and conception. The Aborigines asserted that a young girl could not bear children; after puberty conception only occurred when a man, generally her husband, found a spirit-child. Questioned on the function of sexual intercourse natives admitted that it prepared the way for the entry of the *djinganara:ny*. 'Him make 'em road belonga picaninny: young girl no got 'em road.' Most women believed that the semen remained in the vagina, and had nothing to do with the child. 'Him nothing,' was the trenchant reply, when after circuitous inquiry I finally suggested the facts of the case.

* In East and South Kimberley (but not at Forrest River), *djinganara:ny* were sometimes associated with material objects and even with dances. A woman might become ill on handling a dilly-bag, or when a corroboree was being performed, or when her husband was fashioning a *tjuruna*. This then became the totem of the child, since it was connected with conception.

† There were only three cases of this in my genealogies. For a similar belief see the writer's report in *Oceania*, 6, 1936, 395. These facts should be noted by those who deny individual parenthood among the Aborigines.

Several women thought that the semen, *ŋandö*, entered the uterus, and that the embryo floated in it 'like a water-lily', as one expressed it. Natives with a hint of ridicule for the illogicality of the white would declare impatiently—'All day me bin sleep along him. Me no more bin catch 'em picaninny.' A Forrest River woman whose child was born some months after her husband's death advanced this as evidence of the irrelevance of sexual intercourse which all natives, apart from its preparatory function, regarded simply as an erotic pastime. My inquiries into the causes of procreation at Forrest River suggested only one other alternative to them—namely, that the woman might find the child; and this they brushed aside with an emphatic denial: 'lubra can't find 'em meself.'

Another belief that the natives possess might be cited as further evidence in this matter. A spirit of the dead may follow a woman about who is wearing string around her neck in mourning for the deceased. It may transfer its attentions to another woman who receives food from the mourner, and enter her to be born as her child. A woman who does not desire pregnancy will refuse to take tea, tobacco, etc., from such a woman. This actually occurred twice during my stay. The attitude towards half-castes should prove a crucial instance, but here again the system proved water-tight. It was asserted that the white man was the father, since the woman was living with him at the time, and that he must have found a spirit-child. The *djeriŋ* was some European food; the *guniŋ*, dream totem, which a person inherits from the father, was open to doubt: 'Might be him whitefellow tucker—tomato, pumpkin, lolly: him no bin tell me.' Pressed about the reason for the resemblance of the child to its father in colouring and features, lubras would say: 'Too much me bin sleep along a him,' and the same explanation was given in the case of full-bloods. By this, my informants meant that it was the constant proximity of the man that externally moulded the child within the womb.*

At Moola Bulla only two old men had some inkling of the facts but their version was not held by the generality of natives. *Kaleru* made the *djinganara:ny* from his semen in the Time Long Past, and then placed them in the pools. Both denied, however, that the semen of a living man had anything to do with conception.

These two men were exceptions. After eighteen months contact with over 500 natives, my conclusions were that they had no empiri-

---

* Spencer in *Native Tribes of the Northern Territory of Australia*, pp. 25–6, mentions that the natives gave as explanation for half-castes: 'too much me bin eat 'em white man's flour'; and he comments that the chief difference in the contact with the white men was not the fact that they had intercourse with (them) instead of blacks, but that they ate white flour and that this naturally affected the colour of their offspring.

cal knowledge of the facts of procreation. This means that a child's relationship with her father is a derivative one; he is the husband of her mother; he has most probably found her as a spirit-child; he rears and protects her; arranges her marriage and bestows on her rights to his horde country and his dream totem. The absence of an explicit recognition of the physical tie does not interfere with the establishment of a strong bond of affection between them.

Apart from their bearing on the mother- and father-child relationship, these beliefs have another context in totemism. . . . Here they are significant for the attitudes they engender towards the child even before it is born. Her background is a spiritual one, for she was a *djinganara:ny* created by *Kaleru*; she was a denizen of the Time Long Past and has now become a human being in the present. The pool in which she was found is one by which her parents have often camped, and which she will now regard as peculiarly her own—her *wanyegoara da:m*. *Ngaruŋgani* provides a sanction for custom and belief; its reality, confirmed by the finding of the *djinganara:ny*, is brought within reach of the individual consciousness or awareness. The story of her finding, the possession of a *djeriŋ* and a specific pool forge a personal link between her and the Time Long Past: a link that is more immediate than that among the Arunta, for the child is not the reincarnation of individuals stretching back in a long line to the *Alchera*. In the Kimberleys she was a *djinganara:ny*, who had been created long ago by one of the totemic ancestors. However, once she has entered a woman she becomes a human being, is called *dja:rgil*, most probably embryo, and after birth is referred to as *guna:l* or infant.

No matter who finds or gives the conception-totem to the mother, and no matter what form it takes, whether food, churinga, or dance, it is the spirit-child, *djinganara:ny*, in the conception totem, *djeriŋ*, that produces conception, and this can be achieved only when the father dreams it or, on occasion, when the mother does so. A man who is not the husband of the mother cannot dream it, and hence cannot be the father of the child.

The great similarity of these North-Western beliefs to those of the Northern tribes described in the previous chapter is striking.

In connection with the belief in reincarnation, we must accept Professor Elkin's statement that the Nyul-Nyul actually have such a belief, though the last word upon this subject has probably not yet been said. The majority of the North-Western tribes would seem to be unacquainted with the doctrine.

NOTES

1 'Some notes on scientific travel amongst the black population of tropical Australia in 1904, 1905, 1906', *Report, 11th Meeting of the Australian Association for the Advancement of Science*, 580; 'Schlussbericht über meine Reise nach Australien in den Jahren 1904–1907', *Zeit. Ethnol.*, 39, 1907, 649–52.

2 J. R. B. Love, 'Rock paintings of the Worrora and their mythological interpretation', *J. Roy. Soc. W. Aust.*, 16, 1929, 4.

3 D. M. Bates, 'Social organization of some Western Australian tribes', *Report, 14th Meeting of the Australian Association for the Advancement of Science*, 389–90.

4 A. P. Elkin, 'Totemism in North-Western Australia (the Kimberley Division)', *Oceania*, 3, 1933, 265–6.

5 Ibid., part ii, *Oceania*, 3, 1933, 438–9.

6 Ibid., 444–7.

7 Ibid., 449–50.

8 J. R. B. Love, 'Rock paintings of the Worrora and their mythological interpretation', 3 sqq. On the rock paintings of the Aborigines, see D. S. Davidson, 'Aboriginal Australian and Tasmanian rock carvings and paintings', *Memoirs of the American Philosophical Society*, 5, 1936, 108–20.

9 A. P. Elkin, 'Totemism in North-Western Australia (the Kimberley Division)', part ii, *Oceania*, 3, 1933, 460–4.

10 A. Lommel, 'Notes on sexual behaviour and initiation, Wunambal tribe, North-Western Australia', *Oceania*, 20, 1949, 162.

11 Ibid., 163–4.

12 A. Lommel, 'Modern culture influences on the Aborigines', *Oceania*, 21, 1950, 16–17.

13 H. Schuermann, 'Über die Zunahme männlicher Fertilitätsstörungen und über die Bedeutung psychischer Einflüsse für die zentralnervöse Regulation der Spermiogenese', *Medizinische Klinik*, 43, 1948, 366–8; H. Gantt, 'Disturbances in sexual functions during periods of stress', in H. G. Wolff *et al.* (eds), *Life Stress and Bodily Disease*, Baltimore, 1950, 1030–50; H. Stieve, *Der Einfluss des Nervens Systems auf Bau- und Tätigkeit der Geschlechtsorgane des Menschen*; H. G. Wolff, *Stress and Disease*, Springfield, Ill., 1968; H. Selye, *Stress*, Montreal, 1950; W. B. Cannon, 'Voodoo death', *Amer. Anthrop.*, n.s. 44, 1942, 169–81; W. H. R. Rivers (ed.), *Essays on the Depopulation of Melanesia*, Cambridge, 1922; D. H. Stott, 'Cultural and natural checks on population growth', in Ashley Montagu (ed.), *Culture and the Evolution of Man*, New York and London, 1962, 354–76; W. Schumer and Richard Sperling, 'Shock and its effect on the cell', *J. Amer. med. Assn*, 205, 1968, 215–19.

14 Ashley Montagu, *The Direction of Human Development*, rev. ed., New York, 1970 and (ed.), *Culture: Man's Adaptive Dimension*.

15 See references in note 13.

16 J. R. B. Love, *Stone-Age Bushmen of To-day*, 113–15.

17 A. P. Elkin, 'Totemism in North-Western Australia (the Kimberley Division)', part ii, *Oceania*, 3, 1933, 472–3.

18 T. Hernández, 'Social organization of the Drysdale River tribes, North-West Australia', *Oceania*, 11, 1941, 219.

19 Ibid. (Elkin's note), 220.

20 T. Hernández, 'Children among the Drysdale River tribes', *Oceania*, 12, 1941, 123.

21 Ibid., 125.

22 A. P. Elkin, 'Totemism in North-Western Australia', *Oceania*, 4, 1933, 57.

23 P. M. Kaberry, 'The Forrest River and Lyne River tribes of North-West Australia; a report on field work', *Oceania*, 5, 1935, 416–17. A more detailed account of these beliefs is given by Miss Kaberry in 'Spirit children and spirit centres of the North Kimberley Division, West Australia', *Oceania*, 6, 1936, 392–400.

24 P. M. Kaberry, 'Totemism in East and South Kimberley, north west Australia', *Oceania*, 8, 1938, 278–9.

CHAPTER VII

The procreative beliefs of the native tribes of Western Australia

By no means now may one parley with him of descent from stock and stone.—Iliad, 22, 126.

The following interesting account of the beliefs of some of the native tribes of Western Australia relating to conception has been given by Mrs Daisy M. Bates.

Totems in the south [of Western Australia] appear to be always given from some circumstance attendant on the birth of children. . . .

'Beyoo' means swollen. 'Beyooran', a female, was so called from the fact of her father missing the whereabouts of a kangaroo he had killed, and finding it in the afternoon all swollen from the sun's heat. The girl's *oobaree* or totem was a kangaroo. Put-bee-yan, a female, was named after a tame opossum which used to make a noise like put-put when coming for its food. Put-bee-yan's totem was an opossum. Baaburgurt's name was given him from his father's observing a sea mullet leaping out of the water and making a noise like Brrr-Baaburr. The kalda or sea mullet is Baabur's totem. Baabur's father and his father's brothers also had 'kalda' as their totem, but his grandfather had different totems.

Nyilgee was named after a swamp wallaby (called Woorark) which her father was about to kill, but in the act of raising his spear the little wallaby escaped. '*Yal'gy yook'an*', the father said, 'if he had only stood a moment longer, I should have got him,' and he called his daughter 'Nyilgeean'; her totem is the Woorark.[1]

When I visited the natives at Beagle Bay (north-west), the women told me that their dead children used to take the form of birds, and frequently come to the mother's camps. These little spirits were supposed to wander among the trees for certain periods.[2]

In various parts of the south there were certain *winytch*, or sacred places, so to speak the dwelling-places of certain *Janga*, or *Kaanya* [the spirits of the dead]. These *winytch* places might be only trees, or rocks, a sandbank, a hill, etc. Whatever they were, the natives in passing them were always careful to strew rushes or boughs near them, thereby propitiating the spirits dwelling there. Any native neglecting this ceremony was sure to die.

In some of these *winytch* places the *Kaanya* took the form of a bird, whose voice was always heard in the vicinity, but whose form no native had ever seen. A standing stone near York had a bird as its *Kaanya*, and a part of the river near Busselton (south-west) was supposed to be inhabited by a Wogal, or mythical snake, and was *winytch* in consequence.

There was a *winytch* place in the Chapel district (south-west), where loud noises, 'like the sound of a fire with a strong wind blowing on it,' were frequently heard. Baabur told me that a native on hearing the noise once ventured near this place, but he only saw the smoke circling round the spot, the smoke being the *Kaanyas*, or spirits, who used this means to conceal the place from whence the noise had proceeded.[3]

According to this account it appears probable that the belief in the incarnation of spirit-children, as well as conceptional totemism, existed among the tribes examined by Mrs Bates, the spirit associated with some animal (or plant?) being incarnated in a woman and born as a child.

It is not altogether clear whether the doctrine of reincarnation was held by the tribes investigated by Mrs Bates. The *winytch* are certainly totem places in which reside the *Kaanya* or spirits of the dead. Each *winytch* is chiefly, however, the abode of a particular totem ancestor. Whether he sends out the spirits of the dead to be reincarnated or not is uncertain, and whether the spirits of the dead children which wander for certain periods among the trees undergo reincarnation subsequently is likewise uncertain; but that children are born as the result of an act of incarnation, at least, would seem to be certain.

The following facts were collected amongst a number of Western Australian tribes by A. Radcliffe-Brown during the year 1911.[4]

The tribes quoted all have totemism with inheritance in the male line. Each totemic clan or group possesses not one, but several totems, that are all equally the totems of every member of the group. A man may eat or kill his totem. The members of a totemic group, men and women alike, take part in certain localized ceremonies (here called *talu*, *tauara*, or *nuka*), which are supposed to produce an abundant supply of the particular totemic animal, plant, or other object with which each ceremony is connected. These ceremonies are similar in many respects to those of Central Australia called by Messrs. Spencer and Gillen *intichiuma*. Only men and women whose totem it is can take any active part in the ceremony for any particular totem. In almost all the tribes quoted it is usual to give a child a personal name that refers in some way, often very obscure, to one or other of his or her totems. There is no trace of any belief in the reincarnation of the dead or of totemic ancestors.

In the Ingarda tribe, at the mouth of the Gascoyne River, I found a belief that a child is the product of some food of which the mother has partaken just before her first sickness in pregnancy. My principal informant on this subject told me that his father had speared a small animal called *bandaru*, probably a bandicoot, but now extinct in this neighbourhood. His mother ate the animal, with the result that she gave birth to my informant. He showed me the mark in his side where, as he said, he had been speared by his father before being eaten by his mother. A little girl was pointed out to me as being the result of her mother eating a domestic cat, and her brother was said to have been produced from a bustard. It may be noted that the girl (the elder of the two) was a half-caste, probably, from appearance, of a Chinese father, and had a hare-lip. The younger brother was a typical blackfellow boy. The bustard was one of the totems of the father of these two children and, therefore, of the children themselves. This, however, seems to have been purely accidental. In most cases the animal to which conception is due is not one of the father's totems. The species that is thus connected with an individual by birth is not in any way sacred to him. He may kill or eat it; he may marry a woman whose conceptional animal is of the same species, and he is not by the accident of his birth entitled to take part in the totemic ceremonies connected with it.

I found traces of this same belief in a number of the tribes north of the Ingarda, but everywhere the belief seemed to be sporadic; that is to say some persons believed in it and others did not. Some individuals could tell me the animal or plant from which they or others were descended, while others did not know or in some cases denied that conception was so caused. There were to be met with, however, some beliefs of the same character. A woman of the Buduna tribe said that native women nowadays bear half-caste children because they eat bread made of white flour. Many of the men believed that conception is due to sexual intercourse, but as these natives have been for many years in contact with the whites this cannot be regarded as satisfactory evidence of the nature of their original beliefs.

In some tribes farther to the north I found a more interesting and better organized system of beliefs. In the Kariera, Namal, and Injibandi tribes the conception of a child is believed to be due to the agency of a particular man, who is not the father. This man is the *wororu* of the child when it is born. There were three different accounts of how the *wororu* produces conception, each of them given to me on several different occasions. According to the first, the man gives some food, either animal or vegetable, to the woman, and she eats this and becomes pregnant. According to the second, the man when he is out hunting kills an animal, preferably a kangaroo or an emu, and as it is dying he tells its spirit or ghost to go to a particular woman. The spirit of the dead animal goes into the woman and is born as a child. The third account is very similar to the last. A hunter, when he has killed a kangaroo or an emu, takes a portion of the fat of the dead animal which he places on one side. This fat turns into what we may speak of as a spirit-baby, and follows the man to his camp. When the man is asleep at night the spirit-baby comes to him and he directs it to enter a certain woman who thus becomes pregnant. When the child is born the man acknowledges that he sent it, and becomes its *wororu*. In practically every case that I examined, some forty in all, the *wororu* of a man or woman was a person standing to him or her in the relation of father's brother, own or tribal. In one case a man had a *wororu* who was his father's sister.

The duties of a man to his *wororu* are very vaguely defined. I was only told that a man 'looks after' his *wororu*, that is performs small services for him, and, perhaps, gives him food. The conceptional animal or plant is not the totem of either the child or the *wororu*. The child has no particular magical connection with the animal from which he is derived. In a very large number of cases that animal is either the kangaroo or the emu.

In one part of the Injibandi tribe I came across another interesting custom. When a woman is in labour the woman who is attending to her mentions one after another and at intervals the names of the pregnant woman's brothers. The name that is mentioned as the child is brought forth is that of the child's *kajadu*. I unfortunately only discovered this custom just as I was concluding the season's work, and was unable to make further inquiries. The custom exists side by side with the *wororu* relationship.

In several tribes I found totemic groups that claimed babies as their totem, and performed totemic ceremonies, the avowed object of which was to provide a plentiful supply of children. I found one such totemic group in each of the following tribes: Baiong, Targari, Ngaluma, Kariera, Namal, and two in the Injibandi tribe. One such group in the Injibandi tribe performs its ceremony at a spot near the Fortescue River, where there is a sort of small cave. According to a legend, in the times long ago, the men and women once left the camp to go hunting, and left all the babies in the camp in the charge of one man. After the others had been gone some time the babies began to cry. This made the man in charge of them very angry, so he took them all to the cave and put them inside and lit a big fire of spinifex grass at the entrance, and so smothered them all. An essential part of the totemic ceremony consists in lighting a fire at the entrance of the cave.

There is a very interesting totemic group in the Kariera tribe. The group has a number of edible objects for totems, and also *wanangura*, whirlwind, *kambuda*, baby, and *puna*, sexual desire. A man who belonged to this group told me when it was decided to attempt to produce an increase of children, the men and women of the totemic group first proceeded to Kalbana and performed the ceremony of the increase of sexual desire, which seems to have consisted of setting fire to the bark of a tree. After this, but only after it, they moved on to Pilgun and performed the ceremony of the baby totem. There is thus perfectly clear evidence, dating back to a time before the coming of the white man, that there is a distinct association in the native mind between sexual desire and the birth of children amongst people who, at the same time, by their *wororu* custom, associated pregnancy with the eating of food. Those who believe that the beliefs of savages are strictly logical will, of course, be shocked at such inconsistency. Those of us, however, who, by actual contact with savages, have learnt that even if they do not heed logical consistency less than uneducated Europeans (or even the educated when their religious beliefs are in question), yet certainly do not heed it more, find in such an inconsistency nothing to surprise us. Finally, it may be noted that there are traces of a belief that the small whirlwinds so common in these parts of Australia may cause a woman to become pregnant. This would explain why the whirlwind, sexual desire, and babies are all associated by being the totems of a single clan.

I may add, to complete the account, two other answers I received to the question, 'Where do babies come from?' One was, 'From the moon', and another, 'The magicians make them and send them into women.' One old man, a magician, and a member of a baby-totem clan, nearly got killed a few years ago because a young woman of the same tribe died in child-birth.

There are several features in this account of the beliefs of the Western Australian tribes investigated by Radcliffe-Brown which appear to be so unusual as to require to be examined here in some detail.

In the first place, according to Radcliffe-Brown, there is said to be among the tribes investigated 'no trace of any belief in reincarnation of the dead or of totemic ancestors'. Children, therefore, do not come into being as the result of the incarnation of a pre-existing being who has already led an earthly existence, but, among the Ingarda, are considered to result directly from the consumption by the mother of a portion of some animal or plant which in some way gives rise to a child. The animal or plant thus concerned is not the totem of the child, the totem being inherited from the clan into which it is born.

The facts as given by Radcliffe-Brown are somewhat meagre, but the associated looseness of the totemic organization of the Ingarda, and the obvious over-simplification of their procreative beliefs, raises the question whether these beliefs were not at one time better organized and more closely integrated with the totemic system than when they were studied by him. The disruptive influences of the white contact would be amply sufficient to explain the condition, especially as some of the Ingarda were already quite willing to believe that intercourse played a significant part in conception. The fact that a child with hare-lip was allowed to live is an anomaly so exceptional that it may be taken to serve as a good indication of the extent to which the integrity of the native beliefs has broken down.

Among the tribes farther north of the Ingarda in which 'the conception of a child is believed to be due to the agency of a particular man, who is not the father', the *wororu* of the child, pregnancy it is believed may be produced either by a man giving a woman some edible object to eat which produces the pregnancy, or when out hunting, the man kills an animal, and as it is dying he tells the spirit or ghost to enter a particular woman, or he may take a portion of the fat of an animal which turns into a spirit-baby which he then directs to enter a certain woman. When the child is born he acknowledges that he is its *wororu*. In almost all cases examined by Radcliffe-Brown the *wororu* stood in relation to the child as father's brother, own or tribal. But in one case, it is of importance to note, 'a man had a *wororu* who was his father's sister', from which bare statement it would appear that a woman who stands in the relation of tribal father's sister to the child can bring about the birth of a child to another woman, generally her brother's wife.

The fact that an individual can cause the spirit or ghost of an animal to enter a woman would suggest that these tribes do believe in the reincarnation of spirit-children, at least of the dead animals who have provided them with their spirit parts. The beliefs described by Radcliffe-Brown indicate, however, that the spirit-part of the dead animal undergoes a complete transformation in the body of the woman, for the conceptional animal or plant is not the totem of the child nor its *wororu*; and there is in no way any connection between them after the child is born. It should be quite clear then that upon such a theory there can be no question of a belief in reincarnation. It does not, in fact, exist.

The baby totems and the increase ceremonies performed in connection with them are interesting because they suggest that babies are still regarded, in these tribes, as primitive beings, who are definitely subject to magical control.

Sexual desire is everywhere regarded as a powerful force capable of working considerable effects upon the individual. In Australia it has a wide, though sporadic, distribution as a totem, being found in the extreme west and in the extreme tip of Cape York Peninsula in the north-east. The fact that the increase of sexual desire ceremony is performed immediately prior to the increase of babies ceremony does not, as Radcliffe-Brown states, necessarily prove 'a distinct association in the native mind between sexual desire and the birth of children', although it may well be that there actually exists such an association in the native mind, but the bare fact that the one ceremony is followed by the other does not prove that such an association exists, and in any event, since the native does not understand the teleology of what he experiences as sexual desire it is difficult to see what association of any import of a sexual nature he can make between the one thing and the other. Whatever, if any, association he does make between the two ceremonies it is definitely not of a sexual nature, for above all things else the native is not usually inconsistent in his beliefs, and certainly it would be for him a difficult matter to attempt to reconcile his procreative beliefs with a knowledge of such a sexual association as Radcliffe-Brown suggests. Totemic increase ceremonies are throughout Australia thoroughly self-contained procedures, and their purpose can only be achieved by the performance of the specific procedures associated with the particular totem; the performance of ceremonies associated with some other totem, even though that performance celebrates events which are in tradition historically connected with another, are quite independent and without the power either to control or to be controlled by that other. In the present instance, however, this does not seem to be the case, and we are bound to assume that there may be some connection between the totem of sexual desire and the totem of babies, but, as I have already said, the connection is not necessarily of a sexual nature. We must not be led astray by the term 'sexual desire'. For the native 'sexual desire' represents a merely propulsive force which enables him to satisfy his impulses, and to enjoy a certain amount of pleasure in doing so, and nothing more.

In connection with this discussion it is of interest to note that among the Arunta, according to Róheim, 'when a man wants to get sexually excited, he will kneel in the same position as the father knelt and stick the porcupine grass into the rock[5] or rather into the earth beside the rock. He will also rub the rock with a stone and then the unborn children will come out of the rock and incarnate themselves in their prospective mothers.'[6] There does not, however, appear to be any connection between the sexual excitement and the emanation of the spirit-children.

NOTES

1   D. M. Bates, 'The marriage laws and some customs of the West Australian Aborigines', *Vict. Geogr. J.*, 23, 1905, 49.
2   Ibid., 57.
3   Ibid., 58–9.
4   'Beliefs concerning childbirth in some Australian tribes', *Man*, 12, 1912, 180–2.
5   That is, the totem stone or *knanja*.
6   G. Róheim, 'Psycho-analysis of primitive cultural types', *Int. J. Psychoanal.*, 13, 1932, 66.

The procreative beliefs of the native tribes of Southern, South-Eastern, and Eastern Australia

In order to understand this economy of Nature, imagine to yourself, Sir, that the whole extent of the air . . . is full of the seeds of everything which can live on earth—BENOIT DE MAILLET, *Telliamed: or the World Explained*, Amsterdam, 1748.

Of the Southern tribes Elkin writes as follows:[1]

The dream totem in all the tribes of the western group in South Australia is the *djugur*; that is, if a person dreams of a *djugur* or local totem, a person belonging to that totem will soon come along to the dreamer. But just west of the north-western corner of this state, the dream totem is the species associated with a person's conception as described below.

All the western tribes of South Australia believe that a definite place (or, perhaps, a few places), called Yualanya, is the abode of pre-existent spirit children. This has nothing to do with the totem of a child. Children of different totems may all come from the one Yualanya. Having left there, some of them are believed to play about on the flowers of the mulga trees. The spirit-home is described as a rock-hole, possibly a cave, containing water, with a sand-hill near by. Women must be very careful how they approach and obtain water at that place, or else child-spirits may enter them.

In the north-eastern part of the area the spirit child changes its sex at incarnation. Thus a woman who dreams that a girl-spirit has entered her womb will give birth to a son.

The tribes of south-east central Western Australia who visit Laverton and Mt. Margaret believe that spirit children enter women in the guise of food. If after having eaten something a woman is sick, and later on dreams of a spirit child, she realizes that when she thought she was eating food a spirit-baby had entered her. Some years after birth the child is informed of its mode of entry into the mother's womb, that is, of the particular article of food (some animal or plant) associated with the mother's first sickness of pregnancy. This animal or plant then becomes the child's totem, that is, his symbol in another person's dream. As far as I could ascertain, no ritual attitude is adopted towards this dream totem.

Informants told me that conception could not take place apart from eating 'child-food'. *Djugur* myths explain the association of spirit children with the foods concerned.

We have only to notice here that in this account there is no evidence of a belief in reincarnation among the tribes of south-east central Western Australia, but among the western South Australian tribes it does not appear from this description whether the belief in reincarnation is present or not.

Writing of the Aborigines of the Ooldea region of western South Australia, Drs Ronald and Catherine Berndt state that they 'believe at the same time in both physiological paternity and in spirit children'.[2]

According to informants there is a water-hole somewhere to the north in the Spinifex country, about which are gathered numbers of spirit children. There is probably one such water-hole to each tribal country, several different names being given by various informants. In each case the children are standing round a fire. These children are visible from a distance; but when the traveller comes closer nothing can be seen.

Married women coming to the rock-hole for water would, if they desired children, sit with legs and feet apart. The unmarried, and those who did not want children, would take care to stand up with their legs close together. One informant said that on occasion a spirit child would follow a woman home to her camp, waiting for a suitable opportunity to enter her. All were sure that each child knew definitely to which woman it should go, but continued further enquiries resulted only in puzzling the women, whose reply was that they 'just knew'.

The spirit children are termed *'di:di* (or *'di:dji) ju'lala* (or *'julan*). It was stressed that a spirit child serves to give life to a child which has already commenced to form in a woman's womb as the result of sexual intercourse.

Since the natives of the Ooldea region have had considerable contact with whites over many years it is difficult to say whether or not they acquired the belief in physiological paternity, to the extent that they have done so, from such influences or whether the belief antedates the appearance of white men.

Mountford writes of the Pitjandjara tribe of western South Australia, that all the surrounding country was linked with the legend of the mythical woman, Kutunga, mother of the spirit children, and her unwanted lover, Milbili, the Lizard-man.[3]

Milbili had pursued Kutunga for some time. He finally caught and raped her at the Niunya rock-holes, where, before he took her away to the north-west, she gave birth to quadruplets, two normal and two deformed infants. Those infants are now boulders; two of them, egg-shaped, contain an inexhaustible supply of spirit children, the little silvery-haired *yulanya*; the other boulders, similar in shape, but more irregular in outline, are the source of all the misshapen babies.

If more children are required by the group, the men strictly shunning the transformed bodies of the deformed infants, go to the *yulanya* stones, and, while chanting a song, place short green twigs between the boulders. The little spirits, stimulated by the chants, leave their home, carrying the *kuran* of a twig, not the twig itself, and visit the camps of the aborigines, looking for desirable mothers. Having made their choice, each *yulanya* waits until the woman is off her guard, enters her body and begins life as a human being. The little spirits are so small that they can only be seen by the medicine-men, who, in fact, sometimes help the spirit children to find mothers. It is practically certain [Mountford adds in a footnote] that these are child increase centres associated with the other ancestral beings, although we did not gather information as specific as as that relating to the *yulanya* (child spirits) of Kutunga.

The legend of Kutunga bearing children following her rape suggests, Mountford thinks, that the Aborigines are, to a limited degree, aware of the facts of procreation, but that they consider these to be relatively unimportant. Mountford continues:[4]

The day Jabiaba took us to see the *yulanya* stones, we asked him to show us how the little child spirits were coaxed from their homes. Although the old man did not refuse, he was very half-hearted about the matter, complaining, as he laid some green twigs between the two boulders,

'Too many *idi* (babies) 'bout camp already; man can't get no sleep night-time.'

The belief of the Pitjendadjara in the supernatural origin of their children tended to confirm the conclusions reached by other workers and myself, that the aborigines did not understand physical paternity; that is, they did not associate the father with the birth of the child. In fact, I have met aborigines who, even though they have been in contact with our civilization for three generations, still hold to their original beliefs.

Mulili, an old lady of the Flinders Range tribe, told me that their spirit children, the *muri*, came from two great mothers, the *maudlanami*, who lived above the blue vault of heaven. The *muri* flew down to the earth like tiny butterflies, fed on the nectar of the gum-tree blossoms during the day, and slept under loose pieces of bark by night, until they found the mother they wanted.

When old Mulili had finished her explanation of human origins, I said to her:

'Well, that's the blackfellow's story of how you came into the world, but do you really think it is the right one? You know what the white-fellow says about it?'

'Yes,' agreed Mulili, 'I know what the white-fellow says, but I don't think he's right. If he is, then married women should be having babies all the time, for they're always living with their husbands.'

'But they don't,' she went on; 'some women have many children, some have few, and some have none at all. The white man can't explain that, but the blackfellow can. If one of our women has a lot of babies, we know she is a favourite of the *muri*, the little children from the sky; if another has only a few children, then only an odd *muri* wants her for a mother; and if a woman hasn't any, then everyone knows that the little spirit children don't like her, and won't use her body to become a human being.'

'No,' concluded the old lady, 'I don't think the white-fellow is right, because he can't explain those things, and we can.'

Mountford concludes:

Old Mulili's argument, coupled with the teachings of the Pitjendadjara people about the spirit children in the *yulanya* stones, indicated that the aborigines were not aware of the true nature of conception and birth. Nevertheless, the incident in the legend of Kutunga and Milbili, where Kutunga had borne children after she had been raped, a direct connection between sexual intercourse and birth, made me wonder if the hypothesis was quite so watertight as I had first thought. It is possible that the aborigines are aware, to a limited degree, of the facts of procreation, but as they are at variance with the doctrines laid down in the legendary stories, the native people consider those physical facts as being relatively unimportant, and accept only their philosophical beliefs, as indeed we do in many phases of our own religious life.

The following account of the procreative beliefs of the Nimbalda tribe who lived (and perhaps still live) in the extreme north of South Australia in the vicinity of Mount Freeling, and are thus neighbours of the Central tribes, is of importance because in the first place it represents the fullest report of the procreative beliefs of an Australian tribe available up to the time of the publication of Spencer and Gillen's first book in 1899, and because, in the second place, it represents one of the most interesting accounts of these beliefs that we have. Published exactly twenty years earlier than Spencer and

Gillen's record of the Arunta beliefs, Smith's account of the Nimbalda beliefs seems to have been completely unnoticed by those who were in a position to suggest the proper interpretation. Smith writes:[5]

They believe that two old women called 'Yammutu' live towards the east a long way (*paldrupa*), and that when rain comes they lie down on their backs with their legs open, and the water runs into their person and causes them to bear a lot of young blacks called Muree; who, as they grow up, start westward, always throwing a small waddy, called *wretchu*, before them, till one of them meets a blackfellow with his *lubra*. The Muree, being invisible, then walks in the blackfellow's tracks to make him or her look like the blackfellow, and then throws the small waddy under the thumbnail or great toenail, and so enters into the woman's body. She is soon pregnant, and in due time gives birth to an ordinary child.

The two old women who live in the east, the Yammutu, are probably the mythical ancestors of the Nimbalda, standing, possibly, in the same relation to the latter as Numbakulla does to the Arunta. The *muree*, who result from the entry of rain into the Yammutus' bodies, are obviously spirit-children, and the *wretchu* is doubtless a *Churinga*. The presence of *Churinga* suggests the existence of a totemic organization, and the fact that a *muree* elects to enter a woman whose husband meets with his or her approval indicates, though it need not necessarily be so, patrilineal organization of the tribe. There is no evidence of a belief in reincarnation.

Very similar beliefs are held by the Adnjamatana or Wailpi of northern South Australia. Mountford and Harvey write of them:[6]

The Adnjamatana believe that their children originate in two mythical women as the *maudlaŋami* (*ŋami*—mother), who live in a place in the sky called Wikurutana. They are described as large beings who have sat still for so long that they have become the colour of grey weathered rock. Their long hair almost covers them, and on their pendulous breasts are swarms of spirit children who gather their sustenance therefrom. These women are the source of all life within the tribe, each producing spirit children (*muri*) of their own moiety, Araru or Mathuri.

When the number of *muri* on the breasts of the *maudlaŋami* becomes too many, some are told to go to the world beneath and find a suitable mother. The spirits either descend on a string as fine as a spider's web or fly down in the same manner as butterflies. They are so small that only the *wuŋi* (magician) or the old women can see them.

[There] is a pencil drawing by an old aboriginal woman illustrating this belief. One *maudlaŋami* is shown in the upper left-hand corner, and below her is a multitude of spirit children who have left her breasts and are travelling to the world beneath. On the upper right is a bush of *Jasminum lineare*. Some of the *muri* are feeding on the grape-like fruit as well as the blossoms of the gum tree (lower right). The spirit-child is always on the lookout for pleasant faced and kindly mothers, particularly those with large breasts, and when a suitable woman comes near the habitat of the *muri*, it will enter, by creeping painlessly under the thumb nail, and travelling up the arm, will move downwards into the womb, there to start life as a human being. Until this happens the *muri* spend their days seeking food from the gum-blossoms and the *ŋumaruka*, and their nights asleep under the loose bark of the tree-trunks.

According to our informants late winter and early spring were the favourite times for these little beings to visit the earth. Their arrival was known by the presence of yellow fungi on the damp logs of the creek. These growths are believed to be the vomit of the spirit children, and when the aborigines see these they believe that someone will soon be pregnant.

The father is not in any way associated with the entry of the spirit-child into his wife, and there is good evidence that there is a non-recognition of physiological maternity.

The following passages culled from Howitt's *The Native Tribes of South-East Australia* represent all that is to be discovered relating to the procreative beliefs of the tribes described in that work. It is not much, but Howitt was chiefly interested in what he considered to be the social organization of the tribes with which he came into contact, and apparently the procreative beliefs of these peoples did not interest him.

Howitt states of the Tatahi and Keramin that 'they believe that the daughter is of the father solely, being only nurtured by her mother'.[7]

Of the Wolgal he says that 'a Wolgal man of the Malian class, in speaking to me of the practice of betrothal, said that a father could do what he liked with his daughter, because the child is his, and "he only gives it to his wife to take care of for him".'[8]

Concerning the Wurunjerri Howitt writes, 'The line of descent runs through the males. As it was put to me, "The child comes from the man, and the woman only takes care of it." Berak [Howitt's informant] said in regard to this, "I remember what old Boberi, the brother of Billi-billeri, said at Dandenong, when some of the boys were grumbling and would not mind him. The old man got vexed, and said to his son, "Listen to me! I am here, and there you stand with my body." '[9]

These statements clearly indicate that the mother of a child is regarded among these tribes, as among all other Australian tribes' accounts of which we have thus far had, as a relatively unimportant agent in the procreative process. 'The child comes from the man and the woman only takes care of it.' The difference here would appear to be that whilst among the tribes which we have thus far considered neither one nor the other parent is considered to stand in a directly genetic relationship to the offspring, among those southern tribes, upon the other hand, there would appear to be a recognition of the existence of the relationship between father and child. 'The child comes from the man.' What, it may be asked, is the meaning of these words? And what are we to understand by the remark of Berak who said to his son, 'Listen to me! I am here, and there you stand with my body'?

The obvious implication of these remarks, especially of the latter, is that the father, the social father, is recognized to be the actual genitor of his child. In reality this is far from being the case; in fact among these tribes it is quite impossible to determine who the actual father of a child is, for the form of marriage known as '*pirraurau*' which prevails among these tribes, whereby a man enters into a form of marriage with a number of women, and a woman likewise enters into a similar relationship with a number of men, would render it somewhat difficult to determine the physiological father of a particular woman's child. The relationship between father and child cannot therefore be more, at most, than a purely social one. What Boberi had in mind when he said to his son: 'There you stand with my body', it is impossible to tell; it may have been some such idea as we have seen to have obtained among the Nimbalda, that is to say, the idea that the child as a still unincarnated spirit models its body after that of its prospective father, but for this suggestion there is no evidence; what, however, is the most likely explanation of this remark is that since among the Wurunjerri the clan totem is inherited and descends in the male line a man's children will all necessarily be of the same 'body' as their father, if we equate 'body' here with 'totem', as I think it is permissible to do, for everywhere in Australia an individual's body and his totem are closely identified. Upon this view, then, what old Boberi probably meant when he remonstrated with his son was that it was shameful to be disrespectful and unminding of one who was of the same body, the same flesh, that is, of the same totemic origin as himself.

That the father was considered to be only the social father of his child among the Dieri has been conclusively shown by Professor A. P. Elkin who, in 1930, investigated the tribes of the Lake Eyre region and who most illuminatingly writes as follows:[10]

The tribe is divided into two matrilineal moieties, called *Matari* and *Kararu* respectively, each of which includes a number of totemic social clans, called *Madu*. These are also matrilineal, being divided between the moieties so that the same clan does not appear in the two moieties of any one tribe. Now, according to Australian thought, a person does not inherit his flesh and blood from his father or through his father's line, but from his mother and her mother. The father generally 'finds' the pre-existent spirit of his unborn child in a dream or vision, and henceforth is its social, spiritual and ceremonial parent, but he is not one flesh and blood with it. Blood relationship is only traced in the maternal line. Thus, a man shares the one flesh and blood with his brothers and sisters, his mother and her brother, his mother's mother and her brother and so on, because they have all ultimately been incarnated through the womb of one woman, that is, a maternal grandmother in the '*n*th' degree. Now, in the Dieri and associated tribes, all these persons belong to a man's own totemic clan, and so, when he refers to his relations, he means, in the first instance, the members of his own totemic clan, for this includes these blood relations just referred to. He therefore speaks of them as his 'flesh', just as the totem itself is frequently denoted by the word for flesh, and being one's own flesh, is neither killed nor eaten.

As far as the father's relationship to the child is concerned then, the position is clear, he is its social father; they are both of different flesh. Elkin's use of the terms 'blood' and 'flesh' are, of course, perfectly legitimate if they are understood to mean what they are apparently intended to mean, namely, that since each individual is born into a matrilineal totemic clan his relationship to the clan totem and to other individuals is determined by and can be traced through the maternal line alone—since all members of the same totemic clan are in common descended from the same ancestral totem, or flesh—and since one's flesh is transmitted from the ancestral totem through the female line one must clearly be of the flesh of one's mother's totem. Descended from a common human ancestress through the mothers and sisters of the group, the matrilineal social totem symbolizes this social and physiological bond.

'The question is,' writes Elkin, 'can we regard as physiological a bond between mother and child which is not generative in nature, but is based only on the provision by the mother (as a "host") of that which enables a body to be formed in her womb for the pre-existent spirit or being? Ashley Montagu says "no". I believe that in spite of inconsistencies and difficulties in their thinking, the Aborigines regard this as a physiological (flesh and blood) bond, a bond which is reflected and made the centre of sentiments in matrilineal social totemism and in the descent of such social groups as sections and subsections. It is a bond not of physical generation, but of physiological contribution.'[11]

The distinction between 'physical generation' and 'physiological contribution' is a good one, and I should think, on the evidence, probably valid.

The father 'finds' the child, cares for it, and is head or a senior of the local horde to which it belongs. He is concerned with the initiation of a son and with the arrangement of the marriages of his children. To his fully initiated son he hands on 'his ceremonial local totem which is patrilineal in descent and includes a sacred myth, site, and ritual, possibly associated with the increase of the totemic species.'[12] This totem, of course, is quite different from the matri-lineal clan totem.

It may be noted here that among the South-Eastern tribes the belief seems to be general that after death the spirit leaves the body and goes to live up in the sky, from which there is no return.[13] Howitt states definitely that he has 'not been able to find that the Dieri have the Arunta belief in reincarnation of the ancestor, nor', he adds, 'have I found any trace of it in the tribes of south-east Australia.'[14] Elkin, we have seen, speaks of the *incarnation* of spirit-children among the Dieri. It seems fairly certain, therefore, that among the tribes investigated by these students, and reported upon by Howitt's correspondents, the belief in reincarnation is non-existent. Such a statement, however, does not preclude the possibility that the belief may exist among some, at least, of the uninvestigated tribes of this region.

Of the *Mura-muras* Howitt writes:[15]

At the present time they are said to inhabit trees, which are, there-fore, sacred. It is the medicine-men alone who are able to see them, and from them they obtain their magical powers.

Some of these legends identify natural features of the country with the *Mura-muras*; for instance, the thermal springs near Lake Eyre with the *Mura-mura kakakudana*, and certain petrifications to the south-east of Lake Eyre where some *Mura-mura* women were turned into stone. Professor Baldwin Spencer has told me that the equivalents of the *Mura-muras* occur with the Urabunna, and the places are pointed out where they died and where their spirits still are . . .

This evidently connects the *Mura-mura* beliefs of the Dieri with the *Alcheringa* beliefs of the Arunta . . .

With Howitt's brief remarks it is of interest to compare those of two more recent observers, one of whom lived in the territory for more than twenty years, on the tribes inhabiting the same region as that described by Howitt. The Wonkonguru, who live between the Warburton and Diamantina Rivers east of Lake Eyre, are, in respect of their procreative beliefs, thus described by these authors:[16]

The Wonkonguru group, which includes amongst others the Dieri, Yaurorka and Ngameni, seems to have a sort of ancestor worship, the ancestors being the mooras.

A moora sometimes appears to have been a master-mind who was the first to discover anything, or through whom anything was first discovered or done. They were the first to fashion human beings out of lizards, and they formed the sun. To them is attributed the making of *mardus* or totems, and ceremonies or corroborees invariably have the moora behind them, instigating or appointing, and thus giving them authority. The old men maintain their influence partly by receiving communications in dreams from the mooras. They thus tell where to sink for water and where game may be found. Animals, as well as inanimate things, have their mooras, and, as Dintibunna said, 'Every man has a moora,' a remark that was another day repeated to me verbatim by Koodnacadie.

Sometimes one may originate a whole tribe by leaving potential spirit children in rocks or in trees, whence children are born to women who come in contact with them. For that the father has anything to do with conception is absolutely foreign to the native mind.

Sometimes two, three, or more may be the ancestors of the tribe. This is the case with the Dieri. Rarely has a man a definite moora to himself, as has Dintibunna, 'the maker of the *kirra*' [boomerang], and in his case the name is handed down through his mother.

The moora, one hears them say, cannot die, but yet many of their legends turn on the death of the individual moora. It seems that though dead they yet live, and in this 'spirit' existence they appear far more to be feared than if really alive. One reason, old Nutatacullie told me, for the *kurdaitcha* shoe being worn was *not* to prevent its being tracked—that would be easy—but rather to cause the uncertainty of knowing *what* was being tracked. It might be a moora. What would happen if they did meet one, nobody could say . . .

Stones often appear to commemorate the death or disappearance of a moora. Trees sometimes spring and seem to have grown up where the moora first came or last went. These trees are, of course, never cut down, nor are those into which their ancestors have been metamorphosed. All these objects are endowed with magical force, and are often avoided as *kootchi* (uncanny) if they represent the moora and have his powers. The reverence paid to mooras is largely the reverence of fear, and anything strange or unusual is set down to them. The Aurora Australis in this way creates great alarm, and to appease the moora indiscriminate intercourse is practised. This is, of course, quite against the old men's advantages and may therefore be looked upon as a sacrifice on their part.[17]

The *mooras* are obviously the tribal or totemic ancestors of the Wonkonguru. The remark that 'every man has a moora' may be variously interpreted to mean that (1) every man has some totemic affiliation with a *moora*, or (2) that every man is himself the reincarnation of a *moora*, or that (3) the *moora* is a sort of spirit-double, very much like the Arunta Arumburinga. This last would seem to be the most likely interpretation.

The statement that 'Rarely has a man a definite moora to himself, as has Dintibunna, "the maker of the *kirra*", and in his case the name is handed down through his mother', is not unsuggestive of a belief in reincarnation, but the significance of the statement is not at all clear, and it may simply mean that Dintibunna and his mother happen to be the sole representatives of a particular totem.

It is important to note here that it is definitely stated that stones and trees in some cases arose to mark the spot where a *moora* either died or disappeared (went into the ground) or first appeared, and that in other cases the ancestors themselves were directly metamorphosed into trees. It will be recalled that in considering the related Arunta beliefs there was some doubt as to whether or not some ancestors, as Strehlow asserted, were actually metamorphosed into trees. Spencer held that he had never encountered the belief. The present report would, however, lend some support to Strehlow's statement, though it must, of course, be borne in mind that the Wonkonguru are situated an appreciable distance from the Arunta.

That the Wonkonguru have no knowledge of physiological parentage is clear, and that children are regarded as emanating from totem centres to undergo incarnation in women is also clear, the totem being matrilineally determined.

Writing of the Euahlayi tribe of north-western New South Wales, Mrs K. Langloh Parker gives the following account of their procreative beliefs:

To begin at the beginning, Bahloo, the moon, is a sort of patron of women. He it is who creates the girl babies, assisted by Wahn, the crow, sometimes.

Should Wahn attempt the business on his own account the result is direful; women of his creating are always noisy and quarrelsome.

Bahloo's favourite spot for carrying on the girl manufacturing is somewhere on the Culgoa. On one of the creeks there is to be seen, when it is dry, a hole in the ground. As water runs along the bed of this creek, gradually a stone rises from this hole. As the water rises it rises, always keeping its top out of the water.

This is the Goomarh, or spirit-stone, of Bahloo. No one would dare to touch this stone where the baby girls' spirits are launched into space.

In the same neighbourhood is a clear water-hole, the rendezvous of the snakes of Bahloo. Should a man go to drink there he sees no snakes, but no sooner does he drink some of the water than he sees hundreds; so even water-drinkers see their snakes.

The name of the hole is Dahn.

Spirit-babies are usually dispatched to Waddahgudjaelwon and sent by her to hang promiscuously on trees, until some women pass under where they are, then they will seize a mother and be incarnated. This resembles the Arunta belief, but with the Euahlayi the spirits are new freshly created beings, not reincarnations of ancestral souls, as among the Arunta. To live, a child must have an earthly father; that it has not, is known by its being born with teeth.

Wurrawilberoo is said to snatch up a baby spirit sometimes and whirl it along to some woman he wishes to discredit, and through the medium of this woman he incarnates perhaps twins, or at least one baby . . .

Babies are sometimes sent directly to their mothers without the Coolabah-tree or whirlwind medium.

The bronze mistletoe branches with their orange-red flowers are said to be the disappointed babies whose wailing in vain for mothers has wearied the spirits who transform them into these bunches, the red flowers being formed from their baby blood. The spirits of babies and children who die young are reincarnated, and should their first mother have pleased them they choose her again and are called millanboo—the same again.

They can instead, if they like, choose some other woman they know, which seems very accommodating in those presiding over the reincarnation department.

Sometimes two baby spirits will hang on one branch and incarnate themselves in the same woman, who as a result is the mother of twins and the object of much opprobrium in the camp. In fact, in the old days, one of the twins would have been killed.

No wonder the women cover themselves under a blanket when they see a whirlwind coming, and avoid drooping Coolabah trees, believing that either may make them objects of scorn as the mother of twins.[18]

Bahloo [the moon], too, has a spiteful way of punishing a woman who has the temerity to stare at him, by sending her the dreaded twins.[19]

The point to be noticed in this account of the Euahlayi beliefs is that the doctrine of reincarnation is limited only to the spirits of children who have died young, a belief which is almost invariably present in all those tribes in which the more general doctrine of reincarnation is absent.

NOTES

1   A. P. Elkin, 'The social organization of South Australian tribes', *Oceania*, 2, 1931, 70–1.
2   R. and C. Berndt, 'A preliminary report of field work in the Ooldea region, western South Australia', *Oceania*, 14, 1944, 236–7.
3   C. P. Mountford, *Brown Men and Red Sand*, 158.
4   Ibid., 159–60.
5   H. O. Smith, 'The Nimbalda tribe in the Far North at Mount Freeling', in G. Taplin, *The Folklore, Manners, Customs, and Languages of the South Australian Aborigines*, 88.
6   C. P. Mountford and A. Harvey, 'Women of the Adnjamatana tribe of the northern Flinders Ranges, South Australia', *Oceania*. 12, 1941, 156–7.
7   p. 195.
8   Ibid., 198.
9   Ibid., 255.
10 'The Dieri kinship system', *JRAI*, 61, 1931, 493.
11 Review of the first edition of this book, *Oceania*, 8, 1938, 376–8.
12 'The Dieri kinship system', 496–7.
13 A. W. Howitt, *Native Tribes of South-East Australia*, 434–44.
14 Ibid., 482.
15 Ibid.
16 G. Horne and G. Aiston, *Savage Life in Central Australia*.
17 Ibid., 124–6.
18 K. Langloh Parker, *The Euahlayi Tribe*, 50–1.
19 Ibid., 53.

CHAPTER IX

A summary account of the procreative beliefs of the Australian Aborigines

Yes, sir, but a man is to guard himself against taking a thing in general.—
SAM JOHNSON.

In the foregoing pages the first-hand accounts of the procreative as well as the related beliefs of the various tribes of Australia have been given in the words of the investigators themselves. From these accounts, I think, it is evident that what has been reported in the majority of instances represents the orthodox doctrine of each tribe, and, with the exception of the aberrant tribes to the north and north-east, it is held according to this doctrine that children are the result of the immigration into a woman of a spirit-child which is of an origin going back into the far distant mythological past. From the variety of contexts in which we have seen these beliefs to function it is clear that their chief sociological purpose is to associate a child with a definite *pater*, actual or classificatory, that is, with the mother's husband, whether or not he is the actual *genitor*. Thus it is that by means of this belief in the immigration of spirit-children into women the proper totemic and moiety membership of the child is secured. More importantly, an individual is by this means always associated with a definite locality regardless of where he may have been born, especially, as we have seen, is this the case where the individual is linked to the patrilineal group. There are, of course, local variations in the manner in which these beliefs function, but it is clear that they are essentially similar in nature wherever they occur.

It is evident, then, that these beliefs form a fundamental feature not alone of Aboriginal cosmology, but also of Aboriginal social organization, and, as such, it is also evident that these beliefs occupy a dominant place in the native mind, although, as we shall see later, it is not for these reasons alone that they do so.

When, then, the investigator endeavours to discover what the Aboriginal beliefs are relating to the process of coming into being he is, of course, naturally given the orthodox account of the matter. When he inquires whether intercourse has any connection with pregnancy or childbirth he is in most cases informed that intercourse serves to prepare the woman for the entry of a spirit-child into her but that this preparation is not in itself the cause of pregnancy or of the entry of the child into the woman. Intercourse is always declared not to be the cause of conception, for according to orthodox teaching and belief children are produced by other means.

This is essentially the information which Spencer and Gillen obtained in 1896 from the Central tribes and which they reported in 1899, and it is essentially the kind of information which the majority of subsequent investigators who have worked among the tribes of Australia have obtained, and as such it may be regarded as constituting the faithful record of Aboriginal orthodox belief. From these findings it has been concluded by almost all the investigators themselves and by numerous students of their recorded observations that the Aborigines are ignorant of the relationship which exists between intercourse and pregnancy, that they are unaware of the fact that intercourse is the direct cause of conception (we may, of course, omit the 'scientific' efficient cause, namely, fertilization). As far as orthodox belief is concerned we have seen that that relationship is ignored, although in no case entirely so, for in practically every instance intercourse is regarded as having some connection with pregnancy; in some cases this connection is of a very vague nature, in others the connection or relationship is regarded as a necessary one since, as a rule, a spirit-child will not enter a woman who has not been prepared by intercourse. In other words, intercourse prepares the way for that factor to become operative which is the cause of pregnancy, but intercourse is not either alone or in conjunction with other factors the cause of pregnancy. It is clear then, that by whatever term we may describe this relationship, a certain association is recognized to exist between intercourse and the entry of a spirit-child into a woman, but that this association is not of a causal nature. All this is orthodox belief, but a number of investigators have shown —Róheim in respect of certain Central tribes, Purcell, Warner and others of the far northern tribes, Thomson of the Cape York tribes, Chaseling and Berndt of the Arnhem Land tribes, and Douglas, Mountford and Goodale of the Tiwi of Melville Island—that a much more definite connection is recognized to exist between intercourse and pregnancy than this. Róheim has claimed that a true knowledge of the facts exists in secular belief side by side with the spirit-conception beliefs of orthodox teaching, but that the former is simply repressed in favour of the dominant orthodox beliefs. Upon the basis of his own findings Warner independently arrived at a similar conclusion, and Thomson made a similar suggestion.

It may at once be said that all this is possible particularly in view of the fact that the field-worker does not generally succeed in obtaining any information other than that which is orthodox. Secular belief is for the most part determined and dominated by orthodox religious teaching, and it is unusual for the investigator to obtain any data relating to the genesis and development of belief in primitive cultures. We do know, however, that many of the childhood beliefs of the

Aboriginal undergo an appreciable modification by the time he becomes a fully initiated member of the tribe, and there is no particular reason to believe that his ideas concerning the nature of procreation should not be among those affected. There is, however, no positive evidence that this is so, but it is a possibility to be borne in mind, for it may be pointed out that there is no necessary reason why the native should not pass from a childhood belief in the virtues of intercourse to the adult belief in the virtues of spirit-children, just, for example, as we ourselves advance from the uninitiated childhood belief in the stork to the esoteric adult belief in intercourse as the true cause of children. But we must be on our guard against such analogies. It is no longer possible to conduct investigations on Aboriginal peoples uncontaminated by white influences, but on the evidence as we have it from the recent past, we can say that the tribes that had been least subjected to white influence appear to have been ignorant of physiological paternity, while those peoples who had experienced much white contact were not so ignorant.

It should be remembered that the reports of field studies of aboriginal cultures are generally almost entirely concerned with the report of observations; these observations represent the records of the investigator's experiences in a particular colligation of phenomena. As far as is possible within the time at his disposal the investigator attempts to make these records as comprehensive and as complete as he can. Whatever his own views may be concerning the theoretical implications of the data collected by him, there can necessarily be very little room for the expression of them in the documentary presentation of his evidence. When the investigator has succeeded in putting into the terms of one language what has been told him, generally through the medium of a native interpreter, in terms of another language what, according to the natives' notions, is the meaning of the ceremonies, customs, events, etc., which he has observed or been told about, his record becomes a source from which students of man and society draw the material for their studies. It often happens that the observations of the field investigator stand glaringly in opposition to the tenets of the theory of which a particular student may have become enamoured. In such a case it becomes necessary for the theoretician to analyse the observations of the field investigator in the attempt to show where they may be at fault, or where, when properly interpreted, they are not actually in opposition, but rather in agreement with their critic's general theory.

To the subject of the procreative ideas of the Australian Aborigines there has been devoted a fairly considerable amount of 'higher criticism' of this sort. The controversy received a new lease on life with the publication in *The Sexual Life of Savages* of Malinowski's findings on the procreative beliefs of the Trobriand Islanders.

Before proceeding with the discussion of the significance of these beliefs in relation to these various criticisms, it will be convenient here to summarize the procreative beliefs of the Aborigines as we have had them placed before us by the various authorities for the five great regions of Australia.

THE CENTRAL TRIBES

Among the Central tribes we find a belief in eponymous ancestors who 'in the beginning' transformed various natural objects, and certain half-formed creatures, into men and women. In the beginning, the ancestors deposited numbers of *Churinga*, with each of which was associated a spirit or soul, at certain spots, and themselves entered the earth at various other places. At each of the spots where these *Churinga* were deposited, and where the ancestors themselves entered the earth, there immediately arose some natural feature such as a tree, or rock, water-hole, etc., to mark the place. At each of these places a number of ancestors belonging to the same animal or plant group from which they had been originally transformed are always to be found. Should a woman of the proper tribal moiety and class pass in the vicinity of these totemic spirit-abodes, and providing that she is considered sufficiently pleasing by one of the spirit-children, who are always on the lookout for the proper women, she will be entered in the form of a diminutive spirit-child, and thus be rendered pregnant. The totem associated with the territory or totem centre in which the spirit-child entered the mother becomes the totem of the child there incarnated in her. This manner of obtaining the totem has been called by Frazer *conceptional totemism*, since the totem of the individual is determined by the place at which the mother happened to be, or believes she was last at, or by the victuals she ate last, at the moment when she first felt the child within her.

The term *conceptional* is perhaps unfortunately chosen to describe such conditions, for the notion of *conception* is one that is utterly foreign to the native mind. When he speaks of the entry of a spirit-child into a woman the native means something quite unlike anything that we may understand by the term *conception*. What he understands by these words is that a spirit enters a woman, undergoes an autochthonous development within her, is born of her, and is in no way physically connected or engendered either by her or by any other person. This, of course, is the exact converse of what we understand by 'conception'. The Central Australian Aborigines, in fact, had no idea of conception at all, and it is for this reason unfortunate that a term should be used the meaning of which is patently contrary to the significance of the conditions it is supposed to describe. The term has, however, assumed a definite place in the literature of ethnology, and it would be the cause of needless confusion to attempt to substitute some other for it at this date.

When an individual dies, according to Spencer and Gillen, his spirit returns to the totem abode from which it emanated, and the *Churinga* with which his spirit was associated is placed in the sacred storehouse. The *Churinga* is variously supposed to be thrown at the woman by its spirit-owner or dropped by it as it enters its chosen 'mother'. According to all other investigators the spirit at death leaves the body and departs never to return. The spirit-child is apparently perfectly free to choose the woman it will enter, and though it can be encouraged to do so, it cannot be coerced, as when a man surreptitiously visits a totem abode and by the performance of a simple ceremony causes a spirit-child to enter some woman.

In all the Central tribes a frequent means by which a spirit-child enters a woman is through the agency of some part of an animal or plant with which the spirit-child is associated.

The dream is a common medium through which the fact that a woman has been entered by a spirit-child, as well as its origin, is announced either to herself, or to one of her relatives.

The spirit-children mostly represent beings of *Alchera* origin; some, however, are identified with the spirit-parts of famous old men, who were noted for their learning in tribal matters. There is no evidence of a general belief in reincarnation, but only in the incarnation of spirit-children of *Alchera* origin, and the occasional incarnation of an *Alchera* ancestor himself. The spirit-part of an individual is not regarded as eternal and does not undergo repeated incarnation.

The body is recognized as distinctly separate from the spirit. The body is always derived from an *Alchera* ancestor, and in many cases the spirit originates from the transformed body of such an ancestor, although in most cases the spirit has an independent *Alchera* origin.

Intercourse is considered usual among the Arunta, and necessary among the Loritja, as a condition preparatory to the entry of a spirit-child into a woman, but intercourse is not in any way regarded as a cause of pregnancy.

In every tribe the mother is regarded as the passive medium through whom the child is transmitted into the tribe; there is no conception of any physical or blood connection between the mother and the child, nor is such a connection recognized to exist between father and child. There is thus an ignorance of physiological maternity as well as of physiological paternity.

Descent of the totem is counted neither in the male nor in the female line among the Arunta, Loritja, Iliaura, Unmatjera, Kaitisha, and is generally reckoned in the paternal line among the Warramunga. In the Urabunna tribe in which descent is counted in the maternal line, the same beliefs hold equally as strongly. In all these and the neighbouring tribes the belief in spirit incarnation represents the orthodox doctrine.

THE NORTHERN TRIBES

Among the tribes of the Northern Territory the cosmogonic myths and the procreative beliefs are essentially of the same nature as those that are to be found among the Central tribes, except that whilst among the Central tribes a relatively few individuals bear the names of totemic ancestors, among the Northern tribes every individual is, according to Spencer and Gillen, known to be the reincarnation of a totemic ancestor.

All the tribes of Arnhem Land and further north of Melville Island are aware of the fact that intercourse and seminal fluid are related to the production of pregnancy, but this belief is held concurrently and quite harmonically with spirit procreative beliefs which are of the same nature as those found elsewhere in Australia.

THE TRIBES OF NORTH-EASTERN AUSTRALIA

Among the tribes of North Queensland it is believed that a woman may be rendered pregnant in any one of the following ways: (1) by being told to be entered by a spirit-child by a particular man, (2) by sitting over a fire upon which she has roasted a particular edible object that has been given to her by the prospective father of the child, or (3) by having a spirit-child directly inserted into her womb by one of the nature-spirits. There is no evidence of a belief in reincarnation.

Among those Cape York tribes whose beliefs relating to procreation have not undergone appreciable modification as the result of the influence of extra-Australian contacts, there is a belief in the existence of spirit-centres from which children are sent out to enter women. The child generally inherits the totem of the clan into which it is born, and since this is organized upon a patrilineal pattern, the totemic descent may be said to be indirectly patrilineal.

Among these tribes sexual intercourse is usually associated with the sending out of children from the totem centres and their entry into women, but sexual intercourse is not regarded as the cause of conception.

THE NORTH-WESTERN TRIBES

Among the North-Western tribes children are regarded as emanating from totemic centres following which they undergo incarnation in a

woman. The entry of the spirit-child into the woman is always associated with a dream in which the father 'finds' the child; among the
Nyul-Nyul and among the Bardi the spirit-child is usually just simply
'found' by the father while out hunting. The totemic territory in
which the father 'finds' the spirit-child, which is, of course, usually
his own totemic territory, normally determines the totem of the child
when born. Thus patrilineal totemism is the rule among these tribes
too. The belief in reincarnation is to be found among these two tribes
according to Elkin, although there is no evidence that it exists among
the other tribes that have so far been investigated in the north-west.
The belief of the Ungarinyin and Worora tribes to the effect that
the father always 'finds' the child in a dream or in waking life in
association with water, and that spirit-children were made in the
ungud, or remote past of mythical times, and are brought by the
rainbow serpent, or *wondzad*, is of particular interest; as also is
the belief that the latter's mate, *wondzina*, is causally connected with
the rain, and with the increase of the human race, as well as with the
increase of other natural species. Here, too, the totem of the child is
determined by the territory from which the child emanated, usually
the father's *bor* in which it was 'found'.

THE TRIBES OF WESTERN AUSTRALIA

Among the southern tribes of Western Australia conceptional totemism and the belief in the existence of spirit-centres from which spirit-
children emanate and undergo incarnation in women is found widely
distributed. With the exception of the belief in the reincarnation of
children who have died young there is no evidence that the more
general doctrine of reincarnation exists among these tribes.

Patrilineal totemism is most probably the rule among these tribes.

Among the more northern tribes of this region the child is regarded
as the product of the plant or animal food partaken of by the mother,
and given her by a particular individual, who generally stands in the
relation of father's brother, and occasionally, father's sister, to the
husband of the woman of whom the child will be born. Such an
individual may also cause the spirit of some animal which he has
recently killed to enter a particular woman. The child treats the
individual who has thus acknowledged his relationship to him much
as he does his mother's husband, but apart from this there is no well-
defined or special relationship between them.

The totem is not inherited in the paternal line but from the clan
into which the child is born, but since these clans are strictly patrilineal, the father determines the totemic affiliation of the child.

Among these tribes there is no belief in reincarnation.

THE TRIBES OF SOUTHERN, SOUTH-EASTERN, AND EASTERN AUSTRALIA

Among the tribes of the south (Pitjandjara and neighbouring tribes) the consumption by a woman of any article of food given to her by a man is generally regarded as the causative agent in the production of pregnancy and the birth of a child.

The western tribes of South Australia believe in the existence of spirit-abodes from which children emanate. Curiously enough, however, children of different totems may originate from the same spirit-centre. The totem of the child is announced in a dream. The facts of physiological paternity appear to be known to some of the tribes in this area, an area in which there has been a great deal of contact with whites.

In the North, spirit-children are associated with the rain (among the Nimbalda) which entering the bodies of two supernatural women, the Yammutu, are born as young spirit-blacks who undergo incarnation in the woman at whom they have chosen to throw their waddies. There is no evidence of a belief in reincarnation. The available data indicates the existence of indirect patrilineal totemism.

Among the South-Eastern tribes the belief is general that the spirit-child emanates from a spirit-centre and is directly incarnated in a woman when she happens to pass by one of these. The spirit-child is newly created, and there is no evidence of a belief in reincarnation. Patrilineal totemism is probably the rule.

Among the tribes of the eastern part of Australia in the New South Wales territory, of whom very little is known, spirit-children are believed to be manufactured by supernaturals who send them along to the women in whom they are incarnated and born as children in due course. There is a belief in the reincarnation of children who have died young, but there is no evidence of any more general extension of the belief in reincarnation.

With this brief summary of the procreative beliefs of the Aborigines of Australia the preliminary part of this work has been brought to a conclusion, the chief purpose of which has been to present the classical and other authoritative accounts of these beliefs in order to enable us to judge the evidence for ourselves. From the evidence presented, several conclusions emerge. First, is the remarkable likeness of the procreative beliefs of the Australian Aborigines throughout the continent as well as Melville Island. This striking likeness surely points to a common origin for these beliefs. Second, is the fact that while ignorance of physiological paternity is widespread, the nearer the tribes are to the coastal regions the less likely is such ignorance to occur. This suggests that the ignorance is original, and that knowledge of physiological paternity has been acquired from contact with other peoples. The peculiar geographic distribution of such knowledge seems to me highly significant. Third, it is clear that the procreative beliefs of the Aborigines constitute the foundation stones of their cosmogony, kinship system, religion, and social organization and possess a significance the ramifications of which far exceed in importance any question as to whether or not the Aborigines are in some cases ignorant of the facts of procreation.

In the chapters which follow, the body of critical exegesis which has been devoted to Aboriginal conceptional beliefs will be critically examined, and the attempt will be made to clarify the conditions which have been instrumental in determining the character of those beliefs.

The following discussion is arranged in a manner designed to lead progressively to a clearer understanding of the actual dynamics, in so far as that is possible, of the bases of Aboriginal procreative beliefs, as exemplified especially by the Arunta of Central Australia.

CHAPTER X

The critical theories relating to the procreative beliefs of the Australian Aborigines

The anthropologist gets as near his primitive man as he can, far enough away.—ANDREW LANG (Edward Clodd, *Memories*, London, 1926, p. 214)

J. G. Frazer in the second part of his classical studies entitled 'The Beginnings of Religion and Totemism Among the Australian Aborigines'[1] presented a clearly reasoned interpretation of the significance of the available data relating to totemism in Australia. He argued that the evidence suggested that group marriage and maternal descent of the totem preceded the establishment of individual marriage and the paternal descent of the totem, and that group marriage had in turn been preceded by 'a still wider sexual communism',[2] while maternal descent had likewise been preceded by 'an even older mode of transmitting the totem which still survives among the Arunta and Kaitish',[3] that is, local totemism, in which the totem of the child is determined by the local origin of the spirit which has incarnated itself or undergone incarnation in the mother, 'without any regard to the totem either of the father or of the mother'.[4] This form or manner of acquiring the totem Frazer regarded as probably the most primitive, 'For it ignores altogether the intercourse of the sexes as the cause of offspring and, further, it ignores the tie of blood on the maternal as well as the paternal side, substituting for it a purely local bond, since the members of a totem stock are merely those who gave the first sign of life in the womb at one or other of certain definite spots.'[5] Local totemism, according to Frazer, with its implied ignorance of paternity, could hardly have arisen from hereditary totemism, but it is easy to see, argues Frazer, how the former could have given rise to the latter—a spirit of the father's totem simply incarnates itself in the mother, wherever she may be and however distant from the spirit-child's totem centre.

The explicit denial that children are the fruit of the commerce of the sexes is a piece of ignorance of natural causation which Frazer believes 'cannot but date from a past immeasurably remote'.

In explication of this ignorance, Frazer continues, there is first the relatively considerable interval which elapses between intercourse *cum* fertilization and the first symptoms of pregnancy, an interval which is of sufficient duration to prevent the native from perceiving

231

the connection between the two events. Second, there is the unrestricted sexual licence which is customary between individuals who have not yet attained puberty, and whose unions are necessarily sterile, conditions which clearly contribute towards the belief that intercourse can have no essential connection with the birth of children. The native is therefore driven to account for pregnancy and childbirth in some other way. Nothing would seem more simple than that the spirit-child has entered the mother at the moment when she first felt it stirring within her womb, and it is not unnatural that 'in her attempt to ascertain what the thing is she should fix upon some object that happened to be near her and that engaged her attention at the critical moment'.[6] This would most likely be some animal or plant, or some food of which she had recently partaken. Hence, the spirit of that animal, plant, or object would determine the *nature* of the child, and eventually its totemic affiliation.

The exogamy of the totem stocks, and the institution of the class and section marriage regulations Frazer believes to be a reform introduced at a much later date than the totemic principle. Why this reform should have been introduced Frazer acknowledges to be a matter beyond his power to determine—probably, he suggests, some superstition may have been responsible which led to the belief that marriage between close relatives was injurious to the health.

That the exogamy of the totem is a late reform would, to Frazer, appear certain from the fact that according to Spencer and Gillen the Arunta *Alchera* traditions make no reference whatever to the totemic regulation of marriage, and 'such evidence as there is points towards the normal existence of marital relations between men and women of the same totem'.[7] Thus, for example, in the Achilpa tradition, 'The natives are quite clear on the point that in the case of all the Knanjas originated by Numbakulla, men and women of the same Knanja, or totem, were arranged in pairs as mates, and married one another.'[8] We have already seen that among the Arunta of the present day the totem has nothing to do with the regulation of marriage, which is determined by moiety, section, and subsection rules, and that the characteristic local exogamy is really the result of the regulation of marriage by relationship.

In any event it is difficult to see why that state in which marriage was not regulated by the totems, or before the 'introduction of the marriage classes' constitutes evidence that at one time sexual communism and later, group marriage, must have been the rule. There is nothing in the myths and traditions relating to the totems and the marriage regulations of the Arunta which would suggest the necessity or even feasibility of such an hypothesis. These myths and traditions render no other assumption necessary than that the earliest form of marriage was *individual*. In the passage just quoted regarding the Achilpa tradition we saw that men and women of the same *Knanja* or totem were arranged in pairs as mates, and married one another. Never, in any of the traditions or myths, is there the slightest indication of the former existence of either sexual communism or of group marriage.

Among other Australian tribes, such, for example, as the Dieri[9] and the Worgaia[10] whose traditions appear to indicate the former existence of a time when sexual unions were completely promiscuous, the existence of the marriage regulations is explained as being due to the desire of their ancestors to overcome the ill effects produced by the union of nearly related kin. Such an explanation might be considered strong evidence of the former existence of these conditions. However, it seems more likely that these myths and explanations constitute the purest rationalizations.

The existence among most Australian tribes of ceremonial promiscuity at certain celebrations during which individuals of the forbidden classes may have access to one another, and of the normal custom of lending one's wives to individuals within the privileged classes, the 'marriages' of the *pirraurau* type of the Dieri, in which one individual is 'married' to a group of individuals of the other sex, and, finally, the terms of the relationship system in which an individual calls all women who may potentially have been his mother as well as his actual mother by the same term, and similarly with respect to the terms denoting the relationship of fatherhood, wife, etc., all these things have been interpreted as evidence of the former existence both of promiscuity and of group marriage.

It is impossible here to enter into a discussion of this matter, to which many volumes have in the past been devoted, and which has been most exhaustively discussed in the scholarly works of Frazer,[11] Thomas,[12] Rivers,[13] Westermarck,[14] and Briffault,[15] not to mention others. It would take a volume far larger than the present one to discuss this matter at all adequately, and to present the various arguments for and against the hypothesis of sexual promiscuity and group marriage. It may, however, be noted here that Frazer, Rivers, and Briffault are supporters of the hypothesis, whilst Thomas and Westermarck are very definitely opposed to it.

Whatever the truth of the matter may be, it makes little or no difference to our study of the procreative beliefs of the Australian Aborigines, although the hypothesis of promiscuity and group marriage would perhaps make it easier for some to apprehend something of the nature of the primitive ignorance of the relationship between intercourse and pregnancy. In view of the evidence, however, I am strongly inclined to the belief that sexual promiscuity and group marriage were never more prevalent in Australia than they are today, and that individual marriage, as the Australian understands it, represents the truly primitive condition.

It is here of interest to recall the remarks of an early exponent of the promiscuity and group-marriage hypothesis, namely A. W. Howitt:[16]

I doubt whether even under an 'undivided commune' there could have been anything more than a limited promiscuity, excepting when the whole community occasionally reunited. The general conditions of savage life on the Australian continent would not permit an entire individual commune to remain united for any length of time in the same locality. The Dieri practice may show us, in a modified form, what might take place. The commune 'pirraurau' right exists, but it cannot be fully exercised excepting when the whole tribe assembles.

Frazer assumed or inferred a chronological sequence in the development or appearance of these conditions as, first sexual communism or promiscuity; second, group marriage; and, third, individual marriage.

At this point a strong protest must be entered against the use of the term 'group marriage'. The term is a complete misnomer, for it implies the actual marriage of groups of individuals to one another, whereas in those tribes in which it has been described, most notably among the Dieri of south-east Australia, it is in reality a ceremonial arrangement decided upon in council, of which the individuals concerned are by no means compelled or even expected to take advantage. The decision of the elders in council merely makes known to everyone those who may and those who may not by reason of class and kinship become *pirraurau* to one another. Such individuals always stand in the relationship of those who are *Noa* to one another, that is, who might, other things being equal, normally contract an individual marriage with one another. The *pirraurau* arrangement merely gives a certain number of individuals rights of sexual access under certain conditions to a certain number of others, rights which, as Howitt has pointed out, 'cannot be fully exercised excepting when the whole tribe assembles'. But it should be obvious here that neither the privilege nor the usufructuary right it bestows in any sense constitutes marriage.

In view of these considerations it is somewhat difficult to understand how Briffault arrived at the conclusion that 'Of actual "group-marriage" relations in the sense of regular, recognized, and habitual sexual cohabitation, we have evidence only in the "*pirraurau*" and similar institutions'.[17]

Recognized these relations certainly are, but regular, habitual? Briffault has himself written:[18]

A large proportion of the misconceptions and futile discussions regarding the extent of the actual relations between intermarriage classes in Australia arises from overlooking or ignoring the fact that, owing to unalterable economic conditions, an Australian tribe is never a territorial community forming a single group; it is invariably fragmented into a number of 'camps' or very small communities. So that 'class promiscuity' can never, in fact, be other than 'ceremonial', for it cannot take place except at periodic gatherings of the whole tribe.

Briffault then proceeds to quote with complete approval the statements of Howitt already given above. How then, in view of these facts, is it possible to speak of these group relations as regular and habitual? It is precisely these things that these relations are not, unless by 'regular' is to be understood 'periodic', and by 'habitual', 'occasional'.

It is very strange that while at the present day individual marriage and group relations co-exist side by side in Australia, the co-existence of these conditions in former times should have been implicitly denied by all students of the subject who, on the other hand, have, like Frazer, assumed or inferred a chronological sequence in their development or appearance. But for the reasons already stated it seems highly probable that individual promiscuity and group relations were from the earliest times co-existent with the individual relationship. This view would seem to me to be more consonant with the facts as they exist at the present time than any other with which I am acquainted, and, moreover, possesses the advantage of being in perfect harmony with the myths and traditions of the various Aboriginal peoples relating to their early history.

When, then, Frazer writes that it is 'practically certain that in Australia individual marriage has everywhere been preceded by group-marriage, and that again by a still wider communism',[19] I believe this to be an inaccurate interpretation of the facts. In the first place, I cannot accept, and in this I agree with Thomas[20] and Malinowski,[21] the term 'group marriage'. Group marriage does not and never has, as far as we can tell, existed in any Australian tribe. As I have said, socially sanctioned privileges of the kind involved in the relationship which passes by the name of group marriage do not constitute marriage. The term 'sexual communism' is as objectionable as the term 'group marriage', for there is not the slightest evidence of any kind that there ever was anything in the social organization of any Australian tribe which merits such a description. In point of fact it is doubtful whether sexual communism is ever practised in any Australian tribe, even upon ceremonial occasions. Upon such occasions *ceremonial* licence is the rule. During the normal group relations between families, the actual husband of a woman may, of his own volition or in response to a request from an individual entitled to the privilege, lend her or permit access to her to another man, but these things do not in any way minimize the importance of the fact that the woman is the possession solely of her actual husband, and never in any sense the possession of anyone else after her marriage to him. While her relations to her actual husband are of a permanent nature, her relations to her social 'husbands' and her partners upon ceremonial occasions are of the most transient nature. In the latter relationships no question is involved of a possession held or shared in common with the actual husband who, indeed, is the only and actual possessor of his wife. There is no communism whatever in these extraneous relationships, since communism implies common ownership, and in these relationships there is no common right to enjoy a woman upon an equal basis with her husband; that basis is indeed very unequal. In any case, a socially sanctioned right to enjoy anything whatever does not give the enjoyer a right of property in the thing he enjoys; he may enjoy the thing but it remains the property of its owner. If a *pirraurau* 'husband' upon occasion feels that he has certain ownership rights in a particular woman of which he desires to take advantage, he is far from feeling that he owns those rights in common with her actual husband, for to her actual husband she is bound permanently, and to her *pirraurau* she is not bound at all, for she is not compelled to yield to his advances, nor, if she be willing, may her actual husband permit her to do so.

As Elkin has put it, 'the institution of *pirauru* is a regularizing of wife-lending, and not a mutual combination of marital rites, duties and life between a group of men on the one hand and a group of women on the other.'[22]

In brief, it should be quite clear that in all these relations there is no appearance whatever of communism in sexual relations within the permitted degrees, and certainly none without them.

As for the ceremonial licence which prevails at certain times during the year when the whole tribe is assembled, perhaps a half dozen times during the year, the general promiscuity which occurs, except among those of near kin, lasts no more than about four hours at most upon each occasion. But here, too, sexual promiscuity is not sexual communism. We must be careful here to make the proper distinction between our terms. In the literature dealing with the subject these terms have often been used quite interchangeably, the 'hypothesis of sexual communism' and the 'hypothesis of sexual promiscuity' are phrases which have frequently been used as equivalent in meaning, as meaning one and the same thing. But even according to the lexical meaning of the terms they do not possess the same connotation, for communism means the common holding or sharing of property, and promiscuity, indiscriminate or unrestricted mingling. With reference to the sexual customs of the Aborigines, communism and promiscuity have, in their strictest senses, meant respectively, the common owner-ship of sexual rights in a group of women by a group of men, and the indiscriminate (excepting with respect to near kin) sexual licence on certain ceremonial occasions.

It does not appear to me to be justifiable to speak of the kind of ceremonial licence we have described as sexual communism, for so fleeting and irregular an experience cannot to the participants possess a more extended meaning than both the occasion and its infrequency would suggest. Such licence simply constitutes a ceremonial practice in which, on the appropriate occasions, it is one's obligation as well as one's privilege to participate. If this be so, then I think it is in-correct to describe an impermanent occasional ceremonial practice, in which all the members of the tribe participate equally, by a term which implies the existence of a permanent condition, and *communism* is a term the principal meaning of which is that the common owner-ship be permanent. If we use the term 'ceremonial promiscuity' we shall, I believe, be nearer the mark.

The argument that the present-day existence of ceremonial pro-miscuity constitutes evidence of the former widespread existence of sexual communism preceding individual and even group marriage would appear to me completely specious. That sexual promiscuity was customary whenever the tribe assembled in earlier times is an inference which I believe the evidence warrants, but as has already been pointed out, such relations are improperly described when they are spoken of as 'communistic'.

The fact is that the fundamental social arrangement in Australia is represented by cross-cousin marriage, and it is easily seen how the so-called marriage classes came into being as a result of this arrange-ment. Thus, where the four-class system is established an individual marries his immediate cross-cousin; where there is an eight-class system, as among the Arunta, he marries a cross-cousin once removed. A further consequence of this simple marriage rule is the division of the tribe into moieties and/or semi-moieties. This, together with the marriage classes naturally follows upon the rule of cross-cousin marriage, and it may well be that these conditions represent the primitive ones as far as Australia is concerned. It is, at any rate, quite impossible to go beyond or behind these, for we have no evidence of the existence of earlier conditions anywhere in Australia.[23]

In the light of the above discussion, then, it becomes equally impossible for us to accept Frazer's statement that group marriage and maternal descent of the totem preceded the establishment of individual marriage and the paternal descent of the totem. Of the first matter we have already briefly disposed; of the second there is this to say, namely, that there is nowhere in Australia a particle of evidence to show that maternal preceded paternal descent of the totem. In view of the actual evidence such an assumption is quite unwarranted.

D. S. Davidson has, I think, in spite of some faulty analyses, demonstrated[24] that

there is nothing throughout the original social structure of the Australian local group system which would indicate that matrilineal descent had ever been known. In fact, if we were to eliminate from Australia the moieties, classes, and totemic sibs, leaving just the local group organization, there would be no matrilineal organization on the continent. As a starting point in Australian history, therefore, we would have the local group system with patrilineal tendencies due to the very nature of a hunting occupation and its related organization.

In this passage Davidson refers to the fact that throughout Australia all land and hunting territorial rights of the local group are controlled by the male head of the family and are inherited in the male line.[25]

The local group system is characterized by patrilineal tendencies. The local groups and their subdivisions, the family hunting territories, are patrilocal; when information is at all detailed it is often to be noticed that they are also patronymic. Marriage generally takes place between certain reciprocating localities. Land is inherited in the male line. There is nothing about the entire aboriginal organization which would indicate for a minute that matrilineal institutions are present, ever had been known, or, left to their own resources to develop social progress and intensification, ever would become known.

A similar conclusion is to be drawn from Radcliffe-Brown's comprehensive study of the social organization of Australian tribes.[26]

Radcliffe-Brown has pointed out the error of crudely distinguishing between the terms 'patrilineal' and 'matrilineal descent'. He writes as follows:

It is common to speak of some Australian tribes as patrilineal and others as matrilineal. This, to say the least, is misleading. In the first place in every Australian tribe what is really the most important social group, the horde, is patrilineal. But some tribes, in addition to these patrilineal groups, have a system of matrilineal groups, which are necessarily not localized and are usually, if not always, totemic.[27]

So far as descent goes, therefore, we must divide Australian tribes into two groups, those in which there are only patrilineal descent groups, and those in which there are both patrilineal and matrilineal descent groups.[28]

There is no evidence anywhere in Australia that patrilineal descent ever developed from or was preceded by matrilineal descent, but such evidence as we have just considered, namely the geographical distribution of patrilineal and matrilineal descent together with the moiety system and the universal patrilineal organization of the local group, renders it practically certain that patrilineal descent is basic—that the fundamental primitive organization of the Aboriginal family, horde, and tribe is paternal, and in essentials still remains so everywhere in Australia.

In view of these considerations it seems extremely unlikely that matrilineal descent of the totem ever preceded patrilineal descent of the totem. Frazer, indeed, does not altogether deny the possibility, for he writes:[29]

Finally, I have to point out that, if the present theory of the development of totemism is correct, the common assumption that inheritance of the totem through the mother always preceded inheritance of it through the father need not hold good. If the transition from the conceptional to the hereditary form of totemism was effected in the manner in which it seems to be actually taking place at present among the Central Australian tribes, it is clear that the change could be made just as readily to paternal as to maternal descent. For it would be quite as easy to suppose that a spirit of the husband's totem had entered into his wife as that a spirit of her own totem had done so: the former supposition would give paternal descent of the totem, the latter would give maternal descent.

Frazer's statements that the Arunta belief 'ignores altogether the intercourse of the sexes as the cause of offspring; and further, it ignores the tie of blood on the maternal as well as the paternal side',[30] and that the theory 'derives implicitly, and the natives themselves deny explicitly, that children are the fruit of the commerce of the sexes. So astounding an ignorance of natural causation cannot but date from a past immeasurably remote',[31] immediately upon their appearance called forth the criticism of Andrew Lang,[32] a criticism which he repeated and elaborated subsequently in many places.

The tenor of Lang's objections may be gauged from his opening remarks:

Now when the Arunta 'ignore the tie of blood on the maternal side', they prove too much. They ignore that of which they are not ignorant. Not being idiots, they are well aware of the maternal tie of blood; but they do not permit it to affect the descent of the totem, which is regulated by their isolated superstition, the doctrine of reincarnation combined with the *churinga nanja* belief. Nor do they ignore father-hood . . . in affairs of inheritance of local office and totemic rites.[33]

But they *do* deny that the intercourse of the sexes is the cause of birth of children. Here the interesting point is that tribes much more primitive, the south-eastern tribes, with female reckoning of descent, inheritance in the female line, and no hereditary local moderator-ships, are perfectly well aware of all that the more advanced Arunta do not know. Yet they, quite as much as the Arunta, are subject to the causes which, according to Mr. Frazer, produces the Arunta nescience of the facts of procreation. That nescience, says Mr. Frazer, 'may be explained easily enough from the habits and modes of thought of savage men.' Thus, 'first, the sexual act precedes the first symptoms of pregnancy by a considerable interval.' *Je n'en vois pas la nécessité.* Secondly, savage tribes 'allow unrestricted licence of intercourse between the sexes under puberty', and thus familiarize him (the savage) 'with sexual unions that are necessarily sterile; from which he may not unnaturally conclude that the intercourse of the sexes has nothing to do with the birth of offspring'. The savage, therefore, explains the arrival of children (at least the Arunta does) by the entrance of a discarnate ancestral spirit into the woman.

The conspicuous and closing objection to this theory is, that savages who are at least as familiar as the Arunta with (1) the alleged remoteness in time of the sexual act from the appearance of the first symptoms of pregnancy (among them such an act and the symptoms may be synchronous), and (2) with licence before puberty, are not in the Arunta state of ignorance. They are under no illusions on these interesting points.

The tribes of social organization much more primitive than that of the Arunta, the south-eastern tribes, as a rule know all about the matter. Mr. Howitt says, 'these' (south-eastern) 'aborigines, even while counting descent—that is, counting the class names—through the mother, never for a moment feel any doubt, according to my experience, that the children originate solely from the male parent, and only owe their infantine nurture to their mother.'[34] Mr. Howitt also quotes 'the remark made to me in several cases, that a woman is only a nurse who takes care of a man's children for him'.[35]

Here, then, we have very low savages among whom the causes of savage ignorance of procreation, as explained by Mr. Frazer, are present, but who, far from being ignorant, take the line of Athene in the *Eumenides* of Æschylus. I give Mr. Paley's translation of the passage:—

'The parent of that which is called her child is not really the *mother* of it, she is but the *nurse* of the newly conceived fœtus. It is the male who is the author of its being, while she, as a stranger for a stranger (i.e., no *blood* relation), preserves the young plant. . . . ' *Eumenides*, 628–631.

These south-eastern tribes, far more primitive than the Arunta in their ceremonials, and in their social organization, do not entertain that dominant factor in Aruntadom, the belief in the perpetual reincarnation of the souls of the mythical ancestors of the *Alcheringa*. That belief is a philosophy far from primitive. As each child is, in Arunta opinion, a being who has existed from the beginning of things, he is not, he cannot be, a creature of man's begetting. Sexual acts, say Messrs. Spencer and Gillen, only, at most 'prepare' a woman for the reception of a child—who is as old as the world! If the Arunta were experimental philosophers, and locked a girl up in Danæ's tower, so that she was never 'prepared', they would, perhaps, be surprised if she gave birth to a child.

However that may be, the Arunta nescience about reproduction is not caused by the facts which, according to Mr. Frazer, are common to them with other savages. These facts produce no nescience among the more primitive tribes with female descent, simply because these primitive tribes do not share the far from primitive Arunta philosophy of eternal reincarnation. If the Arunta deny the fact of procreation among the lower animals, that is because 'the man and his totem are practically indistinguishable', as Mr. Frazer says. What is sauce for the goose is sauce for the gander.

The proof of Arunta primitiveness, the only proof, has been their nescience of the facts of generation. But we have demonstrated that, where Mr. Frazer's alleged causes of that nescience are present, among the south-eastern tribes, they do not produce it; while among the Arunta, it is caused by their system of philosophy, which the south-eastern tribes do not possess.[36]

The burden of Lang's criticism is, of course, directed against Frazer's notion that conceptional totemism among the Arunta is an extremely primitive condition and that their nescience of the facts of procreation is a proof of pristine ignorance. Lang believes, on the contrary, that the procreative beliefs of the Arunta, their nescience of the facts of procreation, are the product of an elaborate philosophy which is a quite late development and far from primitive; one, moreover, which has superseded an earlier condition in which the facts were known.

Lang is, of course, perfectly justified in arguing that the procreative beliefs of the Arunta are the product of their 'peculiar philosophy', but it is quite another matter to imply, as I take him to do, that they must once have been aware of the facts, which this peculiar philosophy has now overlaid and made it necessary to deny. Whether the Arunta were ever aware of the facts it is quite impossible to say, and can be matter for speculation only. To us it seems more probable that the nescience and the dogma of which it is a part were historically contemporaneous in their development, and that neither the one nor the other need ever have stood in a relation of priority to the other. The fact is that everywhere in Australia, whatever the nature of the orthodox doctrine or dogma may be, whether the belief in reincarnation be present or not, the nescience of the facts of procreation is the rule. We now know Lang to be in error when he states that the 'more primitive' South-Eastern tribes, who do not share the alleged Arunta belief in reincarnation, are not characterized by a similar nescience; the fact is that, as Elkin has shown for the Dieri, Yantsuwanta and related tribes of north-eastern South Australia, they are quite as ignorant of the facts of procreation as the Arunta are. Among these tribes we have already seen that children are held to come into being in much the same way as they are among the Arunta, for example, by dreaming, by the consumption of 'child-food', by the entry of a spirit-child into a woman from some specific spirit-centre, and by 'finding'. Neither the father nor the mother is believed to play any generative role in the production and birth of a child.[37]

What the meaning of the remark quoted by Lang from Howitt may be, namely that even in tribes with matrilineal descent of the totem the children are said to originate solely from the male parent it is impossible to determine with any degree of certainty. Since it is always the social father who 'finds' the child in a dream or a vision, the 'originate' of Howitt's phrase may mean no more than that. The male who 'finds' the child is held to be closely associated with that child and he will, of course, be its father. The father, however, does not 'originate' the child physiologically, for the child is of purely spirit origin, but it is he who is, in a way, responsible for the entry of the spirit-child into the woman by virtue of his association with that woman in marriage, for a spirit-child will not enter a woman who is unattached. In any event, there exists not a particle of evidence which indicates that either one or the other parent among these tribes believes that he or she in any way generates the child, a child which is, always, unequivocally conceived to be of spirit origin.

The abundant well-documented evidence from every other part of Australia in which the belief in reincarnation is absent likewise proves that ignorance of physiological maternity and paternity is, with the exceptions noted, widespread in Australia. It must, therefore, I think be clear that the Arunta nescience of the facts of procreation is not, as Lang believed, a unique 'consequence and . . . corollary of the Arunta philosophy of reincarnation'.[38] This became clear to Lang after he read Roth's description of the conditions among the Tully River natives of north Queensland,[39] a people who do not possess a belief in reincarnation, and who believe in the spiritual origin of men. In the very work, however, to which these remarks were contributed (Mrs Langloh Parker's *The Euahlayi Tribe*), it will be recalled that the belief in reincarnation was stated to be absent among the Euahlayi, except in so far as it relates to children who die young and who may undergo reincarnation subsequently in their first mother, it is made clear that the entry of a spirit-child into a woman depends chiefly upon the will of the spirit itself normally entering a woman only who already has a husband, who will, of course, be its father. But it will be recalled that in Mrs Parker's account there was no statement made concerning physiological paternity, although it was stated that in order to live a child must have an earthly father, but this, clearly, in no generative sense whatsoever; it was, in fact, made clear that a child might have no earthly father, and might be born to a woman who was completely unattached, an event which is considered highly discreditable. Whatever the conditions may have been among the Euahlayi physiological paternity is not considered an essential of the parturitive process.[40]

In considering the Tully River beliefs Lang writes.[41]

In most references to Dr Roth which I have seen, the details of his discoveries were not fully discussed. I therefore discuss them; they show that an animistic philosophy, differing in many points from that of the Arunta, colours and even causes the North Queensland denial of procreation. When North Queensland people say that the lower animals have no spirits or souls, and they may be and are the result of procreation; whereas, mankind, having spirits, are not and cannot be procreated, but are made or created, then we have to confess that, in the case of mankind, the North Queensland psychology has clouded the Queensland physiology. The North Queensland tribes know the method of procreation of the lower animals. What they deny is that physical procreative processes can produce man, who has a soul, who is a living spirit . . .

Dr Roth says, 'Animals and plants are not regarded as having any *Koi*—spirit or soul.' Although sexual connection as a cause of conception is not recognized among the Tully River blacks so far as they themselves are concerned, it is admitted as true for all animals;

indeed this idea confirms them in their belief of superiority over the brute creation. Connection can make a brute; 'to make a man's beyond its might,' as Burns says, for man is a living spirit.

These passages prove, I hold, beyond possibility of doubt, that the animistic or spiritual philosophy of these blacks, *and nothing else*, causes them to deny that sexual connection is the agency in the making of man. They have to invent other ways.

We may here, in the first place, ask what actually are we to infer the nature of the Tully River belief to be from the statement that sexual connection as a cause of conception is admitted as true for all animals? Do these Tully River natives really know that sexual intercourse is a cause of pregnancy in animals, as Roth's statement suggests? Something of the sort they have unquestionably said and believe, but what actually is their understanding of the connection? A statement made by Roth in an earlier study of the natives in the Boulia district in north-west central Queensland may serve to convey some idea of what these natives really understand about the matter. Roth states that the station managers had often assured him 'that only with great difficulty could their "boys" be made to understand, if ever they did, the object of spaying cattle'.[42]

This may merely mean that the natives are unaware of the fact that the gonads are the seat of the male generative element, or it may mean that they have no notion of any such thing as a male generative element either in men or in animals. That the latter is by far the most likely is rendered most highly probable from the only thorough-going account of the nature of very similar conditions which have been described for the north-western Melanesians of the Trobriand Islands.[43] The social organization of the Trobriand Islanders is matrilineally biased. They believe that the child is of the same blood as the mother, although it is conceived as entering her in the form of a spirit-baby. The father of the child is regarded as having nothing whatever to do with its generation, he is simply its social father, and bears no other relationship to the child. Pregnancy is caused by spirits who are the reincarnations of former members of the tribe. A virgin is regarded as being unable to conceive, she must first be opened up, since no spirit-child will be either willing or able to enter a closed woman. Since every child, both male and female, begins its sexual life at a very early age, the opening up will, of course, normally have been brought about long before the girl has reached a marriageable age. This method is simply the most convenient one, any artificial means would, however, be quite as effective. After the opening up has once taken place, the sexes, it is believed, need never come to-gether again in order for a child to be born. The Trobriand Islanders know that animals copulate, but they do not believe that the copulation is the cause of conception, or even a condition thereof; copulation among animals, as among men, merely serves the purpose of vaginal dilation, but a female will breed without the co-operation of a male, once she has been opened up.

Among the Trobrianders the bush pig is considered to be far inferior to the native domestic pig, yet, as is the case in so many other Melanesian communities, they take no precautions to keep the domestic breed pure, but instead they castrate the domestic hogs, and allow the sows to wander whithersover they will. As one of Malinowski's informants put it, 'From all male pigs we cut off the testes. They copulate not. Yet the females bring forth.'[44] This, of course, as far as the Trobriander is concerned, constitutes a perfect argument in support of his belief that intercourse has no connection with pregnancy and parturition. Since it is very unlikely that the act of copulation between a domestic sow and a bush pig is ever observed by the native, he has no difficulty in dismissing intercourse as at all a possible cause of, or even a matter of relevance in the discussion of the causation of pregnancy.

In an earlier study[45] Malinowski had quoted the remark of one of his informants concerning pigs, obtained early in the course of his field work. 'They copulate, copulate, presently the female will give birth.' Malinowski's comment was, 'Therefore copulation appears to be the *u'ula* (cause) of pregnancy.' In his later report on the same subject he writes,[46]

This opinion, even in its qualified form, is incorrect. As a matter of fact, during my first visit to the Trobriands, after which the article was written, I never entered deeply into the matter of animal procreation. The concise native utterance quoted above, cannot, in the light of subsequent fuller information, be interpreted as implying any knowledge of how pigs really breed. As it stands, it simply means that vaginal dilation is as necessary in animals as in human beings. It also implies that, according to native tradition, animals are not subject in this, as in many other respects, to the same causal relations as man. In man, spirits are the cause of pregnancy: in animals—it just happens. Again, while the Trobrianders ascribe all human ailments to sorcery, with animals disease is just disease. Men die because of very strong evil magic; animals—just die. But it would be quite incorrect to interpret this as evidence that the natives know, in the case of animals, the natural cause of impregnation, disease, and death; while in man they obliterate this knowledge by an animistic superstructure. The true summary of the native outlook is that they are so deeply interested in human affairs that they construct a special tradition about

245

all that is vital for man; while in what concerns animals, things are taken as they come, without any attempt at explanation, and also without any insight into the real course of nature.

The difference between the Trobrianders and the Tully River natives is that whereas the former deny that there is any necessary relationship between intercourse and pregnancy in the lower animals, the latter affirm it. For Lang this affirmation constitutes something of the greatest consequence. Actually the affirmation is neither more nor less significant than the Trobrianders' denial. Among the Tully River natives animals do not possess a *Koi*, or soul, such as man does, nor do they among the Trobriand Islanders possess a spirit or *baloma*. Among both peoples men possess spirits or souls, among both peoples animals do not; yet among the one intercourse among the lower animals is affirmed as a cause of conception, while among the other people it is denied. Thus, with essentially similar 'philosophies' they have arrived at divergent conclusions as to the conditions obtaining among the lower animals. Among the Trobrianders connection cannot make a brute, nor can it among the Arunta or any other known Australian tribe with the exception of the Tully River blacks. Among the Arunta we have already seen that animals come into being in precisely the same manner as men do; to the Trobrianders the subject is of little interest, they take things concerning animals, as Malinowski has said, just as they come, but that intercourse has anything to do with conception either among men or animals they deny. Among the Tully River people connection does make a brute, though 'to make a man's beyond its might'.

In the case of animals, according to Lang's interpretation, there is nothing to prevent the Tully River natives from perceiving the connection between copulation and birth, whereas the spiritual philosophy which obtains for men precludes the possibility of such percipience. But there can have been nothing in this sense to prevent the Arunta, or the Trobrianders, from arriving at the same conclusion. It so happened that the particular inferences which they drew from the world about them eventually resulted in the conclusions of which so many of their beliefs and customs are the embodiment, and which were arrived at with reason as well as imagination.

It is much more difficult to observe or infer a connection between copulation and birth in animals than it is in human beings living together in more or less continuous association. The only animal the Aborigines have 'domesticated' is the dingo, the half-wild dog found in every Aboriginal camp; there is no evidence that the Aboriginal has ever attempted to domesticate any other animal. Certainly no one would claim that animals living in the wild would provide much opportunity for the observation of the processes of reproduction. Furthermore, the sexual behaviour of dogs under domesticated conditions is, as is well known, so erratic, and must of necessity be even more so under Australian camp conditions where there are generally a very large number of these dogs in a single camp,[47] that from the pell-mell and irregularity of their behaviour it would be something of an achievement to determine that sexual intercourse was in any way connected with the birth of young.

Among animals there is not observable the series of so-called *emphatic* experiences which Read[48] and others have claimed link, among the human species, intercourse to labour and birth, such, for example, as cessation of the menses, euphoria, morning sickness, the quickening, etc., for with the exception of the swelling of the mammary glands and of the abdomen, none of these phenomena can possibly be observed in animals.

It seems to me probable, therefore, unless the Tully River belief represents a faint reverberation of an extra-Australian influence similar to that we suspected to have influenced the form of the procreative beliefs of the not far distant Cape York tribes, principally the Koko-Ya'o and Wik-Munkan, who, it will be recalled, held a belief in the relationship between the father's semen and the child, that the Tully River belief represents no more than an adventitious rationalization calculated to explain the superiority of men over animals, for it is to be doubted whether the Tully River natives can have arrived at an actual knowledge of the relationship on purely empirical grounds.

Upon such a view, then, it would hardly be necessary to assume, as Lang does, that these natives actually 'know' that intercourse is necessary for reproduction to take place, and that in so far as they themselves are concerned they invent another way for this process. The truth more probably is that the Tully River natives have no more idea of the nature of the connection between intercourse and reproduction among the lower animals than they have for themselves.

At any rate, whatever the conditions may be among the Tully River people, it is hardly justifiable to attempt to equate them with the conditions prevailing among any other Aboriginal people. What these natives actually believe we do not know, but even if we grant that they do know that physical connection is the cause of reproduction in animals, it by no means necessarily follows that they ever knew this to be similarly true for themselves. The discovery of the conditions for the lower animals, if such a discovery was ever made, may have come long after the development of the spiritual beliefs, restricted as they are solely to mankind. Though animals may be taken for granted man never can take himself or others so. I do not for a moment see that because these natives may know the 'facts' for animals they must therefore either know or have known them as relating to themselves, or that finding them incompatible with their spiritual doctrines have, therefore, repressed them.

The Tully River nescience of the facts of human procreation is not a function of Tully River philosophy, it *is* that philosophy. There is no question of psychology obscuring physiology, unless these words be understood in the sense of ignorance obscuring knowledge, for the crude physiology simply does not exist, and there is consequently nothing to obscure or repress. Men are specially created, that is religious doctrine affectively acquired and empirically confirmed; animals are animals, they breed and just reproduce, that is profane knowledge profanely acquired, and between the two beliefs there is no contradiction and no cause for obscurantism.

If the Tully River philosophy is associated with a nescience of the facts of human procreation that association does not constitute a reason for assuming that that philosophy produced the nescience, and nothing else. As a matter of fact, the one dominant although not universal belief encountered in Australia is a nescience of the facts of procreation, whereas an appreciable variability is to be found in the philosophies which are associated with this nescience; this being so, might it not be argued with even greater cogency, that such evidence constitutes fairly strong proof of the fact that the nescience preceded the development of the philosophies? Such a claim is not being made here, but I do think that the opposite view is a much less valid one, and that the truth probably is that the nescience and the philosophy were historically contemporaneous in development, and that the separation of the one from the other is a device resorted to by the intellectual analyst for his own arbitrary purposes, but is one which in reality has no counterpart in the context in which these philosophies function.

In the present work our purpose is to determine what the Aborigines actually believe concerning the nature of human procreation. We are interested also in the manner in which those beliefs are maintained. We are *not* concerned with the manner in which those beliefs may have come into existence. Here we may profitably conclude this rather tedious discussion of Lang's views with the statement that as far as human procreation is concerned, the north Queensland tribes would appear to be as unaware of the facts as the Arunta are, and that as far as animal procreation is concerned it is extremely doubtful whether they have any real understanding of the bare facts or, rather, whether they know the bare facts at all.

Lang's chief point is that a knowledge of the relationship between intercourse and conception probably co-exists together with the orthodox beliefs, but that since the latter play so important a role in Arunta life the material facts are merely obscured by the more vitally important spirit-beliefs. I cannot claim, in the course of my examination of Lang's arguments, to have offered any really serious objections to this viewpoint. As we have already seen, Róheim, Warner, Thomson, and others have independently arrived at a similar view concerning the manner in which the evidence is to be interpreted but, as I have pointed out, the evidence these students have cited is far from conclusive, and until further material bearing upon this matter is forthcoming it will remain quite impossible to say whether or not the Aboriginal nescience of the nature of procreation is as complete as it is generally believed to be. If we are to judge from the nature of the orthodox beliefs I think it is fairly evident that these render a knowledge of the facts quite superfluous, and, as I shall endeavour to show, there does not exist anything in the world of the Aboriginal which would necessarily render the discovery of the relationship between intercourse and pregnancy either inescapable or inevitable. At any rate, it will be shown that this is not an unreasonable view to take.

The non-relation of intercourse to conception was, apparently, also at one time the orthodox view in Micronesia. Schneider and his colleagues reported on the Yap Islanders that:[49]

In spite of the fact that the connection of intercourse and reproduction is familiar to the natives, the aboriginal belief was that coitus had nothing to do with getting pregnant. Even today, there is enough confusion in this matter to deserve a few paragraphs. The older people especially are skeptical about the role of coitus, and even the educated and Japanized natives feel some conflict over it.

Older people reason as follows . . . some women have intercourse and do not get pregnant, while others do. In addition, the case of a virgin was cited, but the details and gossip on the matter had to be kept quiet because the child's not having a father was very rude and unmentionable.

The analogies to pigs and other animals were countered by the argument that pigs were animals and not human beings. The human means of reproduction is through patrilineal spirits which watch out for the welfare of their living relatives. If these spirits are happy, then one of them will intercede with the spirit which presides over the menstrual area and over the female functions which are associated with that area. This spirit will make the menstrual fluids congeal in a particular woman and she will become pregnant.

This theory is fitted to the system of double descent, since it neglects neither the mother's nor the father's place in the genesis of the child. A woman alone can have a baby, with her patrilineal spirits working on her behalf, but this is somewhat unusual and a little abnormal. She may also try magically to persuade her spirits to act. Ordinarily, however, it is the spirits of the husband which prevail on the mother's spirit in charge of this matter.

Should the husband's patrilineal spirits fail to cooperate, the pregnancy cannot ordinarily take place, since patrilineal spirits are the functional equivalent of coitus. The belief in the efficacy of the spirits of the husband's lineage is the equivalent of the belief in the biological efficacy of coitus for validating the husband's share in the genesis of the child.

When informants were asked how a child was actually made, the matter of a woman's fluids came up. The reason why a *buliel* (little girl) could not have a child was because she had no milk (like semen). Later on, however, when she had passed her first menstruation and became a *rugod*, she would have this fluid, whose name, like that of semen, is *f'ud*. The woman's fluid is like semen but more watery. Her fluid flows when she has an orgasm, and without this orgasm there can be no child. This orgasm is supposed to be twice as good as a man's, and lasts twice as long to make up for the future pains of childbirth.

I do not know what Lang would have made of the Yap Islanders' procreative beliefs, but it seems to me evident that they were until recently, as Schneider and his colleagues assert, unimpressed by coitus as a cause of pregnancy. Their observational powers are clearly well developed, to which their recognition that the female orgasm is twice as powerful as that of the male should constitute sufficient testimony.

We may now turn our attention to those students of the subject who are in sympathetic accord with some, at least, if not with all of Lang's views.

Goldenweiser, in a brilliant critique of Hartland's *Primitive Paternity*,[50] makes the statement that 'ignorance of the physiology of conception no doubt once pervaded mankind; but no proof is forthcoming that such was the case in a state of society at all comparable to that found among primitive peoples we know.' Upon an earlier page Goldenweiser agrees that the proposition that at one time all mankind was ignorant of the true nature of conception 'is indeed obvious and must be accepted even without hundreds of pages of evidence.'

But the crucial question [he goes on to say] clearly is: Would the generalization apply to savages as we know them, from ancient and modern descriptions? No proof is offered that it would. The evidence as to tribes now living is very scanty indeed. Perhaps the Australian facts may be accepted, with some reservations, for in Central Australia, at least, as Andrew Lang and others have often argued, the beliefs in spiritual conception are clearly a late development superseding an earlier condition when, for all we know, there were no such beliefs.

I think that it may at once be agreed that, to keep to a particular example, the beliefs of the Arunta, for instance, are 'a late development superseding an earlier condition', when they did not possess their present beliefs. What condition then, we may well ask, and what beliefs, if any, did this later development supersede? A belief, possibly, in the causal connection between intercourse and childbirth? Let us, for the purpose of this discussion, assume that such a belief did precede the later contrary development: What then? We are still faced with the fact admitted by all sides that at one time all mankind was ignorant of the true nature of conception. It therefore follows that the remote ancestors of the Arunta may at one time have been ignorant of the relationship. This does not, of course, necessarily mean that the Arunta as a particular people need ever have been characterized by such a nescience. But if we pause here to consider the Australian evidence, we are faced with the fact that among most of the Aboriginal tribes investigated there exists a nescience of the facts of procreation. Is it at all credible that such a belief was at one time preceded by its contrary without leaving the slightest trace of its former existence?

In answer to this question it may be replied that it is not only credible but also, on the basis of what we know of the development and history of the beliefs of numerous other peoples, demonstrable that there are no limits to the modification which beliefs may undergo in the course of social development. This is a truism. Moreover, it may well be argued that in the Aboriginal notion that intercourse serves as a preparer of the woman in anticipation of the entry of a spirit-child into her we have evidence of a possible former belief in its single efficacy in producing childbirth. This is, of course, a possibility, but clearly not a demonstrable one. It perhaps requires to be pointed out here that the knowledge that intercourse is the sole cause of pregnancy is quite a late achievement of the human mind.

The large amount of evidence now available to us from every part of the world, and from every time of which there is any record, renders it certain that among every people of whom we have any knowledge, where an awareness of the relationship between intercourse and childbirth exists, that awareness is unexceptionally accompanied by beliefs and practices which, in the first place, prove that intercourse is not regarded as the sole cause of childbirth, and in the second place would, at least, strongly suggest that this limited awareness was once preceded by a still more limited awareness, in which intercourse played no part in the production of children. I do not propose to cite here more than a few examples of the large amount of evidence which is now available in support of this statement, much of which is to be found in the five volumes by Sidney Hartland,[51] in Frazer's great work,[52] and in the essays by Reitzenstein[53] and Nieuwenhuis,[54] and still more in the numerous ethnological treatises which have been published during this century.

The orthodox belief among the pre-Homeric Greeks appears to have been that they were descended from the spirits incarnate in oak trees and rocks.[55] The same belief is referred to in the Old Testament in the passage (ii, 27) in which Jeremiah describes idolaters as saying to a stock, 'Thou art my father'; and to a stone, 'Thou hast brought me forth.' The enlightened belief of Pan-Hellenic Greece is well illustrated in the passage from *The Eumenides* of Aeschylus, to which, as we have seen on an earlier page, Andrew Lang has already made reference. I give the passage here in what may be considered a more satisfactory version:[56]

> She who is called the mother of the child
> Is not its parent, but the nurse of seed
> Implanted in begetting. He that sows
> Is author of the shoot, which she, if Heaven
> Prevent not, keeps as in a garden-ground
> In proof whereof (Apollo exclaims), to show that fatherhood
> May be without the mother, I appeal
> To Pallas, daughter of Olympian Zeus,
> In present witness here. Behold a plant
> Not moulded in the darkness of the womb,
> Yet nobler than all the scions of Heaven's stock.

It was generally believed that men were supposed to have sprung from the stones dropped by Deucalion and Pyrrha, while the men of Aegina believed themselves to be descended from ants.[57]

With respect to the beliefs of the Egyptians, Diodorus Siculus reports: 'They hold the father alone to be the author of generation and the mother only to provide a nidus and nourishment for the fœtus.'[58] The afterbirth was regarded as the physical or spiritual double of the child.[59]

For the Jews we have the belief in the asexual generation of Adam and Eve, and the belief expressed in the Talmud that 'there are three partners in every birth: God, father, and mother'.[60] 'Remember, I beseech thee,' exclaims Job, 'that thou hast made me as the clay; and wilt thou bring me into dust again? Hast thou not poured me out as milk, and curdled me like cheese? Thou hast clothed me with skin and bones and sinews. Thou hast granted me life and favour, and thy visitation hath preserved my spirit.'[61]

According to Arabian belief as expressed in the Koran, God created the human species from earth, which was first turned into semen and then into a mixture of blood and semen. The beasts were created out of water.[62] At the present day, in Arabia, certain tribes such as the Beni Sohkr regard themselves as descended from the sandstone rocks about Madain Salih.[63]

The connection between intercourse and childbirth was, of course, clearly recognized by the few peoples of antiquity cited here, but the nature of their beliefs points to the fact that that connection was not very profoundly understood. The same statement could be made concerning the beliefs of the Aboriginal, the differences in the beliefs of the peoples of antiquity and those of the Aborigines being chiefly a matter of degree, and this is, of course, the important point. The Aboriginal does not regard intercourse as the cause of pregnancy, whatever the mechanism of the latter is interpreted to be; on the contrary the peoples to whom I have referred did regard intercourse as the primary temporal cause of conception, although the character of their beliefs was such as to suggest that the idea of the super-natural nature of pregnancy was once the dominant one among the cultural ancestors of these peoples.[64] Of this there can be no proof, and this is Goldenweiser's point, with which I am in entire agreement, but there is, I think, in view of the evidence a strong presumption of the existence of such more primitive beliefs among these peoples—it is not intended to claim anything more than this.

Among the reasons that have prevented many students from accepting the alleged nescience of the Aborigines concerning the nature of procreation, one of the chief of these has been the difficulty of imagining any people so naturally unobservant as to fail to recognize what would seem to be so impressively and inescapably evident as the relationship between intercourse and pregnancy.

As we shall shortly have occasion to see, this difficulty arises chiefly from certain pre-existing prejudices, entirely unselfconscious, which the various students of the subject have been unable to resist, and in this way have been forced to pre-judge what they were quite clearly in no condition to judge. The analysis of their arguments, therefore, should not be altogether unilluminating.

The most cogent and at once the most representative discussion of the procreative beliefs of savages from this standpoint is that of the late Professor Carveth Read,[65] who was for many years Professor of Logic in the University of London, and a brilliant contributor to the discussion of anthropological problems.

Read opens his discussion with the avowal that what natives say in Central Australia and in the Trobriands is not in question. But, he queries, what state of mind do such declarations on the part of the natives indicate? Are they actually unable to make the connection and draw the inference, or do they, perhaps not all of them, know the truth, and that the dogma contradicting such knowledge has caused its repression and expulsion from consciousness?

Essentially, it will be observed, this is the view earlier put forward by Lang.

Read then proceeds to quote Strehlow to the effect that the old men among the Arunta knew that cohabitation was to be considered as the cause of children, but that they say nothing about this to the younger men and women. The statement, from the same source, is also quoted that both the Arunta and Loritja are aware of the relationship between copulation and offspring in animals, and that even the children are enlightened upon that point. Since the first statement was afterwards corrected by Strehlow himself, and the second statement alone reaffirmed by Strehlow, we need concern ourselves with the latter only so far as to repeat what we have already said, namely, that in view of the Aboriginal beliefs as reported by Spencer and Gillen to the effect that animals come into being in precisely the same way as men do, it is highly probable that these Aborigines were in this connection influenced by white beliefs. Read concedes that Strehlow's work may possibly be unsatisfactory in certain respects, but he suggests that what Strehlow says is not intrinsically improbable. 'The keeping of knowledge by elders secret from the rest of the tribe is a very common thing; and if not only is the truth concealed but an untruth inculcated, there is evidence enough that dogmas taught by elders or priests may be accepted in opposition to immediate and unmistakable fact.'[66]

The last point, I think, is in a provisional way indisputable, every group of elders or priesthood has its esoteric knowledge which it keeps from the multitude, and every pious Catholic woman believes that her child is chiefly the result of an act of God; the notion that it may be the result of the material act of intercourse is of itself felt to be a painful perversion of the truth and a blasphemy.

But nowhere here, nor in any other context with which I am acquainted, are the beliefs taught by the elders, priests, or dogmas for exoteric consumption in opposition to 'immediate and unmistakable fact', for the relationship between intercourse and childbirth is nowhere in the world, neither now nor could it have been at any previous time, either immediate or unmistakable. And this, after all, is the crucial and important point. If these facts are neither immediate nor unmistakable, then it is quite easy to see how other 'facts' can take their place, or be superimposed upon them, and this precisely is quite possibly what may have happened in the case of the Arunta in particular, and all other peoples having similar beliefs, in general. It is precisely this point which it is our task to render clear in the following pages.

The argument which has it that since there must have been a stage during which universal ignorance of the facts of procreation prevailed it is therefore possible that the Arunta may not have got beyond that stage, Read counters with the statement that the level of intelligence which could have entertained such a belief must have been considerably lower than that which the Arunta are known to possess. To borrow a phrase from Lang, *Je n'en vois pas la nécessité.* We have seen something of the beliefs of the peoples of antiquity in this connection, and as far as the procreative beliefs of many individuals among ourselves are concerned these are in many cases, as Hartland and others have pointed out, quite as primitive as those of the Aborigines themselves.

Far from any of the physiological facts of conception being immediately and unmistakably relatable to childbirth, the truth is that even in civilized societies quite a sizable number of individuals grow up without any knowledge whatever of the relationship between intercourse and childbirth. Almost every obstetrician, gynaecologist, urologist, and marriage counsellor of any experience has encountered patients who were entirely ignorant of the relationship between intercourse and childbirth. Writing in 1888 Joseph W. Howe, Professor of Clinical Surgery in Bellevue Medical College, New York, stated: 'Married women, and men too, of much experience in other matters pertaining to the management of their physical natures, have informed me that when they entered the marriage state, they were totally unaware of the nature of the sexual relation, and that many days and nights were passed in the midst of curious sensations, doubts and fears and ridiculous performances before the marriage was consummated. Neither did they comprehend the immediate or remote results of the new relation.'[67] Dr D. E. R. Kelsey reports the case of a south of England married woman of twenty-eight with two children, 'who seemed to have no understanding at all of the significance played by the male and female in reproduction . . . She had apparently no knowledge of the existence or function of the umbilical cord. The navel was "something which happens when you are born". She was under an anaesthetic when her children were born and was therefore unable to say whether anything but the child emerged from her. I am quite sure she had no knowledge of spermatozoa or ova, or the process of conception.'[68]

Dr Sheldon C. Reed tells of 'a teen-age brother and sister of one of the "best" families in the Twin Cities [who] had been so carefully shielded from the viciousness of the outside world that they were completely innocent of any sex education whatever. At least, they were able to convince the social worker that they had no idea that a baby might result from their sexual intercourse.'[69]

Drs J. P. Semmens and W. M. Lamers, Jr, two obstetricians of great experience, write that the teen-age girl 'may think that she is pregnant even though she has not had sexual relations. Despite the progress made in recent years in the field of family life education, there are a few girls who honestly believe they can become pregnant through kissing or mild petting.'[70] Professor Read is, indeed, ready to admit that 'a great deal of the knowledge of savages and even of civilized men, is not of the discriminated, relational, propositional, texture to which, under the influences of formal logic, we are apt to confine the name.'

The further argument that between events so far apart as intercourse and childbirth the relation cannot be observed, but must be inferred—and the conditions are such as to make the inference a matter of difficulty—Read replies that we are not here concerned merely with a simple relation between intercourse and childbirth, but with a series of emphatic experiences, namely: (1) intercourse, (2) from one to six weeks later, cessation of the menses, (3) at about four and a half months from intercourse, the quickening, (4) in another four and a half months, labour and birth. 'Nor is this all,' Read adds, 'for the series is fused together by further impressive changes, the swelling of the breasts and of the abdomen, and by still subjective, very variable phenomena, such as euphoria, nausea, sick fancies and longings. These experiences, each deeply impressive, are not far apart: to connect them needs no great reach of memory; events much farther apart—even many years apart—are connected by savages.'[71]

It will repay us here to examine these so-called 'emphatic experiences' in some detail in the endeavour to discover to what extent, if any, there is any real connection between them, and in how far this may be recognized by the natives.

INTERCOURSE

Intercourse is among all people everywhere regarded essentially as a pleasure, and among the Arunta, who are not exceptional in this respect, there is no evidence that it is invested with any more meaning than that. As an urge the libido must be satisfied, and once satisfied its immediate interest comes to an end, only to be reborn again in the form of a renewed desire, and so on in a virtually endless cycle. One hunts, eats, drinks, has intercourse when one can and will, and sleeps. Of such is the stuff of life. As soon as one is able, as a young child, one learns to indulge in intercourse—it is amusing, and it is a pleasure. From such activities, of course, offspring never result. One has intercourse continually, and that is the beginning and end of the matter. Children do not have offspring because a spirit-child will not normally enter an unmarried girl. It is the act of marriage in the sense of obtaining a social father for the child that makes it possible for a female, under normal circumstances, to be entered by a spirit-child. Of course, sometimes an unmarried female does give birth to a child, and since the child has no father it is regarded as a very shameful thing to have borne a child under such circumstances, for it is not proper that a child should be born which has no father. Thus, for example, Malinowski relates that one of his early informants in the Trobriands lived together with a girl to whom he was going to be married, but, unfortunately, she gave birth to a child, whereupon her lover abandoned her, for it is wrong for an unmarried girl to give birth to a child. The unfortunate girl's lover 'was quite convinced', writes Malinowski, 'that she had never had any relations with any other boy, so, if any question of physiological fatherhood had come into his mind, he would have accepted the child as his own, and married the mother. But, in accordance with the native point of view, he simply did not inquire into the question of fatherhood; it was enough that there was pre-nuptial motherhood.'[72] Both in the Trobriands and in Australia in such cases it is quite clear that someone who has wished to injure the woman's reputation has caused a spirit-child to enter her. It may have been a member of her own tribe, or a medicine-man from another tribe, or a mischievous spirit in an unkindly mood who was the responsible agent. It is, however, a very unfortunate and discreditable thing. Lest it be for a moment thought that there is involved in this situation a recognition on the part of the natives of the physical necessity of a father, it may at once be said that what the natives mean, as Malinowski has pointed out for the Trobrianders, is that the father, in this connection, is the social father only—in fact, the word has no other meaning among these peoples. Before a woman can bear children she must marry, enter into a new family arrangement, and have a husband who will help her to educate the children. As Malinowski has said, 'The sociological role of the father is established and defined without any recognition of his physiological nature.'[73]

In any event, the phenomenon of a pregnant girl who has not yet reached puberty is a relatively rare one in primitive communities. Since, as a rule, girls give birth to children only after they have been married, that is, after they have attained to social puberty, it is evident then that they must grow up in the midst of sexual experiences which they know to be perfectly unconnected with such a phenomenon as childbirth. In any case, they know perfectly well that children come in quite categorically different ways. In the experience of the child, then, there is absolutely no reason why intercourse should be associated with childbirth.

Whether children, among the Aborigines, ever witness sexual intercourse between adults is a matter concerning which we have very little information; that they may occasionally witness it is probable. In general it is, however, likely that intercourse is regarded as a private act which children as well as other adults do not, as a rule, observe. Some evidence for this was obtained by Ronald Berndt from informants of the Anta'kirinja tribe who were gathered at Ooldea soak in South Australia. These informants 'stated that sexual intercourse between husband and wife is never indulged in when children are present. These are either sent to a relative's *wiltja* [shelter, or *mia-mia*], or the husband and wife retire outside the boundary of the camp.'[74]

Abbie, however, states that 'there is no privacy in a *wurley* and children very soon learn all about the marital doings of their parents.'[75]

Read, however, considers the sterile pre-pubertal and pre-nuptial sexual relations as quite unimportant, since, he asserts, the change of sexual life at puberty is deeply impressive and well known to savages. It is difficult to follow Read's meaning here. The important point *is* that the native grows up and develops during his most impressible years in the most intimate association with an experience which he looks upon merely as a pleasure, and which, for him, positively has no connection with childbirth, and is as unconnected in his own mind with such a phenomenon as is the fact that it is necessary to reach physiological maturity before one can conceive. Indeed, puberty is not regarded so much as a sexually maturative phenomenon as it is regarded as a socially maturative one. It is the stage in the development of a girl at which among other things, she is taken over by, and goes to live permanently with, her husband. Puberty is in no way associated with either intercourse or parturition, or the ability to conceive, as it is for the most part erroneously associated by all but a handful of students living in the Western world today. There is, as we shall see, no real reason why these things should be associated.

It has long been known that puberty is not necessarily coincident with the development of reproductive capacity, that in the girl menstruation may long precede ovulation, and that in the youth ejaculation may appreciably precede spermatogenesis. In spite of this knowledge it has been almost universally tacitly assumed that puberty represents the physical sign of the ability to procreate. This assumption is not in agreement with the facts.

This brings us to the particular consideration of the general problem which has perplexed so many students of nonliterate peoples, as well as those biologists to whose attention the matter has been brought. I refer here to the phenomenon presented by the extreme disparity in the fertility[76] of the unmarried and the married in the communities of the simpler peoples. Although among such peoples sexual intercourse is quite free and unrestrained before marriage, pregnancy among the unmarried females is a relatively rare occurrence. This observation holds true for societies in which marriage takes place at or shortly after the onset of menstruation in the female as, for example, among the Aborigines of Australia, as well as for such societies in which marriage takes place some years after the onset of the menarche, as among Melanesians generally. In those societies in which marriage takes place at or shortly after the establishment of the menarche, as in Australia, there is no difficulty in explaining the existing premarital infertility, since prepubertal fecundity, or the physiological capacity to participate in reproduction, is, as I have already pointed out, normally non-existent, for without ovulation, which practically never occurs before puberty, there can be no fecundity and hence no fertility. The matter is, however, very different in those societies in which marriage does not take place until some years after the establishment of menarche, and it is because the situation is so illuminating among such peoples for the vastly more complicated situation among the Aborigines, that we shall devote some space to a consideration of the problems among the former before returning to the Aborigines.

In communities of the Melanesian type the post-pubertal adolescent girls indulge quite freely in sexual intercourse without, as a rule, becoming pregnant. Infertility, indeed, among the unmarried women is the rule and pregnancy the exception. It is to be observed that I speak of *pregnancy* and not *childbirth*, this I do deliberately in order to emphasize the fact that we are here dealing with a natural phenomenon which is quite uncomplicated by such extraneous influences of conscious human agency as abortive or abortifacient practices, which would render the development of pregnancy abortive, and thus, whilst pregnancy might, childbirth would not, occur. We may also exclude the possibility of contraceptive practices here for, in the first place, among the peoples we are considering there is a complete absence of knowledge concerning the role coitus and its accompanying processes actually play in procreation, so that there is no occasion for the use of contraceptive measures, and in the second place even if there were it can be conclusively shown that none of the measures which are commonly employed by the peoples of Oceania is capable of securing the end desired.[77] I do not wish to give the impression that abortive practices are altogether unknown, or that they are not on occasion resorted to, indeed, such an impression would do violence to the facts, but what it is desirable to emphasize is that pregnancy is of such rare occurrence among the unmarried women that whether or not effective abortive measures are resorted to when it does occur is a matter of relevance only in connection with childbirth and not with pregnancy. It is the rarity of pregnancy among the post-pubertal females that is our chief concern. This is a problem which was given deserved prominence by Malinowski in *The Sexual Life of Savages*, in the following words:[78]

it is very remarkable to note that illegitimate children are rare. The girls seem to remain sterile throughout their period of licence, which begins when they are small children and continues until they marry; when they are married they conceive and breed, sometimes quite prolifically. . . . I was able to find roughly a dozen illegitimate children recorded genealogically in the Trobriands, or about one per cent. . . .

Thus we are faced with the question: Why are there so few illegitimate children? On this subject I can only speak tentatively, and I feel that my information is perhaps not quite as full as it might have been, had I concentrated more attention upon it. One thing I can say with complete confidence: no preventive means of any description are known, nor the slightest idea of them entertained. This, of course, is quite natural. Since the procreative power of seminal fluid is not known, since it is considered not only innocuous but beneficent, there is no reason why the natives should interfere with its free arrival into the parts which it is meant to lubricate. Indeed, any suggestion of Neo-Malthusian appliances makes them shudder or laugh according to their mood or temperament. They never practise *coitus interruptus*, and still less have any notion about chemical or mechanical preventives.

But though I am quite certain on this point, I cannot speak with the same conviction about abortion, though probably it is not practised to any large extent. . . .

So the problem remains. Can there be any physiological law which makes conception less likely when women begin their sexual life young, lead it indefatigably, and mix their lovers freely?

It is one of the great merits of Malinowski that he has been able to recognize the essence of the problem and to state it so clearly: this, unfortunately, has not always been the case, the problem being frequently obscured by the manner in which it has been stated. Thus, Rivers in his account of the Eddystone Islanders writes:[79]

The very free relations existing before marriage might have been expected to lead to the birth of many children and to the existence of definite regulations for assigning such children to their proper place in society. Such births seemed, however, to be extremely rare, and in the whole of the pedigrees collected by us only one such case was given, and that many generations ago. We did not hear of any such birth either during our visit or in recent times; and so far as we know there was no one on this island who was the child of pre-marital intercourse. It was said that such births occurred, however, though no actual recent instances could be given . . .

Rivers goes on to say: 'It is quite certain that births before marriage were very rare and two causes were given to account for this, abortion and a process resembling the other magico-religious rites of the island, called *egoro* meaning "barrenness", which is believed to prevent conception'.[80]

Abortion was produced by mechanical means or by the process of rubbing a certain heated leaf on the belly, and then holding four leaves of another kind under the vulva, when the child, so it was believed, would come out.

Now, it is quite clear from Rivers's description of an *egoro* rite, into the details of which it is unnecessary to enter here,[81] that the rite is purely magical, and could have no actual physical effect. The rite is believed to be quite as efficacious in producing sterility in the woman when it is performed upon her husband alone.[82] Rivers, to some extent, recognizes the magical nature of the rite, but considers it quite possible that the concoctions used may be effective in producing some pathological condition of the uterus. As an explanation of the condition of infertility among the unmarried women, apart from the married women, this will certainly not do. For it is obvious that a large number of the Eddystone Islanders must be fecund, and I think, too, that it must be fairly evident that the rarity of births among the unmarried must, at least in part, be due to the fact that though there may have been much intercourse there have been relatively few pregnancies resulting from such intercourse. This is a possibility that does not seem to have occurred to Rivers.

An illuminating account of conditions prevailing among the natives of Wogeo, one of the most northerly of the Schouten Islands, off New Guinea has been published by Hogbin. Among the natives of this island sexual life does not begin until about the age of sixteen or seventeen, or even later, but is then particularly free:[83]

261

Single girls do sometimes have children, but illegitimacy is not nearly so common as one might have expected. Just why this is so it is impossible to say. Professor Malinowski, it will be remembered, found the same situation in the Trobriands. I observed one fact that bears directly upon the problem, namely that it is extremely rare for women to have children until they are, I judge, more than 21 years of age, by which time most of them are safely married. I have noticed that even when a girl is married directly after her first menstruation, which does not regularly take place until almost certainly after the seventeenth year,[84] it is most unusual for her to have a child for several years. One Dap girl had a child within about eighteen months of her first menstruation—fortunately for herself she was married—and this was so unusual that she was described as a coco-nut putting forth a shoot before it had fallen from the parent tree. The comments on this girl, in fact, brought the whole matter to my notice.

The account of this people renders it quite clear that when a girl is married and begins continuous intercourse with her husband directly after the onset of the menarche she does not normally conceive until several years have elapsed. There can be no possible objection to a recently married woman giving birth to a child, but this is so unusual a phenomenon that it has given rise to a belief that it is not a normal thing for a young pubertal married woman to be able to bear children, and certainly not normal in an unmarried woman. In this belief these natives show themselves far in advance of the Western world, for their belief reflects the possession of knowledge based upon observation which owing to a fortunate colligation of phenomena which does not exist among ourselves enabled them to arrive at a knowledge of facts which was not ascertained elsewhere in the world until 1929 when Crew described the phenomenon in mice.

Since, then, it appears that between the onset of menstruation, at whatever age that may occur, and the conception and birth of the first child an interval of some years elapses despite frequent intercourse with mature males during that interval, the question arises as to what can be the explanation of this phenomenon, this apparent sterility? What, if any, can be its physical basis?

As a result of researches published in the thirties and since, we are now in a position to be able to return a satisfactory answer to these questions.[85]

Let us commence with a lower mammal, the mouse. In an experiment carried out on 100 female mice at the first oestrus, Crew found that 20 per cent of the animals refused to mate, while of the remaining

80 per cent of matings only twenty-four cases, or 30 per cent, were followed by pregnancy. Later, however, when the same mice were three to six months old, the fertility ratio—that is, the percentage of pregnancies following matings—was not less than 80 to 90 per cent.

It is seen, therefore, that though pregnancy can occur at the time of the first œstrus, it is relatively uncommon. Furthermore, of the 24 animals which became pregnant following first mating and first œstrus, 7 of them died, whilst 4 others ate their young soon after birth. In our experience it is not uncommon to find that the mother which destroys her young is herself physically unfit to rear them, and that in a great majority of such cases the mother herself dies shortly afterwards. It is seen, then, that not only is pregnancy relatively rare after mating associated with first œstrus, but it is also relatively dangerous.[86]

Professor C. A. Mills and his collaborator, Dr Cordelia Ogle, confirmed these findings by a number of ingenious experiments carried out under a variety of controlled conditions, chiefly of temperature. Whatever the conditions it was found that the lag in sterility between menarche and conception, the sterility interval, was never absent. Moreover, it was found that while the length of the sterility interval may be increased by varying the temperature of the environment in which the animals live, it has, however, not so far been possible either to reduce or to eliminate it. To summarize Mills and Ogle's results:

Mice with first oestrus at	Exhibited a sterility interval lasting
24–32 days	33·4 days
33–41 days	32·5 days
42–50 days	29·5 days

Thus, it would seem clear that in the mouse the sterility interval existing between menarche and maturity is to be regarded as a natural phenomenon.[87]

The next mammal for whom reliable information is available is the catarrhine monkey, *Macacus rhesus*. In an important communication published in 1931,[88] C. G. Hartman briefly reported his observations on fifteen rhesus monkeys whose every menstrual cycle had been from its inception carefully observed. As a result of this study Hartman found that between the onset of the first menstruation and the first conception, despite frequent matings with mature males during the interval, a period of about one year elapsed. In a monograph on the reproduction of the rhesus monkey published a year later Hartman made it quite clear that the failure to ovulate during this interval is 'the probable cause of the relative sterility of adolescent females', for he found 'a very high incidence of non-ovulatory cycles in young animals'.[89] In this communication Hartman suggested that such facts probably explained the infertility of the Trobriand girls which had so puzzled Malinowski.

The only other mammal, with the exception of man, for whom a certain amount of reliable evidence is available with reference to the problem of adolescent sterility is fortunately a close ally of man, namely the chimpanzee.

In a communication published in 1935 R. M. Yerkes reported the first recorded case of a second-generation captive-born chimpanzee whose first menstruation occurred on 10 July 1933, when she was seven years and four months old.[90] She was caged with a mature male from May 1933 onwards (that is from some two months before the onset of the first menstruation) and she became pregnant on 9 August 1934 ($\pm$ 5 days), at the age of eight years and five months. Thus, the interval between the first menstruation and her first conception, despite frequent intercourse during the interim with a mature male, lasted one year and one month. The sterile interval thus being not very significantly greater in duration than that Hartman found for the rhesus monkey.

Tinkelpaugh has reported a chimpanzee who conceived only four months after the first menstruation appeared, her age at the time of conception being approximately nine years.[91]

In the chimpanzee reported by Fox conception did not occur until two years after the onset of menstruation. In this case, however, a mature male was not continuously present during this interval. The approximate age of this animal at conception was seven and a half years.[92]

In the chimpanzee reported by Schultz and Synder conception did not occur until one year and one month after the onset of menstruation, although a mature male was present during the whole of this period. It is to be noted, however, that he did not attempt intercourse with this animal, owing to the presence of another and more recently introduced animal, until she had passed her seventh menstrual cycle, or approximately eight months after her first menstruation.[93]

In the chimpanzee reported by Wyatt and Vevers menstruation regularly occurred for some three years before a mature male was admitted to her society, when conception followed almost immediately after the establishment of sexual relations. The age of this animal at conception was estimated to be about ten years.[94]

These five records for the chimpanzee are obviously of great interest;[95] three of these cases prove the existence of a sterility interval in this animal whilst the two others, though experimentally unsatisfactory, support its existence in this particular animal, showing that when a sufficient length of time has elapsed following the first menstruation the animal is capable of conceiving promptly when put together with a mature male—conditions paralleling those existing among ourselves, where marriage and effective intercourse does not take place until a considerable interval after menarche when the promptitude with which conception generally follows intercourse altogether obscures the fact of the possible existence of an adolescent sterility interval in human beings.

The evidence for the mammals thus far investigated indicates the existence in the adolescent organism of conditions which prevent the immature animal from undergoing an experience which it is not yet viably equipped to undertake. As Crew has pointed out in connection with the mouse, 'not only is pregnancy relatively rare after mating associated with the first oestrus, but it is also relatively dangerous.' There is every reason to believe that similar conditions normally exist in the human adolescent, and that Crew's remark applies with equal force to human beings as to mice. For example, in the United States —and these conditions are everywhere the same—the maternal and infant death rates are highest when the mother is below fifteen years of age than at any other period. When the mother is between fifteen and twenty maternal and infant mortality is higher than when the mother is between twenty and twenty-nine. Maternal mortality is lowest between twenty and twenty-four (5 per 1,000 live births), next lowest between twenty-five and twenty-nine, rising rapidly after thirty by five-year groups from 7·4 to 10·3 to 13·1 to 19·2 at forty-five years.

Infant mortality is at its highest in the years below eighteen with a death rate of 160 per 1,000 infants; between eighteen and nineteen it is 129, between twenty and twenty-four it is 109·5, between twenty-five and twenty-nine it is 101·4, and between thirty and thirty-four it is 104·7. At forty years the rate once more climbs to 129.[96]

These figures abundantly testify to the relatively great danger to the mother and her offspring when conception takes place within the first three or four years following menarche, as compared with any other period. The full growth of the human female is not attained until 23 ± 2 years, and it is from this period until the age of twenty-nine that the optimum conditions for reproduction exist, approximately from between ten and fifteen years after the onset of menarche, taking the latter to occur at 13 ± 2 years. Above and below this age infant and maternal mortality constantly increases, but it is never so high as in the adolescent female below the age of eighteen years.

It would seem fairly clear, then, that the adolescent female is not naturally viably prepared to undertake and to bring to a successful conclusion the process of reproduction.

Among ourselves the belief that at puberty a girl arrives at the capacity to bear children is, of course, a notion bequeathed to us from past generations. We have ourselves had no opportunity of checking the truth of this belief for there has never been the slightest reason to doubt its truth. In the same case were all the generations which preceded us. Since girls arrived at menarche some years before they married, and since they generally conceived at variably different intervals after marriage, this fitted perfectly with the accepted menarche–fecundity relationship. Moreover, for the last hundred years the 'child-mothers' of the East and of primitive peoples who have been described and photographed by so many travellers have, of course, abundantly testified to the truth of a belief which no one has ever dreamed of questioning. We have all seen photographs of these 'child-mothers' bearing in their arms children almost as large as themselves, and their condition has frequently been described. In one such widely read book, Mrs Katherine Mayo's *Mother India*, the author stated: 'The Indian girl, in common practice, looks for motherhood nine months after reaching puberty, or anywhere between the ages of 14 and 18. The latter age is extreme, though in some sections not exceptional; the former is well above the average.'[97]

The facts with which Mrs Mayo does not seem to have concerned herself are that cohabitation begins at 'puberty' or, more correctly, menarche, and that in the great majority of cases the first child is born in the *third* year of effective marriage.[98] Furthermore, the average age of menarche in the Indian girl is $14 \cdot 21 \pm 1 \cdot 66$ years. These figures would give us an approximate age at first delivery[99] of sixteen years and some months. Pillay gives the age of the mother at the birth of the first child as between fourteen and fifteen years,[100] while according to A. H. Clark's statement of the figures obtained from the Maternity Hospital at Seva Sada in Amednagar, in which Presidency early marriage is more prevalent than in any other part of India, the average age of the mother at first delivery is $18 \cdot 3$ years. In Bombay the age is $18 \cdot 7$ years, and in Madras $19 \cdot 4$ years.[101]

The imaginative order of Mrs Mayo's observations is, I think, fairly clear. The fact is that white observers almost invariably underestimate by years the ages of native children who, owing to undernourishment and a variety of other factors appear to be so much less developed than our own children at similar ages. Professor C. A. Mills tells me that during his widely extended investigations among native peoples in various parts of the world it was invariably his experience that when he was able to check his own estimate of the age of an adolescent or a child by some official birth record, he always found his own estimate to be too low.[102] Such a fact would account for the lowness of the age at first menstruation, etc., which, in the absence of reliable records, white observers have generally given for primitive peoples as well as more advanced peoples for whom records were not available. Actually it is extremely doubtful whether there exists any people among whom the mean age at menarche is less than twelve to thirteen years.

It is, of course, perfectly well known that some girls in India, as everywhere else in the world, are capable of bearing children at a *chronological* age of less than thirteen years, but there can be very little doubt that the *physiological* age, that is to say the actual developmental status of such girls as measured against chronologic time, is commensurate with that of the chronologically older normal girls. Arbitrary chronological standards of age do not here concern us.

Owing to the fact that nonliterate peoples do not keep exact records it is virtually impossible to obtain reliable data concerning such events. Conclusive data on adolescent sterility in the human species are, for obvious reasons, difficult to obtain, yet such evidence as is available speaks strongly for the existence of such a period in most adolescent human females.

One of the first investigators to collect and to report upon such data was A.-T. Mondière, a physician and anthropologist who, during the latter part of the last century, spent some six years working among the inhabitants of Cochin China. His results were reported in a study published in 1880,[103] and later summarized in a short article.[104] It was from this latter work that Hartman quoted Mondière's figures in his 1931 communication to *Science*. I quote Mondière's findings from the earlier communication which is somewhat more detailed than the later article. The table gives Mondière's findings in an easily understood form.

People	No. of cases	Mean age at menarche Yrs Mths		Number with first child	Age at birth of first child Yrs Mths		Sterility interval* Yrs Mths	
Annamite	980	16	4	440	20	6	3	4
Chinese	106	16	6	15	18	10	1	6
Min-Huong	62	16	9	40	20	9	3	2
Cambodian	96	16	10	45	22	6	4	10

* The calculation of the sterility interval from menarche to *conception* (= −10 months from parturition) has been added by the present writer.

Mondière noted the variation in the duration of the menarche–parturition interval in his four groups and remarked that since the climatic conditions were the same for all these peoples the difference in the intervals must be attributed to racial differences or, perhaps as we would today say, genetic differences. The great duration of the sterility interval in the Cambodian women Mondière attributes to the fact that among this people the husband is, as a rule, more than twenty years older than his wife, an explanation that may not be without some virtue, though it is of doubtful value. I propose here to do no more than suggest that taken as they stand Mondière's findings indicate that among the peoples of Cochin China investigated by him a period of adolescent sterility normally exists.

Professor J. Preston Maxwell, Professor of Obstetrics and Gynaecology at Peiping Union Medical College, China, was good enough to send me his unpublished data collected in 1907 on 103 Chinese women from Yung Chun in South Fukien; these data relate to menarche, marriage, and first delivery. Professor Maxwell found that there is a mean interval of three and a half years between marriage and the birth of the first child. His findings, as supplied to me, on analysis yield the following distribution for the duration between marriage and the birth of the first child:

	−	+	+	+	+	+	+	+	+	+	+	*No*
	1 yr	1 yr	2 yrs	3 yrs	4 yrs	5 yrs	6 yrs	7 yrs	8 yrs	9 yrs	12 yrs	*pregnancy*
Cases	(2)	(13)	(17)	(17)	(8)	(4)	(8)	(5)	(5)	(2)	(1)	(20)
Per cent	1·9	12·6	16·5	16·5	7·9	3·9	7·9	4·9	4·9	1·9	0·9	19·4

These figures are striking. In only 2 out of 103 cases were children born to women within the first year of marriage, the vast majority of children being born considerably after marriage. Of these 103 women 31 married before the onset of menarche, but in no case did any of these women bear children until after the establishment of menarche. The important figures are yielded by an analysis of the distribution of the intervals between *menarche* and first delivery or birth of the first child. The figures are as follows:

	−	+	+	+	+	+	+	+	+	+	*No*
	1 yr	1 yr	2 yrs	3 yrs	4 yrs	5 yrs	6 yrs	7 yrs	8 yrs	9 yrs	*pregnancy*
Cases	(3)	(6)	(17)	(11)	(15)	(7)	(8)	(5)	(3)	(4)	(20)
Per cent	3·0	6·0	17·0	11·0	15·0	7·0	8·0	5·0	3·0	4·0	20·0

These figures show that only in a very small percentage of cases is menarche followed by pregnancy within the first year, and that an interval between two and three years generally elapses following menarche before the first child is born. It is also to be noted that in 27 per cent of cases birth took place five or more years after menarche, and that in 20 per cent of cases no birth had taken place at the time of the record in spite of the fact that many of these women had been married for a considerable time.

Professor Maxwell informed me that at the time when these observations were made, 'pre-marital intercourse was almost unknown and there was no such thing as contraception'.[105]

Chau and Wright in a report of an investigation on 2,291 Chinese women living in sub-tropical Canton (N. Lat., 23° 7′ 10″) and surrounding districts, state that the mean age at menarche was 14·5 years, the mean age at marriage (683 cases) 17·6 years, and the mean age (596 cases) at the birth of the first child 20·5 years—which suggests a sterility interval of six years. Only one girl became a mother at the age of thirteen years, five at the age of fifteen, and twelve at the age of sixteen.[106] No further details bearing upon these matters are supplied.

Without entering here upon a discussion of the very wide implications of such facts, it seems probable that in the human female, and in the mammals, which have thus far been studied, varying according to race, etc., there is generally an interval of anything up to five years or more between menarche and the ability to procreate, during which the female is functionally sterile and unable to reproduce. This sterile interval has been shown by Hartman to be due, in the monkey at least, to the non-ovulatory character of the adolescent menstrual cycle. And as Hartman has pointed out puberty, which is signalized by the onset of the first menstruation, merely marks the 'early manifestation of a train of events (adolescence) which only after three or four years on the average lead to ovulation and conception, the proof of maturity'.[107]

It is such facts as these, as Hartman has also suggested, which may possibly explain the infertility of the unmarried women in nonliterate societies; and there is, of course, not the slightest reason to doubt that these facts hold as good for Australian Aborigines as for any other people.

As we have already seen, the evidence derived from laboratory experiments with mice, macaques, and chimpanzees conclusively points to the fact that the adolescent sterility interval is a perfectly natural and normal phenomenon. In man, possibly, social factors exert a modifying influence upon it.

It seems, then, very unlikely that puberty could be physiologically associated with parturition by the Aborigines and Read's argument, therefore, that the deeply impressive change of sexual life at puberty is well known to the savages will not, upon such grounds, bear examination.

If it is Read's meaning that upon marriage, that is, at or shortly after puberty, the girl is removed from a loosely characterized sexual life and placed in a situation where the sexual ordinate is of a more constant character, the nature of which renders it a fairly simple matter to educe the necessary relation between intercourse and pregnancy, there is this to say in respect of it: in the first place the girl will not normally conceive for a considerable period of time following her marriage. Definite evidence of this is now available for more than one Australian tribe. Thus, Mountford and Harvey write of the Adnjamatana of northern South Australia, that 'marriage takes place at puberty. But enquiries as to the approximate age of the mother at the birth of the first child revealed the fact that several years normally elapsed before this event took place. The old women of the tribe were quite emphatic and positive on this point.'[108] The fact that young married females fail to bear children in spite of constant and fairly consistent intercourse with the same man, and that there is much variation in the time that elapses from marriage to the birth of the first child, renders the relation between intercourse and childbirth anything but clear. In short, there will be a great deal of variation in the duration of the intervals between puberty–marriage and pregnancy or childbirth, and since the Aborigines with all their accomplishments, are not biometricians, clearly this irregularity in the marriage–parturition interval is something which is hardly calculated to provide that serial history of correlates from which the proper inference could be drawn. Further, there are always a certain number of sterile women in the tribe who although given to frequent intercourse with their husbands never bear children. Then there are the 'old' women who, after a time, cease to bear children, although they continue to have intercourse as frequently as ever. These are facts which may be observed without difficulty and which are incontestable.

In explanation of the sterility in the young women the Arunta say that the condition is brought about by the fact that in her youth the girl tied a man's hair waistband about her, which owing to its great power had the effect of cramping her internal organs and thus rendered them incapable of the necessary expansion in order to accommodate a spirit-child.[109] The reason, it is maintained, why old women fail to have children is because they are so ugly, and spirit-children have a very definite predilection for comely women.[110]

Among the Trobrianders there are certain women who are so ugly that no man, it is declared, has ever had or ever would have intercourse with them, yet these very women have given birth to children,[111] a clinching proof of the fact that intercourse has nothing whatever to do with childbirth.

In view of all these facts it is, I think, really demanding too much of the human mind, however natively powerful, to expect it to draw an inference from premises which are so conspicuously lacking. The effects of intercourse after the attainment of 'puberty' (menarche) and marriage will generally be of such a mixed character, and experientially so clearly unrelated to pregnancy, not to say childbirth, that it would be nothing short of a miracle were the Aboriginal to discriminate, in the face of his deeply felt beliefs and of his own experience, in favour of coitus and pregnancy, made possible by pubertal changes which are in no demonstrable way related to the former, against the perfectly reasonable and efficient system of causes and effects which he has learnt both from experience and by instruction are the two causes of pregnancy and childbirth.

Parturition, as we have seen, will not, in any event, generally occur until between one and five years after effective marriage. A man may have a number of wives with whom he has intercourse frequently, with some perhaps more often than he does with others, yet, if they be normally fecund, they will bear children at the most irregular intervals, and in their fertility in no possible distinguishable relationship to intercourse.

It may be observed here that there is now available a certain amount of evidence which would indicate that the average physiological maximum fecundity frequency in women, that is to say the modal interval between the children that a woman can conceive, is twenty-four months. This has been demonstrated by Aberle[112] for the Pueblo Indian, by March and Davenport for colonial Americans between the years 1700 to 1850,[113] and according to Aberle an analysis of the modal interval between births based upon 1,714,261 children born of 1,695,217 women in the registration area of the United States was found to be also twenty-four months,[114] a similar interval was also found by Pearl for American women of suspected high fecundity.[115] The fecundity potential, or the number of pregnancies a woman is capable of sustaining, is, among the Aborigines, something of which we have absolutely no knowledge, and it may be added here that we have not much more for any other ethnic group. Aberle found that among the San Juan and Santa Clara Pueblo Indian women, who used no contraceptive measures whatever, the average number of pregnancies sustained by them by the time they had reached the menopause (at forty years) was 9·4.[116] Among the Ogala Sioux the average was 8·8.[117] In Australia where the family is necessarily limited to a small number of children, infanticide is practised immediately upon the birth of a child, but only when the mother feels that she is still too heavily burdened with another child to be able to rear the newcomer properly,[118] or for any other pertinent reason. It is possible, then, that the number of pregnancies which a woman, under such conditions, can undergo is somewhat greater than in those peoples among whom infanticide is not practised. If this be true, then we have here yet another complicating factor, since the reduction of the interval between pregnancies thus made possible would render it quite impossible for anyone to make any sense out of the bewildering profusion of phenomena thus presented to the mind.

A factor of quite a different and contrasting character which may be mentioned here is the influence of the lactation interval. It has, for example, long been known that many mammals, including monkeys and apes, neither ovulate nor menstruate during the period when they are suckling their young (the lactation period). It is now known that suckling is the chief cause of the sterile lactation interval, for when the young are removed from their mothers œstrous follows shortly afterwards.[119] A similar sterile lactation interval also exists in lactating women, and since in Australia it is the usual thing for a woman to suckle each child for a period of two or three years and even more, the chances of pregnancy being produced in such a woman early in the course of this period are greatly reduced.[120]

There would appear to be little, then, in intercourse, or in anything associated with it, that would necessarily cause the Aboriginal to perceive that in some way intercourse is connected with pregnancy. The premises from which the inference could be made appear to be wanting.

MENSTRUATION

Read's second emphatic experience is: from one to six weeks following pregnancy there is cessation of the menses.

This 'emphatic experience' can be disposed of very shortly.

Assuming for the moment that the connection between cessation of the menses and pregnancy is in a vague sort of way understood among the Arunta, I fail altogether to see how a woman who has just become aware that she has been entered by a spirit-child, that is, in our terms, at the quickening, four and a half months after conception, and who can at the most have missed but three periods, a number which is often exceeded under normal conditions, should connect that cessation with intercourse. The woman who has particularly noticed the cessation of her menstrual flow may have had intercourse on that very day, or she may not have had intercourse for some days or weeks. Her sexual activities are not regulated according to any definite or indefinite schedule, so that if we grant the totally unwarranted assumption that the woman knows that her menses cease to flow at more or less regular intervals, periodically—most certainly it is clear that *this periodicity stands in no observable relationship to a variable number of sexual acts*. Only one sexual act could normally have produced conception, but what is there to lead the woman to deduce the fact that her menses have ceased to flow as the result of one act out of a multitude, with this or that man? Where are the constant relationships it is necessary to trace before the truth can be determined? As a matter of fact menstruation would appear to be a very irregular condition among the Arunta, and not recognized among them as a periodic occurrence. With respect even to the recognition of the physical signs of puberty, menstruation occupies the least important position, the signs most relied upon, according to Róheim, being 'the development of the pubic hair, the breast and, *in a minor degree*, the first menstruation'.[121] It is surely very significant that menstruation is not regarded as more than a minor secondary sign of puberty.

Strehlow informs us that menstruation is very irregular among the Arunta, and that the flow is much less than that of the white woman. Being so irregular, it is by them regarded as a sort of disease, which is attributed to the fact that the woman has been walking about in a cold wind, or to the fact that she has been drinking very cold water.[122] Róheim corroborated this.[123] One of Róheim's informants told him that she had menstruated all the time during her pregnancy, in flat contradiction to which some of the Arunta women declared that the Luritja women do not menstruate at all. Other women declared that the Pitjandjara women only menstruate when they are very young and that once they are married they do not menstruate again. 'According to the belief of the Yumu and Pindup, a demon called Inyutalu (Hair big) is the cause of menstruation. He is covered all over with long hair and goes into the vagina which he scratches and pulls with his nail to make it bleed. The *piri* (nail) of the *mamu* makes the women menstruate.'[124]

Among the Drysdale River tribes of north-western Australia, writes Hernández, women had not 'the least knowledge of the connection existing between menstruation and conception; and when they became pregnant, they seldom were aware of the fact until gestation was very far advanced. I know of a case where a woman did not realize that she was enceinte till she gave birth.'[125]

From all this it is quite clear that the periodicity of menstruation is not recognized, and that its nature is not understood, essentially, it would appear, because of the extreme irregularity of the flow, and its non-periodic and extraordinary character. It would also seem to be perfectly clear that menstruation is in no way connected with pregnancy. Róheim, however, writes:[126]

It is generally known that the cessation of menstruation indicates pregnancy. Ilpaltalka explained how it began when menstruation ceased and said that vomiting was the next sign of pregnancy. From the men's point of view old Moses, the patriarch of the Mission Natives, declares that the connection between pregnancy and menstruation was always more or less known, but there was a tendency on the part of the old women . . . to keep these facts . . . hidden from the men. This is, of course, in flat contradiction to the official doctrine of incarnation.

In the light of the foregoing accounts of the natives' beliefs regarding menstruation it would seem highly probable that Ilpaltalka and Moses were retailing information which they had received from the missionaries. Moses's statement that the connection between pregnancy and menstruation had always been 'more or less' known may be placed on a par with Strehlow's statement that according to the natives the connection between intercourse and pregnancy has always been 'more or less' known by the old men, but kept secret from the young. If we may rule out here the well-known desire of the native to be always accommodating in his answers to the white observer, we have still to reckon with the strong human tendency to claim as having always 'more or less' known that which may formerly have been as obscure as an Egyptian night. A mission native would be particularly prone to make such a claim with all the urbanity of one learned in the ways of the Mission world. Even if old Moses's statement were true, which is greatly to be doubted, I do not see that it is, as Róheim says, in flat contradiction to the official doctrine of incarnation. It may have been that the cessation of the menses was regarded as a kind of preparation for the entry of a spirit-child into the woman, and in such a case the idea would be perfectly compatible with that doctrine. But this is mere speculation and it would serve no useful purpose to continue the discussion of this matter here.[127] I believe that the orthodox beliefs are correctly represented in the accounts which I have given above, and these unequivocally show that neither the periodicity nor the relationship of pregnancy to menstruation were understood among the pre-Mission Arunta.

Thus, it would seem to be far from true to say, as Read does, that the cessation of the menses constitutes an emphatic experience of an inescapably evident nature,[128] or that it is in any way connected with intercourse or even pregnancy, for as we have seen, the Arunta, in spite of the Mission influences to which they have been exposed, still retain the vaguest notions concerning the nature and meaning of menstruation.

THE QUICKENING

Without doubt, Read's third emphatic experience, 'at about four and a half months from intercourse, the quickening', is the most emphatic experience in the whole process of pregnancy, but it is also the first and the last such experience until labour and birth. In other words, it is the only experience, emphatic or not, which the native recognizes as the first sign of pregnancy; all the experiences which follow, if they ever do, are merely ancillary to this. Thus, the quickening is recognized as the moment of conception and the onset of pregnancy, it is the time at which the spirit-child has entered the woman who will be its host, its social mother then and for so long thereafter.

An important point which may be referred to here is that while the time of quickening is often spoken of as occurring some four and a half months from intercourse, the quickening in reality often occurs very much later (early occurrence of the quickening being considerably less frequent than its late occurrence). When to this fact we add the occurrence of premature births of which the offspring are viable, and such children are viable from the seventh month onwards, we may actually have a child who is born a month or two or three after it had entered its mother. This, of course, would contribute still further towards obscuring the fact that a child is generally born at a certain definite time after a certain definite occurrence. Since the moment of quickening will occur at different times in different women, and their children will thus be born at different times in relation to that experience, it becomes evident that the quickening does not even tell a woman exactly when she is to give birth to a child. Children may be born at any time following the quickening; it would seem to depend entirely upon the spirit-children themselves, upon their own free-will, when they may choose to be born. Such a view is in perfect harmony both with the orthodox doctrine and the physical facts, which are thus confirmatory of all that the native believes.

We may summarize this discussion, then, by saying that the Arunta have no knowledge of the relationship between intercourse and the cessation of the menses, nor have they any knowledge of the connection between the cessation of the menses and the quickening; that the quickening, and this alone, is recognized as the first sign of pregnancy; and, finally, that the time of birth does not necessarily stand in any comparatively constant relation to the quickening, as Read seems to think. Read seems wholly to have forgotten that the duration which he gives for the various stages of the reproductive process and its associated effects has been worked out thoroughly only within comparatively recent times.

We have seen above that in the native's experience there is no possible reason for connecting any of these events, and that Read's *emphatic experiences* are not emphatic experiences to the Arunta, whatever they may be in other social groupings, with the exception of that one upon which Read writes that 'too much stress has been laid', namely the moment of quickening, which is in reality the sole emphatic experience which is recognized by the Arunta as connected with pregnancy.

With respect to the 'impressive changes' enumerated by Read, namely 'the swelling of the breasts and of the abdomen, and by still other subjective, very variable phenomena, such as euphoria, nausea, sick fancies and longings', it may be said that the swelling of the breasts and of the abdomen becomes apparent only during the latter half of pregnancy, that is *after* the quickening, while the remainder of these 'very variable phenomena' may not occur at all.[129] Unquestionably some of these subjective experiences do frequently occur early in the pregnancy of some women, but they need not necessarily occur in a serial manner, and, in any event, these experiences, when they do occur, are of so erratic a nature, some women experiencing them not at all, others experiencing perhaps but one of them and then only in very attenuated and hardly noticeable form while others occasionally experience them in all their intensity, whereas still other women who are not pregnant and are incapable of having children are not infrequently affected by similar experiences, that, it seems to me, in view of all this variability there can be no sensible reason for inferring that such experiences, which may or may not occur, and which in any case occur equally among pregnant as among nonpregnant women, can have anything whatever to do with intercourse, menstruation, or pregnancy.

Read agrees that 'the most irregular part of the series from intercourse to birth is the first stage—from intercourse to the cessation of the menses'. But he precedes this statement with the words: 'After the loss of the seasonal rut, and amongst all extant peoples',[130] words which we may take to mean that Read believes, and as Westermarck thinks probable,[131] that man was at one time subject to a rutting season, a condition which would have rendered it fairly easy to discover that intercourse was followed by pregnancy after a definite interval, thus leading to the conclusion that the earliest men were acquainted with the relationship between intercourse and pregnancy. Since this is a point of some importance and moreover has a considerable bearing upon our subject, it will be worth while to inquire into the matter here.

THE ALLEGED HUMAN PAIRING SEASON IN PRIMITIVE TIMES

Westermarck has, in modern times, been chiefly responsible for introducing the theory of the existence of a human pairing season in primitive times. In the first volume of his *History of Human Marriage* he devotes the whole of his second chapter to a discussion, supported by some two hundred citations from the relevant literature, calculated to establish this theory, a discussion which leads him to believe that the prehistoric ancestors of modern man[132] were characterized by a definite pairing season.[133] A similar opinion has been expressed by a number of other writers, but by none more vigorously than Professor A. M. Carr-Saunders.[134] This notion has even crept into the physiological literature,[135] and has been noticed in a very widely used and most excellent purely general treatise on physiology.[136]

In actual fact the evidence is completely against this theory, and quite as completely against it in respect of the 'half-human' ancestors of man.

The argument for a human pairing season in primitive times usually proceeds along the following lines: almost all the lower mammals are characterized by a pairing season, so, too, are all the monkeys and anthropoid apes, whilst in certain groups of primitive people a pairing season has also been recorded by various travellers. Moreover, the periods at which the greatest number of births take place in the human species indicate the survival of a primitive human sexual rhythm associated with 'annual changes in the human organism especially connected with the sex function'.[137] Furthermore, the practice of certain fertility and erotic ceremonies at certain times of the year, usually in spring and autumn, would tend to support this idea.

As far as the other, or non-primate, mammals are concerned, these, of course, are only indirectly and very remotely related to the order of mammals of which man is a member, so that there can really be very little point in citing the evidence for such groups in connection with the problem as it is related to man; there is more point in citing the evidence for the primates, the order of mammals to which man belongs, and here only in respect of the catarrhinæ, the monkeys and apes of the Old World, for it is to the catarrhine group of primates alone that man is phylogenetically closely linked. This is not to say that the study of the sexual functioning of the lower mammals is pointless in connection with any light it may serve to throw upon the behaviour of higher mammals, but that the citation of the sexual seasonal behaviour of the lower mammals in support of the possible pre-existence of such behaviour in human groups, and as suggestive of the existence of a pairing season in primitive man, can be of no very great pertinence when there is now not the slightest evidence of the former existence of such seasonal behaviour either in groups of apes or of men.

The information at our disposal concerning the Old World

monkeys is limited chiefly to the rhesus monkey or macaque of India, and to the baboons, chiefly of Africa.

According to Hartman, who has thus far published the most exhaustive study of reproduction in the macaque, 'it is now possible to state definitely that the rhesus monkey breeds in winter and is sterile in summer.'[138] This statement was based upon a study of the weekly and monthly distribution of the conception rate in 48 animals studied by himself, and 81 animals for whom there were reliable records from other sources, a total of 129 cases. Hartman's own animals showed that 'by far the greater majority [of conceptions] fall in the November-December-January quarter'. Now, when Hartman's data are subjected to analysis it is found that the conceptions are distributed during each month in the following frequencies; the total number (it is to be remembered) being 129:

Jan.	Feb.	Mar.	Apr.	May	June	July	Aug.	Sept.	Oct.	Nov.	Dec.
11	7	5	8	8	1	1	6	8	21	29	24

From these figures it would appear that the relatively sterile months in the rhesus monkey fall in June and July and that thereafter, beginning in August, there is a gradual increase in fecundity through September to a very considerable increase in October, which increase reaches its peak in November, and is all but maintained in December, gradually declining in January to about one-fourth of the maximum fecundity potential in April and May, until in June and July the lowest fecundity level is reached. The number is seventy-four, or 57·8 per cent, in the quarter January-February-March; sixteen, or 12·4 per cent, in the two months April-May, and two, or 1·5 per cent, in June-July—the months characterized by the lowest number of conceptions,whilst in August-September there are fourteen, or 10·8 per cent of conceptions. These figures would tend to show, therefore, that the rhesus monkey is capable of conceiving at any time of the year, though much less frequently in summer than in the winter months. In the months of June and July it may be accepted as a general fact that the greater number of rhesus monkeys are relatively sterile, for Hartman has shown fairly conclusively that ovulations are of comparatively rare occurrence in summer. But these animals are not altogether sterile, as a species, during these months, as is shown by the two recorded conceptions, and as is also indicated by Hartman's statement that he found definite evidence of ovulation in one of his animals during the summer, and in another case the presence of 'a fairly large follicle with little likelihood of rupturing'. If we eliminate the latter case we may regard the former as a possible conception, which would make a total of two cases of actual and possible cases of conception in Hartman's colony of forty-eight animals, or 4·2 per cent of conceptions, both in the month of July which is probably an estimate nearer the truth than the 1·5 per cent of conceptions reported for the 129 cases.

In spite of the lower frequency of conceptions in the months not of the winter quarter (it should be remembered that the order of the numbers we are here dealing with is very small, and that were the total number of animals increased, the actual numerical differences would not appear so striking, though we assume that the percentage differences would remain the same), it is to be noted that the deviations from the mean number of the conceptions never falls below one-fifth (excepting in June-July) of the mean, whilst the mean conception frequency rate for the months from January to the end of May is 8, giving a mean deviation of −17 conceptions, or 68·0 per cent of conceptions per month less than in the high fecundity period, or only 4·0 per cent of actual conceptions per month, a figure which is very close to our estimate of 4·2 per cent for Hartman's own data.

Thus, it is clear that the rhesus monkey is able to conceive, and therefore to breed, at any time during the year,[139] though much less successfully during summer than in the winter months. Hartman's statement, therefore, that 'the rhesus monkey breeds in winter and is sterile in summer' is, upon his own showing, not altogether correct, for, as we have seen, 32·0 per cent of rhesus conceptions take place during the period from January to the end of May, and 4·0 per cent in the so-called sterile months of June-July.

That there are periodic fluctuations in the conception rate of all primates not excluding man, there can be no doubt,[140] but such fluctuations do not make it at all necessary to conclude that that period which is characterized by the greatest number of conceptions represents the breeding season or even the last vestige of such a season in the species in which it occurs. As Zuckerman has conclusively shown: 'The essential difference in breeding-habit between those primates about which there is definite information and apparently the majority of non-primate mammals is that the monkeys can and do breed at all times. Variations in their birth-rates are without doubt significant phenomena, but they are secondary to this important fact'.[141] That there are maximum and minimum conception periods in the annual life of every mammal there can be very little doubt. It is also the case that in some mammals the conception period is restricted to a definite time of the year when the animals are said to be in rut, or in a state of sexual excitement and preparedness. During this period the animals pair and conception occurs, whence this period has come to be variously known as the *rutting*, *pairing*, or *breeding season*. But such a state of affairs does not exist among any of the catarrhinæ, not even in the rhesus monkey which is very far removed from any of the apes or man. In all primates copulation goes on throughout the year. Though there is a tendency during the hot summer months for sexual activity to be diminished, the phenomenon of rut is not limited to any particular time of the year, but physiologically, in the monkeys, occurs each month with the swelling of the sexual skin, or during the period following each menstruation, whilst psychologically sexual excitement may obtain throughout almost every moment of the year with hardly a break. 'Monkeys', writes Zuckerman, 'that copulate in captivity do so at all times, but copulation occurs most frequently during the period of maximum sexual skin activity.'[142] On the other hand Hartman writes of the rhesus monkey that 'as a rule the females will accept the male whenever given the opportunity . . . the stage of the menstrual cycle has nothing to do with their refusal or acceptance'.[143] There is thus, among the primates, no form of behaviour which may be described as indicating the existence of a *rutting, pairing,* or *breeding season,* for, among the catarrhinæ at least, rutting, pairing, and breeding take place more or less continuously throughout the year, although, of course, it is true that during each month when the sexual skin activity is at its highest, the sexual activity of the animals is heightened; but in all this there is no periodicity of either pairing or breeding. Among the catarrhinæ that have been investigated up to the present the fact has clearly emerged that they are capable of breeding at any time, though in some cases much more so at certain periods than at others, a fact that does not in any appreciable way modify the copulatory behaviour of these animals. It is of just this point, however, that the proponents of the theory of a human pairing season in primitive times seem to be completely unaware. Among the catarrhinæ there is no such thing as a pairing season, not even among the group of monkeys I have chosen to discuss at some length because of the favourable evidence that they would seem to afford in support of the breeding season theory, namely the rhesus monkeys. Before leaving this matter here I should like to quote Zuckerman's carefully considered conclusion with respect to the breeding habits of the primates. He writes: 'the evidence indicates clearly that monkeys can conceive at any time in captivity, and presumably, therefore, like the baboon, at any time in the wild.'[144] His field observations 'prove conclusively that the chacma baboon of the Eastern Province of South Africa has no demarcated breeding season in its wild state'.[145] By this last statement, of course, Zuckerman means that the baboons observed by him manifested no pairing activities of a seasonal nature, the statement does not refer to number of conceptions, but Zuckerman, who has had considerable experience in this field, is definitely of the opinion that monkeys can conceive at any time during the year.

THE SEXUAL BEHAVIOUR OF THE GREAT APES

The anthropomorpha, or man-like apes, consist of the great apes, the orang, the chimpanzee, and the gorilla, but it is only with the latter two animals that man can be said to stand in any close relation. I know of no observations on the sexual life of the gibbon, but for the orang the observations of Fox prove that the sexual behaviour of this group of anthropoids is not in any way limited by the oestrus. 'The sexual act', writes Fox, 'is practised daily, without relation to the sexual cycle.'[146]

For the chimpanzee we have the observations of a number of different investigators. Montané states that among the captive animals observed by him copulation took place consistently throughout the year, and quite as often during the period of pregnancy as at other times.[147] Sokolowsky states that 'repeated intercourse every day' was the rule among the captive chimpanzees under his observation.[148] A similar inference is no doubt to be drawn from Köhler's remark that 'this extreme frequency of sexual effects implies a certain trivialization of this sphere of life, rather than its intensity'.[149] Fox writes of a pair of chimpanzees which were under his observation for some time that 'although the act was practised frequently, day and night, during the interval between the heat periods, it was more prolonged and apparently more interesting to both animals, the female especially, during these periods. "Heat period" means the duration of the perineal swelling. The greater the swelling the more frequent the sexual act'.[150] Köhler similarly remarked about his chimpanzees: 'After the cessation of the flow, there is an excess of sexual desire, accompanied by a pronounced swelling of the whole external genitalia'.[151]

Schultz and Snyder report of the Johns Hopkins colony of chimpanzees that coitus between the pairs of animals under their observation occurred fairly regularly three and more times a day, adding that, according to the records, intercourse between the animals studied did not appear to be markedly influenced by the menstrual cycle of the female. These observers do not appear to have noted any increase in sexual desire in the female following the cessation of the menses.[152]

In gorillas the evidence points to a lack of a preferential breeding season.[153] The evidence would strongly suggest that the sexual life of the gorilla in nowise differs from that of the chimpanzee.[154]

In summarizing the significance of the foregoing observations one could not do better than quote Gerrit Miller's remarks in this connection.[155] In the primates, he writes,

the sexual psychology of the female as well as that of the male has been liberated from strict periodical oestrous control; or, what amounts to the same thing so far as behaviour is concerned, the physiological stimuli to mating, though they may be stronger in the female at some times than at others, appear to be rarely if ever completely absent in either sex at any part of the year. The behaviour patterns are not necessarily uniform at all seasons; but conspicuously marked physiological rhythms are no longer the nearly exclusive regulating factors in the mating behaviour of either sex. Mating behaviour becomes established as part of the play activities of young individuals, and from this early period onward until senility makes it impossible, it may occur at any time, even during pregnancy, when not inhibited by some unfavourable factor such as fear, fatigue, hot weather, moult, injury, or ill health. Throughout its course it tends, in both sexes, to assume more nearly the form of an ever-available amusement activity than that of a periodic blind submission to an inescapable racial force.

Finally, as Zuckerman has put the matter, 'The matings of the lower mammal are confined to short periods circumscribed by the activity of the follicular hormones. The matings of the primate are diffused over the entire cycle, paralleling the continued action of the follicular hormone, but varying in frequency according to the varying degrees of activity of that hormone.'[156] We may also note here Hitzheimer and Heck's conclusion, which is based upon the analysis of the reports of field naturalists and explorers, that 'in every troop of monkeys young ones of every age are found at all seasons', that 'in their reproductive activities [they] are not confined to any definite season'.[157]

Both Zuckerman[158] and Hartman[159] have pointed out that such evidence is of uncertain value since it is so often conflicting and not based upon carefully observed and recorded facts. A preferential mating season has been observed in several species of macaques and in some cercopitheques. But these are far removed from anthropoids and man.

In the light of the foregoing evidence, then, it becomes clear that for the anthropoids there does not exist a particle of evidence which would suggest that they are or have ever been characterized by a rutting, breeding, or pairing season, on the other hand all the evidence is entirely opposed to the possibility of such conditions ever having existed among them. If this is so, and it is indisputably so, what then becomes of the pairing season hypothesis of man's half-human ancestors?

Lest, however, it may be thought that there may be some evidence for recent man himself which might justify such an hypothesis, let us briefly consider this evidence before we leave this subject altogether. It is by no means uninstructive.

Westermarck begins his citation of the evidence in support of the breeding or pairing season hypothesis in primeval man with the statement:[160] 'According to Mr. Johnston, the wild Indians of California, belonging to the lowest races on earth, have their rutting season as regularly as have the deer, the elk, the antelope, or any other animals.[161] With reference to some of these Indians, Mr. Powers says that spring "is a literal Saint Valentine's Day with them, as with the natural birds and beasts of the forest"!'[162] Carr-Saunders also quotes this statement with complete approval as indicating the former existence of a condition in which conception could take place only at one season during the year.[163]

These statements are typical of the majority of those cited both by Westermarck and by Carr-Saunders, but unlike these many others, there is a modicum of truth in them, but of a totally different nature from that imagined by these two authors, for when we consult our greatest authority on the California Indians, namely Professor A. L. Kroeber, we find him writing of the Yurok, for example, who dwell along the reaches of the lower Klamath River, a people who are characterized by an excessive desire for wealth and the great regard in which they hold money, which among them circulates in the form of dentalium shells:[164]

The significant fact is that they hold a strong conviction that the dentalium money and the congress of the sexes stand in a relation of inherent antithesis. This is one reason given for the summer mating season: the shells would leave the house in which conjugal desires were satisfied, and it is too cold and rainy to sleep outdoors in winter . . . Births occurred among the Yurok and their neighbours chiefly in spring. This was, of course, not because of any animal-like impulse to rut in a certain season, as has sometimes been imagined, but because of highly specialized ideas of property and magic . . . Since dentalia and other valuables were kept in the house, a man never slept there with his wife . . . The institution of the sweat house rendered this easily possible. In summer, however, when the cold rains were over, the couple made their bed outdoors; with the result that it seems natural to the Yurok that children should be born in spring.

Alas for the rutting season of the wild Indians of California!

With respect to such statements as Oldfield's, quoted by Wester-marck, concerning the Watchendies of Western Australia, 'Like beasts of the field, the savage has but one time for copulation in the year. About the middle of spring . . . the Watch-an-dies begin to think of holding their grand semi-religious festival of Caa-ro, pre-paratory to the performance of the important duty of procreation',[165] these are quite clearly generalized misinterpretations of the signifi-cance of certain Australian ceremonies, with many of which we have already had occasion to become partially familiar. In any event, we have Curr's succinct and emphatic denial of the existence of any-thing like a sexual season among any of the Australian Aborigines,[166] and likewise, Spencer's statement that Oldfield's remark holds true for none of the Australian tribes known to him.[167] It would be strange indeed if there had been anything conceivably resembling a mating season among the Aborigines that such observers as Fison, Howitt, Basedow, Spencer, Gillen, Brown, and the many modern students of the Australian Aboriginal should have failed to have become aware of its existence. The great inherent improbability of the existence of such a season or anything approaching it, among any people whatsoever, really renders any further discussion of this matter quite unnecessary.

Fertility festivals and other ceremonies with which sexual licence may be associated have never been demonstrated to be associated with any periods of increased sexual desire, and there is not the slightest evidence to support the view that such an association may exist; this is a point which Westermarck has himself made and accepted,[168] it need not be discussed here.

There is one final matter in connection with man that must be disposed of before we may proceed further. Westermarck is at great pains to show, by means of the citation of statistics of births from various parts of the world, that there would appear to be substantial evidence in support of the belief that 'an annual increase of the sexual desire or of the reproductive power, generally in spring, is of frequent occurrence in mankind'.[169] The evidence upon which this statement is based consists of reports of various writers on the in-cidence of births for various months which indicate, on the whole, that the greatest number of births occur in the early spring with another maximum in or about December. Westermarck admits that 'the periodical fluctuations in the birth-rate may no doubt be due to various causes. But,' he thinks, 'there is every reason to believe that the maximum in February and March (in Chile, September) is, at least to a large extent, due to an increased tendency to pro-creation in May and June (in Chile, December).[170] Heape has expressed a similar opinion in connection with Cuban conceptions.[171] 'If,' adds Westermarck, 'we thus find in man, even to this day, an increase either of the sexual desire or of the reproductive power in spring or at the beginning of summer, I think we may look upon it as a survival of a pairing season among our early human or pre-human ancestors. We are the more justified in doing so as a sexual season occurs among the man-like apes, and conditions similar to those which led to it in their case may be supposed to have produced the same result in the case of primeval man.'[172]

We have already had occasion to see how far from the truth these statements are concerning the man-like apes. We have now briefly to show that while it is perfectly true that seasonal periods during the year when the number of births is greatest do occur, these, however, have no connection whatever with 'an increased tendency of procreation', but are instead due chiefly to meteorological factors, and that instead of 'an increase either of the sexual desire or of the reproductive power in spring or at the beginning of the summer', the evidence is on the contrary quite conclusive that where the temperature rises above 70°F. there is a gradual decrease of the reproductive power in these months, culminating in summer when it is at its lowest ebb.

Mills and Senior have shown that variations in conception rates in different localities are very significantly correlated with climatic factors. An analysis of the birthrate of very many different climatic regions shows that both low and high temperatures are not conducive to the successful production of conception, and that human fertility is highest in any given population at a temperature of 65°F. In Japan, to take but one example, the climatic effects are most striking. 'The spring months of April, May, and early June are almost perfect as far as temperature is concerned, but from the middle of June to early September the humidity is almost constantly high, day and night, while the mean temperature rises to 95°F. There is a 50 per cent fall [of conceptions] during their tropical summer period! Calculation has shown that not over 10 per cent of this spring rise in conceptions here could be attributed to the increase in the marriage rate'.[173]

Evidence, in the form of statistics, obtained from the houses of prostitution, shows that there is no significant depression of male sexual activity during the hot summer months.

The authors conclude that 'since Japan shows the most marked seasonal variations in conceptions, the inference is that a biologic reduction in fertility is produced by heat.'[174]

Everywhere in the world the story is the same, low conception rates are correlated with the months with high or low temperatures, and high conception rates with the months characterized by an optimum temperature of about 65°F.

It is known that the elevation of the temperature of the testicles by two or three degrees will have the effect of inhibiting spermatogenesis. Reduction of the temperature to a low level probably has a similar effect. Thus, it is very probable that temperature changes act directly or indirectly upon the sex glands during the hot and the cold months, and inhibit their activity, at least, to some extent. Experimental investigations carried out by Dr Cordelia Ogle[175] to test just these points have yielded the most striking corroborative evidence of these observations. White mice were the subjects used in the experiment. Two constant temperature rooms, identical in construction, were erected. One was kept at 60–68°F. with a very short temperature cycle so that the mean temperature of 64°F. predominated most of the time. The other was kept at 88–92°F. with the humidity near 75 per cent. The control room had a temperature range of 70–80°F.

A single strain of white mice bred in the control room were at twenty-one days of age separated from the mothers and placed in the various rooms for observation. As a result of this experiment Dr Ogle found that the mice subjected to a warm humid temperature exhibited a low degree of fertility in three ways, namely, a low percentage of matings that result in pregnancy, small litter size, and low vitality of offspring. The mice, however, kept in the steady cool environment showed the highest degree of fertility, the greatest number of matings resulting in conception, large litters of lusty offspring born, and earlier onset of sexual life and fertility. Here then is a striking demonstration of the dependence of fertility, in mice, upon temperature. There is reason to believe that similar conditions hold good for man. There can be little doubt, as Dr Ogle says, that the climatic factors here involved act either directly or indirectly upon the sex glands.

It is also probable that changes in the nature, intensity and duration of the light during the various months or seasons play a significant role in influencing sexual behaviour. The influence of light upon plant and animal tissues is still far from being completely understood, but that light exerts specific kinds of action upon such tissues is well known. English,[176] for example, has shown that tropical birds in general lay far smaller clutches of eggs than even quite nearly related species nesting in the northern hemisphere. Rowan has demonstrated the effect of light on the gonads, the breeding, and the migrations of birds.[177] Bissonnette has demonstrated the effects of various components of light on the breeding behaviour of mammals.[178] Here, too, may be mentioned the fact that ozone tends to destroy vitamin E, the vitamin of reproduction.[179] Inactivation of vitamin E invariably results in sterility,[180] a result which may occur organically in a variety of different ways.

Hartman found that ovulation was inhibited during the summer months in his macaques, that during this season there was a greater irregularity of menstruation, a greater incidence of amenorrhoea, reduced sexual skin colour, and a somewhat lessened intensity of the menstrual flow, whilst both the males and the females were sexually much less ardent.[181]

Engle and Shelesnyak, in a study of 3,140 menstrual cycles in one hundred girls from the Hebrew Orphan Asylum of New York, found a distinct seasonal incidence in the occurrence of menarches. Only 18 per cent of the total occurring during the summer months of June, July, and August. Further, these investigators found that the long intervals of amenorrhoea initiated by a period in July were twice as long as those initiated in any other two months of the year, and that, finally, periods of amenorrhoea are especially frequent during the summer months although they occur throughout the year.[182]

Similar records on the disturbance of the menstrual cycle during the summer months have been fully reported for medically normal adult women by Allen,[183] Fluhmann,[184] and King.[185]

With such evidence before us taken in conjunction with the evidence of the human birthrate, which proves that the least number of conceptions occur during the summer months and, interestingly enough, the greatest number of abortions have been shown to occur during these months also,[186] it would appear quite certain that both in the subhuman primates and in man the reproductive powers are at their minimum functional levels during the summer. That this minimal functioning is to a significant extent determined by meteorological factors is indicated by the fact that the incidence of conceptions in the macaque is the same in the northern hemisphere as in the southern hemisphere, where the months but not the seasons are reversed,[187] thus beautifully demonstrating the dependence, other things being equal, of the fertility rate upon climatic factors.

In the primates including man there is every reason to believe that such climatic factors have always been operative, and have had no more influence in producing behaviour of a rutting kind, or increased sexual desire, than they have today. Were it necessary, it might even be plausibly argued that during the various ice ages both the subhuman primates and man functioned sexually and reproductively at their maximum level throughout the year, and that the primeval ancestors of modern man could not upon these grounds alone have been characterized by a rutting or pairing season. The point, however, is hardly worth arguing here, for it must be abundantly clear that neither the man-like apes nor primeval man can have been characterized by a rutting, pairing, or breeding season.

Since this is so it must also be equally apparent that primeval man was completely devoid of this suggested means of determining the periodic nature of the relationship between intercourse and childbirth.

At this juncture we may return to our discussion of Read's analysis.

CUMULATIVE EXPERIENCE AND THE KNOWLEDGE OF PATERNITY

Read has expressed the opinion[188] that

The knowledge of paternity . . . does not depend upon deliberate observation but upon cumulative experience age after age; in the course of which it appears that, although A (intercourse) often happens without B (the rest of the series to childbirth), B never happens without A. This generates a belief that B is dependent on A; but also that B is not dependent on A alone, or else it would always follow. What else B depends on is unknown; so it may be magic or the agency of spirits . . .

In the case of the Arunta and the Trobriand Islanders Read believes that we are dealing with extreme examples; these peoples instead of regarding the magical or spiritual agencies as auxiliary, as other peoples do, regard them instead as the sole operative causes. 'We must expect,' remarks Read, 'to meet with extreme cases.'

As a logician Read has quite clearly been unable to escape the formal inevitability of the method of concomitant variation, and his argument here represents a pretty effective illustration of the inefficacy, which F. C. S. Schiller has for so many years been urging, characterizes the mere verbalism of such modes of thought. Einstein has somewhere said that pure logical thinking can give us no knowledge whatsoever of the world of experience—all knowledge about reality beginning with experience and terminating with it. What Einstein here had in mind was the experience of the mathematical physicist. But for the mathematical physicist as well as for the most unsophisticated native, experience is a function of the content of consciousness. Experience is most generally accepted to mean *something consciously lived or undergone*, and consciousness as *awareness*, but it is clear that the awareness is inseparable from a context which, indeed, conditions its nature, namely the background of experience culturally interpreted which has in the past been transmitted through the consciousness to the mind. There is, however, no dualism involved here of content and consciousness, for it is quite impossible to be aware without a content which, if it does not generate that awareness, at least forms the foundation upon which it rests; the separation between content and consciousness which is usually made is merely a linguistic or, rather, a verbal one, but actually has no real existence. The 'whatness' of any object of experience obtains its form only from the content of the experiencer's consciousness, and the objects of experience are the raw experiences which are worked up by the content of consciousness into more or less definite forms. It depends, therefore, entirely upon the nature of the consciousness, upon its content, which we may collectively speak of as the mind, what particular form the data of experience will be given by any particular individual. It so happens, as we have already had occasion to show in an earlier chapter, that the nature of the mind is something which is culturally determined, and since the meaning with which we invest the data of experience is inevitably a function of our minds, it is obvious that what experience *is*, for the practical purposes of living, is something which is culturally determined also. Experience is *never* something that is merely given, but rather something to which something else is given. *Homo additus naturae.* Thus, the 'cumulative experience' of which Read speaks can only be interpreted to mean the traditionalization of the meanings which the past has bestowed, and the present maintains, upon the raw data provided by the phenomenalistic world in which the individual lives. But no social individual lives in a purely phenomenalistic world, indeed, he lives only in a social world and his knowledge of what the world of nature is he learns not from nature itself but from the culture in which he lives. Among nonliterate peoples, apart from what the existing body of communal knowledge has to say about the processes of the natural world, the phenomena of nature are taken very much for granted, hardly any distinction, indeed, being recognized between what is purely social and what purely natural. As far as we know the equivalents of these concepts do not even exist among the Aborigines, indeed, the world of the Aboriginal would seem to consist of but a single continuum uncomplicated by such abstractions as the distinction between what is cultural and what is natural. For the Aboriginal all things are natural, but only in the sense of being socially so, the converse, however, is not true. If, then, the world of the Aboriginal is the world which his culture makes, what point can there be to speaking of his 'cumulative experience age after age'? His cumulative experience is exactly what his culture determines it to be, with all the authority that age after age can bestow upon that determination.

Disregarding, however, the authority of tradition and the teachings of society, what can be the meaning of the statement that 'the knowledge of paternity does not depend on deliberate observation, but upon cumulative experience age after age'? If the knowledge of paternity does not depend upon observation, how then can anything be experienced which would lead to such knowledge, for observation is a *sine qua non* of the kind of experience that leads to knowledge? Read believes that in the course of ages it would become apparent that intercourse and pregnancy were somehow related as a result of this cumulative experience. This, of course, is a very naïve assumption and certainly an entirely gratuitous one, for the experience of the ages consists in no more than the experience of particular generations extended over an arbitrary period of time during which many such generations have come, experienced, and gone. But what has been experienced, the data of experience, has been much the same in each generation. Isolated peoples, removed from contact with foreign peoples and cultures, and given a fairly consistent environment, are generally characterized by a very considerable cultural stability, and though in the course of time changes do take place, these will on the whole occur only very gradually. To a certain extent the desire to account for the origin of themselves upon this earth served to give rise among the Aborigines to their peculiar system of beliefs. Once established these beliefs would be transmitted, from generation to generation, as the official doctrines of the tribe, the official view of the world and of man's place in it. Such doctrines, of course, represent the syncretic expression of the tribal interpretation of experience. And so long as these doctrines exist, cumulative experience means no more than the repetition of the same experiences in each generation. As soon as an altogether new experience crosses the horizon of such a culture, it is immediately made to fit into the existing system of beliefs. For example, the appearance of the white man in Australia in no way disturbed orthodox beliefs, for when one burns the dead body of a member of the tribe, or leaves his body exposed in the open for some time, the skin becomes depigmented and turns white, thus, with the assistance of the belief in incarnation, not the slightest difficulty was presented in assuming that white men were merely the incarnations of some deceased members of the tribe, being peculiar only in having retained the pigmentless character of the skin which manifests itself after death. Again, the light skin of half-caste children is, as we have seen, assumed to be due to the mother's consumption of the white flour obtained from the missionaries or traders.

Under the circumstances we have already discussed above there can be nothing in the experience of each generation which would render it necessary that one such generation should recognize the true nature of what is in the first place abysmally obscure and, in the second place, is most thoroughly and satisfactorily accounted for not only by existing knowledge, but by the everyday actual experience of the individual. Indeed, if cumulative experience plays any role here at all, and unquestionably it does, it is to conserve the traditional beliefs and to render them incontestable and invulnerable.

Let it not be forgotten here that the conclusion that intercourse is associated with pregnancy was provided with an irrefutable basis only in the middle of the last century, when Newport discovered and described the phenomenon of the penetration of the ovum by the spermatozoon under its own movements,[189] and that until that time almost any theory, no matter how fantastic, concerning the process of coming into being, was sure of gaining a hearing.[190]

NOTES

1 *Fortnightly Review*, n.s. 78, 1905, 452–66, later incorporated in the 3rd edition of *The Golden Bough*, and in *Totemism and Exogamy*, i, 159–62.
2 Ibid., 452.
3 Ibid.
4 Ibid., 453.
5 Ibid., 455.
6 Ibid., 450–5.
7 *The Arunta*, i, 311–12.
8 Ibid., 369, cf. also 71 and 318.
9 S. Gason, 'The manners and customs of the Dieyerie tribe of Australian Aborigines', in J. D. Woods, *The Native Tribes of South Australia*, 260 sqq.
10 B. H. Purcell, 'Rites and customs of Australian Aborigines', *Zeit. Ethnol.*, 25, 1893, 286–9.
11 *Totemism and Exogamy*.
12 N. W. Thomas, *Kinship Organizations and Group Marriage in Australia*.
13 W. H. Rivers, *Kinship and Social Organization*.
14 E. Westermarck, *The History of Human Marriage*.
15 R. Briffault, *The Mothers*.
16 A. W. Howitt, 'Australian group relations', *Rep. Smithsonian Inst.*, 1883, 807 n.
17 *The Mothers*, i, 763.
18 Ibid., 750–1.
19 Frazer, *Fortnightly Review*, 78, 1905, 452 n.
20 *Kinship Organizations and Group Marriage*, 128 sqq.
21 *The Family Among the Australian Aborigines*, 119 sqq.
22 A. P. Elkin, 'Kinship in South Australia', *Oceania*, 9, 1938, 76.
23 For a full discussion of these matters see A. R. Radcliffe-Brown, 'The social organization of Australian tribes', *Oceania*, 1, 1930–1, nos 1–4.
24 *The Chronological Aspects of Certain Australian Social Institutions*, 112–13.
25 Ibid., 84–9.
26 A. R. Radcliffe-Brown, 'The social organization of Australian tribes', *Oceania*, 1, 1930–1, 34–63, 206–46, 322–41, and especially 426–56.
27 Ibid., 443.
28 Ibid., 444.
29 *Fortnightly Review*, 78, 1905, 462.
30 Ibid., 453.
31 Ibid., 455.
32 *The Secret of the Totem*.
33 Ibid., 190.
34 'Notes on the Australian class systems', *JAI*, 12, 1882, 502.
35 *The Native Tribes of South-East Australia*, 283–4.
36 *The Secret of the Totem*, 191–3.

37   See chapter VII.
38   A. Lang, Introduction to K. L. Parker's *The Euahlayi Tribe*, xix. Moreover, it is as we have seen, extremely doubtful whether the doctrine of reincarnation exists among the Arunta; in any event it would make very little difference for Lang's point.
39   'Superstition, magic, and medicine', N. Qld Ethnography, *Bulletin* no. 5.
40   Cf. p. 220 above.
41   'Australian problems', in *Anthropological Essays Presented to E. B. Tylor*, 203–18.
42   W. E. Roth, *Ethnological Studies among the North-West-Central Queensland Aborigines*, 179.
43   B. Malinowski, *The Sexual Life of Savages*. I am, of course, fully aware of the methodological danger of citing the conditions among one people to explain the nature of those prevailing among another; in the above passages, however, it is intended to do no more than to suggest what cannot, at present, be proven.
44   Ibid., 162.
45   'Baloma: the spirits of the dead in the Trobriand Islands', *JRAI*, 46, 1916, 353–430.
46   *The Sexual Life of Savages*, 163–4. It seems to me that Malinowski has here involved himself in a contradiction, for while on the one hand he writes that it would be incorrect to assume that man obliterates any knowledge that he may have of the facts of procreation by the creation of an animistic superstructure, he proceeds on the other to explain that they construct a special tradition about all that is vital for man. Is not this what is meant by an animistic superstructure?
47   'The animals are kept both by man and woman—in a single *wurley* one might count as many as fifteen dogs living with the human occupants.' H. Basedow, *The Australian Aboriginal*, 118; cf. Horne and Aiston, *Savage Life in Central Australia*, 31–2.
48   C. Read, 'No paternity', *JRAI*, 48, 1918, 146–54.
49   D. M. Schneider, N. R. Kidder, E. S. Hunt, Jr, and W. D. Stevens, *The Micronesians of Yap and their Depopulation*, 182.
50   A. Goldenweiser, Review of Hartland's *Primitive Paternity*, *American Anthropologist*, n.s. 13, 1911, 598–606.
51   Cf. *The Legend of Perseus* and *Primitive Paternity*.
52   *Totemism and Exogamy*.
53   'Der Kausalzusammenhang zwischen Geschlechtsverkehr und Empfängnis in Glaube und Brauch der Natur- und Kultur-Völker', *Zeit. Ethnol.*, 41, 1909, 644–83; *Das Weib bei den Naturvölkern*, Berlin, 1923.
54   'Die Ansichten der primitiven Völker über das Geschlechtsleben des Menschen', *Int. Archiv Ethnog.*, 28, 1927, 139–52.
55   M. W. Wisser, *De Graecorum diis non referentibus speciem humanam*, Leyden, 1900; L. Preller, *Philologus*, 1852, 1 sqq.; F. G. Welcker, *Griechische Götterlehre*, Göttingen, 1857, i, 777 sqq.; G. F. Schumann, *Opuscula*, ii, 125 sqq.; A. B. Cook, 'Oak and rock', *Classical Review*, 15, 1901, 322–6; J. L. Myres, 'Herodotus and anthropology', in *Anthropology and the Classics*, Oxford, 1908, 128; Homer, *The Iliad*, 22, 126; *The Odyssey*, 18, 163; H. J. Rose, *Primitive Culture in Greece*; A. C. Vaughan, 'The genesis of human offspring: a study in early Greek culture', *Smith College Classical Studies*, no. 13, 1945.
56   Æschylus, *The Eumenides*, World's Classics, Oxford, 218.
57   Myres, loc. cit.
58   Cf. J. Needham, *A History of Embryology*, 25.
59   J. G. Frazer, *The Golden Bough*, ii, 162.
60   Talmud, *Kiddush*, 30*b*.
61   Job, x, 10–12. The language here is, of course, metaphorical.
62   Koran, xxxiii, 12 ff., xxiv, 44.
63   Doughty, *Travels in Arabia Deserta*, i, 17.
64   H. J. Rose, *Primitive Culture in Greece*, 165–7.
65   C. Read, 'No paternity', *JRAI*, 48, 1918, 146–54.
66   Ibid., 147.

67 J. W. Howe, *Excessive Venery, Masturbation, and Continence*, New York, 1888, p. 18.
68 'Phantasies of birth and prenatal experiences recovered from patients undergoing hypnoanalysis', *J. Mental Science*, 99, 1953, 216–23.
69 *Counseling in Medical Genetics*, Philadelphia, 1955, 36–7.
70 *Teen-Age Pregnancy*, Springfield, Ill., 1968, 13.
71 'No paternity', 147, 148.
72 *The Sexual Life of Savages*, 165.
73 Ibid., 172.
74 'Aboriginal sleeping customs and dreams, Ooldea, South Australia', *Oceania*, 10, 1940, 288.
75 *The Original Australians*, 202.
76 The terms used in the following discussion have the following definite meanings: *fecundity*, physiological capacity to participate in reproduction; *sterility*, the lack of physiological capacity to participate in reproduction; *fertility*, fecundity expressed in performance; *infertility*, absence of fertility, synonymous with childlessness; *menarche*, the first menstruation period.
77 For a discussion of the evidence see N. E. Himes, *Medical History of Contraception*, 3–56.
78 pp. 166–8.
79 *Psychology and Ethnology*, 76.
80 Ibid., 77.
81 Ibid., 77–9.
82 Ibid., 78.
83 I. Hogbin, 'Native culture of Wogeo', *Oceania*, 5, 1935, 320–1.
84 Hogbin was able to check this age estimate quite satisfactorily by a variety of means. To some it may appear that seventeen is rather a late age for the onset of menstruation, especially in the tropics, but the demonstrable fact is that menarche generally occurs later among girls living in the tropics than among those living in cooler climes. The widely held opposite notion is quite incorrect (H. Fehlinger, *Sexual Life of Primitive People*, 118 sqq.; C. A. Mills, 'Physiologic sterility of Adolescence', *Human Biology*, 8, 1936, 607–15; E. Baelz, 'Anthropologie der Menschen-Rassen Ost-Asiens', *Zeit. Ethnol.*, 33, 1901, 211; R. Neuhauss, *Deutsch Neu-Guinea*, 1); in connection with other Melanesian peoples the investigations of Otto Reche on the Matupi of New Pomerania (now New Britain) are of great interest. He found that among this people no girl who had not arrived at the age of seventeen had menstruated ('Untersuchungen über das Wachstum und die Geschlechtsreife bei melanesischen kindern', *Korrespondenzbl. deutscher Gesellschaft Anthrop.*, 41, 1910, 48–55).
85 For a complete account of these researches see Ashley Montagu, 'Adolescent sterility', *Quart. Rev. Biology*, 14, 1939, 192–219; *Adolescent Sterility*, Springfield, Ill., 1946; *The Reproductive Development of the Female*, New York, 1957.
86 F. A. E. Crew, 'Puberty and maturity', *Proc. 2nd Int. Congr. Sex Research*, London, 1930, 9–10.
87 C. A. Mills and C. Ogle, 'Physiologic sterility of adolescence', *Human Biology*, 8, 1936, 607–15.
88 C. G. Hartman, 'On the relative sterility of the adolescent organism', *Science*, 74, 1931, 226–7.
89 'Studies in the reproduction of the monkey *Macacus (Pithecus) rhesus*, with special reference to menstruation and pregnancy', Carnegie Institution of Washington, 1–161; *Time of Ovulation in Women*.
90 'A second-generation captive-born chimpanzee', *Science*, 81, 1935, 142–3.
91 O. L. Tinkelpaugh, 'Sex cycles and other cyclic phenomena in a chimpanzee during adolescence, maturity, and pregnancy', *J. Morphol.*, 54, 1933, 521–46.
92 H. Fox, 'The birth of two anthropoid apes', *J. Mammalogy*, 10, 1929, 37.
93 A. H. Schultz and F. F. Snyder, 'Observations on reproduction in the chimpanzee', *Bull. Johns Hopkins Hospital*, 57, 1935, 193–205.
94 J. M. Wyatt and G. M. Vevers, 'On the birth of a chimpanzee recently born in the Society's gardens', *Proc. Zool. Soc. Lond.*, 1935, 195–7.

95 For a full discussion of other cases see Ashley Montagu, *The Reproductive Development of the Female.*
96 *Causal Factors in Infant Mortality*, Pub. 142, 1925; *Maternal Mortality*, Pub. 158, 1926, Children's Bureau of the U.S. Department of Labor.
97 K. Mayo, *Mother India*, 22.
98 *Indian Census Report for 1921*, Appendix VII.
99 Curjel, 'The reproductive life of Indian women', *Indian J. med. Research*, 8, 1920, 366–71.
100 A. P. Pillay, 'Marriage and divorce in India', *Proc. 3rd Sexual Reform Congress*, 77.
101 A. H. Clark, 'Is India dying? A reply to *Mother India*', *Atlantic Monthly*, 141, 1928, 271–9.
102 Personal communication.
103 A.-T. Mondière, 'Sur la monographie de la femme de la Cochinchine', *Bull. Soc. Anthrop.*, 3, 1880, 250–61.
104 A.-T. Mondière, 'Nubilité', *Dictionnaire des Sciences anthropologiques*, ii, 823–4.
105 Letter to the author dated 13 June 1936.
106 K. T. Chau and J. M. Wright, 'Gynecological notes; Canton Hospital', *China med. J.*, August 1925, 684 sqq.
107 C. G. Hartman, *Science*, 74, 1931, 227.
108 C. P. Mountford and A. Harvey, 'Women of the Adnjamatana tribe of the northern Flinders Ranges, South Australia', *Oceania*, 12, 1941, 157.
109 *The Arunta*, i, 39.
110 Ibid., 272.
111 *The Sexual Life of Savages*, 157–8.
112 S. B. D. Aberle, 'Frequency of pregnancy and birth interval among Pueblo Indians', *Amer. J. phys. Anthrop.*, 15, 1931, 63–80.
113 A. W. March and C. B. Davenport, 'The normal interval between human births', *Eugenical News*, 10, 1925, 86–8.
114 Aberle, loc. cit., 77.
115 R. Pearl, 'Contraception and fertility in 2,000 women', *Human Biology*, 4, 1932, 363–407; 'Contraception and fertility in 4,945 married women, a second report on a study of family limitations', *Human Biology*, 6, 1934, 355–401.
116 Aberle, loc. cit., 75.
117 A. Hrdlička, 'Fecundity in the Sioux women', *Amer. J. phys. Anthrop.*, 15, 1931, 81–90.
118 *The Arunta*, i, 39.
119 A. S. Parkes, 'Observations on the œstrous cycle of the albino mouse', *Proc. Roy. Soc. B*, 100, 1926, 151–70; *The Internal Secretions of the Ovary*; F. A. E. Crew and L. Mirskaia, 'The lactation interval in the mouse', *Quart. J. exper. Physiol.*, 20, 1930, 105–10; R. Deanesley, 'The corpora lutea of the mouse, with special reference to fat accumulation during the œstrous cycle', *Proc. Roy Soc. B*, 106, 1930, 578–95; S. Zuckerman, 'The menstrual cycle of the primates, part iv: Observations on the lactation period', *Proc. Zool. Soc. Lond.*, 1931, 593–602.
120 Ploss and Bartels, *Women*, iii, 173–83.
121 G. Róheim, 'Women and their life in Central Australia', *JRAI*, 63, 1933, 230–1; *italics mine.*
122 *Mythen, Sagen und Märchen des Aranda-Stämmes in zentral Australien*, 33.
123 Róheim, loc. cit., 233.
124 Ibid., 233–4.
125 T. Hernández, 'Children among the Drysdale River tribes', *Oceania*, 12, 1941, 125.
126 Loc. cit., 234.
127 It is of interest to note that among the Trobrianders a woman is believed to be closed to the entry of a spirit-child until the menses have ceased, but they do not count the onset of pregnancy from the cessation of the menses but from the time that the breasts begin to swell, the previous months during which the menses had ceased to flow being not considered at all; thus

pregnancy is counted from the fourth or early fifth month. Cf. Leo Austen, 'Procreation among the Trobriand Islanders', *Oceania*, 5, 1934, 103.

128 It may be noted here that the *men* of Manus in the Admiralty Islands believe that menstruation is produced only after an act of intercourse, and that otherwise their women do not menstruate! M. Mead, *Growing Up in New Guinea*, 124; R. F. Fortune, *Manus Religion*, 82–3.

129 Thus, of the New Guinea Arapesh, Mead writes, 'Morning sickness during pregnancy is unknown', *Sex and Temperament*, 32.

130 'No paternity', *JRAI*, 48, 1918, 149.

131 E. Westermarck, *The History of Human Marriage*, i, 76–102; *The Future of Marriage*, 10.

132 Ibid., 100.

133 Ibid., 81, and maintained in the same author's work, *The Future of Marriage*.

134 *The Population Problem*, 92–4.

135 F. H. A. Marshall, *The Physiology of Reproduction*, 672.

136 S. Wright, *Applied Physiology*, 198.

137 H. Ellis, *Studies in the Psychology of Sex*, ii, 88 sqq.

138 C. G. Hartman, 'Studies in the reproduction of the monkey', 38.

139 S. Zuckerman, 'The menstrual cycle of the Primates', pt. vi, *Proc. Zool. Soc. Lond.*, 1933, 1059–75.

140 See p. 287, in which a parallel seasonal variation in the menstrual cycle of women is discussed.

141 *Proc. Zool. Soc. Lond.*, 1933, 1066–7; also the same author's *The Social Life of Monkeys and Apes*.

142 'The menstrual cycle of the primates, pt. i: General nature and homology', *Proc. Zool. Soc. Lond.*, 1930, 749.

143 'The period of gestation in the monkey, *Macacus rhesus*: First description of parturition in monkeys, size and behaviour of the young', *J. Mammalogy*, 9, 1928, 185.

144 'The menstrual cycle of the primates, pt. iii: The alleged breeding season of primates, with special reference to the Chacma baboon (*Papio porcarius*)', *Proc. Zool. Soc. Lond.*, 1931, 339.

145 Ibid., 341.

146 H. Fox, 'The birth of two anthropoid apes', *J. Mammalogy*, 10, 1929, 41.

147 L. Montané, 'Notas sobre un chimpancé nacido in Cuba', *Mem. Soc. Cubana Hist. Nat. 'Felipe Poey'*, 1, 259–69; 'Histoire d'une famille de chimpanzes: étude physiologique', *Bull. Mem. Soc. Anthrop. Paris*, 1928, 14–35.

148 A. Sokolowsky, 'The sexual life of the anthropoid apes', *Urol. Cutan. Rev.*, 27, 1923, 612–15.

149 W. Köhler, *The Mentality of Apes*, 1973, 302.

150 H. Fox, loc. cit., 50.

151 Loc. cit., 303.

152 A. H. Schultz and F. F. Snyder, 'Observations on reproduction in the chimpanzee', *Bull. Johns Hopkins Hospital*, 57, 1935, 197.

153 G. B. Schaller, *The Mountain Gorilla*, 289.

154 R. Yerkes, 'The mind of the gorilla, pt. ii: Mental development', *Genetic Psychology Monographs*, 2, 1927, 520–2; pt. iii, 'Memory', *Comparative Psychology Monographs*, 5, 1928, 69; J. van Lawick-Goodall, *In the Shadow of Man*.

155 G. S. Miller, 'The primate basis of human sexual behaviour', *Quart. Rev. Biology*, 6, 1931, 385.

156 Loc. cit., 1930, 748.

157 Brehm and Strassen, *Tierleben*, vol. 13, 436.

158 Loc. cit., 1930, 694.

159 'The breeding season in monkeys', *Mammalogy*, 12, 1931, 130.

160 *History of Human Marriage*, i, 81–2.

161 A. Johnston, 'The California Indians', in H. R. Schoolcraft, 'Historical and statistical information', *Archives for Aboriginal Knowledge*, 4, 1860, 224.

162 S. Powers, *Tribes of California*, 206.

163 *The Population Problem*, 94, 96, 100.

164 A. L. Kroeber, *Handbook of the Indians of California*, Bureau of American Ethnology, Bulletin 78, 1925, 41–5.
165 A. Oldfield, 'Aborigines of Australia', *Trans. Ethnol. Soc.*, n.s. 3, 1865, 230.
166 E. M. Curr, *The Australian Race*, i, 310 sqq.
167 Personal statement made to Westermarck, *The History of Human Marriage*, i, 83.
168 Ibid., 92.
169 Ibid.
170 Ibid., 96.
171 W. Heape, 'The proportion of the sexes produced by whites and coloured peoples in Cuba', *Phil. Trans. Roy. Soc. Lond.* B, 200, 1909, 296 sqq.
172 Loc. cit., 97.
173 C. A. Mills and F. A. Senior, 'Does climate affect the human conception rate?' *Arch. intern. Med.*, 46, 1930, 921–9.
174 Ibid., 927.
175 C. Ogle, 'Adaptation of sexual activity to environmental stimulation', *Amer. J. Physiol.*, 107, 1934, 628–34.
176 T. M. S. English, 'On the greater length of the day in high latitudes as a reason for spring migration', *Ibis.*, 11th ser., 5, 1923, 408–23.
177 W. Rowan, 'On photoperiodism, reproductive periodicity, and the annual migration of birds and certain fishes', *Proc. Boston Soc. nat. Hist.*, 38, 1926, 147–89; *The Riddle of Migration*.
178 T. H. Bissonnette, 'Modification of mammalian sexual cycles: Reaction of ferrets (*Putoris vulgaris*) of both sexes to electric light added after dark in November and December', *Proc. Roy. Soc.* B, 110, 1932, 322–36. For a summary of the literature dealing with photoperiodism the reader may consult Bissonnette, 'Sexual photoperiodism', *Quart. Rev. Biology*, 1936, 371–86.
179 H. S. Olcott, 'Vitamin E. II: Stability of concentrates towards oxidizing and reducing reagents', *J. biol. Chem.*, 107, 1934, 471–4.
180 H. M. Evans and G. O. Burr, 'Vitamin E', *Mem. Univ. California*, 8, 1927.
181 'Studies in the reproduction of the monkey', 38–9.
182 E. T. Engle and M. C. Shelesnyak, 'First menstruation and subsequent menstrual cycles of pubertal girls', *Human Biology*, 6, 1934, 431–53.
183 E. Allen, 'The irregularity of the menstrual function', *Amer. J. Obstet. Gynec.*, 25 (5), 1933, 705–8.
184 C. F. Fluhmann, 'The problem of irregular menstruation', *Amer. J. Obstet. Gynec.*, 26, 1933, 642–6.
185 J. L. King, 'Menstrual intervals', *Amer. J. Obstet. Gynec.*, 25 (5), 1933, 583–7.
186 W. Millar, 'Human abortion', *Human Biology*, 6, 1934, 297–9.
187 C. G. Hartman 'Studies in the reproduction of the monkey', 39.
188 'No paternity', 149.
189 The discovery was made on 18 April 1853. See F. J. Cole, *Early Theories of Sexual Generation*, 194.
190 C. B. Aldrich writes: 'When one comes to think of it, the discovery that no woman gives birth to a child except when she has been impregnated by a man is truly a triumph of scientific observation.' *The Primitive Mind and Modern Civilization*, London, 1931, 155.

CHAPTER XI

Phallic ceremonies and so-called phallic worship

Modest Doubt is call'd
The Beacon of the wise, the tent that searches
To th' bottome of the worst.

Hector, *Troylus and Cressida*, SHAKESPEARE.

Perhaps the most disconcerting piece of evidence with which the student of the procreative beliefs of the Aboriginal must reckon is the evidence that has at various times been adduced, generally quite unrelated to any discussion of the procreative beliefs of the Aborigines of the existence of phallic cults and ceremonies in Australia. So strongly contrary does this evidence appear to the generally accepted belief that the Aborigines are ignorant of the facts of conception, that Basedow, who was acquainted with a large variety of Australian tribes, and who for many years was a firm believer in the reality of the Australian nescience of the nature of procreation as a fact, was in the face of this evidence forced to adopt the opposite view. Since his is at once the most exhaustive as well as the most cogent account of the subject it will be given here in his own words:[1]

One often reads, and I was under the same impression myself until I became better acquainted with the tribes, that the Australian natives do not connect the knowledge of conception with any intercourse which might have taken place between the sexes. This I find is not altogether correct, although usually the younger people are kept in complete ignorance on the subject. No doubt strangers are treated similarly when they put any pertinent questions to the old men on matters of sex. The old men believe in the duality of human creation, the spiritual and the material; sexuality is regarded as the stimulus of corporeal reproduction, but the spirit quantity is derived through mystic and abstract influences controlled by a 'totem'-spirit or Knaninja. Under these circumstances, it is not surprising to note that the ceremonies of the phallus are transacted principally by the old men of the tribe who aim at the rejuvenation of their waning powers.

It is interesting to see the old men preparing for a ceremony which is to be dedicated to a Knaninja or Spirit of Sex, because they all endeavour to conceal the white hairs of their beards by rubbing charcoal into them. The bark of the cork tree (*Hakea*) is used for the purpose; pieces of it are charred, crushed between the palms, and applied where needed. It is astounding what a difference this process makes to the appearance, and some of the old grey-beards really look as though they had been made twenty years younger by magic.

In the eastern MacDonnell Ranges stands a cylindro-conical monolith whose origin is believed to be as follows: Many generations ago, the paternal ancestors of the Arunndta walked from a district situated, as near as one can gather, somewhere in the neighbourhood of Ediowie; they were known as the '*Kukadja*', and were characterized by the enormous dimensions of their organs. These old men or Tjilba of the tribe migrated northwards to beyond Tennant's Creek and settled in the productive '*Allaia*' country which surrounds the Victoria River. In that same district one finds, even at the present day, cave drawings of human beings with the anatomical peculiarities

2 Ochre drawing of Kukadja men, north of Wic River, Northern Territory (× ⅓)

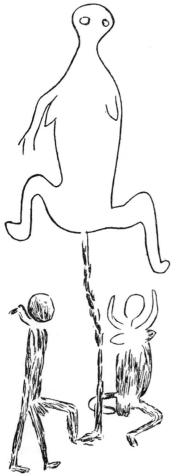

3 Charcoal drawing of a Kukadja man named garrapungja dancing at a sacred fire wi ancestral female. Pigeon-Hole, Victoria (× ⅓)

298

referred to (Fig. 2). At a later time, the head-man of the Kukadja, named '*Knurriga Tjilba*', returned southwards to the MacDonnell Ranges. While roaming the hills, he espied two young women sitting on the side of a quartzite cliff, and without deliberation began to approach them. He was in the act of making lewd overtures when the guardian of the girls, a crow ancestor, caught sight of him and hurled a boomerang at him. The missile struck the great man and cut off the prominent portion of his body, which in falling stuck erect in the ground. The force of the impact was so great that the man bounced off the earth and fell somewhere near Barrow's Creek. He bled so profusely that a clay-pan soon filled with his blood. Thus his followers found him, and overcome with sorrow they opened the veins of their arms to mix their blood with his. Then all the members of the party jumped into the pool and disappeared for ever.

The severed portion of the old man's body, however, remained just where it fell and turned to stone. It has long been known as '*Knurriga Tjilba Purra*'.

The two young women can also still be detected in the cliff as prominent rock formations.

The stone has been protected by the tribe as long as the old men can remember, because they realize that it contains an inexhaustible number of unborn tribes-people. These mythic, fœtal elements are generally recognized to exist in certain objects of phallic significance, and are called '*rattappa*'. The medicine men maintain that they can at times see the dormant living matter in the stone. It is on that account that it is regarded as sacred, and every now and then very secret and worshipful ceremonies are transacted near its base, the main objects of which are to multiply the future membership of the tribe and to preserve the sexual powers of the old men.

The Tjilba Purra naturally figures prominently in some of their ceremonies. In fact, it is reproduced and worn upon the head of the leading man during the functions. The sacred effigy consists of an upright column, about two feet high, composed of a stout bundle of grass stalks, in the centre of which the tjuringa is contained. It is decorated with alternating bands of red and white down throughout its length. This upright column represents the '*Tjilba*' or revered ancestor whose spirit is invoked to 'sit' in the tjuringa; at the top of it a plume of wiry emu feathers well powdered with charcoal ('*unjia*') to give it a youthful appearance, takes the place of the fore-bear's hair and beard. Standing at an angle with the central column a similar though slightly smaller structure is intended for the '*Purra*' or phallus; it carries a plume of white cockatoo feathers at its end to represent the glans.

A landmark, of similar significance as the Tjilba Purra of the

Arunndta, exists on the Roper River in the Northern Territory; it is a pillar of sandstone known as 'Waraka'. Waraka is also the name of the great Spirit Father of the tribe. In very early times this man came to earth in a semi-human form, and made the country abound in game, animals, birds, and fish. Then he found a woman on the shores of Carpentaria Gulf who remained with him as his wife. Many children came of the union; and Waraka's mate has since been looked upon as the mother of the tribe. The woman's name was 'Imboromba', and to this day the tribe takes its name after her. Waraka had an enormous sex characteristic which was so ponderous that he was obliged to carry it over one of his shoulders. Eventually the organ became so huge that Waraka collapsed and sank into the earth. His burden remained, but turned to stone, and is now looked upon by the local natives as the great symbol of Nature's generative power which first produced their game supplies and then the original children of the tribe; it is revered accordingly.

The Kukata have a somewhat similar legend of the origin of a stone of phallic significance, the name of the possessor of the large organ being 'Kalunuinti'.

In the extreme north-western corner of Australia, in the Glenelg River district, the natural stone is replaced by an artificially constructed one which possesses the true shape of a phallus. The stone is about three feet long and stands in a vertical position in the ground commanding a ceremonial cirque as if intended to watch over the proceedings which are instituted there.

On the shores of Cambridge Gulf, a grotesque dance is performed by the men, during which a flat, wooden phallus is used, shaped almost like a tjuringa, about seventeen inches long and three inches wide at the middle. It is painted in alternate bands of red and black, running transversely across the two flat surfaces, which are, in addition, decorated with the carved representations of the male organ of generation. The dance takes place at night and is too intricate to describe in detail. It is introduced by the following chant:

> Wa, la, ja-la-la-
> Wa, la, ja-la-ja-
> Wa la gori wau!

The verse is repeated three times, and then the performers stamp the ground with their feet, about ten times in quick succession, the action suggesting running without making headway. Presently, and with one accord, the whole party falls upon the knees. The phallus is seized with both hands and held against the pubes in an erect position, and so the party slides over the ground from left to right, and again from right to left. An unmistakably suggestive act follows, when the men jerk their shoulders and lean forward to a semi-prone position, after the fashion generally adopted by the aborigines. Still upon their knees, the men lay the phallus upon the ground and shuffle sideways, hither and thither, but always facing the object in front of them. After several repetitions of this interact, the performers raise their hands, in which they are now carrying small tufts of grass or twigs, and flourish them above their heads, while their bodies remain prone. Then follow some very lithe, but at the same time very significant, movements of the hips. When, presently, they rise to their feet again, the phallus is once more reclaimed and held with one of the pointed ends against the pubes in an erect position. A wild dance concludes the ceremony, during which the men become intensely agitated and emotional; very often, indeed, their excitement verging on hysterical sensibility, evokes an orgasm. . . .

The Dieri have a number of long cylindro-conical stones in their possession which are supposed to temporarily contain the male element of certain ancestral spirits now residing in the sky as their recognized deities. These are on an average about fifteen inches long and an inch and a half in diameter, circular in transverse section and pointed at one end. The old men have these phallus in their custody, and are very unwilling to let them get out of their reach because they believe that the virility of the tribe is dependent upon the preservation of the stones. Should one of them be accidentally lost, the mishap is calculated as little short of disastrous; should a stranger find the object, the old men maintain that evil will come to him, and if he keeps it he will die. The stone is used principally during religious ceremonies connected with sex-worship, but it is also produced during some of the initiation practices. After he has submitted to the 'gruesome rite' in his initiation, a novice is required to carry the stone, firmly pressing it against his body with his arm, until he is overcome by the exhaustion occasioned by the painful ordeal. By so doing, the young fellow's virile powers are supposed to receive considerable stimulation through the agency of the phallus he carries. The object drops into the sand beside him; and, when he recovers, he returns to the men's camp without it. Two of the old men thereupon track the lad's outward course and recover their sacred stone to take it back to a place of safety.

The tribes inhabiting the great stony plains of central Australia and those adjoining them, and also the Victoria Desert tribes, are occasionally in possession of nodular ironstone and concretionary sandstone formations, of the 'natural freak' kind, which simulate the *membrum virile* to a marked degree. These are believed to have been left them by a deified ancestor and are kept by the old men as a sacred legacy; they answer in every way the purpose of an artificially constructed phallus.

Closely allied to the phallic significance given to natural pillars of rock and smaller imitative specimens, is the idea that natural clefts in the earth represent a female character. Killalpaninna is the name of a small lake lying about fifty miles east of Lake Eyre in central Australia, it being the contracted form of the two words '*killa*' and '*wulpanna*', which stand for that typical of woman. It is the conviction of the Dieri tribe that when a person, especially one stricken with senility or enfeebled by sickness, at a certain hour passes from the water of the lake into the open, and is not seen doing so by the women, he is reborn and rejuvenated, or at any rate cured of his decrepitness. In this sense Killa-Wulpanna has from time immemorial been an aboriginal Mecca, to which pilgrims have found their way from far and wide to seek remedy and solace at the great matronal chasm which has such divine powers to impart. This fact is of particular interest, since a native, generally speaking, is superstitious about entering any strange water, and does so very reluctantly, thinking that, by doing so, the evil spirit will foist disease upon him through the medium of the water.

A singular stone exists in Ellery Creek, a short distance south of the MacDonnell Ranges, which is called '*Arrolmolbma*'. It was at this place that a tribal ancestor, named '*Rukkutta*', a long time ago met a young gin, '*Indorida*', and captured her. The stone at the present time shows a cleft and two depressions which are supposed to be the knee-marks of Rukkutta. On account of the intimacy which took place, the stone is believed to be teeming with rattappa, which entered by the cleft. The ancient Arunndta men used to make this stone the object of special veneration, and during the sacred ceremonies which took place at the spot, they used to produce carved slabs of stone which they called '*Altjerra Kutta*' (i.e. the Supreme Spirit's Stone or Tjuringa). These inspirited slabs of stone, being of the two sexes, were allowed to repeat the indulgent act of Rukkutta and Indorida, while the natives themselves rubbed red ochre over the sacred stone of Arrolmolbma, and engaged in devotion. The act of rubbing red ochre over the surface of the stone was supposed to incite the sexual instinct of the men and to vivify the virile principle of the tribe. By this performance the men believed they took from the pregnant rock the embryonic rattappa which in the invisible form entered the wombs of the gins and subsequently came to the world as the young representatives of the tribe they called '*Kadji kurreka*'.

Among the cave drawings of Australia, designs are here and there met with depicting scenes from ceremonies having to do with phallicism and other sex-worship. In the picture reproduced from the

Pigeon-Hole district on the Victoria River (Fig. 3), one notices a man of the Kukadja type who was named '*Mongarrapungja*' in the act of dancing around a sacred fire with an ancestral female. The organ of Kukadja, it will be observed, passes into the flame, whence a column of smoke is rising to find its way to the body of a gin which is drawn in outline above the dancers. Here we have the representation of a traditional ceremony associating the Kukadja's phallus with the impregnating medium supplied by fire, which, we have already learned, may be looked for in the column of smoke.

The fact that Spencer and Gillen, Howitt, Strehlow, and by far the majority of other field investigators of the tribes of Australia have failed to remark upon the existence of such phenomena as Basedow has described in the foregoing passages is not a little strange, although Spencer and Gillen did make the statement that 'it is doubtful how far phallic worship can be said to exist amongst the Australian natives'.[2] Basedow's positive statements, however, are more important than the inexplicable silence of these investigators. Moreover, Basedow's statements are strongly supported by the independent observations of Etheridge,[3] and of E. G. Mjöberg[4] who reported the existence of similar phallic cults in Australia. Róheim who has discussed the evidence from the psychoanalytic standpoint is convinced that the *Churinga* are to be regarded as phallic symbols.[5]

We may now well inquire as to what the significance of all this evidence is for our understanding of the procreative beliefs of the Australians in general and the Arunta in particular.

In the first place we may note Basedow's agreement with Strehlow and with Róheim that the older men are aware of the nature of conception but that they keep this knowledge from the younger people. Basedow's statement that among the old men sexuality is regarded as the stimulus of corporeal reproduction, apparently refers specifically to the Arunta, and clearly it means that the Arunta believe that intercourse is essential before a child can come into being. More particularly it is clearly intended to mean that intercourse is regarded as the stimulus which leads to physical being. What the term 'stimulus' may mean here is not altogether clear, but I suspect that the term reflects some uncertainty in Basedow's mind as to the real facts. The qualification in Basedow's statement that the idea that the Australian natives do not connect intercourse with conception 'is not altogether correct', possibly, refers to the the fact that the ignorance of the relationship holds true, according to Basedow, only for the younger people, though it may be intended to mean that the ignorance holds true for the tribe as a whole with the exception of the small number of old men who are the possessors of all esoteric knowledge and who know the 'truth' but keep it hidden from the younger members of the tribe. It is to the old men that Basedow specifically refers as believing 'in the duality of the human creation, the spiritual and the material', and who regard sexuality as the stimulus of corporeal reproduction, the rest of the tribe, we may assume, remains ignorant of such ideas. Basedow's use of the word 'stimulus' must in this connection be interpreted to mean that intercourse excites to activity all those processes which result in the development of a human being—minus a spiritual part, the spirit part being derived from the spirit abode in the manner with which we are already familiar. This interpretation of Basedow's statement, which I think faithfully reflects his meaning, is identical with Lang's interpretation of the evidence, for Lang, it will be recalled, considered that the native is aware that intercourse plays a physical part in the generation of a spirit incarnated, but that the material act was alone insufficient to effect the incarnation of the spirit or soul, and that therefore it had to come from without.

We have already seen that Spencer and Gillen, Strehlow, and Fry, had received statements to the effect that intercourse assisted or was necessary for the entrance of a spirit-child into a woman. These statements, we endeavoured to show, did not really indicate a knowledge of the relationship between intercourse and pregnancy, but on the other hand simply proved that intercourse was regarded among the peoples holding these views, as a condition and not as the cause of pregnancy. We may, however, recall with reference to this the account given by Schulze for the Middle Finke River Arunta, in which it was stated that 'the souls of the infants dwell in the foliage of trees, and that they are carried there by the good mountain spirits, *tuanjiraka*, and their wives, *melbata*. The nearest tree to a woman when she feels the first pain of parturition she calls *ngirra*, as they are under the impression that the *gurunna*, or soul, has entered from it into the child'.[6] Such a belief would suggest that the individual obtains only his spirit part from a totem abode and his body from some other and immediately anterior source—a view of the matter, which it will be recalled, characterizes the beliefs of the north Queensland natives. From Spencer and Gillen's account of the native description of the spirit-child, its colour, form, and various characters, and of its entry as such into the woman, it is quite clear that it enters both as a body and as a soul, but chiefly as a soul which develops its characteristic body subsequent to its entry into the woman's womb. Strehlow's account of the Central Australian's beliefs in this matter, in spite of apparent disagreements, may essentially be reduced to the same system of ideas. And as far as Schulze's statements are concerned there is no reason to assume that they stand in any way opposed to those of either Spencer and Gillen or of Strehlow. What in each case enters the woman is, part and parcel, soul and body, derived from an ancestral source. Such a view is, however, thoroughly opposed to that credited to the Arunta by Basedow, who asserts that the former represents the exoteric doctrine of the tribe alone, whilst the esoteric beliefs make full recognition of the fact that intercourse is the responsible agent in producing conception.

It may at once be said that the existence of phallic cults in any group does not signify that such groups necessarily possess a knowledge of the relationship which exists between intercourse and pregnancy.[7] This should be obvious, yet, strangely enough, Basedow at once hastens to the conclusion that such cults constitute *prima facie* evidence of such knowledge. Since the phallus is a great source of pleasure to the native it is of small wonder that he performs ceremonies in celebration of it, and with the object of preserving its powers of pleasure-giving benefits. As Aldrich has said, 'The primitive sees in sex an immediate personal satisfaction and an immediate matter of religious importance.'[8] It is of interest to note that it is only the old men who take part in these ceremonies, for one of the chief objects of these ceremonies would appear to be the rejuvenation of their waning powers. This seems to be the obvious and chief reason why 'the ceremonies of the phallus are transmitted principally by the old men of the tribe', and not, as Basedow suggests, because they alone are aware of the meaning of sexuality.

In other words, the sex totems identified with the various phallic-shaped monoliths described by Basedow are the abode of the powers of sexual strength, or of ancestors, who were notable for their sexual prowess as is evident from the enormous dimensions of the organs they are believed to have possessed. These ancestors, having entered the earth at such spots as are now marked by the presence of their organs, are a source of the production of sexual strength in others. Actually, it is quite clear from Basedow's account that there are no special sex totems, but that every totemic abode which is associated with the ancestors of the large sexual organs is especially associated with the power of being able to produce sexual strength in others, as well as itself carrying a supply of spirit-children, in the same way as any other totem abode does.

The *Tjilba Purra* ceremonies of Basedow's account have been exhaustively described by Spencer and Gillen,[9] who seem to have been quite unaware of any phallic significance which they may have possessed. Basedow's terms *Tjilba Purra* are suggestive of something of the confusion into which one may fall during a cursory sojourn among a native people. What Basedow is apparently referring to here are the great Achilpa ceremonies which take place during the

Engwura celebrations, when the *Parra* (Basedow's *Purra*), a mound on the ceremonial ground intended to represent the track of the original *Inkata* of the Achilpa totem of the *Alchera*, figures largely during the ceremonies. What Basedow calls the *Tjilba Purra* is actually known as a *Nurtunja*, an upright pole especially made for use at sacred ceremonies, and said to be emblematic of the animal or plant giving its name to the totem in connection with which the ceremony is performed.[10] These *Nurtunja* are identical with those figured by Basedow in his book as *Tjilba Purra*. Of course, these objects may be interpreted as having a phallic appearance but such an interpretation does not necessarily make them so. According to Spencer and Gillen's detailed descriptions of these objects each of which represents 'for the time being the animal or plant that gives its name to the totem',[11] each particular part of these *Nurtunja* is intended to represent the special distinctive character by which the animal or plant it is supposed to symbolize may be recognized. It should be pointed out here that it is only the northern Arunta who make these *Nurtunja* of this peculiar shape, for among the southern Arunta, and the tribes extending as far down to the south as the coast at Port Lincoln, an elongated pentagonal-shaped object called a *Waninga* takes the place of the *Nurtunja*; it would be difficult to imagine a phallic significance for these objects although it may be stated here that Róheim has not failed to detect such a sexual significance in these *Waninga*. But given Róheim's methods I believe it is possible to detect any kind of significance in anything whatever. A specimen of Róheim's discussion of these matters may be given to illustrate to what lengths his method enables him to go:[12]

When we see that the aboriginals have certain more or less mystic decorations made for the ceremonies and discarded when this season is over, we shall be tempted to draw a parallel between these cermonial decorations and the secondary sexual characters that the animals develop for, and discard after, the rutting season. If we accept the view that these ornaments are a sequel of the assertion of the natives that the ornaments represent a part of the body of their semi-human and half-animal ancestors . . .

The origin of the secondary sexual characters of animals cannot be said to be quite clear. At any rate, they stand in close connection to the primary ones, as they are absent in castrated animals.[13] Hesse inclines to the view that they are 'Überschussbildungen aus den Ersparnissen bei der Bildung der Geschlechtsprodukte'[14] (which is about as much as to say that they are phalloi coming out at the wrong place), the male giving less sexual energy out in the sexual act than the female. If this is true, then these crests, manes, and all sorts of ornaments of the rutting season may be described as the physiological pre-formations of certain unconscious mechanisms that we are well acquainted with, or rather the displacement upwards is a 'psychical' survival, a reduced repetition of the biological process manifested in the secondary sex-characters. The helmet of the ceremonies is a Churinga transposed upwards and the Churinga itself a symbolic penis. That is why we see a return of the repressed elements when the Churinga, which radiates its creative faculties on the wearer, is put into the head-dress, and that is why even the latter develop-ments of this head-dress have conserved traces of their ancient connec-tion with the male organ of generation.

With respect to the existence of a rutting season in the progenitors of man, I think that it has already been adequately shown how little such a point may be relied upon to assist arguments such as those of Róheim. It is, of course, perfectly incorrect to assume that such a period ever existed at any time in the developmental history of man, and it is greatly to be regretted that Róheim was unable to resist drawing his incredible parallel, for such reasoning is calculated to injure rather than to advance the cause of the psychoanalyst in ethnological studies.[15]

There can be no doubt that phallic ceremonies exist among many of the tribes of Australia, if not among all of them, but these have actually never been very satisfactorily described, so that it is not altogether a simple matter to judge of their nature. Such an account as Basedow's, however, renders it perfectly clear that as far as the Aborigines are concerned such phallic ceremonies as he has described do not demonstrably involve any knowledge, on the part of those who participate in them, of the relationship between intercourse and childbirth. And this, of course, is the important point. In this respect, whether certain ceremonial objects are to be regarded as of phallic significance or not is of purely secondary interest.

The phallic dance performed by the Cambridge Gulf tribe, described by Basedow, at the conclusion of which an orgasm some-times occurs in some of the men, would suggest that this is a dance primarily performed for the production of a ritual sort of sexual pleasure. It may even represent a form of ritualized quasi-mastur-bation, but whatever the purpose of these dances may be, it is difficult to see what connection they may have with the procreative beliefs of the participants.

Basedow's account of the singular stone at Ellery Creek which is supposed to mark the spot at which a tribal ancestor named Rukutta met and captured a young *gin* named Indorida, is quite another matter. According to Basedow, it is believed by the natives that it is on account of the intimacy which took place at this spot that the stone is teeming with *ratappa*. There can be little doubt that by 'intimacy' Basedow here means intercourse, and since, as we know, intercourse is considered necessary in order to prepare a woman that she may be ready for the entry of a spirit-child into her there is nothing very remarkable in this statement, excepting, perhaps, the emphasis placed on the 'intimacy', but this may probably be due to Basedow's manner of making the point. There are many Arunta myths which tell of the capture of a *gin* by a tribal ancestor and of their living together, and of the subsequent birth from these *gins* of many individuals, such, for example, as the important myth relating to Illapurinja and Lungarinia which has already been noted upon an earlier page in this book. Women are generally necessary in order that a spirit-child may undergo incarnation—it is not on account of any intimacy between the sexes that children are born, but because a child can only be born through the medium of a woman. There can be little doubt that Indorida gave birth to many children, and that these all entered the earth at a spot now marked by the 'singular stone' at Ellery Creek, and that that is the reason why it is now teeming with *ratappa*, and not because of any intimacy that occurred at that particular place. It should be remembered that everywhere in Australia children are thought of only in relation to the family; a man or a woman alone does not have children—children are simply not thought of in such non-familial contexts. In order that a child may come into being above all things else it must have a father, thus a woman can normally only give birth to children if she is married, and there can be little question that it was because Rukutta captured and made Indorida his wife that spirit-children were able to enter Indorida, and that the place where either the one or the other eventually went into the ground is now marked by a *ratappa*-stone or totem abode. Intimacy is here of little significance for Basedow's point.

As for the rubbing of the *Churinga*, this is a well-known and frequently practised method of increasing the virtue or power of the *Churinga*. Rubbing of the *Churinga* is much indulged in during the increase ceremonies,[16] and also in association with the emanation of spirit-children from the *ratappa*-stone.[17] Róheim thinks that 'the rubbing is but a symbolic repetition of the friction produced by coitus'.[18] Actually the virtue that lies in any *Churinga* is for the most part derived from the original ancestor with whom it was associated in the *Alchera*, and also, it should be noted, with the virtues, to some extent, of those into whose possession it has at various times temporarily passed. It is to this original and accumulated virtue of the *Churinga* that an appeal is made during the increase ceremonies. Of itself there is no evidence that a *Churinga* is able to give rise to another being, it merely represents the material abode of the spirit part of an individual, and, as such, it is obviously of great importance in determining the totem of the individual as well as supplying him with a guardian spirit. For the period during which an individual is in actual possession of his *Churinga* he is said to be endowed with the additional power which is normally lodged within it,[19] whilst an old man suffering from some illness will often scrape some dust from his *Churinga* and swallow it, believing that by so doing and by this means he will be strengthened.[20] But there is no evidence of the existence of any procreative or reproductive powers on the part of the *Churinga*. I do not consider that the rubbing of a *ratappa*-stone can be likened to an act of coitus. It would appear, however, that in some way rubbing excites to activity the power within the objects so rubbed, but I cannot, I must repeat, see that this is to be regarded as similar in any way to an act of coitus.

The cave-drawings from the Pigeon-Hole district on the Victoria River depicting 'scenes from ceremonies having to do with phallicism and other sex-worship' are also, I think capable of bearing an interpretation other than that which Basedow has given them. And here we may appropriately voice an objection against the use of such terms as 'sex-worship'. In none of the phallic ceremonies described by Basedow is there any evidence of 'worship' of any kind. Indeed, as far as the available evidence permits us to speak with any definiteness upon the matter, there is no evidence anywhere in Australia that the natives behave at any time, whether ceremonially or otherwise, as if they worshipped anything. Certainly they do not worship their eponymous ancestors; they hold them in great respect, and ceremonially commemorate their lives and deeds, but such ceremonial observances do not constitute what is generally understood by the term 'worship'. Likewise, the phallic practices of the Aborigines represent merely ritual ways of obtaining sexual power, such practices do not constitute the worship of the source of that power.

Fig. 3 (p. 298) shows a representation of a tribal ancestor of the type characterized by a large copulatory organ dancing with an ancestral female around what appears to be a fire from which rises a column of flame or smoke which proceeds directly into the vagina or perineal region of the *gin*. Into the base of the column is projected the large organ of Mongarrapungja. This drawing Basedow looks upon as 'a representation of a traditional ceremony associating the Kukadja's phallus with the impregnating medium supplied by fire'.[21]

In none of the ceremonies which Basedow reports, however, is fire or smoke associated with the idea of an impregnating medium. What Basedow had in mind here is the 'smoking' ceremony to which the girl is usually subjected during the process of her initiation among the Larrekiya and the Wogait. This ceremony consists in allowing the smoke of a dampened fire to play upon the genitalia of the novice until they have been thoroughly permeated by it. Following this ceremony the girl is led away into the bush by the old women, there to stay for some days, during which time she is forbidden to partake of certain foods.[22] There is nothing in this ceremony nor in the account which Basedow gives of it, which would indicate that it is in any way connected with the alleged impregnating action of smoke. The girl, it should be remembered, is as yet unmarried, and at this stage of her initiation has not yet undergone the operation of subincision which will, among these tribes, render her 'marriageable'. We may therefore, more properly, I think, regard the smoking ceremony as a preparatory treatment prior to the operation of subincision. It should be recalled in this connection that immediately following the ceremonies of circumcision and subincision the male novice is made to hold his mutilated organ over a similar smoking fire, the smoke it is believed possessing the property of being able to relieve the pain, the smoke also being possessed of curative powers assists the wound to heal. It is possible that the female smoking ceremony is similarly merely calculated to assist in reducing the pain at the ceremony of subincision which is to follow it.

Basedow has, however, described a myth among the Wogait which may throw some light upon the meaning of the Mongarrapungja drawing. According to this myth and to Wogait belief, it is believed that their 'evil spirit' makes a big fire and from this he takes an infant and places it, at night, in the womb of a *lubra*, who must eventually give birth to it.[23] Among the Arunta there is a myth relating to the origin of fire which tells how it was first obtained by an *Alchera* euro man from the greatly elongated penis of a euro.[24] The Mongarrapungja would seem to combine elements of both these myths. By a stretch of the imagination the drawing may then be taken to mean that the fire which is emanating from the ancestral Mongarrapungja's penis, which carries with it or in it a spirit-child, is entering the body of a *lubra*. It is somewhat difficult, however, to account for the entry of the smoke into the genital orifice of the *lubra*, for nowhere in Australia, curiously enough, do children gain entry through these parts, but it may well be that the artist intended it to be understood that the smoke was entering the *lubra* in the general region of the loins, whatever his intention may have been, at least, the drawing would have been so understood by the natives beholding it. Upon the above interpretation all that this representation would mean is that Mongarrapungja is the source of spirit-children, just as the figure of *wondzina*, in the north-west, is connected with the increase of spirit-children,[25] it would not mean, however, that such children are the result of an act of intercourse, in reality the drawing supports the belief that children are definitely not the result of such an act, a point which I do not think it necessary to press any further.

NOTES

1   *The Australian Aboriginal*, 284–92.
2   *The Native Tribes of Central Australia*, 101.
3   *The Cylindro-conical and Cornute Stone Implements of Western New South Wales and their Significance*; 'Ancient stone implements from the Yodda Valley goldfield, north-east British New Guinea', *Records of the Australian Museum, Sydney*, 7, no. 1 1908.
4   'Vom Phalluskult in Nordaustralien', *Archiv Anthrop.*, 19, 1923, 86 sqq.
5   G. Róheim, *Australian Totemism*; 'Psycho-analysis of primitive cultural types', *Int. J. Psychoanal.*, 13, 1933, 1–224.
6   L. Schulze, 'The Aborigines of the Upper and Middle Finke River', *Trans. Proc. Roy. Soc. S. Aust.*, 14, 1891, 237.
7   In New Guinea, for example, among the Iatmul of the Sepik River, 'phallic symbols are to be regarded, not simply as symbols of the genital organ, nor as symbols of fertility, but rather as symbols of the whole proud ethos of the males.' G. Bateson, *Naven*, 163.
8   *The Primitive Mind and Modern Civilization*, 155.
9   *The Arunta*, 175–303.
10 Ibid., 622.
11 Ibid., 74 n. 2.
12 *Australian Totemism*, 242–3; cf. also 'Psycho-analysis of primitive cultural types', 68.
13 Hesse-Doflein, *Tierbau und Tierleben*, i, 498.
14 Ibid., 496.
15 The excesses, one might almost say the orgiastic excesses, of reasoning committed in Róheim's book, constitutes the sole reason why I have not been able to make use of it in this study. It will, I suppose, be useless for me to protest my sympathy with the psychoanalytic movement, or to state that my comment upon Róheim's book is in no way motivated by the usual type of prejudice with which psychoanalysis has generally had to contend. This very explanation will, no doubt, be immediately interpreted by the orthodox, as bearing witness to an obviously sinister intention! This criticism, it should be made quite clear, does not apply to Róheim's later valuable field reports, to which reference has already been made.
16 *The Arunta*, 377.
17 Ibid., 143, 150.
18 *Australian Totemism*, 220.
19 *The Arunta*, 142.
20 Ibid., 133–4.
21 *The Australian Aboriginal*, 292.
22 Ibid., 253.
23 H. Basedow, 'Anthropological notes on the western coastal tribes of the Northern Territory of South Australia', *Trans. Proc. Rep. Roy. Soc. S. Aust.*, 31, 1907, 5.
24 *The Arunta*, 348–9.
25 See pp. 184 sqq.

CHAPTER XII

Subincision and its alleged relationship to procreation

Subincision[1] is a rite which, as we have already learnt, is associated with the latter stages of initiation. The rite is practised over a very great part of the Australian continent, its distribution being indicated in Fig. 4. All things considered the evidence would appear to point to an origin for this rite somewhere in the centre of the continent, from whence it probably diffused. Such a statement, however, does not preclude the possibility of the rite having been introduced from some source outside Australia. Davidson has studied the distribution of this trait in some detail,[2] and Rivers,[3] and Basedow[4] have independently discussed its possible significance.[5]

In Central Australia, as well as in many other parts of Australia, the female as well as the male is subjected to a similar operation at initiation. In the male the operation consists essentially in slitting open the whole or part of the penile urethra along the ventral or under surface of the penis. The initial cut is generally about an inch long, but this may subsequently be enlarged so that the incision extends from the glans to the root of the scrotum, in this way the whole of the under part of the penile urethra is laid open. The latter form of the operation is universal among the Central tribes. As one proceeds outwards the intensity of the operation becomes reduced, until we meet with forms which strongly resemble the condition of hypospadias, that is, forms in which a small slit is made in the urethra towards either the glans or the scrotum, or both. In the female the operation takes a variety of forms ranging from extensive laceration of the vaginal walls and clitoridectomy to the slightest laceration of as much of the hymen as may be present.

As we have earlier in this book already had occasion to note, the operation of subincision has by many writers been regarded as a practice devised in order to insure the limitation of the numbers of the tribe. In other words, the practice is by these writers regarded as a contraceptive measure. If this were so, it would very strongly suggest that the relationship between intercourse and pregnancy was, at least at the time when the operation was originally introduced, fully understood. Those who hold this belief are of the opinion that since the spermatic fluid normally passes through the urethra to the external orifice to be received by the vagina, the object of slitting the urethra is to cause the loss, through the incised portion of the urethra, of the spermatic fluid before it could reach the external orifice, so that during intercourse it would thus fail to reach the vagina.

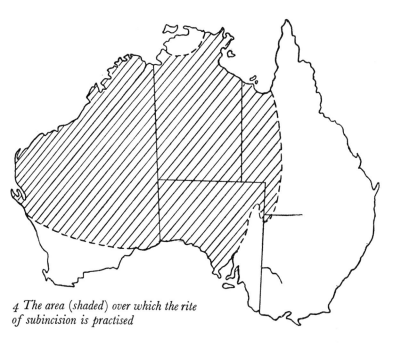

4 *The area (shaded) over which the rite of subincision is practised*

To anyone acquainted with the anatomy and physiology of the male genital system this theory, and the alleged facts upon which it is based, are so patently absurd as hardly to deserve serious consideration. But since in the culture in which this book is being written it is the custom to be least informed upon the subject which each individual should naturally know most about, namely the structure and functions of his own body, it will perforce be necessary to enter into a discussion of the perhaps not altogether patent absurdities of this theory.

In the first place, it is to be noted that the force with which the spermatic fluid is launched into the penile urethra is very great.[6] As far as I know this force has never been measured, but it is, at any rate, well known that the ejaculated fluid is capable of proceeding in space for a distance of as much as 4 feet or more after it has left the urethra, so that even with a considerably lacerated urethra it would be not unreasonable to suppose that some of this fluid, if not the greater part of it, would be projected through the external orifice. Certainly in that form of subincision which is most commonly practised in some parts of Western Australia, in which a small incision is made in the urethra immediately anterior to the root of the scrotum, it is exceedingly unlikely that any but a small quantity of the spermatic fluid would find its way out through such an aperture, for the orifices of the ejaculatory ducts leading into the urethra are situated in the prostatic portion of the urethra, but a little distance posterior to the position which such an artificially made aperture would occupy; it is certain, therefore, that the force with which the spermatic fluid is normally projected through the ejaculatory ducts into the urethra would carry, at least, the greater part of it past this aperture without causing more than a little of it, if any, to be expressed through the latter. Those students who have concerned themselves with this subject and who are under the impression that during coitus the spermatic fluid is ejected through this aperture *extra vaginam*[7] must therefore be acquitted of any but the most innocent knowledge of the facts.

In the second place, even if the greater part of the spermatic fluid were to be expelled through the lacerated urethra during coitus, certainly most, if not all, of it would enter into the vaginal canal. It should be recalled here that the vagina of the female has generally also been lacerated, so that it forms quite a commodious chamber, which, together with the rhythmical muscular contractions of its walls, is capable of catching and holding all the spermatic fluid that is likely to escape in its proximity. The peculiar position adopted by the Aborigines during intercourse is calculated to ensure this. The position is thus described by Basedow:[8]

When a couple is about to indulge, the female, by request or habit, always takes her position by lying with her back upon the ground. The man squats between her legs, facing her, and lifts her thighs on to his hips. Leaning forwards, he steadies his body with his knees on the ground and accommodates the parts with his hands. This accomplished, the woman grips him tightly around his flanks or buttocks with her legs, while he pulls her towards his body with his hands around her neck or shoulders.

The evidence indicates that this method of coition is practised throughout Australia, in Central,[9] Northern,[10] and North-Western Australia,[11] and in Queensland.[12] Such a method of copulation would ensure the ejaculated spermatic fluid reaching the parts for which it was intended. Roth, for example, writes:[13]

The peculiar method of copulation in vogue throughout all these tribes does not prevent fertilization, notwithstanding the mutilation of the male. The female lies on her back on the ground, while the male with open thighs sits on his heels close in front: he now pulls her toward him, and raising her buttocks drags them into the inner aspects of his own thighs, her legs clutching him round the flanks, while he arranges with his hand the toilette of her perineum and the insertion of his penis. In this position the vaginal orifice, already enlarged by the general laceration at initiation, is actually immediately beneath and in close contact with the basal portion of the penis, and it is certainly therefore a matter of impossibility to conceive the semen as being discharged for the most part anywhere but into its proper quarter.

Basedow writes:[14]

It is obvious that through the position adopted by the man, a fair proportion of the rejected spermatic fluid will find its way into the vagina. In a state of erection, the mutilated organ becomes very wide; it is only natural that after the lower connecting wall of the urethral canal has been severed, the *corpus penis* in this condition spreads itself laterally. . . .

Through this lateral distension, the receiving vagina will gape more than it would under normal conditions, and so there is greater facility for the fluid to enter. And more, the tribes who practise subincision in most cases also submit the female to a corresponding mutilation, which further dilates the passage.

Since, then, it must be very apparent to the Australian that the spermatic fluid enters the vagina of the female, it is hardly credible that were he aware of the nature of that fluid and were he anxious to avoid the consequences of its action, that he would have continued the use, had it ever been devised for the purpose, of a method at once so extremely painful and so utterly ineffectual in attaining the object attributed to it by those in whose imagination alone it seems ever to have had such an object. Here, once more, I may quote Roth:

There is no tradition whatever, and I have made searching inquiry, to the effect that introcision is any preventive to procreation. When asked for an explanation, or the origin of the ordeal, the aboriginals invariably plead ignorance or if pressed will answer somewhat to the effect that '*Mulkari*[15] make him first time'. In this connection it is interesting to note that even the possibility of taking artificial means to prevent fertilization, etc. (I am not speaking of abortion), is apparently beyond their comprehension: thus I have reports from station-managers who assure me that only with great difficulty could their 'boys' be made to understand, if they ever did, the object of spaying cattle.[16]

Basedow writes, 'So far as my own observations go, I can positively state that the singular form of penile urethrotomy we are discussing [subincision] is not intended, nor anywhere regarded, by the Australian natives as a method of birth-control.'[17]

The alleged object of the practice of subincision as a method devised to secure the maintenance of a proper balance between the food supply and the numbers of the population, represents a purely fanciful speculation. Unfortunately for this theory there are vast areas in Australia that are well capable of supporting a much larger number of individuals, under normal native conditions, than are ever found in such territories. Further, it should be noted that the rite of subincision is not limited to the hunger-stricken desert region tribes, but is found away to the north and to the south among the tribes where food is plentiful and the population not, oftentimes, as large as among the desert tribes. Moreover, as Roth pointed out many years ago for the tribes of north-west Central Queensland,[18] the alleged object of this practice is already met by the universally strict observance of the laws regulating the sexual union of individuals belonging to one or other moiety, class, and totem, whereby the quantity of food available to parents is in no way immediately affected by the number of offspring. In all Australian tribes the consumption of every article of food is strictly regulated. Thus, the totem plant or animal of an individual is only on very rare occasions eaten by him, and then only very sparingly. A man will eat articles of food which are forbidden to his wife, and old men will eat many articles of food which are entirely forbidden to the younger people. In this way a most efficient balance between the food supply and the number of individuals in the group is maintained, although it could hardly be called an equitable distribution from our point of view; but that is not the point.

Thus, it would seem clear that we must look elsewhere for an explanation of the meaning of subincision, that it has no connection with procreation or its control is abundantly clear, and with this demonstration the *pis aller*, one of the strongest of the evidences which have been cited as tending to disprove the Australian nescience of the relationship between intercourse and childbirth vanishes, and with this statement we might well bring this discussion to a close. But this would not be quite satisfactory, for until some endeavour has been made to show as positively as is under the circumstances possible what the significance of subincision may most likely be the foregoing discussion might not altogether unjustly be criticized upon the ground that what the originators of the practice of subincision originally thought its virtues to be may have had some relation to procreation of a nature which it is now not even possible to guess at. In the discussion which follows I propose to meet any such possible objections, not by speculating upon the possible intentions of the originators of the practice, but by offering concrete evidence which would seem to me to give this practice a meaning which it may very probably have originally possessed. In such matters, of course, there can be no question of proof or even of adequate demonstration; all that can at most be hoped for, or expected, is that the evidence produced be so pertinent and the conclusions to be deduced from it so cogent and reasonable as to afford the explanation thus obtained a degree of probability greater than that which any other explanation has heretofore succeeded in achieving.

It may at once be said that no theory which has thus far been advanced to account for the meaning of subincision has achieved even a remote degree of probability. This has by no means been the fault of those students who have devoted their attention to the subject, for although a certain number of clues were available to them, there was nothing in their nature which could have enabled anyone to single them out from the mass of bewilderingly complicated details associated with the practice, in preference to certain other possible details which invited attention because of their similarity to those found in association with those non-Australian peoples among whom various forms of subincision are also practised. Among these peoples, chiefly the Fijians, the Tonga Islanders, and the natives of the Amazon Basin of Brazil, subincision is carried out chiefly as a therapeutic measure, and it is this possible therapeutic function of subincision that was seized upon as a clue to the significance of the practice among the Australians. Had the clue, which did not really become available until March 1935, been accessible to those students who had concerned themselves with this subject, there can be little doubt that the explanation which is shortly to be offered for the significance of subincision would have been proposed before now.

THE SIGNIFICANCE OF SUBINCISION

Among the Fijians it is believed that subincision is a preventive of many diseases, and that unless the individual submits himself to this operation he is likely to fall a victim to them. The operation is also performed as a remedy following the onset of any of these diseases. It is also said to remove the evil humours of the body. Performed as a cure for tetanus among the Tongans, it is also resorted to in a variant form by passing a reed tube into the urethra, in cases of general debility, and in the operative form with the object of removing the blood from the abdominal cavity produced by wounds in the abdomen.[19] From these practices and their various motives Rivers has concluded that 'the operation acts as a counter-irritant and as a means of evacuating blood and possibly other bad humours, which are believed to be producing or helping to produce disease'.[20] Hence the motive for the practice is obviously therapeutic, a conclusion with which I think there can be no disagreement. Among the Amazon Basin River natives of Brazil subincision is upon occasion practised for the purpose of removing the diminutive fish which sometimes gain entry into the urethra while the natives are bathing in the waters in which these fish abound.[21] Here, too, it is therefore evident, the operation is purely of a therapeutic nature.

Such facts have led Basedow to suggest that the rite may have originated in Australia for similar reasons, since all sorts of crawling and burrowing crustaceans, insects, and other vermin, not to mention such things as splinters, burr, grass-seed, grit, and so forth, might easily gain entry into the urethra among the Aborigines. Moreover, Basedow suggests that in tropical Australia, particularly in the north, where he thinks the practice may have originated, 'acute inflammation of the prepuce, glans, and urethra might periodically have seriously affected many of the male members of the tribe.'[22]

Such a view of the origin of subincision in Australia may, of course, not be impossible, although it is somewhat strange that the operation is never practised for such reasons among the natives of the present time, but is instead regarded by them as a purely ceremonial rite. Rivers, however, has seen in the one factor common to the Fijians, the Tongans, and the Aborigines, namely the effusion of blood, a possible common origin for the practice. He offers two possible explanations for the appearance of subincision in islands so far removed from one another as Australia and Fiji. One is that the procedure of subincision belongs to the culture of a people who once occupied the whole of this part of Australia, and that the practice has only persisted in Fiji and certain parts of Australia, undergoing divergent lines of evolution which, in one place or in both, have greatly modified its original purpose. Thus, it has become a purely therapeutic measure in one place, and a purely magico-religious rite in the other. In favour of this view Rivers states that very similar skulls occur in Viti Levu and Australia, skulls which bear a close resemblance to the ancient Neanderthal skulls of Europe.

The alternative hypothesis is that some migrant people, who practised subincision, either as a therapeutical practice or a ceremonial rite introduced it into Fiji and Australia, and that in the process of assimilation into the indigenous culture of the two places, it has undergone such transformation as now gives it its wholly different purpose in the two places. The special form of this hypothesis which seems the most likely to be true is that a migrant people introduced the use of a urethra seton as a remedy for disease, and that this has largely maintained its original purpose in Fiji, while in Australia it has taken on the special magico-religious purpose, characteristic of the aboriginal Australian culture. Having wholly lost all trace of its therapeutic purposes, it has become a purely ceremonial rite. There still, however, remains the effusion of blood, common to the two practices, which in the one place is the immediate motive, or one of the motives, of the therapeutic measure, while, in the other, it brings this rite into line with many other Australian rites in which the effusion of blood plays so important a part.[23]

Neither of the hypotheses proposed by Rivers is inherently improbable, and, indeed, his first hypothesis derives some support from the fact that subincision has recently been described for two separate tribes in New Guinea, namely the Banaro of the Sepik area[24] and the inhabitants of Wogeo, in the Schouten Islands.[25] What I believe to be the most promising clue to the original meaning of subincision is afforded by the reasons which the natives give for the practice among the latter people.

Against Rivers's hypotheses many objections have been urged, chief among which is the absence of subincision among the marginal tribes of Australia, and the great intensification of the practice as one proceeds towards the centre of the continent. The only marginal area in which subincision is found is in the south, but no one has so far been venturesome enough to suggest that any foreign influences may have come through that part of Australia! Davidson, who thinks that the evidence of distribution is entirely against Rivers's first hypothesis,[26] cannot agree that the form of urethrotomy practised among the Banaro is akin to the form of subincision practised among the Aborigines. The difference, however, in the manner in which the urethrotomy is produced does not, in my opinion constitute a sufficient reason for denying a common origin for them. Had Davidson been willing to grant such a possibility he might not have argued as strongly as he has against the possible introduction of subincision into Australia by way of Melanesia in general and New Guinea in particular. The fact that subincision is unknown in the extreme north including Melville and Bathurst Islands, I do not consider to constitute any objection to such an hypothesis, for it is quite possible that the peoples of these territories may have once practised the rite, which may have been adopted from some migrant people, and subsequently discarded it. It must never be forgotten that these marginal peoples have probably been subject to more than one influx of foreigners and, like the reaction of rocks to disturbing influences, their responses to these migrating influences must either have been comformable or non-comformable, thus, what at one time they may have adopted, they may well, at another time, have given up in favour of some other practice.

These suggestions are all possibilities; whether any one of them is true or not it is impossible to say, and I do not here propose to discuss the probabilities, but will at once proceed to the discussion of evidence for what I consider to be the most likely explanation of the meaning of subincision among the Aborigines.

THE ORIGIN OF SUBINCISION

The element common to all forms of subincision is the inevitable effusion of blood. This, as we have seen, has already been noted by Rivers, but it seems never to have occurred to him that the peculiar means adopted to produce this effusion, namely the characteristic urethral incision of the male copulatory organ might in some way be connected with the analogous natural effusion of blood in the female from a similar source. Briefly, the suggestion here is that male subincision or incision corresponds, or is intended to correspond, to female menstruation. Indeed, I may at once state the hypothesis which I am about to offer as an explanation of the probable origin of subincision in Australia; it is that *subincision in the male was originally instituted in order to cause the male to resemble the female with respect to the occasional effusion of blood which is naturally characteristic of the female, and possibly also with respect to producing some feminization in the appearance of the male organ.* As it stands the theory must appear somewhat fantastic, I therefore hasten to produce the evidence upon which it is based.[27]

We have already seen that among the Aborigines menstruation is not regarded as a periodic occurrence, but that it is somewhat confusedly regarded as being a quite natural phenomenon though of irregular occurrence, or as due to a cold in the head or other illness, or to the scratching of a *mamu*. Such are the beliefs regarding menstruation that have been reported for the Arunta of the present day.[28] Among the Kakadu natives of the Northern Territory menstruation appears to be regarded as a normal occurrence which is said to proceed from something which breaks near the heart and accumulates in the form of blood in a special bag inside, and it is when this bag bursts that the blood flows.[29] The taboos which in Australia are placed upon menstruating women and menstrual blood indicate that menstruation has always been regarded as a phenomenon to which some degree of mystery attaches. Menstrual blood is everywhere in Australia regarded as unclean and as an element of danger. Menstruating women must at such times everywhere be avoided, until they have got this dangerous element out of their bodies and are once more clean. It is the menstrual blood which is a sign of the uncleanness of the woman, and it is not until this noxious matter has been completely voided that the woman is thoroughly clean again. Menstrual blood is a noxious humour of mysteriously strong potency, this much is clear. Is it not possible, therefore, that judging this to be the natural or normal or the most efficient way of getting rid of the bad 'humours' within one's body,[30] some early aborigines upon the principle of like producing like, essayed to produce an artificial menstruation within their own bodies, and seeing that the blood came in the female from the vulva, what more natural than to make it likewise come from the organ in one's own body which most closely corresponds to that organ in the female?

Significantly enough the only etymology which I have been able to trace for the meaning of the various words which are used to describe the subincised penis in Australia is that supplied by Roth for the northwest central Queensland tribes of whom he writes: 'it is interesting to note that in the Pitta-Pitta and cognate Boulia district dialects the term used to describe an introcised penis denotes etymologically one with a vulva or "slit".'[31] Roth considered that female laceration preceded male subincision and that 'on the principle of a form of mimicry, the analogous sign was inflicted on the male to denote corresponding fitness' for the purposes of copulation. In this he came very near to the theory which is here being proposed, but fell somewhat wide of the mark because of his altogether unjustified assumption of the priority of female laceration. That the subincised penis is referred to as a vulva may or may not be of significance for the present theory, I offer the interesting fact here merely for what it may be considered to be worth. Any value that may be placed upon it may perhaps be increased by the following interesting corroborative evidence.

Hogbin in his report on the Dap tribe of Wogeo, which it will be recalled is the most northerly situated of the Schouten Islands, makes the following illuminating remarks:[32]

Perhaps the most fundamental religious conception relates to the difference between the sexes. Each sex is perfectly all right in its own way, but contact is fraught with danger for both. The chief source of peril is sexual intercourse, when contact is at its maximum. The juices of the male then enter the female, and vice versa. Women are automatically cleaned by the process of menstruation, but men, in order to guard against disease, have periodically to incise the penis and allow a quantity of blood to flow. This operation is often referred to as men's menstruation.

All contact with a man or woman who is 'menstruating' has to be avoided, and they themselves have to take a number of precautions. Thus they may not touch their own skin with their fingernails, and for a couple of days they have to eat with a fork. The penalty for touching a menstruating woman is death by a wasting disease, against which there is no remedy whatsoever. The 'menstruating' man has also to avoid sexual intercourse until his wounds are healed, at least two months being allowed for this. Should this prohibition be broken both parties are liable to die, though they may save themselves by confessing their guilt and carrying out a magical rite.

Men also incise the penis after they have performed certain tasks which for magical reasons are held to be very dangerous. These include the erection of a new men's house, burying a corpse, taking part in an expedition with intent to murder someone, and initiating a youth. All these tasks are held in some mysterious manner to contaminate those who take part in them, and the flow of blood is necessary for cleansing purposes.

Similar beliefs and practices have been reported for the Kwoma of New Guinea. Whiting and Reed write:[33]

Menstruation is rationalized in accordance with their beliefs about blood and growth. Women are thought to be provided with a natural mechanism for purging themselves of bad blood. A woman remains in the house during her period of menses, allowing the blood to flow on to a piece of bark which she carries out into the bush and empties from time to time. During her period all adult males of the household must absent themselves and spend their nights in the house of a relative.

The men believe that to preserve their health and strength they, too, must purge themselves similarly. At periodic intervals they go to a stream where they make light incisions in the glans. The flowing water carries the bad blood out of the tribal territory so that there is no danger of its return to their systems.

Among the natives of Wogeo and the Kwoma it would appear quite clear that the penis is incised on the analogy of female menstruation for the purpose of permitting the bad humours within the body, and such as are likely to be produced during the performance of certain tasks with which a great deal of power is associated, to be liberated and voided. Thus, the operation is here of a therapeutic and prophylactic nature, but it is at the same time a strongly magico-religious procedure. Thus, the elements that were missing in Basedow's and Rivers's theories are here supplied, and it seems highly probable, therefore, that whether or not the practice of subincision originated in Australia, whatever the reasons assigned by the natives for the practice, the rite as it is today practised in that continent was originally performed for reasons similar to those given by the natives of Wogeo and the Kwoma for the practice of the rite of incision.

There is some evidence to suggest that circumcision is conceived to have originated in a similar manner as subincision. There is, for example, a legend relating to the origin of menstruation among the Adnjamatana of northern South Australia, which relates how the semi-human bird Jurijurilja, who was uncircumcised, had two wives. 'At Mount Chambers gorge he threw a boomerang which, when returning, circumcised himself and entered the vulvae of his two wives, cutting them internally so that they bled. This caused their monthly periods.'[34] It is of interest that no tribe subincised that did not also circumcise.

Objection has been offered to this theory on the origin of subincision on the ground that a similar operation is performed on women.[35] To this the reply is that, first, the operation performed on women in no way resembles that performed on men, and second, even if it did, that would in no way be incompatible with the theory proposed here.

It is likely that subincision was once widely practised throughout Australasia and Oceania, but whether or not the rite is of indigenous origin in Australia is a matter with which we are not here concerned. It is sufficient for our purpose to have arrived at a conclusion which renders any association between subincision and procreation highly unlikely at any time in the history of the former. It would be impossible to leave this subject here without referring briefly to Arunta traditions associated with the practice of subincision.

Among all the Central tribes there is a tradition that the rite of subincision was introduced by the ancestors of the men of the Achilpa totem. According to this tradition many of the original Achilpa men, during the course of their wanderings, developed a disease known as Erkincha.[36] This disease affects the glands in the region of the perineum and anus, and sometimes the axillæ and the angle of the mouth. It is a disease to which the young people are at the present day particularly liable. Many of the Achilpa men died from the effects of this disease, and where they went into the ground Knaninja arose to mark the spot. Wherever, on their wanderings, the Achilpa men rested there they performed Arilta or subincision upon the young men and sometimes the old men as well. Whenever and wherever Arilta was performed a special Nurtunja was erected.[37] It is curious to note, however, that those young men who were already suffering from Erkincha were not operated upon,[38] at least this was so at one place where the Achilpa men rested.[39] Throughout the wanderings of the Achilpa men *Erkincha* and *Arilta* are always and with uniform regularity associated together. This continued emphasis upon the association in the Achilpa tradition is significant, for it suggests that subincision was performed as a preventive measure against the contraction of *Erkincha*. It is likely, too, that the operation may have been performed upon the women for the same reason, for the Aborigines at the present time believe that a man suffering from *Erkincha* conveys a magic evil influence, which they call *Arungquilta*, to the women, and by this means it is conveyed as a punishment to other men.[40] It is possible that the operation was originally introduced to guard against just such magical effects. If the Achilpa tradition rests upon any factual basis, such an interpretation then becomes quite possible.

In an Arunta myth reported by T. G. H. Strehlow, namely the myth of the 'great chief Ntonionunga', the eldest son of the 'chief' performs subincision on his father out of sexual jealousy, in order to prevent him from interfering with another Achilpa woman, the father and the woman both having belonged to the same subsection, which would have made their relationship incestuous.[41] Strehlow thinks that this myth may throw light on the origin of subincision, but I must confess myself completely unable to see how, and in what sense, such a myth could be taken to throw any light on the subject.

As a rule wherever any myths or traditions are found associated with the rite, these indicate that the practice was instituted in order either to prevent or to overcome the effects of disease and its magical influences. Thus, for example, among the natives of King Sound in the north-west it is believed that the operation was introduced by a stranger who came to earth from above, at a time when an awful scourge, due to the poisonous exhalations of a green monster, was threatening to exterminate the tribe.[42]

Such beliefs are perfectly consonant with the view of the origin of subincision which has been outlined above, and with this statement we may well leave our discussion of the matter here.

NOTES

1 A confusing variety of terms have been used to describe this operation, such as introcision, division, *urethrotomia externa*, terrible or gruesome rite, Sturt's rite, artificial hypospadias whistle, *mika, kulpi, arrilta, yerrupa*, etc.
2 *The Chronological Aspects of Certain Australian Social Institutions.*
3 *Psychology and Ethnology.*
4 'Subincision and kindred rites of the Australian Aboriginal', *JRAI*, 57, 1927, 123–56.
5 See also N. Himes, *Medical History of Contraception.*
6 As Rabbi Schlomo Izchaki (Rashi) said in commenting upon Genesis xlix, 26, 'The seminal fluid spurts out like an arrow from its bow.' See C. J. Brim, *Medicine in the Bible*, New York, 1936, 316.

7   See H. Aptekar, for example, who accepts this as a fact without making any attempt to discover whether there can be any basis for it; *Anjea*, 124.
8   H. Basedow, 'Subincision', 153.
9   Loc. cit.
10 Loc. cit.
11 Loc. cit.
12 W. E. Roth, *Ethnological Studies*, 179.
13 Quoted in Basedow, 'Subincision', 153.
14 'Subincision', 154–5.
15 *Mulkari* is the supernatural guardian who makes everything which the Boulia district natives cannot otherwise account for; he is a good beneficent individual and never harms anyone. Roth, op. cit.
16 Ibid., 179.
17 'Subincision', 150.
18 Op. cit., 179.
19 W. Mariner, *An Account of the Natives of the Tonga Islands*, ii, 254; B. S. Corney and B. A. Thomson, *The Fijians*.
20 W. H. R. Rivers, *Psychology and Ethnology*, 67.
21 K. von Steinen, *Durch zentral Brazilien*.
22 'Subincision', 144–5.
23 Loc. cit., 68–9.
24 R. Thurnwald, *Die Gemeinde der Banaro; Zeit. vergleich. Rechtswissenschaft*, 38–9, 1922, 21–2.
25 I. Hogbin, 'Native culture of Wogeo', *Oceania*, 5, 1935, 320–1.
26 *Chronological Aspects*, 45–58.
27 For striking supporting evidence see Bruno Bettelheim, *Symbolic Wounds*.
28 G. Róheim, *Women and their Life in Central Australia*, 230–4.
29 B. Spencer, *Native Tribes of the Northern Territory of Australia*, 320.
30 Blood-letting has among most peoples been practised for the same reason, and is still so practised down to the present day among the peasantry of Europe. At one time, particularly in the seventeenth and eighteenth centuries, the treatment of almost every disease began with a phlebotomy or 'cupping'.
31 W. E. Roth, *Ethnological Studies*, 180.
32 'Native culture of Wogeo', *Oceania*, 5, 1935, 330.
33 J. W. M. Whiting and S. W. Reed, 'Kwoma culture: report of field work in the Mandated Territory of New Guinea', *Oceania*, 9, 1938, 192.
34 C. P. Mountford and A. Harvey, 'Women of the Adnjamatana tribe of the Northern Flinders Ranges, South Australia', *Oceania*, 12, 1941, 161.
35 C. Simpson, *Adam in Ochre*, 216.
36 *The Arunta*, 384–6.
37 Ibid., 388.
38 Ibid., 385.
39 Ibid.
40 Ibid., 385, n. 1.
41 'Ankotarinja, an Aranda myth', *Oceania*, 4, 1933, 193.
42 H. Basedow, *The Australian Aboriginal*, 283.

Note The following contributions came to my attention too late to be discussed in this chapter: I. H. Jones, 'Subincision amongst Australian western desert Aborigines', *Brit. J. med. Psychol.*, 42, 1969, 183–90; J. Morrison, 'The origin of the practices of circumcision and subincision among the Australian Aborigines', *Med. J. Aust.*, 21, January 1967, 125–7; J. E. Cawte, N. Djagamara and M. J. Barrett, 'The meaning of subincision of the urethra to Aboriginal Australians', *Brit. J. med. Psychol.*, 39, 1966, 245–53; J. E. Cawte, 'Further comment on the Australian subincision ceremony', *Amer. Anthrop.*, 70, 1968, 961–4; J. E. Cawte, 'Why we slit the penis', reprinted in G. E. Kearney, P. R. de Lacey and G. R. Davidson (eds), *The Psychology of Aboriginal Australians*, 380–94.

CHAPTER XIII

Maternity and paternity in Australia

I dare say little with an air of finality about black peoples; I have lived too much with them for that. To be positive you should never spend more than six months in their neighbourhood; in fact, if you want to keep your anthropological ideas quite firm, it is safer to let the blacks remain in inland Australia while you stay a few thousand miles away.—K. LANGLOH PARKER, *The Euahlayi Tribe*, 141.

Among the most important facts which have been brought to light during the course of the preceding discussion stands most prominently the fact that in Australia *maternity* and *paternity* are viewed as essentially non-biological, exclusively *social* concepts. There is an absence of any notion of blood relationship between mother and child as well as between father and child—a fact which has been generally completely overlooked. It is not difficult to understand how this nescience of the blood tie between mother and child came to be overlooked by students of Australian ethnology, for in the first place, the bias which had been given to the discussion by the controversies of the 'mother-right' and 'father-right' schools had turned exclusively upon the ignorance of physiological paternity, and, in the second place, the blood relationship between mother and child was considered to be so inescapably obvious, that any suggestion that a real 'ignorance' of physiological maternity could possibly exist among any people, however lowly, would have been received, as it was by Lang and others, with frank incredulity. Lang's objections to the alleged ignorance among the Arunta of the tie of blood on the maternal side have already been mentioned. The relationship, argued Lang, was far too obvious for them not to be aware of it, they merely did not permit it to affect the descent of the totem, which is regulated by their doctrine of incarnation. It cannot perhaps be too often remarked that the categories of thought peculiar to ourselves are not necessarily refined enough to enable us to use them with any degree of success as effective instruments in the analysis of Aboriginal thought. The difficulty is, I think, much greater than is customarily supposed, as those who are possessed of some knowledge of the structure of the languages of nonliterate peoples will agree. Lévy-Bruhl has shown something of the nature of the difference involved in the mental functions of nonliterate peoples, and has emphasized their essentially mystical nature. The mind of the Aboriginal is no more pre-logical than that of the modern educated man or woman. Essentially the mind of the native functions in exactly the same way as our own. The differences perceptible in the effects of that functioning are due only to the differences in the premises upon which that functioning is based, premises which represent the logical instruments of the native's thought, and have their origin in categories and forms of judgment which are to some extent different though quite as rigorously organized as our own. Had Aristotle and Kant been born into an Arunta group their categories and forms of judgment would have been quite different from what we know them to be. It is for this reason that it is so difficult for one who has been educated in the Western tradition to judge or evaluate the meaning of certain native beliefs and practices, and unless such a one has divested himself of as many of his own prejudices as he is able, he will never succeed in arriving at an understanding of such beliefs and practices. According to the categories of thought in which Lang was educated it is quite impossible to escape the observation of the fact that there exists a *physical* connection between a mother and her child. Whatever pagan or Christian doctrine may allow as possible in the Western world, when all other facts have been eliminated in the consideration of the nature of maternity, there remain the two irreducible correlates which alone make the physical or psychical relation possible, namely the relation between the woman and the child to which she has given birth.

Among ourselves a child is the effect of certain causes operating in a given system of conditions, the first and most indispensable of which is a woman, called the mother, who will bear the child, and who will be socially known as its sole mother thereafter. As stated, this view hardly differs from the view held by the Aborigines, it is only in the interpretation of the nature of the causes and conditions that there exists any difference between our own and the Aboriginal belief. The logic by which the Aboriginal arrives at his conclusions in this matter is as faultless as our own, it is the difference in the nature of the premises which produces the difference in the conclusions in each case. Both recognize the necessity of a woman in order that a child may be born, but while our own system of beliefs tells us that a child is the immediate product of the fertilized ovum of the woman who bears it—its physiological mother—among the Aborigines there is no such recognition of any essential physiological relationship between the woman and the child that 'comes out' of her. The child born of a woman is believed to be a being much older than anyone living in the tribe at the time of its birth, the incarnation of an ancestral being or sage, and, thus, an entity perfectly independent *in origin* of any physiological causes operating at the time of its incarnation or birth into the tribe. The spirit-child merely enters a woman whom it considers sufficiently attractive and who is of the right moiety. The same spirit-child could have entered and have been born of any number of different women. The spirit-child does not acquire a new body from its host, the woman in whom it is incarnated, but is already associated with a body which needs only to undergo an 'unfolding' during its sojourn within its host, from a *ratappa* or *kuruna* to a new-born baby. It is clear that there is and can be no physiological connection between a woman and the child which comes out of her. The only purpose of the woman in the whole cycle of events leading to childbirth is to act as the means of transmission of a spirit-child into the proper moiety, class, and section of the tribe. There is no more connection between her and the child transmitted through her than that. Certainly it is quite clear to every Aboriginal that every child passes into the world through the medium of some woman, and there is no one who would or could deny that this elementary fact is quite clearly recognized by the native. What the native does deny, quite possibly as a result of his lack of awareness of the fact—and that is quite another thing—is that there exists any tie of blood between a child and woman out of whom it has come. We, with our prejudices find it difficult to understand such a state of affairs, but this in no way affects the conditions as they exist among the Aborigines. Each individual is an independent entity, and has been so from the beginning of time, no one is dependent upon anyone else for his or her appearance upon this earth. If a mother or father kill their child, it will certainly make its re-appearance at some future time, either to its late parents or to some other parents. There is no question of *physical generation* on the part of any woman or man, there are no physiological conditions to be fulfilled before one can be reborn. Sexual intercourse between a husband and wife acts as a socially sanctioned announcement to the proper spirit-children that the woman is now available for their transmission into the tribe, though the mere fact of marriage is quite sufficient to produce this effect. But these conditions are not construed as physiological ones, but as purely social ones. A child must have a family, a 'father' as well as a 'mother', without a 'father' it is an anomaly, something that does not fit into the structure of society as it is—in such a society it can have no place. Whether the 'father' is the actual husband of the 'mother', or is some other individual not so related, such as the *wororu* of some of the Western Australian tribes, these elementary 'family' conditions must be fulfilled. It is not so much that society demands it, as that it is clearly the natural condition of things that a child should be born into a family, for it is only in exceptional cases that a child is born out of wedlock, and thus outside the family. Such an exception is regarded as the effect of some malign influence either on the part of a mischievous spirit, or a medicine-man, or some other malignant individual, who may have incited a spirit-child to enter the unfortunate girl. In neither the normal nor the abnormal cases is any physiology involved as between the spirit-child and its mother or father. As I have already had occasion to point out, these terms, 'mother' and 'father', are used in a purely social sense. There is nothing in their meaning that denotes any relationship of blood with anyone or anything else. In fact, the concept of blood relationship in our sense does not and cannot exist among the Aborigines—there are only *social* relationships. To recognize, or to become aware of the existence of such a thing as *blood relationship,* one individual at least must be regarded as in a particular sense the cause of another, it must be recognized that some part of the one has contributed to the formation, to the genesis, of the other. An awareness of such things the Australians do not have, nor, I believe, have they ever had, thus, the recognition of the concept of blood relationship or consanguinity is impossible to them. It is probable that prehistoric man failed to recognize blood relationships. This last suggestion is supported only by such evidence and arguments as have been presented in the preceding pages of this book. Upon the basis of these it seems fairly evident that such a suggestion is more likely to be true than otherwise. However, in the present work we are concerned only with the conditions among the Australian Aborigines as we know them, the suggestion for prehistoric man has been introduced here only because I believe that it is a consideration which deserves rather more attention than has thus far been given it in discussions of the evolution of concepts of kinship and kinship terms. The confusion originally introduced into this subject by Morgan, who believed that all systems of kinship were based on a recognition of community of blood through procreation, that is, consanguinity,[1] has to a large extent persisted down to the present day.

Malinowski, who has been responsible for a valuable discussion of kinship in Australia,[2] failed to say the last word upon the subject because of his failure to recognize that not only was there no recognition of the blood tie between father and child, but that there was also the more important non-recognition of such a tie between mother and child. Instead, Malinowski began his analysis of the concept of kinship on the basis of 'the existence of the individual family as a social unit, based upon the physiological facts of maternity . . .'[3] and throughout his discussion assumes that 'the existence of this physiological and social basis of kinship may be taken as granted'.[4] From this standpoint he then proceeds to discuss the subject in relation exclusively to paternity. Had Malinowski correctly interpreted the evidence relating to Australian Aboriginal maternity his discussion of kinship would, I think, have been unimpeachable. That

Malinowski was not altogether unconscious of the possible significance of the facts relating to 'maternity' in Australia is clear from his comment made in connection with 'the well-known fact that physiological maternity is much more easily ascertainable than physiological paternity. Paternal kinship,' he writes, 'therefore, will much more frequently differ from what we called consanguinity than maternal kinship. But,' he adds, 'some of the Australian examples and our previous general considerations should make us cautious in laying down *a priori* any assertion of the purely physiological character of maternity.'[5]

A study of the factors which in the past have caused ethnologists who occupied themselves with this subject to overlook the nescience of physiological maternity among the Australians would in itself provide an illuminating chapter in the history of ethnological thought. Frazer, once having stated the fact seems completely to have forgotten it, except only in so far as it related to his theory of totemism.[6] Gomme who seems to have been fully aware of this peculiar nescience,[7] and came nearer than anyone else to a realization of its significance, did not, however, work out in detail the full implications of this nescience, while van Gennep,[8] like Hartland[9] and Malinowski,[10] as well as numerous others, restricted his discussion to the ignorance of physiological *paternity*. Indeed, as I have already pointed out, it was this preoccupation with the ignorance of physiological paternity that served to divert the attention of students of the subject from the more important, but apparently less obvious, ignorance of physiological *maternity*.

Radcliffe-Brown in a valuable general survey of the social organization of Australian tribes went quite out of his way, it seems to me, to perpetuate this error, an error which has, however, rarely been so positively stated:[11]

In Western civilization we normally think of genealogical relationships in terms of what are commonly called biological, but may perhaps better be called physiological relationships. There is an obvious physiological relationship between a woman and the child to which she gives birth. For us there is also a physiological relationship between a child and the man who is the genitor. The first of these is recognized by the Australian native, but the second is not recognized. In some tribes it seems to be denied that there is any physiological relationship between genitor and offspring. Even if in any tribes it is definitely recognized it is normally, or probably universally, treated as of no importance.

Upon what grounds Radcliffe-Brown attributes a knowledge of physiological maternity to the Aborigines I do not know, certainly there is nothing either in the organization or in the beliefs of any Australian tribes which has thus far been described which would lend the slightest support to such a statement. Radcliffe-Brown's statement can only be explained upon the ground that the physiological relationship between a woman and her child seemed so obvious a thing to him that he considered, or rather assumed, that it could not fail to be equally obvious to the Aborigines. Nowhere, however, has he, nor for that matter has anyone else, been able to produce any evidence in support of such a statement. On the other hand, Radcliffe-Brown has clearly shown, in his own words,[12] that

The father and mother of a child are the man and woman who, being husband and wife, i.e. living together in a union recognized by other members of the tribe, look after the child during infancy. Normally, of course, the mother is the woman who gives birth to the child, but even this is not essential as adoption may give a child a second mother who may completely replace the first.

In a final section of the same study Radcliffe-Brown, having demonstrated the misleading nature of the kinship and genealogical terminologies of earlier writers, goes on to say: 'They [the earlier writers] distinguish between "blood" and "tribal" relationships. In the first place the term "blood" is misleading. The Australian aborigines do not recognize physiological but only social relationships as was mentioned in Part I of this essay'.[13]

If, as Radcliffe-Brown here states, Aborigines do not recognize physiological but only social relationships, how, then, can they be aware of a relationship between two individuals, a mother and child, which Radcliffe-Brown has himself declared to be of a nature which is not recognized? Obviously, they cannot be aware of such a relationship. Clearly, while recognizing the essentially social nature of maternity and paternity in Australia, Radcliffe-Brown's own Western prejudices have unconsciously caused him to interpolate the wholly unknown and unnecessary concept of physiological maternity into this scheme.

There is a difference between the recognition of the fact that a child develops from an egg produced by the mother, and the idea that a child develops from a 'spirit-child' which is produced by, and enters her from, an external source. A recognition of the first fact constitutes an awareness of the essential physiological nature of maternity, while a non-recognition or rejection of this interpretation of the nature of maternity and an acceptance of the second notion obviously constitutes a non-physiological, spiritistic interpretation of maternity.

Many millions of eggs are every day hatched in incubators, but no one believes that the incubator is genetically or physiologically related to the chick in the sense in which the hen is that gave it birth. While studying the literature descriptive of the procreative beliefs of the Australian Aborigines, the evidence gradually forced upon my attention the probability that the Aborigines conceptualized the actual generative process in much the same terms as those in which we think of the relationship between incubator and chick. The incubator enables the egg, in which the already predetermined undeveloped chick lies, to develop into a chick, but it has no more connection with the generation of the egg than it has with the predetermined character of the chick.

As I have already said, a consideration of the Australian material suggested to me that it was much in this way that the Aborigines looked upon the development and birth of a child. The mother was merely the incubator of a spirit-child (*pace*, egg) which very definitely originated from a source *physiologically* quite unrelated to her own body. This is what I mean by 'ignorance of physiological maternity' among the Australian Aborigines.

When a group or an individual affirms belief that in the generation of a child the female, who subsequently gives it birth, plays no role other than that of housing it and supplying it with nutriment during the time of its 'unfolding', such a belief can only be pronounced as unphysiological. In reality the word 'unphysiological' is quite unsatisfactory here, since the notion that the predetermined externally originating spirit-child is supplied with nourishment during its stay in the mother's womb is certainly a physiological conception, and in so far as this belief prevails in any group the woman who gives birth to a child must be said to be physiologically related to it in the sense that she supplied it with nourishment during its sojourn in her womb. In this sense the incubator is physiologically related to the chick hatched from the egg which was placed within it for that purpose by some external agency. There is no *genetic* relationship between either egg, chick and incubator, or between spirit-child, mother and offspring, and it is in this genetic sense that a physiological relationship between mother and child can be said to pass unrecognized among the Australian Aborigines. This is what I mean by ignorance of physiological maternity.

Since several critics have taken me to task for asserting what I have never stated, and since 'evidence' has recently been produced to prove the existence of facts and knowledge concerning the relationship between mother and child which I have myself asserted to exist, it would seem that some further discussion of my views concerning the ignorance of physiological maternity is necessary.

Professor Radcliffe-Brown,[14] Dr Géza Róheim,[15] Dr Phyllis Kaberry,[16] and Dr Ralph Piddington[17] have criticized my views on the grounds that to say that an Aboriginal child does not know its own mother is ridiculous. 'We need not take the trouble even to refute such a view.'[18] I thoroughly agree—all the more so since I have never stated that an Aboriginal child does not know its own mother. Every child unquestionably knows its own mother. In this book I had written (p. 328)—and Radcliffe-Brown quotes the passage —'Certainly it is quite clear to every Aboriginal that each child passes into this world through the medium of some woman, and there is no one who would or could deny that this elementary fact is quite clearly recognized by the native. What the native does deny . . . is that there exists any tie of blood between a child and the woman out of whom it has come.'

Upon this passage Radcliffe-Brown comments as follows: 'Since this is precisely what my statement means, I am completely at a loss to understand why the author should censure me for saying what he says himself.'[19] He goes on to say: 'One has to try to guess what "tie of blood" may mean, and more particularly what it might mean to an Australian black fellow, since this is what he is declared to deny.'[20] In the first sentence the reference is to my criticism of Radcliffe-Brown's statement: 'there is an obvious physiological relationship between a woman and the child to which she gives birth.'[21] I maintained, as I still do, that it is difficult to see upon what grounds such a knowledge of physiological maternity could be attributed to the Aborigines, since as Radcliffe-Brown had himself shown in the same essay, 'The Australian aborigines do not recognize physiological but only social relationships.'[22] In a footnote to this sentence (p. 313 n. 2) I suggested that 'this statement would indicate that our disagreement here resolves itself purely to a matter of definition.' And that is clearly to what the misunderstanding is due. Before proceeding to discuss this matter, it is necessary to point out here that Radcliffe-Brown's statement that 'one has to guess what "tie of blood" may mean', is hardly justified in view of my statement, and the discussion which follows it, that 'to recognize, or to become aware of the existence of such a thing as *blood relationship*, one individual at least must be regarded as in a particular sense the cause of another, it must be recognized that some part of the one has contributed to the formation, to the genesis, of the other.' Only between individuals recognizing such relationships could a 'tie of blood' be said to exist. Surely, this is a clear enough definition of what I mean by 'tie of blood'? In the succeeding sentence I stated that the Aborigines had no conception of such operative *causes*, and hence that the concept of consanguinity was impossible to them. This is the notion of 'tie of blood' which the blackfellow was held, not so much to deny, as to ignore, and of which he has no awareness.

Where the misunderstanding has arisen is quite evident from Radcliffe-Brown's statement: 'I should have thought that it was evident that the physiological relation to which I referred as being obvious is the fact that a child comes into the world out of the body of the mother and is not found under a gooseberry bush.'[23]

Of course, everyone knows that 'a child comes into the world out of the body of the mother', but no one for a moment believes that the child was *produced* or *created* in the body of the woman from which it has issued. The belief is rather that an already *pre-formed* spirit-child has entered her from some external source, generally, but neither always nor necessarily associated in some way with her husband. A child is not physiologically produced in a woman, and physiologically the male has nothing to do with its production—the latter is merely the means of causing a *particular* spirit-child to migrate *into* a woman. Children are not *physiologically produced* by anyone; they are conceived to have been created at a far distant time, and human beings play absolutely no physiological part in their generation. Such a view of the process of coming into being is certainly both non-genetic and unphysiological.

I have shown that intercourse is everywhere in Australia considered a necessary factor in bringing about the immigration of a spirit-child into a woman, but that it is nowhere considered a cause of pregnancy. Similarly, a woman is a necessary part of the process of pregnancy and childbirth, a necessary condition in the same sense as intercourse, and some specific man—usually the husband—are necessary conditions. Neither the role of the male, nor of intercourse, is the crucial factor in any judgment concerning their awareness of physiological paternity and physiological maternity.

Neither intercourse nor childbirth is considered as the *cause* of a child's appearance in the group. Both intercourse and childbirth are necessary factors before it can be born. In this sense a child is no more *physiologically* related to a certain man than it is to a certain woman, merely because the one had intercourse with the woman and the other gave birth to the child. Certainly while the child always looks upon the woman out of whose body he came as his own mother, the man with whom she had intercourse prior to conception is not necessarily regarded as his own father. This is in itself only a recognition of the fact that he is so related to his 'mother'. But this does not imply any necessary recognition of a *physiological* relationship between them. The child is nourished while in her womb by whatever the mother eats, and particular items of diet may injure it during its sojourn there, but for all that the child is not regarded as having in any way been generated by the mother. She stands in the same physiological relationship to her child as the chick does to the incubator which hatched it. The real mother and father of the child is in the one case the eponymous ancestor who created all the spirit-children in the long distant 'dream-time', and the barnyard hen in the other. Without the hen there would be no eggs. Without the ancestors there would be no spirit-children. Without an incubator there would be no chicks. Without a mother there would be no means by which a spirit-child could be born. The hen is the ancestor of the egg, but an Aboriginal mother is not the ancestor of the egg which enters her from a totem centre, an egg which she only serves to incubate.

As one of Howitt's informants put it, the mother is nothing; she is only a kind of wet-nurse.[24] If this is what they believe, then those Aborigines who do so are ignorant of physiological maternity.

In criticizing my interpretation of the evidence relating to the ignorance of physiological maternity, Radcliffe-Brown has commented that when it is necessary to ask an informant for the name of his or her own or some other person's mother, 'the natives uniformly give the name of the woman from whose womb the person in question entered the world.' Radcliffe-Brown then goes on to say:[25]

For the Australian the essential feature of the social relationship between mother and child is that the mother *feeds* and cares for the child during infancy. . . . the general rule is that the greater part of the task of feeding and caring for the child in its earliest years falls to the woman who gave it birth. If a woman dies in childbirth the baby, even if alive, is buried with her. Thus it does in fact happen that the physiological relationship between a woman and the child she bears becomes the basis of the social relationship of *own* motherhood through the fact of suckling. In the sign-language of N.E. Australia the gesture denoting 'mother' is to point to or touch the breast.

The fact, if it is a fact, to which I have sought to draw attention, could not have been better illuminated. The mother of a child is the woman from whose womb it has been born, the woman who suckled it. These events are seen as social and not as physiological. The child is not derived from the mother's body, but issues from its temporary lodging within it. Having passed through the woman's body he is *socially* related to her, *not* physiologically.

Dr Phyllis Kaberry has offered criticisms similar to those of Radcliffe-Brown of my views relating to physiological maternity. Dr Kaberry convincingly shows that I have underrated the impression made by the physical, emotional, and behavioural events associated with pregnancy upon both the mother and others, that the birth of a child is, in fact, no less impressive an event for the Aboriginal than it is for the civilized woman. These criticisms are well taken. 'It is the native belief', she goes on to say, 'that the child is nourished by whatever the mother eats, and that, therefore, particular items of diet may injure it within the womb. What closer physical association could there be than this?'[26]

Communication appears to be the most difficult of all the arts, and I am afraid I have again failed to make myself clear. It is, of course, perfectly possible for an Aboriginal mother to nourish her infant in the womb, and choose its diet carefully in order to avoid injuring it in any way. The mother cares for the umbilical cord until the child is able to walk, she observes various taboos after childbirth, siblings are recognized on the basis of their common mother, and so on. The emphasis is on the physical tie with the mother.

Of course. But a physical tie is not the same thing as a physiological tie. The chick hatched from an egg in an incubator has a physical tie with the incubator, and may even become imprinted with it as its 'mother', but the tie remains physical, though it may become social. The one thing it is not, is physiological. Everything Dr Kaberry says about the physical relation between mother and child may be quite true, without in the least constituting a rebuttal of the view that the mother does not consider herself or is considered by anyone else the physiological genitor of the child.

As far as I am aware the only field-workers who have inquired into the matter of the ignorance of physiological maternity among the Australian Aborigines are Mountford and Harvey, who write of the South Australian Adnjamatana:[27]

We would suggest that certain features of the Adnjamatana conception theory point to non-recognition of physiological maternity as a corollary to their undoubted nescience of physical paternity. This is suggested by the following beliefs: first, the spirit child which enters the woman is an already existent, complete and self-directing being that originated from a super-earthly source. It is able to find its own food and shelter. It also has the ability to choose for itself an earthly mother, and exercises freedom of choice among the women, subject only to the moiety rules. Stress is laid on the spirit's liking for fat and comely women. The second belief is that the *muri* is independent of the mother during the period of gestation, this being indicated by the statement that after birth, it still has sufficient supplies of *namaruka* to sustain it for a period of equivalent to eight hours before suckling takes place.

We have seen in the foregoing pages that everywhere in Australia whether the tribe be organized upon a patrilineal or upon a matri-lineal basis the relationship the mother bears to the child is regarded as being, from the physiological standpoint, none at all, whereas the relationship between father and child is practically everywhere emphasized, but, of course, in no physiological sense, but only in a strictly social sense. This, however, has not always been allowed to be the case. Such statements as those quoted by Howitt for some of the South-Eastern tribes have, as we have already seen, been taken to mean that there is some consanguineous relationship between father and child. Malinowski, for example, writes of these tribes:[28]

They seem to know that conception is due to copulation. But they exaggerate the father's part. The children are begotten 'by him exclusively; the mother receives only the germ and nurtures it; the aborigines . . . never for a moment feel any doubt . . . that the children originate solely from the male parent, and only owe their infantine nurture to their mother'.[29] This theory is not a logical and consistent one, but none of the aboriginal views possess these qualities! But this theory of procreation is quite clear and categorical in acknow-ledging exclusively what seems to the native mind important for the formation of consanguineous ties in the act of procreation. Let us adduce the examples in detail, as they are very instructive. The Wirdajuri nation[30] believe that the child 'emanates from the father solely, being only nurtured by its mother'. There is a strong tie of kinship between the child and the father; the latter nevertheless has not the right to dispose of his daughter in marriage; that is done by the mother and the mother's brother. We see here that curiously enough strong paternal consanguinity coincides with weakening of the *patria potestas* (provided the information be accurate on both points). For disposal of the daughter is one of the chief features of a parent's authority over the child. Among the Wolgal the child belongs to the father, and he only 'gives it to his wife to take care of for him'.[31] This is probably an interpretation of the facts of procreation. In this tribe the father disposes of his daughter; in fact 'he could do what he liked' with her on the ground of his exclusive right to the child. Here, apparently, the ideas on kinship enhance the paternal authority. A strong proof of the unilateral paternal consanguinity is given in yet more detail in the case of the Kulin tribes. There, according to a native expression, 'the child comes from the man, the woman only takes care of it'.[32] And when once an old man wished to emphasize his right and authority over his son he said: 'Listen to me! I am here, and there you stand with my body.'[33] This is clearly a claim to kinship on the basis of consanguinity. It is interesting to note that in the examples just quoted this consanguineous kinship seems to give some claims to authority. Analogously amongst the Yuin the child belonged to his father 'because his wife merely takes care of his children for him'.[34]

However, Malinowski remarks:[35]

Withal this information leaves us in the dark about the detailed working of these ideas. Especially we are not quite clear whether the assertions of 'being of the same body', of 'belonging to him', etc., do actually refer to the act of procreation, whether they form an interpretation of this act, or whether they have quite a different basis. . . . We are not at all sure whether all these ideas, instead of being theories of the act of impregnation, have not some mystic, legendary basis like the beliefs of the Queenslander dealt with above.

These last doubts expressed by Malinowski are very much to the point, fortunately it is today possible to resolve them more or less definitely.

It is fairly certain that the beliefs of the South-Eastern tribes regarding parentage merely represent particular examples of the case which is general in Australia, namely the belief that the father is in many ways socially more significant than the mother. Actually, there can be little doubt that the South-Eastern tribes place little more emphasis upon the paternal relationship than the Central tribes do. Howitt and Cameron emphasize the role of the father; Horne and Aiston assert 'that the father has anything to do with conception is absolutely foreign to the native mind'.[36] Thanks to the investigations of Elkin among these tribes we know that in no case is the father or mother regarded as playing a causative or generative role in procreation. A child originates neither from the father nor the mother but from a purely spiritual source, either by being 'found' in a dream or vision by the prospective father, or by the prospective mother's eating 'child-food', or from a spirit-centre.[37] It will be recalled in this latter connection that according to Horne and Aiston the *Mura-muras* sometimes left potential spirit-children in the rocks or in trees, and that these entered the women who came in contact with them.[38] What the meaning of such statements as those made by the informants of Howitt and of Cameron might be I have already attempted to explain (p. 215). It was there suggested that since among the Wurunjerri the clan totem is inherited and descends in the male line, a man's children will all necessarily be of the same 'body' as their father, 'body' here being taken to mean 'totem', for as we have already had abundant occasion to learn everywhere in Australia, an individual's body and his totem are closely identified. It is probable, therefore, that what old Boberi meant when he remonstrated with his son, who must necessarily have been of the same clan totem and therefore of the same descent as himself, was that it was shameful to be disrespectful or unminding of one who was of the same body, the same flesh, that is, of the same totemic origin as himself. It is equally possible that old Boberi's remark may be explained by an appeal to some such belief as that which was held among the Nimbalda of the extreme north of South Australia (pp. 212–13). It was apparently the belief of this tribe that a *muree* (*mura, moora, mura-mura*), or spirit-child, before undergoing incarnation in a woman formed itself to look like the blackfellow whom it wished to have for a father. This was achieved by following and walking in the blackfellow's tracks, and by then throwing a *wretchu* or waddy under the thumb-nail or great toe-nail of the blackfellow's *lubra*, in this way enter her body. There is no question here of childbirth being regarded as due to intercourse; the child was of spirit origin and merely modelled its appearance upon that of its prospective father, but the father was not himself regarded as the direct cause of the resemblance, for he constituted only an unconscious model, as it were, upon which the spirit-child looked in order that it might resemble it. If we make use of a rather lame analogy here, we may say that there is as much connection between the spirit-child and the prospective father as there is between a well-known beauty and her innumerable apes or imitators; all these are in origin distinct and separate individuals, and their existence is quite independent of one another, but owing to an accepted convention it becomes desirable and even necessary for one to resemble the other. Since they do, to some extent, resemble each other there is this much in common between them, namely, that they form a class or group linked to one another by similarity of looks. Among the Nimbalda the knowledge that a *muree* models itself upon its prospective father naturally makes it clear that the relationship between father and child is somewhat closer than that which exists between mother and child, for the child or *muree* would not have entered a particular blackfellow's *lubra* had not that blackfellow pleased him, his *lubra* has nothing to do with the matter at all. But in forming itself after the blackfellow the *muree* does nothing which would in any way give rise to a conception of *consanguinity* between itself and the blackfellow, for from start to finish they are distinct and separate entities. What, however, can be claimed is that the child owes the appearance of its body to the model after which it was fashioned. If, as is possible, some such beliefs obtain among the South-Eastern tribes referred to by Howitt then the meaning of the words. 'There you stand with my body', might well be interpreted to mean, 'there you stand with the body which you voluntarily fashioned after mine', or 'There you stand acclaiming to all the world by your physical appearance that you are my son, that you chose to become my son of your own volition . . . ' The statement that the South-Eastern tribes never feel 'any doubt that children originate solely from the male parent' may well mean that owing to some such beliefs as those which prevailed among the Nimbalda there was never any doubt that a child belonged to a particular father, for in the sense which has been indicated a child owes its appearance, and in a way its existence, to its father.

Such an interpretation is, of course, perfectly consistent with what we know of the beliefs and the social organization of the South-Eastern tribes, and if in this discussion we have approached anywhere near a true interpretation of the probable meaning of the South-Eastern beliefs, then it becomes fairly certain that the relationship which is held to exist between father and child is based not on consanguinity, on a community of blood between them as we understand it, but upon a tie which constitutes a rationalization calculated to emphasize a relationship between father and child which is not otherwise recognized to hold upon a physiological basis. Such a rationalization approaches very close to the recognition of a physiological tie between father and child, but clearly not a generative tie, and this is the important point, for it is only when a generative relationship is recognized between father and child that it is possible to speak of a consanguineous relationship. This notion obviously had no existence among the Nimbalda, nor can it have existed among the South-Eastern tribes, if, as has been suggested, their procreative beliefs resembled those of the Nimbalda.

In connection with the point we have here been considering, namely, the relationship of the body of the child to that of its father, it would not be wholly out of place here to cite the beliefs prevailing among another people who are characterized by an ignorance of physiological paternity though not of physiological maternity, namely the Trobriand Islanders.

Among the Trobriand Islanders every child is assumed and affirmed to resemble its father.[39]

When you inquire . . . why it is that people resemble their father, who is a stranger and has nothing to do with the formation of their body, they have a stereotyped answer: 'It coagulates the face of the child; for always he lies with her, they sit together.' The expression *euli*, to coagulate, to mould, was used over and over again in the answers which I received. This is a statement of the social doctrine concerning the influence of the father over the physique of the child, and not merely the personal opinion of my informants. One of my informants explained it to me more exactly, turning his open hands to me palm upwards: 'Put some soft mash (*sesa*) on it, and it will mould like the hand. In the same manner the husband remains with the woman and the child is moulded.' Another man told me: 'Always we give food from our hand to the child to eat, we give fruit and dainties, we give betel nut. This makes the child as it is'.

Thus [remarks Malinowski], we see that an artificial physical link between father and child has been introduced, and that on one important point it has overshadowed the matrilineal bond. For physical resemblance is a very strong emotional tie between two people, and its strength is hardly reduced by its being ascribed, not to a physiological but to a sociological cause—that of continued association between husband and wife.

In precisely the same way, and differing only in the details of its form the same artificial link between father and child has been introduced among the Nimbalda. There is reason to believe that similar ideas are at the back of the South-Eastern bond between father and child as expressed in the statements we have had occasion to consider above. Wrenched from their context, they have in the past served to act as so many bogies with which to frighten anyone who may have been innocent enough to suggest that an ignorance of physiological paternity was widespread in Aboriginal Australia. What, we may well ask, would ethnologists have considered to be the nature of the Trobriand state of procreative knowledge if some very proper observer had merely thought fit to report of them that one of their fast cherished doctrines was the belief in the physical resemblance between father and child? Would not most students of the matter have arrived at the 'obvious' conclusion that among the Trobrianders there was clearly a recognition of the physiological relationship between father and child? I believe that this is exactly what has occurred in the case of the fragmentary reports of Howitt and Cameron. Apart from all other considerations it is very difficult to believe, that the South-Eastern tribes should in this matter of physiological paternity differ so radically from the Southern tribes to the west who unambiguously exhibit this nescience,[40] and similarly the tribes to the east and to the north, in fact, all the tribes neighbouring upon the South-Eastern tribes. It is possible, but it is extremely unlikely. In all the neighbouring tribes there is to be found the belief in the incarnation of pre-existent spirit-children together with the host of ideas which are invariably associated with this fundamental belief; that the South-Eastern tribes should form a unique exception to this rule is unlikely.

Until evidence to the contrary is forthcoming, I think we may fairly conclude that the concept of blood relationship is the exception rather than the rule in Australia.

With the problem of the South-Eastern tribes thus disposed of we may now proceed to a consideration of the actual meaning of motherhood and fatherhood in Australia, since this matter is of fundamental importance in any possible fruitful discussion of the procreative beliefs of the Aborigines.

We have already seen that the concepts of maternity and paternity have no place in Aboriginal psychology, for if we restrict the use of these terms to the physiological relationship, employing the terms *motherhood* and *fatherhood* to denote the social relationships, then certainly they do not exist in Australia. The evidence presented in the first part of this book is conclusive upon these points. We have now to consider what the nature of the relationships is that in Australia take the place of these non-existent relationships of maternity and paternity.

At the outset we are immediately faced with the problem of determining whether the Aboriginal conceptions of motherhood and fatherhood as we have come to understand them in the preceding pages had any existence prior to the development of the peculiar procreative beliefs of the Aborigines, or whether they constitute a development immediately following from these beliefs. It should, I think, be obvious that the peculiar nature of the Aboriginal notions of motherhood and fatherhood as we know them take their form from the existent procreative doctrines of the tribe. What we are concerned to determine is whether there existed any concepts of motherhood and fatherhood prior to the development of such procreative beliefs. Such an attempt can only be speculative. I do not propose any elaborate hypothesis concerning the nature of those beliefs.

The conditions under which beliefs relating to procreation would appear are not difficult to imagine. As soon as the nuclear family was established, that is, a male, his wife, and their offspring, the relation in which each individual stood to another would in the the very nature of things give rise to certain emotions, sentiments, and ideas which would eventually crystallize into certain definite concepts which would in a very special sense serve to define those relations, and such concepts would naturally determine the nature of the terms used to describe those relations. Such relations would be recognized not in any terms of blood relationship, but merely as the consequence of the simple fact of a number of people living together in a common group,[41] and of whom it is inevitable that one comes to think of another in certain definitely restricted ways. This is no more than to say that the psychological conditions arising out of the fact of a group of people living together give rise to terms designating relationship. What the character of these terms would be is, I think fairly obvious. There would clearly be a term, first, to denote the position of the head of the family. Let us call it *family headman*. There would then be the woman or women united to this man, his *wife or wives*; there would be children of both sexes, obviously the family headman's children (but in no generic sense), whom we may safely speak of as his sons and daughters. From the standpoint of the latter he would be their family lord or headman, and together with his wife or wives, their family—and here there arises a difficulty. What are we to call these women: *family headwomen*? Such a term would be misleading, for the position of the female in the primitive family must have been one of subservience to the family headman. The position of the headman's wife or wives would generate a constellation of emotions, sentiments, and feelings in the minds of the children of the family group which would be expressed in a term descriptive of the complex of experiences denoting the fact that one has been suckled, nursed, nurtured, and cared for during one's early years by this woman, or group of women. Such women would then be described by the members of the first descending generation of the family by a term having some such connotation as *the woman-who-brought-me-up*. The children of the family would be called by a term meaning *those were-brought-up-by-same-people*, or brothers and sisters. Since the same relationship would hold within each family, the same or similar terms would probably be used to describe the relationships existing between members of different families. Thus a child would call every man and woman of an ascending generation *family headman* and *woman-who-brought-me-up*,[42] and the children of the latter, brothers and sisters. A family headman would call all the wives of other family headmen by a term denoting *wife*, and the women would likewise call such men by a term meaning *husband*, or *family headman*. But these last points are not necessary to our argument. All that I have here wished to bring out is that the relationship between the family headman and his wife or wives and the family children of the immediate family must have been construed in purely social terms, and not in any sense biological ones: that these terms, whatever they may have been, represented a purely social expression of what were esteemed to be the natural facts as given in the social conditions which they were meant to express.[43]

Such terms express the primitive concepts of motherhood and fatherhood. It is probable that they possessed a very different meaning from that customarily given to these terms.

The outcome of this discussion, then, is that it is probable that the primitive conceptions of fatherhood and motherhood were already in existence prior to the development of any doctrines concerning their origin and meaning. These doctrines must have been elaborated at a later stage in order to provide an explanation of how these things came to be. That these doctrines were based upon the conditions as they presented themselves to their makers seems obvious, and that they were elaborated without the slightest notion of anything relating to concepts of community of blood, or the relationship between intercourse and childbirth seems probable, for it is unlikely that any of these things could possibly have been understood by primitive man, for reasons we have already abundantly dealt with. By such a route, then, we arrive at the conditions as we recently found them among Aborigines.

Among the Australian Aborigines the concepts of motherhood and fatherhood were probably of much the same nature as those held by prehistoric man, except that among the Aborigines such concepts were more profoundly developed.

Some support for the view of the original primitiveness of Aboriginal concepts of motherhood and fatherhood, as well as for many other of their concepts, is to be drawn from a consideration of the history of the Aborigines. It is generally agreed that the Australian Aborigines constitute a remarkably, indeed, a uniquely homogeneous group physically,[44] and that they have probably existed physically, relatively unchanged, for many thousands of years, in much the same way as they live at present.[45] At a very early period in their history they seem to have become isolated upon the continent of Australia, where, there is every reason to believe, they have retained, with but little change, their original culture. The striking general likeness of their present cultural structure constitutes strong evidence in support of these statements, a fact which points significantly to the common origin of that culture and to its primitiveness. It is possible, then, that their beliefs relating to motherhood and fatherhood, for example, bear some resemblance to the earlier form of these concepts, and that the Aboriginal doctrines which have been developed with respect to them represent later superimposed developments.

If, in considering the Australian evidence, we eliminate all reference to the beliefs about the origin of children, concerning which we have already seen that there exists no physiological knowledge whatever, nor any question of consanguineous relationship, we shall be able to deal with the fundamental primary facts, which, in any event, are entirely independent of the doctrine which forms the secondary social commentary upon them. At this stage of our discussion it must be quite evident that parentage in the greater part of Aboriginal Australia was a purely social category. As Briffault has put it, 'They do not "start" from a biological fact, which they set aside, because they are not concerned with recording biological, but social facts.'[46] Let us now consider the facts.

Everywhere in Australia the tribe is based upon the family. Each family within the tribe lives in more or less independence of the other, whether such families happen to live together in a local group or separately. In each family the male head is the chief arbiter of its fortunes, and his wife or wives are subservient to his will. When a child is born into a family it is normally left to the woman who gave it birth to nurse and suckle it, a process which usually lasts some four years. Thereafter the 'mother' has to assume the greater part of the responsibility for its upbringing until the age of puberty, that is, social puberty, at which time a girl, who will normally have been promised in marriage either before she was born or in infancy, will go to live with her husband, and a boy will go to live in the bachelor's camp. In all the processes involved in caring for the child the 'father' generally assists as much as he is able. All observers agree upon the extraordinary tenderness which parents display towards their children, and indeed, to all children whether of their own family and race or not. Naturally, the affection, existing between parents and their own children is greater than that which exists between them and children not so related. Indeed, the ties of affection between parents and their children are extraordinarily highly developed among the Aborigines. Malinowski gathered a large number of statements from various sources which bear witness to the universal distribution of this trait among the Aborigines.[47] It is also to be noted that coupled with this great affection which the natives have for their children is a notable leniency in their treatment of them. They look after all their wants and go to the greatest trouble in order to satisfy them. Yet most observers agree that the children are quite unspoilt by this treatment, that, on the other hand, they are very obedient to their parents and greatly respect them, and are altogether very delightful little people.

Until a child is able to walk it is usually carried about by its mother wherever she may go. In the Central tribes when it is quite young it is placed within a *pitchi* or bark carrier, which the mother then skilfully carries under her arm, or atop her head. This utensil also serves the purpose of a cradle which the mother will gently rock with her foot to soothe the child and cause it to fall asleep. When the child is a little older, and able to do so, it is allowed to ride pick-a-back style upon its mother's back, or upon her shoulders, or it will often be allowed to straddle across one of her hips where she will support it with her arm. When at rest or sitting upon the ground at work a *gin* will contrive to make a trough by raising her thighs towards her body in which she will place the child whilst she works with her hands or gossips.

At night time, in order to keep the child warm, the mother will cuddle it closely, and during the day, if it is necessary, she will keep it comfortable by bedding it upon, and sprinkling it with, warm ashes.

As soon as it is able to walk the child is allowed every freedom, but always under the watchful eye of its parents. Much time is devoted by both parents to the entertainment, amusement, and instruction of their children, and admirably enough the Aborigines contrive to make their didactic activities amusing to their children. No opportunity is missed of instructing the young in the arts that will be useful to them as full members of the tribe. In the evenings songs and dances relating to the ancestral traits are performed for their benefit, and these songs and dances they are taught and encouraged to acquire. The notes and calls of various animals are imitated, and their tracks drawn in the sand, these things of course, they enjoy imitating and some acquire a remarkable proficiency in doing so.

The study of animal spoors, [writes Basedow] in all their specific and various intricacies, and especially the art of individualizing the human foot-print, rank among the most important and earliest occupations of the aboriginal child's mind. Parents are required by law to see that the children receive constant instruction and exercise in this department. It is a common thing for a mother to purposely slip away from her children and not to respond to the imploring wail, which follows when her absence is discovered. The only sympathy that some relatives or friends will proffer is to direct the child's notice to its mother's tracks and at the same time urging it to follow them up.[48]

The importance of tracking in the Australian bush is, of course, great, and it is of interest to note that, according to Basedow, the parents are under a *legal* obligation to make their children proficient in this department of knowledge. Whether the parents are or are not under a similar legal obligation with respect to the teaching of other branches of knowledge it is quite impossible to discover, but it would seem highly probable that the practices and customs of the past generations have in this respect gradually resulted in a social outlook which renders such conduct on the part of the parents the normal thing, questions of obligatoriness, doubtless arising only when there is an infringement of what amounts to the customary law of the tribe, that is, when a parent fails in his duty towards his child and therefore in his duty towards the tribe, such a case one may feel reasonably sure would practically never occur. It is the family pattern of the Australian tribe that parents should behave towards their children as they do, their family life characterized as it is by their deep affection for their children makes them solicitous for their well-being and for their acquisition of the various accomplishments which are demanded of every member of the tribe. Again, it is in what the tribe expects of every individual at a certain stage in his social development that it is the task of the parents to instruct these individuals. Up to the time of puberty, which is generally estimated to arrive at between eleven and twelve, but is probably nearer thirteen years of age, it is the function of the parents to educate their children in all those many fundamental arts in which they will later be required to display a high degree of proficiency. At puberty the task of the parents is brought to an end and assumed by the tribe. At this time both the boy and the girl leave their parental family to undergo the first stages of initiation into full membership of the tribe, and from this time forward they live apart from their parental families and pursue their own lives.

Very clearly, from this general account, it is apparent that the parents in the Aboriginal family are not more than the social guardians and tutors of the children, who happen to have been born into the immediate group which they constitute, and whom they hold, as it were, as wards in trust for the tribe. On the contrary, the biological parent of all children among the Arunta is Numbakulla who originally made them all,[49] among the Nimbalda the two old women called Yammutu,[50] Bahloo among the Euahlayi,[51] Anjir among the Koko-Warra,[52] and Kakara among the Proserpine River blacks;[53] there is no question of consanguinity between parents and children then, and such terms as are used to describe the relationships existing between them are, therefore, expressive of purely social relationships. Motherhood and fatherhood in Australia are categories which characterize certain purely social relationships between certain individuals, just as any other social category does. One's father's brothers are fathers, one's mother's sisters are mothers. The difference between the immediate family parents and one's other mothers and fathers is not classificatorily expressed, although qualifying terms may sometimes be added to the usual terms, as mother's elder sister, or father's elder brother, etc., to denote the person spoken of: in all the relationships expressed by the classificatory system of terms it is *groups* of individuals that are involved, although the group terms, of course, apply to single individuals within the groups thus designated. Radcliffe-Brown has put the matter very clearly:

Every Australian tribe about which we have information has a classificatory system of kinship terminology. That is to say, collateral and lineal relatives are grouped together into a certain number of classes and a single term is applied to all the relatives of one class. The basic principle of the classification is that a man is always classed with his brother and a woman with her sister. If I apply a given term of relationship to a man, I apply the same term to his brother. Thus I call my father's brother by the same term that I apply to my father, and similarly, I call my mother's sister 'mother'. The consequential relationships are followed out. The children of any man I call 'father' or of any woman I call 'mother' are my 'brothers' and 'sisters'. The children of any man I call 'brother', if I am a male, call me 'father', and I call them 'son' and 'daughter'.[54]

The only difference recognized between one's immediate family parents and one's other mothers and fathers is that which arises out of the purely psychological condition originating in the intensely close association which we have seen to be characteristic of the life of the immediate parental relationships, otherwise one behaves much in the same general way to one's non-family mothers and fathers as one does towards one's own family mother and father. The affection which the members of the family group naturally bear for one another generally lasts throughout life, even though after puberty a boy may never again speak to his own sister. But the affection which exists between parents and their children has been particularly commented upon by all observers, yet it is an affection based purely upon early sentimental relationships, and the ties which exist between parents and children draw their sustenance from a force no stronger than these sentiments born of their early association.

Both the mother and the father are necessary units in the family organization, but there exists evidence which would serve to prove that the parental relationships are determined solely by the existence of the 'father', and that the mother plays, as has been continually emphasized, a purely secondary, though by no means unimportant, role in the early life and development of the child.

It is natural and socially recognized and the normal order of things that children shall be born only into the socially recognized family, that is, the group which by marriage is thus sanctioned to act as the medium for their transmission into the tribe. A child that is born out of wedlock, as has been frequently pointed out, is an anomalous being, not merely an unusual phenomenon but an extremely unfortunate one, for such a child upsets all the rules. Since it has no father it can have no class nor subsection, and generally no totem, since the totem is usually patrilineally determined. Such children must be disposed of. The importance of the father for the proper functioning of the paternal relationships is very strikingly emphasized by the fact, as has been shown for the Narrinyeri, that 'if the father dies before a child is born the child is put to death by the mother'.[55] There can be no parental relationships without a father, and the existence and organization of the family is dependent entirely upon the presence of the male who is the indispensable condition of its being. The fact that children are required to obey their 'fathers' by law, but their 'mothers' only under the sanction granted by their 'fathers', who may reserve the right to rescind it at any moment,[56] is a fact further illustrative of the importance and indispensability of the father.

We may, in the words with which Malinowksi has summarized the role of the father among the Trobriand Islanders,[57] say of the role of the father among the Aborigines that it is

strictly defined by custom and is considered socially indispensable. A woman with a child and no husband is an incomplete and anomalous group. The disapproval of an illegitimate child and of its mother is a particular instance of the general disapproval of everything which does not conform to custom, and runs counter to the accepted social pattern and traditional tribal organization. The family, consisting of husband, wife, and children, is the standard set down by tribal law, which also defines the functions of its component parts. It is therefore not right that one of the members of this group should be missing.

Thus, though the natives are ignorant of any physiological need for a male in the constitution of the family, they regard him as indispensable socially. This is very important. Paternity, unknown in the full biological meaning so familiar to us, is yet maintained by a social dogma which declares: 'Every family must have a father; a woman must marry before she may have children; there must be a male to every household.'

The institution of the individual family is thus firmly established on a strong feeling of its necessity, quite compatible with an absolute ignorance of its biological foundations. The sociological role of the father is established and defined without any recognition of his physiological nature.

Among the Aborigines the reasons for this indispensability of the father within the family are such as to involve the whole social organization of the tribe. By this it is not meant that the necessity for a father arises out of the conditions of the social organization of the tribe, though this may with great force appear to be so, but that actually the original condition of the 'father' in the primitive family provided the foundation stone upon which the social organization of the tribe was eventually built, and that, if the position of the father were at all modified in respect of that organization, it would obviously very profoundly affect the whole superstructure which is so firmly based upon it. The position of the father is more than that of an integral unit in the structure of the Aboriginal family and of society, for he is the fundamental dynamic unit in the whole scheme, without whom it could not function, he is the centrum about which each family group revolves in an orbit which is determined by the horde or tribe. The wife of a man gains her importance only in his reflection, it is in his light that she is seen as a member of a family group, and without the power and authority derived from him there can be no family existence either for herself or for her children.

The importance of the father and the comparative unimportance of the mother in the social organization of the tribe is clearly brought out in Elkin's account of the groups in the region of Laverton and Mount Margaret in the western part of South Australia:[58]

A man of one section may have at the one time two wives of two different sections—from two tribes with different section systems— and therefore children of two sections, whereas a woman can only have one husband at one time. If she passes to another husband of a different section in another tribe, she herself loses her former section affiliation and normally leaves her children, if any, by the former husband with him or 'his brother' in his tribe. She becomes, as it were, another woman, an integral part of another section organization.

When a family head dies his brother may incorporate his deceased brother's family into his own, and thus give the mother and her children a family social existence once more; or it may happen that the relatives will adopt them. It is certain that such a woman is not left very long unattached, and it is quite probable that the custom of the levirate, whereby a wife or wives of a deceased man pass to his younger or elder brother in marriage may have originated in the recognition of some such social necessity as the indispensability of a father for each family.

The family, upon this view, is not merely a self-sufficient economic unit entered into by the marriage of a man and a woman, even though the purpose of marriage from the standpoint of the individual may be understood in purely economic terms, its sexual aspect being the least important consideration. Socially, however, the function of marriage is the reproduction and maintenance of the tribe, for it is only through the medium of the married members of the tribe, or of a married woman of another tribe whose child entered her in the locality of a particular tribe, that the tribe's existence can be maintained. The second social function of marriage is the raising and preparation of the young during their infancy by the responsible members of the marriage group until the tribe as a whole is ready to assume the completion of the process which results in their full induction into the membership of the tribe.

Thus, we see that the social nature of parenthood, originating in the primitive association of a man and woman and their children is maintained and enforced by custom and justified by traditional teaching. That motherhood and fatherhood in Australia are based

upon and fulfil certain fundamental social needs, that these relationships are of a purely social nature, and that there is nothing of any
biological or physiological nature, nor any concepts of consanguinity
associated with these relationships, should, I think, now be perfectly
clear.

NOTES

1   L. H. Morgan, 'Systems of consanguinity and affinity of the human family',
    Rep. Smithsonian Inst., 17, Washington, 1871, ii, 10 sqq.; *Ancient Society*, 393–5;
    cf. J. F. McLennan, *Studies in Ancient History*, 83 sqq.; McLennan, however,
    allowed that the concept of consanguinity was not understood by *primeval man*,
    op. cit., 83.
2   *The Family among the Australian Aborigines*, chap. vi.
3   Ibid., 173. (In his article on 'Kinship' in the *Encyclopædia Britannica*, 409, this
    becomes 'the personal bonds based upon procreation, socially interpreted'.)
4   Ibid., 174.
5   Ibid., 206, 207, 217.
6   'The beginnings of religion and totemism among the Australian Aborigines',
    Fortnightly Review, 78, 1905, 455; also *Totemism and Exogamy*, i, 159–62.
7   *Folklore as an Historical Science*, 232, 'The Australians, for instance, have no
    terms to express the relationship between mother and child. This is because
    the physical fact is of no significance.' Frazer pointed out that the descent of
    the totem among the Arunta and Kaitish was peculiar in that 'it ignores
    altogether the intercourse of the sexes as the cause of offspring and, further,
    it ignores the ties of blood on the maternal as well as the paternal side, sub-
    stituting for it a purely local bond, since the members of the totem stock are
    merely those who gave the first sign of life in the womb at one or other definite
    spots.'
8   *Mythes et légendes d'Australie*, chs xliv–lxvii.
9   *Primitive Paternity*, ch. viii.
10 *The Family among the Australian Aborigines*, ch. vi.
11 A. R. Radcliffe-Brown, 'The social organization of Australian tribes', *Oceania*,
    1, 1930, 42.
12 Ibid., 43.
13 *Oceania*, 1, 1931, 436. This statement would indicate that our disagreement
    here resolves itself purely to a matter of definition.
14 A. R. Radcliffe-Brown, *Man*, 38, nos 12–14, January 1938, 15–16.
15 Géza Róheim, 'The nescience of the Aranda', *Brit. J. med. Psychol.*, 17, 1938,
    343–60.
16 Phyllis Kaberry, *Aboriginal Woman*.
17 Ralph Piddington, *Man*, 40, 1940, 92.
18 Géza Róheim, review of *Coming into Being Among the Australian Aborigines*, *Brit.
    J. med. Psychol.*, 17, 1938, 379–80.
19 Radcliffe-Brown, loc. cit.
20 Ibid.
21 A. R. Radcliffe-Brown, 'The social organization of Australian tribes', *Oceania*,
    1, 1930, 42.
22 Ibid., 43.
23 *Man*, 38, 1938, 15–16.
24 A. W. Howitt, *The Native Tribes of South-East Australia*, 195.
25 Letter, *Man*, 38, 1938, 15–16.
26 *Aboriginal Woman*, 56.
27 'Women of the Adnjamatana tribe of the northern Flinders Ranges, South
    Australia', *Oceania*, 12, 1941, 159–60.

28   *The Family Among the Australian Aborigines*, 230–1.

29   A. W. Howitt, 'Notes on the Australian class systems', *JAI*, 12, 1882, 502.

30   A. L. P. Cameron, 'Notes on some tribes of New South Wales', *JAI*, 14, 1885, 351.

31   A. W. Howitt, *The Native Tribes of South-East Australia*, 198.

32   Ibid., 255.

33   Ibid.

34   Ibid.

35   *The Family Among the Australian Aborigines*, 230–1.

36   *Savage Life in Central Australia*, 125.

37   A. P. Elkin, 'The social organization of South Australian tribes', *Oceania*, 2, 1931, 70–1; see above pp. 216–17.

38   Loc. cit., 124–6.

39   B. Malinowski, *The Sexual Life of Savages*, 176–7.

40   A. P. Elkin, 'The social organization of South Australian tribes', *Oceania*, 2, 1931, 44–73.

41   This is the point which has been stressed by Westermarck, *The Origin and Development of Moral Ideas*, ii, 197 sqq.; *History of Human Marriage*, i, 255.

42   Basedow states that Australian children in general look upon the *men* of the generation older than themselves as those who *grew them*, their tribal as well as their actual fathers; *The Australian Aboriginal*, 85.

43   A kind of inversion of this situation, designed to obliterate all knowledge of blood-relationship within the community, is to be found in *The Republic* of Plato. Plato proposed to establish *social* kinship relations in the following manner: 'Dating from the day of the hymeneal, the bridegroom who was then married will call all the male children who are born in the seventh and the tenth month afterwards his sons, and the female children his daughters, and they will call him father, and he will call their children's children his grandchildren, and they will call the elder generation grandfathers and grandmothers. All who were begotten at the same time with them will be called their brothers and sisters, and these will be forbidden to intermarry', v, 461; Jowett's translation, Oxford, 1881, 151.

44   Abbie, *The Original Australians*, 45–6.

45   See W. W. Howells, 'Anthropometry of the natives of Arnhem Land and the Australian race problem', *Papers of the Peabody Museum of American Archaeology and Ethnology*, 16, 1937, 8–90; D. J. Mulvaney, *The Prehistory of Australia*; D. J. Mulvaney and J. Golson (eds), *Aboriginal Man and Environment in Australia*.

46   R. Briffault, 'Family sentiments', *Zeit. Sozialforschung*, 2, 1933, 362.

47   *The Family Among the Australian Aborigines*, 234–73.

48   *The Australian Aboriginal*, 72–3.

49   *The Arunta*, 356.

50   In Taplin's *South Australian Aborigines*, 88.

51   *The Euahlayi Tribe*, 50.

52   W. E. Roth, 'Superstition, magic, and medicine', N. Qld Ethnography, *Bulletin* no. 5, 16.

53   Ibid., 17.

54   A. R. Radcliffe-Brown, 'The social organization of Australian tribes', *Oceania*, 1, 1930, 44.

55   H. E. A. Meyer, 'Manners and customs of the Aborigines of the Encounter Bay tribe', in Woods, *Native Tribes of South Australia*, 186.

56   H. Basedow, *The Australian Aboriginal*, 85.

57   *The Sexual Life of Savages*, 172.

58   A. P. Elkin, 'Kinship in South Australia', *Oceania*, 10, 1940, 320.

CHAPTER XIV
Nescience, science, and psychoanalysis

In an ingenious study,[1] Géza Róheim has endeavoured to show that the so-called nescience or ignorance of the relationship between coitus and childbirth exhibited by such native Australian tribes as the Arunta (Aranda) and their neighbours is not due to any failure in their sciential processes, but to a process of repression whereby knowledge of this relationship previously conscious is rendered unconscious, and is in consciousness replaced by a symbolic superstructure.

Why do the Aborigines repress the knowledge of the father as the agent of procreation? Because, explains Róheim, 'The identity in their minds of the child with a being who was killed by the father before the child was born is an expression of the unconscious hostility between father and son, that is, of one aspect of the Oedipus complex. The unborn child protects large game from the father's spear, because in the father's unconscious mind the large game he kills is identical with the unborn child.'[2]

To this explanation we shall return later. Meanwhile it will be recalled that in 1925 Ernest Jones had already suggested that wherever the ignorance of 'procreative paternity' was found to exist it would be found to be motivated by the wish to 'deflect the hatred towards his father felt by the growing boy'.[3] Jones went on to add that 'repudiation of the father's part in coitus and procreation, and consequently softening and deflection of the hatred against him, a consummation desired equally by son and father . . . is what has happened where the institution of mother-right is combined with the denial of paternal procreation.'[4]

In 1927 Malinowski showed that in a culture which was characterized both by matrilineal descent and ignorance of physiological paternity, as among the Trobriand Islanders, anything resembling the phases of the Oedipus complex, upon the existence of which Jones rested his theory, was entirely wanting, thus disproving the basic assumption, at any rate, of that theory.[5]

Money-Kyrle quotes Malinowski's demonstration that the Oedipus complex does not exist among Trobriand children, and refers to Reik's suggestion[6] that the couvade may have as one of its functions the preservation of the child from its father, and Money-Kyrle goes on to ask: 'May not the Melanesian matriarchy serve a similar purpose as well as that of preserving the father from the hatred of his sons, a hatred that is dangerous to society? This is the result which, according to Malinowski, has been achieved. May we not suppose that it was also the reason for the survival and development of such a social system?'[7]

The suggestion here is that in order to 'soften and deflect' the hatred of father and son for one another the institution of mother-right was gradually developed and, in fact, owes its survival to the efficiency with which it reciprocally protected the father from his sons and the sons from their father. This is essentially the view of Jones, who has in addition stated that 'it is clear that any objectionable tendencies the source of which is imputed to the act of birth can most radically be countered by simply denying this act, as is done, for example, in the puberty rites. Now in the analysis of our neurotics we are very familiar with the wish-phantasy in which this happens in regard to the father. Many of them cherish, consciously or unconsciously, the idea that their "father" had nothing to do with their conception or birth, this being a matter entirely between them and the mother.'[8]

It would be interesting to know whether any of these neurotics repress the knowledge of the part played by the father in conception to such an extent that for all practical purposes they are not consciously aware of the facts. If, in spite of the strength of their desires, they do not succeed in bringing about such a state of repression, may not that failure be due to their inability to overcome the resistance offered by the knowledge of the facts which have so frequently been impressed upon them? And which, from the point of view of one who wishes to appear normal, must form a part of his intellectual equipment even though he cannot accept them in his own particular case? I do not know the answer to these questions, and I should strongly doubt whether any individual in our own culture has ever achieved a state of repression so complete that the fact of physiological paternity was denied. The fact is that, with rare exceptions, all individuals of adult age are, in our own culture, acquainted with the role of the father in procreation. If we who hated our fathers so much, and our fathers who hated us so much, have failed to repress the knowledge of our relationship to one another, why should the Australian Aborigines have succeeded where we with all our beautiful systems of make-believe have failed? I do not think that any psychoanalyst has yet attempted an answer to this question.

With respect to knowledge of physiological paternity in our own culture among children, the case is different. As is well known, in our own culture, many children grow to adolescence without knowing anything of the elementary fact that it is necessary for a man to have coitus with a woman before childbirth can occur. I have known several such children intimately, and I have met a fair number of adults who have informed me that they were unaware of the elementary facts of procreation until they were quite grown up. Upon this point I want to make myself quite clear. Concerning the adults who informed me that they were quite old before they became aware of the facts of procreation I can only say that as far as I was able to determine they were perfectly honest and sincere in volunteering this information. I cannot say that they may not have known something of the facts in early childhood and subsequently forgot or repressed what they may have known. In this connection I may say that I do know of a case of a young man who when he was four years of age asked his father to tell him 'how babies are born', the father then and there gave him the facts about procreation which the boy, as he told his father more than twenty years later, promptly forgot, having to re-learn them long afterwards. I do, however, know a number of children varying in age from four to seven who, I have good reason to believe, never at any time in their lives knew, nor do they know now, anything of the relationship between coitus and childbirth. These children are rather better than normally intelligent, but I am afraid that they must be sadly lacking in that 'instinctive intuition' which is by Ernest Jones said to play so considerable a role among infants in enabling them to divine 'the main outline at least of sexual knowledge',[9] for they are completely ignorant of any such knowledge.

Experience has convinced me that in this age of enlightenment a large number of children pass towards puberty without the slightest knowledge of the facts of procreation. In a variety of ways they become aware of these facts later. Someone tells them, or they read about them in a book. I have never heard of any child working the facts out for itself, in spite of Ernest Jones's statement that 'a child of two years old can frame an image of genital coitus, and a year or so later connect it with the birth of another child'.[10] Not only that, to me it seems perfectly clear that no child could upon a foundation of 'instinctive intuition' or upon a purely rational basis work these facts out for itself. With the latter part of this statement Ernest Jones might perhaps have agreed, for he speaks only of 'images' which are presumably formed upon an instinctually intuitive basis, becoming only later more or less fully conscious. If, however, this process of 'instinctive intuition' is postulated as a universal trait of mankind or any particular group of mankind, then I deny it, for in those human beings whom it has been my privilege to assist in developing from birth towards puberty, although I have done everything in my power to discover them, I have detected no signs of such 'instinctive intuitions', or such images as Ernest Jones speaks of.[11] This is not to say that no children exhibit such characters, as Ernest Jones asserts they do. I am merely interested here in establishing the fact that while it may be possible that some children may by the age of two and three years become aware of the relationship between coitus and childbirth, some do not; and that it would be a methodologically unsound practice to assume a universal or even general frequency distribution among children for either the awareness or the unawareness of the facts. But that is just the sort of generalization which some psychoanalysts make in this very connection. Knowledge of the elementary facts of procreation is supposed to characterize all or most children; this knowledge developing upon a basis of 'instinctive intuition' into an 'image of genital coitus'. Róheim, for example, is quite certain that all Aboriginal Australian children possess such knowledge and that this knowledge merely becomes subsequently repressed.[12]

Now, if the fact be accepted as such that some children in our own culture pass through their early years without any knowledge, unconscious or conscious, of the relationship between coitus—or even the fact that such a thing as coitus exists—and childbirth, is it not then probable that awareness of the facts of procreation in children is not a piece of knowledge which is 'divined' with the assistance of a process of 'instinctive intuition'? For without the proper setting the stimuli are wanting which would 'elicit' the proper responses, and the necessary images would not follow.

My own observations on the development of knowledge of the elementary facts of procreation among children, that is to say, that a man and a woman must have coitus before childbirth can occur, have convinced me that this knowledge is in all those cases which I have investigated based upon empirical acquisition of empirical facts. This statement does not, of course, invalidate the generally assumed details of the process of development of the Oedipus complex in some neurotics. I am quite ready to follow Melanie Klein[13] in her theory of the pre-phallic phases of the development of the Oedipus complex. I cannot, however, accept the notion that the complex is of universal distribution even within our own culture area, and certainly not for all mankind. Such an assumption has been likened to that of the chiropodist's that all mankind must at one time have been martyrs to corns![14] They may well have been, though without the necessary evidence we have no right to make the assumption. With respect to the biological determinance of this complex, I think that McDougall has already said all that requires to be said upon that score.[15] And already among the ranks of psychoanalysts belonging to the Freudian school[16] a few heretics have begun to make their appearance. Thus, Karen Horney has been forced to reject the instinctivistic and genetic approaches upon which so many of the alleged 'fundamental' concepts of psychoanalysis are based, and she has come to see that the sociologically based approach is the only sound one.[17] Karen Horney has very strikingly revealed the processes of circularity of reasoning involved in the concept of the Oedipus complex, and has repudiated the concept as either a necessary or sufficient mechanism in the development of many neurotics. She writes:[18]

When character trends are no longer explained as the ultimate outcome of instinctual drives, modified only by the environment, the entire emphasis falls on the life condition molding the character and we have to search anew for the environmental factors responsible for creating neurotic conflicts; thus disturbances in human relationships become the crucial factor in the genesis of neuroses. A prevailingly sociological orientation then takes the place of a prevailingly anatomical-physiological one. When the one-sided consideration of the pleasure principles, implicit in the libido theory, is relinquished the striving for safety assumes more weight and the role of anxiety in engendering strivings toward safety appears in a new light. The relevant factor in the genesis of neuroses is then neither the Oedipus complex nor any kind of infantile pleasure strivings but all those adverse influences which make a child feel helpless and defenseless and which make him conceive the world as potentially menacing.

Dr Horney points out that the 'contention that the Oedipus complex is not of a biological nature seems to be confirmed by anthropological observations, the results of which indicate that the generation of such a complex depends on the whole set of factors operating in family life, such as the role of authority of the parents, seclusion of the family, size of the family, sexual prohibitions and the like.'[19]

On the basis of the evidence relating to the development of the knowledge of procreation, and of the development of the attitudes between parents and children, in our own culture, I think it may fairly be postulated that neither this knowledge nor the attitudes subsumed in the concept of the Oedipus complex are either usual or necessary features in the development of the personality of any but declaredly neurotic individuals. Certainly it has been demonstrated that this complex does not develop among the Melanesian Trobrianders by Malinowski,[20] and among the American Zuñi Indians by Benedict,[21] nor do any evidences of such a complex appear to have been encountered by Margaret Mead among the Melanesian Manus where the father plays the part of 'the tender, solicitous, indulgent guardian, while the mother takes second place in the child's affections.'[22] Among the Trobrianders only avuncular authority exists for the children, among the Zuñi—not even that. These evidences—and a great many more could be cited[23]—are alone sufficient to prove the non-biological nature of the Oedipus complex;[24] they prove that whatever the complex is construed as being, one thing is certain, and that is, wherever that complex is found to occur it is demonstrable that it owes its origin to cultural factors. Moreover, the evidence strongly indicates that the Oedipus complex arises only under certain conditions, and that where these conditions are wanting the complex does not develop. It appears that individuals who grow up in families where the relations between themselves and the parents—whether in a patrilineal or a matrilineal group—are of a happy kind, in a family in which there has been a minimum of situations which would be calculated to create those mental reactions which under other conditions would lead to the formation of such a complex, it appears that such individuals do not, in the absence of such conditions, develop such a complex.

In our own society, in those families in which the father's role is that of a tyrant, these conditions are widely prevalent, but in many primitive societies they are absent; and certainly they are absent among the Australian Aborigines. It is for this latter reason that I strongly doubt the accuracy of Róheim's interpretations with respect to the occurrence of the Oedipus complex among these natives. Everyone who has ever had anything to do with the Aborigines has been greatly impressed by the extraordinarily affectionate relations existing between parents and children. The evidence up to 1913 has been dealt with by Malinowski,[25] and I have brought it up to date in the present book which prompted Róheim's article.[26] Under the conditions existing in the Aboriginal family group, with suckling of the children being continued for at least three years, with no training as to bodily cleanliness, and thus, without the frustration of weaning and the anal frustrations postulated by Melanie Klein as the determining influences in the formation of the Oedipus complex,[27] the conditions necessary for the development of this complex hardly seem to be fulfilled. The fact alone that so many observers have thought it worth recording that the most impressively affectionate relations exist between children of all ages and the father would strongly suggest that at no time are the conditions favourable for the development of any jealousies, unconscious or conscious, between them. Similarly these relations appear to hold true for the female members of the family.

I think, therefore, that there are good grounds for believing that anyone who goes to Central Australia and finds that the Aborigines, in their cultural structure if not in themselves, show evidences of a repressed Oedipus complex, is simply forcing an interpretation of the facts according to the demands of a predetermined theory.

It is these facts which we shall here have to consider, but before doing so I should like to make certain general remarks both in connection with comments by psychoanalysts on this book, and the relation of psychoanalysis to anthropology in particular.

In this book I have been interested in discovering what the Australian Aborigines *consciously* believed and said concerning the nature of their own and their fellows' genesis. As an anthropologist relying, for better or for worse, upon the accounts of anthropologically trained field-workers I could hardly do otherwise. Róheim points out that without the psychoanalytic perspective the anthropologist is here at a disadvantage. With this statement I am strongly inclined to agree; but where, may one inquire, is the psychoanalytic data which I might have utilized in my analysis of the Aboriginal pro-creative beliefs? There is, of course, the outstanding work of Róheim himself. This, I thought I had examined and treated in as impartial and as rigorously scientific a manner as it was in my power to do. In a very kind unsigned review of my book in the *International Journal of Psychoanalysis*[28] the anonymous reviewer states that I have neglected to take into consideration the 'complexities of the unconscious mind', and points out my failure even to 'refer to the psychoanalytical critique of the evidence' published by him.

The only psychoanalytical critiques with which I was acquainted which bear on the Australian problem are those of Róheim.[29] On the general question of ignorance of physiological paternity I knew of only two works written from the psychoanalytic standpoint by Ernest Jones.[30] These latter works I had read at least twice before my book ever came to be written, and during the preparation of my book I must have read them on three or four separate occasions, each time coming to the conclusion that the views there put forward had no direct bearing upon the evidence I was considering. For the same reason I decided against any discussion of Malinowski's *Sex and Repression in Savage Society*, a work to which no reference is made in this book. I need not point out that in the writing of a book such as this very many more works are read and consulted than ultimately find a place in the author's text or list of references. Had I adopted the principle of including everything which others might consider relevant to the problems I was discussing the book would have been swollen to impossible dimensions. It is big enough as it is. The material dealt with and the evidence discussed in various sections and chapters have already been made the subject of separate and more elaborate studies.[31]

But, it may justly be inquired, is the question of the complexities of the unconscious mind, of the possibility of repression, merely of indirect relevance to any treatment of the procreative beliefs of the Australian Aborigines? Are these things of such slight importance as to merit no consideration in a work which claims to be something of a study in the psychology of belief? To these questions I can only answer that I consider that such light as psychoanalysis would be able to throw upon the problems of aboriginal nescience would obviously only assume relevance and importance under conditions which, in the opinion of all informed students, would render it so. I have never for a moment entertained the slightest doubt that when psychoanalytic methods came to be applied to the study of primitive peoples, in addition to the methods commonly employed by the field anthropologist, our understanding of such peoples, and particularly of the individuals comprising them, would be greatly enriched. Róheim's later Australian studies are an interesting beginning, but it would be an uninformed judgment, aware neither of the complexities of the problems involved, nor of the methodological difficulties to be overcome, which would hazard the opinion that Róheim's work represented more than such a beginning.

Cultures are extremely complex systems of phenomena, and not less so are the individual minds functioning within them. To learn to understand fully the culture in which we ourselves are born and live is a difficult enough task, not to mention the difficulty of learning to understand oneself or another individual. How much more difficult is it then to gain even an inkling of the character of a native culture and of a native mind! Those who have had the rare opportunity of studying the languages of several so-called primitive peoples are, in my opinion, the only persons, with the exception of those anthropologically trained investigators who have been able to live among such peoples, who can form any real idea of the extraordinary variety of ways, and the profoundly different manner, in which minds functioning in cultures other than our own are capable of being organized. It is not merely a matter of difference in language, but a profound difference in the orientation and organization of thought.[32] These differences are, of course, merely the reflection of the differences in cultural organization. They have no demonstrable relation to any gratuitously assumed biological differences. It is quite evident that the anthropologist with his usually foreign cultural background is at a great disadvantage when, in the field, he commences the study of the culture of a primitive people. Unless he can acquire the language of the people he is investigating he can at best hope only to obtain a superficial acquaintance with that culture. In order to understand what individuals really think he must be able to think with them. He must be able to take down native conversations, discussions, songs, myths, and so on, in a systematic manner, and in interpreting his texts he must be able to find not so much the right word as the right *meaning*.[33] It is only within relatively recent years that anthropologists have been able to do this in any satisfactory manner.

Concerning such matters psychoanalysts have not often shown themselves to be fully aware. I believe I am correct in saying that it has generally been assumed among psychoanalysts that the method and theory of psychoanalysis which have been developed in our own European cultures are universally applicable, not only to all peoples and cultures,[34] but to all peoples and cultures of all times. *Totem and Tabu* is the best example of this latter assumption. The fundamental assumption is that all human minds are organized upon the same fundamental plan, and operate in much the same way. Whereas the findings of ethnology abundantly demonstrate that among existing peoples, at any rate, cultures and minds are organized in a great variety of different ways. What is profoundly meaningful to the individual in one culture may be, and frequently is, completely meaningless to the individual of another culture; and what may mean one thing to the individual in one culture may mean a very different thing to the individual of another culture, even though they may live cheek by jowl with one another. Meanings and significant relations are clearly the functions of cultural organization. This seems to me to hold true for unconscious as well as conscious mental functions.

When the psychoanalyst applies his European methods of analysis to the Australian Aborigines and their culture, and interprets his findings by a theory elaborated upon the basis of his observations among European peoples, neurotic or normal individuals, he is, in my opinion, guilty of an elaborate process of self-deception. It is an elementary principle of scientific experimentation that results obtained on animals of the same species and strain cannot be assumed to be comparable unless the conditions under which the experiments were carried out were comparable. Of course, the results may eventually prove to be comparable even though the conditions under which the experiments were carried out were not, but such a fact can only be established by repeated experiment—one cannot assume it, for the simple reason that one may be wrong. Psychoanalysts, however, are content to dispense with such experimental procedures and at once assume that whatever the conditions in different cultures psychoanalytic findings hold good for all mankind; and, naturally, if one grants the validity of this premise, everything works beautifully. My point is that this premise requires to be repeatedly tested by dispassionate observers who are interested only in establishing the truth, and not by observers who are anxious to establish the fact that psychoanalysis is or is not applicable to the investigation of primitive peoples.

With substantial modifications adapted to the particular culture to be investigated there can be no shadow of doubt that the psychoanalytic approach could be made to do good service in illuminating the problems revolving about the personality of the individual, as well as about the 'personality' of the culture itself. Anthropologists have too long neglected the study of the individual in primitive cultures, and have paid too much attention, perhaps, to the type. In the study of the individual psychoanalysis will, it is to be hoped, render great service to the anthropologist. But what should we say of the anthropologist who, and of an anthropological approach which, approached the problems of primitive culture with the methods used by the sociologist in the study of European cultures? Precisely, I think, what we should have to say of the application of psychoanalytic method in a culturally untested situation to the study of primitive culture and personality, namely, that being the study of *cultural* effects as reflected in mind and behaviour in a European culture or cultures, the method and the theory were not—as they stand—applicable to the analysis of mental functions and behaviour in any culture other than that in which they were elaborated.

That was my view when I wrote this book, and it is still my view. If I am wrong I shall be only too glad to have the fact demonstrated to me. But until psychoanalysts with a thorough training in anthropology have gone into the field and have tested out the theory and the method of psychoanalysis in situations which are more or less comparable, or for which all due allowances have been made, and which are amenable to scientific treatment, I think it hardly reasonable of them to take the view that they are being unduly neglected when their contributions to European psychology are not taken into account when a student of a field which includes their own happens to be inquiring into the psychology of a people of a totally different culture. Had I, in this book, entered into any discussion of 'unconscious processes' of mind and their 'symbolic' reflections in culture, I should have been committing a scientifically unpardonable error. I would then have deserted the realm of factual data, by which alone I was steering my course, for an adventure in speculation—and that was not my purpose.

As a student of psychoanalysis of long standing my view of the present status of psychoanalysis is that it is still very much in process of development as regards its most fundamental concepts, and that it is still far from being as readily usable a method of investigation in the field as Róheim thinks it is. These remarks will make clear, I hope, my reason for not having devoted more space than I did in this book to the consideration of the problem of Australian Aboriginal nescience of the facts of procreation from the psychoanalytic standpoint. I do not, in short, believe that a method and theory of mind based upon the treatment of European individuals suffering from some form of psychoneurosis, can be uncritically utilized in interpreting the individual and collective phenomena with which we have to deal in primitive societies. Boas stated this position quite clearly more than fifty years ago. I am not aware that any psychoanalyst paid any attention to the challenge of his remarks. He wrote:[35]

While I believe some of the ideas underlying Freud's psychoanalytic studies may be fruitfully applied to ethnological problems, it does not seem to me that the one-sided exploitation of this method will advance our understanding of the development of human society. It is certainly true that the influence of impressions received during the first few years of life has been entirely underestimated and that the social behavior of man depends to a great extent upon the earliest habits which are established before the time when connected memory begins, and that many so-called racial or hereditary traits are to be considered rather as a result of early exposure to a certain form of social conditions. Most of these habits do not rise into consciousness and are, therefore, broken with difficulty only. Much of the difference in the behavior of adult male and female may go back to this cause. If, however, we try to apply the whole theory of the influence of suppressed desires to the activities of men living under different social forms, I think we extend beyond their legitimate limits the inferences that may be drawn from the observation of normal and abnormal individual psychology . . . While, therefore, we may welcome the application of every advance in the method of psychological investigation, we cannot accept as an advance in ethnological method the crude transfer of a novel, one-sided method of psychological investigation of the individual to social phenomena the origin of which can be shown to be historically determined and to be subject to influences that are not at all comparable to those that control the psychology of the individual.

In this book I have devoted a great deal of space to the consideration of Róheim's findings among the Australian Aborigines in so far as they have any bearing upon their procreative beliefs. In other connections I quoted Róheim as my authority more than once. Since, in his article, Róheim offers a single sentence from this book as my 'critical observation' on his account of the enaction by the Pintubi, Pitjandjara, and Nambutji children of the whole process of coitus, conception and childbirth, I may be allowed to repeat the whole paragraph here.[36]

The fact that Róheim observed children enacting 'the whole process of coitus, conception, and childbirth' does not, of course, mean that these children were aware of the fact, as Róheim implies, that intercourse is causally related to conception and childbirth, nor does it even necessarily mean that they recognized that intercourse was in some way connected with childbirth. The observed fact alone that in play they go through the 'whole process' tells us very little concerning their ideas about that process. If, as all observers including Róheim are agreed, it is generally known that intercourse serves to prepare the woman for the entry of a spirit-child into her, the role of intercourse will, in the case of the children's play, be quite clear—it is but the mirror of what is officially believed, namely that intercourse is usually a necessary preliminary condition of the entry of a spirit-child into a woman. Róheim's statements cannot be too easily dismissed. As an experienced psychoanalyst he could be relied upon to discover and faithfully report those nuances of meaning and behaviour which might perhaps escape others. His statements concerning the western central tribes, namely, that they believe the unborn child to enter the mother through the penis are certainly somewhat novel, for no other investigator had been previously able to secure similar statements from the natives. These statements are, of course, not in question, and although they were secured from informants who had never seen a white man it is none the less possible for all that that some white influence had been at work here, though this is to be doubted. If then Róheim's report is to be relied upon it would seem probable that until the native is initiated into the social interpretation of the nature of things he is under the impression that intercourse is closely connected with childbirth; when, however, he has been initiated into the traditional teachings he discovers his former elementary knowledge to have been incomplete, and he gradually shifts the emphasis from a belief in material reproduction to one in favour of spiritual reproduction. The inference from this being that in certain groups the shift in emphasis, the displacement, may become so complete that any connection between intercourse and childbirth may eventually come to be altogether obscured.

Surely, it should be clear from this that what I was saying in this passage, and what I now repeat, is that Róheim's analysis of the nature of the native nescience may be quite correct, but that until further evidence becomes available it would be more compatible with the principles of scientific method to await the further evidence before drawing any definite conclusion.

Róheim has claimed that a true knowledge of the facts exists in secular belief side by side with the spirit conception beliefs of orthodox teaching, but that the former is simply repressed in favour of the dominant orthodox beliefs. Upon the basis of his own findings Warner[37] has independently arrived at a similar conclusion, and Thomson[38] has made a similar suggestion.

It may at once be said that all this is possible, particularly in view of the fact that the field-worker does not generally succeed in obtaining any information other than that which is orthodox. Secular belief is for the most part determined and dominated by orthodox religious teaching, and it is unusual for the investigator to obtain any data relating to the genesis and development of belief in primitive cultures. We do know, however, that many of the childhood beliefs of the Aboriginal undergo an appreciable modification by the time he becomes a fully initiated member of the tribe, and there is no particular reason to believe that his ideas concerning the nature of procreation should not be among those affected. There is, however, no positive evidence that this is so, but it is a possibility to be borne in mind, for it may be pointed out that there is no necessary reason why the native should not pass from a childhood belief in the virtues of intercourse to the adult belief in the virtues of spirit-children, just, for example, as we ourselves advance from the uninitiated childhood belief in the stork to the esoteric adult belief in intercourse as the true cause of children. But we must be on our guard against such analogies.

Until further intensive researches have been carried out with reference to this problem, preferably on Aboriginal peoples uncontaminated by foreign influences, the question as to whether or not the Australian Aboriginal is *completely* ignorant of the facts of procreation cannot be definitely settled.

The above passage is a quotation from the first edition of this book, p. 201. Róheim states that 'the main thesis of Ashley Montagu's book is the ignorance of natives with regard to physical paternity.'[39] Throughout his article Róheim conveys the impression that the book was written to support the thesis that the natives were ignorant of physical paternity.

I may remark that thus far Róheim happens to be the only critic who has detected such a thesis in my book. My book has no thesis. What it claims to be is an impartial and critical analysis of the evidence relating to the procreative beliefs of the Australian Aborigines. Certainly I tried to show that such a complete nescience of the facts of procreation was a possibility not to be lightly dismissed, but that was not my thesis. If anyone has a thesis to support it is Róheim, not I. Róheim is concerned to show that the natives do understand the relationship between intercourse and childbirth. Having examined the evidence I admitted the possibility, and pointed out that there were also other possible explanations for the facts described by Róheim.

I am unable to accept the view that because Róheim states he observed certain children enacting the process of coitus and child-birth that these children were therefore actually aware of the meaning of what they did. In his earlier study Róheim stated that the children enacted the whole process of coitus, conception, and childbirth, now writing from his notes he finds that they enacted the process of coitus and childbirth only. Róheim quotes from his field notes of 5 August 1929:

The realism with which Wili-kutu imitates the process of cohabitation cannot be surpassed. He fits the *kalu kurari* (a paper trumpet I gave them to play with they called *kalukurari*, *i.e.*, penis of a boy. The other objects mentioned in the text—serpent, monkey—are the toys I gave them to play with) to his own penis and adds the ball sideways as an additional *ngambu* (testicle). Then he puts the ball to the opening of the *kalu* (trumpet) and takes it out again. 'This is how the semen comes out,' he remarks. Then he fits the serpent right into the hollow part of the trumpet, pulls it out again and says: 'The child comes out of the penis.' Muluru, a smaller Nambutji boy, uses the serpent as a penis and copulates with the monkey. The monkey, he declares, is a very big woman, a *kunka mamu* (demon woman), and the serpent *tarpangu*, *i.e.*, goes into it, he says when he imitates the movements of coitus, using the serpent as a penis. (This performance of Muluru is interesting because *tarpangu*, the technical term for the final 'going in' of the ancestors, is here used to denote coitus.)

'By this performance,' writes Róheim, 'they proved that they were fully conscious of the rôle played by the penis and by semen as a fecundating agency.'[40] I am not so sure.

From what Róheim reports I still do not know of what the children were conscious or thinking when they did and said these things. As for the Pitjandjara story, one phrase of which goes

Copulate, copulate, children make,
Copulate, copulate children with with

I have quoted several similar instances in this book where copulation is closely associated with the finding of babies. And as I have shown, such sexual activities are not regarded by the Aborigines as the cause of children. The fact that a little Aboriginal boy said that 'the child comes out of the penis' may mean merely that that particular boy had but the most confused of ideas as to the manner in which children really are created. In this book I have pointed out *ad nauseam* that practically everywhere in Aboriginal Australia, contrary to the common belief, intercourse is associated with conception, *but not as a cause of conception or childbirth*. That native boys enact the process of coitus and childbirth is not therefore a matter for surprise. It is what we should expect. What is of interest, however, is that Róheim now clearly states that they did not enact the process of coitus, *conception* and childbirth. This may be significant; that is, that the process of conception was not included in their dramatization. As I have shown in this book, the Australian Aborigines have no notion of physiological conception, but they do believe that a woman must be opened up by the male penis before a spirit-baby can enter her.

Róheim says: 'The facts stated in this paper prove beyond doubt that the rôle of the male in procreation is known to Australian children.' And in a footnote he adds, 'I do not say that they are professors in physiology.'[41]

Róheim's facts prove nothing of the sort. In my opinion all that they prove is what everyone already knows, namely, that children are conscious of the fact that such activities as intercourse and childbirth exist; that semen comes out of the male penis; that one boy said that the child comes out of the penis. But what these children understood or understand beyond all this remains doubtful.

Róheim quotes several cases in which small children from our own culture area rejected the 'real' explanation after having accepted it for a few months. 'Thus a little girl of three rejected the real explanation after having accepted it for a few months. The reason as revealed by analysis was that she desired the little brother to grow in her own stomach and not in her mother's stomach. After a year she had "forgotten" whatever she knew regarding the natural causation.'[42]

What, it may well be asked, does Róheim mean by a little girl of three rejecting the 'real' explanation of the facts of procreation? What can the 'real' facts mean to a little girl of three? Róheim quotes Zulliger's report of 'the case of a little girl of four who first accepted the natural theory, and then, after seeing the picture of the stork with a child in a picture book, reverts to the stork theory. The same child also evolved absolutely "Australian" theories on the subject, for the little girl believed that the father gives the mother something to eat and that is how she gets a child.'[43]

It might be argued that in quoting this case Róheim is putting himself in a vulnerable position, for it may be said that in the case of this little girl he is presenting an argument in favour of the notion that the Australian beliefs are founded upon an early desire to find a a really workable explanation for childbirth!

But the Australian children, according to Róheim, are aware of the role of the father in procreation, and only later repress this childhood belief in favour of a belief in spirit children immigrating into women, and as adults have only 'a latent concept of' the connection. From all this we infer that the adults are consciously unaware of the relationship between coitus and childbirth. If this is what Róheim really means, we may well ask where did the children obtain their knowledge of the facts of procreation which they subsequently repress? By 'instinctive intuition'? By working it out for themselves? Or did some unrepressed individual let the cat out of the bag?

Róheim writes: 'How far the official doctrine succeeds in supplanting this view one cannot exactly say—but it does not go very far. The process is probably merely like repression, a skin-deep repression. "It would be nearer the truth to say that some of them go so far in the acceptance of the official doctrine as to *deny* this connection."[44] I agree entirely with Professor Warner, who remarks that probably the physiological knowledge is not considered important by the native when he is talking to the anthropologist, for it is the official doctrine of spiritual conception that looms large in their thinking.'[45]

We have already seen[46] that the tribes discussed by Warner,[47] and others near-by by Thomson[48] show the clearest evidences of having undergone the most radical changes as a result of contact with at least one Melanesian people. Also they have been for a considerable period of time exposed to contacts with the white man. Their knowledge, therefore, of 'the facts of procreation' may have been acquired from a Melanesian source, or still more recently from a white one. When speaking to an investigating anthropologist it is not unnatural that they should vaunt their knowledge of these 'facts' before him. However this may be, the suggestion that the orthodox teaching looms so large in native thought that it completely overlays the facts when the native is speaking to the anthropologist[49] is, of course, of the greatest interest in itself as showing what the Aborigines do consider important even in a group in which the elementary facts of procreation are said to be understood.

It may be that these facts are everywhere in Australia understood. I should not be surprised to find that they were, but thus far satisfactory evidence has not been forthcoming that they are understood. On the other hand, there is a great deal of evidence which suggests that the relationship between coitus and childbirth is not understood.

Róheim raises the question: 'If the father has nothing to do with the child why must he find it? And why does he place it on his wife's navel? For as we happen to know in the sex theories of European children the navel is the symbol of the vagina, and in Central Australia the *tjalupalupa* (navel) in the songs or ceremonial ground drawings is definitely explained as being a euphemism and meaning really the vagina.'[50]

In the first place it must be pointed out that the 'finding' of the child by the father and his placing it on the wife's navel is a process which occurs only in dreams. In the second place it requires to be pointed out even more strongly that this process is only one of many ways in which babies may come to enter a woman. Thus, for example, a woman may dream that she has been entered by a baby, or another woman may dream the spirit-baby has entered a certain woman whom she will then tell her dream, and only then will the woman thus informed know that she has been entered by a spirit-child. In other cases the woman becomes aware that she has been entered by a spirit-baby only at the quickening which is always taken to be the instant of entry of such a child into the woman. She may be miles away from her own or her husband's horde country. In such a case the conceptional totem of the child may then be that of the locality in which its mother knows it to have entered her. Spirit-children may enter women from whirlwinds which have overtaken the latter; or they may enter women by merely being told to do so by a man, not necessarily the father, or even by a woman. In Western Australia the father of the child is not necessarily the husband of the mother, but the man or woman who 'found' or dreamed it, the *wororu*.[51] In other cases where it is obligatory for the father to 'dream' the spirit-baby there is no shadow of a suspicion of a physiological relationship between them. Nowhere is this better brought out than in a work by Mrs Daisy Bates, who for very many years lived in intimate contact with various tribes of Australian Aborigines. Among the tribes of Broome, in north-western Australia, Mrs Bates describes the spirit-child, or *ngargalulla*, beliefs, which in general follow the usual pattern of these beliefs throughout Australia. She writes:[52]

So firm was the belief in the *ngargalulla* that no man who had not seen it in his sleeping hours would claim the paternity of a child born to him. In one case that came under my observation, a man who had been absent for nearly five years in Perth proudly acknowledged a child born in his absence, because he had seen the *ngargalulla*, and in another, though husband and wife had been separated not a day, the man refused absolutely to admit paternity. He had not dreamed the *ngargalulla*. Should a boy arrive when a girl came in the dream, or should the *ngargalulla* not have appeared to its rightful father, the mother must find the man who has dreamed it correctly, and he is ever after deemed to be the father of the child.

The *ngargalulla* is still a spirit in the first months of its existence, but when it begins to laugh and cry, to touch and talk, and to manifest its personality as a little human being, its link with the dream world is gone, and it becomes *coba-jeera*—in other words, a normal baby. Thenceforward, through its whole life, the fathers who have dreamed its existence are the controllers of its destinies, within the relentless circle of tribal law. There is no glorification of maternity, no reverence of woman as woman, in the dark mind of the aboriginal. Apart from the natural affection between mother and son, sister and brother, and apart from her physical fulfilment of certain dominant needs, a woman is less than the dust. Her inferiority is recognized by the very youngest of the tribe.

From this account it appears clear that these natives have no notion of physiological conception, or if they do that they have succeeded in concealing it pretty thoroughly from Mrs Bates. It is also made quite clear why the father must 'find' or 'dream' the child—whether he be the husband of the mother or not. It is because a definite man must be secured in a socially acceptable manner to stand in the relation of father to a definite child—*pater*, not *genitor*—and to be responsible to it in a socially obligatory manner. This was one of the principal facts which I tried to make clear in this book, the facts that in Australia such a thing as physiological paternity is not recognized, but only social paternity, which is the important thing. I also put forward the view that the same was true of maternity. What Mrs Bates says of the native attitude towards maternity and the lack of regard in which women are held in the tribes with which she is acquainted is in accordance with that view. Róheim[53] finds this latter view absurd, one not even worth troubling to refute. Professor A. P. Elkin, who knows the Australian Aborigines as few anthropologists have ever known them, takes a view of this suggestion of mine which I wish Róheim had had time to consider. He writes:[54]

The point of Dr. Ashley Montagu's book, however, is not just to reaffirm the native nescience[55] of physiological paternity, as a result of a re-examination of the old sources and a critical examination of the more recent evidence of which there is a considerable quantity; he also maintains that the evidence shows that the Aborigines are and were ignorant of physiological maternity. This is a thesis which justifies the vast labour expended by the author, whether we finally agree with him or not. Even those who know the Aborigines well have probably not bothered to analyse or to ascertain the native conception of motherhood. In the light of Dr. Ashley Montagu's thesis, we are now challenged to do this. Possibly the difference between himself and some others will turn out to be one of definition only or mainly, but he will have done a good service if his argument causes clarity of thinking on this matter.

I can only regret that Róheim had not been inspired to clarity of thinking, and that he altogether failed to understand what I meant by ignorance of physiological maternity. I, of course, meant nothing so utterly *imbecile* as that 'an Australian child does not know its own mother.'[56] What I tried to show in this book is that while everyone knows that a certain child was transmitted into the horde or tribe through a certain woman, no one believes or thinks in terms of the child having been actually *produced* by her in connection with a particular man. The belief is rather that a spirit-child already preformed has entered her from a spirit centre, generally situated in her husband's territory, and that in due time it makes its appearance through her medium among them. This view of the process of coming into being is certainly unphysiological, and since the natives are continually asserting that the 'mother nothing', that she acts merely in the capacity, as Howitt suggests, of a wet-nurse,[57] I am inclined to take their word for it.

My point, in brief, is that from the purely physiological or biological standpoint the natives think of the relationship between mother and child in much the same way as we do of the relationship between the incubator and the egg. The incubator makes possible the development of the egg into a chick, and the woman makes possible the development of a pre-formed spirit-baby—*kuruna*—into a fully formed infant—*ratappa*; but neither of them has any connection whatever with the generation of the egg in the one case and of the spirit-baby or the infant in the other. *The mother has no part in the generation of the individual.* This is what I mean by ignorance of physiological maternity. The fact that a child 'comes out' of the body of a woman is socially important, and physiologically without any significance whatever. The woman is a kind of necessary incubator for the spirit child, but biologically no more than that. Socially, of course, the association of a particular woman with the child to which she has given birth is of the very greatest significance. Róheim, like Radcliffe-Brown,[58] assumes that the fact of 'coming out' of the body of a particular woman is a physiological and inescapable fact. Inescapable the fact is to everyone and it is of the greatest importance that it should be so, but physiological it is only to those who think in such terms. My point is that the evidence strongly suggests that the Aborigines do not think of this obvious physical relationship as a physiological one, any more than we think of the relationship between the egg and the incubator as such.

Radcliffe-Brown has stated that 'the Australian aborigines do not recognize physiological but only social relationships.'[59] In an earlier part of the same work Radcliffe-Brown claims that the 'obvious physiological relationship between a woman and the child to which she gives birth . . . is recognized by the Australian native.'[60] These statements are obviously contradictory, but the contradiction is not necessarily a serious one. As I have pointed out in this book,[61] the difference of opinion here may ultimately be reduced to a matter of definition. If it can be agreed that a relationship between a woman and a child which she does not generate but merely gives temporary lodgement until it issues from her does not constitute a physiological relationship in the eyes of the Aboriginal, the contradiction is, I think, resolved.

Among the Aborigines the woman out of whom an individual has issued into the world is that individual's *own* mother, *because* he has issued from her. The notion of generation does not enter into the matter in the least. The process of issuance is a fact, but it is not regarded as a physiological fact, no more than the entry of a spirit-child into a woman is regarded as a physiological fact. This is, however, not really a point of great importance; the important fact is that the woman is not held to play any part in the generation of the child. And this is what I mean by ignorance of physiological maternity. Future researches in the field will show whether such a nescience exists among the Australian Aborigines or not. I can only hope that I have provided a few ideas which may be considered worth testing. Mountford and Harvey appear to have found confirmatory evidence for such a nescience.[62]

I may now briefly refer to Róheim's theory that the native nescience of paternity is due to repression of the knowledge of the father as the agent of procreation because 'the identity in their minds of the child with a being who was killed by the father before the child was born is an expression of the unconscious hostility between father and son, *i.e.*, of one aspect of the Oedipus complex. The unborn child protects large game from the father's spear, because in the father's unconscious mind the larger game he kills is identical with the unborn child.'[63]

This generalization is based upon a single one of the many ways in which children are believed to come into being among the Australian Aborigines. Róheim's theory can at best, therefore, only be applied to a particular belief, it obviously cannot be extended to embrace those cases in which the father actually dreams or finds the child, or to those many other cases in which the child enters the woman independently of any activities on the part of the father, or to those other cases which I have briefly touched upon. Hence, as I see it, Róheim's theory cannot be accepted without doing violence to the facts as a general explanation of the Aboriginal nescience of physiological paternity. I conclude, therefore, that while it is possible that Aboriginal children know, as everyone of course does, that coitus is a necessary factor in the production of childbirth, such children realize after they have undergone initiation into the esoteric beliefs of adulthood that it is by no means an important factor and that it is certainly not the *cause* of conception. What they believe to be the *truth* as adult thinkers is that immigration of spirit-children from a source independent of the bodies of a particular man and woman is the cause of conception and childbirth. Such adult knowledge is really an extension and clarification of the childhood notions relating to procreation, not a suppression or obfuscation of them. There hardly seems to be any necessity to invoke the mechanism of repression here. In any event if children actually know that coitus and/or seminal fluid makes babies how are we to explain the alleged fact that these children have already succeeded in repressing, for this is what Róheim suggests, the knowledge of their physiological relationship to a particular man? Or are we to understand that repression occurs only later, during or after initiation? If the mature Aboriginal is convinced that coitus is not the cause of childbirth whatever he may have believed as a child, and whatever the elements involved in the development of that conviction, we can do no other than accept his own testimony to that effect.

NOTES

1   Géza Róheim, 'The nescience of the Aranda', *Brit. J. med. Psychol.*, 17, 1938, 343–60.
2   Ibid., 343.
3   Ernest Jones, 'Mother-right and the sexual ignorance of savages', *Int. J. Psychoanal.*, 6, 1925, 120.
4   Ibid., 122.
5   Bronislaw Malinowski, *Sex and Repression in Savage Society*, London and New York, 1927.
6   Theodor Reik, *Probleme der Religionspsychologie*, Leipzig and Vienna, 1919, 30–2; 'Die Couvade', *Imago*, 3, 1914, 409–55.
7   R. Money-Kyrle, *The Meaning of Sacrifice*, London, 1930, 36 n. 2.
8   Ernest Jones, op. cit., 122.
9   Ibid., 120.
10 Ibid., 118.
11 A. Montagu, 'The acquisition of sexual knowledge in children', *Amer. J. Orthopsychiatry*, 15, 1945, 290–300.
12 Róheim, op. cit., 359.
13 Melanie Klein, 'The psychological principles of infant analysis', *Int. J. Psychoanal.*, 8, 1927, 25–37; 'Early stages of the Oedipus conflict', ibid., 9, 1928, 167–80.
14 Lord Raglan, *Jocasta's Crime*, London, 1933, 75.
15 William McDougall, *An Outline of Abnormal Psychology*, London and New York, 1926.
16 Members of the schools of Jung and Adler have, of course, never been able to attribute as much importance to sexuality and to the part played by incestuous desires in the development of the individual as the Freudian school has done. Compare Carl G. Jung, *Collected Papers on Analytical Psychology*, London, 1916,

231 ff.; *The Psychology of the Unconscious*, London and New York, 1916, 463; Alfred Adler, *The Practice and Theory of Individual Psychology*, London, 1924.

17 Karen Horney, *The Neurotic Personality of our Time*, New York, 1937; *New Ways in Psychoanalysis*, New York, 1939.

18 *New Ways in Psychoanalysis*, 9–11.

19 Ibid., 84–5.

20 Malinowski, op. cit.

21 Ruth Benedict, *Patterns of Culture*.

22 Margaret Mead, *Growing Up in New Guinea*, 6–7.

23 For North American Indian peoples, see the studies edited by Fred Eggan, *Social Anthropology of North American Tribes: Essays in Social Organization, Law, Religion*, University of Chicago Press, 1937; Robert H. Lowie, *The Crow Indians*, New York, 1935. For South America, see Rafael Karsten, *The Civilization of the South American Indians*, New York, 1926. For the relations between parents and children among primitive peoples generally, see Nathan Miller, *The Child in Primitive Society*, New York, 1928; Wayne Dennis, *The Hopi Child*, New York, 1940.

24 For a very cogent discussion of the Oedipus complex from the anthropological standpoint, see Edward Westermarck, *Three Essays on Sex and Marriage*, London, 1934, iii, 103. Some other writers who have been unable to subscribe to the 'all-or-none' conception of the Oedipus complex are Abraham Myerson, 'Freud's theory of sex: a criticism' in V. F. Calverton and S. D. Schmalhausen (eds), *Sex and Civilization*, New York, 1929; Alexander A. Goldenweiser, *History, Psychology and Culture*, New York, 1933, 201–8; Lord Raglan, op. cit., 70–5; Ernst Kretschmer, *A Textbook of Medical Psychology*, New York, 1937, 78–9; Havelock Ellis, 'Eros in contemporary life' in R. B. Cattell *et al.* (eds), *Human Affairs*, London and New York, 1937, 197; Havelock Ellis, 'Perversion in childhood and adolescence' in V. F. Calverton and S. D. Schmalhausen (eds), *The New Generation*, New York, 1930, 539; William McDougall, op. cit.; William Stern, *General Psychology from the Personalistic Standpoint*, New York, 1938, 350, 356; Gordon W. Allport, *Personality*, New York, 1938, 12–13; W. N. Stephens, *The Oedipus Complex*, New York, 1962—to note but a few. The only anthropologist who seems to have encountered no difficulty in giving his whole-hearted support to the concept of the Oedipus complex as a developmental process among primitive children is my old friend and teacher Professor C. G. Seligman, 'Anthropological perspective and psychological theory', *JRAI*, 62, 1932, 193–228. See also B. J. F. Laubscher, *Sex, Custom and Psychopathology*, London, 1937.

25 Bronislaw Malinowski, *The Family Among the Australian Aborigines*.

26 Ashley Montagu, *Coming Into Being Among the Australian Aborigines*.

27 'The Oedipus tendencies are released in consequence of the frustration which the child experiences at weaning, and . . . they make their appearance at the end of the first and the beginning of the second year of life; they receive reinforcement through the anal frustrations undergone during training in cleanliness'; see Melanie Klein, 'The psychological principles of infant analysis', and 'Early stages of the Oedipus conflict'.

28 Review of *Coming Into Being Among the Australian Aborigines*, *Int. J. Psychoanal.*, 19, 1938, 156–7.

29 Géza Róheim, *Australian Totemism*; 'Psychoanalysis of primitive cultural types', *Int. J. Psychoanal.*, 13, 1932, 1–224; 'Women and their life in Central Australia', *JRAI*, 63, 1933, 207–65.

30 Ernest Jones, 'Mother-right and the sexual ignorance of savages'; review of *Sex and Repression in Savage Society*, *Int. J. Psychoanal.*, 9, 1928, 364–74.

31 Ashley Montagu, 'The origin of subincision in Australia', *Oceania*, 8, 1937, 193–207; 'Infertility of the unmarried in primitive societies', *Oceania*, 8, 1937, 15–26; 'Physiological paternity in Australia', *Amer. Anthrop.*, n.s. 39, 1937, 175–83; 'The future of the Australian Aborigines', *Oceania*, 8, 1937, 343–50; 'Social time: a methodological and functional analysis', *Amer. J. Sociol.*, 44, 1938, 282–4; 'Adolescent sterility', *Quart. Rev. Biology*, 14, 1939, 13–34, 192–219; 'Climate and reproduction', *Science*, 89, 1939, 290–2; 'Ignorance of

physiological paternity in secular knowledge and orthodox belief among the Australian Aborigines', *Oceania*, 11, 1940, 110–13; 'Physiology and the origins of the menstrual prohibitions', *Quart. Rev. Biology*, 15, 1940, 211–20.

32   On this subject see Franz Boas, Introduction to *Handbook of American Indian Languages*, Bulletin no. 40, Bureau of American Ethnology, Washington, D.C., 1911, pt 1, 5–83; 'Language' in Franz Boas (ed.), *General Anthropology*, Boston, 1938, 125–45; Edward Sapir, *Language, an Introduction to the Study of Speech*, New York, 1921; Leonard Bloomfield, *Language*, New York, 1933; B. Malinowski, 'The problem of meaning in primitive language' in C. K. Ogden and I. A. Richards (eds), *The Meaning of Meaning*, London, 1923, 451–510; B. Malinowski, 'An ethnographic theory of language and some practical corollaries' in *Coral Gardens and their Magic*, London, 1935, ii, 3–74; see also A. P. Elkin (ed.), *Studies in Australian Linguistics* (*Oceania* monograph no. 3), Sydney, 1938; Ernst Cassirer, 'Philosophie der symbolischer Formen' in *Die Sprache*, Berlin, 1923, i; E. Cassirer, *Das mythische Denken*, Berlin, 1925, ii; E. Sapir, 'Language' in *Encyclopedia of the Social Sciences*, 9, 1933, 155–69.

33   For an excellent example of this see F. H. Cushing, *Zuñi Folk Tales*, New York, 1931.

34   This is the viewpoint adopted by Ernest Jones in his valuable article on Psycho-Analysis and Anthropology, *JRAI*, 54, 1924, 47–66.

35   Franz Boas, 'The methods of ethnology', *Amer. Anthrop.*, 22, 1920, 319–21.

36   See pp. 98–9 of the first edition.

37   W. L. Warner, 'Birth control in primitive society', *Birth Control Rev.*, 15, 1931, 105–7; *A Black Civilization*, 23–4.

38   D. F. Thomson, 'Fatherhood in the Wik Monkan tribe', *Amer. Anthrop.*, n.s., 38, 1936, 374–93.

39   'Nescience of the Aranda', p. 346.

40   Ibid., 351–2.

41   Ibid., 359.

42   Ibid., 358. Siegfried Bernfeld, 'Über sexuelle Aufklärung', *Zeit. psychoanal. Pädagog.*, 1, 1926, 195. Compare also Hans Zulliger, 'Eltern, Schule und sexuelle Aufklärung', *Zeit. psychoanal. Pädagog.*, 1, 1926, 230, 235; G. H. Graber, 'Zeugung und Geburt in der Vorstellung des Kindes', *Zeit. psychoanal. Pädagog.*, 1, 1926, 278.

43   Róheim, 'Nescience of the Aranda', 358–9.

44   This is undoubtedly what Warner means but it is not, as Róheim suggests, a direct quotation from Warner.

45   'Nescience of the Aranda', 360–1.

46   See pp. 108–9.

47   'Birth control in primitive society'; *A Black Civilization*.

48   'Fatherhood in the Wik Monkan tribe'.

49   This view was first put forward by Andrew Lang, *The Secret of the Totem*, London, 1905 and subsequently independently maintained by Read, Westermarck, Porteus, and others.

50   'Nescience of the Aranda', 348.

51   A. R. Radcliffe-Brown, 'Beliefs concerning childbirth in some Australian tribes', *Man*, 12, 1912, 180–2.

52   Daisy Bates, *The Passing of the Aborigines*, London, 1938, 27–8; see also 'The marriage laws and some customs of the West Australian Aborigines', *Vict. Geogr. J.*, 23, 1905, 36–60; 'Social organization of some Western Australian tribes', *Report of the 14th Meeting of the Australasian Association for the Advancement of Science*, Sydney, 1913, 387–400; pp. 201–2 of this volume.

53   Géza Róheim, Review of *Coming Into Being* . . ., *Brit. J. med. Psychol.*, 17, 1938, 379–80.

54   A. P. Elkin, Review of *Coming Into Being* . . ., *Oceania*, 8, 1938, 377.

55   In this connection, Elkin writes: 'In my own experience, assertions of the procreative effect of sexual intercourse have only been made by men who have been in long and close contact with whites', *Oceania*, 8, 1938, 377.

56   Róheim, Review of *Coming Into Being* . . ., 379.

57   A. W. Howitt, *The Native Tribes of South-East Australia*, 195.

58   A. R. Radcliffe-Brown, *Man*, 38, 1938, 15–16.
59   'The social organization of Australian tribes', *Oceania*, 1, 1930, 43.
60   Ibid., 42.
61   See p. 333.
62   See p. 336.
63   'Nescience of the Aranda', 344.

CHAPTER XV

Tradition, experience, and belief

Man is mind, and the situation of man as man is a mental situation.—KARL JASPERS, *Man in the Modern Age*, 1933.

In the preceding chapters the evidence relating to the procreative beliefs of the Australian Aborigines has been considered at some length, the myths, the traditions, and the beliefs. We have seen what these myths and traditions are, and also something of the source from which they derive. We saw that wherever in Australia generally intercourse is in some way associated with pregnancy it is generally considered to be one of the conditions, not a cause, and sometimes a dispensable condition, of pregnancy. Intercourse, we found is customarily considered incapable of producing pregnancy. The effective cause of pregnancy, *and nothing else*, is the immigration into a woman of a spirit-child from some specifically known external source, such as a totem centre, an article of food, a whirlwind, and the like. The spirit-child is in origin entirely independent of its future parents. Whether or not a woman shall be entered by a spirit-child is generally considered to be dependent entirely upon the will of the spirit-child itself. Whether the belief in incarnation or in reincarnation was dominant or non-existent in any particular tribe we found to make little distinguishable difference to the observed fundamental belief that children were not the result of the congress of the sexes. Where animals are regarded as having souls they are believed to come into being in the same way as humans do, where they are denied any spiritual qualities, as among the Tully River natives of North Queensland, they are said to be the result of intercourse, or what is more likely, simple physical reproduction. This latter view represents a special form of the doctrine of supernatural birth which, in the absence of the belief in the original transformation of animal and plant life into human beings, together with the general totemic beliefs of the Central Australian type, accounts for the birth of men in such a way that animals and plants are necessarily excluded from the process.

It is clear, then, that the conceptional beliefs of the Aborigines in general represent but a special case of the belief in supernatural birth. This belief has virtually a world-wide distribution and assumes a large variety of forms. These forms and their distribution have been exhaustively dealt with by Hartland in his two works, *The Legend of Perseus* and *Primitive Paternity*.

We have also seen how the beliefs of the *Alchera* type, in eliminating or rendering unnecessary any notion of a physiological role played by individuals in the generation of a child, give a non-biological purely social meaning to the concept of parenthood and to the terms 'father' and 'mother'.

Whether the nescience of the causal relationship between intercourse and childbirth is a result of a primitive unawareness of the facts as Frazer, Hartland, and others believe, or whether this nescience has been secondarily produced by a social dogma which has caused a shift in emphasis to take place which completely obscures the part that intercourse may formerly have played in the native conception of procreation, as Lang, Read, Westermarck, and others believe, are questions which it has seemed to us impossible to answer with complete certainty. Whether the nescience gave rise to the dogma or the dogma to the nescience can be matter for speculation only. Such questions, it would appear to us, are falsely posed. Are we not in putting such questions, committing the error of introducing our own categories of Aristotelian thought into a situation in which they do not apply? The nature of the Aborigines' conceptual world is so thoroughly different from that of civilized Western man, it does not readily yield to what Lévy-Bruhl called 'simplist intellectual analysis'.[1] Such intellectual exercises are not only misconceived and doomed to failure but, what is worse, are likely to lead to explanations which, while perfectly congruent with our own patterns of thought, are quite inapplicable to that of the Aborigines. The question as to which preceded the other, the nescience or the dogma, is, I think falsely broached because it altogether fails to take into consideration the possibility that both the nescience and the dogma may actually be historically and culturally one and the same thing; that the dogma is the nescience, and the nescience is the dogma; or, at least, inseparable parts of one another, and in origin and development contemporaneous with one another, since they are part and parcel of one another. I do not see the necessity of assuming the priority of one to the other, and no very good reason has ever been adduced in its support by those who have made the assumption, though much erudition and ingenuity have been expended upon the question. Certainly it is possible to envisage a change in the shift of emphasis during the course of the development of the conceptional beliefs of the Aborigines from a condition in which intercourse was regarded as playing a more important role than it does today in the production of conception to one in which it was finally allowed to play little or no role at all in the procreative process; but this is purely speculative and, as far as we are concerned, unimportant. What the 'facts' may formerly have been there is now no means of telling. What the 'facts' are today it is difficult enough to determine, and our chief concern in this work has been with these latter, and with the attempt to determine their most probable meaning. In the present chapter our task will be to discuss the mechanism, the means by which the particular variety of the Aboriginal conceptional beliefs or 'facts' are maintained and confirmed.

The power of the human mind to transform 'facts', the data of experience, and to reinterpret as necessity arises and occasion demands is one of the most striking of all cultural processes, and there can be little doubt that such processes have played an appreciable part in all that is comprised within any particular Australian Aboriginal culture. A fact, as we see it, an idea or a belief, is essentially a judgment about something, and as such one of the chief characteristics of such judgments is that they are capable of undergoing modification and even complete change. Reason, imagination, emotion, are all brought to bear by the Aborigines upon their experience. By the use of these agencies it is not difficult to see how modifications, and even the reasons for them, may in the course of time bring about changes in social dogma and in individual belief.

In view of these considerations it is quite possible that the Aborigines have gradually succeeded in suppressing or in attenuating the emphasis that may possibly formerly have been placed upon intercourse in relation to conception, in conformity with the development of the official doctrines. It is possible but, as we have seen, there is no adequate evidence that this was ever the case.

Without, then speculating further concerning the possible origin of the conceptional beliefs of the Aborigines let us now inquire into the manner in which these beliefs function, how the individual comes to believe in them, and in what way these beliefs are maintained and reinforced by his own experience.

In an earlier chapter in describing the *Alchera* beliefs and social organization of the Arunta we saw something of the emotionally charged world in which the Central Australians live, a world consisting to a very large extent of spirit forces and influences, of occult powers and magic properties, concerning which there exists a body of traditional teaching which serves to give these phenomena their meaning and value. Into this world the individual is born as an experiencer and heir to the teachings which serve to give his experience its meaning. The variety of ways in which this teaching, the body of traditional knowledge, is acquired must be understood if we are to obtain any understanding of the nature of the process which produces the harmony between tradition, experience, and belief.

The all-pervasive spirit-nature of the Aboriginal world begins to make itself felt almost from the moment of the individual's birth, for from that moment, as well as being the product of spirit factors, he becomes the object of spirit practices and himself becomes closely associated with certain spirit charges and spirit objects with which he soon comes to establish a deeply emotional relationship. Gradually almost every object in the outside world and almost every one of his subjective states assumes a spiritual meaning for him, for he comes to life and grows up in a world which owes its being to spiritual powers and is operated and regulated by spiritual processes in which men seek to participate in order that they may, among other things, have some share in the regulation of that world.

Apart from such early instruction as he receives in the religious doctrines of the tribe, the more serious instruction is left until the time when the individual is considered to be capable of receiving it, which is usually some time after the attainment of puberty. Such instruction is formally concluded after a series of protracted ceremonies and ordeals have been passed through; before this period in his development, the individual is busy acquiring the techniques of living, in learning how to track animals, to read spoors, to distinguish the cries of birds, to make simple weapons, to dig for grubs and burrowing animals, and so on. His secular activities are pursued in an environment that is characterized by a dominant and all-pervasive belief in the operation of spirit forces. There are sacred places which he must never approach and which are shrouded in deep mystery, there are numerous other places which are the abode of certain spirits, the rocks, the gorges, the trees, the waterholes, the clouds, the sky, the sun, the stars, and the moon, all these are associated with spiritual powers, and for well understood very definite reasons.

Writing of the Arunta, Miss Olive Pink puts it very graphically:[2]

No one who has not experienced it can appreciate the vivid reality of the partially historic myths. The whole country through which we passed was apparently only mulga scrub, a few gum trees, a low or high range here and there, or some open plains, yet it is made a scene of much activity by aboriginal history embodied in myths, such as the journeys of 'dream-time' people travelling in various directions, whose roads we bisected or rode parallel with, or who were 'sitting down', that is, camping permanently and performing ceremonies, or 'finishing' and going into the ground . . . So vivid are the tales that the investigator has the feeling of an inhabited area with much activity around: people hurrying hither and thither, or living normal lives like blackfellows did only a few generations ago in this very tribe.

On the march, a woman with her children will at times separate from her husband and take a very roundabout course to reach the same destination; the children eventually learn that this is because the locality which they have taken such pains to avoid is the location of a sacred place peopled by spirits, and so powerful that it is death for a woman or a child to approach it. Additional explanations are offered, and the mythological history of these and similar events to a certain extent illuminated, and for the rest the imagination of the child is relied on to supply what it can. When, as happens at certain intervals during the course of the year, the men depart from the camp to take part in the celebration of their totemic ceremonies, when a youth is to undergo the ordeal of initiation, the children witness and often participate in certain preliminary and subsequent activities which imaginatively interpreted against what background of knowledge they already possess serve to produce in them emotional states which are of lasting duration. When from the distant ceremonial ground the children hear the mysterious sounds which they observe to inspire such awe in the women and other children who have heard them before, and learn that the sounds are made by some great mysterious spirit who is about to swallow or has already swallowed one of the novices who used, perhaps, formerly to play with them; when they observe the difference in the deportment and in the appearance of the returned novice whom they may glimpse in the men's camp to which he is now permanently removed, the nature of the spiritual world becomes more real and more deeply impressive than ever.

Without entering into further detailed discussion of the many other elements of experience that condition the child's mind in Australia, it would seem so far clear in what manner experience is built into the mind, and how deeply it is ensconced in emotion and mystical bases. It should also be evident that under such conditions the play of the child's imagination in relation to the mystical events with which it is everywhere surrounded will form one of the strongest factors in producing a single system of workable beliefs. The fact that everyone else believes the same things in the same way makes the acquisition of these beliefs uncomplicated and inevitable.

As the child passes into adolescence and eventually proceeds through the various stages of initiation he acquires a broader and deeper knowledge of the nature of his world, of the place of the tribe within it, and of the individual within the latter, of the origin of the tribe and of himself, and of the traditions telling of these origins, of the nature of his world as it at present functions. During the course of the protracted ceremonies of initiation, which take place at intervals over an extended period of time, this knowledge is acquired by him in such a manner that it, together with all that he has formerly known, assumes for him a more profound meaning than was ever before possible. The extraordinarily mysterious nature of the rites, the practices, and the ceremonies in which he participates, the ordeals through which he passes, and all that he sees and hears are so sur-charged with spiritual significances, and are emotionally, imagina-tively, and intellectually so impressive, that ever afterwards the effective associations thus established for the structure and function-ing of his universe are to him a living and ever-present reality.

The experiences through which the individual passes during the initiation ceremonies are deeply religious ones during which he comes into the closest touch with the spirit-forces with which his world is filled. The impenetrable veil of the non-appearing which lies behind the appearance which constitutes his experience is raised for him, he is admitted into the inner mysteries, the penetralia of things, and the essence of the non-appearing is made available to him.

Thus does the content of his mind, relating to his view of the world, come to acquire the deeply mystical character it possesses. The content of knowledge thus acquired serves as the measure to which all the data of experience are referred for judgment, and since the traditional teachings consist to a very large extent of judgments and interpretations of the nature of experience, that experience is there-fore already prejudged, and so it comes about that the traditions which give experience its meaning are by that experience, through the medium of the individual, confirmed and supported. Tradition and experience are reciprocally and mutually supporting, and the result is that the individual's beliefs are constantly receiving the confirmation of this dual endorsement.

We must be careful here, however, not to draw too fine a distinc-tion between things that are not quite so finely distinguished by the natives themselves. While it is true for classificatory purposes that there exists a body of traditional knowledge which is in the keeping of the elders and the initiated men of the tribe, the distinction is an artificial one, for what comprises this knowledge is largely lived and experienced by each individual for himself whether what is experi-enced is perceptible to sense or not. We perceive the world according to the kingdom that is within us, and the kingdom that is within us, the content of our minds, is determined by the culture which has constructed and furnished it, hence, what reality is conceived to be is culturally determined. The manner in which this enculturation is produced among the Aborigines we have to some extent been able to see. The traditional teaching, therefore, is no mere body of esoterically idolized doctrines, but it is at once a testament of belief which each individual progressively lives and experiences for himself, a vital force which is inseparable from the life of the individual, an inter-active relationship which maintains the individual and which the individual in turn serves to maintain.

There can have been little conscious speculation involved in the

Aboriginal's acquisition of his knowledge of the world. The Aborigines are as intelligent as any other people—even their spirit-child beliefs attest to that fact—but in the spiritual environment in which they grow and develop, it is not so much with refined intellectual analysis that they are called upon to respond, but rather with the affective responses of emotion and imagination. One is neither encouraged nor required to speculate or critically examine the beliefs in which, like everyone else, one has been reared. Traditional teaching is there ready made to provide the Aboriginal with all that he needs to know. As Boas has said, 'the traditional material with which man operates determines the particular type of explanatory idea that associates itself with the emotional state of mind. Primitive man generally bases these explanations of his customs on concepts that are intimately related to his general view of the constitution of the world . . . the origin of customs of primitive man must not be looked for in rational processes.'[3] This, of course, applies with equal force to the religious beliefs of primitive man.

From the standpoint of its consistency and organization as a workable cosmology, the traditional account of the nature of the Australian world is deeply impressive. It would, however, be an error to assume that because it is intellectually so impressive it was therefore arrived at through the operation of intellectual processes which sought to give a rational explanation of the world in which man has his being. We are not concerned here with the origin of the cosmological beliefs of the Aborigines, but in considering them in their present form there can be little doubt that, as far as the individual is concerned, that form was not arrived at as a result of intellectual processes of reasoning, but rather that it is the result of processes of a nature more or less purely imaginative in character. The mythical environment of spirit-forces in which the Aboriginal lives is the great conditioner of his beliefs. It is the great 'illusory major premise' from which, with entire logic, he deduces his beliefs, the conclusions, that have been drawn out of what has previously been packed into the major premise.[4] That in the course of the historical development of the traditional beliefs individual thinkers, 'wise men' have, within the limits of the spirit-universe of feeling-permeated thought, served to bring about modifications in the traditional beliefs is more than likely, and that these were the result of some conscious reflection. It is also probable that such reflection was largely influenced by the affective-imaginative universe of thought within which it functioned. We know that the Aboriginal in his 'profane moments' dispassionately reflects upon and discusses the traditional beliefs in a rational and logical manner, but his reason and his logic operate upon premises which serve only to sustain those beliefs.

Beliefs upon which the whole of one's existence, as well as that of one's fellows, has been founded do not represent conclusions arrived at in the course of discussion or reflection, but represent rather the bequest of the hard-earned wisdom of earlier generations for the benefit of the group and of the individuals comprising it. Tested by each generation for itself, and by each individual for himself, these beliefs have passed every conceivable test of worthiness. They are beliefs that have been verified repeatedly, and the Aboriginal, a confirmed pragmatist, has every reason to believe that they work, and that therefore they are true. This is the acid test of experience which above all else serves to confirm for the Aboriginal the truth of the traditional teaching and of his own beliefs. Were his objectively patterned experience to fail in confirming him in the beliefs that he has socially acquired he could not and would not believe in them.

Having grasped the *meanings* with which his culture has endowed his world, their truth is confirmed and corroborated for him by his own experience of that world. Thus does the more personal and immediate part of his experience of the world come to enhance the truth, and increase the value, of the traditional view of it. It is in this way that he comes, as an apparently free and independent agent, to confirm for himself the truth of the traditional teaching concerning the nature of things. Since his world is thus finally accounted for at every point, there is, of course, never a necessity for the expression of a serious doubt or opinion concerning the nature of things as he knows them. Nor is there normally any occasion for anyone ever to inquire into things of which no one else knows, for everyone of adult years knows everything there is to know, or, what amounts almost to the same thing, needs to know. The world of the Aborigines is a *closed* and self-contained world in which everything proceeds according to laws which define the boundaries of all that is experienced within it. The beginnings and ends are all accounted for and properly classified in relation to one another. The body of knowledge at the disposal of the individual in such a world comprises for him the principles, the laws, the standards, according to which experience must necessarily function; that this experience is socially biased through and through is not much to the point here; what *is* to the point, however, is that experience can only function in certain ways if it is to be true experience. Experience which does not function according to the prescribed culturally established laws has no place in primitive culture. Normally such experiences could not, in any case, be, for all experience which could possibly fall within the universe of individual apprehension would long ago have been accounted for. Abnormal experiences such as those provided by the strange beliefs of the white man simply do not approach to within the periphery of the closed world of the Aboriginal; such beliefs are outside his world, and thus outside his experience. Once such a foreign element has penetrated into his world it means the loss of its integrity, its dissolution. Unless an experience fits into the pattern of the world as he knows it that experience can have no place in his world, for it is meaningless. If the new experience can be made to fit into the scheme of his system, the traditional beliefs and judgments which are his principles, the new experience is readily incorporated into that system, otherwise it is simply *nonsense*, in the strict meaning of that word. Thus, all experience normally functions within a specific configuration, a configuration always determined by cultural necessity. To these principles the individual is for ever referring his new experiences, and perpetually fitting these experiences to them. Like everyone else he tends very strongly to believe in that which fits in with some pre-existing pattern. The common man of the civilized world proceeds in precisely the same way, The critical thinker proceeds by the converse method of adjusting his principles or beliefs in the light of new experiences. What is already known, what is accepted as truth, 'is held subject to use, and is at the mercy of the discoveries which it makes possible . . . truths already possessed may have practical or moral certainty, but logically they never lose a hypothetic quality.'[5] For the Aboriginal, however, a truth never possesses this hypothetic quality. For him it is an eternal verity, a complete and unchanging certainty. The question of probability never arises, since everything he knows and experiences confirms the validity of his beliefs.

In his own thought the native is perfectly logical, and in relation to his own system of beliefs, his own framework of reference, his conclusions are perfectly valid. Like the philosopher he deduces results in accordance with what is implied in his own standards or measures, and through these he arrives by a logically faultless route at knowledge, or what is the same thing, for him as for ourselves, *justifiable belief*. 'Common sense' is for him what it is for us, that which is in common agreed upon as obvious to sense. It is common sense to the Aboriginal that children are the result of a woman having been originally entered by a spirit-child. Among ourselves it is common sense to believe that children are the result of an act of intercourse. If this is not so, then we are using a meaningless term and common sense does not perhaps have a real but a putative existence. Certainly common sense is demonstrably not the innate quality of the human mind some have imagined it to be, an irreducible 'reality' which causes it to judge all things in a similar manner.[6] Common sense represents a process of inference. What the nature of that inference will be depends largely on what happens during the passage of whatever it is that passes through the alembic of the mind. This is the reason why common sense is so often wrong. It is not that the data are at fault, but the mind through which they are perceived that is at fault. If this is true then it is clear that the inferences of common sense will depend almost entirely upon what is in the minds of those making them, and that the nature of the inferences will vary with the kind of apperceptive equipment with which the process of inference is made. The apperceptive equipment of the Aboriginal with respect to the datum of childbirth constrains his common sense to see only the effects of certain causes, spirit-children entering women in certain ways as a result of certain conditions and causes. The apperceptive equipment of the average bearer of Western culture inclines him to see in the similar datum of experience the effect of a cause which he believes to have been initiated by intercourse and possibly also the will of God. It is perhaps unnecessary to add that as far as his actual knowledge of the matter is concerned, it is quite as much a superstition as the beliefs held by the Aborigines. Common sense, in short, like every other aspect of thought, is a culturally conditioned trait.

But to return more specifically to the question of the interaction between experience and belief. In a valuable study of the relation of the religious beliefs to the everyday life and habits of the Pigeon River Indians, Dr A. I. Hallowell writes:[7]

The authority of tradition, elaborated most specifically in the *mythos* is, of course, the source from which the native belief receives its primary sustenance. But it is a mistaken view, I believe, to assume that any body of religious beliefs is transmitted mechanically from generation to generation with nothing save dogmatic assertion and mythology to support it. Even 'primitive' man can hardly be saddled with so naïve a faith. It is almost tantamount to the implication that religious beliefs are not taken with sufficient seriousness to make them a subject of reflective thinking and discussion. On the contrary, it may be assumed that any system of beliefs, in so far as it involves an interpretation of the phenomenal world, is recurrently and, in fact, inevitably, subject to challenge on empirical grounds. Granting for the moment that this is the case, how do beliefs react in the crucible of experience? In the case of the Pigeon River Indians the men, e.g., are expert hunters. Their knowledge of the habits of animals would excite the envy of any naturalist. Their knowledge of the topography of their country is extremely accurate, and they are constantly observing meteorological conditions. A white man unfamiliar with the country might be subject to illusions regarding the identity of some strange object but dimly perceived in the bush, or he might be inclined to misidentify the source of some unfamiliar sound. But the native has spent his life in these surroundings. He has run the gamut of sights and sound. Moreover, a man subject to delusions and hallucinations would make a poor hunter. His living actually depends upon accurate identifications. Consequently we must reckon with the fact that, although the weight of tradition always conditions the mind of the individual in favour of native belief yet the daily round of life, the first hand knowledge of celestial, meteorological, physiographic, and biotic phenomena, cannot be dismissed as an unimportant factor in the total situation. Experience and belief must be harmonized if beliefs are to be believed. The Indian is no fool. He employs the same common sense reasoning processes as ourselves, so that, if he firmly holds to certain beliefs, we may be sure that they are supported in some degree by an empirical foundation. Thus experience is obviously the crux of religious rationalization. But dogma furnishes the leverage which makes the reconciliation of experience with belief possible. This, indeed, is its sociological function, else a system of beliefs would constantly be subject to disintegration. Since the fundamental assumptions of any religious system are those usually least transparent to its adherents, they are able to retain a relative stability even when the more superficial beliefs of the superstructure are modified. It is in the toils of these implicit underlying tenets that the individual mind is caught. It cannot escape them through the ordinary processes of reasoning because it is uncritical of the assumptions they involve. And unconsciously, much of the experience itself is interpreted in terms of them. Thus it comes about that although experience is consciously recognized by the Indians as a means of verification of beliefs, experience itself is unconsciously interpreted in terms of traditional dogma so that, in the end, specific beliefs receive a satisfying empirical support and dogma and experience are reconciled.

Following a discussion of the types of experience to which the Pigeon River Indians appeal in support of their beliefs, Dr Hallowell concludes that[8]

while from our point of view the body of religious tradition of these Pigeon River Indians is the primary conditioning factor in the beliefs of successive generations of individuals, and that in this sense their beliefs are but the impingement upon human minds of an arbitrary pattern, the result of historical circumstance, yet, in the experience of the believers themselves, the events of daily life and reflective thought offer recurrent proof of the objective truth of their beliefs. It is also apparent that the mental processes involved in this reconciliation of experience with belief are those of normal human reasoning, even though we may grant that this rationalization is naïvely applied. Yet even in this way they are but following the mental procedure of common men. For how else may the truth of religion be demonstrated or belief upheld?

Dr Hallowell has here, it seems to us, given a somewhat restricted view of the nature of the experience which serves to support the traditional teaching and the individual beliefs, for he has omitted all consideration of the role played by the imagination and by affective associations of the kind we have discussed earlier in this chapter, but so far as Dr Hallowell has gone in his consideration of the interrelation between 'objective experience' and belief we may in general agree with him that 'in the experience of the believers themselves, the events of daily life and reflective thought offer recurrent proof of the objective truth of their belief.' Tradition provides the forms of belief, and experience having accommodated itself to the shape, the configuration, of these forms, confirms it, and reduplicates it.

We have now to consider how tradition and belief operate in every-day experience in Australia in relation to the procreative beliefs in particular. In considering this matter we shall restrict ourselves to a consideration of the conditions among the Arunta. With the traditions of the Arunta relating to conception we are by this time fully acquainted, so that it will be unnecessary to restate them here. We are also, I believe, sufficiently familiar with the manner in which the individual comes to acquire the traditional beliefs. How then do these beliefs react in the crucible of experience, and what specifically is that experience? How, in short, are the traditional beliefs confirmed by experience?

In the first place there is the direct personal experience of the natural world and of natural phenomena as the Arunta and as we understand them. In the second place there is the experience afforded by dreams[9] and visions which, for the Arunta, are at least as real as any event of waking life; and in the third place there is the experience and testimony of other individuals who are recognized by everyone to enjoy a range and intensity of experience not normally possible to ordinary men and women, namely, the medicine-men.

In discussing these three categories of experience I shall proceed as if we were discussing as the experiencers fully initiated married members of the tribe only, for it is the individuals who fall into this class who will be in possession of almost all the traditional beliefs that they are ever likely to acquire, and who, in any event, represent the average individual.

Children are normally born to married women only; this is so because, as we have seen every child must have a father. Spirit-children will not under ordinary circumstances enter a woman who does not have a husband to serve as father to the child, whether he be the acknowledged father or not. It is only under the influence of a mischievous or malign spirit, or of an individual who has manipulated the spiritual powers to further his own designs, that a spirit-child will enter a husbandless woman. Such cases are exceptional.

In what manner are these beliefs confirmed by experience? The answer is simple. Experience confirms them in every detail. We have already seen that since a girl marries at puberty it is practically certain that she will not normally bear a child before marriage. It is, in fact, extremely rare for a girl who has not reached the menarche to conceive. Premarital intercourse is therefore necessarily sterile. These facts are unequivocally clear, and well known to everyone. The belief is that only with marriage can children be born. The Aboriginal observes that children are practically never born before marriage; the facts of his own experience tell him that quite clearly, for neither his wife nor any of the married people of whom they have any knowledge ever had any children before marriage. But after women have been married for some time, spirit-children begin to enter them. On the negative side, therefore, it is quite clear to the Aboriginal that intercourse, which for him is something one enjoys for the sheer pleasure of the thing, has nothing whatever to do with pregnancy and, thus, the belief that children must come otherwise than through intercourse is for him confirmed by his own direct experience.

Women know by direct and immediate experience at exactly what time and at what place a spirit-child has entered them, for they become aware of the entry of a spirit-child either then or shortly afterwards in the plainest and most unmistakable of terms, a sharp pain usually, followed immediately by the movement of the spirit child within the womb. What else could possibly cause similar symptoms? The fact that a spirit-child has entered the woman is something which can hardly be doubted, for there can be no other possible explanation of her symptoms. If it were suggested that the child had entered the woman long before she experienced these quickening sensations, the suggestion would be met with the objection that it would be difficult to imagine a *ratappa* lying so long quiescent in the woman's womb, without giving some sign that it had entered her. It is contrary to all experience and to common sense. When something enters something else it usually makes the fact quite plainly known immediately, thus, a fly in one's nose, eye, ear, mouth, or any other place, the moment it enters any of these structures it makes its presence known immediately by producing unmistakable sensations, and so it is with the entry of a *ratappa* or spirit-child into a woman, the woman knows that the *ratappa* has just entered her because she feels it within her.

This, of course, is the most direct possible kind of experience one can undergo, and the most direct proof of the fact that the spirit-children enter the woman from an external source. The source is a totem abode or *Knanja*, and experience confirms this, for the woman will certainly have been in the vicinity of some local totem centre when she experienced the entry of the spirit-child into her, or she will easily recall having been near such a totem centre shortly before experiencing the movement of the spirit-child within her. Thus, the fact that she has been near a totem centre in which spirit-children are on the lookout for likely women to enter, and the fact of her experience of the entry of a spirit-child into her, are two facts obviously causally connected with one another and confirmed by actual experience. A woman never has a child unless she has been near such a centre, hence it is clear that the two events are causally related.

Another way in which a spirit-child may enter a woman is by eating food given her by the man who stands to her in the relationship of husband, either actual or tribal, shortly after which she will feel herself pregnant and will know that the spirit-child is within her. The two experiences are thus clearly and unambiguously shown to be related to one another in the strict sense of cause and effect. The food will be given to a woman if the man, and usually also the woman, desires to have a child. In due course a child will be born. It is natural, therefore, for them to conclude that the ritual act of giving and the consumption of the food were the acts responsible for initiating the entry of a spirit-child into a woman.

The fact that a woman is pregnant or is shortly likely to become so may be announced to her or to her husband, or to the father of the child, who is not necessarily the actual husband of the woman, or to some relative of hers, through the medium of a dream. Dreams among the Arunta are regarded as perfectly natural experiences, and the events therein enacted are regarded not as a counterpart, but as an actual part of reality itself. What more proof, then, could one require of the origin of spirit-children than is revealed, it may be, to a number of relatives of the same woman independently in similar situations in other families than one's own, in dreams? It should be recalled here that the word used by the Arunta to denote the far distant mythological time of their ancestors, the *Alchera*, means literally *the dream-times*. Speaking of such times in relation to himself, a man refers to them as 'my dreaming'.[10] The dream is conceived to possess an even deeper reality than waking life itself. The nature of some of these conception dreams has already been discussed in Róheim's account of them as given in the preceding pages. We may recall one dream here of an Arunta woman named Ngunalpa. Róheim reports her as saying,[11]

In my dream I saw a *rubaruba* (whirlwind) with an *iwupa* (poisonous kind of witchetty worm). Next day I vomited my bread and I knew that I was pregnant. This [adds Róheim] was at Mount Andulja. She had a fight with her husband before the dream. This was because he had *lolkuma* (refused) to give her meat. He did this because she had not fetched water. The child was an *erritja* (eagle hawk), because Mount Andulja is an eagle hawk place and the wild wind blew from there. The *rattappa* was in the *iwupa*, and she had a headache because the cold went in through her head. The *iwupa* becomes a *chapa* or *chimacha*, both being great delicacies of the Aranda menu.

From this dream and the commentary upon it it is not difficult to see that the dream events and those of reality are not distinguished. The headache Ngunalpa experienced was caused by the blowing through her head of the wild wind she had encountered in her dream. Apparently the dream took place at Mount Andulja, an eagle hawk totem centre, hence the child clearly belonged to the eagle hawk totem.

Naturally the content of the dream will follow the pattern in which it is culturally structured. To the Aboriginal, any suggestion that the content of his dreams is determined by the exigencies of his culture would be absurd. To the Aboriginal, the dream itself as well as its content represents a unitary whole; not a by-product of reality but reality itself, and as such it constitutes part of his immediate personal experience. The events occurring in his dream constitute an empirical demonstration and validation of the facts as they are traditionally taught, and confirmation of them.

Still another form of experience in which tradition receives the clearest confirmation is the vision. Thus, for example Ngunalpa's third child, a daughter also of the eagle hawk totem, came to her in a vision. 'She was walking with her husband, near Andulja, when she saw a little girl with *kapita aralkara* (fair hair). The little girl came quite near, and then disappeared. After this she felt the baby. The girl with the fair hair looked like her own sister Nelly when she saw it first. As the vision approached from Andulja, the little girl was an *erritja*. Her own grandfather (*aranga*) and her father's brother are also *erritja*.'[12]

Such visions are, of course, real experiences. They may be eidetically projected structures, or perceptions based on some real object, or purely hallucinatory. Whatever their nature, there is no doubt that they are considered as real events, and the proof, if proof were needed, lies in the events which follow them.

All these personal experiences constitute so many independent verifications and corroborations of the truth of the traditional doctrines. Nothing could occur that could render those doctrines questionable. Hence there exists a perfect congruence between the traditional doctrines and the beliefs of the individual, beliefs which represent no mere bigot's adherence to the traditional teaching, but the self-experienced confirmation of their truth.

Finally, to the evidence of direct personal experience we may add testimony of the medicine-men, whose pronouncements enjoy great respect because of the special powers which enable them to establish direct relations with the spirits of the Arunta world. The medicine-men are able to see the spirit-children, and capable of causing them to enter women. They can describe their appearance down to the last anatomical detail, not to mention their ability to influence their behaviour in various ways.

Thus, to the Aboriginal it is apparent that the traditional procreative doctrines represent a systematic historical account of experience, an experience which the individual is able to confirm, in almost every essential particular, for himself.

The foregoing summary of the manner in which experience is harmonized with the traditional teaching concerning the process of coming into being is in fundamentals applicable to most Australian tribes, only the relatively unimportant details will, as the reader must be aware, differ in various ways. In every case, however, experience is integrated as tradition and confirms it, and the two, experience and tradition, confirm the beliefs of the individual.

NOTES

1   *How Natives Think*, 15.
2   'The landowners of the northern division of the Aranda tribe, Central Australia', *Oceania*, 6, 1936, 282–3.
3   *The Mind of Primitive Man*, 227.
4   W. G. Sumner and A. G. Keller, *The Science of Society*, New Haven, 1928, ii, 786; R. Karsten, *The Origins of Religion*, 22–48.
5   J. Dewey, *Experience and Nature*, 154.
6   See W. J. Perry, for example, 'Theology and physical paternity', *Man*, 32, 1932, 175–6.
7   A. I. Hallowell, 'Some empirical aspects of Northern Salteaux religion', *Amer. Anthrop.*, n.s., 36, 1934, 392–3.
8   Ibid., 404.
9   On the place of dreams in the life of the Aborigines see especially R. Berndt, *Kunapipi*; also B. Pentony, 'Dreams and dream beliefs in Northwestern Australia', *Oceania*, 32, 1961, 144–9.
10 *The Arunta*, 306, 592. See also L. Lévy-Bruhl, 'Le temps et l'espace du monde mythique (Australie et Nouvelle Guinée)', *Scientia*, 57, 1935, 139–49.
11 'Women and their life in Central Australia'.
12 Ibid.

Bibliography

Abbie, A. A. The Australian Aborigine. *Oceania* 22 (1951) 91–100.
The Original Australians. London, 1969.

Aberle, S. E. D. Frequency of pregnancy and birth interval among Pueblo Indians. *American Journal of Physical Anthropology* 15 (1931) 63–80.

Allen, E. The irregularity of the menstrual function. *American Journal of Obstetrics and Gynecology* 25 (1933) 705–8.

Angas, G. F. *Savage Life and Scenes in Australia and New Zealand*. 2 vols, London, 1847.

Aptekar, H. *Anjea*. New York, 1931.

Armstrong, W. E. *Rossel Island*. Cambridge University Press, 1928.

Austen, L. Procreation among the Trobriand Islanders. *Oceania* 5 (1934) 102–13.

Baelz, E. Anthropologie der Menschen-Rassen Ost-Asiens. *Zeitschrift für Ethnologie* 33 (1901) 211.

Barnes, J. A. Physical and social kinship. *Philosophy of Science* 28 (1961) 296–8.

Basedow, H. Anthropological notes on the western coastal tribes of the Northern Territory of South Australia. *Transactions and Proceedings and Reports of the Royal Society of South Australia* 31 (1907) 1–62.

— *The Australian Aboriginal*. Adelaide, 1925.

— Subincision and kindred rites of the Australian Aboriginal. *Journal of the Royal Anthropological Institute* 57 (1927) 123–56.

Bates, D. M. The marriage laws and some customs of the West Australian Aborigines. *Victorian Geographical Journal* 23 (1905) 36–60.

— Social organization of some Western Australian tribes. *Report of the 14th Meeting of the Australasian Association for the Advancement of Science*, Sydney, 1913, 387–400.

Bateson, G. *Naven*. Cambridge University Press, 1936.

Benedict, R. *Patterns of Culture*. London and Boston, 1934.

Berndt, C. H. Women's changing ceremonies in Northern Australia. *L'Homme* (Paris) 1 (1950) 30–42.

Berndt, R. M. Aboriginal sleeping customs and dreams, Ooldea, South Australia. *Oceania* 10 (1940) 286–94.

— Subincision in a non-subincision area. *American Imago* 8 (1951) 3–19.

— Influence of European culture on Australian Aborigines. *Oceania* 21 (1951) 229–35.

— *Kunapipi*. Melbourne, 1951.

— *Djanggawul*. London, 1952.

— and Berndt, C. H. A preliminary report of field work in the Ooldea region, western South Australia. *Oceania* 13 (1942) 51–70; (1943) 243–80; 14 (1944) 220–49. Republished as *Oceania* monograph, Sydney, 1945.

— — *Sexual Behavior in Western Arnhem Land*. Viking Fund Publications in Anthropology, no 16, New York, 1951.

— — *From Black to White in South Australia*. Melbourne, 1951.

— — *The World of the First Australians*. London, 1964; University of Chicago Press, 1965.

— — *Man, Land and Myth in North Australia: the Gunwinggu People*. Sydney, and Michigan State University Press, 1970.

— — (eds). *Aboriginal Man in Australia*. London and Sydney, 1965.

Bertelsen, A. *Meddelelser om Grønland*. 117, no. 1, 1935.

Bettelheim, B. *Symbolic Wounds*. New York 1954; London, 1955.

Bischofs, J. Die Niol-Niol, ein eingeborenstamm in Nordwest-Australien. *Anthropos* 3 (1908) 32–40.

Bissonnette, T. H. Modification of mammalian sexual cycles: reaction of ferrets (*Putoris bulgaris*) of both sexes to electric light added after dark in November and December. *Proceedings of the Royal Society*, Ser. B. 110 (1932) 322–36.

— Sexual photoperiodicity. *Quarterly Review of Biology* 11 (1936) 371–86.

Boas, F. *The Mind of Primitive Man*. New York, 1929.

Bonney, F. On some customs of the Aborigines of the River Darling. *Journal of the Anthropological Institute* 13 (1884) 122–37.

Brehm, A. E. and Strassen. *Tierleben*. Berlin, 1912–20, vol. 13.

Breipohl, W. Untersuchungen über den Menstruationszyklus in der Menarchezeit. *Zentralbalatt für Gynäkologie* 61 (1937) 1335–42.

Briffault, R. *The Mothers*. 3 vols, London, 1927.

— Family sentiments. *Zeitschrift für Sozialforschung* 2 (1933) 355–81.

Brodsky, I. Congenital abnormalities, teratology and embryology: some evidence of primitive man's knowledge as expressed in art and lore in Oceania. *Medical Journal of Australia* 30 (1943) 417–20.

Brooks, C. E. P. *Climate*. London, 1930.

Brown, A. R. *see* Radcliffe-Brown, A. R.

Burridge, K. O. L. Virgin birth. *Man* n.s. 3 (1968) 654–5.

— *Encountering Aborigines*. London and New York, 1973.

Cameron, A. L. P. Notes on some tribes of New South Wales. *Journal of the Anthropological Institute* 14 (1885) 344–70.

Cannon, W. B. Voodoo death. *American Anthropologist* n.s. 44 (1942) 169–81.

Capell, A. The Wailbri through their own eyes. *Oceania* 23 (1952) 110–32.

— Review of W. Schmidt's 'Die Konzeptionsglaube australischer Stämme', *Oceania* 23 (1953) 240.

Carr-Saunders, A. M. *The Population Problem.* Oxford University Press, 1922.

Cassirer, E. *The Philosophy of Symbolic Forms.* 3 vols, Yale University Press, 1953, 1955, 1957.

Chaseling, W. *Yulengor: Nomads of Arnhem Land.* London, 1957.

Chau, K. T. and Wright, J. M. Gynecological notes: Canton Hospital. *China Medical Journal*, August 1935, 684.

Chewings, C. *Back in the Stone Age.* Sydney, 1936.

Clark, A. H. Is India dying? A reply to *Mother India. Atlantic Monthly* 141 (1928) 271–9.

Cleland, J. B., Fry, H. K. and Macgraith, B. J. Notes on the pathological lesions and vital statistics of Australian natives in Central Australia. *Medical Journal of Australia* 2 (1930) 80–3.

Cole, F. J. *Early Theories of Sexual Generation.* Oxford University Press, 1930.

Collins, D. *An Account of the English Colony in New South Wales.* 2 vols, London, 1798, 1802.

Cook, A. B. Oak and rock. *Classical Review* 15 (1901) 322–6.

Corney, B. S. On certain mutilations practised by the natives of the Viti Islands. *Reports of the Australasian Association for the Advancement of Science* 2 (1890) 646–53.

— and Thomson, B. A. *The Fijians.* London, 1908.

Crew, F. A. E. Puberty and maturity. *Proceedings of the 2nd International Congress for Sex Research*, London, 1930.

— and Mirskaia, L. The lactation interval in the mouse. *Quarterly Journal of Experimental Physiology* 20 (1930) 105–10.

Curjel. The reproductive life of Indian women. *Indian Journal of Medical Research* 8 (1920) 366–71.

Curr, E. M. *The Australian Race.* 4 vols, Melbourne and London, 1866–7.

Davidson, D. S. *The Chronological Aspects of Certain Australian Social Institutions.* Philadelphia, 1928.

— Australian throwing-sticks, throwing-clubs, and boomerangs. *American Anthropologist* n.s. 38 (1936) 76–100.

— Aboriginal Australian and Tasmanian rock carvings and paintings. *Memoirs of the American Philosophical Society* 5 (1936).

— The geographical distribution theory and Australian social culture. *American Anthropologist* n.s. 39 (1937) 171–4.

Deanesley, R. The corpora lutea of the mouse, with special reference to fat accumulation during the oestrous cycle. *Proceedings of the Royal Society*, Ser. B. 106 (1930) 578–95.

Devereux, G. Mohave paternity. *Samsha, Journal of the Indian Psycho-Analytic Society* 3 (1949) 162–94.
— *A Study of Abortion in Primitive Societies.* New York, 1955.
Dewey, J. *Experience and Nature.* New York, 1929.
Dixon, R. M. W. Virgin birth. *Man* n.s. 3 (1968) 653–4.
— *The Dyirbal Language of North Queensland.* Cambridge, 1972.
Doughty, C. M. *Travels in Arabia Deserta.* vol. 1, Cambridge, 1888.
Douglas, M. Virgin birth. *Man* n.s. 4 (1969) 133–4.
Douglas, W. O. Jiberabu. *Colliers* 134 (26 November 1954) 28–31.
Duguid, C. *No Dying Race.* Sydney, 1964.
Durham, M. E. *Some Tribal Origins, Laws and Customs of the Balkans.* London, 1928.
Earl, G. W. On the Aboriginal tribes of the northern coast of Australia. *Journal of the Royal Geographical Society* (London) 16 (1846) 239–51.
Elkin, A. P. Rock paintings of North-west Australia. *Oceania* 1 (1930) 257–79.
— The Dieri kinship system. *Journal of the Royal Anthropological Institute* 61 (1931) 493–98.
— The social organization of South Australian tribes. *Oceania* 2 (1931) 44–73.
— The social life and intelligence of the Australian Aborigine. *Oceania* 3 (1932) 101–13.
— Totemism in North-Western Australia (the Kimberley Division). *Oceania* 3 (1933) 257–96, 435–81; 4 (1933) 54–64.
— Beliefs and practices connected with death in north-eastern and western South Australia. *Oceania* 7 (1937) 275–99.
— Kinship in South Australia. *Oceania* 9 (1938) 41–78; 10 (1939) 196–234; 10 (1940) 295–349.
— Elements of Australian Aboriginal philosophy. *Oceania* 40 (1969) 85–98.
Ellis, H. *Studies in the Psychology of Sex.* 2 vols, London and Philadelphia, 1897, 1900.
Elwin, V. *The Baiga.* London, 1939.
— *The Muria and Their Ghotul.* Bombay, Oxford University Press, 1947.
Engle, E. T. and Shelesnyak, M. C. First menstruation and subsequent menstrual cycles of pubertal girls. *Human Biology* 6 (1934) 431–53.
English, T. M. S. On the greater length of the day in high latitudes as a reason for spring migration. *Ibis,* 11th ser., 5 (1923) 408–23.
Etheridge, R. Jr. Ancient stone implements from the Yodda Valley goldfield, north-east British New Guinea. *Records of the Australian Museum,* Sydney, no. 1, 1908.

— *The Cylindro-conical and Cornute Stone Implements of Western New South Wales and Their Significance*. Sydney, 1916.

Evans, H. M. and Burr, G. O. Vitamin E. *Memoirs of the University of California* 8, 1927.

Eylmann, E. *Die Eingeborenen der Kolonie Südaustralien*. Berlin, 1908.

Fehlinger, H. Vom Sexualleben der Australier. *Zeitschrift für sexual Wissenschaft* 11 (1915–16) 137–41.

— *Sexual Life of Primitive People*. London, 1921.

Fluhmann, C. F. The problem of irregular menstruation. *American Journal of Obstetrics and Gynecology* 26 (1933), 642–6.

Ford, E. Notes on pregnancy and parturition in the D'Entrecasteaux Islands. *Medical Journal of Australia*, 16 November 1940, 498–501.

Fortune, R. F. *The Sorcerers of Dobu*. London, 1932.

— A note on some forms of kinship structure. *Oceania* 4 (1933) 1–9.

— Manus religion. *Memoirs of the American Philosophical Society* 3 (1935).

Fox, H. The birth of two anthropoid apes. *Journal of Mammalogy* 10 (1929) 37–51.

Frazer, J. G. The beginnings of religion and totemism among the Australian Aborigines. Part 2. *Fortnightly Review* 48 (1905) 452–66.

— Beliefs and customs of the Australian Aborigines. *Man* 9 (1909) 146–7.

— *Totemism and Exogamy*. 4 vols, London, 1910.

— *The Golden Bough*. London, 1935, vol. 11.

Fry, H. K. Body and soul: a study from western Central Australia. *Oceania* 3 (1933) 247–56.

— Aboriginal mentality. *Medical Journal of Australia* 12 (1955) 353–60.

— and Pulleine, R. H. The mentality of the Australian Aboriginal. *Australian Journal of Experimental Biology and Medical Science* 8 (1931) 153–67.

Gason, S. The manners and customs of the Dieyerie tribe of Australian Aborigines, in J. D. Woods, *The Native Tribes of South Australia*, 257–307.

Gennep, A. van *Mythes et légendes d'Australie*. Paris, 1906.

— Les idées des australiens sur la conception. *Mercure de France* 61 (1906) 204–20.

— Questiones totemicae: a reply to Mr. Lang. *Man* 6 (1906) 148–9.

Goldenweiser, A. Primitive paternity: a review. *American Anthropologist* n.s. 13 (1911) 598–606.

Gomme, L. *Folklore as an Historical Science*. London, 1908.

Goodale, J. *Tiwi Wives: A Study of the Women of Melville Island, North Australia*. London and Seattle, 1971.

Granquist, H. *Birth and Childhood Among the Arabs*. Helsingfors, 1947.

Gregory, J. W. *The Menace of Colour.* 2nd ed., London, 1925.

Grey, G. *Journals of Two Expeditions of Discovery in North-West and Western Australia.* 2 vols, London, 1841.

Haddon, A. C. *Reports of the Cambridge Anthropological Expedition to Torres Straits.* 6 vols, Cambridge University Press, 1901–35.

Hallowell, A. I. Some empirical aspects of Northern Salteaux religion. *American Anthropologist* n.s. 36 (1939) 389–404.

— *Culture and Experience.* University of Pennsylvania Press, Philadelphia, 1955.

Hamlyn-Harris, R. Some anthropological considerations of Queensland and the history of its ethnography. *Journal of the Royal Society of Queensland* 29 (1917) 1–44.

Hartland, E. S. *The Legend of Perseus.* 3 vols, London, 1894, 1895, 1896.

— The secret of the totem. *Man* 6 (1906) 27–8.

— *Primitive Paternity.* 2 vols, London, 1909, 1910.

— *Primitive Society.* London, 1921.

Hartman, C. G. The period of gestation in the monkey, *Macacus rhesus:* First description of parturition in monkeys, size and behaviour of the young. *Journal of Mammalogy* 9 (1928) 185.

— The breeding season in monkeys. *Journal of Mammalogy* 12 (1931) 129–42.

— On the relative sterility of the adolescent organism. *Science* 74 (1931) 226–7.

— Studies in the reproduction of the monkey *Macacus (Pithecus) rhesus,* with special reference to menstruation and pregnancy. *Contributions to Embryology* no. 134, Publication no. 433, Carnegie Institution of Washington, 1932.

— *Time of Ovulation in Women.* London and Baltimore, 1936.

Heape, W. The proportion of the sexes produced by white and coloured peoples in Cuba. *Philosophical Transactions of the Royal Society* (London) Ser. B. 200 (1909) 296sq.

— *Sexual Antagonism.* London, 1913.

Henderson, J. *Excursions and Adventures in New South Wales.* 2 vols, London, 1851.

Herbert, X. *Capricornia.* Sydney, 1938.

Hernández, T. Social organization of the Drysdale River tribes, North-West Australia. *Oceania* 11 (1941) 211–32.

— Children among the Drysdale River tribes. *Oceania* 12 (1941) 122–33.

Hesse-Doflein. *Tierbau und Tierleben.* Vol. 1, 1914.

Hilliard, W. *The People in Between: The Pitjantjatjara People of Ernabella.* London and New York, 1968.

Himes, N. E. *Medical History of Contraception.* London and Baltimore, 1936.

Hirschfeld, M. *Men and Women*. London and New York, 1935.

Hogbin, I. Native culture of Wogeo: report of field work in New Guinea. *Oceania* 5 (1935) 320–1.

Horne, G. and Aiston, G. *Savage Life in Central Australia*. London, 1924.

Howells, W. W. Anthropometry of the natives of Arnhem Land and the Australian race problem. *Papers of the Peabody Museum of American Archaeology and Ethnology* 16 (1937).

Howitt, A. W. Notes on the Australian class systems. *Journal of the Anthropological Institute* 12 (1882) 496–512.

— Australian group relations. *Reports of the Smithsonian Institution* (1883) 797–824.

— *The Native Tribes of South-East Australia*. London, 1904.

Hrdlička, A. Fecundity in the Sioux women. *American Journal of Physical Anthropology* 16 (1931) 81–90.

Johnston, A. The Californian Indians, in H. R. Schoolcraft, 'Historical and Statistical Information', *Archives for Aboriginal Knowledge* (Washington, D.C.) 4 (1860).

Jolly, A. T. H. and Rose, F. G. G. The place of the Australian Aboriginal in the evolution of society. *Annals of Eugenics* 12 (1943) 44–87.

Jose, A. W., Carter, H. J. and Tucker, T. G. (eds). *The Australian Encyclopaedia*. 2 vols, Sydney, 1927.

Kaberry, P. M. The Forrest River and Lyne River tribes of North-West Australia: a report on field work. *Oceania* 5 (1935) 408–36.

— Spirit children and spirit centres of the North Kimberley Division, West Australia. *Oceania* 6 (1936) 392–400.

— Totemism in East and South Kimberley, north west Australia. *Oceania* 8 (1938) 265–88.

— *Aboriginal Woman, Sacred and Profane*. Routledge, London, 1939.

— Virgin birth. *Man* n.s. 3 (1968) 311–13.

Karsten, R. *The Origins of Religion*. London, 1935.

Kelsey, D. E. R. Phantasies of birth and prenatal experiences recovered from patients undergoing hypnoanalysis. *Journal of Mental Science* 99 (1953) 216–23.

King, J. L. Menstrual intervals. *American Journal of Obstetrics and Gynecology* 25 (1933) 583–7.

Klaatsch, H. Some notes on scientific travel amongst the black population of tropical Australia in 1904, 1905, 1906. *Report of the 11th Meeting of the Australian Association for the Advancement of Science*, Adelaide, 1907.

— Schlussbericht über meine Reise nach Australien in den Jahren 1904–1907. *Zeitschrift für Ethnologie* 39 (1907) 635–90.

Köhler, W. *The Mentality of Apes*. London, 1925; reprinted, Routledge & Kegan Paul, 1973.

Kroeber, A. L. *Handbook of the Indians of California*. Bureau of American Ethnology, Bulletin 78 (1925).

Krzywicki, L. *Primitive Society and its Vital Statistics*. London, 1924.

Landtman, G. *The Kiwai Papuans of British New Guinea*. London, 1927.

Lang, A. *The Secret of the Totem*. London, 1905.

— The primitive and the advanced in totemism. *Journal of the Anthropological Institute* 35 (1905) 315–36.

— Introduction to K. Langloh Parker, *The Euahlayi Tribe*, ix–xxvii.

— Questiones totemicae. *Man* 6 (1906) 51–4.

— *Mythes et légendes d'Australie*: A review. *Man* 6 (1906) 123–6.

— Questiones totemicae: a reply to M. van Gennep. *Man* 6 (1906) 180–2.

— Australian problems, in *Anthropological Essays presented to Edward Burnett Tylor in Honour of his 75th Birthday, October 2nd, 1907*, Oxford, 1907, 205–18.

Le Souëf, W. H. D. *Wild Life in Australia*. Christchurch and London, 1907.

Leach, E. R. *Rethinking Anthropology*. London, 1961.

— Virgin Birth. *Proceedings of the Royal Anthropological Institute* (1966) 39–49.

— Virgin birth. *Man* n.s. 3 (1968) 655–6.

Lefroy, C. E. G. Australian Aborigines, a noble-hearted race. *Contemporary Review* 135 (1929) 222–3.

Leonhardi, M. von. Über einige religiöse und totemistische Vorstellungen der Aranda und Loritja in zentral-Australien. *Globus* 12 (1907) 285–90.

Lévi-Strauss, C. *The Savage Mind*. London and Chicago, 1966.

Lévy-Bruhl, L. *How Natives Think*. London, 1926.

— *The 'Soul' of the Primitive*. London, 1928.

— *Primitives and the Supernatural*. London, 1935.

— *La Mythologie primitive*. Paris, 1935.

— Le temps et l'espace du monde mythique (Australie et Nouvelle-Guinée). *Scientia* 57 (1935) 139–49.

Lipmann, E. *Urzeugung und Lebenskraft*. Berlin, 1933.

Lockwood, D. *I, the Aboriginal*. Adelaide, 1962.

Lommel, A. Notes on sexual behaviour and initiation, Wunambal tribe, North-Western Australia. *Oceania* 20 (1949) 158–64.

— Modern culture influences on the Aborigines. *Oceania* 21 (1950) 14–24.

— Traum und Bild bei den Primitiven in Nordwest-Australien. *Psyche* (Paris) pt 3 (1951).

— Die Unambal, ein Stamm in Nordwest-Australien. *Monographien zur Völkerkunde*, no. 2. Hamburg, 1952.

Love, J. R. B. Rock paintings of the Worrora and their mythological interpretation. *Journal of the Royal Society of Western Australia* 16 (1929) 1–24.

— *Stone Age Bushman of To-day*. London, 1936.

Lyons, A. P. Paternity beliefs and customs in Western Papua. *Man* 24 (1924) 58–9.

McCarthy, F. D. *Australia's Aborigines*. Adelaide, 1957.

McConnel, U. The Wik-Munkan tribe, pts 1 and 2. *Oceania* 1 (1930) 97–104, 181–205.

— A moon legend from the Bloomfield River, North Queensland. *Oceania* 2 (1931) 9–25.

— Totemic hero-cults in Cape York Peninsula, North Queensland. *Oceania* 6 (1936) 452–77.

— Mourning ritual among the tribes of the Cape York Peninsula. *Oceania* 7 (1937) 346–71.

— *Myths of the Munkan*. Melbourne University Press, 1957.

MacGaffey, W. Virgin birth. *Man* n.s. 4 (1969) 457.

MacGillivray, J. *Narrative of the Voyage of H.M.S. 'Rattlesnake'*. 2 vols, London, 1852.

McLennan, J. F. *Studies in Ancient History*. London, 1886.

Madigan, C. T. *Central Australia*. Oxford University Press, 1936.

Maine, H. *Dissertations on Early Law and Custom*. London, 1883.

Malinowski, B. *The Family Among the Australian Aborigines*. London, 1913.

— Baloma: the spirits of the dead in the Trobriand Islands. *Journal of the Royal Anthropological Institute* 46 (1916) 353–430.

— *The Sexual Life of Savages in North-Western Melanesia*. Routledge, London, 1929; reprinted 1968.

— Kinship. *Encyclopaedia Britannica* 13, London, 1929, 409.

— Parenthood—the basis of social structure, in V. F. Calverton and S. Schmalhausen (eds), *The New Generation*. New York, 1930, 112–68.

March, A. W. and Davenport, C. B. The normal interval between human births. *Eugenical News* 10 (1925) 86–8.

Marett, R. R. and Penniman, T. K. (eds). *Spencer's Scientific Correspondence*. Oxford, 1932.

Mariner, W. *An Account of the Natives of the Tonga Islands*. 2 vols, London, 1817.

Marshall, F. H. A. *The Physiology of Reproduction*. London, 1922.

Massola, A. *Bunjil's Cave: Myths, Legends and Superstitions of the Aborigines of South-East Australia*. Melbourne and New York, 1968.

Mathew, J. *Eaglehawk and Crow*. London, 1899.

Mathews, R. H. *Folklore of the Australian Aborigines*. Sydney, 1899.
— Ethnological notes on the Aboriginal tribes of New South Wales and Victoria. *Journal and Proceedings of the Royal Society of New South Wales* 38 (1904) 203–381.
— *The Aboriginal Tribes of New South Wales and Victoria*. Sydney, 1905.
— Sociology of some Australian tribes. *Journal and Proceedings of the Royal Society of New South Wales* 39 (1905) 104–23.
— Ethnological notes on the Aboriginal tribes of Queensland. *Queensland Geographical Journal* n.s. 20 (1905) 49–75.
— Notes on some native tribes of Australia. *Journal and Proceedings of the Royal Society of New South Wales* 40 (1906) 95–129.
— The totemistic system in Australia. *American Antiquarian* 28 (1906) 140–7.
— Notes on the Arranda tribe. *Journal and Proceedings of the Royal Society of New South Wales* 41 (1907) 147–63.
— Notes on the Aborigines of the Northern Territory, Western Australia, and Queensland. *Queensland Geographical Journal* n.s. 22 (1907) 74–86.
— Marriage and descent in the Arranda tribe, Central Australia. *American Anthropologist* n.s. 10 (1908) 88–102.
Mayo, K. *Mother India*. London and New York, 1927.
Mead, M. *Growing Up in New Guinea*. New York, 1930, London, 1931.
— *Sex and Temperament*. New York and London, 1935.
Meggitt, M. J. *Desert People: A Study of the Walbiri Aborigines of Central Australia*. Sydney, 1962; University of Chicago Press, 1965.
Meyer, H. E. A. Manners and customs of the Aborigines of the Encounter Bay tribe, in J. D. Woods, *The Native Tribes of South Australia*, 183–206.
Millar, W. Human abortion. *Human Biology* 6 (1934) 297–99.
Miller, G. S. The primate basis of human sexual behavior. *Quarterly Review of Biology* 6 (1931) 379–410.
Miller, M. D. *Child Artists of the Australian Bush*. London, 1952.
Mills, C. A. Geographic and time variations in body growth and age at menarche. *Human Biology* 9 (1937) 43–56.
— and Ogle, C. Physiologic sterility of adolescence. *Human Biology* 8 (1936) 607–15.
— and Senior, F. A. Does climate affect the human conception rate? *Archives of Internal Medicine* 46 (1930) 921–9.
Mjöberg, E. G. Vom Phalluskult in Nordaustralien. *Archiv für Anthropologie* 19 (1923) 86–8.
Mondière, A. T. Sur la monographie de la femme de la Cochinchine. *Bulletin de la Société d'Anthropologie* 3rd series, 3 (1880) 250–61.

— Nubilité. *Dictionnaire des Sciences anthropologiques*. Paris, 1886–94, vol. 2, 823–4.

Montagu, Ashley. Infertility of the unmarried in primitive societies. *Oceania* 8 (1937) 15–26.

— The future of the Australian Aborigines. *Oceania* 8 (1938) 343–50.

— Adolescent sterility. *Quarterly Review of Biology* 14 (1939) 13–34, 192–219.

— Physiology and the origins of the menstrual prohibitions. *Quarterly Review of Biology* 15 (1940) 211–20.

— Nescience, science and psychoanalysis. *Psychiatry* 4 (1941) 45–60.

— The acquisition of sexual knowledge in children. *American Journal of Orthopsychiatry* 15 (1945) 290–300.

— *Adolescent Sterility*. Springfield, Ill., 1946.

— *The Reproductive Development of the Female*. New York, 1957.

Montague, S. Trobriand kinship and the virgin birth controversy. *Man* n.s. 6 (1971) 353–68.

Montané, L. Notas sobra un Chimpance nacido in Cuba. *Mémoires de la Société Cubana Histoire Naturelle 'Felipe Poey'* 1 (1926) 259–69.

— Histoire d'une famille de chimpanzees: Étude physiologique. *Bulletins et Mémoires de la Société d'Anthropologie de Paris* (1928) 14–35.

Morgan, J. *Life and Adventures of William Buckley*. Hobart, 1852.

Morgan, L. H. Systems of consanguinity and affinity of the human family. *Reports of the Smithsonian Institution*, 17 (1871) 10sq.

— *Ancient Society*. New York, 1877.

Mountford, C. P. *Brown Men and Red Sand*. Melbourne, 1948.

— *Records of the American-Australian Scientific Expedition to Arnhem Land*. I. Art, Myth and Symbolism. Melbourne University Press, 1956.

— *Ayers Rock*. Sydney and Honolulu, 1965.

— *The Tiwi, their Art, Myth and Ceremony*. London, 1958.

— and Harvey, A. Women of the Adnjamatana tribe of the northern Flinders Ranges, South Australia. *Oceania* 12 (1941) 155–162.

Mulvaney, D. J. The prehistory of the Australian Aborigine. *Scientific American* 214 (1966) 84–93.

— *The Prehistory of Australia*. London and New York, 1969.

— and Golson, J. (eds). *Aboriginal Man and Environment in Australia*. Canberra, 1971.

Mundy, G. C. *Our Antipodes*. London, 1854.

Murdock, G. P. *Social Structure*. New York, 1949.

Myres, J. L. Herodotus, in *Anthropology and the Classics*, ed. R. R. Marett, Oxford University Press, 1908.

Needham, J. *A History of Embryology*. Cambridge University Press. 1934.

Needham, R. Virgin birth. *Man* n.s. 4 (1969) 457–8.

Neuhauss, R. *Deutsch Neu-Guinea.* Vol. 1, Berlin, 1911.

Niewenhuis, A. W. Die Ansichten der primitiven Völker über das Geschlechtsleben des Menschen. *Internationales Archiv für Ethnographie* 28 (1927) 139–52.

Nilles, J. The Kimbu of the Chimbu Region, Central Highlands, New Guinea. *Oceania* 21 (1950) 25–65.

Oberländer, R. Die Eingeborenen der australischen Kolonie Victoria. *Globus* 4 (1863) 278–82.

Ogle, C. Adaptation of sexual activity to environmental stimulation. *American Journal of Physiology* 107 (1934) 628–34.

Olcott, N. S. Vitamin E. II: Stability of concentrates towards oxidizing and reducing reagents. *Journal of Biological Chemistry* 107 (1934) 471–4.

Oldfield, A. Aborigines of Australia. *Transactions of the Ethnological Society of London* n.s. 3 (1865) 215–98.

Oliver, D. L. *The Pacific Islands.* Harvard University Press, 1951.

Oparin, A. I. *The Origin of Life.* New York, 1938.

Palmer, E. Notes of some Australian tribes. *Journal of the Anthropological Institute* (London) 13 (1884) 276–334.

Parker, K. L. *The Euahlayi Tribe: A Study of Aboriginal Life in Australia.* London, 1905.

Parkes, A. S. Observations on the oestrous cycle of the albino mouse. *Proceedings of the Royal Society*, Ser. B. 100 (1926) 151–70.

— *The Internal Secretions of the Ovary.* London, 1929.

Pearl, R. Contraception and fertility in 1,000 women. *Human Biology* 4 (1932) 363–407.

— Contraception and fertility in 4,945 married women: a second report on a study of family limitation. *Human Biology* 6 (1934) 355–401.

— Biological factors in fertility. *Annals of the American Academy of Social and Political Science*, November 1936, 1–12.

Pentony, B. Psychological causes of depopulation of primitive groups. *Oceania* 24 (1953) 142–4.

— Dreams and dream beliefs in Northwestern Australia. *Oceania* 32 (1961) 144–9.

Perry, W. J. Theology and physiological paternity. *Man* 32 (1932) 175–6.

Phelan, G. Aboriginal children in New South Wales schools. *Integrated Education* (Chicago) 3 (1965) 36–41.

Pickering, C. *The Races of Man.* London, 1851.

Pillay, A. P. Marriage and divorce in India. *Proceedings of the 3rd Sexual Reform Congress*, Routledge, London, 1930.

Pilling, A. R. *Aborigine Culture History: A Survey of Publications 1954–1957.* Wayne State University Press, 1962.

Pink, O. The landowners of the northern division of the Aranda tribe, Central Australia. *Oceania* 6 (1936) 275–305.

Ploss, H. H., Bartels, M. and Bartels, F. *Woman: An Historical, Gynaecological and Anthropological Compendium*, 3 vols, London, 1935.

Porteous, S. D. *The Psychology of a Primitive People*. London, 1931.

— Mentality of the Australian Aborigines. *Oceania* 4 (1933) 30–6.

— *Primitive Intelligence and Environment*. New York, 1937.

Powell, H. A. Virgin birth. *Man* n.s. 3 (1968) 651–3.

Powers, S. *Tribes of California*. Washington, 1877.

Preller, L. *Philologus*. Berlin, 1852.

Purcell, B. H. Rites and customs of Australian Aborigines. *Zeitschrift für Ethnologie* 25 (1893) 286–9.

Rabaud, É. Telegony. *Journal of Heredity* 5 (1914) 389–99.

Radcliffe-Brown, A. R. Beliefs concerning childbirth in some Australian tribes. *Man* 12 (1912) 180–2.

— Three tribes of Western Australia. *Journal of the Royal Anthropological Institute* 43 (1913) 143–94.

— The social organization of Australian tribes. *Oceania* 1 (1930–1). 34–63, 206–46, 332–41, 426–56.

— The diffusion of culture in Australia. *Oceania* 1 (1930–1) 366–70.

— Letter. *Man* 38 (1938) 15–16.

Rainwater, L. *And the Poor Get Children*. Chicago, 1960.

Rashleigh, R., *see* [Tucker, James]

Read, C. No paternity. *Journal of the Royal Anthropological Institute* 48 (1918) 146–54.

Reche, O. Untersuchungen über das Wachstum und die Geschlechtsreife bie melanesischen Kindern. *Korrespondenzblatt deutscher Gesellschaft für Anthropologie* 41 (1910) 48–55.

Reed, S. C. *Counseling in Medical Genetics*. Philadelphia, 1955.

Reitzenstein, F. von. Der Kausalzusammenhang zwischen Geschlechtsverkehr und Empfängnis in Glaube und Brauch der Natur- und Kultur-völker. *Zeitschrift für Ethnologie* 41 (1909) 644–83.

Riesenfeld, A. Ignorance of physiological paternity in Melanesia. *Journal of American Folklore* 62 (1949) 145–55.

Rivers, W. H. R. *Kinship and Social Organization*. London, 1914.

— *Psychology and Ethnology*. London, 1926.

Robertson-Smith, W. *Religion of the Ancient Semites*. London, 1927.

Róheim, G. *Australian Totemism*. London, 1926.

— Psycho-analysis of primitive cultural types. *International Journal of Psychoanalysis* 13 (1932) 1–224.

— Women and their life in Central Australia. *Journal of the Royal Anthropological Institute* 63 (1933) 207–65.

— The nescience of the Aranda. *British Journal of Medical Psychology* 17 (1938) 343–60.

— *The Eternal Ones of the Dream*. New York, 1945.

— The western tribes of Central Australia: their sexual life. *Psychoanalysis and the Social Sciences* 5 (1958) 221–45.

Ronhar, J. H. *Het Vaderschap by de Primitieven*. Groningen, 1933.

Rose, F. G. G. *Classification of Kin, Age Structure and Marriage Amongst the Groote Eylandt Aborigines*. London and New York, 1960.

Rose, H. J. *Primitive Culture in Greece*. London, 1925.

Rose, R. *Living Magic*. New York, 1956; London, 1957.

Roth, W. E. *Ethnological Studies among the North-West-Central Queensland Aborigines*. Brisbane and London, 1897.

— Superstition, magic, and medicine. North Queensland Ethnography, *Bulletin* no. 5, Home Secretary's Department, Brisbane, 1903.

— Notes on government, morals, and crime. North Queensland Ethnography, *Bulletin* no. 8, Brisbane, 1906.

— Marriage ceremonies and infant life. North Queensland Ethnography, *Bulletin* no. 10. Records of the Australian Museum 7 (1908).

— Transport and trade. North Queensland Ethnography, *Bulletin* no. 14. Records of the Australian Museum 8 (1910).

Rowan, W. On photoperiodism, reproductive periodicity, and the annual migration of birds and certain fishes. *Proceedings of the Boston Society of Natural History* 38 (1926) 147–89.

— *The Riddle of Migration*. Baltimore, 1931.

Sarasin, F. *Ethnologie der Neu Caledonier und Loyalty Inselaner*. Munich, 1919.

Schaller, G. B. *The Mountain Gorilla*. University of Chicago Press, 1963.

Schelling, F. *The Ages of the World*. New York, 1942.

Schmidt, P. W. Die Stellung der Aranda unter den australischen Stämmen. *Zeitschrift für Ethnologie* 40 (1908) 866–901.

— Die Konzeptionsglaube australischer Stämme. *Internationales Archiv für Ethnographie* 44 (1952) 36–81.

Schneider, D. M. Virgin birth. *Man* n.s. 3 (1968) 126–9.

— Kidder, N. R., Hunt, E. E. Jr, and Stevens, W. D. *The Micronesians of Yap and their Depopulation*. Report of the Peabody Museum Expedition to Yap Island, Micronesia, 1947–1948. Harvard University, Cambridge, Mass., 1949.

Schultz, A. H. and Snyder, F. F. Observations on reproduction in the chimpanzee. *Bulletin of the Johns Hopkins Hospital* 47 (1935) 193–205.

Schulze, L. The Aborigines of the Upper and Middle Finke River.

Transactions and Proceedings of the Royal Society of South Australia 14 (1891) 210–46.

Schürmann, C. W. The Aboriginal tribes of Port Lincoln, in J. D. Woods, *The Native Tribes of South Australia,* 207–52.

Schwimmer, E. G. Virgin birth. *Man* n.s. 4 (1969) 132–3.

Semmens, T. P. and Lamers, W. M. Jr. *Teen-age Pregnancy.* Springfield, Ill., 1968.

Sharp, L. Social organization of the Yir-Yoront tribe. *Oceania* 4 (1934) 404–31.

— Ritual life and economics of the Yir-Yoront of Cape York Peninsula. *Oceania* 5 (1934) 19–42.

— Letters to the author, 16 June, 3 July 1936.

— An Australian Aboriginal population. *Human Biology* 12 (1940) 481–507.

— Steel axes for Stone Age Australians, in E. H. Spicer, *Human Problems in Technological Change.* New York, 1952, 69–90.

Simpson, C. *Adam in Ochre.* Sydney, 1951.

Smyth, R. B. *The Aborigines of Victoria.* 2 vols, Melbourne and London, 1878.

Sokolowsky, A. The sexual life of the anthropoid apes. *Urologic and Cutaneous Review* 27 (1923) 612–15.

Spencer, B. *Native Tribes of the Northern Territory of Australia.* London, 1914.

— *Wanderings in Wild Australia.* 2 vols, London, 1928.

— and Gillen, F. J. *The Native Tribes of Central Australia.* London, 1899; reprinted, New York, 1968.

— — *The Northern Tribes of Central Australia.* London, 1904.

— — *The Arunta.* 2 vols, London, 1927; New York, 1966.

— — *see also* Marett, R. R. and Penniman, T. K.

Spiller, G. The mentality of Australian Aborigines. *Sociological Review* (London) 7 (1913) 348–53.

Spiro, M. E. *Kibbutz.* Harvard University Press, 1956.

— *Children of the Kibbutz.* Harvard University Press, 1958.

— Virgin birth, parthenogenesis and physiological paternity: an essay in cultural interpretation. *Man* n.s. 3 (1968) 242–61.

— Virgin birth. *Man* n.s. 7 (1972) 315–16.

Stanner, W. E. H. The Daly River tribes: a report of field work in North Australia. *Oceania* 4 (1933) 27–8.

— A note on Djamindjung kinship and totemism. *Oceania* 6 (1936) 441–51.

— Murinbata kinship and totemism. *Oceania* 7 (1936) 186–216.

— Aboriginal modes of address and reference in the north-west of the Northern Territory. *Oceania* 7 (1937) 300–15.

— On aboriginal religion. *Oceania* Monograph no. 11, 1969.

Steggerda, M. *Maya Indians of Yucatan*. Publication no. 531, Carnegie Institution of Washington, D. C., 1941.

Steinen, K. von *Durch zentral Brazilien*. Leipzig, 1886.

Stieve, H. *Der Einfluss des Nervens Systems auf Bau- und Tätigkeit der Geschlechtsorgane des Menschen*. Stuttgart, 1951.

Strehlow, C. *Die Aranda- und Loritja-Stämme in zentral Australien*, ed. Moritz von Leonhardi. 7 parts, Frankfurt, 1907–21. Part 1, *Mythen, Sagen und Märchen des Aranda-Stämmes in zentral Australien*.

Strehlow, T. G. H. Ankotarinja, an Aranda myth. *Oceania* 4 (1935) 187–200.

— *Aranda Traditions*. Melbourne, 1948.

Strong, W. M. Papua: physical paternity. *Man* 33 (1933) 24.

Sutherland, J. M. and Landing, B. H. Failure to demonstrate antibody to sperm in serum of prostitutes. *Lancet* ii (1961) 56.

Suttie, I. D. *The Origins of Love and Hate*. London, 1935.

Taplin, G. *The Folklore, Manners, Customs, and Languages of the South Australian Aborigines*. Adelaide, 1879.

Tauber, E. *Molding Society to Man*. New York, 1955.

Thomas, N. W. *Kinship Organisations and Group Marriage in Australia*. Cambridge University Press, 1906.

Thomson, D. F. The hero cult, initiation, and totemism on Cape York. *Journal of the Royal Anthropological Institute* 63 (1933) 453–537.

— Fatherhood in the Wik Monkan tribe. *American Anthropologist* n.s. 38 (1936) 374–93.

Thurnwald, R. *Die Gemeinde der Banaro*. Stuttgart, 1921.

Tindale, N. B. Survey of the half-caste problem in South Australia. *Proceedings of the Royal Geographical Society, South Australian Branch*, Session 1940–1, 66–161.

Tinkelpaugh, O. L. Sex cycles and other cyclic phenomena in a chimpanzee during adolescence, maturity, and pregnancy. *Journal of Morphology* 54 (1933) 521–46.

[Tucker, James]. *Adventures of an Outlaw: the Memoirs of Ralph Rashleigh*. London and New York, 1929.

U.S. Department of Labor, Children's Bureau. *Causal Factors in Infant Mortality*. Publication no. 142, 1925.

— *Maternal Mortality*. Publication no. 158, 1926.

Vaerting, M. and Vaerting, M. *The Dominant Sex*. London, 1923.

Vaughan, A. C. The genesis of human offspring: a study in early Greek culture. *Smith College Classical Studies*, no. 13, 1945.

Ward, T. *Rambles of an Australian Naturalist*. London, 1907.

Warner, W. L. Birth control in primitive society. *Birth Control Review* (New York) 15 (1931) 105–7.

— Malay influence on the Aboriginal cultures of north-eastern Arnhem Land. *Oceania* 2 (1932) 476–95.

— *A Black Civilization*. London and New York, 1937; rev. ed., 1958.

Westermarck, E. *The Origins and Development of Moral Ideas*. 2 vols, London, 1917.

— *The History of Human Marriage*. 3 vols, London, 1922.

— *The Future of Marriage*. London and New York, 1936.

Wheeler, G. C. *The Tribe and Intertribal Relations in Australia*. London, 1910.

Whitaker, W. L. The question of a seasonal sterility among the eskimos. *Science* 88 (1938) 214–15.

Whiting, J. W. M. and Reed, S. W. Kwoma culture: a report of field work in the Mandated Territory of New Guinea. *Oceania* 9 (1938) 170–216.

Wilhelmi, C. Manners and customs of the Australian natives, in particular of the Port Lincoln District. *Transactions of the Royal Society of Victoria* 5 (1861) 164–203.

Wilkins, G. H. *Undiscovered Australia*. London, 1928.

Williams, F. E. Physical paternity in the Morehead District, Papua. *Man* 33 (1933) 123–4.

Wilson, P. J. Virgin birth. *Man* n.s. 4 (1969) 286–7.

Wolfe, A. B. The fertility and fecundity of early man. *Human Biology* 5 (1933) 35–60.

Woods, J. D. *The Native Tribes of South Australia*. Adelaide, 1879.

Woolard, H. H. The growth of the brain of the Australian Aboriginal. *Journal of Anatomy* 65 (1931) 224–41.

Worsley, P. The Changing Social Structure of the Wani Ndiljaugwa. Typescript, Australian National University, Canberra.

Wright, S. *Applied Physiology*. Oxford University Press, 1934.

Wyatt, J. M. and Vevers, G. M. On the birth of a chimpanzee recently born in the Society's gardens. *Proceedings of the Zoological Society of London* (1935) 195–7.

Yerkes, R. The mind of the gorilla. Pt II: Mental development. *Genetic Psychology Monographs* 2 (1927) 520–2.

— The mind of the gorilla. Pt III: Memory. *Comparative Psychology Monographs* 5 (1928) 69.

— A second generation captive-born chimpanzee. *Science* 81 (1935) 542–3.

Zuckerman, S. The menstrual cycle of the primates. Pt I: General nature and homology. *Proceedings of the Zoological Society of London* (1930) 691–754.

— The menstrual cycle of the primates. Pt III: The alleged breeding season of primates, with special reference to the Chacma baboon (*Papio porcarius*). *Proceedings of the Zoological Society of London* (1931) 325–43.

— The menstrual cycle of the primates. Pt IV: Observations on the lactation period. *Proceedings of the Zoological Society of London* (1931) 593–602.

— The menstrual cycle of the primates. Pt VI: Further observations on the breeding of primates, with special reference to the suborders Lemuroidea and Tarsioidea. *Proceedings of the Zoological Society of London* (1933) 1059–75.

— *The Social Life of Monkeys and Apes*. London, 1932.

— The physiology of fertility in man and monkey. *Eugenics Review* 28 (1936) 37–50.

Additional References

Cawte, J. E. Further comment on the Australian subincision ceremony. *American Anthropologist* 70 (1968) 961–4.

— Why we slit the penis, in *The Psychology of Aboriginal Australians*, G. E. Kearney, P. R. de Lacey, and G. R. Davidson (eds), 380–94.

— Djagamara, N., and Barrett, M. J. The meaning of subincision of the urethra to Aboriginal Australians. *British Journal of Medical Psychology* 39 (1966), 245–53.

Jones, I. H. Subincision amongst Australian western desert Aborigines. *British Journal of Medical Psychology* 42 (1969) 183–90.

Kearney, G. E., de Lacey, P. R., and Davidson, G. R. (eds). *The Psychology of Aboriginal Australians*. Sydney and New York, 1973.

Lawick-Goodall, J. van *In the Shadow of Man*. Boston, 1971.

Montagu, Ashley (ed.). *Culture and the Evolution of Man*. New York and London, 1962.

— (ed.). *Culture: Man's Adaptive Dimension*. New York and London, 1968.

Morrison, J. The origin of the practices of circumcision and subincision among the Australian Aborigines. *Medical Journal of Australia* 21 (January 1967) 125–7.

Rowley, C. D. *The Destruction of Aboriginal Society*. London, 1972.

Index